BEYOND JUDGMENT

by
Gene Wall
and
Michael Schon

Published by
Nevada Sierra Publishing Co.
Sparks, Nevada

Published by Nevada Sierra Publishing Co.
1165 Exchange St.
Sparks, Nevada 89431

Printed in the United States of America

CHAPTER 1

"Sure wonder at times what the hell God wants us folks to do Helen, you know it? Especially if you use me as an example of what I'm talkin' about, 'cause here I sit, an old man now, and wealthy like precious few people on this earth ever know." He shook his head slowly, staring into the fire. "But you know what, Babe? I can't seem to get fired up anymore. Don't much care about nothin', not since Momma left us. Talk about your money, power and prestige? Got lots of that. Question is what do I do with it now? Well what the hell." The old man sniffed. "Anyway, you know anybody who really cares!" Followed by bitter laughter. "S'pose lots of folks would though, huh Babe, 'cept you and me. Somethin', ain't it? The money's mine and it just don't matter anymore!"

The crusty old man put his arm around his companion, continuing. "For damn sure you couldn't care less either. Am I right or what?"

Helen, sat beside him at rigid attention on their favorite leather couch. Alex George, one of the wealthiest men in the world was sitting alone in his favorite darkened "Shed", chatting easily, naturally, with the beautiful Doberman Pincher. The intense creature with her piercing eyes never left his side, whether sitting in this their favorite place, walking in the primitive beauty of the huge lawn or sleeping in his upstairs bedroom. She was his constant companion, motionless when he spoke to her, appearing to understand every word. She was gorgeous, her majestic head and face sculpted to absolute perfection. Listening to her personal God, as on this occasion, her eyes never left his ancient face until he wandered away in his thoughts.

"Yeah, yeah, yeah...end of a long ass road. A down home wild ride it's been too, you know it? Money! Power! All that razzamatazz, but who cares! Without Momma there just ain't...."

He broke into tears at the mention of his now dead wife, the palm of his broad gnarled fist covering most of his face while he wept. Helen stirred, sliding her long muzzle onto her old friend's shoulder, pressing against his neck.

"There I go feelin' sorry for myself again, huh Babe? Sure do a lot of that lately don't I?" He put his arm around the sensitive dog, hugging her tight. "You probably miss her more than I'll ever know, don't you?" Adding with a sigh. "Yeah, yeah. She was your lady all right." Followed by sudden laughter. "And you were hers too, 'ya know it? Christ, I thought Momma'd lost her mind when she brought you home, ears all bandaged up in that white tape. Knew for sure you'd lift right off the ground in a high wind. Looked for all the world like a king size mouse, but boy how she loved you right off the bat, yeah. 'Course we all loved her, didn't we?" His breathing came hard as he fought for control. "Damn! Just to know that lady was to love her."

They sat motionless for a while, lost in thought.

"Aw nuts Helen, let's go on down to the bayou, see if she's there. We had some good times down there you know."

He thought about it for a while, his face brightening as he rose from the couch slowly.

"Yeah, let's get outta here and pick up the boat. Beats sittin' in the dark anyway. How 'bout it? Sound good?"

Helen responded instantly jumping down from the couch, stretched, shaking out her ears to the soft flapping sound which always amused him. Then she pranced excitedly about the huge room, darkened by the shuttered French doors. This very old man was her only reason for being, now that their beloved Momma was gone, and any offer to go outdoors was always met with wild enthusiasm.

"All right! All right!" He laughed. "Don't go wettin' the floor. I'll just get my sweater and we'll fire up the truck. OK?"

It was OK, and the two of them drove the short distance to the water in the battered old white truck. They were a sight these two, the white haired man driving and the regal creature pressed tight against his side looking for all the world like she was in command. The citizens of LaFayette knew them though, giving the shabby white vehicle wide berth, as the two friends went seeking Momma.

They drifted aimlessly in the sluggish current. It was quite cold, and very humid. The old man and his companion seemed oblivious to the weather, sitting motion-less in the boat. He was utterly out of touch with his surroundings, as he stared into space, analyzing his life. The boat, and this special place on the bayou, had been a source of great pleasure to his wife of all those many years. They came often to enjoy the beautiful scenery together, and it was proper that Helen should be with him now.

Water was everywhere, glass like, motionless, broken now and then when a bass shattered the surface, arcing and twisting through the air, carving great slashes through the water while walking on its tail. Simply to catch a glimpse of these unbridled creatures, the object of so many sport fishermen's efforts, was an exciting treat and delight to the old couple.

The old man and his wife were especially grateful, in a spiritual sense, when lucky enough to see the deer. They were absolutely exquisite in their timid, graceful ways as they approached the water. Wary, with nerves and reflexes tuned to the maximum. Listening, sniffing. Freezing in mid step. A dainty foot suspended gracefully, one with their surroundings.

His beloved Momma's eyes always filled with tears when they came upon their most sacred sight of all, a doe with her new fawn. The air virtually crackled with the intensity of the new mother, testing every step of the way, guarding the beguiling creature in her care with it's sweet, oversized features.

They never spoke when this rare, cherished sight unfolded, conversing rather with a gentle touch or a nod of the head in the direction of the soft colored scene. It was definitely sacred this special event, and what more stunning place in the whole world to share it than amidst the lush beauty of the Bayou Teche.

Everything, everywhere, was shades of green, some subtle, some profound, endless varieties all produced by the water and its lighting. No matter which way one looked it was there, bright under direct rays of the sun, dark almost to black in deep areas of shade. It started at the water line, moving, changing everything it came in contact with. The old man wondered from boyhood which way they were growing, from trees to the water, or water to trees. Another which came first riddle he thought. Well whatever, they were there, elegant with the Spanish moss swaying in the wind. This delicate growth draped over the limbs of the trees, exhibiting a beauty and grace he never tired of seeing. He thought too that no less than God Himself must have finished off this sensuous beauty with the endless varieties of lush, thick green grasses, adding to the stunning tableau.

'Must have looked like this, at creation,' he thought, when the weather grew dark and ugly with the often times violent, swift storms boiling out of the Gulf. Greenish clouds laced with black rolled in off the Gulf of Mexico, a few short miles away, accompanied by howling wind and eerie darkness.

Alex loved storms, hurricanes most of all, but his wife was exactly opposite, wanting to hurry for cover whenever they came. That this sweet and gentle woman was so fearful of violent weather didn't escape him.

Momma was gone now and while the old man had no problem admitting this hard fact, it was simply beyond his ability to accept. Through powerful forced concentration, he tried to capture her essence if only for a moment, spending great periods of time talking to her, just as though she was still with him. Not sure what death was all about, even though it had escorted him all his life, he felt it must simply be a passing to another sphere of existence, and so maybe there was an outside chance Momma might be able to hear him.

He was out here now because she was easier to visualize sitting in the end of the boat, where the large Doberman sat now. His heart warmed thinking of her in her old, wide brimmed straw hat, constantly updated with bright colored ribbons and her cotton print dresses, comfortable and much lived in. Faded and sewn Momma called them. Beat up and washed out he said, but only to Momma. He teased her lovingly about her outfits, down to the white anklets thrust into faded blue canvas shoes.

God how he'd loved her. In view of the fact she could have anything in the world money could buy, he found it both touching and amusing she chose instead to be sensible, plain Momma, holding to those things most comfortable for her.

She called herself "a little Cajun gal, lucky enough to have married her wild Cajun who turned out to be Mr. Alex George." Although life dealt her much pain, she knew she'd been fortunate in her choice of husbands. A wild, exuberant product of Cajun country, his days full of joy and the promise of excitement, he was truly a human dynamo, and she wouldn't have missed her life with him for anything in this world.

One of his cherished memories was the time he got in serious trouble with Momma and her ancient car they had dubbed "old blue". It was a faded, blue 1967 Chrysler Newport she loved, felt comfortable in, and refused to part with. This irritated him immensely because she insisted on driving the old car when she could have any vehicle in the world, but no amount of pressure from him could change her mind.

On this occasion she'd gone to New Orleans for a short stay, and Alex thought he'd take care of the old blue turd once and for all. Wicked glee in his heart he took the aging vehicle to town, replacing it immediately with a sleek Mercedes.

"Wholesale the old shitter, Mr. George?" The man from the dealership asked before driving the faded car away.

"No, man no!" He always kept an ace in the hole, no matter the situation. "Park it in back or something, Charlie. We've been all through this before, you and me, and haven't pulled it off yet. Momma buys it, you can burn the damn thing. She doesn't? Hey, what the hell?" He shrugged his shoulders, and walked away.

Alex always wanted her to have only the very best there was, and this gorgeous new vehicle certainly was that, so they put it in the most beautiful setting possible, centered in front of the large white house. Even though he wanted to give her the nicest things his money could buy, and it could buy almost anything on earth, he also knew she liked what was comfortable and wanted no unnecessary changes in her life. He held his breath and waited.

The gorgeous car stood in front of the house, when she arrived, brilliant in the sun. Her eyes slid momentarily over the car, as she stepped from his chauffeur driven vehicle. He winced when her back stiffened as she looked around for her Chrysler and didn't see it, and he knew Old Blue was coming back to Momma's house.

"Alex!" She called, exiting the car. "Did "you" get a new car, sweetheart?"

'Oh shit!' Alex thought. 'She knows! She knows!'

"It's a pretty one, Cher." He was right, she knew.

"You like it, Momma?" Allowing some hope.

"Why yes, it's so pretty. Certainly a man in your position needs a nice car like that to ride in." Her tone of voice grated, like chalk screeching on a blackboard. "Does it have a telephone?"

She knew exactly what had happened without asking, and what's more she knew he was aware of her knowledge. True to her love and respect for this powerful colossus of the business, political and financial world, she thought she at least owed him a graceful way out.

"You having "Blue" serviced, and washed for me?"

Momma asked in the saccharine tone specially reserved for wives admonishing husbands. Her husband nodded.

"Well would you ask whoever has it to bring it right over, Alex? I have things to do at St. Johns. Need to be there soon." Continuing in exaggerated sweet tones. "I'll go up and take a bath now, which should give you time to get "Old Blue" back here." This was the code of the long married, asking him nothing but telling him everything.

"Hey Charlie, twenty dollars to your lot boy," he whispered in the phone to the salesman who had just taken the car away, "if he gets that boat scrubbed cleaner than it's ever been, and back here in one hour. Tell him to make it shine too. He cast a furtive glance around him for Momma. "If it don't son, I'm in a world of hurt!"

"Boy, howdy damn Helen!" He blurted to the startled dog sitting watchful in the end of the boat. "'Bout ripped my britches on that one!" He chuckled remembering how he evaded the issue, giving the new car to one of his top executives, an act of generosity common to him.

Alex George was as tough a negotiator as there was in the world, some said the toughest. He held no man in awe, and widely acclaimed for his skills handling captains of industry, financial giants, heads of foreign governments. No one bested him in hard headed mediations. No one but Momma. She was the Boss where they lived, hands down going away, and the ferocious old oil tycoon would have it no other way.

Staring at her in the boat he thought of the tumultuous times they had, good and bad, rich and not so rich, and always their wild inventive love making when young. God how he'd tried to induce her to partake in sex with him only to be denied until their marriage. Then, after their marriage the confusion, wondering who the aggressor really was. To his absolute amazement and delight, she was the one with the insatiable appetite for lovemaking. Alex often times wondered if she might have invented sex. It was so unbelievably good with her, all the more beguiling because of her total lack of shame marked by a sensual, innocent abandon captivating him completely, all the while fervently trying to meet and satisfy her needs and wants.

'God damn what a life I've had with this woman.'

If there was anything to reincarnation, the old man knew who he'd spend his next lifetime looking for.

'Wonder why was I given so much, while others seem to have nothing but the toughest of tough luck?'

He had this woman who owned his heart. A massive financial empire. His health. So many things to be grateful for. He wondered if it was attitude, for his life with Momma had not been without profound sorrow and anguish. Survival would have been difficult some of those times had it not been for the steadying influence and deep spirituality of this strong woman.

Their daughter Mary was taken from them at the age of six, scarring him forever. Like most families consisting of parents, a boy and a girl, his favorite was Mary. Momma's was the near metaphysical attachment of mother for son, especially when the son is the first born.

Mary died in 1936 and it was the first time Alex George understood how little money and power meant, when it came to the basics.

His feeling of utter helplessness standing in the hall of the hospital while his beloved Mary lay dying, would remain with him forever. Alex had been a barroom brawler of great renown in his youth. A powerful man physically, fighting through the oil field boom towns, taking on all challengers. He knew only one response to anyone foolish enough to try him, and that was savage counterattack. That never changed, whether it was brawling in his younger days, or later in life in the business world. All aggressive comers withdrew from Alex George bloodied, knowing they had tangled with the best, in this man.

It was different though, so different, when the Catholic priest came into Mary's room that night, to administer the last rites of the Church. His helplessness in the face of death was too much to bear. Momma and he got through it somehow, mainly on the strength of her unshakeable faith, another brilliant facet of her character.

'Where in the name of God did that sweet simple South Louisiana country girl get strength like that?'

Could it have been in the genes from the Acadians who fought and died during their passage from Canada when the British dispossessed them in the 1700's? Maybe it was simply her beautiful faith and trust in a loving, caring God?

He was ravaged beyond caring unable to stand the anguish of Mary's death, raging even more at the thought of his beloved wife having to bear the same pain. He'd spent much of his life deluding himself his was the strength in this family. In truth it wasn't that way at all.

He escaped the pain of Mary's loss through a combination of drink, and terrible brawling characterized by savage brutality. Whether the situations were created by him or not was vague, but when his pain was beyond his ability to endure anymore he kissed Momma goodbye, and departed for the oil fields. Her prayers for his safe return always went with him. She knew him like the back of her hand, this lady, totally aware he was going to drink himself into oblivion and try to escape the inescapable, himself, and reality.

Drinking and whoring in the boomtown toilets that passed for saloons he waited like a wounded animal. His inner being screaming for any opportunity to vent his rage. He fought with total abandon for his own personal safety, and God have mercy on whatever fool stood up against him.

His was an unbelievably powerful body, short at five foot seven inches, immense at 220 pounds. Massive deep chest, broad shoulders, and heavy muscular arms. His friends teased him saying his forearms looked like Popeye's.

Built close to the ground as he was, Alex was like a bull when challenged and many found out, to their everlasting sorrow, he was absolutely the wrong man to meet in a fight. His low center of gravity and phenomenal strength, a result of wrestling pipe and chain on the decks of the drilling rigs of his youth, made him an awesome opponent indeed.

His actions of those darkest days, always left him mystified immediately afterward at his animal like rage. Many of his opponents in "the bad old days" were hospitalized, the last nearly dying as a result of the ferocious beating handed him by the violent, deranged creature he'd become. He came to his senses on that occasion, recognizing his attempt to purge his terrible anguish and anger at God, by devastating someone else. Momma was the great power on his road to recovery though, pulling him through his long, dark tunnel of despair.

'Jesus,' he thought, 'the mystery of woman.'

This one especially, who could still praise the goodness of God after such a stunning loss.

Alex could see Mary's gorgeous blond hair dancing in the sunlight many times, over the years. What a lovely illusion it was, since she would always remain a child in his mind, no matter how long he lived. It was a pleasant way to remember her.

Mary and her many pets, were a hauntingly beautiful memory but in particular the dog called Phideaux, her last and constant companion. He could watch them play together for hours, impressed most by their awareness of one another on a completely different plane from his. Their activities could be quite different, his daughter coloring in her book with great concentration while Phideaux was busy sniffing out every tree, bush and blade of grass. Somehow in tune with one another, they were conscious of what the other was doing without looking. The budding oil tycoon loved these interludes because of the near mystical quality he saw in their relationship.

Alex George was a rare exception to the usual rule most hugely successful businessmen of this world have in common. A strange indefinable separation from family, physical, mental and emotional. His love for family was well known, and he respected the same feeling in anyone else.

He wasn't always in the driver's seat while influencing things around him, and had to work and fight his way up from the poverty he was born to. Utilizing to the fullest his natural gifts received at birth, Alex George fought all the way up, ultimately achieving membership among the top ten wealthiest men in the United States.

He was born in 1900, to Gaston and Louise George, a typical South Louisiana Cajun family. They were what they were, which was dirt poor, never asking how it was fate put them in their position. Typical of their sturdy breed though, through great good humor they rose above the situation, living each day with joyous gusto.

Gaston, like all of his contemporaries, did many things to provide for his family, and was master of them all. Trapper, fisherman, hunter. He worked on the big plantations at harvest time for the two main crops, sugar cane and rice but no matter what the effort, there was money only for the barest, most immediate needs.

Alex was born at home, in country more or less equidistant from LaFayette on the north, New Iberia on the south and St. Martinville on the east. His favorite memories were those of his youth spent in the area.

"Gods chosen land," Gaston called it, "and who better to love it than us Cajun's."

The countryside lends much to the character of the land, its lush primitive beauty accentuated by wandering bayous. No current, almost without movement in the flat countryside, they just seem to be there.

Before the Gulf of Mexico, lies the vast marshland where Alex's father did most of his trapping. To the east stood the great swamps of the Atchafalaya Basin, a land of continuing fascination to Alex all the days of his life.

His memories were all good, thinking back on those youthful days even with, or perhaps because of, the knowledge that his family was quite poor. There were especially warm recollections of his father Gaston, a typical Cajun, weaving a tapestry of episodes most pleasant to him. His first chance to go with Gaston down the wildly exciting waterways leading into Vermillion Bay to join in the fishing, a mainstay in their lives, was among his earliest recollections. It was only after great efforts at persuasion, and his father was good at it, that they received his mother's approval, who was most reluctant at first to let her only child go out in the wild.

Excitement pounded in his small heart, when the nets went down for shrimp, because of the variety of marine life that came up, with the myriad of odors all fighting for dominance. Seagulls followed the boats so close he could almost touch them, marveling at their flying skill in pursuit of anything tossed their way, yet never colliding. Then there was the explosive action of hooking a barracuda while fishing for the succulent red snapper. This experience stuck with him in parable form, while negotiating with particularly difficult people later in his business life. Especially those from the Middle East with their unpredictable turns of temperament.

"Lead 'im." Gaston shouted over the noise of the gulf, after his young son hooked one. The boat bobbed on the surface, with cold spray blowing in his face but all he felt was pure excitement. "Let 'im run 'til he's done, Cher!" He ran to his son's side. "Oh God damn son ain't he beautiful, yeah? Give him enough line boy, to fly across the Gulf if he wants. If they can't go they'll run straight at you, down under the boat, and goodbye barracuda."

The big payoff was bringing home whatever they bagged, fish, fowl or animal. They'd turn it over to his mother to perform her extraordinary culinary magic, filling the tiny house with magnificent odors indicating serious South Louisiana cooking was going on. This simple woman could turn out a gourmet dish with practiced ease.

Alex recalled with warmth one particular meal Louise prepared when her hunters returned with a fat Canadian goose, after a day in the cold windswept marshes. They brought ravenous appetites too, a result of biting cold temperature, and energy expended wading through the marsh. Then the excitement and satisfaction over watching what they'd brought down turned into dinner on the table.

Youthful fascination ran high as Gaston made quick work of cleaning the fat goose, followed by his mother going through her mesmerizing cooking ritual. Alex wondered all his life how she regulated the heat in that wood burning stove, but regulate she did. Then followed the pleasant, near musical sounds of heavy iron cookware sliding about the surface as she labored for her loved ones. His heart soared, boy and man, remembering those exquisite odors tantalizing his sense of smell as they gently enveloped him. He tried valiantly to stay awake through the preparation, but it wasn't easy. He moved in and out of consciousness because of his exposure to the long cold day followed by the cozy warmth of her kitchen. Dining on the finished product was pure ecstasy, followed by deep sleep in his warm bed.

The next morning was cold and damp, the countryside clothed in a delicate mist, part ground fog, part smoke. Some of the smoke was created by the few houses about, but most came from the sugar cane refinery, adding yet another striking scent to an area teeming with rich odors too numerous to count.

Alex rode in the wagon with his father, oblivious to the swaying, bouncing ride, thinking only of the marvelous meal his mother had prepared the night before. Unable to contain himself anymore he asked Gaston in his native French.

"Papa, where did Mama learn to cook like she does?"

Gaston exploded with laughter. He loved to tease his son, always on the alert for any opportunity.

"Why? What's the matter son?" Gaston knew full well what he meant. "You don't like your Mama's cooking, no?"

Neither understanding Cajun humor, nor realizing he was being lovingly teased, Alex was quick to reply in his beautiful lilting French.

"No, no, Papa!"

It wouldn't do for his father to misunderstand and transmit this back to Louise, the creator of the gourmet feast the boy was trying so hard to praise.

"Mama surely must be the best cook in the whole wide world. I just wondered how she ever learned to do that?"

The boy hoped his admiring words would clarify what he was trying to say, also removing possible embarrassing implications about his mothers cooking.

Gaston George threw his right arm around Alex's shoulder catching him up in a great hug, crushing him against the rough fabric of his heavy coat.

"Son, son! All coonass girls are just naturally born knowing how to cook better than anyone in the world."

His booming laughter delighted Alex utterly, but the mood shifted instantly as Gaston dropped his voice to a low, mock confidential tone.

"Why my very own Mama could scrape a three day old cow turd off the road, and with a roux, onions, celery, tomatoes and spices that only she knew," his words were coming faster and faster, conveying tremendous excitement over the event, "would you believe Cher," hugging the boy to his side, "she could turn that cow turd into a feast fit for the President of the United States himself, yeah!"

Well, this was fabulous news indeed for his small mind and heart to handle. He was especially excited about his Grandmama being able to cook up a three day old cow turd. That was big news itself, but that the President of the United States would enjoy it too, simply overwhelmed him.

It was then the delighted boy asked his laughing father the long awaited question. He would never, all of his life, ever forget not only the answer he got, but the outrageous manner in which it was delivered.

"Papa?" The small Alex asked with great caution. "Papa, you say coonass? What's a coonass, Papa?" There was deep, serious thought involved here. "Am I one?"

Gaston had been waiting for this question for some time, and the time was exactly right for his two part reply. Feigning exaggerated seriousness he looked straight into his son's eyes.

"Oh son, I'm glad you asked me that question instead of some of these men around here. Most of them won't tell the truth for two reasons, because they're ignorant, and don't want you to know it." He looked around furtively lest they be heard, even though they were alone bumping through the huge field. "Others lie to be lying, and because you are a child think they can pull something over on you." He pulled his son closer to him to share in the private news. "Ah but you're the smart one, Cher! Coming to your Papa and that's good yeah, because you know I will tell you the truth for sure!"

Alex swore Gaston became larger as he continued.

"A coonass is...." a pretentious pause, "are you listening to me little Alex?"

"Yes sir!" Wide eyed.

Gaston took the reigns firmly, shifting his weight on the hard wooden seat. His face was grave, eyes staring intently.

"A coonass is...." the small boy thought his father was having a terrible time of it. Obviously it was of great importance. "Do you think you're ready boy?"

"Oh yes Papa!"

"I don't know son." Gaston murmured gravely. "It might be too much."

"No, no Papa." Eagerly. "I'm big now. I can take it!"

His father looked at him once again. "I don't...."

"Tell me Papa!" He shrilled. "I won't tell anyone! Tell me!"

"All right son." Grave concern. "But your Mama musn't know I told you."

"I promise Papa!"

He looked all around in a outrageously exaggerated manner, making sure no one in the empty field they were riding through was listening. The words came in a slow, deliberate manner.

"A-coonass-is-the-little-round-hole-you-find-when-you-lift-up-a coon's-tail!"

His voice rose sharply during the short statement, reaching a thunderous crescendo on the word, tail. Alex's father slapped his thigh roaring with laughter. He couldn't stop laughing, continuing harder and harder eventually falling from the wagon. He lay face down, spread eagle, laughing, sobbing, pounding on the ground, riveting this scene in the young boy's mind. It was to remain forever. Never, even in old age did Alex forget this spectacle, employing the experience many times over the years to his own purpose.

Gaston eventually regained his composure, after losing himself completely in the ridiculous hilarity of the moment. He climbed back up on the wagon seat, laughing, wiping away the tears generated clowning for his son. Finally, in an earnest manner he delivered the 'piece de resistance'.

"Actually Cher," he stared straight ahead stone faced, "a genuine coonass is a person who can look over a ten acre field of rice and tell you how much brown gravy it would take to cover it!" Alex observed an almost imperceptible flaring of his fathers nostrils, which led him to believe the truth was being violated.

Eventually he learned "coonass" was a vague term meaning Cajun, some of the most exciting and charming people in the world. Nobody seemed to know how the word originated but it was what this marvelous breed of people were nicknamed.

This man, like most Cajuns, worked hard and played hard. There was no better hunter, trapper or fisherman in South Louisiana, and when it came time for a "fait-do-do", dancing to wildly exciting string bands far into the night, he danced with the best, and drank everything in sight while doing it.

There were no baby sitters in those days for which Alex was forever grateful. He could attend these joyous gatherings with his parents, dancing with anyone available, imitating the adults in their uninhibited ways. Joy throbbed in his young heart when he danced with his mother because he thought she was the best human being in all the world, and being with her like this was as close to heaven as he could imagine.

Wild Cajun music, and dancing feet enhanced by the sound and feel the dancers created as they swung by on the wooden floors caused a syncopated impact in the pit of the boy's stomach. Most buildings were raised off the ground by blocks to keep them from the water of this flat semitropical country, thus creating an amplified reverberant sound.

And the rides home from those evenings with him lying in the back of the wagon, while Gaston and Louise rode on the bench behind the horse, hugging, kissing and feeling all the way home. He warmed thinking of his mother scolding, slapping Gaston's hands, turning aside all advances made by her earthy, inebriated romantic. Falling off to sleep upstairs, he heard the melodious laughter and raucous whispering of their love making. Curiosity over being their only child was considerable, aware as he was of their shared passion. He concluded something must have gone wrong with his mothers reproductive powers coincidental with, or some time after his birth.

All the marvelous Cajun traits of character were his, enhancing them with a personal intensity. A natural born hard worker, he gave all out effort, no matter what the task at hand. Gaston watched in amazement, at the pace the small boy set for himself, attacking the work with wild abandon no matter what the job. Unloading cane into giant presses, hitching horses to the wagon, or helping his father pull up the fishing nets, he did willingly and on the run.

The boy either walked or rode an old horse to the school in St. Martinville his mother attended, insisting Alex do also. She wanted him to have a strong Catholic background, knowing the nuns would give him a quality education second to none, and they did. The holy women did a good job providing him with a solid religious foundation. They demanded his best efforts, insisting he learn how to think for himself, habits that stayed with him all his life.

No one prepared him for the emotional shock of his father's accidental death at the sugar cane refinery, one October day during the cane harvest. Alex came home from school that afternoon to find a crowd of neighbors gathered at his house. He learned the details of his fathers death, beset immediately with the thought if only he'd been with Gaston that day something might have been different. His death might have been avoided somehow. It was his first exposure to death, and he had difficulty understanding how someone could be gone so quick.

"Say a prayer for me today, Cher!"

It was the last thing his father ever said to him, accompanied by his great laugh as they parted at the fork in the road, traveling on to their separate destinies. Gaston reached out catching his son up in a great bear hug, pressing his small face against the cold, rough wool coat. It was no different from most of their partings but Alex never forgot how the man smelled that morning. To this boy who loved, enjoyed and admired his father, it was the finest smell in the world. A rich mixture of tobacco, coal oil, smoke from the cooking vats of the refinery, and manly sweat. He thought it was beautiful then, and would think so forever.

The year was 1912 and his formal education stopped with the death of Gaston, much to his mother's sorrow. She had no choice but to give in to the harsh realities of the times though, and Alex set forth on his personal odyssey. He did all he could, following exactly in his father's footsteps providing for his mother with what was available to him. The cane harvest, rice fields, hunting, fishing and trapping. It was his turn now and he did exactly as Gaston had taught him, as all previous generations had been taught by their fathers.

Short of stature he developed into a powerfully built boy, acclaimed for his physical strength, and since most work was performed by the strength of ones back, employment was no trouble for this lad. His reputation as a worker without peers was already well established.

The next five years went by routinely until 1917 and America's entry into the war, a war talked of as if it were on some other planet. Soon more of Alex George's qualities of leadership were to become apparent.

His enlistment in the Marines was natural enough given his innate sense of adventure. Excitement and action were his hallmarks, all of his days.

The Marines were exciting stuff to this 17 year old boy and in his enthusiasm and natural salesmanship he convinced Louise to let him join.

His company consisted of men from many different parts of the country, and he found their speech fascinating. There was a cacophony of pronounced accents from the young boy-men, who had never heard anything other than their own dialect. His was the most pronounced of all, turning all the jokes about it aside with his infectious good natured laughter.

He hadn't been there but a short time when his attention was drawn to a group of four rough boys who seemed to take pleasure in pushing people around. Alex couldn't understand why they acted this way, but learned soon enough they were members of a New York City street gang.

Myron Cohen was from New York too, but a very different part. Almost nothing about him was like the others. His speech, clothing, manner of dress and hair, before it was shaved off, was different. It seemed something was wrong with his background too because that's what the trouble was all about. Alex had never heard the names the four toughs kept calling Myron. It started innocent enough the first night in camp, their leader jumping down from his bunk after lights out, asking in a loud voice.

"Any reason why we should have a Cohen in here?"

The barracks was silent except for the snickers of his cohorts. Alex noticed how the other three toughs followed their leaders example in every way. If he laughed, they laughed. If his humor became foul, so did theirs. They even smoked when he did. When the leader raised the question about Cohen his three man admiration society chimed in with busy choruses.

"Yeah, yeah! Cohen! How come we gotta have him? God damn Jew! Who needs him? Thought the Marines wanted men! How'd this chickenshit kike get in?"

Myron tried to ignore the insults staying away from the hostile four, but the barracks and training fields were simply not big enough to keep them separated for long. Their DI was no help either, a whiskey soaked corporal, 40 years of age, enjoying the bigotry and hostility shown Cohen.

The young Cajun noted with alarm that instead of them accommodating Cohen's presence, what started out light enough was obviously developing into an ugly situation. He didn't like it. The terms, yid, kike or sheeney didn't exist back home and he was somewhat surprised when Cohen told him they were slurs meant to hurt and insult.

Alex asked why they were so angry, and Myron replied there was no reason really except bigotry toward his Jewishness. Alex didn't want to display his ignorance, since he didn't know what bigotry meant, thinking it best to keep his mouth shut and drop the subject, but it was not to be.

Their hostility toward Myron, and belligerent attitude regarding the company as a whole was so obvious, Alex thought to befriend the Jewish boy, and restore peace to the company. Myron needed a friend, so his buddy became Pvt. Alex George, coincidentally beginning his first experience with real hostility and prejudice.

"Hey boys!" Alex hollered at the New York toughs who were badgering Myron especially hard. "Boys! How come you don't leave my friend Cohen alone, yeah? He's not doing anything to you?"

They turned like a pack of dogs diverted from an intended victim, although cautious, on the powerfully built boy from the bayous.

"What business is it of yours?" The leader of the group sneered. "What's the matter with you anyway, and how come you talk so dumb?" Strutting for his friends. "I never heard anyone talk like you. What's your name?"

"Alex! Alex George, yeah!" Alex replied smiling. "I'm from Louisiana swamp country. Why man, we hunt grizzly bears with switches, and catch barracuda with our bare hands down there, yeah! We got mosqeets big as sea gulls, and we all speak French. That's why I talk this way."

He was laughing in an abandoned way, which concerned the group of toughs. They knew he wasn't afraid of them, and they didn't know what to do about it.

"Why hell boys I thought you were the ones who talked funny! I never heard anyone sound like you before! Where you from?"

"New York, Frenchman! Biggest, toughest city in the world! Hells Kitchen! Mean place, and you're lookin' at the toughest four guys there! So don't give us any of your smart ass lip at all." They advanced a step on the short powerful lad from the swamps as they talked. "You hear what we're saying?"

"Yeah! Ok boys! I was only joking. I don't want to make you mad, no!" His smile suddenly disappeared. "But how you say...." He was groping for the word. "Oh yeah," his face darkened, "don't mess with my friend Cohen, no. If you do I'm goin' to get mad, and I'd a whole lot rather be your friend. You hear?"

The impending explosion was delayed by the DI calling them to fall in, and Alex pretended not to hear the threats hissed in his direction. The showdown was not long coming, and did so when they were least apt to be disturbed. After taps and lights out, everybody settled in for the night. Alex was curled up in his bunk drifting in the state that precedes sleep, when he was awakened suddenly by his friend Myron going to the head. He dozed, waking with a start, aware instinctively the toughs were also gone. Myron was in trouble! Alex jumped down from his bunk moving swiftly in the direction of the head, thinking Cohen might need help. He was right.

It was impossible to make out what was happening, due to poor light and the tightly knit group of bodies, but as his eyes adjusted it was apparent his friend was taking a severe beating. His anger became rage when he saw Myron curled on the floor warding off the blows. The pack continued beating him, oblivious to the newcomer.

"Hey boys!" Alex's voice boomed, startling the four. "I told you boys once, don't touch my friend, not even one more time! Didn't I tell you that?" The group stood stunned, more in shock at his audacity than anything. "Don't you remember? Didn't' I tell you if you hurt my friend, I'm gonna have to hurt you? I didn't want to do that!"

The pack turned from their fallen victim as one, facing Alex while Red screamed.

"Why you stupid son of a bitch! I'll beat the shit outta you personally." He lowered his head, screaming as he charged the squat Frenchman. "This's none of your God damn business!"

Red smashed into Alex's massive chest, bouncing against the wall, and the angry Cajun dropped to one side quickly, instinctively. Thrusting his right arm through the boys crotch area, he grabbed him across the shoulder and back with his left. Alex emitted a guttural, growling sound as he snatched Red off his feet. He swept him off the ground exactly like the hundred pound sacks of rice at the mill. The difference was he never grabbed or threw a sack of rice in anger, and he was angry now. Hurling him into his group of supporters he knocked two of them down, stunning them and their leader.

The last man ran for the door as Alex swung in a low crouch smashing him in the lower rib cage with a powerful blow causing him to rise on his toes and freeze in his tracks, paralyzed by the stunning pain of the blow. This was followed by another short, crushing punch flush on his cheekbone and temple area. He was unconscious before hitting the floor.

It was a tangled group of survivors trying to get up when they saw their fourth go down like a stone, looking into the eyes of this strange apparition from the swamps. Swinging around in a low crouch looking like nothing they had ever seen before, veins, muscles and tendons standing out from his neck Alex hissed.

"Get up now, boys. Get up. We're not through, no." His voice was low. Soft. "I told you and I told you, don't mess with my friend Myron and guess what? You didn't listen! Why? Why didn't you listen? Did you think I was fooling with you? Well I'm not fooling now. I'm mad! God damn mad! You hurt him! I'm gonna hurt you!"

The fight was over, the thugs gathered themselves up, running out into the night leaving Alex, Myron and the unconscious lad. Alex saw quickly that Myron was all right, suffering slight nicks, minor cuts and bruises. His concern now was for the unconscious boy, having never knocked anyone out before. The Frenchman turned his attention to reviving the victim, washing his face off, helping him back to his bunk.

The whole affair lasted but a few minutes, establishing Alex immediately, and irrevocably, as the undisputed leader of the company. He also earned the undying gratitude and friendship of the young Cohen who was to play such a gigantic role in the future of his new found friend.

The seventeen year old Cajun boys romantic dreams of war ended abruptly, while charging a German machine gun position hidden in the wheat fields of a place in France he'd never heard of. He was to learn for the second time in his young life, how quick death comes.

'Train with these boys. Eat, drink, laugh and fight with 'em.' He thought. 'Ride a boat, run into a wheat field together, watch 'em get cut to pieces by machine guns. Remember that DI saying, you people will learn to fight together or you'll die! And if you don't fight together, I guarantee you're dead.'

They believed it was a wild story the Marine Corps or their rummy DI invented.

'Wasn't kiddin', even a little bit.' Alex thought as he ran in a deep crouch through the wheat. 'Hard ass too, yeah! Tryin' to keep us alive and they're tryin' to kill us. Only way we can stop 'em, is kill 'em.'

Alex ran to the left and slightly behind the leader of the Hells Kitchen gang, experiencing the bizarre things that run through a mind at times like these. The raging sounds of war were all new to him. The discordant sounds of killing machines assaulted his ear drums, while they ran for their lives and country.

'There's old tough guy Red. Never did learn how to wrap leggings. Runs funny too.'

He remembered the exact shade of his red hair, as a burst of machine gun fire caught the boy full in the chest. The impact of the bullets jerked him violently off his feet. His rifle continued on a line, straight ahead.

Alex knew the lad was dead before he hit the ground, amazed how quick the transition from alive, young and strong, to instantly dead.

It was only a short distance further, twenty feet or so it seemed, he found Cohen lying in the wheat. Alex yelled at him.

"Get up Cohen! Come on and fight boy!"

He was angry for a split second because Myron looked as if he might be sleeping, his head cradled on his arm. The gaping hole behind his ear told him all there was to know. His brilliant young friend was dead.

Sobbing, in the state of stunned temporary insanity men reach in battle, he grabbed his rifle ever tighter running hard toward the German lines.

'You two boys ain't gonna' have any more trouble between you now, no.' Addressing the departed souls of Myron and the tough kid. 'Sorry it had to end this way but you know something,' laughing sardonically, 'I loved you boys! Yes I did. Even you, bad ass Red.' He ran harder, lower, machine gun bullets whining. 'Maybe you see my Papa up there?' Thinking 'Hey, tell him for me, will ya'? I loved him too. Can't remember if I ever did.'

The squat marine hit the German trenches like a man possessed, his fury coming from some unknown place. He fought hand to hand, vaguely aware of the animal like grunts he emitted, and the screams of those he killed. It was hard, hard manual labor murdering in the close confines of the trenches but the child warrior went about his work like what he was, an animal of a higher order temporarily deranged by grief, terror and rage.

Through the deaths of higher ranking noncoms and his natural gifts of leadership, "Frenchy George" rose swiftly to be the youngest master sergeant in the Marine Corps at the time of his discharge in early 1919. He became a marine's marine in the effort.

Alex was one of the lucky ones too, he survived. Luckier than many not to be affected in a negative way. He viewed it as the apocalyptic event in his life, and while at no time would the veteran ever forget it, neither would he allow it to bog down his thinking or future.

He returned in the spring, decidedly not the naive country boy who left only two short years before. Two brief years that seemed to him like an eternity. Neither was he the sophisticated man in the ways of the world he was destined to become. His arrival was accompanied by the usual confused emotions of most returning combat veterans. At once profound feelings of joy over being home, and vague disquiet because of the deeper emotion of guilt. Alex could not reconcile the fact he was alive, when so many of his buddies were gone forever.

"Damn, damn!" He commented many times. "How come it is I'm here alive, when so many of my boys are over there, dead. How many times was I right next to one of those boys, when all of a sudden they were dead. Some clean, a bullet in the head. Some in pieces, brains blown out...insides laying on the ground." His emotions were hard to handle, as he spoke through tightly clenched teeth. "Lousy war! Killed my boys. MY BOYS, and I'm standing right here talking about it."

He never forgot Myron Cohen nor the tough kid. Two lads with their stupid ancient differences, dying instantly, and together. It seemed remarkable to him they should enter eternity literally side by side. He wondered about differences there.

"Man, man, hot damn! Alive one minute and so dead the next! Makes you think a whole lot, yeah! How come them and not me?" Tilting his head in the Gallic fashion listening for a silent reply. "Not my time? Yeah, yeah but how come?" Adding thoughtfully. "How come it is Cohen dies and George don't? Then the tough guy goes with Myron, yeah! Buddies in death, if not in life. All these boys and men, they go to see their God and Alex don't!"

Tears filled his eyes, thinking about what they were going to miss.

'Ain't gonna have any welcome home parties with bands, people cheering and all that good shit, no! Lots of families won't be celebratin' their returning warriors. Yeah,

and the sweethearts who'll miss the parade my dead buddies won't be marching in
...." Then whispering. "And the babies? How 'bout the babies of these same dead lads
and their sweethearts, that don't get born? What about them? They don't get a chance
either? Other plans have to be made about their souls, huh?" He always ended these
thoughts with bitter emotion. "Yeah, well so what?"

The questions were ever present, but not the answers. The war and his dead
buddies with their nonexistent futures never left his mind. He thought about them
most of all, because of the guilt he suffered for having survived them. The jut jawed
marine swinging down off the train bringing him home, was indeed a much changed
person who stood looking at his beloved "coonassville".

"Jesus!"

He stood by the side of the train, all five of his senses absorbing the beauty of his
south Louisiana home, especially the incredible odors.

"Jesus! There's no place in this whole wide world so beautiful, or smells so good
as this place, right here!"

Alex refused the many offers for rides extended from passersby in their buggies,
wagons and new automobiles which were now appearing in ever increasing numbers.
They seemed to understand his desire just to look at his gorgeous LaFayette, all except
the one woman somewhere around his mothers age. She would haunt him forever.

As her buggy slowed to a stop, she got down gracefully, walking toward Alex. She
smiled a distant smile, and as she neared held out her arms to him, her beautiful dark
eyes shimmered through crystalline tears. Alex dropped his sea bag without a word,
taking her in his arms gently, very gently. He felt her tremble as she sobbed. Finally
she stepped back, her face glistening.

"Welcome home, Cher."

Holding him at arms length, looking deep in his eyes for the spirit of her own dead
son, she released him and returned silently to her husband sitting in the buggy, with
bowed head. She never looked back as they rode away but if she had would have seen
the rugged warrior standing ramrod straight, arm raised in salute, blinded by tears.
He knew without a word being spoken her son would never see the extraordinary
beauty of this place again.

It was beautiful walking down the road past the new St. Johns Cathedral. The
flowers were in full bloom. He paused to look at the massive oak tree standing in front
of the church, idly wondering if it had always been there. Alex continued his trek
home, past the city hall building. He wanted to look at it too.

His walk took him down through the center of town, and then south into the
countryside he loved so much, resplendent in its riot of colors, presented for his
review. A strange reflective state of mind possessed him, alternating between
intensified awareness of the extreme beauty of the area, and the loathsomeness of
the shattered, muddy European battlefields of his immediate past.

Sighting Louise long before she saw him, Alex lowered his bag on the dirt road
to watch while she hung the wash. There had been many times in the immediate past
he was sure he'd never see her again.

'Not like when Papa was alive.' He was hesitant, unsure, the moment charged with
intense emotion. 'Took two lines then...not much now.' He picked up his sea bag and
drifted closer to his mother.

Louise put her hand to her mouth in shocked disbelief, when her son walked around the corner of the house, dropping a freshly washed sheet to the ground.

"Alex! Alex!" She sobbed running toward her son.

"Hey Mama!" He answered holding out his arms, swallowing hard. "Hey Mama! Look, I'm home!"

It wasn't much of a greeting, but it was the best he could do at the time. He swept her off her feet in a crushing embrace, both crying openly. After kissing her only child many times Louise stood back to look at him. Yes, she thought, the boy she once knew, was no more. He had been replaced with something quite different.

She went about doing what all good mothers do if they're the lucky ones whose sons return, trying to feed him gently, lovingly, to the bursting point. One after another of his favorite dishes were prepared along with new ones she had only heard about, her extraordinary culinary skills heightened by the occasion. Alex laughed as he watched her, envisioning wheels going around in her head as she tried to think up another dish to surpass the last one.

"Hey Mama!"

Alex protested feebly after a huge meal of chicken sauce piquant, hot fresh baked French bread and sumptuous desert. His father's words recalled, that coonass cooking was good enough for the President of the United States, or any man who'd ever lived.

"Mama! Stop! Please! I'm gonna bust! I'm not used to eating like this."

"Hush Cher," Louise laughed, "look at you son, nothing but skin and bones. Well I'm going to put some meat on those bones before the next hurricane comes. One big wind," puffing out her cheeks to demonstrate, "and my beautiful Alex is gone again.

Even though she was only teasing, her eyes filled with tears instantly at the words, "gone again".

Alex wasn't home long before deciding it was time to get on with his life, involving changes in direction and expectations of a much broader scope than before. This was a concern to his mother who had been accustomed to the lives of her grandfather, father and husband. They had been sufficient making it difficult for her to understand why Alex would want, or need, to change anything. She listened attentively to him though while they sat talking in the kitchen after meals.

"Oh, Mama!" His eyes danced with excitement. "You should see the places I've been! New York City! It's somethin', bigger even than New Orleans, with the same mix of people. My friend Myron said most of the people from Europe landed in those two cities and lots of 'em stayed." His heart warmed remembering his friend's words. "He said that's why people living in New York City sound like those in New Orleans."

His mother was wide eyed at his tales of travel, having never left the immediate area, not even to see New Orleans. She loved his descriptions of the many European cities he'd visited, especially Paris. That city held a mystique among the Cajun's of Louisiana, and she'd heard many stories, obviously generations old, of its splendor.

She laughed when Alex told her of his experiences as an interpreter, pressed into service because he was a Frenchman from South Louisiana, speaking the language since birth.

"Oh hey Mama!" Laughing. "I couldn't understand those people hardly at all, no!"

"Why Cher?" Her face a question mark. "We speak French! Why not?"

"'couldn't figure that out Mama, 'til I was told us coonass's," they laughed, "talk different from pure French." Returning to his dead friend. "Myron said when the British threw us Cajuns out of Canada, we started drifting and traveling all down the east coast 'til we got here, picking up different words and phrases on the way."

Her son the marine was an amazing source of information. Louise was proud of him indeed.

"So it was real different when it came out the end of the pipe down here. I could understand 'em Mama, but I had to redo their sentences to do it."

Louise was receiving an education of sorts through the experience and travels of her only child. Using the sixth sense mothers have, she refrained from asking him about what happened on the battlefields of Europe. She knew one thing for sure, her handsome, fun loving, hard working boy full of "joie de vivre", had been changed forever in two years away from home. This was brought home vividly one day shortly after his return. He'd gone hunting, returning sooner than normal, empty handed.

"What happened, my soldier son." Louise laughed. "You forgot how to hunt, no?"

Her comment was made in pure innocence, so she was totally unprepared for his stunning answer, drifting from the recesses of his mind.

"No Mama." He spoke softly, crushing his hat in powerful hands. "It's just that I'm so damn tired of the killin'...you know what I mean? Always, always in the presence of death. It was ugly and it stunk Mama. It stunk real bad." Her sons beautiful dark eyes took on a horrifying, deadly look.

His soft tone turned to a whisper and Louise knew instinctively he wasn't speaking to her at all. She was listening to his mind.

"You know, I've been with some of the best, yeah. Good boys like me, and some of those old boys simply went out and died," snapping his fingers, "just like that."

Louise didn't like the soft laugh, followed by the most stunning thing she had ever heard, and never, ever, wanted to hear again.

"They killed us and we killed them." The distance grew as he drifted further back. "Oh yeah, and I had to get 'em too, those Germans who destroyed my friends. Yeah, yeah, shot 'em, stabbed 'em, ran bayonets through 'em."

His mother's mind reeled in horror.

"Strangled 'em with these two hands."

His voice could barely be heard, as he stared down at his only weapons left from the time of the slaughter.

"The best those Germans had, I killed." Still drifting. "And killed, and killed some more. I am a killer Mama, and I'm so sick of it, I can't do it anymore. I won't do it anymore! I saw those animals in my sights and I couldn't pull the trigger. Didn't wanta' kill 'em. Don't wanta' kill nothin' anymore Mamma."

Her son appeared to be losing control and Louise anguished over ever starting this. She was unaware in her compassion it was the best possible thing he could do to purge his mind and soul of his actions. Actions done at the behest of his government. He was at the point that needed to be reached, a total release of all the pent up emotion to help him quickly on the road to recovery. His mother's soul ached with compassion for the son she adored, and her heart was filled with profound gratitude God had allowed him to live.

It was to be the only time she would ever be allowed to see that far into her son's soul, and the following morning an entirely different Alex appeared for breakfast. Her heart soared at the welcome sight.

"Hey Mama!"

Yes, this was the old Alex. No mistaking that.

"Mama, make me a big breakfast, will you? One with all the good things you know how to make?"

Her heart raced with joy as he swept her off the floor hugging her. She'd cried herself to sleep because of her soldier son's anguish of the previous evening, but her joy was short lived as plans for his future tumbled out. Drinking his coffee, dark like tar, filling the tiny house with a beautiful aroma, he went on excitedly.

"Mama, how many times I told you of my good friend Myron Cohen?"

"Many, Cher." She acknowledged quickly, nodding, afraid of opening more wounds.

"We became real good friends after I kept him from gettin' hurt one night, and used to talk a whole lot. He was the smartest fella I ever did meet."

She was relieved his conversation seemed to be free of pain, listening attentively as he continued, blowing on his coffee.

"Loved to listen to him talk. Why do you know he even went to college! Must have studied everything there was including us Cajuns. Well anyway, we sat around and talked every chance we got, which was all the time on the boat going to France. We talked about a lot of stuff but it always came around to what we were going to do after the war. You know what he told me?"

Louise's heart fairly sang, Alex was so alive and enthusiastic.

"No, no Cher. What?"

"He told me," the words couldn't come fast enough, "the future of the whole world was going to be in oil and gas, and whoever finds it's going to be some kind of rich, yeah." Indicating without either of them knowing, what his course was to be for the rest of his life. "Myron told me to come home and get in the oil business because there was lots of it down here." His eyes clouded, adding. "Said he'd be here soon's the war was over to get in...how'd he say...on the ground floor?"

The news wasn't received cheerfully, but it was okay. Her boy was home now. Nobody was trying to kill him here.

"Where do you find these oils Cher?" She asked with concern, knowing there wasn't any around these parts.

His forehead wrinkled. "He said north, up north, around Shreveport."

Her heart sank, tears appearing in her eyes over the possibility of seeing her son trudge off in the distance after just getting him back. She was sad over the prospect, but her sadness was tempered by his enthusiasm. She listened in wide eyed attention.

"Use big...umm, derricks he called 'em. Said they put 'em over the ground." She watched him grapple with his memory. "Drill far down in the ground to get the oil...." Trying to remember Myron's words, they seemed so hard to believe. "Said it's been down there millions of years!" The thought obviously impressed him. "I wish Myron had made it home Mama." There was no bitterness in his voice. "You know, show me what to do. Where to do it. Why a dumb coonass like me don't even know where to start."

"Don't say that Alex! You're not dumb, no. It wasn't your fault you couldn't finish school when your Papa died!"

Her temper flared somewhat as she rushed to his defense. She whipped the pancake batter furiously, taking her anger out on the ingredients.

"No, no Baby, the good nuns at St. Martin's said you were one of the brightest boys they ever had." Beaming at the words of praise from the holy women. "They said you were good at everything, quick to learn. Why they said you were smart enough to be anything you want to be, and I think so too!" Her words dared anyone, including her much loved son, to disagree.

"Myron said the same thing and I liked to hear it, him going to college and all. I didn't know what he meant though, so I asked him one day, hey Cohen, how come you think I'm so smart when I only go to school 'til I'm twelve years old?"

"So? What'd he say?" Louise wanted to know.

"He said the amount of time you spend in school ain't important, it's what you learn from life. He said he knew I would learn a lot." Alex grinned from ear to ear, his New York friend obviously held in the highest esteem. "You know why Mama?"

She was most attentive, sliding his breakfast from pans to dishes.

"No, why Cher?"

Alex laughed harder and harder, his broad handsome face bulging with the good things she had prepared. He could see his father acting the fool, rolling off the wagon, stretched out pounding the ground in response to his innocent question of many years ago. "Papa, what's a coonass?"

His eyes filled with tears created by his sudden wild abandoned behavior.

"Because, Myron said I asked so many questions." He nearly lost control, laughing. "Hell Mama all Cajuns ask questions, it's in our blood Cher! Why only the other day I heard two guys talking about it in town...." He started laughing again, happy, noisy. "One of 'em says this guy sees his coonass friend pulling a chain behind him and even though it's drivin' him crazy wonderin' why says to himself, 'I will not ask that son of a bitch anything! Nothing at all. That's why he's pullin' the chain! He wants me to ask him why so he can give me some kind of a smart answer.'

But the guy keeps on walking by his house, day after day draggin' the same damn chain. Finally he can't stand it any more so he breaks down and says.

'Hey Alcide, how come it is you keep pulling that damn chain there, son?'

Alex was hysterical, laughing so hard the tears ran down his cheeks.

"You know what Alcide says Mama...."

She was leaning against the counter, doubled over because of his infectious laughter.

"Alcide says, hey! What the hell you want me to do son, push it?"

His face turned beet red from laughter, as he tipped his chair back, roaring like some hidden damn had burst, and indeed it had, until he fell flat on his back still seated, staring at the ceiling.

Mother and son were delirious in their wild, abandoned laughter.

CHAPTER 2

Louise didn't object too much upon learning of Alex's determination to go north and "find the oils". Her gratitude was such given his survival of the great war, that she felt the least she could do as an expression of her thanksgiving was to let him go. Shreveport's location remained a mystery to her even after looking at a map, but his continued presence in the state of Louisiana was truly consoling.

"Hey Mama! I know I'm gonna' do real good in that oil business, yeah!" Alex was leaving for Shreveport. "I know I am, and when I do I'm going to buy you a fine house one day. One with a bathroom inside! I'll be sending you money right along too, so don't worry about a thing."

Louise wasn't at all sure about that but it sounded good.

Boarding a train at the LaFayette station the young veteran embarked on a trip that would defy predictability, and a future few men experience. Riding north through the center of the state he watched the land change dramatically in a short distance. Changing from his lush semitropical French country filled with massive oak trees, festooned with their graceful trappings of Spanish moss, interlaced by rivers and bayous enhanced by the many shades of green Alex found so fascinating.

The red dirt of central Louisiana was different too, and interesting. It was his first exposure to this country. He remained glued to the window, mesmerized, as the thick pine forests rolled into view. The smell was sensational. Even though he was a battle hardened veteran his heart was full of excitement and enthusiasm at this time, just thinking about what life had in store.

The forests turned darker and darker, as night fell, disappearing finally from view, replaced by visions of his future. Drowsiness became fantasies and then gave way to dreams, lulled to sleep by long mournful whistles coming from the engine. Awakened by the lurching of the train as it pulled into Shreveport, Alex was pleased to remember his friend Myron had been in his dream.

'Hey Myron, don't know whether you can hear me or not son, but I'm going to pretend you do. If you do know what's goin' on, my friend, I'd appreciate your help. I don't have any idea what I'm doin', or where to start.'

It didn't seem unusual to Alex, talking to a dead person this way. He was to carry on conversations with his friend Myron all the rest of his life, referring to him as "my silent partner."

Alex entered the oil business like everything he did, with boundless energy and enthusiasm, starting the morning after his arrival in Shreveport. Directed to a supplier of oil field equipment, he appeared at the gate before sun up, waiting impatiently for someone to open up. He was in a hurry to learn the business. Impatience reigned supreme, and the chance there might not be a job available, simply did not exist for this eternal optimist.

The yard boss arrived first, mildly curious at what the short, powerful young man was doing at the front gate so early in the morning. Alex greeted him with an enormous smile, asking in his broad French accent.

"Hey boss! My name's Alex George! I'm from down south, LaFayette. I want to be in the oil business, yeah! Got off the train last night, asked where's a man go to get a job?"

The yard boss stared at him in wide eyed wonder.

'Where the hell'd this one come from?' He thought. 'Talks funny too.'

The short, bull like youth smiling all through the conversation, reached out his hand taking the boss's in his crushing grip, pumping it vigorously, continuing.

"This guy said nothing happens in the oil...." An obvious question forming in his head. "What'd he say...patch?"

The boss shook his head in affirmation.

"Don't know patch, but anyway until you boys," the still silent boss was astonished by his aspiring employee unable to take offense at being called "you boys," "until you boys sent 'em the stuff to get those oils out of the ground and you know what? My friend Myron," not pausing to identify his dead friend, "told me the very same thing." Laughing, he held the mans hand while grabbing him by the forearm with his equally powerful left hand. "So by God boss, here I am! I'm ready to go!"

It finally occurred to him the man might not have any work, he hadn't said a word, but Alex reckoned without his yet unknown powers of persuasion. As luck would have it, or maybe intervention of a higher order, a yard man had quit only the day before, thus creating a spot for entry into the field of his choice. He thought about this, moving on from one stroke of good fortune to another, marveling at the random ways a life seems to unfold.

'What if that guy in Shreveport hadn't quit? Who was he? What happened to him? How come he quits the day I'm riding north?'

His excursions into "what if," usually wound up with a laugh, head cocked, and the question spoken aloud.

"You have anything to do with this Myron?"

His approach to the new job that first morning was more assault than anything else. He literally ran from one task to another, like in the old days helping Gaston as a boy, to the wide eyed amazement of his bosses and fellow workers. It was even suggested he slow down a bit. No one was expected to work that hard, and besides it was making the rest of them look bad.

"No, no, Cher!" He replied, still using the idiom of his native French. "I don't want to make anyone look bad no, but you know what?" Not waiting for a reply. "My God man, I'm just real glad to be alive yeah, and have a good job like this too. I want to do it all! You understand what I'm saying?"

None among them ever understood what drove Alex but they were aware of his bull like strength and were more than reluctant to bring it to his attention. Even the most vocal detractors were won over by his joyous approach to the back breaking manual labor, making games of the difficult jobs. Handling forty foot lengths of pipe, a mind numbing job, became sport when Alex showed them techniques handling the heavy pipe based on teamwork, joy, and rhythm.

Singing his wild Cajun tunes, to the utter delight of workers, bosses and owners, the men were driven by his infectious tempos. Their all time favorite moment was when Alex became overwhelmed by his music, dancing, pirouetting with wild abandon between the long rows of pipes. Because of his short stature the crotch of his bulky coveralls hit him at knee level, adding to his comic look, but he was much too happy and uninhibited to care.

They called him "Crazy Frenchman", but saw immediately he wasn't the ass kisser they might have taken him for. All of them soon fell under the spell of his "joie de vivre." His place in the yard assured, these sober North Louisianians learned quickly the ways and attitudes of their exuberant fellows from the southern part of the state.

Management was impressed instantly, and they especially liked his driving spirit, anxious to reward him for his efforts. The only promotion possible though would be the job of the man who opened the gate for him the first morning, the yard boss. Alex did not want that to happen however, and was forced to take the next step of his long journey.

"Hey boss!" He hailed the worried man. "I appreciate you letting me work here yeah, but do you know what my friend? It's time to move on." A look of relief crossed the man's face at the news. "I could sure use your help which should be a lot, 'cause you seem to know everybody in the business." A natural at persuasion even then. "You hear somebody needs a man on one of the rigs, I'd sure like to go."

This was good and bad news to the yard boss who was genuinely fond of this exciting man from the swamps. After all not only was an excellent worker about to be lost, but a forceful influence on the rest of the men, leading them to heights of effort never before approached in this yard. However the nagging pressure of Alex's aggressive spirit would not be denied.

"You know my friend Myron told me to get up here and learn.... Let's see now, what he said.... Oh yeah! Facet! Every facet of this business." Alex laughingly added. "And you know what? I know how to stack, load and unload pipe, right now, about as good as I'm ever gonna'. I need to get out to the fields now, and see what happens next." His eyes lit up in a joyous vision, continuing. "Why hot damn man, I want to be there when one of those suckers, how you call it, comes in!"

Alex joined one of the drilling outfits they supplied, with a strong recommendation from the yard boss. When told there was a job waiting for him as a roughneck his now relieved boss was delighted one last time by the Cajun as he said.

"Oh hey, Boss. I like to have fun and maybe get carried away a little bit, but I'm no roughneck, no!"

Alex moved to the oil fields learning "roughneck" was a job description, not an indication of behavior, although for many of them it wasn't far off. Everyone on the rig was surprised at how the greenhorn adapted to the work but none more than his new boss, the driller. This was an older, tough, no nonsense oil man who'd been around a long time and had seen a lot of men come and go. He was also very fair, like so many of this type.

"Listen kid, I'm taking you on as a favor to your old boss, a damn good friend of mine." Squinting over his cigar clamped in the middle of his teeth, aimed directly at Alex. "Ain't no grab ass around here, when we drop that pipe we go from can to can't, and we expect...." pausing, then emphasizing, "expect shit! We demand every man works on this rig puts out 100 per cent. Understand?"

"Yeah, yeah! My boss said this was no picnic out here, everybody goes hard or the rig slows down." Checking the drillers reaction while speaking. "Said nothing better slow, or stop the work, 'cause it costs too damn much money to have one of these suckers shut down. Right?"

"You got the idea kid!"

"Said the work goes as fast as the slowest man on the rig." A big grin on his face. "How'm I doin', Boss?"

The driller started to feel better, as he became aware this wasn't some dumb kid who was all brawn and no brains. Most men he took on as a favor to someone, were usually gone in short order because they couldn't stand the physical demands of the work.

"You're damn right kid! You got the story." The driller was pleased because this enthusiastic young man seemed so different from the usual oil field drifter. "I'm gonna tell you this only one time boy." The hard eyed old timer said. "You gotta be fast on your feet around here because we don't stop movin' 'til we hit oil, or run out of pipe. Heavy iron's always movin' 'round. Watch what you're doin' all the time!" Warming to the task of trying to scare the shit out of the newcomer, unaware of his recent marine corps experience, the veteran oil man drawled slowly so the boy wouldn't forget. "They's only two kinds of people around these rigs kid. The quick and the dead."

"Got'cha Boss." Alex replied, smiling. "Just left a place like that. There were lots of both."

What the man said was exactly right, and over the years Alex was to see many a man killed as the result of these very things. Accidents caused by slippery footing while pulling many feet of pipe out of the hole, chains loose, whipping about the rig, all contributing to the hazardous work. However as bad as it could get, it didn't escape him that at no time was anybody intentionally trying to kill him. The odds of staying alive in the "oil patch" were at the very least considerably better than the blood soaked wheat fields of France.

"Okay boss," the broad smile flashed, a special endowment never to desert him, "you better tell those old boys up there," nodding toward the platform and derrick man standing high in the top of the rig, "that Frenchy George, from the swamps of Louisiana is here, and I'm some kinda fast! Real fast! Why man I been outrunnin' them bayou alligators since I was a puppy, to keep those sons of bitches from tearin' me clean up. German bullets couldn't find my Cajun ass either and they were tryin' real hard so you better believe I know how to move!" Grabbing the rail, swinging up on the platform, his enthusiasm brought smiling confidence. "What I don't want, is any of those old boys up there on the rig slowin' me down," slapping himself on the chest, "'cause while I don't know what it is you do here, I am gonna find out pretty quick, yeah! Shit Boss, I'm gonna' be the best man you got out here, you know that? And do you know why? 'Cause I want to, that's why! I don't know how much time

I got Chief, but I ain't got none to waste! So how 'bout it? Show me what to do, and let's roll."

Always good to his word, Alex assaulted the job with gusto, heightened the more because while the yard was a place to break in, opportunities there were extremely limited. Looking at the rig for the first time the novice could see at least three different jobs and obviously income too. It was a whole different work story on the rigs too. Constant action kept his interest honed to a fine edge, and though previously warned of the work tempo he wasn't slightly prepared for the coordinated effort called for from every man on the job. Every move by each man, was directly influenced by whatever action took place immediately before. The rig operated with the fine precision of a ballet troupe. His Marine Corps experience recently behind him, Alex understood thoroughly the meaning of, and the necessity for, men working together with a single purpose.

Stacks of pipe were familiar enough, he'd been on the other end of the supply line that got them here. From that point on though, everything was new. He was fascinated with the operation of the rig and its monstrous equipment, and with his natural intelligence and desire to pursue his education, nothing could stop him.

The driller was right, it was truly a case of every man not only doing his own share but also contributing to each other's effort. Alex's statement to the driller was correct too, the rest of the men were hard pressed, as promised, to keep pace with him. He was also amazed at the teamwork necessary to make it operate as it should. The coordination between roughnecks, derrick man, and driller inspired him. Simply being part of this was heady stuff.

"Those rigs are really somethin', Mama!" Expounding to his wide eyed mother on a visit home. "Some wood, some steel! Why they stand as high as a fifteen story building!"

This was impressive news to Louise, who had no idea how tall a fifteen story building was. She'd never seen one. She thought it must be at least as tall as the steeple on the new St. Johns church in LaFayette though.

"What do these...what you say...derricks...look like Cher?" She asked, her eyes shining. She wanted to share in these exciting new things, swept along by the fervor with which he told his stories.

"They're tall Mama! Real tall! Big across the bottom, down on the deck where I work, and get smaller as they go up. Makes 'em strong to hold the pipe." He searched for something to describe, so Louise could understand, suddenly his eyes lit up. "I know Mama. They look like a big windmill with no blades! Damn! I'll tell you somethin's happenin' all the time. Pipe comin' up, pipe goin' down. Me and this other old boy workin' fast as we can, slapping this big iron collar around the joints, screwing or unscrewing those suckers, changing bits. Boy hot damn they're something, and all this going on over the roar of the engines, rig floor shaking like crazy. Everybody's working hard, and that driller? Man damn, you should see that one! He's the main man, makes everything go. You know how much everybody thinks about Justin Arceneaux? How good he plays?" The best fiddler in the area, highly revered for his music. "Justin can't play his fiddle half so fine as my driller plays that rig. Why he sends that pipe humming up inside the derrick, slams on the brakes and shuts it down with the next joint bobbin' right there in front of me and my partner. We clamp that

sucker Mama! Lock it up, and unscrew 120 feet of pipe at a time. Then the man in
the derrick, way up close to the top, stacks it. That's somethin' to see too. Grabs the
pipe with a big hook and walks it around up there...you know stackin' it, and we keep
doing that 'til we've got it all up."

Louise tried to stay with her sons rapid fire conversation. She enjoyed these
moments, sharing what was happening in his life.

"What's really something though, is watching that driller work all them levers,
listening to every noise the rig makes. Engine's roarin', bolts strainin', wood creakin',
chains rattlin'." He slammed his massive fist into his palm. "Hot damn, ain't that
somethin'! All that racket and he don't miss nothin'! I love to watch him sitting there,
head cocked over to one side, eyeballin' the hole while the pipe goes up or down."

His conversation incorporated a tone of amazement as his story continued.

"He knows what's going on down there too, clean down at the bottom of that hole!
Knows what we're in, soft stuff like mud, or hard like granite. We really earn our
money when we hit that rock. Why I've seen those bits go down, drill just a tad, and
have to pull a couple thousand feet of pipe to change the bit. Couldn't believe it at
first, but that's how hard some of that rock is. I watch him watch that hole, while the
rig's jumpin'! Damn Mama, it's exciting, yeah! I love it!"

Louise missed the boy that she, Gaston and God produced, but was also happy
he loved his work.

Alex learned his trade quickly, seeking help along the way from the other men.
Most were proud to show this intense young man all they knew. His persistent quest
for knowledge was such that all who knew him, succumbed to the charismatic spell
of this man of the bayous and none would ignore his questions. He worked diligently,
mastering whatever the job at hand, moving swiftly to the next.

The men lived on the rig sites in the early days before good roads, sleeping and
eating in a metal hut called the shed. Myron Cohen had insisted his education should,
and could, be continued by reading, and he did exactly that. He arrived at the rig sites
with the customary gear, plus a box full of books. Questioned about this, Alex told
them they were for his education. Besides, he enjoyed reading because he had so much
to learn. While there was lots of good natured kidding about his books, discretion was
always observed because of his unbelievable strength, and his ability to turn them aside
with outrageous humor.

The oil business was booming and Alex went where the work was, mostly in the
triangle created by the borders of Louisiana, Texas and Oklahoma. It didn't take him
long to learn each job on the rigs, advancing rapidly from grunt, to roughneck, to
derrick man, and on to driller. That was as far as most oil field workers ambitions
would take them. His income was always excellent and true to his word built Louise
some of what he'd promised. She wouldn't move from the house that had been hers
since marrying Gaston, but she did let him build the indoor toilet.

His reputation as driller was overshadowed only by renown as the premier barroom
brawler in the oil patch. Like most reputations it started quite by accident, immediately
and convincingly established by the violent, lightning like manner in which it happened.

Alex was sitting with his crew in a large, rough, wooden building that passed for
a saloon, relaxing after a hard week. They were involved in small talk when suddenly
a big drunken oil field worker shouted at him from across the floor.

"Hey short boy!" Staring intently at Alex leaving no doubt who he meant.

"You mean me?" Alex replied, smiling.

"Yeah you! You the guy they call Frenchy the coonass driller from Louisiana?" Followed by a raucous laugh, glancing around the room to see how his audience was reacting. "Or could that be, dumbass driller?"

Having experienced many dangerous situations already in his young life, Alex recognized this as a bad one. He answered smiling.

"Hey yeah partner! Oh yeah you bet! Name's Alex George from LaFayette, Louisiana." He turned in his chair still smiling." How 'bout you friend, what might your name be?"

"Well I'll tell you somethin' right now dumbass," followed by more mean laughter, "my name is none of your God damn business! And I'll tell you somethin' else, you sure as shit ain't no friend of mine!"

The big man rose from his chair, heading toward their table as Alex moved smoothly out of his, standing clear of everything. He held out his hand to shake that of this new found enemy, asking.

"Let me buy you a drink? Sit here with me!" Pointing toward his now empty chair. "Who knows, we might become friends?"

The man swept Alex's outstretched hand away, growling.

"Fuck you dumb ass. I don't want your drink or your silly coonass shit!" Leering for the crowd. "What I do want though is some of your smart ass, right here and now."

"Whoah now Cher." Laughing, his mind raced ahead to the hazards confronting him. "I don't know what made you mad at me no! I don't even know who you are, but I do know I'm not mad at anybody. Why don't you let me buy you that drink. How 'bout it? Maybe we can talk over the problem."

His men started to come out of their chairs as the big man advanced. Alex motioned them back with a wave of his hand, making a mental note where everything in the room was, furniture and people.

"What you might have done?" Playing to the bar, rather than Alex. "Did you say what you might have done, you stupid fucker? I'll tell you what you might have done! You might have knocked me, or some of these other boys who've been in the oil patch a helluva lot longer than you, out of a shot at that drillers job, that's what!"

'So,' Alex thought, 'that's it. Money.' It was to be the first of many fights in his life for the same reason, money, although most future rivals would be far more dangerous than this dolt.

"Me and a lot of these boys," suggesting with a broad wave of his hand the entire room, "have been humping it long before you crawled out of your hole!" The tough was losing control, seething, staring down at the short Frenchman. "I deserve that job a lot more'n some stupid swamp rat!"

He was screaming, clenching his fists.

"Well now wait a minute pardner, don't blame me for that. I'm just a hard working boy too, and the bosses know I can get the job done. That's all! I didn't mean to take anything away from anybody. I hope you get the very next one of them driller jobs that comes open, wherever it is."

Alex moved slowly between the tables as he spoke, consigning every man, every piece of furniture to memory. He moved with fluid like motion. One witness said he thought of smoke, watching the strange transformation taking place before his eyes, in the usually light hearted Cajun.

Everyone in the saloon knew this was going to end in violence. None had any idea to what degree.

"I don't like you Frenchman, and I'm sendin' you back in a sack to whatever swamp whore gave you birth." He screamed turning a dark color, lunging at Alex and swinging his right fist in a great sweeping roundhouse.

No one in the room had ever witnessed such an awesome explosion of rage from anyone, much less this otherwise fun loving man. The man called him the son of a whore. He called Louise George a whore.

Alex easily stepped aside from the initial rush ducking under the first and last punch thrown by the vicious tough. He swung around gracefully, but with awesome intensity, striding into the drunk hooking his massive right arm, rigid as a piece of curved steel. His broad fist smashed his antagonists lower ribs with incredible power.

The big man's eyes bulged in agony from the impact of the tremendous blow, as his ribs snapped with sickening sound. He hung momentarily, stunned disbelief etched on his face as Alex followed with an equally powerful blow flush on the bottom of his jaw, shattered teeth flying after the impact. As the troublemaker fell to the floor Alex drove his knee into his face, smashing his nose, whipping the back of his head viciously into an empty chair. It was over in seconds, utterly savage in its brevity. His man lay unconscious on the floor, bleeding from nose and mouth.

They could hear Alex's labored breathing, the only thing heard in the split second after the annihilation. He was out of control with rage, speaking in a tone barely heard.

"No man calls my Mama a whore! No man!" Staring down at the unconscious form that had just been his attacker. He shook his head as if the conversation was only in his mind. "I'll kill any one who does! Nobody does that! Not my Mama! Nobody does that!"

Alex looked up from his devastated victim, as he swept a heavy chair off the floor, smashing it across a nearby table with terrifying sound. Cords in his neck bulged to the bursting point, his black curly hair hung over crazed eyes.

"Anybody else!" He screamed at the stunned faces. "Anybody want some of Alex George, come on!" No one dared look directly at him. "Get off your ass, now! Help yourself!"

There were no takers that night, only tense silence.

News spread quickly, as it does in all fields of work involving heavy manual labor and the men who do it. His fame as a brawler was instantly established that night, when details became known of the ferocity and swiftness with which Alex demolished his opponent, a man of considerable reputation. As a result he was forced to fight many times in the future for no reason, usually by someone with a sense of power, wanting only to say they'd whipped Frenchy George. Failing in attempts to talk the glory seekers out of their folly, Alex gave them the beating of their lives, and while not coming through this period in his life unscathed, he was never beaten.

CHAPTER 3

After bringing in a well in East Texas in 1923, Alex took time off before starting his next job. He returned home to visit Louise, and met the girl who was to become, and endure, as his beloved "Momma." So many times over the years he thought about their chance meeting, forever grateful for the way fate had controlled his life.

Louise asked him to drive her into St. Martinville so she could shop and show off her successful son, and his new automobile. Alex sat smiling in his new Model T, not unaware of the admiring stares from the males, young and old, when she appeared for the very first time. His attention was drawn immediately to her walk. It was different, a spring in each step, much the way many athletes move. After analyzing her unusual gait the young driller let his eyes drift over the lovely figure responsible for it.

The girl was blond, most unusual for this country with its French population, and dark haired women. She looked bright, freshly scrubbed in her dazzling white blouse, filled to heavenly capacity with what Alex called "Gods own gift to man". The picture was finished to perfection by a dark blue skirt, plain, tasteful.

There was nothing coy about this girl though as she boldly returned his stare with a dancing smile revealing stunning, sky blue eyes. Alex thought she was absolutely the most breathtaking girl he had ever seen and his emotions were taking over.

Louise was still in the store while her son's concern grew quickly to panic, lest this lovely girl walk right out of his life without so much as an introduction. His anxiety soared, hoping she would return immediately so he could meet this lovely vision, because his mother knew everyone in these parts. She made it her business to do so. Desperation crept into his heart as he swept the street with his eyes for Louise, as this newly discovered beauty walked by his car with not so much as a second glance in his direction. Alex knew something had to be done and quick, or she might disappear forever, so he jumped out of the car hurrying after her, trying to think of something to say. She stopped suddenly, whirling around looking him full in the face.

"Now I know who you are!"

It startled him so, she laughed out loud causing the corners of her eyes to crease in beguiling wrinkles, catching his heart up in them as she rushed on with her conversation.

"You're Louise George's son, the oil man!"

Something about the way she said it made him envision a picture of himself covered with oil, not a new experience. He was totally charmed.

"I just said hello to your Mama in the store and she was so excited about your being home from the oil fields. She's hoping you can stay for awhile to feed you real good! You know, fatten you up when you go back to...what did she say, Oklahoma?"

The words came in torrents, but Alex heard almost nothing. He was completely captivated by this small town Cajun girl, fascinated by her wholesome, healthy good looks. The memory of their first meeting made him smile many times through the years.

'Sure didn't need to worry about what I was going to say, to get the conversation started...never got a chance to say anything at all.' Alex always remembered thinking as she kept up her rapid fire conversation. 'How does she do that? How does she keep that up, without breathing.'

"...you can probably live a long time off the fat she's going to put on you."

Alex was hypnotized, she still hadn't inhaled.

"I wonder if that's so? They say bears live all winter long with nothing to eat. You know, living off the fat they stored before hibernating, but I'm not so sure about people. What do you think?"

Finally she stopped, inhaling, to his immense relief. He was sure she might pass out otherwise. She lit up his heart and mind with a radiant smile as she held out her hand.

"Oh, I forgot to tell you! I'm Marie Comeaux. I know your Mama, Louise, real good. You're a mighty lucky man to have her for your Mama too, you know. Anybody who knows her, loves her. She's such a sweet person."

That did it. The final qualification, not that one was needed but the final one capturing his heart completely. They were in agreement that Louise was truly a lovely person. That this charming girl could have such considerate thoughts about a woman older than her own mother impressed him because girls this age were usually interested only in themselves. How they look, and how the boys think they look? Are they the most popular girl in their class? This vision of beauty seemed different in the respect she was able to include someone in her thoughts besides herself.

Alex took her outstretched hand in his, briefly. He never shook hands with a woman before. He was impressed by her firm grip and soft hand. Marie, on the other hand, looked the oil man straight in the eye, equally affected by the great physical power she saw standing in front of her, with such a gentle grip.

Her laughing eyes lit up again, and Alex felt his heart slipping away observing her changing expression, assuming correctly impishness was at hand.

"Louise! Your Mama! She didn't say whether you could talk or not? Probably took such good care of you, you haven't had to, up to now, huh," laughing out loud, "or have I given you a chance?"

He was still holding her hand, he did not want to let it go. Alex George, celebrated as the most ferocious barroom fighter in the oil patch, was being handled with ease by this vivacious school girl, and it was happening right now.

"Marie you say? Marie is it?" Breaking out of his trance. "Well OK Marie, let me see if I got what you were saying. Yes, I do know how to speak, but I was raised by a good woman who told me ladies should always go first."

He exploded with laughter, anticipating what he was going to say, enchanted by simply being with this girl who'd taken instant control of his heart.

"She said always let the ladies go first, especially talking, because they had a tendency to run out of breath quick and when that happens a man can get a word in edgewise. If he's quick." Heeding his own advice he hurried on. "Yes I am Alex George, son of Louise and real glad to hear you say you like her. Any friend of Mama's is a friend of mine, so I guess that makes us friends, right now!"

It seemed his heart stopped momentarily as he saw Marie flush a little, realizing her hand was still in his. He released it with great reluctance.

"Yeah, she is trying to fatten me up." He pinched his sides. "But I know I'm not going to find food anywhere, and I do mean anywhere, as good as hers."

Alex was grateful when Louise walked toward them. Even though they were doing very well without her, there would be more comfort with her presiding over the conversation. She did that, immediately. Her eyes glittering with joy seeing these two young people standing together.

"Marie Cher, I see you found my son! Do you know him?"

"No ma'am." Marie replied, hardly taking her eyes off Alex.

"So how is it your standing here chatting together like old friends? My boy didn't chase you down did he?" Casting a gimlet eyed look in his direction. "If he does with the girls like everything else in his life, maybe you should look out Marie, pretty as you are."

The words rolled out while she schemed that these two could get to know each other much better.

"Marie," Louise asked, "are you going to the dance at the hall tonight?" She started plotting.

"Yes ma'am. Wouldn't miss it. We don't have too many social events around here." Her eyes lit up in their special way, adding. "It's the only way we can look the boys over in a bunch without having to talk to them. Some of them are very dumb you know, and don't know how to act when they're around girls."

She looked invitingly at Alex while talking to Louise, adding with enthusiasm.

"You're coming too aren't you, Miss Louise? You know how much fun we have at these affairs," staring at Alex, "and we always enjoy having any friends you'd like to bring along."

Bouncing over the rutted dirt road on the way home, Alex had a great many questions to ask about this exciting girl who suddenly appeared in his life. One after another they rolled out, and Louise new exactly of the magic that had just happened to her son.

'Poor boy's been swept away by the charm, vitality, and very good looks, of young Miss Marie Comeaux.' She thought.

She was struck by her rare stroke of good fortune being lucky enough to witness their first meeting. Romantic thoughts of her first encounter with Gaston crept into her consciousness. She drifted for awhile, wandering through her memory recalling what an exciting thing young love was. She fought the tears, wanting nothing to spoil the magic mood of this second most loved man in all her life.

Wild animals couldn't have kept Alex away from the dance that night and his mother was charmed down to her toes with his obvious excitement. She was taking her time increasing his anxiety, and because of her femininity enjoyed every minute of it. He, in turn, was trying every subtle ruse possible to hurry her.

The dance was held in the parish hall, a building for all functions, from wedding receptions to the following baptismal parties, to meetings of the Knights of Columbus. Because almost all the residents in the surrounding area were Catholic, the hall was the center of their social lives. This was another favorite recollection of his, conjuring up haunting memories involving all five of his senses.

Justin Arcenaux and his band were at their best that night, apparently part of the conspiracy to steal Alex's heart. Marie danced to all the fast numbers skillfully, and even though she wasn't long out of childhood she knew her movements were followed everywhere as she swung around the floor. The young oil man wouldn't join her in the fast numbers but made sure she danced with him to the slower ones. Alex had never fainted before in his life but there were times that night it seemed possible, dancing with this lovely, Cajun girl. The small of her back was damp with Alex acutely aware of the firm muscles of that back, especially the long graceful indentation of her spine.

'My God, my God.' He thought prayerfully. 'How did You think up these marvelous creatures? Tough! Oh yeah tough, yet so gentle.'

It had not escaped his notice when Marie danced to he fast numbers, that no part of her body shook like the older women.

'To make their voices like music,' his prayer continued, 'whatever gave You these thoughts? Oh and yes, Lord God, the way you put the rest of them together is far, far beyond my ability to express.'

His eyes teared, continuing.

'Woman is so wondrous, full of giving, caring and forgiveness. And their capacity to love? Dear God they overwhelm me! You overwhelm me! Did You put them here to keep the rest of us animals from killing one another?

As if everything else wasn't enough, the smell of this girl was almost too much. Whatever her perfume, it worked with stunning magic on this man who simply couldn't have been more receptive on this lovely spring night. Its warmth accompanied by the many exotic fragrances floating on the soft breeze of the bayou country. The ever present mustiness and perfume of the flowers in full bloom combined, producing an unforgettable evening.

Justin and his music makers stood down from the platform later, for a much deserved break, and Alex asked Marie if she would like to take a walk and catch whatever breezes were available. His heart stood still waiting for the yes he received.

Marie, confident in her new found power, with the most natural motion of all, reached out taking his hand and his heart as they left the building. She chattered on in her usual rapid fire way, while her escort heard little, struggling for control, dominated completely by this lovely girl.

Strolling down the street, hand in hand, Alex felt a powerful mix of emotions. There was everything from a deep feeling of love to a strong physical desire to have this girl in bed, making love together as long as either were capable of continuing. A strange feeling of warmth and desire overwhelmed him as his fantasy drove him to the edge of control, thinking what a beautiful thing it would be to share the same bed with this child. To hold her naked against his body, for the extreme sensual pleasure of feeling this exquisite creature against his skin.

Alex was no stranger to physical love making, he lost his virginity in a small town in France to an experienced prostitute. She knew the young boy warrior had never had a woman before, and took exceptional sensual pleasure in introducing him to every marvel of fornication she knew. She was teacher, and Alex the wide eyed, eager, attentive student trying his best to hold on and learn all that was being offered. This lady accomplished what she'd set out to do. Knowing she was the first woman in his life, she wanted it to be a memorable experience to remain forever, so that she would be at least remembered for as long as he lived. Firsts of this order are always remembered. In this she succeeded.

While still in France the young marine sought out these sensual pleasures wherever they were to be found, and to his delight discovered it was possible to practice this newest and best pastime almost anywhere. Very handsome, black curly hair and ever present smile, the ladies found him irresistible in a mischievous little boy way, endearing him to their hearts and bodies. His powerful physique didn't go unnoticed either, and most went willingly to bed with him seeking momentary escape from the harsh realities of war. As long as the love making held out they pretended this was the man they loved, and were fervently loved in return.

It was an absolute delight discovering even more willing females in Shreveport, the returning veteran spending many an evening and dollar in a bordello discovered with the help of some friends. The fact they were prostitutes had no effect on his consideration for them. He understood for the most part they were aggressive fun loving people who made him feel relaxed and comfortable, and why not? There were no cat and mouse games played here, what with the nature of the house. Everyone knew why they were there, lessening the strain of the chase.

Alex developed a strong bond with one girl in particular. He admired her candid attitude toward her craft while enjoying the pleasures of her company and enhanced physical skills too.

Her name was Sue, a good looking sandy haired girl from a destitute lumber town in Arkansas. She had a stunning figure, and absolutely superb breasts. They had great fun laughing together not only while talking, before or after their sexual encounters, but sometimes right in the middle of their love making. They were constantly amused, and amazed, at the positions they found themselves in at the end of these sessions, noting they were quite different from where they began. His favorite bedroom roughhouse play, was laying in bed naked with this exciting, fun loving country girl. During the course of their pillow talk Sue would invariably grab Alex by his ears, pulling his face to one of the voluptuous breasts he found so unbelievably soft and warm.

"Enough talking Frenchman." She'd whisper. "Rest on this 'til we think of something else."

Wild salacious laughter always followed, and then silence followed by their combined heavy breathing. Yet more intense action and silence again as they drifted off to sleep, each to private dreams.

"God damn Sue!" Alex pontificated one rainy Sunday afternoon while resting after a particularly exhausting session between the sheets. He thought rainy afternoons were specially made for fornication. "How come you have to make your living this way?"

Sue raised up in bed, propped on her elbow, looking deep in his eyes, creating a mind boggling dilemma for the hot blooded Frenchman. He really was interested in what she had to say, but was terribly distracted as one of her gorgeous breasts was exposed by her languid movement, interfering with his train of thought.

"Jesus Baby, you ought to be able to do something besides screw for a living, shouldn't you?" He wore an expression of real concern for this girl which she recognized immediately. She was touched. She knew he wasn't passing moral judgment on her, but truly interested in her well being.

"Oh Alex you sweet thing!" Again pulling his head to her magnificent breasts, with a great hug, releasing him suddenly. "Baby, what the hell do you think I'd do if I wasn't doing this?" She didn't wait for an answer. "Well in case you haven't given that any thought, let me give you a little clue, my Cajun friend. If I wasn't screwing for a living, I'd probably be a waitress in some low class beanery in this town. I'd have to work my ass off," she giggled, the thought amused her as opposed what she now did with that part of her anatomy, "for no money until some jerk showed up and convinced me he was just the guy to take me away from it all." She laid back in the bed staring up watching the imaginary saga play out on the ceiling, continuing. "Mr. Stiff Dick would get me all knocked up and suddenly I've got two problems, a kid I don't want plus an asshole for a husband." Sue was getting into this and while the man in her vision didn't even exist, she disliked him anyway. "And I mean a kid every nine months, so the son of a bitch could stand around the saloons and tell all his friends what a stud he was, the old lady was knocked up again." Smiling, she picked up the thought, milking it for all it was worth. "Do you know what the son of a bitch would do then?"

"No, no Cher! What?" Alex frowned with concern for this girl he loved in his own way, fully aware of what she was.

"He'd come home drunk from that same God damn saloon he hangs out at all the time, and beat the shit out of me." She was really having fun with her fiction. "Regular!"

His frown deepened. He didn't want any one to lay a hand on this exciting woman. 'The son of a bitch better not touch her and have Alex George find out!' He thought. 'I'll break his God damn head.'

"You know why?" She knew Alex was suckered because of the expressions playing over his face. This was great fun. "Because the dinner I fixed the son of a bitch while he's out telling everybody about his studhood...."

'Studhood?' Alex thought. 'Studhood?' That was a new one on him. Strange. "You say studhood, Cher?"

"Yes!" Laughing. "You know, same old shit. Who's got the longest dick and how many times a night can they do it? Important stuff you guys talk about standing around the bar." She punched him in the arm in mock anger. "Don't tell me it's not so, because that's all I hear down there! Anyway it's either that or back to the same God forsaken town I came from. The same drab bullshit for a life my Mom's had, and will have 'til the day she dies, and I'll be God damned if I'll do that!" Defiance shimmering in her eyes.

"OK Cher," he replied, "but how the hell'd you get in this business in the first place?"

She beamed, a wicked look in her eye.

"You know Alex it was the strangest thing but there was this boy back home who was forever chasing me around. You know, when we were kids? Well he kept trying to pull my pants down out there in the barn, and I fought him all the way. Don't even know how it happened but one fine day, we were bigger then, 'course it was time for something to happen. Anyway he got to rubbing everything exactly right and it dawned on me pretty quick it'd be great fun to get our pants off right then and find out what the hell we were trying to do." Alex and Sue were smiling broadly, excitedly reliving her magical first time. "And you know what? "

"No Cher. What?"

"That's just what we did."

"So?" Alex was on his elbow gazing into her smiling face. "How'd you like it?"

"Well, it was fun and after we got to doing it more, we got to doin' it better." She started giggling, building quickly to outrageous laughter, out of control. "I was wondering why the hell I'd been running from him because by this time I thought it was a whole lot of fun."

"So how did you decide to become a...do this for a living?"

"What, a whore? You can say it Alex. How come I decided to become a whore? Well because. We kept at that screwing business, out in the barn, for a long time after that. Sometimes when he wasn't ready, and I was, I had to get him ready." Defiance in her voice. "I enjoyed that. In time I got good at those kinds of things. Anyway, he sure thought I was."

Sue was being WOMAN now, playing to a captive audience, relishing the emotions displayed on Alex's face. She felt a strange mixture of anger and love for this compassionate Frenchman in her bed, although still the mischievous lady Alex liked so much.

"It wasn't too long before I learned a girl could get paid for screwing and figured if it was that much fun, you know, doing it for nothing, it must be absolutely marvelous getting paid for it."

Sue rolled over, her nude body on top of Alex as she looked into his eyes, whispering.

"And you know what?"

"No, what Cher?" Wide eyed.

"Why don't you know if I hadn't gotten into this business I never would have met you, and wouldn't have known the thrill," her hand darted under the covers grabbing his now soft penis causing him to jump involuntarily, "of your big Cajun dick!"

They burst into wild laughter, wrestling as they fell out of bed in a soft tangle of sheets and blankets.

CHAPTER 4

"I'm tellin' you Mama that's all it was, just a walk around the square! Nothin' more!" Alex implored. Louise had suggested there was indeed a good deal more to their disappearance. She knew how long to the minute they'd been gone.

"Fifteen minutes you were out there, my oil man son!" She giggled. "A whole lot can go on in fifteen minutes." She loved teasing him.

"Mama, you gotta' be thinking 'bout something I'm not. Fifteen minutes will only get you from the parish hall to the feed store at the end of the square, across the street and back, and no time for any foolin' around."

Impatient anger registered in his voice with the renewal of the walk in his mind. He didn't have the time to try and kiss the girl, knowing that wouldn't be right anyway, but he sure wished he had. And he knew deep down, especially in view of what the nuns taught, that nothing aggressive should take place with this lady at this time. But one thing he knew for sure and that was she created feelings of such a different nature in him, she might be the one for him.

Their conversation was light enough, with Marie completely at ease as she took his hand while walking in the dark of the huge Evangeline Oak tree. Its colossal branches running in every direction made all the more melancholy by long strands of Spanish moss wafting like ghostly spirits in the soft wind.

"I hope you don't mind my taking your hand, Mr. George." Undue emphasis on "Mr. George". "I'm not too brave in the dark."

"No, no Cher!" He said it without thinking. "And please, don't call me Mr. George. I want you to call me Alex, and I'll be damned if I'm going to call you Miss Comeaux."

She smiled in the dark, knowing beyond any doubt she had this man right where she wanted him. Her new found wiles made her feel very powerful.

'Christ.' His meditation, 'I've been in lots of bad places in my life. People trying to do everything from beat me up to kill me. Made love to women from Paris to Tulsa. Whipped all comers in the oil patch and now ain't this somethin'. This sixteen year old baby is walkin' me right down the road like she's in charge.'

He was even more surprised, mindful that enjoyed being led around like a puppy on a string, by this beauteous creature.

In that short walk Marie learned many things about him, except what he didn't want her to know. She knew parts were being left out, but it was all right that special night.

They laughed so when Alex told her about his wild and crazy father Gaston, that magnificent clown of a man, who held such a unique place in his heart. Alex fought the tears back when he described his death and how much he'd loved his father. Marie stopped him only once during his story, that was about quitting school at the age of twelve. It seemed unusual this man seven years older than she, had four years less formal education. She asked about that.

"Well Marie" He liked her name. It had a melodious ring to it and seemed to fit her quite nicely." I didn't have any choice in the matter, not that it matters too much, 'cause I make more money right now than most men. When Papa died, Mama and me were on our own. We could've gotten along with the help of friends and relatives." Marie couldn't see the dark look crossing his face as those thoughts struck a discordant response in the mind of this fiercely independent man. "I already knew how to work, hunt and fish though, so we always had food on the table. Papa taught me that. Anyway we stayed alive, Mama and me," finishing his sentence through clenched teeth, "and never asked nobody for nothin'!"

She felt his grip tighten as he uttered those words, equally impressed how gentle his touch was upon finishing his statement.

"Anyway I had this good friend in the Marines during the war." Suddenly remembering this sixteen year old girl would only have been eleven when the war was over and probably didn't know a thing about it. "Jewish boy from New York."

Marie thought this was interesting news. Her knowledge of Jews consisting of what the nuns taught her, and they had few good things to say about these mysterious people. After all they crucified Christ, but the fact that Jesus was also a Jew put to death by his own people, bothered her and made her wonder why the nuns got so worked up. She had never seen a Jew in her whole life, but felt sure they would be easily recognizable.

"His name was Myron Cohen and you know what? I'm beginning to see that except for my own crazy Papa," he laughed whenever the memory of Gaston danced across his mind, "he's been the biggest influence in my life."

"But why?" Great curiosity at this uncomfortable disclosure. "Why is he such a big influence? How long have you known him?"

The barrage of questions was natural enough Alex decided, and took no offense, aware of the basis for her concern. He too had been taught by these same well intentioned but sometimes misguided nuns.

"Probably why Cher," there it was again, and so natural, "is because he was such a smart man. The only college man I've ever known."

"Was?"

"Oh yes Baby." He answered softly, unaware what he'd called her. "I left him there in France." He struggled for control, drifting. "...dead, last time I saw him. Runnin' across a wheat field. Very first day in battle."

He caught himself, realizing this beautiful girl was too full of the joy of life to hear any of this. She shouldn't know anything of the killing fields of France. He finished by saying.

"I went to see his grave later. It had what they call a Star of David on it. Cross sort of thing with two triangles reversed on it. Right there in the middle of a lot of regular crosses he was. I got to wonderin', it was so quiet and peaceful there. I was wonderin' if God didn't love all those boys exactly the same, Jew or Christian?"

She knew Alex loved this Myron but never having to endure what these men had, would never understand to what degree.

Alex picked up the tempo immediately not to appear maudlin or emotional, yet because of the Latin blood flowing in his veins, there wasn't much else he could be.

"Anyway I learned many things from him, and we talked about a lot more." Suddenly laughing. "Boy what a talker! Wanted to be a salesman. Promoter he said. Figured he could, because he sure could get excited about an idea. You can believe this or not but Myron's the man who got me started in this oil business, mainly because of his excitement. Why you know Marie, he said the future of America was going to be tied up in oil!"

"What made him think so?"

"'Cause, he said probably every family in the country was going to have an automobile some day. I guess you know that'd be a lot of cars. They won't run without gas, oil and grease in 'em and that's where I come in. I get that stuff up out of the ground, put some in my Ford and go lookin' for more."

Marie wasn't unmindful her young man was driving his own car. She made a big issue of it while telling her mother about meeting Alex. There weren't too many men of any age who could say the same, and she was justifiably impressed he did so at such an early age.

"Oh but that's only the beginning, Miss Marie. He said most of the homes and businesses in the country, would be heated by gas, what they call natural gas. You can't see it but you sure can smell it."

Chuckling as his mind crossed connections remembering what Sue had to say when he told her how you couldn't see, but sure could smell the natural gas.

"Damn, does it ever burn. Fact is we got to be real careful when we bring one of those suckers in because any sparks out on that rig and we could light the whole thing up, and burn it to the ground. There are so many places where gas and oil are going to be used it makes you wonder how much money they're going to get for it in the future."

"Boy!" She was excited, falling victim to his natural ability to stimulate people with his enthusiasm. "Where do you find it?"

"Geologists find it! Guys trained to look at rocks. You know, how they're shaped, where they're laying, what they're made of. Then they've got to convince somebody else they know what they're talking about. Finally, in comes a guy they call the land man, to talk farmer Brown into lettin' them drill for oil on his property. When he says okay, they holler my guys up. We come in, drop a big string of pipe in the ground and look for oil."

She was enjoying the walk with this good looking young man, and learning about an interesting business. Both were fascinating.

Their courtship was a hectic affair sandwiched in the short time he had at home between drilling jobs, driving long hours to be with her. They had marvelous fun, like most young lovers, and got special dispensation from Marie's parents to let her stay out past her normal curfew time. This was easily accomplished because everyone was part of the gentle conspiracy to steal Alex's heart away, and make it a permanent arrangement.

The main conspirator though was Louise, an impossible romantic but loving mother, who simply wanted her son happily married. She could see he was hopelessly smitten with Marie, which delighted her. She'd entertained dark fears Alex would one day come home with one of those girls from up north. She did not want that to happen. Rumor had it that none of those people were Catholic, so no matter what it took she would do everything possible to save him for the Church.

Alex pushed his men hard that year, who tried to keep the pace set by the love crazed Frenchman. They did though, and for the good reason of the handsome bonuses available for bringing wells in early. Bonuses paid cheerfully by the company because each day's drilling was a considerable expense. The sooner they brought them in, the less money spent, and that money was shared with the men. His men also had great respect for him, enjoying the notoriety of being a part of "Frenchy Georges" crew. There was magic in that distinction, something that meant a lot to each man after being indoctrinated with the special brand of "Esprit de Corps" he instilled in all who would ever work for him. This wasn't exactly what he'd learned from the Marine Corps, although their efforts were obviously successful.

"Pussycats going in, wildcats coming out." Alex said in his broad accent. They proved it for the world to see in their actions on the European battle fields they fought and died on, but most important, to a man, they believed they were the best. Alex liked being part of the best.

"God damn!" Alex told his men time and again. "If you're going to do something, anything, what's the use of doing it any other way than the best you know how? You know what I'm saying boys?" He always got nods. "Hey, I don't care what you're doing out there, pulling pipe, fighting chain, or me watching that hole, listening...listening to that son of a bitch hum. Whatever you're doin', if it's digging a ditch, you owe it to yourself and God, to dig that ditch straight and true, the best you can every time? You know, sort of a thank you for giving you your life in the first place."

Alex always provided this parable illustrating the reason for trying.

"Let me ask you this. What you think you'd do if God, or one of his boys came to you in the morning and said, hey Alcide...." This always brought the laughter. His men thought the name about the most outrageous they'd ever heard. "Alcide, I have a special message for you this morning, from the Man yeah, so get ready! Listen up! Good news or bad news, today's the last day you have on this earth. I'm coming for you tonight, yeah. Sorry to tell you but there's a restriction on this deal too. You can't do anything different today from any other day in your life! Do you know what I mean?"

His audience usually was hysterical having an angel portrayed in this manner.

"And this angel would tell Alcide, 'What I'm saying my man is you can't be having no big party's with booze and girls, you know.' Accompanied by exaggerated finger shaking. 'Oh, no, no, no!'

His listeners never tired of hearing him say that, no matter whether they were roughnecks on a drilling rig, or an Arabian sheik in his sumptuous palace years later. It had such an engaging ring to it, the emphasis on the first no going down, the rest coming up.

'The only thing you can do this day son, is exactly what you'd do in any normal day.'

"Do you know what Alcide would do that day, boys?"

His audience was in the palm of his hand shaking their heads in unison because he was telling them something they'd never thought of before, in an engaging manner.

"Why boys, boys! Don't you know what Alcide would do that day is work, eat and laugh each minute of the day like what? Like his last? You God damn right he would! The Man gave him the word he was all washed up in this living business! I'll absolutely guarantee you, Alcide would savor every second of that day. Doing everything to the absolute best of his ability, and you know why? Well why not? Wouldn't you? Wouldn't I? You damn betcha! Okay then let me ask you this? How come it is, I wonder, we don't put out like that all the time anyway. Who knows which day's gonna be the last!"

This was new theory to his fellows, most climbing life's ladder doing whatever it took to keep the job, and little more. Simply being around Alex was incentive enough to make them drive as hard as they could with few mistakes, because errors on the rigs could be costly, fatal, or both. That would have been reason enough for any man to want to put out his best effort, but people working with Alex sought also to please him. They were anxious for his approval because this exciting Cajun had an undeniable magic about him.

The courtship went smooth enough in spite of the frustration Alex felt, unable to have his beautiful Marie in bed, especially when that's exactly where both wanted to be. Many a night of heavy petting ended in exhaustion and frustration, but the nuns taught her well and she would not give up her virginity until after the wedding vows. It was obvious however through their impassioned caressing, that when he did get this beautiful daughter of Evangeline in their nuptial bed, she would be worth the wait.

Many times that year after taking leave of Marie with his powerful physical desires churning, Alex would head north to the next drilling job, stopping in Shreveport to see Sue.

"Jesus Christ, Alex!" Sue begged. "I'm not going to lose that thing over night you know! Slow down! Won't that damn thing of yours ever go down? What the hell's happened to you anyway? You were always good in bed but this is much, much more than usual?"

Alex had grave difficulty telling her of his impending marriage but finally managed to get it out, grateful she took it so well.

"So, you Cajun son of a bitch, you fall in love with one of those dark eyed swamp country beauties who won't go to bed with you and then come up here and take your passion out on me! That's some kinda deal for old Sue here, huh?"

She didn't mean it but knew she'd get mileage out of it. A woman in her profession met this situation many times. They understood the role of surrogate, but this woman knew she was going to miss her Cajun, loving him as much as a whore is allowed.

"Hey, I couldn't help it! It just up and happened one day while I was home and I met this...what did you call her, a dark eyed beauty? Would you believe Miss Marie Comeaux is a blond Cajun lady with light blue eyes? That's different, huh? Anyway I don't know what happened, but the first thing I knew the hook was set and I couldn't...." pausing, "no wouldn't...shake it loose. That ever happen to you?"

Sue scoffed at the idea suggesting a woman in her profession had no business falling in love. She was selling her willing body a man could love for a little while. Her eyes softened as she pulled Alex to her, whispering.

"Hey coonass." Hugging him tight. "I could never be mad at you. Not for long anyway. You're too good a man for that. How is it you say? No, no Cher! I'm just thinking what a lucky lady your new wife is, getting a man like you." Then laughed, adding. "If that girl is smart, she'll love you to death and never give you any trouble at all. What's her name again? Tell me about her!"

They were sitting in bed facing one another, conversing like the lovers they were. Sue wanted to hear all about his future wife.

"SIXTEEN YEARS OLD!" She screamed. Alex thought the bouncer from downstairs might come up, thinking she was in trouble. "SIXTEEN YEARS OLD! JEEEESUS CHRIST!" Cocking her head in the beguiling way Alex loved. "Virgin too I suppose? What the hell are you trying to do, get a young one and break her in your way?"

"Oh yeah but she's gonna be seventeen by the time we're married." He begged.

"And a virgin?"

"I think so. Bad's I want to, and she does too, we haven't done anything yet. She says not until she's married and she ain't kiddin'! I'll tell you something though, she's one of those gals that's sixteen going on thirty, and if anybody knows what I mean by that, it's you!"

She did and sent him on his way with her blessing and a solemn promise from him to come back and see her whenever he could, and for whatever reason.

"You're a mighty special man, Alex George." She looked intently into his eyes adding. "You're going places and do things in this life. I don't know where you're going, or what you're going to do when you get there, but before you're through, a whole lot of folks will know who you are. I'm going to be damn proud to say I knew that coonass, way back when." She was smiling, her eyes full of tears. "Now give your Shreveport lady one last big hug and don't forget to come and see me whenever you can."

He almost squeezed the life out of the woman with a powerful hug showing what she already knew. She liked the comforting feel of his body anyway.

"You're a great sport and a wonderful gal," holding her away while studying her face, "and not bad at all in bed." Thundering laughter while fending off the blows following that remark. He'd told her so many times she was the most exciting woman he had ever had. "But I'll tell you one thing for damn sure, sweet thing! Alex George won't ever forget you, no!"

Good to his word, he never did.

*   *   *

The wedding was a huge affair by St. Martinville standards, considered a smashing success by all in attendance. The ceremony took place in the time honored St. Martin's church, with the reception and wedding party holding forth in the parish hall.

Decorations were arranged with great enthusiasm under the carefully negotiated stewardship of Louise, and Marie's mother. They had a genuine appreciation and liking for one another, but each wanted things to be done her way, thus requiring exaggerated diplomacy.

Alex thought Marie was about the most beautiful...no that wasn't right, she was absolutely the most beautiful thing he had ever seen in his life, when she walked down the aisle on her father's arm. He was in a state of complete awe all through the ceremony. The organ played the wedding march, reverberating through the church's high ceiling and hard walls. Alex's breathing was labored, he had difficulty swallowing as he watched his much loved woman approach the altar.

Her dress was a gorgeous, dazzling white. She'd earned the right to wear it, much to the frustration of the man waiting at the altar. He even thought it was a good idea now, happy in the knowledge he didn't have much longer to wait. It was a long gown with train, supported by Marie's two giggling nieces. He swallowed again with difficulty. The high neck, see through lace accentuated her well shaped bust line suggesting a tantalizing hint of promised sensual delight. A local lady renowned for her dress making ability made the dress, and it fit Marie's body like a glove, falling gracefully to her waist, made smaller yet by the line of the dress from shoulder to floor.

When Marie and her father arrived at the foot of the altar Alex, overcome by great emotion, felt swift uncontrollable tears spring to his eyes. She raised the veil, kissing her father in the symbolic gesture signifying the end of a relationship with one man, and the beginning with another. Alex was to attend many weddings in his lifetime, always deeply affected by this powerful tradition.

Her father was still holding her arm as she turned, looking at Alex with a hauntingly beautiful misty eyed gaze. Taking his extended arm gently, oh so gently, they ascended the three steps to the altar. The celebrated bull of the oil patch wasn't sure he could handle the charged emotion of the moment. He heard absolutely nothing of what Father Girard had to say.

'Hey God.' Alex prayed during the nuptial mass. 'Don't know why You've chosen this coonass boy to give all these good things to, but I want You to know I'm mindful of Your generosity.' His emotional state was at its highest, able to keep himself under control only by taking deep breaths, then holding them until it seemed his chest should explode. 'Please God, I want to be a good husband to this beautiful girlwoman You've given me. I want to take care of her and love her always, as much as I do right now. Thank You for one more of your special favors.' He prayed on. 'I don't understand what You've got in mind for me God, You know it, but I know somethin' for sure, yeah. I know how lucky I've been so far, and I believe You've allowed it to be. Life's a two way street God, maybe our relationship is too. Hope You won't think me out of line but if ever there's anyway I can return the favor, I'd appreciate the chance.'

Justin Arcenaux and his band inspired by the occasion played with extraordinary fervor, and most of the community turned out as usual, since nearly everyone was either related or had known one another since birth. Weddings were the highlight of social life, in that place, at that time.

Tables literally groaned with all kinds of marvelous food cooked by the ladies, each trying to outdo the other, resulting in unbelievable aroma's. Gumbo's. Seafood. Game. Beef. Dishes of all descriptions. Some floating in rich broths, tomatoes, onions and peppers bobbing seductively on top. Others with golden brown gravies, steam curling up creating frenzied enthusiasm in any male within smelling distance. Jambalayas' and sauce piquantes defied description, with pungent spices that not only seasoned the food but also drove the waiting diner to distraction with anticipation. As much as Alex wanted to try everything, he couldn't resist stuffing himself on his mother's crawfish 'etouffee. It made him curl his toes while eating.

Gaston called the crawfish "mud bugs", followed by Louise's scolding. It was a disgusting thing to call them, she said, and then laughed as she told her small, big eyed son, they were really lobsters. Well anyway they were lobsters once upon a time, but when the British ran them out of Canada those lobsters had to swim all the way alongside their boats, which caused them great loss in size and weight. That's why they were so small now. It was to remain one of his favorites, that story, because it showed him the delightful Cajun sense of humor and besides, those "mud bugs" were so damn good to eat. Yes and his amusing Papa was right. A good coonass lady could make a sumptuous feast out of any cow turd, no matter how old it was.

'My God I must have died and gone to Heaven already.' He thought, adding prayerfully. 'Is it this good up there Myron.' He never considered Myron to be any place else.

Theirs was the table of honor, and it was a glorious day of eating, drinking, and dancing into the evening. Alex and Marie made an extremely handsome couple, his black curly hair and dark eyes contrasting sharply with her blond hair and sky blue eyes. The ladies chattered excitedly about how many children they would have, and how beautiful they were going to be. As Alex held this lovely girls hand and watched the dancers go whirling by, he was transported immediately back to the nights when Gaston and Louise went to the 'fait do do's. He still loved to hear the rhythmic beat of the dancers feet.

There was plenty to drink too, at these affairs, but Alex was careful, he wanted nothing to interfere with what was immediately ahead. He was having a perfectly marvelous time and felt good about being one of the center pieces in this event. Most of all however, he ached over every square inch of his body for the new Mrs. Alex George. His mother was having great fun too, all at his expense. She was enchanted at every moment of his anxiety from the time he stepped up to her side and asked.

"Hey Mama, when do the bride and groom get to leave?"

"I don't know Cher. Why?" She answered with a look of feigned innocence. "Aren't you having a good time with us? Look at all these people, they're having such fun. Don't you want to stay with them?"

As though magically transformed, standing before her was her precious little boy Alex, who did so want to please his mother but who also wanted what he wanted, when he wanted it. Her heart nearly left her chest as she threw her arms around him whispering in his ear, so no one else could hear.

"Soon Cher! Soon! Oh and beautiful son of mine." She released him, her eyes full of tears, remembering her own wedding night and all its marvelous discovery, looking now into the eyes that were the result of their lovemaking. "It will be worth the wait."

Finally allowed to leave by the fun loving guests the bride and groom departed. New Orleans was the destination but they made it only as far as LaFayette, a distance of twenty miles. Neither thought further travel advisable lest they do something very foolish. They were married now and because they'd restrained from sex this long, they felt that a proper bed was no more than right.

They checked into the hotel and were given the best room in the house, at Alex's request, but it could as well have been the broom closet. This couple didn't need much room, on this special night.

Alex was totally charmed, consumed with intense desire as Marie walked out of the bathroom wearing only a worried smile.

"Well, this is what we've been wondering about. I don't know of any reason why we should have to wait any longer." Her eyes brimmed with tears as she laughingly added. "And I don't mind telling you one little bit either, I'm scared to death."

Alex picked her up in his arms, never to feel such total love at any other time in his life. He would love this girl for some sixty years, but that moment was different from anything he would ever know.

Their love making was tenuous at first as to be expected, she was giving up her virginity. Their beginning was followed by greater and greater enthusiasm on her part however, with Alex utterly amazed at what he'd gotten hold of in this surprising woman. No sooner catching their breath from one session, Marie urged him on to the next. Her new husband wanted desperately to fill her wants and needs, finally becoming concerned he might not be able to meet the drive elicited in his astonishing child bride.

"God damn Cher!" His breathing was labored, causing her to giggle. "We're gonna' be married for the rest of our lives you know. At least that's what Father Girard said this morning. Maybe we ought to save a little for some time in the future." He was struggling trying to normalize his breathing. "Where, oh where Baby, did you get all this energy?"

Marie was in control, knowing intuitively you could enjoy sex and pillow talk too. "Why? What's the matter with my strong oil man?"

The room was dark but Alex felt sure he could see her eyes dancing with merriment, visualizing her beautiful laugh lines as she doubled up with laughter?

"Have you run out of gas?"

They were hysterical. Marie at his obvious plea for mercy and he from her newly discovered, earthy sense of humor.

"No, no!" Pleading. "It's simply that you're much more woman than I expected." That pleased her. Aware as she was that Alex had been many places in his life, she also suspected he'd shared a few bedrooms in those travels.

"But Cher," she said, "don't you know we French women are supposed to be the most exciting in the world?"

She was thrilled with his heartfelt, diplomatic answer.

"I don't know about that Cher, but I do know you are just about all the excitement this Cajun can stand right now."

He pulled her close in a strong embrace, he fervently hoped would serve a dual purpose. To hold this woman he loved with all his heart close to his body, and at the same time keep her off so he could get some sleep for the gathering storm of sexual demands he knew he would have to meet.

CHAPTER 5

Alex was promoted to "Land Man" the year they were married, and with Marie's enthusiastic support. She knew of the danger on the drilling rigs and Alex learned quickly to be selective with respect to what he said to his new bride regarding his activities. He told her, while still courting, about the wildest well he ever brought in and had a rapt audience as he described the dramatic scene, trying to paint a word picture that could do justice to the violence with which some wells come to life.

"The business end of that string of pipe is far, far down the hole, and even with all the stuff we've got to work with you never really know what's happening down there. You know what I mean?"

She nodded with great curiosity, wanting to hear the rest of the story this exciting man had to tell about his wild, unpredictable business.

"So me and my boys...."

"Alex, you should say, 'My boys and I'."

"Yeah? OK" Accepting his first lesson from the woman who was to teach him so much in life. "Listen Cher, I appreciate you telling me that. I want you to help me whenever I mess up will you? I need to speak better than I do." This pleased her, she didn't know how he might take criticism. "Myron said so too, you know. He said the better you talk, the more the big money boys listen. You have to out smooth those guys if you're gonna' use their money." Alex chuckled. "He even told me I should get a genuine Jewish boy to deal with the money guys when I do hit it big, because they were the best in the world at it. Anyway my boys and I," bowing in her direction, "were down as far as anybody had gone in that particular field, and everything we drug up from the bottom looked real good."

"Does it look like oil, when it comes up?"

"No, no Cher. What it looks like is one hell of a mess. You get sand, rocks, water, mud but after spending time on those rigs you understand what you're looking at. Well like I say, we were down there bringing all this stuff up that meant we were getting close to oil. You know what they say, if it walks like a duck, quacks like one and has feathers, why chances are real good it's a duck." His look of earnestness charmed her. She called it his little boy look.

"What duck?"

"None," he laughed, "it means if all the signs are there, probably whatever you're looking for is too."

"Did you find it?"

"Did we find it? More like did it find us? Oh hell yes! We kept drilling and drilling getting more nervous all the time, when one day we get a disgusting little gurgle and that pipe spits up just enough water to overflow, wet the outside, and pool up a little on the rig floor. Hell I've seen puppies pee bigger puddles than that! I looked at the boys, they looked at me, and we all wanted to sit down and cry."

"Why?"

"Because, we thought that was it! When you work hard as we do to get something out of the ground and nothing happens, you get upset." Arched eyebrows inquiring if she understood. "Then the God damn thing says 'Burp', and we get a big, dumb looking bubble, right behind the water."

"What were you looking for?"

"More'n a sick little dribble like that."

He shot a look of impatience her way. "Well we're standing around feelin' sad when all kinds of weird noises start deep in the hole. Scary noises."

"What do you mean, scary?" She simply could not imagine this man being afraid of anything.

"I don't know how to describe it Hon', but it sounds like the Devil himself trying to get his breath."

"The Devil?"

"Nobody else, and we're edgy! It's like shrimpin' in the Gulf, you don't know what's coming up when you pull up the nets, you know what I mean? You drop 'em down there hoping to get some shrimp and 'voila' what a surprise when you pull that sucker up. Sometimes you're staring at a bunch of real weird lookin' critters."

She shook her head in agreement. She'd been in the gulf many times with her father, amazed at the creatures that appeared every time the nets were pulled in.

"So the hole's wheezin' and blowin' and the rig starts to rumble and shake. I screamed at the boys, specially the man up in the derrick, 'Get off! Get off the God damn rig.' And we all ran for it! We made it! Even the guy in the top. I swear to Christ I don't know how he got down, we didn't have hardly any time, but another minute and he'da been dead. That thing simply exploded."

"Blew up?"

"No, not that way. What happened was it started blowing pipe right on out of there, which is enough to scare you half to death because of the force needed to push 'em. Sections slammed into everything, smashing whatever they came in contact with to splinters."

"What'd you do?" Her wide eyed question.

"Nothin'. Kept down tryin' to stay away from all that stuff flyin' through the air. It shredded that derrick like it was nothin'. Chains snappin', whippin' around. Mud, water, rocks, sand, everything you can imagine was blowin' out of there at the same time with a noise like you never heard." He paused momentarily. "You know, what it sounds like when you blow across the top of a big bottle with a small neck?"

She nodded affirmation.

"Well that's kinda what it sounded like, only many, many times more powerful, because of the gas pushin' it. It's blowing through that pipe making a forty foot flute out of each section. Meanwhile the pipe's twistin', turnin', sections comin' out straight's an arrow then trying to turn around sideways and the rig won't let it, so it whips around in there smashing everything. I want to tell you it's enough to make you say a few prayers. Damn! Damn! I heard a lot of noise when I was in France, cannons and machine guns and all, but that was nothin' compared to this. This thing sounded and felt like an earthquake must. I never heard anything like it, because what happened was Momma nature seemed to come unglued."

Alex paused, staring straight ahead, reliving the moment.

"Then you know what?"

"No Alex, what?"

"Just like that, she quit!"

"That's all? Only the pipe?"

"For then! She wheezed some more and we're haulin' ass away from that sucker. Now then's when I thought we'd really screwed up because along came another...explosion sort of. The whole platform blew to pieces, followed by the wildest gusher I'll probably ever see all the rest of my life."

"What was it like?" She was right there, in her imagination, standing beside him in that field.

"A huge fountain of oil with pressure pushing it way up. My God it was something Marie! I'd sure like to see it again, only not so scared. That stream must've been a couple of feet in diameter, and when it blew as high as it could go it bent at the top and spread out in a wide pattern covering everything with that ugly stinking stuff men kill for nowadays. We were real lucky we got off under our own steam instead of getting blown off." Followed by the statement she didn't like and wouldn't forget. "Some boys in the oil patch haven't been as lucky."

She remembered that story well, and although it was exciting she realized then her husband was in a hazardous job, happy when he switched to something less dangerous.

Nothing happens until the land man does his job. The process starts with geologists probing the terrain for oil, eventually ending up in the pumps at the gas station. The land man is the super salesman of the oil business, many corporate heads coming from these ranks. He contacts the farmer, whose property contains the suspected black gold, then must convince him to sign a lease with the company he represents, for a percentage of the royalties.

With his devilish good looks, personal drive and engaging Cajun accent, Alex's success was assured, because everyone who met him soon fell under his spell. His charm consisted of his fun loving ways and ability to joke with his prospects, putting them at ease. He could speak on a one to one basis on any subject, from kids to crops. It wasn't long before Alex understood he truly had the magic of persuasion, which was something his friend Myron saw immediately. As fate would have it a meeting was about to take place with an even more persuasive personality that would change his life dramatically.

Alex was weaving his magic with a farmer in north Louisiana, regaling him with stories about his beloved south Louisiana and the crazy characters who lived there, real and imagined. He had a routine consisting of serious talk about the financial possibilities for the man and his family, interspersed with wild Cajun jokes. They loved his finish with the definition of a coonass his father had told him years ago, after which he'd go into Gaston's act of losing himself completely in hilarious laughter. It worked, time and time again.

This day he wound up his routine, slapping the farmer on the back, falling against the barn convulsed in laughter. He was most receptive to Alex's sales pitch, and after signing all the papers, told him.

"You know for a Coonass man," furtive check to see if that was okay for him to say, "you're one hell of a talker. Matter of fact I think you're the second best talker I ever heard in all my life."

"Second best!" Alex howled. "Second best you say! Who the hell's first best?"

"Guy's comin' to town tonight." His face lit up. "You know what? If you're gonna' be in the area you ought to hear him."

"Yeah. What's his name? What's he selling?" He was interested, wanting to perfect his skills.

"Name's Huey Long. Politician! Ex-salesman. Came through these parts selling stuff, some time back. Why he broke down right out there in front of the house once, and asked to use my tools to get going again." He laughed good naturedly.

"Know what he did?"

"What?"

"Got to sweet talkin' me and my wife. Talks his way inside the house and before you know it he's baking a cake for her, using some kind of special lard he was peddlin'. Son of a bitch is sweet talkin' her inside and I'm outside in the boiling sun fixin' his car." Laughing. "But if you think that's funny, listen to this! He's got this guy with him for a driver. He's sittin' on the porch drinking a long cool lemonade, watching me sweat my ass off in that red dirt."

"Didn't he help?"

"Asked him, and he told me the only thing he knew about cars was drivin' 'em. Huey couldn't even do that."

"So what'd Huey do?"

"Sold shortening, organized baking contests. Put that product on the market in these parts. What's more he got to know a lot of folks up here he's coming back to see, cause he's a politician now. Wants us to vote for his friend who's running for governor."

"I don't know. I'm not much into politics." Alex replied.

"Yeah, I know," the farmer agreed, "I felt the same way but you really owe it to yourself to go hear this guy. I'll guarantee you ain't never heard nothin' like him in your whole life."

"What's he do now?" Alex was looking for some avenue of graceful escape.

"Railroad Commissioner. Guess old Huey's really heatin' that sucker up too. Never heard of the job myself, 'til he got it, but he's fired that thing up and now lots of folks know about it."

"Yeah, well I don't think I'd be too interested in listening. I don't have much to do with railroads now that I've got my car."

"You know that's the same thing I said to him, last week while he's setting this thing up. He laughed and said his job had to do with a lotta things besides trains."

Leaning into Alex the inarticulate farmer reversed roles unaware, becoming persuasive salesman.

"What else?"

"Well, he said the most important thing besides regulatin' trains up here, and ships in the gulf, is going to be making policies for the transportation of oil and gas."

Alex snapped to attention because next on his list of things to learn about his industry, was pipelines. There was unbelievable talk about pipelines carrying oil and natural gas, way up north so people could burn it in their furnaces, replacing coal.

"What time and where?"

Just like that, he could kill two birds with one stone learning something about pipelines, and some new tricks about selling.

"In town, at the courthouse. Circulars all over the place. You can't miss it. Quarter to five. Seems like a strange time to me but I'm tellin' you that's the way he is. Different. Then too, he might have other places to go. You gonna be there?"

"Yeah, yeah. Are you?" There was no other place Alex was going to be that afternoon.

"Oh hell yes," laughing again thinking of the upcoming experience, "I wouldn't miss it for the world. Why he's the damndest character we've had around here since the civil war. I'll be right down front." Adding sheepishly. "That's where my wife wants to be, in case he says something nice about her."

The hour arrived and so did Huey, exactly as the farmer said, but Alex's heart sank when he saw the politician for the first time. The man simply wasn't what he expected to see. He was looking for a forceful character like himself, only maybe taller and thin with prominent features. But this?

"Jeeeeeesus!" He breathed, watching the main event unfold.

Huey rode into the square breaking to a stop in a cloud of dust blowing his horn, which he did for the rest of his life, only in a different fashion. Alex knew he was the guy who wasn't driving, suddenly wishing he'd gone to Monroe as originally planned. Huey didn't look like much to him, much less a dynamic politician. What he saw was a nondescript looking person of about 30, dark curly hair, soft round face. Look though he might, Alex couldn't see any features about the man that would make him stand out in a crowd. The car came to a halt, and Huey left it like he was shot from a gun.

'Damn!' Alex thought as he watched him leap into the crowd pumping hands, slapping people on the back. He made a political constituent forever by grabbing the farmers wife, kissing her on the cheek while telling everyone within hearing distance that this woman was the best cook he had ever run across, with the exception of his own dear mother.

'Slick.' Alex acknowledged, bemused. 'Nailed her with praise, and smoothed all the rest of 'em. Didn't say she was the best cook there was, only the best he'd run across. They all know in their hearts, they could out cook her on their worst day. That quick! Baits the hook, only took a minute, then grabs every man, woman, and child with his remark about his mother.'

The magic had only just begun however, hidden completely until he ran up the steps two at a time. A whole new Huey sprang to life. The fleshy, shapeless face took on a different set, a shock of reddish brown hair hanging down in his face. His piercing eyes were hypnotic, and the words came sometimes in torrents, others in deliberately paced monosyllables, screaming, or whispering.

In the middle of his speech a train rolled into town, directly across the square, causing a mild disturbance as it came to a stop. It sat only long enough to load and unload and with a short whistle slid down the tracks and out of sight. When they could hear, Huey apologized to the crowd.

"You folks remember when I first came and asked you to vote for me?" Heads shook in assent. "Anybody remember that train came thundering through town, while I was talking?" More nods. "Why I was so sorry and embarrassed about that train coming through here, what with all the noise and dirt, I could have just about cried. Shucks, if I'da known their schedule, there'd been no problem at all. We could have held that get together another time."

'Feeling. Concern.' Alex thought. 'Shows his feelings, and puts the whole crowd in his pocket while he's doing it.'

"Who'da thought that train'd be so noisy anyway." Huey continued in a soothing voice. "Now wouldn't you think it'd come rolling in nice and slow, stop for passengers, and ease on down the track without all the noise and dirt. Y'all remember that?"

The farmers wife Huey cooked for years before, found her voice blurting. "That was the problem. We couldn't get 'em to stop here. If we wanted to go on a train we had to go to the next stop!"

Her timing couldn't have been better had they planned it. Alex swore Huey got bigger somehow, upon hearing this remembered news. His eyes took on a special strange light as his anger resurfaced. "You mean to tell me that train don't stop here," the grammar chosen specially for the rednecks, "and you folks can't get the railroad to do nothing about it? Isn't that what I asked you that day?" He was breathing hard, his face growing darker.

'Oh Christ.' Alex thought. 'He's getting all worked up over something that took place six years ago.' He felt relieved though that he wasn't the target of Huey's wrath. His voice was rising to a shrill scream, not waiting for an answer.

"You folks had to go miles in either direction to get on that thing, or ship anything? Am I right?"

All heads were nodding yes, none daring to speak.

"Well let me tell you something," his head was shaking with rage, nearly out of control, "I came down here to ask you folks to vote for my friend today, and do you know why?" No one knew why. "Because I am a man of my word, that's why!" He was nodding in response to his own statement. So was everyone in the crowd including Alex. "Yes that's why I came here then, to "DEMAND" you vote me into the Railroad Commissioners job." He ripped off his coat, throwing it over a railing. "Then we'd see how quiet that train could roll in and out of your town because," his voice dropped almost to a whisper adding with stiff necked rage, "I'd see to it they stopped that thing here everyday, and do you know what?"

All heads now shook in the negative.

"I didn't care if I slept in the office of those railroad big shots to do it!"

Instant recovery by the crowd. They nodded yes again.

'Boy', Alex thought, 'I've been mad before, but why's he getting so worked up over what happened back then.'

"You're saying yes aren't you?"

They were saying yes.

"That's what I promised you back then and now what? Well let me tell you what. You see that train coming in here nice's can be." He was getting expansive, thumbing in the direction of the tracks. "Wasn't that sucker quiet?" Heads nodding. "Well wasn't it?" Screaming, all heads pumping up and down. "Well I'm back, and I want you to know Huey Long keeps his promises! I'll do what I tell you! Didn't I do what I told you?"

"YES. YES" The crowd chorused.

'OK. Now here's what I expect you to do. We got a governor's race going here and I expect you to vote for my man, 'cause he'll do what he says he will, and I'll stake my reputation on it! Vote for him now and I'll be back in four years asking for you to vote for me, 'cause folks your are looking at your future governor."

A cheer went up and the crowd milled around Huey slapping him on the back.

"Atta boy Huey. You got my vote!"

"You got those railroad guys Huey, just like you said!"

Then the cry went up that was to become the future magic for the modern day legend.

"Show 'em! Show those big shots who you're for Huey! Us! The little guy! They can't push you around! Show 'em who you're for!

'Wow.' Alex thought. 'He's not running for anything and these people are acting like he's running for president.'

It was a small crowd and Alex was swept right along with them. He had no experience in politics and the art of moving people with oratory, and didn't realize he was witnessing the beginning of an American phenomenon. A man who was to generate fear in the consummate politician in the nation at that time, Franklin D. Roosevelt. A charismatic leader accepting in earnest the mandate of his people of the state of Louisiana, not only to overpower his opposition but destroy them in every real political sense of the word.

"God damn man!" Alex grabbed his farmer friend. "I see what you mean. That son of a bitch is something! Where's he from? Naw forget it! Do me a favor, though! Introduce me! Jesus, I never saw anything like him?"

Alex had a barrage of questions, mesmerized as he was by this strange new political force rising out of the red dirt of northern Louisiana. He didn't realize he had the farmer in his steel grip, surely not aware of how he sounded.

"Get me up there!" It was an order not a request. "I've got to meet him!"

The introduction was handled by the proud farmer, and Huey detected genuine interest in himself and his candidate by this magnetic man from the Cajun country. He was most receptive to meeting Alex at a spot convenient to both.

"Where you going to be tomorrow night?" Alex pressed after the introduction. "I'm real flexible and would like to buy your dinner. I'm working the northern part of the state. I can be anywhere you say."

Huey was equally impressed with Alex, recognizing immediately many of the characteristics they shared in common. He suggested they meet the following night in Shreveport, to pursue their mutual admiration, and see what benefits might accrue for both.

"I have some bankers and lawyers to meet tomorrow afternoon and then I'll be free for the evening. What say we meet at your hotel at six PM?"

"I'll be waiting, Mr. Long."

"Huey's my name. Call me Huey, and I'll call you Alex. O.K.?"

'What the hell kind of magic is going on here.' Alex wondered. 'This guy's talking about three things Myron said were absolute musts if you're going to make it to the top. You got to know the power boys. Bankers. Lawyers. Nothing happens without 'em. They're as much a part of the business and industrial makeup of this nation as paper and pencil. You need good ones. He also said you have to think of, and speak to, the big shots of the world as absolute equals.'

They met as scheduled.

"Get the advantage and keep it." Huey's eyes bulged with a mouthful of steak, and his ever present state of excitement. "The secret to life is simply that. All the world flocks to a winner and that's what it takes to win. Put your opponent down and go for the jugular, you know what I mean?" Pointing at Alex with his fork.

"Think I do, Huey." There, he said it. Equals. "Kinda like when I'm out there trying to get leases signed, stringing a big line of bullshit." He startled himself. "Oh I'm sorry Huey, I didn't mean...."

"Bullshit's the word, Alex! Don't worry about your language around me 'cause I don't hold with any holier than thou...." Searching for the word, smiling when he found it. "Bullshit! Holier than thou bullshit! Somebody talks to me, I want 'em to talk like they think, then I got a chance to understand 'em!"

"Stringing 'em along," they laughed knowing the subject had been covered, "and I'm doing everything I can to get 'em coming my way." Huey nodded understanding. "I'm trying to get acquainted and put them at ease."

"Yes, yes?" Huey had a way of pushing conversations with his impatience.

"We talk crops and weather, family and kids, and when they see I'm sincere they start listening and leaning my way."

"Are you?" Huey shot back quickly.

"Am I what?"

"Sincere?"

"Yeah, I am." Thinking it over as he answered. "Then I give 'em my coonass jokes and that gets 'em every time. When we quit laughing...."

"You laugh every time you go through your routine?" Huey interrupted.

"Yes. Yes I do."

"No matter how many times you've told the story?"

"Yes. Why?"

"'cause that's great. That's exactly what you have to do. Make it sound like it's the first time, every time. Spontaneity!" Concerned lest this bull from the swamps wasn't up to his education level. "You know what I mean? Right now! You know Alex, there's a saying about the whole world is a stage and we're all actors."

Now it was Alex's turn to stun the politician.

"And in our lifetimes we play many parts."

"I thought you had to quit school as a kid." Huey was genuinely impressed at this gem of wisdom from such a diamond in the rough. "Where the hell'd you learn that?"

"I did, but I had a buddy in the marines who taught me a lot, and that was one of his favorite sayings. Anyway," Alex continued, "if anyone around knows about spontaneity, it has to be you."

"Why'd you say that?" Huey waved his coffee cup.

"Because I've never seen anything like what you did when that train came into town yesterday interrupting your speech." Alex wondered why Huey was smiling so broadly. "Christ, if that'd happened to me I don't know what I would've done, but I'da been plenty mad."

The explosion of laughter that followed confused Alex. He didn't like it either. He didn't know if he was laughing at him, or with him.

"You like that, did 'ya?" Huey was out of control laughing, slapping the table.

'Remember now, stage and actors.' Alex thought. 'Don't get hot.'

"God damn!" People in the restaurant were staring as Huey's face turned beet red. "Oh thanks, Alex. I know you meant that as a sincere compliment, but the fact of the matter is I planned my speech for the exact moment that train went through. This time and the first time I spoke to those folks. I knew from our mutual friend it was one hell of a sore spot with everyone around there, and how much they appreciated the work I did for them."

A grin started spreading across Alex's face.

"The only thing I worried about was the sucker being on time to interrupt the meeting. Thank God they ran on schedule."

They dissolved in laughter slapping table, knees, anything in sight, over what seemed to be an accidental happening. Huey had planned it all along, to achieve his goal.

"You are a slick one." Alex was wiping his tears away. "Set up all the time, and took us for a ride."

"True. True enough Alex, but it's the old story of the end justifying the means."

Alex's ham like fist shot across the table grabbing Huey by the arm, a look of shock on his face.

"Where'd you hear that?"

"What?" Huey thought he'd said something wrong.

"End justifies the means."

"Hell I don't know." Relief in his voice. "Why?"

"Because that was another of my dead friends sayings, and you two are the only ones I ever heard say it."

"He must have meant a great deal to you Alex to be such a big part of your life now. Tell me about him."

When Alex finished, Huey was obviously moved, acutely aware of the emotions involved in the telling. He noted especially the part about Alex coming to Myron's rescue, pounding four men into submission in the process. It appealed to him because Huey was not known for his physical bravado, and while he would never admit to that he admired the man that could meet his adversary with words or blows. He also knew he could never charge into machine gun fire under any circumstances, and admired those who could.

"He was the smartest man I ever knew, Huey. He always told me to do whatever necessary to get where I wanted to go."

"End justifies the means?"

"Exactly!"

There was a long silence for respect and reflection, finally broken by Huey.

"I appreciate your interest in me Alex, and I wish you could have voted for me when I ran in this district. That alone would have meant a lot to me. Since you couldn't, then or now, maybe we could ask you to work for, and support, my candidate for governor."

"I will! You know I will. How else can I help? Money?"

"I couldn't accept your money Alex, but our campaign sure could."

"Five hundred dollars help?"

Huey was speechless at an offer of this magnitude made by a relative stranger. A young one at that.

"God's been mighty good to me Huey, and so have the people I've worked for. I've made good money in the oil patch and would like to invest some in you, and your man. Anyway it goes along with what we've been saying."

"What's that?"

"The end justifies the means."

"In this case meaning?"

"Meaning I like you." That certainly appealed to Huey's abundant vanity. "You tell me you want to help the little man? I like that 'cause I come from a long line of those folks, and I'd like to put some money on you. You know what I mean? Like bettin' on a horse."

Huey sat back, as close to speechless as he could ever be.

"And I'll tell you something else!" Alex was in charge now as he leaned across the table staring straight into Huey's wide eyes. "I'm gonna' get something out of this too."

"What? What do you want?"

"An education about part of my business I don't understand, but I'm told it comes under the Railroad Commission."

Huey beamed at this display of confidence.

"What?"

"The only thing I don't know about the oil business is pipelines. I want to call you when I'm in town, so we can get together for dinner, which I'll buy. Hell, it'll look good to the big guys in the home office anyway, where it says on the expense account, Railroad Commissioner, State of Louisiana. They'll like the hell out of that, but they won't know what it's really for."

'I do like this boy!' Long thought. 'Four square, true blue, and a scheming son of a bitch to boot. I like him.'

Huey's man lost the election, which didn't seem to bother him in the least, and Alex saw him often, following their initial meeting. Their friendship grew out of mutual respect and trust, and the pleasure of the others company. The Cajun oilman was one of the first people Huey told of his serious intention to run for Governor.

"But God damn, Huey." Alex responded fearful his pipline education might go by the boards. "You just got over an election. Now you're going to start running for Governor?"

"Yes, but I can do both. I can work my law practice and the job of Railroad Commissioner with no problem. Matter of fact I intend to make this office my stepping stone, my source of publicity, to put me in the public eye and I'll do it with pipelines."

"How?"

"I'm declaring war on the big guys, the big money boys that come to this state, suck up our natural resources, and laugh all the way to the bank. They pay our people jackshit and sit in their offices in Wall Street, laughing at the dumb assed hicks down here that let 'em do it!" He was starting to breath fast again.

'Oh shit.' Alex thought. 'Here we go again. He's gettin' excited.'

"Pipelines are my territory! They are my God damn business!" Stabbing his chest with his finger. "I can put the heat on anybody that has anything to do with 'em, and I'm fixin' to turn that heat up! You know who I'm going to start with, Alex?"

"No who?"

"Just only Mr. John D. "Robber Baron son of a bitch" Rockefeller that's who!" He loved inventing middle names.

"What do you mean?"

"I mean those bastards are going to pay, and pay, to make up for what they've already stole." Huey could mangle the language or caress it, whichever was called for at a given time. "They'll wish I'd never been born before I'm through." The light started to come up in his eyes.

"Why?"

"Because, they're the ones sucking up our natural resources and then run off to their high falutin' homes and clubs in New York snickerin' as they go. God how they must laugh at us down here! Don't you know how clever they think they are?"

"Don't guess I ever thought of it, Huey."

"Exactly!" His hand slammed on the desk. "Exactly! That's exactly what those assholes want!" Staring intently at this lone witness to his wrath. "No offense to you Alex for not knowing about this, but that's exactly what those thieving son's o bitches want. Our apathy! They know most of us down here, not on their dole, don't think about the deal, don't give a shit, which is precisely what they want. You understand?"

"I think I get your drift, Huey."

"Don't rock the boat. Don't wake those sleepy southerners up, they might want a piece of the action. You know Alex, if anything, we should hang our politicians and news people in this state because they're supposed to be the watchdogs. If the truth were known I'll bet some of those watchdogs have been given a few bones to gnaw on to keep 'em content."

Alex wasn't familiar with what Huey was suggesting and had a slight suspicion this master of the hustle might be putting it on him a little bit, but whatever, it sure was convincing.

"Oh yeah, every once in a while one of our windbag politicians will swell all up like a...like a...stinkbug! Like a big stinkbug!" Spotting a quizzical look, adding. "Stinkbug Alex! Somethin' upsets 'em they get all swole up." He loved inventing words, acutely aware of their impact. "They look ugly and stink. That's all, they don't do nothin' else 'cept sit there and stink. Sounds like some of our illustrious politicians, don't it?"

Innocent in political matters, soon to be taught by the master of them all, Alex could only agree.

"Right!"

"Guess how many miles of paved road we have in this swamp of a state, Alex?" He had no idea.

"I give up."

"Three hundred lousy God damn miles, that's how many! About enough for one skinny assed road from here to New Orleans." His voice rose in volume. Huey was aroused. "And no place else. That silly assed road wouldn't go no place else, 'cause that's all there is!"

"Wow!"

"You bet, wow! And how 'bout the bridges we need, especially down in your country, to tie this swamp together." Laughing sarcastically. "Why hell Alex, I was talking to one of your coonass friends during the campaign, and he told me he's screwed right now when it comes to moving crops to Baton Rouge and New Orleans. What with all the rivers and bayous he's got to cross to get there, he can't do it. Oh he can, but he can't drive like the crow flies and he ain't got no pontoons on his truck. If he's going to make the trip he's got to go by way of Dallas to St. Louis to Birmingham and then down to New Orleans."

Alex loved to hear him exaggerate in his outrageous manner, a well calculated tact on Huey's part, because it worked. It made him think, and he knew it was designed to make anyone who heard it do the same.

"No doubt about it Huey. Every time I go home I have to wait for ferries, dodge cattle, and get off the road for the lumber wagons. It takes a heap of doing simply to get there. Matter of fact, you almost can't get there from here."

Huey liked the sound of that last remark, made a note of it for future use and rushed on.

"Right and how about our schools. What do the kids do about school books?" He didn't wait for an answer. "They don't do shit, that's what! None of these red neck hicks or your web foot folks from the swamps, got the price of books for their kids."

"My folks didn't."

"Right again, so what do they do? They scrounge around and maybe come up with a couple of books for the whole damn classroom and all the kids. Well that's bullshit! No, no, my friend, Mr. John D. has had it his way all too long now, but I'll absolutely guarantee you one thing." Huey sputtered excitedly. "No I'll do better than that." Reaching for the bible. "I'll swear on this bible, and my mothers grave."

'His mothers grave?' Alex thought. 'She's still living.'

"...that Standard Oil, and all the big moneyed boys up there on Wall Street are fixing to go into their pockets and buy us those roads, bridges and school books. Yeah, and for good measure we'll let 'em buy us the schools too!"

"Jesus Huey, can you do that?"

"Oh hell yes son, and that's only for openers. When I get rolling there's going to be a whole lot more."

"How?" The young man was earnest. He knew he was talking to no fool.

"Only one way. I've got to have the power of the Governors office, but even more important than that is after I get elected, I've got to get that legislature by the balls...." He paused, concluding that wasn't strong enough. "No, I've got to have their balls in my pocket! I don't want them working with me, I want them working for me," jabbing his index finger in the table, "then I'll have the power! I'll be able to do anything I want!" His voice dropped to a whisper. "I'll have something special figured out for my enemies, the people I don't like...," His face changed suddenly from a look of malevolence concerning his enemies, to one of benevolence for this intriguing young bull from the swamps adding, "and I can do anything for those who helped me on my way by believing in me."

"That's great Huey! I count myself as one of those. I hope you do too."

"I do. I do indeed. I like you. I like your style. The world's going to hear much from both of us, and I hope we can always work and pull together, because I think we would make a hell of a team." He continued more or less thinking aloud. "I hope we can always be friends Alex, because I don't think either of us would want the other for an enemy."

"I don't know how I can help, except contribute campaign money, but if I can...."

"Oh hell yes you can, Alex." Emphatically.

"How?"

"I'm weak in the south and before the next governors race I've got to put together strength down there, and I mean real strength."

Alex felt his heart quicken. He knew he could help his friend immensely in the bayou country.

"You know I supported that dumb bastard for governor in the last election, simply because he's from your country, and I wanted some political IOU's. Everybody knew he didn't have a chance, but I was thinking ahead four years. Hell yes, you can help me a lot down there."

"How!"

"Well for one thing you speak the language and I don't. You can sure as hell help there. Then there's this damn religion thing that always comes up whenever you have candidates running for state office."

"Religion?"

"Yeah religion." He paused looking intently at his young friend. "How old are you Alex?"

"Twenty four."

"Jesus Christ, I didn't know you were that young, I thought you were more my age."

"What's that?"

"Thirty one."

"Well I'll be damned. I thought you were more my age." Both laughed, the point was so well made.

Huey had a cherubic face, one he used to advantage when feigning innocence, while Alex definitely looked the older of the two.

Sidetracked momentarily, Huey asked. "How the hell have you done everything you've done, in such a short time. Growing up, helping your mother, quitting school to do it, although that's no big deal, never got a high school diploma myself."

"How'd you get to be a lawyer? I thought you had to go to high school to do that?"

"Went to high school, didn't graduate. The law degree is a whole other story." Waving his arm dismissing the subject. "Anyway you fought in the war and all those jobs in the oil field...married and only twenty four?"

"Married and soon to be a Papa!" Alex beamed, joined by his friend upon hearing the news, who was familiar with the details of the courtship and marriage. He knew how very much the man loved his new wife.

"Oh Alex that's great! Kids are great!" He grew distant adding. "The only problem is they come at the wrong time in our lives."

"How's that?"

"If a man's going to do anything with his life, he's going to be busting his ass when his kids need him the most. You know what I mean?"

Alex nodded, tears suddenly appearing in his eyes because he missed Marie. Leaving home to travel up north was tough enough now, he knew it would be terrible leaving her and a new baby.

Huey didn't want to dwell on it, embarrassed by the emotion he caused.

"How the hell'd we get sidetracked? Where were we?"

"You were talking about religion."

"Yeah, right. I asked you how old you were because I didn't know how many elections you've voted in, but I s'pect the answer to that is none. Right?"

"Right."

"OK! The problem is the state's split politically right across the middle. Draw a line straight through Alexandria, from Mississippi to Texas you'd have a pretty good idea of the religious boundaries of the northern and the southern halves. For sake of discussion you could say the top half is Baptist, and the bottom half is Catholic."

Alex looked at him.

"What are you Alex?"

"Catholic."

"OK. I'm Baptist. See what I mean?"

"Yeah but what's the big deal? I mean who gives a shit?"

"That's just it, nobody should, but lots of folks do and I think it's because of a couple of things. The politicians who are always going to make hay out of anything, especially anything as strong as religion, and now you have the God damn Ku Klux Klan to boot. I hate those chickenshit bastards about as bad as I know how!"

"How come?"

"Because they're such cowardly assholes hiding behind their silly dime store masks, attacking everyone in sight. They hate Jews, Catholics and niggers." He busted out laughing. "Jesus I wonder what they'd think about a Catholic nigger? That'd probably be too much for 'em to handle."

"We got lot's of black Catholics around our country." Alex laughed.

"Well for Christ sake, don't tell those KKK freaks because it would upset 'em real bad, and cause 'em trouble trying to figure who to hate the most. Anyway I need help down in your Catholic country. I need it from the locals, and when the governors race comes around I'll need you. Can I count on you?"

"You bet! Let me know when and where."

"I will Alex, as a matter of fact I've got some guys coming up from LaFayette tomorrow. Pretty big politicians. We're going to put our heads together and see if we can't work up an alliance. They want the Railroad Commission to do some things for them now. I've got some things I want them to do for me, in four years."

"I don't know too many people from LaFayette, my home's south of there, down by St. Martinville."

"Yeah, well you need to know these guys. One's a banker, the other's a hot shot lawyer. Didn't your friend Myron say those are the people you need."

"He did that." Alex nodded agreement.

"Well OK then, we start now." Huey's brow wrinkled in concern. "Although I've got a problem right now with our banker friend."

"What kind of a problem do you have?"

The question puzzled Huey, because of the ominous tone and somber look. He laughed nervously, because he was seeing a side of Alex he didn't know existed.

"Seems our money man likes the ladies. According to his friend the lawyer, he doesn't like to put his shoes under any bed that doesn't have a pair of ladies slippers right next to them. Sort of obsessed about it."

It was Alex's turn to throw back his head and laugh, moving around Huey's desk. He put his arm around his shoulder giving him a powerful hug.

"Well now, what you know my friend? It looks like I get to help you sooner than I thought, because it so happens I have a real good friend who lives in this town and her name is Sue." Huey's eyes widened noticeably. "I guarantee your banker friend is going to like this lady, a whole lot!"

All three men were fascinated by Sue, when Alex appeared with her on his arm, because she was so different from the ordinary lady of the night. She dressed with taste and kept her conversation at a minimum. She didn't want to disclose her ignorance on matters these men were discussing. She excelled at light conversation however, delighting them when the discussion turned that way and included her. The banker was extremely attentive to Sue, and Huey made certain the seating arrangement was such as to place her between Alex, and her lover for the night. Huey was also impressed at the cunning Alex revealed in not wanting the banker to know specifically where he came from in South Louisiana, afraid the man might shy away from his liaison of the evening because of potential risk.

"See what I mean, Huey?" Alex explained. "You want your political IOU's and intend to get them. Well maybe, down the road a piece, I'll need some of this guys money, in the form of a loan. It wouldn't be a half bad idea to know some things about him that are...how you say, compromising? Might make the loan easier to get."

Huey's laugh was infectious anyway, but he was beside himself with joy over this comment.

"Oh Alex, Alex! The first time I met you I had a hunch you were a real sharp operator, but by God you are just impressing the shit clear out of me daily with your scheming, conniving ways, and I love it." Adding "Are you sure you never thought of going into politics?"

"Not only no, but hell no!" Alex emphasized. "I'll leave the political bullshit to the artists," nodding toward Huey who was still enjoying the humor of the moment, "and I think I'm sitting with the master of them all."

Alex meant that as a sincere compliment, without the slightest idea how far this legend to be, was going to travel down America's political highway.

CHAPTER 6

Louise delighted in telling anyone who would listen that her new grandson, a beautiful baby boy, was born nine months and thirty seconds after Alex and Marie were married. She wasn't far off the mark. She was thrilled with his arrival and could not have been more pleased than to take this new baby into her heart. He was a good looking little fellow with much black hair and a sturdy body. It was a foregone conclusion his name was to be Alex, Jr.

"God damn Huey!" Alex beamed, a big cigar clamped in his teeth. "You ought to see that little bugger. Why I swear I think his chest's bigger'n mine."

Huey doubted that, looking at his friend's massive chest, but would give any new father all the bragging rights he wanted.

"Boy I'll tell you something for sure though," Alex said looking disconsolate, "it ain't easy to leave home with the both of them just getting to know one another. Makes me want to quit and go home so's I can be with them."

"Yes Alex!" Huey rushed around his desk. "I hear you! I know what you're saying but you can't do that yet! There's nothing the matter with wanting to be with them, but all in good time."

"What do you mean?"

"You've got to learn the oil business first Alex," Huey was pacing the floor, instantly at his impassioned best, "before you can go back down there to live, and that means you'll have to be traveling back and forth. Your background's excellent, especially for a man your age, but you can't give it up now to be with your family. That's not good thinking. You want them to have everything you can provide don't you?"

"Yes.!"

"Well all right then, get your education and save all the money you can because soon you'll have to go in business for yourself. That's what your friend Myron said didn't he?"

"Yeah, he said it was the ultimate goal."

"Your God damn right it is, and when I'm governor I'll have lots of information that'll be a big help to you." His sincerity was intense. "You know what I mean Alex?"

"Not exactly."

"You probably already know lots of folks suspect what oil's been taken out of south Louisiana is a drop in the bucket to what's really down there. Why they think the next big oil boom could be right down there in your area!"

"Yeah I heard about that but how do I get into the act, unless I get a job as roughneck on a rig down there?"

"No, hell no man! Screw the roughneck job. Drill your own. Your rig, your leases, the whole damn thing yours. Wildcattin'!"

"That's what I want to do Huey, but how? How do I get started?"

"I'll tell you how my boy!" Waving the cigar around expansively. "What you do is let your good friend, the future governor of Louisiana," accompanied by an exaggerated bow and flourish, "extend you a small consideration. I'm going to put you in touch with a man who owes me a very big favor." The wheels were turning in his head, as he picked up momentum. "By the way, you got any money?"

"Sure, some. Saved much as I could. I've made damn good money, what with wells I brought in early, and the bonus money I got for that."

"Good! Listen Alex, I saved this guys ass in a big lawsuit last year. He thought he was going to lose everything, maybe even go to the penitentiary and he didn't. Your's truly with a little of this, and a lot of that, got him off with almost all the skin on his ass." His eyes glowed as he worked out the conversation in his mind. "The son of a bitch owes me, so let's see what I can do in the way of making you a deal...maybe some kind of lease arrangement on one of his rigs. Hell you know the business Alex, and you're young enough to take a gamble with the money you've got, so what do you say, do I put the heat on him?"

There wasn't any other logical course of action and Alex knew it, for he had been following Myron's instructions ever since he got home from France. Like Huey said, what the hell did he have to lose besides his money and while he was not unmindful it was a considerable sum he did agree with his thought. If he crapped out, he had much time in life to get another bankroll together.

"Okay Huey! Whatever it takes, let's go! But for the record what, do you want out of the deal?"

The moment he said it he was afraid he'd hurt Huey's feelings. Afraid he might have offended him, but nothing could have been further from the truth. This man knew how to deal and was in his element when the action was hottest, never offended at the suggestion of any arrangement. He might not accept it, but he certainly wasn't offended.

"Nothing my boy. Actually it's me that owes you because of what you did for my man from LaFayette and how that worked out for me. I got everything out of him I wanted, but so you don't think you're getting off Scot free on my end, I'm going to let you contribute whatever you can to my campaign. Maybe even do some advance work for me down in coonassville." Extending his hand. "Fair enough?"

"Fair enough and it's done, the part about helping you in...." he laughed, "what'd you call it, coonassville? Who knows, I may split my drawers wildcattin' and need a job running interference for you, or cutting cane, or some damn thing."

"Bullshit!" He was adamant. The preacher light was in his eyes again. "I see nothing but success for you and me! I mean it Alex! I want you to mean it and believe it right along with me. For some reason I've always felt like a child of destiny, and I see that same quality in you."

Huey was right. He was right about a lot of things.

The next few years were tumultuous ones for these two fast friends, Alex in his beloved oil business and Huey in the world of politics. As he had predicted they were as wildly successful as they had hoped and worked for, each driven in his own way, their paths crossing many times.

Alex got his deal on the drilling rig, with the help of his politician friend. It was up to him to see that it paid off by arranging concessions to the owner of the equipment, then making whatever kind of long deals on leases he could to get property owners to sign with him. He didn't have too much trouble with that part, because his reputation as a square dealer preceded him. A man's word was worth something in those days.

He didn't try to pull the wool over anyone's eyes trusting instead to his down home style and the ability to talk, one on one, with these poor scrub farmers. He'd learned a great deal from Huey, and wasn't above using some of the master politician's practices to convince people to do business with him. Huey had discovered the magic button accidentally many years before, watching another politician. The lesson was, you could badger the poor by pointing out to them what fools they were for letting the rich get over on them, deserving all they'd get.

"The have's against the have nots," he enthused, "and I'm their champion. That's the juice it'll take to get me where I'm going."

"Oh yeah!" He would assault his small town audiences with great emphasis, rolling his eyes. "You're the ones the big shots love to stomp on, do you know that? Yes I'm talking about you." He would point directly at someone in the audience who had nodded vigorously in agreement at everything he said. "A dumb bunch of redneck hicks, but do you know what?" He would scream. "Huey P. Long ain't goin' to allow it no more! No sir! No way! Those high falutin' Yankee boys have had it their way long enough. It's time they come down off their pedestals and let us poor folks share in the good things!" He always had them going at this point, adding. "And if they won't come down," he would scream, "we'll, by God, drag them down, and do you know why? BECAUSE WE ARE THE PEOPLE! WE ARE THE POWER!"

This always brought his audience to a screaming frenzy and he could do anything with them from there.

He looked like an avenging eagle, matching rich against poor, with his electrifying gestures and expressions that not only swept his followers along with him, but also frightened off all but the most stout hearted foes.

"That's what those high toned money boys want you know, is to keep us dumb hicks down on the farm, while they lolligag around in their fancy cars with their fine, fine clothes, and those purty looking sweet smellin' women." His arms flailed in the wind like a chicken with it's head cut off.

The really amazing thing was, he got away with insulting his followers by convincing them he was not only one of them, but was their savior and only hope. He moved them with his evangelical fervor from the political stump. It was said later he was one of the five most powerful speakers in the world, in the first half of the twentieth century, and versatility was his hallmark, able to speak on any subject, anytime, anyplace.

Alex was a natural born salesman too, and with lessons learned from Huey, became unstoppable. Dark curly hair outlining a powerful, broad smiling face, and thick French accent that made listening to him such a pleasure. He knew he had all these things going for him and used them to his great advantage, emphasizing to the maximum whatever it took to get the men laughing and leaning his direction. He also utilized to the fullest his Gallic charm for the women when they were present.

"If you don't sign up with me, why the first thing you know some slick dude from Standard Oil, or one of those other high falutin'," that was Huey's very special word, making it sound like a vile disease, "New York oil boys is going to come sashaying right on up here." He would swing his hips outrageously. "Man what I mean, right up the path here to your house, with his slick hair and cute little mustache. Wearing a pretty white suit with pointy toed shoes, and you know what he's going to be thinking?"

"No! What?" The answer always the same.

He'd twist his face into a most disdainful look, like he'd smelled something real bad.

"Huh, he'd think, I got me another one of those dumbass country boys right here yeah. Think I'll flim flam this hayseed and see if I can steal his underwear right off his backside...." followed by salacious laughter playing to the big eyes staring at him. "Heh, heh and see if the dumb shit ever knowed what hit him!" It worked for Huey, and it worked for Alex, using homespun tactics with very unsophisticated people.

"Jesus Huey, where'd you get these?" He asked with amazement during a visit with his friend. "These things cost a hell of a lot of money and are guarded like gold."

He had surveyors reports, indicating the possibility of oil in a particular area, given to him by Huey after he'd arranged the deal on the rig.

"Call it providential Alex, but given the circumstances of their acquisition it'd be best for all concerned if that was my secret. Okay?"

It was okay.

The oil business was swinging into a fever pitch in the triangle created by the adjoining corners of Texas, Oklahoma and Louisiana. There were land men behind every bush, trying to out hustle the competition for whatever leases were to be had. Luck, or Alex wondered if it was something beyond luck, Myron maybe, was with him on his very first effort. Nothing could have been more welcome because by the time they hit oil he was almost broke, investing every cent he had in the effort, plus running up debt as far as his creditors would allow.

His first well hit in Oklahoma with his coerced rig and a lease from a widow with a nine hundred acre trash farm that wasn't good for raising much of anything except scrub brush. When Alex arrived to talk lease, he found an interested and amazing listener.

"Mrs. Tate," he told the lady, "if you let me drill on your property I think we'll have a winner here. Want to know why I say that?"

"Yes? Yes I would."

She was listening carefully, squinting slightly as they sat on rickety chairs on an even more dilapidated porch.

"This'll be my very first attempt at drillin' on my own, as an independent operator that is, although I've done everything there is to do on a well site, as far as the actual work's concerned. I know what I'm doing when it comes to drilling, Mrs. Tate. I believe there's oil under your property and some geologists think so too. Sound interesting?" He hoped she couldn't hear his pulse pounding in his ears.

"Go on sonny." She replied, eyes half shut.

"OK. Now what I propose is you and me go into business together, and see if we can bring us in a good one." She laughed out loud, thinking Alex wanted her to invest money. "Oh Alex, you know that all sounds real good but for one thing."

"What's that ma'am?"

She was a big, strong, good natured woman, exactly the kind it took to be on a piece of property like that, and while she was poor, very poor, there was nothing wrong with her sense of humor.

"You know son, Mr. Tate was a real fine man, in his way. We had a pretty good life together, starving to death out here in this Godforsaken country." They laughed together. "Well bless his dead old heart, he did the best he could you know, but really the only thing he ever did worth a shit, was to outrun a bunch of other idiots on the day they opened this God damn territory to the homesteaders."

This caused her deep thought.

"Come to think of it Alex, when you look around this scrub you gotta think maybe the rest of those runners wasn't the idiots, maybe just old Mr. Tate was for claiming this place." She had a real twinkle in her eye and Alex knew he was being included in a special family joke. "Maybe," her eyebrows arched, "the dumb son of a bitch simply passed out here from all his running, somebody found him laying here and figured it was his claim."

Alex was amazed at the torrent of words from this woman, doing all he could to keep a straight face. He didn't know if he was being jerked around or not.

"Anyway, other than a few scraggly assed chickens, two milkin' cows, couple of no account dogs and some hogs," she spoke in an exaggerated nasal tone, "why honey Mr. Tate didn't leave me a pot to piss in, nor a window to throw it out."

Alex loved to laugh anyway, and felt his control slipping away.

"Why do you know if it took a nickel to get to Dallas, sweetheart I couldn't get out of sight. I'd love to be in business with you honey, but the fact is I'm poor! I don't have any God damn money!"

Her face was frozen in the sweetest, most insipid smile he could ever remember seeing. Alex lost his self control, laughing so hard the tears were rolling down his face. He thought for better or worse, this was certainly his kind of woman. He loved her candid observation of life, Mr. Tate and this farm she was stuck on, and he was dead certain she did not have the means to leave it. After wiping his tears away he explained she wouldn't have to put up any money.

"You mean not even a red cent, honey?"

"No, ma'am Mrs. Tate. The only thing you have to put up is your signature right here on the lease. I do the rest."

"What's the rest, Alex?"

"Well ma'am, getting a crew, movin' the rig in here, settin' up, buyin' supplies. You know, drill stem and bits, casing, chain and cable, and find some place to bed and board me and my crew."

"How much would that be in money?"

"When all's said and done Mrs. Tate, you're usually talking twenty five thousand dollars. We go deeper now and you figure a well on so many dollars a foot. You multiply one by the other."

Mrs. Tate stopped rocking, and looked at Alex in concern.

"Baby, this whole God damn place, chickens and all ain't worth shit, much less any twenty five thousand. Who's gonna put up that kinda money?"

"I am." Swallowing hard as he said it.

"You are! Where'd you get all that money?" She was really squinting now, directly at Alex. "How the hell old are you anyway?"

"Twenty four goin' on a lot older ma'am. What I have, I've earned in wages plus bonuses as a driller. I worked for some people Mrs. Tate, who showed their gratitude for wells brought in early with big bonuses, and I saved 'em. I got about eighteen thousand cash and a deal on this rig. I know where the deals are on pipe and supplies, so I think we can make it."

"You get oil every time you go looking?" She asked with concern because she liked this interesting young man and did not wish to be responsible in any way for spending all his money without finding oil.

"Wish that were so Mrs. Tate," very serious, "but it doesn't work that way. Matter of fact that's what causes wildcatters to go broke, hittin' dry holes." He shook his head. "'cause then what you got is a real deep hole with a lot of money stuffed in it."

"Well, what's our chances and what do we get out of it?"

"About one in three drilled are dry holes Mrs. Tate, and what you'd get out of that would be a real deep, skinny hole you could dump shit in." He thought after what she'd said and the language used, he could take a few liberties of his own. "You know Mrs Tate," he started to lighten up, "if we get a duster you might even be able to move your outhouse over it and become famous for having the deepest privy in the county!"

She liked the thought, exploding with laughter.

"I'd sure have to be careful if that were to happen, cause I have a tendency to hold my breath 'til I hear the splash." Pausing to do her mental calculations. "How deep would that thing be, sweetheart?"

"Maybe three thousand feet."

"Oh my God! Well then we couldn't put the privy over that 'cause my neighbors might find me sitting on that thing dead, with a blue face from holding my breath 'til I heard her hit!"

Alex felt in his heart this effort was going to be a success because this outrageous character, Mrs. Tate, simply could not be anything but a harbinger of good luck, and she was.

"How much do I get out of this thing if we," she was already in the deal mentally, "come up with a bunch of oil?"

"Well you'll get a bonus for signing the lease and one eighth of whatever's down there."

"What might that be in money?" Accompanied by her sweeter than sugar smile.

"Well say we got one that produced five hundred barrels a day."

"That much?" She interrupted.

"Yes ma'am. They've brought in ten thousand barrel a day producers. The first one down in Spindletop, that's in Texas, was that big and there've been others. There was a field up Tulsa way had some big ones too."

"Well sweet Jesus!" She sighed.

"Anyway let's be conservative and say five hundred barrels a day. What they call crude oil is going for around two fifty a barrel now, so that would be twelve hundred and fifty dollars a day." He did some arithmetic "Your share'd be around a hundred fifty a day."

Her eyes were like saucers, as she was tried to project these numbers. Alex came to her rescue.

"'be about four thousand five hundred a month Mrs. Tate." Almost whispering. "What would you do with that kind of money?"

She sat there trying to take it all in, calculating even what it would mean in a year, her eyes growing ever larger as the numbers added up.

"I've got kids all over Oklahoma and Texas, Alex," she brushed away a tear at the thought, "and the first thing I'd do is send 'em all some money to make things easier." She was staring into the future, various expressions matching her visions. "You know, those babies of mine had to leave, they couldn't make a livin' 'round here. Now wouldn't it be somethin' if this old farm up and produced lots of money, so's maybe their lives'd be nicer than mine was." She grew thoughtful adding. "You know what though Alex?"

"No ma'am."

"Except for having no cash money, me and old Mr. Tate had one hell of a life together!"

"I'll bet you did, Mrs. Tate."

"Mabel!"

"What?"

"Alex, you and me is going to be partners and so I want you to call me Mabel, 'cause that's my name."

"Okay. Mabel it is!"

"Anyway, I tease about Mr. Tate a lot, but only because he teased about himself and enjoyed doing it. I'll tell you something for sure though, if I had it all to do over, I sure would try and find him again." Real tears filled her eyes.

"That's about as fine a statement as you could make about a man, Mabel. I'll bet he felt exactly the same about you. You seem like one hell of a woman to me."

She shook off the nostalgic mood, returning to her normal state. "When's the money start comin' in, honey?"

"Soon's the oil comes up."

"Well then get the God damn rig in here and let's either get some oil, or one hell of a deep shithouse!"

They signed the lease, celebrating with some of Mr. Tate's "corn squeezin's" as she called it, which was as close to liquid fire as Alex had ever come. He didn't know as it scorched his throat, nose and stomach going down whether he was going to survive. He was assured, only a little, because Mabel was having a healthy blast too.

When he found his voice again, he rasped. "What'll we call the well, Mabel?"

"You mean you put names on 'em?"

"Yep!"

"Christ honey I don't know. Got any ideas?"

"Oh yeah, I got just the name for it." He was wiping the booze generated tears away.

"What? What's it going to be?"

He was smiling broadly, thinking. 'Shit son, this partnership's goin' to be a winner.' Mr. Tate's brew was already at work, altering his brain.

"Let's call it The Mabel Tate Number 1"

"Would you do that Alex, honey?"

"I would, and since I'm the majority stockholder in this deal," declaring with alcoholic expansiveness, "that's what it's going to be!"

"By God Alex, I like that!" His exultation dimmed as she added. "Let's have a tad more of Mr. Tates squeezin's to seal the deal."

He remembered for years, the drive away from her farm and the emotions that went with him. First there was his mental state which was almost drunk, a result of the powerful moonshine booze. Elation about the signing of the lease. Excitement over beginning a career as an independent oil producer, or possibly ending one. He was also nervous thinking about the risks and responsibilities he was undertaking, and yet knew without any doubt, it was what he had to do.

*   *   *

After arranging transportation for the rig from Shreveport to the Tate farm, Alex was drinking his last night away. He'd stopped in to see his friend Huey for some company and last minute pep talk, but found he was out of town, leaving Alex with no one to talk to. More drinks resolved that when he found himself at the house where Sue worked.

"God damn baby, I don't mind tellin you, I'm scared!" He offered earnestly. "Every cryin' assed dime I've got's on the line, and we're digging a deep hole in the ground."

Sue had never known gloomy thought from this positive man, and tried to turn his thinking around. She listened attentively, shocked at his attitude, but pleased to see him. He'd not been to see her since his marriage to Marie and she was excited for him when he told her, with the freedom the booze imparted, all about Alex, Jr. Sue paid close attention to the details, a tear appearing now and then during his discourse. It was a bittersweet experience. Alex was the love of her life, but she knew he was absolutely unattainable.

"Alex," she whispered after having sex with her Cajun lover, "I know you've got the magic sweetheart. You must believe that too, don't you? You can make it happen! You will make it happen. Please Baby don't worry, it's going to turn out good. I know it!"

"Christ I hope so Sue, but anyway it sure is great having people like you and Huey and...." he stopped.

"And Marie!"

"Yes...." his tone changed.

"Alex you're conscience isn't going to be hurting over this when you go to Oklahoma, is it?"

"Probably."

She rose up on one elbow, distracting him again by the exposure of her breast, truly a beautiful sight.

"There's something you should know. I don't ask, or even suggest you understand, but I want you to know." She put her arms around him pulling his head down against her breasts, holding him tight. "For better or worse Alex you have two women who love you. Your beautiful child bride and your own private whore."

He started to pull away in protest but she held him tight against her, causing him to lessen his struggle.

"No, no. I am a whore, Alex! I know that. I chose this life and it's okay with me, but before that I'm a human being susceptible to all human conditions, one of which is falling in love. Under no circumstances do I want to hear you say you love me to make me feel good. I know who you love, and that's your Marie down there in the swamps." Her eyes were full of tears, sweet loving tears for this man she loved so much. She knew she could never have him but felt no malice toward Marie because she did. "I only ask one thing of you Cher, please come to see me whenever you can, anytime you can, and with no remorse. You know I'll do you no harm. I love you and love being with you, if only for awhile."

She was very talkative while Alex was dressing, trying to buoy up his spirits and hers too.

"Are you going to see Huey while you're in town?"

"No, he's gone to Baton Rouge. His secretary doesn't know when he'll be back, but I'm leaving in the morning anyway. No, I only wanted to say hello and have him pump me up for the job. You know, generate enthusiasm," smothering her in his great bear hug of an embrace, "but I like the way you do it a hell of a lot better."

"I'll tell him hello for you." She offered. "Your friend from LaFayette seems to have a lot of business up here now, and Huey calls me every time he comes in."

"Oh ho, so you're serving our future governor, eh!"

"No, no," she laughed, "you might say in service for the governor. He's one more special guy Alex, and I enjoy helping him however I can. Besides, what the hell, if his LaFayette friend likes the ladies and is willing to pay for their company, I might's well be that lady."

*   *   *

The Tate farm became a beehive of activity with the arrival of Alex, his crew, and the endless stacks of exotic equipment they brought with them. He moved everything he owned to the site, and after getting situated set about the drilling operation, driving his crew very hard. They responded well, knowing all his marbles were down on the operation, inspired by his indefatigable fervor.

Mrs. Tate did everything she could to help. She knew what a gamble this young man was taking and wanted desperately to be part of the effort. When the crew showed up to begin drilling, they were amazed at how livable she'd made the barn, turning it into a more than adequate bunkhouse. She added even more to the effort by keeping the spirits of the crew at a high level with her incessant and thoroughly delightful chatter. To a man they felt knowing the departed Mr. Tate would have been an experience but after listening to Mabel chatter on about him, he seemed to be part of the job.

"How much further do we have to go, Honey?" She'd ask Alex every night, listening attentively as he explained their progress.

One day, after they'd been drilling for weeks, Alex ran onto the porch shouting, "Mabel! Mabel! Come see Cher!"

"What?" She ran to the door wiping her hands on her apron. "What is it Alex, have we struck oil?"

"No, but we're getting close!" He was clearly beside himself with excitement. "Come see what we got!"

They bounced out to the site in Alex's Model T, it was located on a raised mound about a half mile from the house. Mabel watched Alex closely, while he animatedly described where they were in the drilling process. She was deeply concerned about him, watching his strain build with each passing day, doing whatever she could to give him relief. She was truly an outrageous character and she knew it, using any opportunity to reduce this intense, hard working, Frenchman to a mass of laughter and tears.

'Oh dear God,' she prayed on the bumpy ride, 'if it's Your will, please let this boy succeed in this thing he's doing.' She continued with tears of concern in her eyes, casting a glance at the intense man behind the wheel. 'Please sweet Jesus, this boy's got everything he owns riding on this, and I know the chance of failure is really gettin' to him. So please, please God help him find the oil, so he can go back to his family rich instead of poor.' She paused and then continued. 'Hope it's okay God, if I ask for wealth for Alex? Isn't that what we mean when we pray, give us this day our daily bread? If that is okay, then I'm asking you now.'

"What the hell's the matter with you Mabel?" Alex glanced at her, her eyes brimming with tears. "You all right?"

"Just one of those damned flying varmints hit me in the eye, sweetie." She answered, ever true to her hard ass reputation, adding with her pasted up smile. "And why don't you watch where you're going anyway. Don't be watchin' me!"

He laughed, and that pleased her.

'Listen Heavenly Father,' she continued, 'long's I'm asking, I'd like You to know I got nothing against old Mabel here being rich either, soooooooo....'

"See!" Alex commanded after they'd mounted the rig, holding out a handful of ugly, wet, black sand. "See what I told you!"

"Jesus!" Feigning disgust. "Did you bring me out here for this?" She was playing straight man to Alex's intensity. "Whatever it is, I've seen cow poop that looked and smelled nicer than that ugly mess!"

"No, no, Mabel! Listen to me! We're close!" He insisted, bypassing her attempt at humor.

His visible strain, made her hurt for Alex and she wanted to come up with something, anything, to break the tension.

"That's sand from the bottom of the well!" He shouted over the noise of the rig. "The black color's caused by oil! God damn it hon', it's down there! We're close!"

"Here, smell it!" He held the handful of ugly, wet, black sand under her nose. "You know what that smells like, don't you?"

"No!" She screamed over the rig noise.

"It smells like money!" His reply.

Mabel bent forward inhaling deeply, straightening up with a terrible expression on her face, announcing in a shrill scream.

"Might smell like money to you sweetie, but it smells like nothin' more'n one of Mr. Tate's beer and hard boiled egg farts, to me!"

She did it again, cutting through Alex's strain, reducing him to helplessness he laughed so hard.

The Mabel Tate #1 came in shortly after the sand episode and just before Alex was completely broke. He spent every cent he had and more on credit right down to the discovery of oil, but when she came in he knew his financial troubles were a thing of the past. He and Mabel danced around the platform, each of them aware all of their dreams were going to be realized.

"I told you Mabel. Dammit I told you!" He exulted. "I knew this'd work! The first time we met, I knew you were the kiss of fortune I needed!"

"Yes baby, and you know how too don't you? Lots of hard work and faith. Oh Alex, I'm so happy!" Then she asked with her special squinty eyed look. "How much will it make?"

"The way I see it right now Mabel," his smile radiated, "we're looking at a thousand barrels a day!"

The effect obviously stunned her, which upset Alex. He'd never seen a person have a heart attack, but he'd heard of them.

"You okay, Mabel?"

"Yes. Yes Alex. Let me catch my breath a little. Did you say a thousand barrels a day?"

"Looks like that now."

"Why honey, that would mean double everything you told me. What am I going to do with all that money?"

Alex was his old gregarious self now and then some. He was a rich man and knew it, producing a generosity of thought and spirit he hadn't enjoyed since the gamble started.

"Looks to me like you can do anything you want, because we're talking lot's of money. Those kids of yours? I s'pect they're all going to be wealthy! Probably their kids too! They'll all share in this Hon', because what you get out of this well ain't going to be nothin' compared to what you're gonna get!" He stopped, afraid it might be too much for her at one time.

"What the hell are you saying Alex?"

"Your farm's nine hundred acres. Even drilling conservative, there'll be lot's more wells on this property."

All of this was beyond her ability to understand. How she could be dirt poor one day, and an extremely wealthy woman the next?

"Alex sweetie, when you and the boys get this thing under control let's go over to the house and drink the rest of Mr. Tate's lightnin' to celebrate."

Ordinarily this would have been terrifying news for Alex, more of Mr. Tate's fiery "Panther Piss", but he joined this celebration gleefully.

The last Alex ever saw of Mabel Tate was when she left the farm, turning everything over to him, to do with as he saw fit.

"Going to Dallas sweetie." She gave Alex a big kiss on the mouth. "Don't know what I'm going to do after I set the kids up, but dammit Alex, I've still got some spark left in me. Why shoot, with the kind of money I've got, I should be able to buy any kind of husband I want. I don't think Mr. Tate would mind, do you?"

"Mabel, from what you've told me about Mr. Tate I think he'd be jumping for joy up in heaven right now. Joy for you and joy for finding this piece of shit farm back there. Makes him look pretty smart right now doesn't it? I'm sure anything you'd want to do with your money would be okay by him."

With that he swept her up in one of his great Alex George hugs, nearly squeezing the life out of her. He watched her bounce down the road in the Model T he'd given her, wearing a blue and white figured cotton print dress, with a stiff brimmed straw hat conjured up from some strange place. He knew he would never, ever, forget Mabel Tate.

CHAPTER 7

The years rushed by for Alex because of his involvement in so very many ventures, each making great demands on his time. His wealth was assured with the income from Mabel Tate's farm alone, but like most oilmen the excitement of the hunt meant far more than the money itself. He drilled everywhere, but in financial comfort produced by his original strike. At least now the inevitable dry holes encountered in drilling became welcome tax deductions instead of utter catastrophe, as it would have been on his first try.

He kept his promise to Huey too, contributing great sums of money to his campaign for governor plus organizing appearances in the bayou country. It was during one of these that Huey saw, for the only time in their friendship, what a terrible foe Alex was when angered and what a ferocious brawler he really was.

Alex, who was a capable speaker in his own right, was warming up a crowd for Huey in New Iberia, a neighboring town to his own LaFayette. He was feeling expansive, joking and having fun with the people when a group, discovered later to have been planted by the opposition, started heckling and jeering.

"Tell it in English!" One of the hecklers shouted, after a burst of laughter from the crowd at the finish of one of his jokes. Alex knew they were not from the area because everyone there spoke French. He didn't take kindly to the interruption.

"Oh but everybody here speaks French, yeah. We like stories in our own language, my friend." He was trying to be cordial.

"What's the matter with American, you got something against that?" Alex felt a strange tingling sensation along the back of his neck, that always suggested to him what a dog must feel, when their fur stands up in anger.

"Oh no, no, pardner." Alex was smiling but Huey noted it wasn't his usual smile at all. To accommodate them though he proceeded to tell the joke to the hecklers, in English. They didn't like it and neither did Alex. Suddenly he stopped.

"You know something boys? It ain't even funny in English."

The group of three, big, rough looking men, edged closer until they were standing right in front of Huey when Alex introduced him. He had spoken only a short time when the heckling started again. Alex knew they had been hired for this disruptive purpose.

It was Huey's custom to tell a few jokes too, with which he loved to illustrate points.

"Why don't you tell it in French, asshole." The biggest one in the group asked. Huey paused. Alex knew he was upset, because almost nothing ever slowed him down during a speech.

"Oh how I wish I could, friend. I love these people and their beautiful language, but I'm afraid if I tried, it'd sound real dumb."

"Sounds pretty God damn dumb no matter how you two assholes say it, so why don't you just shut up and...."

Huey's mind couldn't function fast enough to comprehend what happened next. He saw the huge fist smash into his hecklers face, blood and teeth flying every way. He had a look of stunned disbelief in his eyes as he went down.

'What the hell....' He thought, instantly aware the devastating fist was attached to the massive arm of his friend Alex. Alex pushed Huey aside while slamming another of the group with his elbow, catching the man under the nose with an unbelievable noise. He dropped to the ground without uttering a sound. The third tough was trying desperately to make it through the crowd but didn't. He was caught by the shoulder and spun around, catching a momentary glimpse of the broad fist smashing into his jaw. The whole affair lasted 10 seconds.

"Jesus Christ Alex, I've seen some fights, but I've never seen anything like that in my whole life. You know I couldn't figure out what was happening when you hit that first guy. I simply could not comprehend what was happening."

Huey was badly shaken, not sure whether it was because of what might have happened to him, or what did happen to the three imported toughs.

"One minute I'm talking away, and the next a big arm with a fist on it whistles past my ear and right into this face in front of me. How the hell'd you know it was time to nail him?"

"Aw shit Huey, when you've been in as many fights as I have, you just know when it's time. I saw this asshole easin' up in your face, fixin' to bust you good." Shrugging his shoulders. "I beat him to it."

"Where in the name of God did you ever learn to hit with an elbow like that?" Still wide eyed, "I'm telling you I've never seen or heard anything like that. Jesus Christ Alex, I thought from the sound, you hit him with a ball bat."

"Guy in a saloon in East Texas laid one on me, and while I've been hit a lot, I never in my life saw stars like that night." Alex laughed. "It was all I could do to hang on and keep him from killin' me 'til I could think."

"What happened?"

"I got 'im, finally! Knocked him out! Then I waited for him to come to, so he could teach me how to do that. I'll tell you somethin', you hit a guy with one of them, and do it right? I guarantee the fights over!"

"Son of a bitch!" Huey shook his head in disbelief. "How much you worth now Alex?"

Laughing, knowing the shock he caused his friend and aware he was going to be teased, Alex answered.

"Hell I don't know Huey. Lots, thanks to you. Why?"

"Don't s'pose you'd come work for me full time so's you could discourage people from stompin' my ass, would you?"

He knew the request was out of the question, but he had to ask. Huey was grateful for his rescue and longed to have a bodyguard like this.

"Huey, fighters like me come and go. They're a dime a dozen." There was no way Huey believed that. "So what you gotta' do is find a good one, and I wouldn't waste any time about it. You do have a way with words that seems to piss off lots of folks. Why hell, I've read and heard they're taking tickets and standing in line for a chance to bust your ass good."

Huey wasn't in to fighting. He had a real aversion to it but he was thinking it over as Alex continued.

"Unfortunately Huey, although I'm kidding you right now, what I say is the truth. I'm all for you and unless you do something to change my mind I think I always will be. I believe you want to help the little man. I think you do want better schools, and roads, and bridges. I don't think you're shittin' when you say we gotta do all we can for our kids."

"I do mean that, Alex."

"Yeah, well that's great and I'll guarantee you, you got my vote and my money," he leaned across the table taking Huey by the forearm, "but Huey you're getting into the most dangerous waters of all when you get in the rich guys pockets. They're no patsys, not those bastards. They ain't going to lay down, roll over, stick their feet in the air and let you take nothin' away from them. And if you think they're not up to killin' to protect what they got, you better think again."

Huey's eyes grew larger, he never gave the possibility of being killed serious consideration.

"You're right Huey, you need a bodyguard. Now for Christ's sake do yourself a favor and don't go gettin' any fancy type who gets up on his toes and dances around. You know what I mean, punch and jab real sweet like? No bullshit man, get yourself a brawler that can clean out a room anyway possible, with his fists or a table leg. A man devoted to you and you alone, one you can trust. Oh, and one more thing Huey."

"What's that?"

"Make sure he can shoot!"

*   *   *

Huey was inaugurated as governor in 1928 and Alex was standing close by. They basked in the adulation accorded him.

"Damn Alex, ain't it something. I've been working for this a long time, you know it? Ten years to be exact. Now it's mine and I'm having a hard time realizing it."

"It's yours all right Huey. You fought for it and you won it. You got the ball my friend. Now run with it!"

*   *   *

Alex slowed down long enough to build a beautiful home for his beloved Marie and their young son in LaFayette, backing it up to a bayou in exquisite surroundings of grass and trees decorated with the ever present, gorgeous Spanish moss. Marie was afraid it was too pretentious, a couple their age having a home as grand as it was, but Alex prevailed and they moved into their first and last home.

1930 saw two pivotal events in Alex's life, starting with grave financial reversals. Oklahoma was experiencing a serious glut in oil supplies caused by over production. Few understood the value of conservation. Everyone in the oil business was trying to get as much out of the ground as possible with no consideration for the consequences until prices slid from $2.50 to .10 cents a barrel. They soon learned the consequences.

"God damn Huey, it's tough up there, but I swear I admire what the governor's done about it."

"Yeah, I do too Alex. Old fart marched the National Guard in there and shut you boys down, didn't he? That took some guts, huh. Governor of Texas did the same thing?"

"Oh yeah. They say they're going to keep her down 'til the price goes back up. That's okay, but what ain't okay is I've got some ball busting expenses going right on. Something better give soon or I'm in deep shit."

"That serious for you, Alex?"

"It's that serious. Lots of money going out and nothing coming in."

A look of deep concern came over Huey's face as he thought of the possibilities facing his friend.

"How much can you lose?"

"All of it!"

"What about the house in LaFayette?"

"No, no. I'm safe there, paid cash for it and it's in my mothers name. Did that just in case. You remember our old friend the banker who was so sweet on Sue? Well he suggested that. Said oil men have a way of splittin' their drawers real quick like. You know, goin' broke over night. I also got some start up money in a bank account in her name, so if I crap out in Oklahoma and Texas I got somethin' nobody can get to, to fire up again."

"Christ that is bad." Feeling for his friend, wondering how he could help this man who gave him so much support when he needed it. "By the way Alex did you know Sue was in town now?"

"What town?" The magic had never left.

"Baton Rouge. You know, the state capital of Louisiana? This town."

"God I'd love to see her Huey, how long's she stayin'?"

"For good I guess. That lady's no dummy you know." Huey was beaming, he understood the deep bond between them. "There's lots of action down here and since she does know the governor, having done some things for friends of yours truly, she thought she might be able to clean up. I s'pect she's right."

"I'm glad to hear that. That's a real special lady in my life."

"I know you think a lot of her Alex and don't take offense when I tell you I think it's a damn shame we don't all have what she does to sell, there'd be a lot less people starving."

"True, there's hard times all around and lots of folks have nothing at all, so no matter what happens it could always be worse."

"Oh shit, Alex, I really feel bad about this. Tell you what though, hang tough, something is bound to come up to turn this around for you."

"Yeah? Well that luck may have already shown up."

"How? What do you mean?"

"Marie's pregnant again. I'm going to have a beautiful blonde daughter. She's going to be my own personal good luck charm."

"How the hell do you know that? How you know its going to be a girl, much less a blonde girl?" Huey asked suspiciously, aware of many tales of voodoo that came out of the swamps.

"Aside from yourself, you know anybody in your whole life, lucky as me?"

Thinking about it, Huey decided he was right.

"Well then, do you think after having a barrel chested dark haired baby boy I could have anything but a carbon copy of Marie? Hell no! She'll be here in a couple of months and her name's Mary."

*   *   *

Mary showed up on schedule exactly as Alex had suggested, bringing with her the winsome smiles and soft noises to steal her fathers heart away, and she did it totally.

"Alienation of affection!" Marie laughed.

"What Cher?"

"Alienation of affection. I read that's a big reason for divorces, and when I get mine it'll be because this little lady took you away from me!"

Alex put Mary down and with an expression of great tenderness in his eyes took his beloved wife in his arms.

"Nobody will ever take me away from you, Marie. God maybe, but no one else. Yes, I do adore this beautiful baby because she is a new version of you. Oh Cher, I'm so grateful to God for letting me have all three of you, but you know how it is, the men are always going to love the girl child in a special way."

It was that way in their family too, Marie had a special bond with her first born, while the tiny blond was the center of Alex's attention. He spent a lot of time at home after she was born because he wanted to. He missed his sons infancy, and there was nothing to go back up north for now, the situation was so dreary.

It stayed that way long enough to create an unbelievable financial strain on Alex, forcing him to sell his holdings and equipment, for a fraction of their worth. All that is, except the rig he used to bring the Mabel Tate #1 in. He would not sell that one, viewing it as another of his good luck pieces, so he had it shipped back to LaFayette and stored, waiting for better times.

"Boy you were right Huey, those big bastards will tear your ass up real bad if they get the chance. They knew I was down and out, extended as far as I could stretch, so they just naturally ate me right up."

"Well you came away with something, Alex."

Huey suggested as they walked down the hall accompanied by Huey's ever present bodyguard. He took Alex at his word hiring a man built much like him, short, dark, 'probably Italian,' Alex thought when he saw him, with a powerful deep chest, heavy arms. There was a difference however, and that was disposition. He had only one and it was bad. Huey and Alex were grateful for his apparent lack of good humor though, because he would never be distracted by normal things or light banter.

"I want you to meet Sam Battaglia, Alex. He's decided to come to work for me. Sort of be a jack of all trades."

He wanted to laugh at first, but didn't as he shook the mans hand. Battaglia was an extremely hostile looking man, wearing a wide snap brim hat and a double breasted suit with the coat unbuttoned. Alex knew why. His arms were extra long giving him the appearance of a member of the ape family. He had a round shouldered posture which made his hands hang side by side in front of his body, instead of at his side.

Alex bristled only a bit when he shook hands with Battaglia, but dismissed the feeling when Huey explained. "They say he got messed up in the war Alex, and he hasn't been right since, but he's really something."

"What you mean?"

"I mean this guy watches after me like a dog. And you talk about loyal? I think he'd do anything, and I do mean anything, I asked him and never blink an eye. What you think of him?"

"I'll say you listen good." Alex laughed.

"What do you mean?"

"Well, he looks like a bowling ball with feet. I s'pect it'd take a truck to knock him down. I'll bet he don't know shit about fancy fighting. I'll also bet he could clear out a room pretty quick, and that's real good, but you know the best part of all?"

"What?" Wondering what extra bonus Alex saw in this man.

"He obviously doesn't like anyone...no one at all, to get near you." He paused for a minute, adding. "Probably more accurate to say he doesn't like anyone at all, period!"

"How can you tell?"

"When we shook hands, he was staring in my eyes and he wasn't smiling. I know what he was thinking."

"What?"

"He was figurin' if he could whip my ass, and I got no problem with that, 'cause that's exactly what you need. One more thing though, can he shoot?"

"We're working on that." Huey smiled.

Sam Battaglia got behind the wheel of the car as Alex and Huey took their seats in the back.

"Going over to see how they're coming on the new state capital building." Huey explained

"What about the old one?"

"Outgrew it. Jesus son, don't you read the papers?"

Alex laughed, "I love you Huey, but you're in a business I think is the absolute shits. I steer way wide of anything in the paper that looks like politics."

"You mean you don't like to read about me, Alex?"

"Only to make sure nobody's killed you." Then leaning into Huey's ear whispering. "But long's you've got that God damn ape up there," indicating Battaglia in the front seat, "I don't think anybody could get close enough to do it."

Huey laughed pleased with his choice, especially since Alex was impressed too.

"What you need a new capital for Huey, toilets quit workin' in the old one?" He was aware of his disdain for personal comforts.

"Symbol, Alex. Symbol. We're gonna yank this sleepy God damn state right out of civil war times and shove it into the twentieth century, whether those high falutin' rich boys that been running things all these years like it or not. No 'count assholes never done an honest God damn days work in their lives, livin' on name and reputation. Well screw em', I got 'em on the run now. Tried to impeach my ass, they did, and I busted their balls!"

Alex felt uncomfortable when Huey started ranting about personal power, fearful he might forget why he wanted the job.

Huey continued, his eyes glittering.

"Those all powerful sons of bitches, and Mr. Standard Oil, thought they were going to bury me!" He struck his chest for emphasis. "Well we'll see about that. We'll see who pays for what!"

"So how's things with you Alex," instantly changing directions, "anything opening up?"

"We're okay, but it's not time to step back into action yet. We've got enough money to live on, so I'm gonna sit things out for awhile. Doing nothing 'cept having a ball playing with the baby."

"And the baby's momma?"

"She's fine."

"That's not what I meant." Huey said with a nasty snicker.

"What do you mean?" Alex queried.

"Didn't you say you were having a wonderful time playing with the baby."

"Oh I see, you cagey bastard. You want to know if I'm playing with the baby's momma too!" Alex gave him a playful punch, noticing Sam Battaglia's eyes slide over him in the rear view mirror. "Well while it's none of your God damn business, the answer's yes to that too."

They laughed raucously.

*   *   *

Those were the sweetest years in Alex's life, serving as a time of renewal. They brought Louise up to live with them, only after much discussion to assure no one was going to feel pressured. Louise, because of her status as grandmother and motherinlaw, was afraid Marie might feel intimidated by her presence. Marie in turn was concerned lest Louise think she was being invited to be a baby sitter. Alex was the sounding board for all parties concerned, laughingly calling a meeting in which all five people involved attended. Alex Jr, now six years old, gave a strong yes when asked if Grandmama should come and live with them. He loved this funny lady, and delighted in her company. Mary gurgled in her high chair, enjoying the whole scene with dancing eyes and bouncing golden hair, when Alex asked her.

"Ok Mary, now it's your turn to vote." He picked her up out of the high chair. "I know you can't talk Baby, but you can sure give us some kind of sign whether Grandmama Louise should come live with us or not."

The sign was immediate. His angelic looking daughter noisily expelled a great quantity of gas followed by a radiant smile, all the more lovely because of it's innocence. They laughed themselves into tears with Alex finally announcing.

"That's it Mama, what more kinda sign could you ask for? You are definitely voted in."

This was a blessed time in Alex's life, and a genuinely romantic period between he and Marie. There were no more heirs born to the family however, due to the loss of her ability to have any more babies, following a difficult birth with Mary. Raised in the French Catholic tradition of large families and able to afford many more children was a source of great concern to Marie.

"Oh but Cherie," Alex would breathe into her ear exaggerating the French accent, while making love to her, "I am so sorree' they had to take away the babee' carriage yes, but isn't it wonderful they left the play pen for Papa?" Which usually resulted in a gentle fight between the sheets.

They had it all. A boy for Marie, and what Alex thought was one of Gods own mistakes in Mary.

"You know Mama," running through the situation in his mind with his mother, "I love little Alex with all my heart yeah, so much that I asked God in my prayers to help me find yet more love for this new baby, but either my prayers were unnecessary or it's not the same with her." His eyes filled with tears of love at the thought of his beautiful baby girl. "You think God screwed up Mama? Maybe he sent us this child he meant to be an angel?"

"Hush son." Louise scolded. "God doesn't make mistakes. He knew what He was doing."

"Yeah, yeah. I know that too Mama, but I simply don't understand how we could have been so lucky to get this one."

"The grace of God, Alex." Her eyes glistening with happiness over her sons joy.

"What's that?"

"You heard that all of your life haven't you?"

"The nuns used to say it all the time."

"Do you know what grace means?"

"Not really, Mama."

Looking at the chortling object of the conversation, thinking maybe Alex was right, she said, "When we say, 'Through the grace of God', the word grace means an undeserved favor."

"Wouldn't argue with that Mama. I know damn well I never did anything good enough to deserve this one."

He especially loved to stare into those bright blue eyes and wonder what she was thinking. Her expressions were endless, running the complete gamut from supreme joy when everything was all right to great distress when it wasn't. Intrigued would have been the better word because this was the happiest baby he had ever seen. He couldn't understand why she was either smiling all the time or at the very least wearing a pleasant expression.

"She's got a pretty Mama and a rich Papa." His mother offered.

"Used to be rich, Mama," he corrected.

"Huh," she sniffed, "I sure don't see any candidates for the poor house around here. Anyway as lovely as she is, you've got to admit she's pretty well liked."

They laughed, because it was such an understatement.

It was Mary and the dog, Alex went to great lengths to watch. The little stray certainly didn't look like much of anything but they were at least grateful for his short hair, which helped eliminate much of the odor found in long hair dogs.

He walked up the driveway the same day Louise moved in, and it was apparent from the moment of his arrival he intended to stay.

"Only thing wrong with this guy is he didn't bring a suitcase." Alex said as the whole family stood on the top step of the porch looking down at the new arrival. He stared back with equal interest.

"Can we keep him, Papa?" His son asked, walking down the stairs to a joyous licking by their guest.

"What if he's somebodies dog, Cher?" Alex replied.

"Well if he is they sure don't watch him good." Louise offered. Alex knew where his mother stood if her grandson liked the critter. She'd push it all the way.

"He's cute Alex." Marie was moving for the 'coup de grace' while little Alex was struggling with the licking from this small creature with the wagging tail.

Louise was holding the baby watching, when she made a delightful gurgling sound. The vagrant pups ears snapped to attention, forgetting everything else in the moment of discovery. Leaping up the steps he ran to Louise, placing his front paws on her hip stretching his utmost to more closely inspect this small new person. It was complete love at first sight, Mary as enchanted as the new dog.

"Well, that's it!" Louise chimed in laughingly. "These two seem to know each other, so I guess he moves in." This was in the form of a statement, with a beseeching glance at her son.

He frowned momentarily thinking the situation over, then settling it in his mind chuckled. "Why not, he doesn't look like he'd eat too much, and he'll even up the balance here."

"Balance? What balance?" Marie joyously asked. She'd fallen in love with the pup the minute she saw him.

"Three females and now three males, we're all even so any votes in the future will have to be on some basis other than sex."

Since Alex had all the time he wanted, to do anything that came to mind, he immediately set about building a nice dog house at the foot of the back stairs, utilizing the well intentioned but misguided help of his small son.

"What'll we call him Alex?" his father asked.

"Dog!"

"Oh come on now, we can do better than that." They ran through a series of names, each with its objections.

"I've got it!" Alex announced. "Get me a board, son. I'll put his name on it and hang it right over the door. That way he won't have any trouble figuring out which house is his."

This mystified his son. He could not understand why that was necessary since this was the only dog house around. He was also amazed to learn from his father that the dog could read.

"PHIDEAUX" appeared on the board, Alex explaining.

"What we got here is a coonass dog, moving in with a coonass family, so what better name than a coonass version of Fido."

They loved it, so it stuck, but the dog house wound up as a playhouse, for little Alex first and then Mary. It was totally ignored as a doghouse from the very first night.

The pup had been fed, petted and played with extensively then led out the kitchen door down the steps and around to his new house, which he marked immediately by hoisting his leg.

"Gave it his shot of approval." Alex commented, but it didn't work out that way at all. Marie was awakened in the night by scratching on the back door and went quickly downstairs to quiet him before he woke up the master of the house, possibly resulting in serious trouble.

She opened the back door, instantly charmed by the new arrival sitting so proper with his head cocked in a beguiling manner, creating a rush of affection in Marie for the appealing stranger.

"Go back puppy, get in your new house." She whispered but nothing happened except Phideaux twisted his alert little head to the exact opposite side, listening intently.

"Do you want a drink of water, maybe?" Was Marie's next question followed by enthusiastic tail wagging.

When she opened the screen door, a streak shot by her accompanied by clattering toe nails flying across the linoleum in the kitchen, down the long hall, picking up speed because of the stability of the carpeting, with Marie in hot pursuit. She saw his tail disappear around the corner of the stairs, hearing the soft patter as he sped up them. When she found him he was laying on a small throw rug in front of Mary's bed, looking for all the world like it was exactly where he belonged.

It was there too that Alex would spend hours watching their beautiful display of togetherness. With the exception of when the dog was let out to perform his bathroom duties, they were bound commonly by some invisible thing, intriguing Alex no end. Mary was as delighted with her new friend as he was with her and it was on these warm sunshiney days, after she had started walking, Alex felt as close to paradise as he could get, without being there.

Each exquisite color surrounding them would have been an extraordinary elegance, but placed in the same setting became a kaleidoscopic event of stunning proportion.

The blue sky was given its special tone by the proximity of the gulf, he thought, because it was a different shade than up north or over in France, and the lustrous greens defied description. Everything was green, six feet of rainfall a year the average, south Louisiana was green all over. The massive dark oaks, front, side and back, balanced this tableau perfectly.

Gardenias, dazzling white, heavily perfumed, fragile Mimosa trees with their dramatic star burst blooms, all shades of orange and pink. Roses of every color and variety, each with their own breath taking scent accented by the sensual color emphasizing the even more gorgeous "piece de resistance" the azaleas. When in bloom their beauty was simply overwhelming, a riot of vivid colors set against the ever present and intense green of the bush.

Those unforgettably precious days he spent sitting for hours on the broad front steps surrounded by all this sensual beauty, which was was in turn punctuated by Mary and her constant companion. Marie and Louise clothed her mostly in white dresses, which were utterly brilliant when contrasted by this lush verdant setting. Then finishing the picture were her glossy black patent baby shoes that intrigued Alex so, and all this kaliedescopic luciousness crowned by Mary's golden blonde hair so pure as to seem unnatural.

'Lot of women pay big money getting their hair to look like that.' He thought. 'Wonder why God puts stuff like that on kids and they don't even know how beautiful they are.'

All this, and the dog. Hours he spent just watching Mary and her shadow, unaware of anything except each other. They might not pay attention to one another, doing different things, seeing different sights, but never more than a few feet apart, and yet in some unexplained way totally aware of the presence of the other.

He was especially captivated when these inseparable friends sat on the lush grass surrounded by silence broken only by her tuneless humming, all the while watched by her self appointed guardian lying his customary few feet away. With eyes half closed turned into lustrous pools of deep liquid brown, his black button like nose constantly working, he savored all the scents in the air, especially the most sacred scent of all, that of Mary.

'Isn't it something,' he thought, 'that dog's sitting right there, right now, looking at his God. The only creatures on earth that get to do that.'

CHAPTER 8

"So, it's been Senator Long for what, two years now?" Alex was visiting his old friend.

"Yup, two years it is. If you remember way back there in the woods when we first met, I told you that's where I was going, and that's where I got."

"Yeah, but can you do a better job for Louisiana in Washington, than here?"

"Yes Alex, I can. I know I can. I've already got most of my programs rolling at the state level. It's been one hell of a fight all the way, but we're looking at more progress these few years than the previous sixtyfive, or whenever the hell they quit fighting that stupid civil war."

It was fought 30 years before he was born, but he never approved of it.

"With the power and influence of the senate behind me I can get a whole lot of federal money coming this way. So yes! The answer is yes! I can do a hell of a lot more for Louisiana up there than down here." He was rolling a seldom lit cigar in his mouth. "How 'bout you Alex, back drillin' yet?"

"Nope but I'm ready to get on with it, I'll tell you that. I'm just trying to figure out where."

"Need any help?" Pointing at Alex with the wet cigar.

"All I can get. Got any ideas?"

Alex knew this man had access to all sorts of information, much more than most politicians, and for two reasons. He actively sought every conceivable type of information available, plus being blessed with a prodigious memory.

"Alex, I found out when those bastards tried to impeach me that the less direct communications I have with people, on things like this, the better off they are. You know what I mean?"

"I think so."

"I don't want those vicious sons of bitches draggin' your ass before a squinty eyed committee some day, so to be on the safe side I'll give you Sue's address and phone number." He appreciated the pleased expression on Alex's face. "I think she might have some interesting information for you."

"Great! Where is she?"

"Here, in Baton Rouge. Doing real well for herself too I might add. She's operating as a high line lady with some damn prominent clients."

"Politicians?"

The Senator nodded.

"And oilmen. Oilmen of all kinds, from locals to the fancy guys from back east. Big shots in geology and exploration." He leaned toward Alex, adding confidentially. "You get my drift?"

"Oh yeah," Alex smiled, "I get your drift all right." He lost no time getting to Sue's house after saying goodbye to Huey.

Sue was absolutely thrilled to see her old lover when he arrived, giving him a long kiss in welcome.

"Well, it's about time you came to see your first great love." Hugging him again, then holding him at arms length.

"Where the hell have you been all these years?"

He told her of all that happened to him since his strike in Oklahoma. Sue was especially tickled over his lengthy story about Mabel Tate.

"Sounds like my kind of woman." Sue laughed. "Last time you saw her, she was headed to Dallas to buy a real purty husband. I like that!"

"Yes, well I expect she'd say the same about you. Two no bullshit ladies, looking life right square in the eye."

"Tell me about your family, Alex." Sue led him to a settee. "I bet the baby's a big guy now. Does he look like you?"

"Yes ma'am he does, but he's not the baby anymore."

Sue was thrilled for Alex, giggling, wondering if his vest buttons would hold as he told her all about the new baby Mary, and the rest of his family.

"You really adore her don't you Alex?"

"Who?"

"Mary! The new one."

His big smile lit up the room again, seeing Mary in his minds eye sitting on the grass humming to her four legged friend.

"Yeah I do in a strange special way. Jesus Sue I love 'em all." Suddenly remembering where he was. "Just like I've always loved you, but this one's got a special hold on me."

His comment startled her momentarily but she didn't pursue it. He told of all the developments after the Mabel Tate find, including his great losses, bringing her up to date on his life.

"What now Alex?"

"Back to the oil patch, Cher."

"Jesus, I love to hear you call me Cher again." Then smiling. "We'd better get down to business right now sweetheart. I'm only a little bit before ripping your clothes off and attacking you seriously."

He laughed, adding. "You look pretty good to me too and you know what they say. I love my wife, but oh you kid!"

Her information about new surveys and locations was astonishing in both quality and quantity, prompting him to ask how she'd come by this wealth of knowledge.

"Huey and I have kept in close touch these years Alex. He calls me his private Mata Hari, because I get real inside information from those politicians and oil boys, by being a good listener. Hell I've even made some money in the stock market, since the crash, buying stocks I'm told about on the hush hush."

'Christ,' he thought, 'I do love the beautiful, wide open smile on this girl.'

"A guy'll tell you things with his head on a pillow, laying down, he'd never tell you with his pants on standing up."

"That's for damn sure kid. If a guy's just scored, or fixing to, he's got a whole different set of conversational rules between those sheets."

"Well that's where I got almost all my information. You know Alex, the guys I'm dealing with generally have two things down, their guard and their pants. They're all here for the same thing but motivated different. Some disillusioned in their marriage, others lonely. I can handle them better than the guys that roll in here drunk and want a little action. Then there's the type I hate most of all. The hairy chested ego maniac who feels he has to have some strange stuff the minute he gets away from home."

"Sounds like you might be down on your profession." Alex followed.

"No." She laughed. "I'm like Popeye the sailor man. I am what I am, and that's all I am." Her gaze distant.

"Ever think of another line of work?" He was serious.

"Not while I've still got my figure, which I have to work pretty hard at, and my looks, which seem to take a little longer to make up. But as you can see by this house, I'm doing okay. None of my clients tries to smack me around, or get out of line anyway at all, because the ones that don't know who my connections are, don't want to find out, and the ones that do, walk..." a sudden burst of naughty laughter, "or otherwise behave very carefully."

Her house was a lovely Louisiana style wooden structure, replete with old fashioned gingerbread decoration. It was all white, with blue trim accentuating the many colors in the carefully groomed lawn she worked hard to perfect.

"I looked everywhere to find the right location, and this was it." Laughing again. "You gotta think about convenience when you set up your lemonade stand or they might not be able to find you. I'm halfway between the downtown hotels and the state capitol, and that's where my business comes from."

"And this information?"

"From Huey's pet hate. The high falutin' oil boys. They're in this town thicker'n flies, lobbying the shit out of our illustrious legislators. When they get through wining and dining, for lots of them anyway, it's time to come see Sue, and they do. Usually they're full of booze, heat and information and I save the stuff I think's important."

"I'll bet you do get a lot of information that Huey needs."

"I do. I'm sure not the only reason he didn't get impeached, but I heard an awful lot that helped him beat those bastards."

"I was kind of out of touch during that deal. Was it really bad?"

Her eyes lit up smiling as she thought about the legal war.

"Alex, I seriously believe had it been anybody but Huey, they'd have nailed him. You know, just run his ass down the road. Well if they didn't know it before, they do now. If you're gonna get the Kingfish, you better get up early in the morning."

They laughed. Sue because of her intimate knowledge of the maneuvering Huey had gone through to break the thrust of the legal effort. Alex in the belief Huey could outfox any adversary who tried to take his measure. He knew Huey P. Long was the master of political chicanery.

Suddenly Sues eyes clouded over with tears.

"What's the matter, Cher?"

"Oh Alex, I'm afraid somebody's going to kill him!"

"Who?" Alex asked.

"I don't know who! If I knew I'd stop 'em, or see to it they got stopped." She was crying which caused that old feeling along Alex's neck. Mixed feelings of compassion, frustration and anger.

"Sue."

He was startled at his reaction which at this moment was icy, controlled rage. It was an entirely new feeling to him, one he didn't understand at all, although over the ensuing years he was to master these feelings, understanding them completely.

"Sue, listen to me careful! If you ever get anything solid, get hold of me instantly, before you call anyone." Taking a piece of paper from his pocket and writing on it. "This is my home phone number in LaFayette, don't hesitate to call if you get anything."

Sam, the jack of all trades bodyguard, was standing in the hall outside the governor's office that Huey obviously still ran, indicating his boss was inside.

"Sam." Alex took his forearm in his strong grip, a grim look on his face. "I'm hearing some bad shit I don't like, and I'm going to ask you real strong like to keep a sharp eye out for the senator."

The same malevolent light danced out from Sam's broad expressionless face.

"What the hell you mean!"

His reason for disliking Alex was jealousy, pure and simple. Alex recognized this, making Sam's animosity at least tolerable.

"I mean watch him! Watch him like a hawk! Watch anybody who gets around him. Look for unusual shit, quick movements, suspicious looks, anything that doesn't look kosher!"

"You done this kind of work before, or maybe you got some hot news?" His expression never changed.

"Not really Sam, only what I've been told."

"Which is?"

'I wouldn't have this asshole around me for thirty seconds,' Alex thought, 'but he's perfect for Huey.'

"I was told somebody's out to kill Huey!"

He had never seen him laugh before, startled by the sinister effort. It made his lips puff out in the center, simultaneously pulling the corners in.

"Is that what's bothering you?"

"Yes! Yes it is!" Alex didn't like this conversation at all. "Ain't it okay for me to worry about him?" He was hoping this unpleasant man would take a swing at him.

"Yeah yeah, but where the hell you been, friend?" That grated even more on Alex's nerves. "Christ we've known for a long time a whole lot of people would like to see him dead."

"Who?"

"Jesus Alex," that was the first time he ever used his name, "list's too long to count. All the way from high offices in Washington D.C., to little ones here in Louisiana."

This was all news to Alex, and it showed on his face.

"Huey's been stomping on toes, reputations, and feelings ever since he became governor...before even, and I can tell you he ain't even started yet. The man's serious.

He really wants to help the little guy get up off his ass, and he will see to it that the big shots quit holding 'em down!"

Alex realized he'd truly been out of touch, whiling away his time during his enforced sabbatical in his idyllic surroundings, paying little attention to what was happening.

"Why we know of a meeting in New Orleans where the main order of business was how to kill Huey Long."

Sam grew distant as he pictured himself in that room. He would gladly have given his life to be in that room, at that time.

"Heard about another up in Alexandria. Same shit. Those are the ones we know about. Christ Alex, they broke into his office in Washington, safe blown, papers stole out of it." He was laughing again. "Well you know old Huey. One thing he ain't, is shy. So he picks up his phone, calls the main man," indicating someone real powerful, "and told him...are you ready for this?" Alex nodded. "He told the man he wanted those fucking papers back in his office the next day. That's the exact word he used, and you know what?"

"What?"

Battaglia was wheezing with dry laughter. "Next day he got his fucking papers."

"So the man with the big balls had his office burglarized. Is that what you're saying?"

Alex was absolutely astonished, detecting a twinkle in the somber man's eyes as he replied.

"Don't know anything about that. All's I know is Huey got his shit back, but you know Alex," the chill was coming off their relationship in the midst of the conversation, "this guy in here," nodding toward the door he was guarding, "is getting to be some powerful man in this country. He's done a whole lot down here in Louisiana, and fast! Now he's showin' the world it wasn't no fluke by going into Arkansas, which ain't his stompin' grounds, and getting that old lady up there elected to the Senate. Shit man, nobody gave her a chance before he showed up. Now he's in the U.S. Senate and rattles lots more cages, and bones in closets, takin' on any of those powerful bastards that want a piece of him. Jesus Alex, if everybody that wanted him dead was to show up all at once, they'd have to take numbers and stand in line to get at him. Least that's what the Senator says."

"Well what are you going to do about it?" Alex knew if he wasn't talking to a friend, he was at least talking to an ally.

"Nothin'."

The twinkle was replaced by the gimlet eyed look of an angry rattlesnake.

"Wait! Oh yeah, I'll wait for 'em right here. The line forms in front of me, Alex. They get to him, right after they get through me," brushing back his coat revealing his ever present pearl handled revolver, "and me and old Bertha here ain't goin' nowhere." He thought a moment adding. "I'll kill any son of a bitch that tries to hurt the man!"

Alex believed him with no reservations.

He saw the strain of the tumultuous years written all over the Senators face, as he paced the borrowed governor's office.

"Sent him on some errands." Huey's explanation for the governor's absence. The subtle but profound gesture amazed Alex, as yet another indication of his extreme power.

'Sent the chief executive officer of a sovereign state on an errand.' Alex thought, considering the idea, trying to comprehend how far this nondescript looking man had come in such a short time.

"Yeah I know all about the rumors Alex," Huey snorted, in reply to his friend's anxiety "and while I'm not unconcerned, nothing's changed."

"Sam learn how to shoot?"

"Hell yes, but don't for a minute think Sam's all the firepower I've got, cause he ain't. I'll never get rid of him though, because loyalty like his is something you can't find just anywhere. I know he ain't the swiftest thing around mentally Alex, but I didn't hire him for his IQ, you know what I mean? You can't bust the shit out of somebody with a Phi Beta Kappa key! Besides, I think he'd lay down his life for me in a minute. That's worth a lot."

Alex nodded agreement.

"You know Huey you look tired, sort of all strung out. Think you ought to slow down some? You know, a rest? That's what I've been doing for four years, and while I don't recommend anything like that, all work and no play can make Huey a dead boy too."

"Yeah, you're right. I know you're right Alex," stabbing the air with his ever present unlit cigar, "but I can't slow down now. I just pinned Roosevelt's ears back with a couple of sweet moves. Lots of people think I ought to be a leading candidate for President of these old United States come 1940."

"Good God Huey! Are you serious?"

"You mean are they serious Alex, cause I'll guarantee you I am! Anyway, what's the matter? You don't think I'd make a good one?" He was laughing, but Alex understood it for the 'you think I'm messin' around but I'm really thinkin', look.

"You'd probably be one of the best we've ever had," he was sincere, and the Senator appreciated that, "but you are talking some real high cotton there. I know you can do it, but you're going to run up against some rough folks in the doin'."

Huey threw back his head, laughing unrestrained. "Alex I know what your concern is and I appreciate it, 'cause I know it's based on our friendship, but don't you worry about the rough folks. I've already run up against the best they got and I got 'em suckin' hind tit, for sure." Then the strange light appeared in his eyes again, adding. "They don't call me Kingfish for nothin', and those people in Washington are beginning to understand that." Suddenly darting in another direction. "Did Sue fix you up?"

"Not the way you think, she didn't!"

"Oh now listen, I wasn't suggesting anything like that!" Huey feigned exaggerated innocence.

"I'll bet, but anyway she had some great information about new fields, places where the experts think there's oil. I'll get some leases and look for that ugly stuff, now we can get a decent price."

"Okay Alex, and I've got something for you too. I'm in on a deal with some people who have first shot at pretty spectacular lease land that's owned by the State of Louisiana." He gave Alex his most innocent look. "We need a good operator to come in and do some drilling for us. He'd be rewarded handsomely of course, with a piece of the pie, plus drilling costs. Sound interesting to you?"

"Are you kidding? Hell yes! How long would it last?"

"What, the oil?"

"No, the partnership."

"Why I'd imagine it would last as long as you live Alex. We're going to set this up where you'll always be in a favored position, I promise you that. Now listen, while you're here I got some people for you to talk with about this. Sam will escort you personally." Anticipating his friends objection. "Don't worry! I got more Sam's outside, and having him with you is sort of like having Huey's stamp of approval."

The months following were a whirlwind of action, with Alex trying to be everywhere at once. He had enough time before starting the Louisiana operation, to squeeze in some frantic and fruitful operations of his own back in the Oklahoma fields, but not without working for it. His first two holes were dusters, putting great pressure on his already strained financial resources. His third try proved successful bringing in a producer of considerable proportions, thus eliminating his money troubles again.

It was hard leaving his family in LaFayette, but he had to and everybody seemed to understand that, even his much adored daughter, now an exquisite five year old replica of her mother. Her rich blonde hair had lost none of its luster, nor had her smiling good humor left, except when she suffered the usual hurts and pitfalls of childhood.

The Louisiana operation followed, and Alex drilled a succession of producing wells. This enabled him to breathe easier in that area, plus forming long lasting alliances with Huey's friends, who would be in power for years to come.

*   *   *

Alex was working on a rig site in the middle of Oklahoma, far from communication of any sort, when he had to go to town for money to meet his payroll. After concluding his business he walked into a cafe to eat before returning, when the voices of two men seated at a nearby table entered his subconscious.

"How'd he last two days?" The first part drifted in.

"Beats me! Heard on the radio, the guy shot him at close range."

"What happened to him?"

"Who?"

"The shooter."

"Bodyguards shot him up so bad they had a bad time identifying him."

"Who was he?"

"Some doctor. Lived right there in town."

Alex's subconscious was at work gathering information, trying to make conclusions. He was involved in so many thoughts concerning the drilling operation. Supplies, progress, costs, manpower, his mind was far, far away from the subject at hand.

"Jesus Christ!" One of the men said. "Look here! It says he was not only becoming a powerhouse in the U.S. Senate, they figured him to be a presidential candidate in 1940."

"Listen to this!"

The words erupted in the oil mans brain.

"GOVERNOR OF LOUISIANA AT 35. SENATOR AT 37. DEAD AT 42...."

Alex exploded out of his chair, shoving the table away with a powerful involuntary motion. The chair fell over, skittering across the floor with a rasping wood on wood sound stopping the two conversants instantly. They were staring up into the wild man's face standing over their table.

Ripping the mans paper away, ignoring the feeble protestations, he stood in the middle of the floor staring at the headline.

HUEY LONG DEAD

"Jesus, Jesus! Oh sweet Jesus!" He sobbed. "They killed him. They killed Huey!"

Everyone; diners, waitresses, the owner at the cash register were so stunned there was no reaction, only silence as the obviously disturbed, powerful looking man swung around in a combative stance subliminally trying to defend against this unexpected sting, ready to ward off the next. He regained control instantly.

"Christ I'm sorry mister!" Alex apologized his eyes filled with tears. "I didn't mean to do that, but Senator Long was a close personal friend of mine. You understand what I'm sayin'? Maybe the best friend I ever had. I didn't know anything about it 'til I heard you reading. Sorry if I acted a fool but it came as such a shock I was reacting, not thinking."

"Oh that's okay. Guess I'd feel the same way." One of the men replied, adding. "A friend of yours you say? What was he like, anyway?"

"I don't know really." Alex had a distant look in his eye. "It'll take lots of time to figure that out, but I'll tell you one thing...."

"What's that?"

"God only made the one like him."

*   *   *

"Sam! Sam what the hell happened?"

A strange mixture of anger and compassion came over Alex as he observed this cold unusual man, crying open and unashamedly at the funeral.

"Where were you?"

"Oh Christ Alex," he sobbed, "I was there, man. I was right with him. Me and some other boys. We were going like hell trying to keep up with him. You know how he walked, like everything else he did. Full speed."

Alex knew this loyal servant of Huey's would play that scene over and over again every day of his life, hoping just one time it would change. Then he could kill the young man threatening his beloved master because that was exactly what Huey Long was to Sam Battaglia. His master, to be served with blind loyalty and at any cost.

"We were coming from the legislature, Huey leadin', the rest of us trying to catch up. Said he had to talk to some newspapermen." Sobbing. "Jesus Alex, there were lots of people there. Highway patrol. Judge. A flock of politicians. All of a sudden this guy steps out from behind one of those big pillars."

"Didn't anybody see him?" Alex was trying to make the scene turn out different too.

"Everybody saw him! Nobody saw him! The son of a bitch just drifted in at an angle, Alex." His tears were flowing freely. "He was on Huey before anybody could do anything. Somebody hit his arm the same time he fired, but it was a split second too late."

"You didn't think Huey was hit bad?"

"I can't explain that Alex, it all happened so fast. Soon's we realized what happened, we started shooting and didn't let up 'til our guns were empty."

"Yeah, I understand he was shot up pretty bad."

"Right! You bet!" He hissed through clenched teeth. "The son of a bitch! We must of hit him 30 or 40 times, but God damn it," he broke down completely, sobbing, "he got off the first one...."

*   *   *

"None of us thought his wound was that serious, Mr. George," one of the inheritors of Huey's mantle of power was saying, "and in that respect, we were right. We simply did not reckon with the complications that followed, especially in view of his lucidity almost to the moment of death."

Alex was listening with his elbows on his knees, staring down at the floor.

"Yeah, well what happens now?"

"If you mean as far as the arrangement Huey set up for you and the others? Nothing will change. That's set."

"That too, but I mean who's going to run the show now. His senate job, the Governors position. Everything. I guess what I'm asking is who's going to run the state of Louisiana?"

"You know Mr. George a lot of people are asking that same question. That's extraordinary isn't it? A magnificent epitaph to the Senator."

"What do you mean?"

"I mean how many men in this country, in nineteen thirty-five, would be considered so prominent.... No, I think indispensable is the word. Indispensable in the operation of our state government as to cause people, local and national, to wonder how a sovereign state with a sizable population is going to carry on."

"Yeah."

"Anybody and everybody who asks that question knows beyond a shadow of a doubt that we will carry on. Maybe not without terrible difficulties in our daily affairs, but we will carry on. I think too it's a wonderful tribute to him, to have the question posed."

"Well he did a lot for this state, and in seven short years. He made the raggedy assed guys in overalls, all over our state, stand up and quit playing Uncle Tom to the rich boys. By the same token, he tightened the screws down on the big money people." Alex drifted, searching his way through his impromptu eulogy. "And he could be a good friend. Hell he took me on as a friend. I'm still wondering why? I didn't have anything. I wasn't anybody."

"Precisely, Mr. George."

"What?"

"He loved you, and loved to regale us with Alex George stories."

"Did he?"

"Yes."

"Like what?"

"Oh how you met. He felt you were one of his first really staunch supporters. He loved to tell about the fix he was in with the amorous banker from LaFayette, and how you came to his rescue with a lovely lady. I think his favorite story though was the campaign speech in New Iberia and your action in coming to his rescue with the toughs." He smiled broadly.

Alex chuckled too, his eyes glistening with tears as he thought of how awed Huey was over the terrible swift, and decisive manner, in which he dispatched the hecklers.

"He was never too good at Cajun accents, but he tried so hard to imitate yours." Suddenly changing the subject in order to lessen the pain. "He did champion the cause of the common man, you know."

"Yeah, and he pissed off the rich guys doin' it. Lot of people said he was only stirring up shit between rich and poor."

"That's more or less the history of the world Mr. George, isn't it? Not always, but often, the rich get that way by the sweat of someone else's brow and stay that way, much of the time, by shedding someone else's blood. When you really scrutinize the situation, you are almost forced to conclude the very rich are quite a distasteful breed. Perhaps it's the nature of the beast, fearful they may lose what they have, and while Huey was not against personal wealth, you could make a strong case for his anger, and impatience, at the never ending exploitation of the many, by the few."

There was silence while Alex struggled with his emotions.

"I'll miss him, I'll tell you that!"

"You loved him, didn't you Mr. George?"

"Yeah, yeah. Oh yeah. There's no doubt about that."

"Then you can take solace, and some lessons, in having known him. You see his genius was complete, in that he had an infinite capacity to thwart the thorns and arrows hurled his way by the opposition. No one day did he have without strife, but didn't he teach us that growth usually comes only after, or through struggle? He knew all problems could be solved...almost none without contention. He was truly a great teacher to us all, and out of it comes the one shining truth."

"What's that?"

"Oh I don't know, it's an idea I have, but it seems as though whenever extremely enlightened men appear on earth, and bring with them a certain magic, a light if you will, trying to help and asking others not to hurt their fellows. Usually, no matter what century they show up, their messages are basically the same. Love your neighbor. Don't take advantage of him. Don't hurt and exploit him and profit from so doing. Sort of like the sermon on the mount. I think it contains what most of these men have had to say, and yet have you ever thought about what these men have most in common, Mr. George?"

"No what?"

"Someone always has to kill them!"

*   *   *

Alex turned to Marie for support in his sorely felt loss of Huey. She was his source of strength, developing from the exuberant fun loving girl she was at the time of their marriage, to a deep, loving, caring person who always saw the other persons suffering. She desperately wanted to help carry whatever burden she could.

"I think I'll go out to the camp for a couple of days Hon', get things sorted out in my mind, then I'll go back and hit it."

Marie's heart was torn by the suffering she knew her husband was going through. She would have done anything in her power to alleviate his pain, since this was such a radical departure from his usual lively, fun loving self.

"What can I do, Mama?" She asked Louise, tearfully.

"Nothing Cher. Let him go. Let him go to the swamp. Men find answers there, they can't find anywhere else."

Oh how she loved this compassionate girl, taking her in her arms, holding her gently.

"That's a place where men go to get in touch with their souls, like some go to a church. It's what he needs now."

Alex drove his pickup to the end of the shell road, pulled his pirogue out of the back, slipped it into the water and paddled silently through the unbelievable surroundings.

Water was everywhere, with every conceivable form of vegetation emanating from it, dominated by strange looking cypress trees. Its leaves are slight in shape, deep green, and always adorned with wispy Spanish moss. In only a few short minutes, he was in water the color of mahogany surrounded by nearly impenetrable growth at the shore line. Because of the dark water, surrounding greens, blacks and browns of the countless trees with the somber gray Spanish moss, the swamp and waterways take on an appearance of gathering darkness, no matter what the time of day.

"It's like being in another world, Alex." Gaston told him in low tones as they entered the area that caused an unexplained awe in the boy, and remained in the man.

He spent three days in the hushed gloom of the huge swamp thinking about his life to this point, and the huge part his friend Huey played in it.

"It's okay Hon'." He whispered to a sobbing Marie upon his return. "I had to think about a few things, which I did, and get all my ducks in a row, which I'm going to, because I know how Huey would feel about it."

Marie's heart danced with joy and relief, at this apparent recovery in her husband. "How would he feel about it?"

Alex thought she was growing more beautiful each day, particularly so at this moment as she smiled at him, her blue eyes intensified by the tears they contained.

"Well if he's anywhere watching right now he's probably real happy about the fuss I'm making over him, but I 'spect he'd want me to know time's a wastin'. I got things to do." He pulled her to him, giving her a great kiss, at the same time feeling her breast in an outrageous manner. "He would also think they should begin with you."

Louise came drifting through the kitchen, in time to witness this salacious act, laughing and winking to her mildly protesting daughter-in-law.

"See Cher what I told you! The swamp will do it every time!"

CHAPTER 9

While Alex pursued his career, drilling, developing, and in the pipeline business too, his holdings grew by leaps and bounds along with considerable liabilities. He'd learned his lessons well from his previous experiences however, careful never to put himself in a totally vulnerable position again. He was willing to adopt the doctrine of two steps forward, and one back.

"When it's the other way around the shit hits the fan," he'd tell his management people, "so remember that. If you do something wrong, but your intentions were right, all's you're going to hear from me is, don't make the same mistake twice. We're in a pressure business that demands we stay on top of everything, all the time, so we have to work fast and smart."

"That Alex George has to be one of the smartest young operators in the oil patch." One of Sue's customers told her, while relaxing over a drink, unaware of any connection but pleased by her great interest in his opinions.

"Who's he?" She asked in mock innocence.

"George? Oh he's something else, Sue. Out of the bayous over LaFayette way. Understand he started out handling iron up in Shreveport and hustled his ass off." Suddenly. "'Scuse me Sue, nothing intended there."

"It's okay, Hon'," she laughed, "I know what I am and what I do. I'm told I do it real good too." Her eyes were sparkling because the conversation was about her old lover.

"You do, that's for damn sure!" Relieved at her quick dismissal of his unintended faux pas. "Well anyway he worked and fought all over the oil patch, in Oklahoma and East Texas. He put together a helluva lot at an early age. Why hell, some say the guy's magic."

"How?"

"It's like he's got a sixth sense. The way he made his first fortune, lost it, laid low for years, drug his old rig out of the swamps and started nailing down leases. He's got some kinda magic with the rural folks. Found oil before the people who hunted it down in the first place had time to move on it. They say he's got some damn good sources of information. Sure wish I had some."

"You do have some, honey." She laughed.

"Some what?"

"Some of all you can handle, right now." Her seductive reply, and her client forgot immediately all about Alex George and the oil business.

Sue told Alex of this conversation, when he stopped to see her next.

"Boy that guy'd feel some stupid if he knew our association." She giggled.

"Yeah, well let's don't tell him Cher." Oh how that word warmed her heart. "That's our secret." Then seriously. "Sue, I came to talk business with you."

She beamed. "Oh Alex, I do hope it's the same kind of business we used to do so much of."

"No Babe." He laughed. "It's simply something I want to do, and strictly on the up and up."

"Up and up? Ooooh I like that." Her retort in an exaggerated sexy voice.

"Dammit, will you behave?" Still laughing. "I'm talking real live money type business here, and I want you to listen."

She knew he was serious, and quit teasing.

"I set up a new corporation with the state, and the bank. It'll be for stuff like exploration, research, all kinds of miscellaneous crap."

Sue stared at him, blankly.

"OK. So what are you getting at, Alex?"

"Well it's kind of hard to say, 'cause I know you're going to give me a lot of sass about it." He was searching for the right way to tell her. "I brought in a big one up there in Oklahoma as a result of that information you gave me just before Huey was killed. That son of a bitch came in like a wildcat." His eyes twinkling. "Something about the way it acted reminded me of you." Receiving a playful jab in the ribs. "Anyway, I've got you down for an eighth share in the royalties, which should be great because I don't think that thing has a bottom to it." Reflecting briefly. "God doesn't that sound familiar?"

He braced himself for the next blow that never came. He turned to look into Sue's face. She wore an expression of total shock.

"Oh Alex, you can't!"

"Oh hell yeah! Sure I can Babe! As a matter of fact, I already did."

"What do you mean, you did?"

"I mean it's on the books, with royalties directed to a new account at the bank. It's done. I need you to sign some signature cards, and papers at the bank, and then the bucks will roll right in."

"Why are you doing this?"

"Why am I doing this she asks?" It was his turn to do the teasing now. "Because sweetie, among other things I love you. I have since I was a pup, and I enjoy doing things for people I love." He could see she was fighting for control, hurrying on. "Also in the truest sense of the word you earned it. You came up with some sensational stuff that proved to be right...."

"Oh sure, I got the information, but that shouldn't put me in for anything. You took all the risk. Drilling expenses were yours. Everything was a gamble and I didn't have a dime on the line."

Alex frowned hoping to convince her of his determination.

"Look Mon Cherie it's done, except for signatures. So why don't you quit arguing with me, put on some street clothes, and let's make the deal final."

"What if I were to take these off, right here and right now?" Indicating the filmy garments she was wearing. "Maybe we could delay the trip to the bank, a little?" Accompanied by her most seductive smile.

"Look Babe, I'm going to wait for you in the car so don't keep me waiting too long or you'll have to walk." He was laughing, but hesitant. "And another thing." Now he was going to preach. "One of these days you may decide to quit doing this for a living, and with what you'll have coming in, you could."

"Anything the matter with my figure, or my looks yet?" Opening the top of her gown, revealing most of one of her breasts.

"Jesus Sue, will you stop that?" He moaned. "No, hell no! If anything, you keep getting better looking. No, I only meant...."

Sue was in control now. She moved toward Alex, putting her arms around his waist, leaning back to look in his eyes.

"I know what you meant Cher." She said softly. "Even though I have always known how much you love Marie, right now I want to love you. Not for what you've done for me, but because I love you with no reservation or claims. Can I do that?"

She could, and they did, and were deliciously tardy for the bank appointment.

*   *   *

Alex was indeed a rising young star in the fast paced oil and gas business, his holdings in Oklahoma expanding by leaps and bounds, plus making great strides in the hotly contested east Texas fields. It was there he met some of the legendary oil men, of that or any other time, who were to dominate the industry for years to come. Sid Richardson, H.L. Hunt, and perhaps the wildest of the wildcatters, Glen McCarthy. He learned from each of these men.

Richardson's contribution was hard work and a never say die attitude. He'd been up and down so many times he felt like a fiscal yoyo, but whenever he was down, he refused to stay. He wound up one of the wealthiest men in the country, ultimately becoming a leading backer of Lyndon Johnson. Alex understood that well, because of his close personal relationship with Huey, he'd learned great wealth made possible the rubbing of shoulders with the politically powerful. They were always more than happy to trade their influence, for a lot of green money.

"I'll tell you what Alex," Richardson avowed, "when you've got serious money, lots of people come see you that wouldn't spit on your grave otherwise. Hell, I don't for a minute have any mistaken ideas these politicians are anything but a bunch of whores. Always have been, always will be, only they don't have the basic honesty most whores do. You get with one of those gals and both of you know positively who's going to get screwed. What's more, y'all know who's going to pay. Am I right?"

"A hundred per cent!" Alex agreed, thinking of Sue.

"Yeah, well it ain't that way with those shifty eyed political dudes, and don't you ever forget it! When you crawl into bed with those slippery sons of bitches, keep one hand on your money and the other over your asshole, then you got a chance. But remember one thing Alex, politics was invented a long time ago, and politicians do the business of politics. You and me, son? We ain't going to change that part, but what we have a chance of changing is legislation affecting our pocketbooks, and that's what it's all about. My message is Alex, grease whatever palms you have to in order to get a better break for yourself, and I don't give a shit if the palm belongs to the President of the United States. What it is, is the end justifying the means!"

H. L. Hunt was natural born to the oil business. He was a professional gambler, and won his first lease in a poker game. He went on to be a giant in the business with a personal fortune estimated over a billion dollars. Alex loved to study Hunt, whenever in his presence, drawing on his observations of this gambling man, many times in future years.

"Son, just don't ever let the other guy know what you got or what you're doing. And for Gods sake never, ever, let him know what you're thinking."

He met Hunt at an industry convention, and never forgot the lessons the man gave him.

"I was a professional gambler over in Arkansas. Don't know how much poker you've played in your life, but I'll tell you one thing for sure and that is if you expect to win, and win consistently, you don't simply sit down there and handle some cards. No, no. What you better do is study your opponent like a hawk. You got to know when to check or raise, put up or shut up! Then, when it comes bluffing time, sometimes you do it with style and grace, and sometimes raw power. You know what I mean?"

"Yeah I know what you mean. Huey Long was a friend of mine. I saw him do exactly that, plenty of times."

"Oh well shit, why didn't you tell me that instead of letting me blow off steam? Christ, when it came bluffin' time, that guy was master of 'em all. Why I've heard tales about that guy that are simply unbelievable." His eyes wrinkled with humor. "Heard one time he headed off a big circus coming to Baton Rouge? It was gonna' be the same day LSU was playing a football game and he asked 'em not to do it. Not that day. That man loved his LSU football team. They said 'up yours Governor, we're scheduled and we ain't changin' it'. He didn't like that worth a shit so he up and made some real quick governor type moves. Then he told those circus boys it'd be okay to come on in there that day, but he wanted 'em to know they had a brand new law in Louisiana that said all animals brought across state lines had to be dipped in some kinda horrible stuff. Ha ha ha, can you imagine what a lion would look like, coming out of a tank full of that nasty shit? Well it didn't sound good to those circus folks either, so once again Huey ran his bluff and got his way. Pretty good lesson I'd say."

It was the kind of business that lent itself to all sorts of colorful characters and Alex was born to the action. He had everything going for him. Rugged good looks, now in his mid thirties. A hard worker, and the main ingredient necessary for any huge success, intelligence far beyond his meager formal education, and he would gamble. So it was he naturally fought his way upward in a ruthless business where no quarter was asked, and none given.

CHAPTER 10

"Jesus Hon'," Alex asked Marie one day after driving in from Oklahoma, "what's the matter with Mary?"

"Nothing's the matter with her, Alex." She looked up. "Why do you ask?"

"Well, I drove up and didn't get my usual big time welcome. She just sat there with the dog and gave me a little smile but didn't get up. I went over to hug her and she was wringing wet."

Marie said nothing, running to the back door with Alex following. She stopped on the back porch, laughing.

"Will you look at that?"

"What?"

"Poor Phideaux, Mary's using him for a pillow again." She was laying with her head on her constant companion, who was lying perfectly still, hardly breathing so as not to disturb her.

"Mary honey!" Marie called. "Mary your Daddy's home. Don't you have a kiss for him?"

There was no response.

Alex moved swiftly, he was frightened. There was nothing right about this. Her dog looked at them with panic in his eyes, as if he knew something terrible.

"Baby do you hear me?" Marie was frightened now too, as Alex reached down to shake Mary gently, causing another look of concern in the dogs eyes.

"Oh Christ Hon', she's burnin' up!" Alex lifted his daughter. "She's got a terrible fever! Let's get her in the house. Call the doctor and tell him to come. Right now!"

Mary whimpered when her adoring father gently picked her up. She was obviously semiconscious. Her cry caused the small dog to take an aggressive stance, which no one noticed.

"My head hurts Daddy." She murmured, as he ran up the steps two at a time.

Alex's panic grew even larger upon seeing his mother's face, when she came into the room.

"What is it, Mama?" He moved around the bed to where she was standing.

"I don't know Cher, maybe it's one of those quick fevers little people are always coming down with."

He knew there was more behind his mother's concern than a quick fever, and felt his world moving away as her eyes filled with tears.

"Oh Jesus! Sweet Jesus!"

The expression on Louise's face terrified him, and fear was a stranger to him. He knew something ominous was threatening Mary, and couldn't stand his helplessness.

"The doctor's coming right over!" Marie said to no one in particular, interrupted by Mary throwing up with great violence.

"We'll take her to the hospital now, Mr. George. The fever's too high to try and break here. We'll take her there to work on it." The reserved doctor talk stopped. Alex had him by the wrist, undisguised fear in his eyes.

"What is it, doctor?"

"I don't know, Mr. George. I do know we have a little girl with a very high fever, and we must do something about that, immediately!"

Alex ran down the stairs sheltering his daughter, trying somehow to place himself between his helpless child and whatever had her in its grip. Marie was right behind him, while young Alex was kept behind by his grandmother. She was crying uncontrollably.

That's what frightened Alex so, the obvious terror in his mother. He knew she thought something terrible was happening to Mary. He also knew country women could diagnose many things accurately, out of generations of handed down information.

"There's nothing you can do, Mr. and Mrs. George, except wait." The nun said with genuine compassion. "They are working on her with everything they've got, in order to break the fever. I suggest you wait here...or, we have a little chapel down the hall if you'd care to go there."

"Sister...I don't mean any offense...."

"Yes, Mr. George?"

"Sister, what if we were to take her to Baton Rouge or New Orleans, maybe? Bigger hospitals? Maybe they have better...I mean do they have more...."

"No, Mr. George they wouldn't have anything more to treat Mary with than we do, but I do understand your concern." She took his hand, gently. "She's a very sick girl and we have to get the fever down. Even if those other hospitals had better facilities, you wouldn't want to defer treatment while moving her."

"What is it, Sister?" Marie asked. "What's the matter with Mary?"

"We really don't know, but it's a high fever and we must stop it. Please, be comfortable. Be together now. The doctors are doing all they can." There was a meaningful pause, as she continued. "Perhaps you would like to ask God, however you wish, to help them."

She moved away silently, leaving the little girls parents lost in their concern. Marie wept quietly, creating a rising tide of passion in Alex. He could not stand to see her cry. There was something about her tears that created an almost uncontrollable rage in him, because of his frustration and inability to do anything to relieve her pain. He paced the hall like an animal, watching Mary's room as the hours rolled by, alert and increasingly concerned over the rush of activity as people went in and out.

"You are Catholic, Mrs. George?" The nun asked softly on her return.

"Yes." She replied with a pleading look. "Why?"

"Do you have a parish priest you would like to call?" It was such a painful question to ask. There was simply no other way to do it.

"A priest? Why a priest?" Alex demanded. "It's just a fever, isn't it?"

"She has a great fever, Mr. George. When children do that, we never know which way they are going to go."

"What you mean, they are going to go?" His voice rising with fear.

"Mr. George," the nun was holding his hand gently, "children as young as your daughter, down to birth, are such delicate creatures. So full of life one minute and simply gone the next. It's almost as if they were on loan here, instead of as we all consider them, permanent fixtures in our lives...."

"Gone the next?" He pulled his hand away, unconsciously forming a fist.

"We have perfectly healthy babies in our nursery, who sometimes simply don't wake up. It's as if they forget to breath, and we don't know why. We never plan on these eventualities, but if one of our patients is in a life threatening situation we suggest, if Catholic, they receive the last sacrament of their church."

"But I'm not gonna give up!" He replied, his fear turning to anger.

"Of course you're not. No one is going to give up Mr. George." She took his hand back, looking directly in his eyes. "We're all going to fight with every means at our disposal and I know you believe that, but we should be prepared for anything, which is why I am suggesting your parish priest."

Alex had never known such searing fear in his whole life. Not on the battlefields of France. Not when drilling his first, and possibly last well. Never when confronted with yet another barroom tough, but he was terrified now and his body became rigid with expectation of the coming battle. The cords stood out from his bull like neck, his chest and back muscles taut. Had the antagonist been human he would have annihilated him on the spot, his feelings were so intense, but he couldn't lay his hands on this insidious thing that was killing his daughter.

The tall, thin priest with the sensitive face of the ascetic, entered the corridor with long graceful strides, accentuated by his floor length cassock. He had the materials for the last sacrament in his hands as he swept by the grief stricken parents. Alex felt his helplessness rise to a state of panic.

'Hey God.' He prayed his prayer of desperation. 'How 'bout it? Let her stay with us, will you? She hasn't had time to do anything yet. She hasn't lived hardly at all, you know what I mean? You want somebody? Need somebody? That's okay, take me! I've seen it all! Done it all! Yeah, I'm thirty six years old, that baby's only six. Give her a chance? If someone's got to go, let me will ya'. Will you let me take her place?' He thought his brain was going to explode, continuing. 'Look, I'll tell you what! I'm a rich man, you know that? You gave me that! I'll swap it all for her. You want churches... hospitals? I'll build 'em! Anything you want, but please let me keep that baby.' He broke down, sobbing. 'Oh please God, listen to me will ya'. Anything! Anything you want! Only please don't take her. I've never begged You for anything but I'm begging You now. Please! Please God, let me keep her!'

When the priest came out of the room after the last sacraments had been given, Alex was like a mortally wounded animal, his eyes rolling in wild desperation. His savage fighting instincts took over as he pressed his back hard, against the smooth tile wall. He was into reaction now, ready for anything in front, using the wall to protect his back. His enemy this time though was death, and his chest and shoulder muscles bunched for the onslaught.

"Would you like to see her?" The nuns voice was so gentle and caring.

Marie was the strength now, leading her devastated husband into the room where Mary lay dying.

"Mary?" She whispered. "Look Baby, your Daddy's here."

"She can't hear you Mrs. George, she's in a coma and isn't aware of anything." The attending nurse said softly.

"She's so hot. Feel her hand Alex." Marie was examining her unconscious daughters hand and arm. "Where did all these little spots come from?"

"It's part of the fever, ma'am."

Alex took his daughters small hand in his powerful fist, hoping somehow to drain her fever into his body. He would never forgot the intense heat he felt at that moment. It would burn in his soul forever.

Louise was sitting on the porch with her grandson, saying her rosary, when Phideaux jumped up suddenly, pointed his nose to the sky letting out a long mournful howl three times in succession. He turned instantly, trotted down the long drive and disappeared.

"Where's Phideaux going, Grandmama?" Her grandson asked, turning to discover Louise with her head in her hands, rosary in her fingers, sobbing uncontrollably.

"It was spinal meningitis." The doctor was explaining to the stunned parents. "It's a fever of such severity and devastation as to be almost unbelievable. We did everything we could, unfortunately we don't know enough about it...." his voice trailing off.

Neither of them heard much of the explanation about the death of their daughter, stunned beyond belief.

"How could it have happened so quick?" Marie murmured.

"Where were you? How come you weren't watching?" Alex didn't even hear his own question.

"Watch what, Alex? There was nothing to watch." She wept.

"What Cher...." He didn't hear the answer either.

They made it through the funeral by holding on to one another, with Alex's moods swinging from sobs to icy silence.

"Help her Alex." Louise said to him after Mary died. "That must surely be a terrible pain to see your own children die. Yes, I know it's bad for you Cher. I know how much you loved that sweet baby and how close you were, but to lose a child of your own flesh would have to be the most painful thing a mother can be asked to bear. All mothers think they will die before their children. The other way is never even considered. Be her strength son! She needs you now!"

Alex stayed around the house after the funeral, trying to support Marie however he could, but was so blinded by his own grief as to be little help.

"Marie." Alex whispered to his wife holding her gently. "I don't know why this had to happen, but it's over with now and no amount of wishing will bring her back." He felt his anger rising as he continued. "I prayed and begged God, to let us keep her, but He took her anyway, and that makes me mad as hell." He held her away, looking down in her eyes. "I'm going now Cher. I got to get things straightened out in my mind. Yeah, I got to figure out why God had to take that baby away from us when I begged Him not to. I'm so angry now Marie, do you hear me? Angry with God and I don't know what to do about it, so I'll be gone for awhile until I can figure this out."

"Where will he go Mama?" Marie asked through shimmering tears as they watched him drive off.

"Back to the swamp. Men have to go there, sweet child, so they can cry with no one to see. The swamp will grieve with him, and between them they may solve his problems."

*   *   *

His screams could be heard only by those creatures close by, vegetation, water, leaden skies and heavy rain muffled everything. In his drunken rage he thrashed around in the vines and weeds on the small island that made up his camp. It was night, the area lit up intermittently by jagged flashes of lightening, followed by long rolling thunder. No human would have approached him, had there been any around, he was so frightening to look at. He was drunk and temporarily insane, as he staggered around with a long double blade ax, laying everything to waste that came within reach.

"Hey, hey, hey, hey!" He screamed. "Can you hear me now God?"

He wailed, staring down the bayou that passed in front of his camp, weaving, hoping in his drunken mind that the Creator might come that way.

"Or is there something wrong with your hearing?"

He stood swaying, his head cocked, listening for an answer. There was none.

"Yeah! Yeah! It's me all right! Alex George! Remember? I'm the guy you just shit on, big time! I want to talk to you!"

His words were intermittent, torn by sobs.

"I asked you.... No, I begged you let me keep that baby, but no, no, no I didn't hear nothin' from you."

He was stumbling, grabbing vines, falling, scrambling to his feet, falling again, taking huge roundhouse swings with his ax, splitting whatever tripped him with terrible force.

"Well okay, you son of a bitch! You got her!"

His anguish enveloped every fiber of his being, as he sobbed and screamed.

"But tell me somethin' though will ya'? Why? What you want with her?"

Falling again, he ripped his shirt going down, tearing it even more as he fought his way back up, exposing his massive chest, muscles accentuated by weird flashes of light filtering through the trees. The glistening combination of sweat and rain made him appear like a creature from another world. His hair was disheveled, hanging across his forehead, and his eyes were maniacal. He knew only exquisite agony, at this moment. Any creatures that might have been on the island this night, would have long since fled.

"Hey! You listening? Do You hear me? This is Alex George down here!"

Falling, he struggled up, swinging his ax again in a great circle.

"How about this Babe? How about coming down and tangle assholes with old Alex here, just one...fucking...time? Why don't You come and get me, yeah?"

He screamed, pounding on his chest.

"Or are You only killing little girls this season? Huh?"

He was in a low crouch, turning constantly. He wanted desperately to kill something, anything.

"Where are you, God damn it? Do you know what you did to Marie? Do you? Do you give a shit? Well let me tell you somethin' big boy! Fuck you! Do you hear me? Write my God damn name down so you know who's callin' you out! Alex George is callin' you out! Alex George says fuck you! How do you like that?"

Blinded by his agony, tears and rain, he screamed.

"Jesus, if I could only get my hands on you. I'd...."

He swung his ax with tremendous power sinking the head deep in a cypress tree, which in the sporadic illumination looked to the drunken madman like a tall figure in a long flowing robe. As he tried to remove it, he fell face down in the mud and passed out.

*   *   *

He tried, through the fog that was his mind, to figure where he was, fading in and out of consciousness. He was in a bed, that he knew, but nothing looked familiar to him. It didn't bother him though in his state of mind. Consciousness finally arrived when he opened his eyes to gentle nudging.

"Alex Baby, are you all right?" He looked up at Sue's worried face.

"Oh shit Hon'. What am I doin' here?" Burying his face in the muddy pillow. "How'd I get here?"

Sue told him he woke her up, pounding on the door at four in the morning, scaring her out of her mind until she could determine the wild looking man outside was him.

"Best I can figure your truck's stuck, back in the swamp. I never could get you to tell me how you got here, but I'm mighty glad you did."

Alex looked at the bed. It was a total mess, covered with drying mud.

"Don't know how I got here? Jesus Sue, I'm sorry about this. Why didn't you call the cops and have them get me?"

She managed a nervous laugh, obviously worried.

"You know I almost did, when I first heard you hollering out there. I didn't even recognize your voice until I heard you call out 'Cher' and even though it didn't look like you, I knew it was. Besides I think you'd have killed any cop I might have called so I let you in, and I sure am glad."

"Oh Baby, look at this mess!" He was focusing on the mud.

"Don't worry about the mess Alex. Everything that's messed up, will wash up. There's no harm done. I just thank God you found your way here."

"He probably didn't have a whole lot to do with it." Vaguely remembering. "I got no time for Him."

"You okay now?" She looked deep in his eyes, ignoring his comment.

"Been much better in my time, but I'm going to live."

"You want to get up now, and shower?"

Looking at the mess he had created in the bed, that sounded reasonable. "Coffee?"

"No Babe, coffee won't get it." Thinking it over, he added. "Wait a minute, you got any whiskey?"

"Yes."

"Give me half a cup of coffee and fill the rest with whiskey. That'll help."

Sue wept openly as Alex told her what happened, her anguish heightened by her love for this man, so deeply wounded by the death of his favorite child.

"What next?" She asked when he finished his story. "What are you going to do now?"

"I don't know." He looked at her like a small boy as he asked. "Could I stay here 'til I find out?"

He stayed with her for a week, drinking himself into oblivion nightly, making a strange, sick, violent kind of love to Sue when he was able. She, in turn, was much disturbed with his change in personality. The fun loving Alex she had known and loved all these years was gone now, replaced by something quite different. Between drunks it seemed he'd had all the light taken out of him. He was distant, cold.

"What about Marie?" Sue asked.

"What about her?" It was the first time the thought had entered his mind.

"Oh Alex, I know how much your beautiful daughter meant to you, and my own great sorrow is that I never got to see her," she reached across the table taking his hand gently in hers, "but can you think for a moment how this must have wounded Marie. Yes she was your favorite, and that's okay, but Alex you didn't carry that baby for nine months. You didn't have the thrill of feeling that warm speck of humanity placed in your arms when you woke up. It was Marie who nursed her, fed her, changed her diapers. Try to put yourself in her shoes? Can you imagine how she must have felt burying her own child?"

Alex was listening carefully to Sue's selfless words, impressed that she was trying to send him back to another woman who loved him. He was deeply touched by her tears.

"Sweetheart, you can stay here forever if you'd like. I'd like that a lot, but you don't have any business here. You belong with Marie. Go to her now, Alex. Help her, and thank God you have another child to love."

She was right and he knew it, so as soon as he could get himself straightened out he went back to LaFayette, and Marie.

"Oh Hon' I'm so sorry I left you like that." He was standing in the kitchen talking to his wife, "I really think I lost my mind. I'm sorry for being so selfish. I was only thinking of myself." He started to cry. "I know how much her death hurt you too."

She looked at him, her eyes overflowing with tears. With a strange, beautiful, distant smile on her face, she took him in her arms listening to him sob.

"I loved her so much Cher, I lost my mind when she left. I was so angry with God for not letting us keep that beautiful child...."

It was then he understood the depth of this remarkable woman. She held him for awhile, both weeping, holding on to one another for the strength they needed. Marie finally pulled back from their embrace, looking straight into Alex's eyes and down into his soul, whispering.

"Yes Alex. Yes I know. I loved her too. The sting is almost more than I can bear, but please Cher don't be angry with God, for if it hadn't been for Him we would never have known her at all. Let's thank Him instead for letting us have her the short time we did," adding with a radiant smile, "for wasn't she truly something?"

Life was never quite the same for either Alex or Marie, each turning their own way after Mary's death. Marie turned inward, devoting her time to the rearing of their son, and to the pursuit of helping others wherever she found them, those who could not help themselves to a better life. She changed, almost overnight, from a gay lighthearted person to one seeking the disadvantaged, trying to ease their burden by whatever means possible. Her support of the church was as much as Alex would allow, and her philanthropic efforts were to be found everywhere in the state. She constantly badgered Alex for money, to give away. As his wealth grew to immense proportions, so did her generosity and her ability to persuade her husband for more and more. In this regard she didn't have to work too hard, because he loved her so he would have honored most any request she made of him.

Their son, was a happy boy with few difficulties that sometimes afflict adolescents, attending local schools instead of being sent off to the pretentious institutions usually associated with children of the rich. This was the wish of both parents who wanted to enjoy and share in his experiences of growing up. He was secure in his relationship with his family, Marie, Louise and a warm and loving Alex, even though Alex's great love was Mary. The boy was subliminally aware of this favoritism but seemed perfectly capable of accepting it, as one of the facts of life. He had no jealousy toward the memory of his sister at all, falling under her spell of love and innocence, convinced too she had truly been a rare example of the generosity of God.

Alex had grave difficulty giving Mary up though, and entered a dangerous pattern of drinking and brawling to vent his anger. Louise spoke to him about this, suggesting he look deep into his soul for the answers to his problems, because he was only hurting himself and those he loved. Nothing really worked to change his approach toward self destruction, until his final brawl which nearly resulted in the death of his opponent.

"Jesus Sue," he agonized on a subsequent visit, "I don't know what the hell's the matter with me. I never used to be this way. Oh sure, I got in plenty of fights in the old days but they weren't anything serious. Contests more like? Most of the time nobody was really mad, just drunk and somethin' to do." His eyes glazed over as he thought aloud. "But now I'm out there looking for trouble. You know what I mean? It's as if...as if...I want the other guy to start the fight, swing first, so I can kill him with my hands, legal. Somethin's bad wrong Sue. I got to get it under control before I do kill somebody."

"Yes sweetheart I know, and you're right, but you do understand what your problem is don't you?" Sue asked, taking his hand in hers.

"Mary?"

"Yes! Yes of course it's Mary!" Her eyes filled with tears of compassion for her old friend and lover.

"Yeah, I know Sue. Marie's told me, so's Mama, and now you. Must be unanimous. The three most important ladies in my life." Her heart ached when he said that, aware of who the most important lady used to be. "They all agree what my problem is, but don't know the answer."

"I think I do, Alex." Her tentative reply.

"What?"

"I don't want to sound like a preacher or anything Alex, but I think the only place you'll find peace is in acceptance."

"What do you mean acceptance?"

"Just that. It doesn't really matter what the situation, there comes a time when we must sit down and carefully figure out what we can do about it." She was holding his hand tightly as she continued. "When you were coming up in the oil business, what did you do to get where you are?" She held her hand to his lips. "Don't bother to answer, 'cause I'll tell you what you did. You worked and you fought for everything you got. Am I right?"

"Yeah and some lucky breaks."

"What did you do when you came across reversals, no matter what kind?"

"Figured out what to do about 'em."

"Yes, that's exactly right. You stopped and sat down to see what could be fixed, and what couldn't, then acted accordingly, didn't you? When the price of oil fell to nothing in Oklahoma, what did you do about it? You sold at a loss, and laid low 'til things were looking up again. You didn't try to beat the system and keep on producing oil when there was no market for it, did you?"

"No."

"In other words you determined what you could do about a situation and if there was a way, you moved. By the same token if there wasn't, you weren't foolish enough to walk through doors that weren't there. Would you agree?"

"Yes, I think so."

"Alex I got something here that says it all. I want to read it to you. It's a prayer some long time ago saint prayed. From an everyday, practical, common sense standpoint it's absolutely profound in simplicity and directness." She looked Alex in the eyes. "You ready to be preached to by a whore?"

"Please don't say that Sue, that bothers me. Maybe you are what you are, but by God I love you and I'll put you up against anybody, anywhere. Besides, what was Mary Magdalene? She was no damn ribbon clerk, I'll tell you that, and whoever Jesus Christ was, man or God, he thought she was good enough to be with him. So if she was okay by him, I'll guarantee you should be too."

"Thanks for the kind words," she nodded, "I know you mean them. The prayer goes like this, Alex."

'God grant me the serenity to accept the things I cannot change. Courage to change the things I can, and the wisdom to know the difference.'

"When you look at those words and think about them seriously, you have to conclude they cannot be argued with. Up to this point in your life you've lived those words without even knowing it. When you had to do something to change a situation you did it. You did it if you could. When your father died you accepted it and went to work to support your mother. When Myron was killed, you accepted that. Huey died and it hurt like hell, but you kept right on keepin' on, doing what you should have been doing. Living!" She kept his hand, looking in his eyes for understanding, as she continued her efforts at reaching this man. "Alex, Mary is gone. You'd give your life for hers and so would I, but it doesn't work that way." The end of her statement came between sobs. "She's gone Alex, she's gone and that you must accept!"

Alex knew they were right. He had been acting like a madman, and if he was to survive, had to do something about the situation immediately, which he did. He accepted the irrefutable fact of Mary's death and got on with the business of living, taking solace in the fact that while she was gone, she was also an integral part of him like his other dead loved ones. The one thing that seemed to help him more than anything was the understanding she would always be with him, in his mind, until the day he died.

'God damn!' Alex thought forever, impressed by the major events of his life. 'I wonder how all these strings get pulled? Lose something, find something. Like the whole thing's staged.'

*   *   *

It was three years after the loss of Mary, he picked up the skinny kid on the dusty Oklahoma road and once again had another major character ushered into his life, through what appeared to be wild coincidence.

Although Alex had become a hard nosed, relentless businessman he did have compassion for others. That was his motivation when he picked Tom up off that desolate road in 1939.

Tom Brooks was the name the kid came with, but no one would ever know if that was correct or not. When they checked into his background, they were stymied by the loss of all records pertaining to his background.

The home he walked away from that day, burned to the ground a few years after he left, so there was no way to check anything. No one could even tell them how he got there.

Christ they'd been through a lot together over the years with Tom, and his family, filling a great void in the lives of Alex and Marie after the death, in a plane crash, of their last remaining child, Alex, Jr. He was in the Naval aviation program, something he could have gotten out of easily with his father's power and influence, but chose not to. His plane went down in the Gulf by the Pensacola Naval Training Center, on a training flight, and was never found. They were stunned by the news, and once again Marie handled it better than Alex, because of her great faith, and devotion to her church.

Tom was in the marines, in the South Pacific at the time, unaware of their loss until his arrival home. Nothing had been planned, as far as Tom playing a central role in Alex's affairs after the war, it simply worked out that way. There were desperate days for Tom, returning from the horrors of the South Pacific after he'd become such an integral part of that action. He lost many friends in that savage conflict. Alex salvaged him for the second time in his young life, pulling him back from the abyss of insanity caused by an especially vicious war, and his savage participation. That barbaric combat was not what the Geneva Convention had in mind, when debating the rules of war.

His devotion to Alex was such that any suggestion from him, was tantamount to gospel in Tom's mind, and that's how he wound up getting the education he did. Alex suggested it.

The years following Tom's return from Harvard School of Business were years of incredible growth for Avro Enterprises. The mushrooming oil industry in South Louisiana and even more prolific offshore exploration and discovery took them to unbelievable heights in the world of commerce. His contacts, set up by Huey years before, were still in effect assuring his meteoric rise because of his favored status in leasing on both state and federal lands.

In the ensuing years Tom was the Old Mans right hand, always at his beck and call, appearing to serve as guardian of the man who drug him off the scrap heap of life. He too became a wealthy man in the process. Many tried to understand the exact relationship between these two men, the answer evading most, but had they been able to see inside their hearts and minds, they'd have found Alex looked upon Tom as a son, while Tom viewed Alex as his own personal idol. His loyalty and devotion, seldom seen in this day and time, was more like that of a medieval knight and his king. Anything, anything at all Alex suggested, was like a command to Tom and as they grew in the pursuit of corporate affairs, Tom's devotion to Alex George was a never ending topic of discussion in many circles.

He was not considered to be only a follower, anything but, because he brought much needed business expertise to the entourage of this south Louisiana magnate. He was responsible for introducing many diversified operations to the Old Man's attention, along with reasons why they should be looked into, then abiding by his decisions. Tom was the one who insisted they get in oil exploration in the middle east, and the one who always sat next to Alex while negotiating with various sheiks, desert kings and princes. They admired what they saw in this strange quiet man. Each of them were attended by bodyguards of every description, but none of them were so sensitive to everything around them as this tall, alert man who seemed to radiate a foreboding of restrained savagery toward anyone who might be a threat to his master. Those who suspected these things, were right.

Alex and Marie grew closer and closer all through the years of their marriage. That impressed the old wildcatter. They didn't discuss these things openly, which he regretted all the remaining years of his life after she died. He thought a lot about how his love had grown over the years, starting with his infatuation with that beautiful blond girl back there so many years ago, on the streets of St. Martinville. That bright, fun loving, energetic, strong, wild sexual girl he married when she was but a child, and how quickly she made the transition from carefree youth to caring and loving mother. It broke his heart that she had to lose both of her children, trying however possible to help ease her pain, after he found his own way. Mary, he never understood. Alex he could. It was wartime. A quarter of a million sets of parents in the United States shared their loss. That was war. He still wept over the six year old child when he saw her blond beauty dancing in his minds eye. Oh but Marie.

'My God, my God.' He wondered how she stood it, honoring her acceptance, strength and faith.

Marie in turn, knew she was loved by her husband totally, and was grateful and happy for him. She turned her energies, after the loss of their son, toward helping the helpless, donating millions of dollars to that end. Her eyes turned in the direction of the loving things in life, and her heart was constantly being broken by ever present evil and cruelty. Alex tried desperately to shield her from these things, after he understood how her mind worked.

Right after the war and the loss of their boy, Alex came home to find her sitting at the kitchen table, sobbing like her heart had been torn from her body. His immediate reaction was the same, rage over whatever was hurting her. It was always the same frustrating, helpless feeling. He wanted to put his hands on the cause and make it stop.

"Oh Cher." He said dropping to his knees pulling her head to his shoulder. "What's the matter? Why are you crying? What is it, Babe?"

"Do you know what they did to the Jews?" She whispered between sobs, staring down at the oil table cloth, wide eyed in horror.

"Who Cher? What Jews?" Myron was a Jew, and he loved him. He didn't want anyone hurting Jews.

"The German's. The Nazi's."

"No, Hon'. What?"

"Oh Alex." She bowed her head and wept unrestrained. "The paper says they killed millions of Jews. Nobody knows how many." She looked up at him, begging silently for it not to be true.

"What! How? Bombing?"

"No. No. They rounded up Jews everywhere in Europe. Whole families...sent them to camps...put them in gas chambers," her words came in choked half whispers, "and killed them."

"What do you mean?"

He raised his voice in anger. He'd never heard of this. There must be some mistake.

'This was 1945, not 1445. People don't do things like that now.' He thought. 'War yes, battlefields yes, but Jesus Christ not slaughter innocent people! Nobody does that! Where did this story come from?'

Alex couldn't help, her sorrow was total, down to the bottom of her soul. She was crushed to think it could be true, while the hideous details of the unbelievable genocide crept to the surface. Guilt somehow manifested itself in Marie's mind. How could all this have happened while we did nothing?

"But why should we feel guilty about it, Momma? Yes, it's the most horrible thing I've ever heard of, but why should we feel guilty? We didn't know anything about it."

She stared wide eyed in horror holding her hand over her mouth, whispering lest someone hear.

"Because we were here. We were on this earth. We should have known. Somebody should have known. How can you keep something like that a secret. How can you kill millions of people on purpose?" Then she grew distant adding. "And all the babies. The beautiful babies."

Alex knew the reason for her agony and made a mental note. It was a reminder he was never to forget.

She asked him for money to give to the Jewish Relief agencies, which he gave in abundance because of his love for her, and his friend Myron. She asked him for money for a wing at the hospital where Mary died, and he gave it to her. She asked him for money for any and all worthy causes that came to her attention, which he either gave her, or reasons why not. Her obsession in life seemed to be people hurting people and although Alex tried every conceivable way to keep the sordidness of life from her, was unsuccessful in his attempts. It was as though she had a strange sixth sense about where cruelty was manifesting itself, demanding her attention. She could not understand why Negroes were held is such contempt by whites, hurt by whites. It couldn't be resolved causing her terrible anguish during the years of the civil rights movement, with the riots, pain, suffering and death. Why all the killing? Why did people as promising as the Kennedy brothers have to be slaughtered? By whom, and for what? Her heart was broken over the murder of Martin Luther King as she felt he was the most outstanding Christian America had produced this century. Not for what he'd done, but for what he wanted to do, and to be murdered for his efforts. Alex thought about that when she told him. He remembered what the official said to him after Huey's death.

"These kinds of men? Someone always has to kill them."

Marie spent the rest of her life trying to help those she could, agonizing over those she couldn't, and it had a profound effect on her husband, causing him to think about things he wouldn't have, ordinarily. His concern about things that hurt Marie, turned to icy rage when her pain was more than she could bear, as on the occasion he found her in a state of despair over a child found clutching a chain link fence in the median way of a west coast interstate highway. Beaten and thrown out of the car like garbage by his parents, left to whatever. It was the words of the child that hurt her more than the deed.

"The boy said he didn't want to live any more." She whispered to her old warrior husband. She always whispered these things for fear God might be listening. "Oh Cher, he's only nine years old."

Vietnam was something else she couldn't fathom, questioning Alex how our military men could ask more boys to go in what was so obviously a totally futile effort. To be shot at and killed, in the most vile circumstances, while we were being lied to at every turn. She agonized over what was happening to everyone in that area following the My Lai massacre story from its beginning, to its inconclusive end.

Our young men were sent into impossible situations where they fought and died over what? If it weren't so tragic, it would be a joke. Could anyone write a scenario, such as existed there, and expect it to be believed? Could it be that our leaders were insane and we didn't know it? Was it possible this savage war was being fought because of the egos of a select few? How many of our boys, who couldn't buy or scheme their way out of the service, were going to have to die? Worse. How many were already dead and didn't know it?"

Alex talked to her endlessly about Sue's theory of acceptance. About accepting things we can't change, changing what we can, and knowing which was which. She always asked why can't we change things? He fought out of desperation to help, because her sorrow was dragging her down physically. It terrified him watching her deteriorate, dying by inches in front of his eyes, and he couldn't do anything about it. They had been together so many years and had grown old sharing the same triumphs and defeats. It was apparent to him many times in the last years of her life, that he only thought he loved her when he married her, concluding he didn't even know the meaning of the word then. Years of married life bringing two souls together, that's what love for this woman came to mean to him.

"Help them Alex. Help the ones who can't help themselves." She begged him before the cancer took her life.

So that's what he decided that misty afternoon in the boat with Helen. It was all over but the shouting for him in this life, but while he was still here and had his vast wealth he would do what he could to help. What he had in mind was decidedly different from what she was thinking, but maybe he could help lessen the pain for others.

He would definitely need Tom for these plans.

CHAPTER 11

"Well shit!"

The response was as sudden and harsh as the jangling telephone demanding his attention from the other side of the room. Tom Brooks thought it was a perfect day for one of his most cherished and elusive of pastimes, reading. He thought for something so pleasurable, he sure didn't get to do much of it. He'd wanted in the worst way, to read a recently published book on the Vietnam experience. He was interested in, and read everything on the subject he could possibly find time for, intrigued by all treatments on the subject, plus having an intense personal interest in anything to do with jungle fighting. Now the God damn phone.

It was a real and totally unwelcome interruption of a brief but balancing respite from his duties as Chief Operating Officer of Avro Enterprises, one of the largest industrial conglomerates in the world. Since Marie George, the beloved wife of the Old Man had died, he was now shouldering most of the responsibilities for guiding this huge entity through its daily affairs.

It was a perfect day for reading. About the only thing he enjoyed watching on TV were football games, and this was the wrong day for that. A slow drizzle precluded golf, and his wife and daughter were gone on one of their infrequent but delightful shopping days together.

The phone was on its third ring when he ripped it off the cradle with a brusque "Hello" to whoever the interloper, at the same time thinking of a harsh reply to the idiot who dialed his unlisted number by mistake. His mood changed instantly by the soft voice of the Old Man, recognized at first sound.

"Tom?"

Something about the way he said it, caused immediate cessation of his previous thoughts. The Old Man was THE OLD MAN and when he spoke, like the commercial said, everyone listened. Bankers listened, knowing he had enormous wealth and didn't need theirs. Industrialists listened, because of his unbelievable track record in every phase of industry he ever entered. Senators and Presidents listened. Governors of the State of Louisiana listened most attentively of all, because his personal power and influence in the Bayou State were such that while his support did not necessarily guarantee election, it came close enough. Anyone who ever came in contact with him after he reached the peak of his power listened, because he was such a formidable man, and had the best top hand in the business world in Tom Brooks.

"Tom?" It was soft, almost whispering. "I hope I haven't interrupted anything important."

"No, Mr. Alex," he lied, "you didn't."

What he was doing wasn't important at all, compared to anything this man wanted of him. His loyalty to the Old Man was absolute, something rarely seen in these times.

Tom was a millionaire now, many times over in his own right, but never lost sight of who put him where he was.

"I was more or less killing time, loafing around until Nancy comes home from her shopping. I'm going to try and talk her into taking me out for a steak, when she does. How about you Boss, would you like to go with us if I can talk her into it?"

Tom wasn't listening to, or thinking about, what he was saying because anytime the Old Man called or in any other way summoned, he dropped everything. His full attention was brought to bear on what Mr. Alex George wanted of him.

"I hesitated to call you. I know it's Saturday...a man needs time away from job and the boss, but I want to talk to you, so if you don't mind...." His voice trailed away.

"You know I don't mind Boss."

He started calling him Boss when he was only a boy, first coming under the influence of this remarkable man, and when speaking directly to him called him either Boss, Mr. Alex, or Mr. George. Never, ever, did he call him Alex, because in that part of the country, at that time, a young man simply did not call an older man by his first name under any circumstances, out of tradition and respect.

"Tell me where and when Boss, and I'm on my way."

He was curious why he'd call on a day usually given over to rest, relaxation, and family functions of one kind or another. Unlike most powerful men of might and means, the one magic word around him was the word "family." Tom had seen him on many occasions release valuable men, some of whom he would have done almost anything to keep, who left because of family. He always sent them away, not only with his blessing but a wide open invitation, heartfelt and sincere, to return to any of his enterprises whenever they could.

"Well Tom," he went on, "if you could I'd like to see you right now, at the shed. I apologize for the nuisance son, but I think you know I wouldn't ask if it wasn't important."

The voice seemed sad, bringing an immediate positive response from Tom.

"Thanks Tom. My apologies to you and Nancy for taking you from her, but as I say...." His voice dropped.

He knew every nuance of the Old Man's behavior better than any human being alive, now that Momma was gone, and because he served this man in a way few could understand, felt an immediate need to be at his side. Alex George was the most powerful person in his life, and he needed him now.

"Be right there Boss, and don't worry about tearing me away from Nancy. She and Mary are trying to spend me into the poor house, right now. Hope you got a few ideas to make some money. Got a hunch I'm going to need it before they're through."

He liked to kid with the Old Man, it helped. Now that Momma was gone he not only didn't laugh like he used to, he didn't laugh hardly at all. Tom would do anything to provide relief from his constant sadness, but this time it seemed to go unnoticed.

"Well fine then. Oh and Tom, when you get here come on around to the shed and let yourself in. Helen and me are back here, so we won't be disturbed."

Helen stayed as close to the Old Man as possible. Her role as self appointed protector put her always within range of his hand, when he reached out to touch her. She was Momma's dog in the beginning. They were inseparable, much like Mary and Phideaux years before. She had "carte blanche" and pretty much did what she wanted, but was always only a step or two from the woman she adored. She slept in their bedroom, most of the time on the bed, which he groused about, but never changed. She would float along on her beautifully muscled legs wherever Momma went, to the store, St. John's, in the yard while gardening which toward the end of her life was a favorite pastime. They communed for long periods of time with Momma talking gently, and Helen listening.

The Old Man was the only one left now, and Helen was with him every waking, moving, moment of the day, and of course slept with him at night. The only time she wasn't with him was when he couldn't take her, for whatever reason. This was not to her liking at all, and she always reacted to it by a very deep and obvious funk, which both amused and touched him.

"I'm leaving now Boss," cradling the phone wondering what this was all about. Whatever, he was moving toward the Old Man. All kinds of possibilities for this call ran through his head. He glanced at the log burning in the fireplace, hoping it didn't roll out and burn the house down. He was irritated that he'd even lit the damn thing.

When they had the house built Nancy insisted on a fireplace in his den. Any home like this, should be liberally sprinkled with fireplaces, she said. Tom said OK and let her have what she wanted, as he did in all matters to do with their family life. This special lady had been places with him most women never go. He could not bring himself to object to her wishes.

So Nancy, Mary, and their architect, had an absolute ball putting the place together. They did it well too, compromising between unlimited funds and exceptional taste. The results were one of the most beautiful homes in the LaFayette area.

Tom pulled on his jacket, thoughts racing through his mind, the fireplace quickly forgotten. He was preoccupied, gathering and sorting ideas. Why'd the Old Man want to see him? Why now? There were no great problems involving the many companies connected with or controlled by Avro. None that might be hanging fire. Even if there were, they had the best top level executives anywhere. Managers perfectly capable of handling anything that came their way. The Old Man taught Tom a long time ago, one of the first rules of business was surround yourself with the best professional managers you could find, pay them according to their talent, and make them perform.

Nothing was coming through until the chilling thought, 'maybe the Old Man's health.' He was truly a great age now, living on borrowed time by anybody's standards. He was born a long time ago.

'That's it,' Tom recoiled at the thought, 'bad health news...wants help on long range planning...what course Avro should take.'

The thought distressed him, because of their unique relationship through the years. Love would have been much too insignificant a word to describe it.

He scribbled a note for Nancy on the outside chance she and Mary might return before him.

"Gone to see the Boss. See you when." He dropped it in the middle of the hall floor, to be sure she didn't miss it, and let himself out the front door.

As Tom pulled out of the driveway, he glanced at the house in the rear view mirror, thinking what a beautiful place it was. Nancy and her architect did a fantastic job, and Tom realized what a truly lucky person he was. Lucky? Anointed was a better word, for his life had been a miracle.

'Jesus Christ, I wonder who puts the twists and turns in a life.' He thought. 'Where would I be now, if I hadn't been on that road up there, that day?"

*   *   *

It was a hot, dusty, chickenshit day in 1939, and the 15 year old kid was drifting down the road. It was a road going nowhere, and he was alone. It wasn't simply that nobody was with him; there wasn't anyone, anywhere, who knew where he was, much less cared. He was nobody, going no place. No plan! No destination! Nothing! The thought terrified the kid. His parents, whoever they were, had long since quit.

He seemed able to conjure up a memory...dim...didn't know even if it was real. Slender sad faced man, ghostlike, in his recollection. Everybody seemed to be crying. He tried, but couldn't get the smoky image to clear up. Too much fog. Got the impression of heavy drinking...never knew whether that was true or imagined. Thought there was a lot of arguing and shouting. Yeah...a funeral too. Must have been his Dad...couldn't even remember him. Remembered his Mom. The marvelous memory of laying with his head in her lap, drifting to sleep. Damn, that was good! Soft. Warm. The reassuring rumble of her voice transferred through her body to his ear. He never knew what happened to her, and in later years spent a small fortune trying to find out. His dim memories included a succession of strange faces...many different places to live. Foster homes he guessed, only dust bowl Oklahoma didn't know foster home from jack shit. They couldn't let a kid die on the road or in a field, so it seemed it was a scrap of food here and a strange bed there until he wound up in the County Home. Yeah, the name conjured up all sorts of Dickensian images, but he knew they did the best they could with what they had, and that wasn't much.

In those days there wasn't any money, much less state organized programs, to support the ever increasing number of kids who showed up needing care. Tom had no hard feelings at any time in his life over the events of those tough days, only everlasting sorrow over what he felt must have been the fate of his parents.

For reasons he didn't understand, he had particular grief for his Father, feeling the man probably had all joy and hope...yes and love too, ground out of him by that miserable dust bowl depression era of sadness, that paralyzed the whole nation at that pitiful time in our history. He knew a lot of men went down the tube with the burdens of those circumstances. He knew it because the Old Man told him of many a good man destroyed by the times, but it bothered him to this day when he thought about his Dad being one of the victims. If only he could have helped, let him know he didn't care what he had, or what he did for a living, but that was all far in the past. So it was that day he walked out of the home and kept going.

Scared? Jesus Christ was he scared! Mighty big world for a fifteen year old kid to be facing on his own.

He was so preoccupied he didn't even notice the Ford bust the top of the hill, a mile or so behind him, kicking up its tall dusty rooster tail. He was so lost in thought as it approached, it took the tremendous noise created by the car to break his concentration. He glanced around first to see what it was, making some sort of hailing action because in his youthful ignorance he didn't even know how to hitchhike. The car bounced to a stop and while the kid was trying to figure out what to do next, the smiling driver pushed open the door.

"Hop in kid!"

Tom pulled back with a shyness to be expected from a kid who'd bummed his first ride.

"Hey look, don't be afraid. Hop in. Bet I'll get you further down the road, and faster, than those bare feet, yeah."

Tom looked down at his feet. He had no shoes but it didn't seem strange to him. The home did the best they could, but they only had so much to work with and he was wearing the only garment he owned, a pair of overalls. No shirt, no shoes, no underwear, only a pair of gray and white striped bib overalls. He climbed in, sitting as far as he could get from the driver, hugging the passenger door after he closed it.

Thinking back Tom knew he had no feelings of fear then, because it was the "Old Man" who'd picked him up. He never had memories of him that were anything but pleasant, except those occasions when he was in for a deserved ass chewing by this same man. He came to know, over the years, that even when he was receiving a bombastic reaming, as soon as it was over, it was also forgotten.

The "Old Man" was in his late thirties then and could be a gentle and charming person, when the occasion called for it. He was shorter than the gangling scarecrow kid seated next to him, but the first thing Tom noticed about him was his arms. The boy thought they were the biggest arms he'd ever seen.

'Funny what a person remembers.' He thought, whenever memories of that day returned. 'Most men with their sleeves rolled up to mid forearm, have considerable slack between the fabric of the sleeve and the arm itself. He had no slack at all. That sleeve was just jam full of arm.'

As soon as Tom closed the door, his benefactor ground the gears and they were caroming down that nameless, Oklahoma road toward a life no one could have imagined.

The Old Man smiled warmly, when he asked where the kid was bound for and picked up instantly on the boys objection to being called "kid".

"Oh by the way, since we're going to be fellow travelers for awhile, I think we should know one another by real names, instead of me calling you kid, and you wanting to call me asshole for doin' it. My name's Alex! Alex George! Sounds like two front names don't it, but that's what it is. What's yours?"

Tom was still hard against the door, boring two holes in the windshield with his eyes. He was too shy and scared to do anything else, but out of his bewilderment he did remember many a sharp blow to the head, when he was slow answering such questions.

"Tom."

It was the best he could do at the time, startling Alex with his deep voice.

"Ok! Gotcha Tom. It's a real pleasure to meet you son. Yeah, yeah. Now what you say, let's get this sucker down the road and see where it goes."

With that Alex stuck his hand out in front of the boy so shy or not, he couldn't refuse it. When he shook hands he was struck, as he was for the rest of his life, with how gentle a grip it could be, yet so firm that it transmitted a feeling of great power. Tom looked into the warm smiling face over the extended arm and had a curious feeling, one he had no way of describing, but he felt comfortable with this man. He tried to figure out the strange accent, because he had taken his initial step onto life's stage, and this was the first of many accents he was to experience over the years.

As Tom remembered, the trip was uneventful except for his terror born out of ignorance about the situation he found himself in, and his desperate attempt to make any sense of anything. He couldn't even begin to fathom his dilemma because he knew nothing of life. It was as though he had only just been born and in the truest sense of the word, he had.

The Old Man had an uncanny ability to know intuitively what people were thinking, rich or poor, powerful or not. He knew the kid was terrified and it tore at his heart because he'd never learned to handle suffering in those unable to fend for themselves. Most of these feelings were underscored by Marie's concern, and there was something both awesome and terrible in his compassion for the underdog. He joked constantly about how you could always tell the American at a bullfight. He was the guy that was cheering for the bull, but in his heart it was no joke, remembering the time in a sleazy beer hall he nearly killed the man who was beating a woman, for whatever reasons men beat women in bars. Alex thought about that much of his life, because his reaction just wasn't normal. He didn't want to punch the man around and let it go at that. No, what he wanted was to kill him with his bare hands. His passion at that moment was such that he could have, and most certainly would have, had he not been restrained by others.

It was a part of the Old Man's character he could never fathom. In moments of self appraisal he knew he was a good man, although unyielding. He had enormous compassion for others, yet was capable of extreme violence, and then deep concern after it had exploded.

How was he to communicate with this dust bowl drifter, baby that he was? Alex felt the pressure in his chest, as his mind raced over the reasons the kid was in this situation. He weighed variables and obviously not one God damn thing could be attributed to the victim. Finally he hit on something, eyeball to eyeball conversation with the kid, over something to eat. All kids his age and size ate, and could do so around the clock. He broke the silence.

"Listen Tom, I'm hungry. Blew out of my room before breakfast. Know a little diner down the road where this gravel strip connects with 66. We'll stop there and get something to eat, then back on the road. What you say?"

Some kind of sound came from Tom the Old Man couldn't hear, for the roaring wind and gravel crashing against the underside of the car. He didn't want to push it, so he said no more until they reached the crossroad diner and he fought the Ford down to a stop.

Alex got out of the car, and headed for Mamie's Diner, when he realized he was alone. He knew instantly why the long, lean and lanky kid wasn't coming, he obviously didn't have a dime, but had an inherent pride about him that would not allow him to ask for help.

"Hey Tom! Come on son, get down! Let's eat!"

Tom wondered instantly what he was supposed to get down from, because he wasn't on anything, rather sitting in the car when Alex opened Tom's door. He was to learn much about Cajun conversation in the future.

"Look, I'll tell you what...."

'There it is again.' Tom thought. 'He does talk funny.'

"I got to eat and don't like to eat alone unless I've got something to read. Don't have nothin' to read, so why don't you come on in and sit with me. Maybe we can think of something to talk about. OK?"

He knew the kid would fall for this line. He also knew once he got him inside, it would be only a formality to get some food in him. He was right, because that's the way it worked out.

Mamie brought the menu's. She was a great frizzy haired, blond character who spoke louder than any woman Tom had ever heard.

"What'll it be for you guys?" The kid shrank into his side of the booth afraid his poverty might become public domain, and because Mamie was so intimidating, at least to this most recent recruit to the human race.

"Mamie!" Alex asked smiling. "You Mamie, Cher?"

"In the flesh. What you think?" Turning around slowly like a model, smiling. "What you guys gonna have?"

Alex was laughing as he gave her his order, after which he uttered some prophetic words.

"My man here's a little on the shy side, so fix him the works? You know what I mean, Babe? Ham and eggs, and he'd probably love the hell out of your hotcakes, 'cause I'll bet you make 'em real good. This here's my new side kick. Tom's his name. We just met up, and I want him fed right so's we can get some work out of him, yeah!"

"Hi Tom." Mamie ruffled his hair, turning her gaze back to the handsome curly haired man. "You one of them Cajun guys, ain'tcha?" Mamie asked, in her wide open way.

"Oh hell yeah, Cher. How'd you know?"

"Cause, I used to know a sweet talking Frenchmen." She was obviously enjoying a pleasant memory. "Boy, hot damn! That's what he used to say all the time. He was a real mess. Loved to talk about his bayous and swamps." She was leaning against the end of the booth enjoying her brief mental trip, pretty much unaware of their presence. "I wonder whatever happened to that sweet thing?"

"Oh hey now Mamie, I'll tell you what," breaking her reverie, "he's probably back down there in those swamps, you know it? Why hell yes, if he wasn't here," arching his eyebrows in the direction of Mamie's figure, "that's where he'd be, yeah! You know, sweet thing, you can take one of them coonass boys out of the swamps, but they's no way you can ever take the swamp out of the boy."

Tom never could figure why that conversation stayed so clear in his mind, except much was being explained to him, on the spot. In a roundabout way, he found out what Alex George was, and where he came from. A Frenchman! No wonder he talked so funny.

"I, uh...."

"What you say, Tom?"

"Uh, I don't have any, er...."

"What.... Money? You worried about money?" He threw back his head and roared with laughter. "Well don't, 'cause I got more money'n there is! You're sittin' with a very rich man, right now! Not that it make's a shit, but believe me when I tell you I am. In the second place you ain't gonna get something for nothin' anyway, 'cause when we get out to my rig you can pay for what you're eatin'. What you think about that?"

Tom thought, in his painfully shy way, that sounded like a good deal wolfing down his breakfast while the Old Man talked on and on. He hurt deeply for this boy, obviously adrift, trying to figure what he was going to do with him.

"Look Tom, I'm not trying to butt into your affairs son, but where're you headed?" Alex was sincerely interested, even this unsophisticated lad could see that.

"Don't know." Replying in his heavy voice.

"Yeah, well that's what I figured. Anybody lookin' for you?"

"Nope."

"Family?"

"No sir."

"How old are you, son?"

"Fifteen, they say."

"Yeah? Well OK, tell you what. Ever had a job before?"

"Only workin' around the home."

He never forgot the tears that suddenly appeared in the Old Man's eyes. He was pulling on his jaw pretending to look around until he could gain control.

"That where you coming from now?"

"Yes sir."

"They know you were going?"

"Nope. Just left. It don't matter anyway, got too many kids now."

"Ever had a job for money before?"

"Never had any money before."

"Tom, how'd you like to work for me? I work a lot of people and I'm on my way right now to one of my drillin' rigs to check things over. What if you worked there, for me, would you like that?"

Through the years Tom thought maybe God himself had intervened in his life at that precise moment, because he had absolutely no place else to go.

"Yes sir, I think I'd like that." Even though he had only known this magnetic character a very short time, he was instantly drawn to him.

Alex George reached a ham sized fist across the table to shake the boys hand.

"OK then, it's a deal! Now let's hit it Tom!"

The boy was as happy as he knew how to be and stuffed with Mamie's culinary delights.

"Hey Mamie, great breakfast!" Alex said at the cash register. "Tell you what, sweet thing! If I see that old coonass boy down there in the swamps, I'm going to give him one more big hello for you."

Mamie looked at him quizzically.

"How the hell you going to know who he is, Cajun?"

"Easy enough Babe! He'll be wearin' the biggest smile in the bayou!"

They walked out the door to her raucous laughter.

Alex loosened Tom up on the remainder of the trip to the rig site, finding out the kid was absolutely rootless. Thinking back to what Sue had told him about being able to change the things we can, he decided to change things for this boy, and right now. The Ford bucked, rattled and crashed out to the rig site from the main road, braking to a stop in a huge cloud of dust.

"Wait here, Tom!"

He watched the Old Man walk over to another man who came down off the rig to greet him. An earnest talk took place with both participants nodding toward him from time to time.

"Hey Tom! Get down son!" Alex shouted to the kid.

"Come shake hands with Mr. Mahoney, he's the man you'll be working for."

Oh how painful that was, for the shy backward kid, walking over, shaking hands. He couldn't even look Mahoney in the eye.

"They teach you much about God, at the home Tom?"

He loved these memories, because he was learning so much about Alex George while they were happening.

"Some."

"That's good boy, 'cause out here Mr. Mahoney is God! We call him the driller and he is the God damn boss, for sure! I told him what your situation is, you need a job now, and a place to sleep! That right Mahoney?"

"Yep. You sure did." The driller replied.

"Tell Tom what we got for him."

The driller didn't appear happy about being nursemaid to the half naked kid. He wasn't smiling when he told Tom what was going to happen.

"We don't really have a job here, 'cept Mr. George said to make one for you and I s'pose we can do that all right. You're going to be sort of a general flunkie around here, kid. You'll clean tools, handle pipe, work in the pits." Indicating an ugly, smelly pit, full of an indescribable black liquid. "Anywhere we need a spare hand. You drive?"

"Yes sir! I was the biggest kid at the home. I drove most everything there."

"Good. There'll be times you'll have to run into town for us. Pick up stuff. You go, we don't have to take a man off the job." Mahoney was running the possibilities of this new man over in his head, liking the idea more and more all the time." Just remember, the Old Man," that's the first time he ever heard him called that and wondered about it at the time, because he didn't think Alex George was all that old, "told you the driller is the head honcho out here, and the man's right. When I tell you to do something, you move! I want to see assholes and elbows watchin' you get to it. Understood?"

"Yes sir." Tom replied in a state of mixed emotions. He was happy to be away from the home and on his own. He was worried about being able to do the job.

"Tom I gotta go into town, and get some stuff." The Old Man spoke up. "You ain't goin' to be able to work around here dressed like that. You know what size clothes you wear? I'll get you shirts and shoes and some more overalls. You got any underwear on under that thing?"

The boy looked very embarrassed.

"No sir, they gave us what they could, but didn't have everything we needed."

Alex whipped around pretending to inspect something about the rig until he could get those 'God damn' hot tears out of his eyes.

'Kid never had shit.' He thought. 'Not a God damn thing, not even a family, and defending the home all the way.'

It was nothing to Tom, apparently seeing things the way they were, but it disturbed Alex George.

"How big are you Tom?" Alex asked looking up at the kid.

"Six feet, last time we measured."

"No shit! Mahoney!" He was very intent. "What size shoe's it gonna take to cover those feet?"

They drew an outline of his foot on a piece of paper and the Old Man went to town in Mahoney's car, telling Tom before he left.

"Okay Tom, you start earning your money right now. Underneath all that dirt, on the Ford there, is paint. Grab a hose and wash that thing down. Let's see if we can get the paint back on top, instead of the dirt."

While he was gone, Mahoney took the bewildered kid aside telling him, "Son, you are one very lucky boy. You don't know that yet, but in time you'll understand what I'm saying." What an understatement it came to be. "The Old Man told me he wants you to make it here, and he meant it. He wants to help you, and when you realize who and what he is, you'll know what a one in a million break you got. He thinks you're a good kid, probably a hard worker, and while it's only a hunch on his part he told me to give you every chance in the world of stayin' on, here with us. Got what I'm saying so far?"

"Yes sir."

"Okay, and so's you know for damn sure who the boss is on this rig, he told me if you can't cut the mustard, I turn you loose and you get on down the road. Understand?"

"Yes sir."

"Good! Now wash the holy hell out of his car and while you're doin' it, you might say a little prayer of thanks to the Man upstairs for the break of your life!"

Alex took the small crew aside before he left the rig site, telling them he didn't expect Tom to receive any slack as far as the work was concerned. He also made it clear he didn't want any of them harassing him simply because he was a new man.

"Life's shit on this kid ever since he was born, and I want to give him a chance. I want him to have a chance here, with us." Alex told the assembled crew before leaving, waving his hands for emphasis. "Don't expect anything to be slowed down by him. Told Mahoney not to baby him, or give him even one extra privilege. I hope you understand that." His conciliatory tone ended abruptly. "Same time boys, if I hear any of you give the kid some unnecessary shit, you know what I mean, picking on him 'cause he's green or 'cause he's a pup, why then you and me's goin' back of the shed and work things out. Understand?"

All nodded affirmative. They understood.

Tom joined the crew with a vengeance, leaving no doubt in anyone's mind he was aware of the break he had received, anxious to please and do whatever necessary to keep his job. Anything Mahoney told him to do, was done without hesitation. There was meager resentment toward Tom, when he first came to work, quickly dispelled by his approach to the work, Mahoney's eagle eyes, and the memory of Alex's threat to whip any man's ass who didn't treat the kid fairly. His reputation as a brawler was intact.

Everything about the job excited the youngster and he was truly grateful, knowing nothing about gratitude, to have the chance to work with these men. He worked, and worked hard, to the satisfaction of Mahoney, and the crew. Each man took an interest in Tom and he went from having no one to care for him, to a kind of unofficial mascot to his fellow workers.

"Jesus Christ!" Alex shouted upon seeing Tom for the first time in a month. "What the hell are we feeding this guy?" He had Tom by the arm facing Mahoney. He wanted to brag on the kid to make him feel good. "He's grown half a foot and looks to me like he could pick your rig up Mahoney, and move it whenever you wanted. Christ, I've only been gone a month Tom and look at you! You look good son!"

He did look good. The combination of good food, hard physical labor, regular hours and a deep tan provided by the hot Oklahoma sun made him look like a million dollars. Nobody knew how much he weighed when he got there, but Alex figured he must have gained twenty pounds in that short period of time, all hard muscle. His shoulders and chest received most of the newly acquired weight, and although overalls aren't meant to flatter a physique, he looked good in his. Slim waisted, tall, deepening chest and developing shoulders foretold of a powerful build in the making. The sun had done an admirable job on his sandy hair, bleaching it to an attractive hue. He was a handsome boy, growing into a man.

The Old Man was beaming, grinning from ear to ear, happy his hopes for the boy were working out. Tom was happy too, but for a different reason. His joy was the same as a stray dog who'd been picked up, cleaned up, fed, petted and allowed to lie down at the feet of his benefactor. He was much too young to realize what was happening to him, but it was simple adoration toward the man who yanked him up from near nonexistence, to become a member of the human race.

"Tom, come over here. I want to talk to you." Alex said during the course of his visit to the rig. They walked over to his car, which he'd washed to a high sheen. "Boy hot damn, you washed the dirt right off this rig, huh!"

The boy's heart filled with these honest words of praise. He'd like to do something really meaningful for Alex. His feelings for this man were love, devotion, a desire to be of service, but he wasn't familiar enough with any emotions to understand them.

"You happy here, son?"

"Yes sir!"

"Good! Yeah that's great! The whole crew thinks you're a good man, and so's Mahoney. That's good enough for me, and I'm real glad you got their approval because I was pullin' for you all the way. I wanted you to make it on your own, and you have."

"Thanks Mr. George."

"No thanks to me." He paused. "Well maybe a little bit, for bringing you out here in the first place, but you're the guy had to do the proving."

"I'm trying hard, Boss." He slid his eyes toward Alex to see if it was okay for him to call him Boss, and upon seeing no reaction whatever figured it was.

"I know you are Tom and I appreciate that, but I appreciate it more for you than me."

Tom didn't know where this conversation was going, afraid it might be goodbye. He heard Mahoney and the others saying it looked like they were getting close to oil, and if so it would only be a matter of time before this job would be wrapped up.

"Mahoney thinks we're just before hitting here, and when that happens we move on." The big kid's reaction wrenched Alex's heart after his statement. He looked sad, staring at the ground. "What kind of plans you got, when we finish here?"

"None, Mr. George. Get on down the road, I guess."

'Get on with it George.' Alex was saying to himself, unable to stand the whipped dog look his words caused.

"Wait a minute! Wait a minute Tom! What I'm asking is, would you like to come with us?"

Tom's heart skipped a beat at the thought.

"Yes sir! I sure would!"

"Hey OK, that's great Tom! I was hoping you'd say that. You're a damn good worker, and that's what we need. I was hoping you'd go with us." Suddenly remembering he hadn't told him where they were going. "Christ Tom, I forgot to tell you where we're going."

The boys reply was almost too much for the Cajun.

"Don't much care where you're going Mr. George, I just want to go with you."

There was another long silence as the short, dynamic oil man looked quickly up in the rig, over at the pond, back to the shed, everywhere except straight at the boy. He dug at the ground with the toe of his boot and Tom noticed while he had his back to him he seemed to be having difficulty breathing. Finally he looked back at the boy.

"Oh hey Tom, I don't know if you realize what you just said but I'll tell you somethin', that's one of the nicest things anyone ever did say to me." He hurried on not wanting to cause embarrassment for Tom or himself. "You ever been to Louisiana son? South Louisiana?"

"Mr. George, the only place I ever been, outside of the home, is right here!"

"Well God damn then!" Regaining his composure. "Boy are you in for a treat! Listen to me!" This was vintage Alex George, bullshitter extraordinaire speaking. "Before we go I want you to look real hard at this miserable hardpan country. Keep it in the front of your mind so's you can compare this with south Louisiana. Why son we're going to LaFayette, Louisiana!" The Old Man was caught up in his descriptive magic, drifting dreamily for a moment. "Man that's got to be the capital of the whole wide world, down there. It's so beautiful you have to see it to believe it." Giving him a pat on the back, unaware what a state of delirious joy he was causing the lad. "I'm sure glad you're going with us Tom. It's a real pleasure sharing good things with people I like."

Tom laid awake nights thinking about what the Old Man said. 'Capital of the whole wide world. Wow, that must really be something. Wonder how big it is.'

He wasn't long in finding out, because when the well came in everything was dismantled, loaded on trucks and they headed south. He was fascinated by the changing countryside, it was so new and interesting to this boy who up to this point in life had experienced nothing, except the monotony of the home. It took three days to make the journey, and while Tom normally enjoyed driving, he didn't want to on this trip, in order to stare at the wondrous scenery passing by. Rolling out of the dusty dry Oklahoma country into the Eastern hills, which he thought were absolutely beautiful would have been enough to make the trip worth while. Then Northern Louisiana followed with its dense pine forests.

'Damn,' he thought, 'this smells beautiful in here. Never saw so many trees. Big, thick, right up to the edge of the highway. Wonder if any wild animals live in there.'

He didn't have long to wonder when he saw the deer, four of them. They seemed to run or glide, maybe even float, across the road ahead of them. He wanted to see them so bad, but by the time they reached the spot where the deer entered the forest, they had disappeared.

He'd seen red dirt in Oklahoma, but not as pronounced as this, and he sure didn't have any trouble seeing how the Red River got its name. It was red. Somewhere south of Alexandria the trees thinned, and crop lands appeared.

"Mostly rice around here Tom." Mahoney told him as they rode along. It was a pleasure to be with the boy, watching this panorama of beauty unfold with someone seeing it for the first time. "Lots of rice down here. We'll be seeing sugar cane pretty soon."

It was after dark when the convoy rolled into LaFayette and the young escapee from the county home was thrilled to be there. He wouldn't know until the following morning what the town looked like, but he was excited by the exotic odors.

"What smells so different?" He asked Mahoney.

"Louisiana, son!" The driller was thrilled to be back too. "Damn, don't it smell good?"

"Yeah, but what am I smelling?"

"Everything on God's green earth! Grass, trees! The Bayou Teche! Flowers? Talk about flowers! Damn, wait 'til you can see 'em! You're smellin' dark roast coffee, and coonass cookin' like what you can't believe. Likely some stale beer! Folks around here like their beer. Spill some of it once in a while! Oh yeah and maybe, just maybe, you got a whiff of a sweet smellin' Cajun lady in there." He was hard put, trying to explain the riot of odors and what they were about. "Hell Tom, you're smelling south Louisiana and I'll tell you one damn thing for sure, there ain't no other place like it, on this earth."

The boy was trying to figure if that's why the Old Man called it the capital of the whole world. It was certainly stimulating, and he was excited being here.

"My old lady's probably put all the pots and pans to bed for the night Tom, so soon's we get all this stuff in the yard, I'll take you to a cafe I know that's still open. We're going to get us some real coonass cookin'. What you think?"

"Guess so, Mr. Mahoney. I'm pretty hungry." Pausing, asking cautiously. "Mr. Mahoney?"

"Yeah, Tom."

"You said something about a...a coonass I think you called it? What's a coonass?" Mahoney laughed loud and long over the question.

"That's a special thing with the Old Man, Tom. He'll tell you. Be sure you ask him tomorrow."

Tom fell instantly in love with the food, eating things he'd neither seen nor heard of before. Some dishes he was half afraid to eat, they looked so discouraging but Mahoney laughed and told him to dig in. One dish he called seafood gumbo and told Tom that really only the gods should be allowed to eat it. He sampled it tentatively, instantly addicted to its pungent odors and taste. Then came shrimp, which he had never heard of, followed by a dish he certainly would not have eaten had he been alone.

"It's called crawfish etoufee' Tom. Spoon some over that rice there boy, and I'm tellin' you, you'll think you'd died and went to heaven."

He tried each dish with the hesitancy of someone eating their last meal, then ate with a gusto that pleased Mahoney immensely.

"You like it?" Laughing as Tom tried to answer, unable because his mouth was stuffed.

The coffee at the end of the meal was as startling to Tom as everything else. It looked like a cup of tar, with an aroma richer than anything he had ever experienced.

"How come such small cups, Mr. Mahoney?"

"Cause son, what you got in that itty bitty cup is enough coffee to put most yankees clear out of the coffee drinkin' business, all the rest of the day, if they drink it in the morning. That's dark roast coffee Tom, and I'll bet you're going to like it as much as you have everything else tonight. What'ya say, you anywhere's close to filled up?"

"Oh yes sir! Anything else and I'd blow up. Damn, I've never eaten anything like this in my life. Does everybody eat like this down here?"

"Maybe not as much, but they would if they'd been away from it long. I know you got a little room for something real special to top it off." Mahoney was happy the kid liked it, and he knew the Old Man was going to be really pleased when he told him about it. "Miss, me and my Yankee friend here would like to have some of that pecan pie."

'Sure enough.' Tom thought drifting off to sleep. 'Maybe I did die and go to heaven.' Musing as sleep crept over him. 'Wonder why they all talk so funny? Oh well, anyway now I know why the Boss sounds the way he does.'

CHAPTER 12

Tom was reviewing his life, en route to the shed, concluding that he too had long ago fallen under the spell of South Louisiana. It had been so many years since he rode into town with the Oklahoma convoy, it was as if he'd been born here, which was true to a certain extent. Before being picked up by the Boss he had no personal history whatever, and while some distant memories did exist, even those blurred because there was nothing to differentiate one from another. He remembered a tornado that came close to the home, but there was no date or age to isolate it. He really only existed, and barely at that, before that day in 1939. He had one hell of a life, after.

He had matured into a distinguished looking man. Tall, over six feet, athletic. He hadn't changed much physically since his younger days, still possessing a narrow waist, and quite broad shoulders. He was well preserved physically, for a man his age, kept at it by constant urging from his wife and daughter. They also kept at his wardrobe, which was not something he resisted. He was neither self centered, nor ignorant, aware of his handsome good looks. He had a full head of hair, mostly white now, with sharp chiseled features. His face was generally impassive, the one notable feature his hooded eyes. When studied closely, which he often was by the many powerful with whom he came in contact, these eyes suggested no one should pursue what lay behind them.

The rain persisted, the high humidity making everything sticky. He snapped on the air conditioner, checking the climate control.

'Seventy two degrees.' He thought. 'Right on.'

Tom let his mind drift, casually observing the gorgeous scenery as the university campus slid by.

'Checked the beauty lately, son?' He thought to himself. 'Looks just like a miniature swamp.'

He asked the question constantly, acutely aware of the fleeting nature of life, all life. The beauty that was south Louisiana should never be taken for granted, even if one had been down the same path as he. Tom was neither believer, nor disbeliever, referring to himself instead as a passive agnostic, curious why some lives take the turns they do, while others seem to be a waste from the beginning.

*   *   *

"Jesus, Mr. Mahoney, you sure were right!" Tom commented the morning after their arrival in LaFayette. "It's beautiful!"

"Where'd you learn that kind of language, my boy?" Mahoney asked, an impromptu sermon developing in his mind.

"What?" Mildly defensive.

"Jesus, and the rest of your vivid expressions."

"Oh! Learned 'em on the rig. Never heard 'em before. Why?"

"Just wondered." Subdued. "Think it's as good as I described?"

"Better! Couldn't sleep this morning, got up about the same time as the sun, and walked around town. I never saw anything like it. Fog hanging everywhere, about treetop height. It was like I was looking through a piece of gauze. You lived here all your life Mr. Mahoney?"

"Yeah, my grandparents got off the boat in New Orleans. They were starving to death in Ireland, left the old sod to see if they could keep from starvin' over here. Made it far's LaFayette. Liked it and stayed. Me and my whole family are what you'd call naturalized Cajun's. We keep marrying these French gals, so even though the name's Mahoney, blood's pretty thick Cajun."

It was decided Tom should work in the company storage yard, that way he could support himself and finish school too.

"Where can we put the kid up, Albert?" The Old Man asked the morning after they arrived, telling his yard boss Tom's life story, which wasn't much.

"Well there's that cabin on the back of my property Boss. You've seen it, back by the bayou? Thinking 'bout it, don't know why I built the thing in the first place, 'cept I was fixin' to screw myself right out of house and home." Followed by salacious laughter. "Anyway, let me talk to the old lady. See if it's okay with her. It'll mean she'll have to cook for another mouth, not that she could tell the difference."

"OK, do that will you? I'll take care of his room and board, but don't tell him. Charge him," he calculated quickly, "say ten bucks a month. Make him think he's paying the whole thing. He'll work after school and Saturdays in the yard, so he can make spending money. No free ride here. Don't want him to have one, and if I read him right, don't think he'd want one."

The Guidry's had a large piece of property backing up to the bayou, with a small cabin at the extreme rear, a few short feet from the dark water. Mrs. Guidry made it quite livable, upon hearing about the newcomer, to welcome him with open arms. She was a small lady, full of "joi de vivre'", with her dark hair pulled back in a bun. She wore rimless glasses and Tom figured she must be about the age, maybe, of his own mother. There were six small Guidrys providing a never ending riot of action for the pert Mrs. Guidry to try and stay abreast of. Her eyes were full of tears as Albert told her of the new arrival, and what was known about his background.

"Oh Alber', bring him on home Cher! Yes! Yes he can stay here! We got so many kids now, one more doesn't matter!"

"Oh but he's a big one, yeah! He might eat a lot."

"I hope so Alber'. I hope so. I'll cook a lot!" She couldn't keep from crying out loud over this fifteen year old boy who had no one, especially no mother.

"He's back at the yard. I didn't know what you'd say, so I left him there."

Mrs. Guidry gave Albert a big hug, smiling through her tears saying. "Well then, husband of mine, how about trotting your behind right on down there and bring me that boy."

It was certainly love at first sight as far as Jane Guidry was concerned when Albert brought the big, shy boy through the back door and into the kitchen, where she was to be found most of the time. All the small Guidry's were there too, to see first hand this newest addition they'd heard about. The kitchen was sizable and Tom, surrounded entirely by Guidry's, towered over the entire assemblage, including Albert. Everyone in the kitchen seemed to be smitten by an inability to speak, with the smallest Guidry's peeking around their parents legs, the larger ones all thumbs and elbows trying to appear nonchalant about everything.

"Tom is it?" Jane Guidry stepped forward taking his hand as she stared up into his serious eyes. She was smiling, but it was hard. The tears were there.

"Yes ma'am." The somber reply.

"Well Tom, my name used to be Jane, but now it's Mama. That's what I want you to call me, because that's what everybody calls me including Albert there. We've got a whole lot of kids Tom, as you can see. This kitchen is just full of Guidry's. Let me introduce them to you."

Jane took Tom by the arm, pointing out each child as she named them.

"The little one hiding behind me is Stevie. Isn't he about the cutest thing you ever did see? Up 'til now he was the newest one."

Tom didn't miss the implication.

"He's two and very, very spoiled. Then over here we have Brenda. Isn't she pretty?" She never paused long enough for an answer.

"She's five, and will be going to school next year."

He could only see one of Brenda's eyes, because she was sharing the safety of her mothers skirt with Stevie.

"That lovely lady over there is Barbara, she's seven and has a new boyfriend."

Many giggles accompanied this announcement.

"The pretty lady at the stove, that's my Nancy. She's a smart lady too, and brings home only the highest grades."

This comment met with a demure smile from Nancy.

"The next one is little Albert, although he's trying hard to be big Albert. He's thirteen. Rough. Likes football, and girls."

Many more snickers from the crowd.

"And last, but the first is Paul." Her eyes softened in a special way for the studious looking boy, short and dark haired. "Paul's fifteen. We hope someday, he'll be a priest. That would be nice, wouldn't it?" There was a special pause as she showered her love, with her eyes, on her oldest son.

"Now come on over here Tom." The small Mrs. Guidry said, noisily sliding a chair around from its position at the table. Pushing it in front of her shy new boarder, she jumped up on the chair before he knew what she was doing, put her arms around his neck and gave him a big kiss right on the lips, to his utter embarrassment and absolute delight of all the kids in the room.

"Welcome to your new home, Cher. We're all mighty happy to have you." Tom noted especially at the time, her dark eyes were full of tears.

'Wow,' he thought, 'how do these things happen? Going from no home, family or love, to the exact opposite.'

When Tom thought those years over, he concluded they were the happiest of his life. He certainly knew now where Jane Guidry was coming from even though she overpowered him at the time. She had so much love to give, and lavished it on this welcome addition to the large family, to the squeals of delight from the others. When he entered the kitchen each morning, she made a great issue of getting a hug from him. The big shy kid was mortified to begin with, but one did not reject Jane, especially when she didn't wish to be rejected.

"Oh ho, my friend," she'd shout when he acted stiff about the hugging, "shy is it? Tell you what Brooks, here's the deal in this kitchen! No hug for Jane, no food for Tom! How do you like them apples?"

She stood there in her apron, one foot balanced on the heel, toe moving vigorously in the air, looking at him. Jane Guidry did not accept turn downs. He recognized later what she was doing, never sure if it was intentional or not, but he thought it was. She was teaching him through example how to love. He had no experience in these matters.

The Guidry kids managed to overcome his shyness quickly, and soon had him participating in many of their activities, such as the impromptu ball games that erupted in their large back yard. He especially loved the balmy nights when the kids came down to his cabin, and sat on the porch talking. They looked up to Tom, as an instant hero. It was his only chance at childhood, and he had it all jammed into two and a half years. They were probably the best years of his life.

The Old Man took great pains to speak with Tom every time he came into the yard, savoring to the fullest the moment when he asked him, "Mr. George, what is a coonass?" The effect was pretty much the same on Tom, as it was on Alex when he was a boy. The part about the hole under the racoons tail wasn't nearly as funny as the exaggerated behavior of Alex, at the end of the story. He fell up against a truck fender laughing crazily, pounding on it with his right hand while cradling his head on his left arm, kicking the tire below. Although Tom was a serious boy, he couldn't help but be caught up in the silliness of the moment. The Old Man thinking, 'it worked'. There was something about this lad that nearly tore Alex's heart out, no doubt the fact he had no family love at all, to this point in his life. This condition was so foreign to him as to be nearly impossible to understand. He'd been born to love with Louise and Gaston, and lived in an area of the country steeped in a long tradition of family love.

Alex had plenty of things to do, in those days, to keep him on the run constantly but compared to where Avro found themselves now, he was still a small oil entrepreneur. When he went to the rigs about operational matters, he took Tom so they could be together and talk. These times were of monumental significance to him because he felt like he was in the presence of God, or at least as much as he knew on that subject. It was hero worship in the extreme, and although he never showed how he felt about this man, knew in his heart he would do anything for him, anything at all.

He worked in the yard, after school and on Saturday as scheduled except during football season. His high school coach nearly swooned with ecstasy the first time he saw Tom, taking pains to see that the big kid played for him. He put it to Alex on the basis of civic duty that this young giant play for them, because any boy his size should definitely be playing for the home team.

In the summer, between school terms, Tom worked on the drilling rigs which he loved. The excitement of the rig, captured many a man before him including Alex George, and it was no different with Tom. He didn't attempt to understand why he felt as he did, he simply loved being out there. Part of his feeling could have been the exotic locations they were forever finding themselves in.

They were drilling this momentous time in a flat, apparently endless, salt marsh. He could see for miles in all directions. The drilling sites are man made islands set in the marsh connected to the main road, by an ingenious method. Marshland is much too soft to support heavy loads, so it's impossible to drive on. A log road is the answer, built with heavy timbers like railroad ties. These are placed side by side to the rig site, after which they nail flat planks to the top for better weight distribution of the enormous loads they must carry.

'Loved those timber roads,' he thought driving over to the Old Man's shed, 'listen to 'em try to jump out of line, wheels squirmin', hell of a racket. I miss that.'

He enjoyed standing on the rig, staring out at the vast expanse of nothingness, marked by the ever present timber road winding its way to the site. The summers were ferocious, heat shimmering off the surface with humidity beyond belief. If anything good could be said about conditions out there, it would have to be the resulting fine physical condition of the men. Whatever fat they had upon arriving at the site, was immediately lost through perspiration.

The swift summer storms rolling in off the gulf were awesome when they screamed over the marsh, creating waves in the grasses like the waters of the gulf. Most of them were violent, roaring in off the water with nothing whatever to stop them. Nearly all brought rain, sometimes gentle, sometimes torrential, dumping what appeared to be much of the Gulf of Mexico on them. The first time Tom saw one of them blowing in, he couldn't believe the color of the sky or the odor the winds brought with them. The mosquitos were something he could do without though, anybody could do without that ferocious breed. They were tough, so tough as to be almost unbearable. He had to apply a smelly solution to whatever part of his body was exposed, to keep them from eating him alive, but mosquitoes or not he loved working in the marshes.

The summer of 1941 marked in a strange way what was to become his life work, that of serving Alex George as few men are.

They were on location in the marsh, Tom working as one of the roughnecks. Physically he could stand in with anyone now, usually bigger than most of his fellow workers. He was over six feet, with well muscled arms and shoulders, and a hard body acquired through the arduous labor involved in oil field work.

It was a day like any other, the rig humming when Tom glanced up to see the Old Man's car bouncing its circuitous way out to the location. He pulled up, giving an exaggerated wave to Tom who returned it in like fashion. He felt good about seeing him anytime, all the more so on these unannounced occasions. He wanted to go down and talk to the Boss, but knew that was out of the question. It was okay with the boy though because Tom knew before the Boss left, he'd make a special effort to come up on the platform. So he went back to his duties wrapping chain, slapping on the collars, pulling long strings of pipe across the deck. He felt so God damn alive and strong, loving the rhythm, feeling as full of life as he ever had. He was where he wanted to be.

He saw the other car out of the corner of his eye, bumping over the rough timber road. Tom wondered casually who it was, he'd not seen this particular vehicle before.

'Not one of the regular oil field supply salesmen's cars,' he thought, 'they don't drive anything that nice. Four guys....'

He watched them for reasons he didn't understand at that time, but it was definitely more than just to see what was happening. Nothing on the rig changed as he worked his big steel hook around the long sections of pipe they were pulling out of the hole, hauling them across the floor of the platform to be stacked by the man in the top. He never would forget that day, and tried to reconstruct it many times, it was almost surrealistic.

The big diesel, providing power for everything on the rig, was bawling its lungs out with a steady roar. The rig pounded and shook and Tom was swinging with the operation. He was part of it! Totally alive. Jesus, he loved the rhythm. Smoke from the diesel smelled good too. God damn rig tryin' to bounce right off the marsh, and he felt strong enough at that moment to hold it down by himself. Slap on the collar, wrap the long chain around the pipe, grab a section, walk it back. He could do it in his sleep and he loved it. He glanced down at the Old Man standing by the shed, hoping in the manner of a sixteen year old that he was watching. Tom loved to showboat for the Old Man, but he noticed Alex wasn't looking at him at all and didn't seem happy to see these visitors.

Tom didn't like anything about this, they approached Alex too fast. It didn't look right. The boy knew instinctively something was wrong when Alex tried to move in such a way as to keep all four in front of him. He couldn't hear any conversation, but he knew this wasn't good. Suddenly one of the men swung on Alex, hitting him on the side of his head with a blackjack, which staggered him. The others jumped in immediately swinging away with fists, and kicking. Stunned as he was, the oil field fighter was fending them off, holding his own. He kept his foes in front with the shed protecting his back.

Tom had never seen a serious fight in his life, but he knew someone was trying to hurt the Old Man, and that wouldn't do.

"Hey! What the hell are you doin'!" He screamed to the group as he flew off the rig. "What are you doin'?"

He was running at top speed as he approached the men. One of them saw him coming and reached into his pocket pulling a gun. The ugly gesture in no way affected Tom, his fear and anger was so great. The thug with the gun started to raise it, as Tom hurled his steel hook with all his might sinking it in his shoulder. He screamed as he went down.

'Fuck him!' Tom flashed as he reacted. Someone was hurting the Old Man. 'Not while I'm here.'

"Get away kid." The man with the blackjack yelled as he swung to face the charging Tom. It was the last thing he ever said as Tom grabbed a short piece of iron pipe swinging it like a ball bat, in a great sweeping roundhouse hitting him on the side of his head. His skull exploded like a melon.

Tom turned to face the others as they jumped off the boardwalk, ran to their car and drove away, leaving their dead mate behind.

There were no words spoken for a moment between Alex and Tom, but the look that passed between them said it all. Alex really understood Tom's feelings for him at that moment, he knew the boy could have killed all four or given his life in the attempt. He also saw love there of a totally different kind than he had ever experienced, understanding it completely. Tom's eyes glittered with tears when he saw the blood trickling from Alex's head.

"You okay Mr. Alex?" It seemed like hours had passed before he answered.

"Yeah, yeah. Little groggy. Never got hit like that before." Tom caught him as he started to lurch off the walk, holding him gently. "Some shit about leases." Answering for his young friend a question he wouldn't have asked, then or ever.

The rest of the crew scrambled quickly down to the scene of the fight, stunned by what they found. Alex George being held by the new young killer in their midst, the dead man laying where he fell, blood splattered on the shed wall from the man impaled by Tom's hook. It was a scene of extreme violence, and the men were shocked.

"What happened?" Someone asked.

His answer came in a wave of Tom's hand indicating now was not the time to talk about that. No one pursued it further because there was an indefinable something about the sixteen year old boy that suggested otherwise.

"What do we do with the body?" Someone finally asked.

"Throw him in the fucking marsh." Tom's stunning reply was spoken softly, as he gently wiped the blood from the Old Man's head.

"No, no. It's okay, boys." The Old Man found his voice. "Put him in the truck. Take him into town...give him to the sheriff. Tell him I'll be in tomorrow to square things."

Tom drove the Old Man back to LaFayette, neither speaking.

"Appreciate what you did for me out there, Tom." The Boss broke the silence. "Sorry that guy had to die, but he should've thought of that before coming." He glanced at the boy sideways. "Where the hell did you learn to fight like that? Why Jesus Christ son, you destroyed 'em."

"Never had a fight before in my life, Mr. Alex. I thought they were going to hurt you, bad." Softly adding. "It scared me. Never been that scared in my life. Can't remember hardly what happened. Couldn't let 'em hurt you."

"Yeah well whatever, I sure am grateful to you. We'll take care of the business with the dead guy tomorrow. Don't worry 'bout it though, I know everybody who runs this state. We'll get it handled. It wasn't your fault, they were out to bust my ass and you were defending me."

"If they ever came back, I'd do it again." Alex was startled at Tom's icy reply. "One thing though Mr. Alex."

"Yeah son."

"I'd sure thank you if Mrs. Guidry didn't have to know about this."

"Don't worry Tom, she won't."

Looking at him in the dim light, Alex George thought Tom looked much older than he was.

Two phone calls the following morning, one to Baton Rouge and the other to the local sheriff's office, and the whole affair was handled. It also served as Tom's first lesson in how big money, and the power that passes to the possessor of that money, gets things done that would otherwise be impossible.

"Wealth gets benefits other people just don't have, Tom. Might not be right, but that's how it is. There's an old saying sums it up. Money talks, and bullshit walks. I didn't know anything about that until after the money showed up, but I like the leverage it gives me. The best seat in the restaurant, an open door to the governor's office, the Bishop saying special masses for my family, 50 yard line seats whenever I want them. That ain't all bad Tom, and while it's not something I flaunt, I guarantee you it's something I'll use whenever it's to my advantage."

Tom continued working on the rigs, the summer and fall of 1941, after graduation from high school. He was by this time, a bona fide member of the Guidry family, enjoying all the love and privileges that entailed, and was the absolute idol of all the small members of Jane's family.

The middle children, ranked by age, had an aura of unstated respect for their big boarder, all except Nancy. Her feelings were more those of an adult, which she had no way of understanding at that time.

CHAPTER 13

"Mr. Alex?" Tom was standing in the office door looking at the Old Man. "Could I talk to you for a minute?"

"Oh hell yes! Just a minute son, let me get these things cleared off my desk."

Alex's mind raced as he busied himself, trying to buy a little time. He knew why Tom was there. He just didn't know what he was going to say when the boy asked the question he'd come for. It was Monday, December 8, 1941. Pearl Harbor, and the world, had just gone up in flames.

"What does Mrs. Guidry think, Tom?" Hoping to get a little help from that quarter.

"She said I should talk it over with you." Closing that avenue of escape.

"You know Tom, I could fix it so's you wouldn't have to go at all. A couple phone calls."

"But I want to go, Mr. Alex." Gazing calmly in his benefactors eyes. "Weren't you in the last war?"

"Yes. Yes I was."

"Would you have stayed out if it had been possible, at that time?"

"No Tom, I wouldn't."

"I want to join the Marines, Mr. Alex. From what I hear, they're the best fighting outfit in the world and I want to be with the best."

Alex didn't want Tom to go, but was pleased with his choice. He told him about his experiences in the first World War, and what he could expect in boot camp. He explained the DI's only seemed to be the biggest assholes in all the world, but were really there to train men to obey and fight together, thereby standing a better chance of coming out the other side alive.

"Don't believe the war movies Tom. There's no romance to seeing one of your friends laying dead next to you. Won't be any music playing when you head for a machine gun nest, unless you figure the sound of bullets whining around you for music. When all those guns start hammering, it's another world out there. Everyone's trying to kill the enemy, and if you're the enemy, they're trying to kill you. I had some real good buddies I lost out there." His eyes glazed over as he looked 24 years in the past. "I loved some of those boys Tom, and when you get where survival is all there is, you'll know exactly what I mean when I use the word love. A man who shares the constant possibility of death with you, becomes far, far more than a buddy. He becomes someone you really love and cherish, because he's right there beside you. You don't want him to die 'cause he's all you got." Hoping his words had been heard Alex added. "You got some time 'til you're draft age. Why don't you wait and see what happens?"

"How old were you when you went in." Tom asked.

"Seventeen." The subdued answer.

"Did you want to wait, Mr. Alex?"

"No."

"I'd like to join tomorrow, and they say you'll have to sign." Looking steady at the Old Man. "Will you sign for me?"

*   *   *

Tom's trip through boot camp was as to be expected, a smooth journey for the tall quiet boy. He cut his teeth on hardships most men grouse about, becoming an unofficial leader of his company in short time. Men were attracted by his cool demeanor, taking in stride everything the Marines had to hand out. He was also an outstanding physical specimen, which in a group of young men is a mark of distinction in itself.

Boot leave was a special time because of the loving attention he received from Jane Guidry and her tribe. The mother of this brood received her surrogate son like he was her own, eyes glistening through tears of joy at seeing him, while standing on her chair hugging him close. The small members of the clan crawled all over him, admiring his uniform, with its buttons and emblems. The whole group, especially Albert an avowed outdoorsman, were much impressed by his sharpshooters badge, oohs and aahs resounding through the house. Stevie, Brenda and Barbara being the youngest swarmed over Tom, and like any other big brother he loved their irresistible enthusiasm. Nancy was different, she stood her ground. Silent, aloof, but with a heart full of love. Young Albert wanted to go back with Tom, and be a marine too, while Paul the one with the special light in his eyes wanted to go right now but was out maneuvered by his mother at every turn.

"Listen Paul, Mama wants you to be a priest." Tom told him while the two of them were sitting on the small porch of his cabin. "Why don't you go to the seminary instead of the service?"

"I think if there's a war Tom, I should be there. You went. Why shouldn't I?"

"Oh yeah but the enlistment lines are blocks long in front of every recruiting office in the country. Soldiers, sailors, marines we got, but I wonder how many boys are standing in front of the seminaries to be priests?" Turning to look at Paul. "You really want to be a priest, Paul?"

"Yes. I hope someday, but not now. Anyway I feel that's pretty much up to God. If there has to be a war, and everybody's going, I should go too. God can wait 'til it's over, then I'm a priest for the rest of my life."

"Yeah but Mama?" Tom had been among this family over two years, acquiring their lilting way of speaking. "What about Mama? She doesn't want you to go, no. You're her oldest and have a special place in her heart. You know that. She wants you to be a priest, Paul. What if you went in the service and didn't make it back? What then? What about her?"

"I have to go Tom." Sudden laughter at the black humor in the situation. "Besides, God's going to get me no matter what. Sooner, on a battlefield, or later, in an ordination ceremony."

They laughed together, Tom couldn't argue with that.

*   *   *

After Tom entered advanced training, the word came down that a special guerrilla combat group was being formed. It would be different from the rest of the Corps, stressing hand to hand combat. They would live off the land operating in small groups, traveling light, penetrating far into enemy lines, engaging in hit and run harassment tactics. A very special group, among the best trained fighters in the world, patterned after the British Commando's. The groups were to be known as Raiders, and they were looking for volunteers.

Alex George was Tom's idol, about that there was no doubt. He wielded tremendous influence over him all of their lives together, including now. Considering his attachment to The Boss, driving to his house, he thought what a natural he was as warrior and student to the man moving into his life, in 1942. His name was Lt. Col. Evans F. Carlson, and this new unit was to be known as "Carlson's Raiders".

Carlson was a unique Marine, taking a different route to where he found himself in 1942. He'd been an officer in the regular army during the first war, received his discharge and soon found civilian life was not for him. He joined the Marines, where he had a most unusual career. Among other things he traveled with the rebel Chinese Army on their celebrated "Long March", and was considered the foremost authority on guerrilla warfare this country had in its military. He was also on special personal and professional terms with President Roosevelt, serving him in his China time as a special advisor which gave him great personal prestige, whether he wanted it or not, and he did not. This relationship earned him the animosity of many in the officer corps, eventually causing him to submit his commission for retirement, which he did prior to WWII. After the outbreak of hostilities between Japan and the U.S., Col. Carlson asked for and received his commission back, and was put in command of the new fighting group.

His background was unusual, the son of a New England preacher, and although he found it necessary to leave home at a young age, unable to get along with his father, he became a student of the Bible like many other outstanding military men over the ages.

Many officers in the Marine Corps felt at the very least, Evans Carlson had definite socialist leanings, while a few considered him to be an out and out communist of whatever hue. This was a result of his time with the rebel Chinese army and his espousal of many of their theories and practices. He spent years with them, and came to believe in many of their goals.

He developed a strange metaphysical theory of survival under heavy fire, believing if you were totally about the business of conducting a battle with only the highest of purpose, if you kept your wits and equipment about you, then you should emerge unscathed. It worked with him, and while not trying to appear heroic he had great indifference to the death and destruction around him. At Tarawa, after losing his Raider command, he walked what was considered the deadliest beach in military history, coming through with two bullet holes in his clothing but none in his body. He was there only as an observer, serving with great courage and distinction even in this lesser capacity.

His was an incredible approach to building a lean, hard guerrilla unit, contrary to everything the Marines were famous for teaching. It was Col. Carlson who introduced the phrase "Gung Ho" to our language, which has been bastardized to mean almost anything except what it truly does. "Working together." He believed in common effort, enlisted men and officers, ending many training sessions discussing the events of the day with both groups, something unheard of in the Marine Corps. To the horror of all career Marine officers, he allowed enlisted men to question the reasons for any command he had given during the course of the day.

He was much more than the marines could fathom, and as usual had to pay the price for being the exceptional man who believed there was another way. The Raiders became victim of the same jealousy and enmity of others in the Corps, those pitiful few that are found in every branch of the service in every war. The detractors asked how could you have a specialized elite in a corps that already considers itself the best fighting group in the world.

Tom felt fortunate indeed, all the rest of his life, for the honor of serving under this man. It was the second time in his young life, he was to come under the influence of such a towering personality. Tom would have followed Alex George into the hubs of hell. He did follow Evans Carlson there.

"Why do you want to be a Raider, Tom?" Carlson asked during the interview. He tried to interview personally as many of his volunteers as possible. He was that kind of man, and commander.

"I understand the Raiders are to be a special outfit Colonel, made up of the best the Marines have. I want to be part of the best."

"That's admirable Tom, but do you have specific reasons for feeling that way?"

"Yes sir, I do. A man in Louisiana taught me I should be the best I can, on a daily basis. He says we owe that much to God and ourselves."

"Your father?"

"No sir. I don't have a father. I never knew him."

He explained, at the request of Col. Carlson, who Alex George was and how their relationship came about.

"Sounds like an extraordinary man to me Tom, and I'm sure you know how lucky you are to have such a friend. From what I see here I'd say we want you in the Raiders, but there is one more thing. Please think carefully before you answer."

He paused to let the import of his words have full meaning.

"Could you kill a man with your hands?"

"Yes sir." Tom's reply was as soft as it was stunning to the career Marine. "I already have."

*   *   *

'Long time ago.' Tom thought wheeling the Lincoln across town to the Old Mans shed. 'Can still see the Colonel. Tall, thin.... No...skinny. Gray hair, crew cut, lantern jaw, long thin nose. Eyes and ways of a preacher. Kind man. Exacting. Got along from the beginning. Wonder why? Maybe because our backgrounds were similar. Sure picked a pair in Alex George and Evans Carlson.'

After the Raiders initial probe on Makin, in the early part of the war, turning what could have been a total disaster into a public relations coup, they went on to a heroic effort stalking and killing Japanese through the mountainous heart of Guadalcanal. Tom's part in that phase of the war, was so savage in nature, it seemed now as though it must have happened to someone else. Had it not been for the Old Man, Miss Marie and Nancy, he felt he could have not have survived on his own. The three of them acting out of pure love, managed to pull him through a headlong rush toward insanity and probable self destruction to an active, productive life.

Upon returning home, in late 1945, the Old Man asked Tom to stay on with him. His business was booming, in part due to the war, and since he and Marie had lost Alex too, he wanted and needed Tom to come into the business. He was going to need a strong right arm in managing what was a prospering, dynamic, growing business, and the sooner the better. When Tom gave him an affirmative answer, the Old Man suggested he go back east to the best business school he could find, and learn everything they could teach him.

"Geologists, engineers, scientists I got. No, what I need is somebody schooled in management, to help me with what we've already got, and aim it toward the future. I don't want all my eggs in one basket Tom, and I 'spect we're going to be entering an era of growth, like this nation never's seen. It's going to be a case of the big getting bigger, and I want in on that action."

"Aren't you a millionaire now?" Tom asked with some incredulity, wondering after having survived what he did why anyone could possibly care about anything as impermanent and meaningless as money.

"Yeah Tom, but that's not the point, nor is money my motivation to keep on, keepin' on. It really never has been. No, it's the thrill of the action itself. That, and what I've always believed. Today's the day, you know the one and only we can live right now, and I think we're supposed to do the best we can with it."

Tom thought seriously about what the Old Man was saying, because he was his patron, and because he was still in a state of disbelief that he had survived the carnage of the South Pacific. Never, all the rest of his life, would he cease wondering how he survived the impossible odds, while so many others of his kind were long since dead. Maybe it was because he listened, and believed with all his heart what Col. Carlson espoused. "Gung Ho." Work together toward a common goal, which for them was the complete annihilation of enemy forces. He went down those savage jungle trails with Carlson, believing in the forceful man and would have followed him into the hubs of hell, which couldn't have been far away. Maybe he endured simply because this mystical man also survived. Tom never quit marveling over the simple fact of his existence.

"What do you want me to do, Mr. Alex?" He asked him in 1946.

"I wouldn't take advantage of our relationship to the extent of telling you what to do, Tom. I'll tell you what I hope you can see your way clear to doing."

"Which is?"

"If you want to throw in with me son, I'd suggest you go back east to Harvard School of Business and learn everything those people have to teach you. We gotta diversify! You know, spread out! Find different ways to go. I don't want all my eggs to be in the oil business, although it's been plenty good to me. I'm mighty grateful to and for that business because it's provided us with a lot of cash money right now, and there'll be a great deal more in the future. Off shore drilling looks like the wave of the future and we're ready, right there with equipment, leases, people, whatever it takes to get in on the absolute ground floor. But Tom, the big boys back east say diversify and that's what I want you to learn about. Listen to those...those...high falutin' guys Huey called 'em. Pick their brains, find out what they know and if their ideas are any good, let's make 'em better."

Tom was fortunate to be there at the time he was, because most of his school mates were veterans too. He stayed away from the usual collegiate foolishness, drinking, parties, nonsense, that seems to be part of getting away from home. He'd been away from home for a long time, and was here because Alex George suggested it. Tom could serve those he believed in, and had been fortunate indeed to have come under the influence of two such hypnotic leaders. He believed in them and followed their directions.

'What an experience.' He thought, drawing closer to the Old Man's house. 'Got to see how the big cats operate, right in their own back yard.' Laughing sardonically. 'Those smooth bastards showed me what ruthless was all about, while turning the wheels of commerce.'

In that august company Tom was treated to first hand observation of some of the wealthiest families in this country, and for the most part did not like what he saw. He felt they had ice water for blood, particularly despising the "old money" he came in contact with.

"Those assholes don't know how to live, Boss." He reported to Alex on one of his trips home. "They seem to be more into trying to slide something past the world. I don't think they know how to enjoy themselves, you know what I mean? How to live life. I'll tell you one thing for sure though. I don't like 'em, and as soon as I get my education they're going to be nothing but memories."

"Yeah, I know what you mean Tom. I get a lot of that when I go back there to deal with 'em. I know they're looking down their noses at me and think I'm some kind of country bumpkin, but they sure do like the color of my money. They're scheming, conniving assholes Tom, and you've got a marvelous opportunity to study 'em, right up close."

Tom remained an enigma to those on campus, one of few exenlisted men. His was a forbidding presence, no one able to fathom what was behind his incredible eyes.

He laughed thinking how difficult it had been, both for him and Nancy, to keep from marriage until he finished his studies, but keep from it they did.

'Jesus,' he chuckled to himself, 'she did do a whole lot of maturing during the war years. Pretty kid when I left, something else when I got back. Like the Old Man said at the time, she filled out real good and turned into a full grown woman.'

He thought of the unbelievable job she'd done helping him return to the normal world, and she did it with her forceful love. It was really all she had, but it was powerful. She told him she fell in love with him the afternoon back in 1939, when her father brought him in the back door. At that moment she decided he was going to be hers and with a combination of the wily ways of her mother, the natural cunning of a woman, and a fierce determination not to be dissuaded, rose to the challenge.

Hers was an especially terrible task because she had to defeat his nightmares, a voyage into completely alien territory. When she slipped out of the house at night, to hold him in her arms, fighting with ferocious innocence the insanity that stalked him, she went, unbeknownst to her, with the prayers of her mother.

He thought. 'Christ, I've been a lucky man.' He was right about that.

The financial fortunes of Avro Enterprises took off immediately after Tom completed his studies and returned to LaFayette, the Old Man called the shots and Tom carried out his wishes. Tom also brought many of their later successes to fruition such as their entry into the infant computer business, in the early '50's.

"These people are a different breed, Mr. Alex. I don't know if I can tell you what they do or not, but I'll try. They say they're developing machines that calculate at the speed of light. A hundred eighty six thousand miles per second and as you say, that's movin' on. These guys think the world of the future is going to be run by these things."

"What do they look like, Tom? How much do they cost?"

"Don't look like much now, cabinets full of tubes and things but the man I'm talking to says the technology's developing so fast that by the time one idea is developed, it's out of date. They're high ticket, but if they'll do what they say, and if they become what these people believe, we need to be in on the ground floor."

The Old Man looked into matters like this with high good humor, and an uncanny eye for possibilities. He had what these entrepreneurs needed, money, and a lot of it. They had what he wanted, an opportunity at a wild ride in the financial world of the budding computer business.

"What are these people selling?" Was the question asked so much of Alex when they first entered the field.

"Beats the shit out of me, except they sure believe in what they're doing. These guys are different from most folks. They're narrow between the eyes, smoke pipes, talk in algebraic equations, and probably wouldn't know how to pour piss out of a boot, but they do make those slide rules hum!"

Tom's expertise and foresight, coupled with the Old Man's money took them into area's Alex hadn't dreamed of, but they had the money to put on the table for development.

'We've come a long way, Baby.' Tom thought as he approached the Old Man's shed. 'Oil, gas, pipelines, hotels, refineries, computers, real estate, clothing stores, shipping, tanker fleet, financial institutions, banking, lumber, fast food, construction companies. The beat goes on.'

The kind of wealth Alex George had multiplies fast and according to Forbes, he'd arrived in the rarefied company of the top ten richest men in the United States.

The Old Man never left LaFayette to surround himself with the usual accouter-
ments of wealth and power. He felt no need to move his base of operation to any
major financial center, figuring the telephone and computer would handle his needs
just fine. When either he, or Tom, or both, had to be somewhere, one of their many
corporate jets were standing by ready to whisk them to any part of the earth, at a
moments notice.

With the opening of the Heymann Oil Center in LaFayette in the early '50's, he
was surrounded by business's of all stripes, involved in some phase of the oil industry,
so he stayed where he belonged, where his home and heart was.

His heart was gone now. It left with Momma. His home and empire was intact,
although there were monumental changes in the wind as Tom pulled into the long
driveway, driving through the now steady rain, around to the back of the main house.

He stopped in front of the shed.

CHAPTER 14

"Why shed?" Marie asked, upon hearing him refer to the new building for the first time.

"Because that's where everything happens around a drilling rig, a little tin building we called the shed. Way back, in the real old days, we did everything there. We slept, ate and did our paper work. It was the center of everything, so I figured that's what I'd call the place out back."

A "shed" this building decidedly was not, done in a style of architecture unique to south Louisiana. It had a low roof line covered with tile instead of wood shingles, the better to withstand the hurricanes that visit that part of Louisiana. The exterior was used brick, a beautiful contrast to the umber colored roof. It was surrounded completely with a low overhang which formed a porch, supported by heavy white barrel shaped columns, short, maybe seven feet from walk to overhang. The exterior walls were made up mostly of French doors opening from floor to ceiling, allowing a stunning view of the grounds. Heavy vegetation had been planted when it was built, in order to shield it from the main house, and so it appeared to be the only building on the property.

Tom pulled up to the front of the building, running quickly to the sanctuary of the porch to escape what had developed into a heavy Gulf storm. He could hear Helen's deep bark, followed by the Old Man's voice assuring her everything was okay.

"Come on in, Tom!" The voice sounded far away.

"Yeah, okay Boss. Listen, does Helen know it's all right for me to be here?" He was kidding, and not kidding.

"Hush Helen, be good now. It's Tom." The Old Man chided as Tom pulled open the heavy screen door.

Helen got down off the couch, her own private and special place, moving with languid grace to the side of the Boss's chair. Her eyes glittered in the half light, a long bright sheen suddenly appearing in her beautifully well groomed mahogany coat, as she faced Tom. She shook her head slowly, obviously displeased with the interruption.

"Hush now Babe." The Old Man was trying to make her stop the low growling, which seemed to harmonize perfectly with the long rolling thunder outside.

"You got her, Boss?"

Tom was laughing, because even though Helen should know who he was, and it was all right for him to be there, he also knew she thought Alex George belonged exclusively to her. She seemed to know of his great age, and considered herself protector, ready, willing, and able to attack anything that might threaten her master. She understood toward the end of his life, that he was somehow impaired in his abilities to take care of himself. Maybe it was because of the loss of Momma, and she was merely hanging on to this lone survivor. Whatever it was, Helen had a heightened awareness, an unusual air of protection. This was her man God, and she wanted no one in any way, to even act like they might do him harm.

The room was dark, illuminated by a small light over a desk to the right of where the Boss and Helen were now sitting. The lightning helped some, at least Tom could see everything between the door he had entered, and where the Boss was sitting. It was a most unusual building in that it was but one large room, furnished in such a way as to make its openness quite acceptable.

This is where the Old Man held court, and while it always surprised first time guests, they came to enjoy the building for its notable uniqueness. All along the outside walls were groupings of large comfortable chairs, some placed to accommodate intimate gatherings, some that would seat twenty people comfortably. Screens and dividers were placed in such a way as to give the impression of many rooms, even the three bathrooms blending smoothly into the corners of the building. An elaborate kitchen was built into the center of the area, the hub of everything and his favorite part of the building. It mixed with the rest of the interior in such a way, as to make it difficult to realize it served as a weight bearing inner wall, allowing the broad open expanse of the room. Like most Cajun men, Alex George was an excellent chef, and enjoyed cooking whenever the opportunity presented itself. There was a pool table off to one side, and a desk with a computer which was always on.

Tom approached the two through the semidarkness, moving with his unusual but highly developed manner of walking in half light. His body automatically turned at an oblique angle, left side leading. He'd lived such an intense, savage period in his life where he used his body as a highly sophisticated instrument, that these movements were forever imprinted in his mind, their purpose on his soul.

"Want me to close some of these doors, Boss?" Tom called. The tall French doors stood wide open.

"No Tom, leave 'em like that will you? I love the sound and the smell of the rain. Had the lights out, except the fire here, 'til I heard your car. Just lookin' at the lightning, listenin' to the thunder." Punctuated at that moment by a clap of thunder, causing Helen to stir. "My main lady here doesn't like it worth a shit though, but she's getting used to it 'cause it's what we do this kind of weather." He nodded toward the fire going in a suspended fireplace. "Hope you don't think I've lost my marbles though, doors open with a fire going."

"No, I don't. What's the matter with that?"

"You know something, Tom?"

"No sir, what?"

"I appreciate that, more than you know."

"What?"

"Oh that. Everything. That's what I want to talk to you about. Everything. Get yourself a beer son, or something to drink. What do you say, you hungry? Want me to make you a sandwich?"

"No thanks, Boss. I'll get a beer. Food I don't need."

Helen's intense head and eyes turned slowly, following his every move, her eyes flashing as they crossed the path of the lone light.

Tom knew the Old Man so well after all these years, and could tell the mood of any meeting they were about to have. He knew this was going to be a heavy one. He opened the beer, threw the top in the wastebasket, walked back to the area the Boss was seated in, sat down in a large easy chair, crossed his legs and returned Helen's baleful stare.

The Old Man said nothing, staring out the window, his mind a million miles away. Tom waited, patiently. This kind of situation always made him think of the time Nancy had the lump on her breast. He was so God damn scared he couldn't think properly, because she was threatened. She had to have it removed, but he was afraid to have it done, afraid of what the results might be. Sitting in the waiting room area, while she was being operated on, his nerves were drawn as taut as a violin string, until the doctor walked in to talk to him. As the doctor approached, Tom's heart was pounding afraid his worst fears would be realized, a malignancy.

'Damned if you do. Damned if you don't.' He thought as he left the hospital walking on air, alternately laughing and crying. The doctor told him exactly what he wanted to hear. "No malignancy."

'If you're there God, thanks. I really want to keep her, you know. I'll never understand how I got her in the first place, but I did and I don't want to let her go. Not now.'

It was about as close to prayer as he got and it was OK by him.

"People! Strange breed of cat, Tom."

Alex was staring at the lightning, groping, trying to find the way. Tom remained silent.

"Wonder what God was thinking of when He put us together? You know.... People!" More silence and staring. "Huh, better yet, wonder how He likes the way we've turned out so far? You know son, a great many people live lives of continuous suffering...." long pause, "suffering of the most exquisite nature, simply because they can't accommodate themselves to the pain and agony that goes on all around them?"

The Old Man's eyes were full of tears, which caused Tom great personal anguish. He wanted to lighten whatever pain this man felt, overcome with a feeling of compassion and desire not to let anything hurt him anymore. Like all people of great age, he'd been through enough. He'd taken the big losses. Gaston, Myron and his other buddies, slaughtered so long ago, in France. Huey Long, perhaps his best friend, a man who taught him so much. It could be said Avro Enterprises were what they were, and the Old Man was what he was, as a direct result of what Huey Pierce Long had done for him, all the way back in the early '30's. Mary, his beloved daughter who died before Tom even entered the picture. Apparently the Old Man almost didn't survive that one. Young Alex? World War II gave his death some reason, although he didn't know what that was except the George's had a lot of company in their grief for the loss of their remaining child. The war made everything understandable, so said the politicians, usually the ones who hadn't suffered personal losses. They always seemed to understand these things more clearly than those whose lives were ripped apart forever by this stupid, periodic exercise in barbaric insanity. Then there was the lady Tom never understood too well, Sue. Not until her death, and the Old Man's reaction to it. Then he did.

'Yeah, yeah, special effort on that one for the Boss.'

Now his most recent, and greatest loss of all. His wife and best friend of many, many years. Momma. What is there to say about a marriage that lasts that long, except after that period of time and what they'd gone through together, their souls seemed to become one. Momma was it though, there weren't any more.

"I hate that Tom. I hate the thought that there is so much evil on the land, it becomes unbearable to these, these...what'll we call 'em, boy...weak? Should we call 'em weak? Life's victims maybe? No I don't think so, not if I understand weak." This was the beginning of a soliloquy, and both men knew it. Tom offered no answers and the Old Man didn't pause for any. "Yeah well, there are many who would you know."

Tom saw the jaw muscles working as the words were pulled from his mind and pushed through tightly clenched teeth.

"...but for the most part those would be the cruel and insensitive motherfuckers that make up so much of this world."

Tom snapped instantly to a much higher degree of alertness, because among other things he knew the Old Man simply did not use this kind of language anymore, unless angry to the point of rage.

Tom turned slightly to put his cigarette out, letting his eyes slide over Alex, startled by the viciousness he saw there.

"I'm old now boy, and one of the richest men in the world, and that automatically makes me one of the most powerful men alive. What power? What have I done with it? Who's going to remember? Well I'll tell you, as it stands right now, almost no one, and who gives a big shit? Oh sure, there's all the charitable things Momma did after Mary died."

The Old Man drifted away momentarily, tears on his cheeks at his mention of Mary. He cried easier at this time in his life, unconcerned about covering his feelings. Helen seemed to know too, moving up from her position at his feet, laying her jaw across his thigh in a gesture of concern, looking first up into his eyes studying him carefully, then slowly turning her magnificent face around to gaze at Tom.

"The wing at the hospital, in Mary's name. Endowments in Alex's name. Yeah Momma left most of her money to the needy and the poor." A sad smile. "She wanted to educate bright young people who wouldn't have a chance otherwise because of no money. No chance because they were born poor. People who might not have the opportunity, or chutzpah, to do what I did."

'That's it.' Tom thought. 'He wants to set up a trust. Something to help others.'

"Problem is though, we don't feel enough. If we did there'd be a whole lot less pain in this world." Followed by a quiet, sardonic chuckle. "Yeah, you know they ought to change that one beatitude. You know what I mean son, all the "blessed are theys". I'd like 'em to change that meek one around. You know the one says they're gonna inherit the earth? Bullshit! The meek won't inherit nothin'! How 'bout this instead? 'Blessed are the meek, for they shall have the shit stomped out of 'em.' That sounds better don't you think?" He lit another cigarette. "Sometimes wonder why God doesn't herd all of us in the direction of absolute sensitivity? What do you think? He should, shouldn't He? Shouldn't we be constantly heading in the direction of God, trying in some huge subliminal way to be better than we are? God damn, don't you hope something like that could be true? Makes sense, doesn't it? Shouldn't mankind be getting better at what we do? Doesn't it make sense that the more we practice at living, each generation, the better we should get? Jesus man that's not too much to ask is it?"

His hand fell on Helen's head, she pointed her nose toward the ceiling, seeking even more attention.

"Yeah well shit, you know that's what I get to hoping Tom. We, mankind, have to be getting better. Then I look around, see what's really going on, and get my answers. You know what I see? I see the savages of the world standing right on the chests of the meek, pissing all over 'em. No I'm not talking about any one individual, although I guess that's where it starts. I'm talking about the whole act from individual all the way up to nations, but as a species we don't seem to feel enough, do we? I mean if I really cared and felt, how could I possibly stand around and watch people hurting people?"

Tom was listening, trying to figure where the Old Man was going. He knew he was being taken down some mental road traveled many times by Alex George, certainly many times before this rainy evening.

"The good religious people of the world tell us what we have to do is pray, and everything's going to be all right. You know something? Lots 'o those folks are sincere. They mean what they say too, most of 'em. I don't know if they know it's bullshit and out of some deep sense of moral right don't want to admit it, or maybe a sort of pious naivete makes 'em think if they pray over bad shit long enough it'll go away. I've thought about that a whole lot, and I don't know the answer. Used to talk about this to Momma, but I never could take my thoughts to the end with her. She was much too good to adjust herself to the real hard facts of life. She cried one time when I tried to tell her how the real world operated. I never tried again."

Tom couldn't tell if the Old Man even knew he was in the room. He seemed to be in his own private world and yet obviously wanted to share it. That's why he called. He had something he wanted to share.

The thunder rolled on endlessly, and Tom thought the storm must extend a long way out in the gulf. There was nothing violent about it, just steady, heavy rain, lightning, each flash followed by long rolling thunder. The Old Man was right, the sound of the rain was pleasant, and the freshly washed smell it brought.

"How we doin', Tom?" The Old Man asked suddenly.

"Sir?"

"You and me?"

"I'm not sure what you mean Boss."

"You and me. Our relationship?"

Tom thought before attempting an answer.

"I probably don't have the right words for that Mr. Alex, because to answer properly you and I would have to walk around inside my mind." He thought a moment, adding. "Yes, and my soul too."

"You been happy with me?" Laughing a dry laugh which was accompanied by an exceptional clap of thunder. "Although it's probably a little late for that question." He leaned forward in his chair upsetting Helen, searching his younger friends face for what he needed to find. "I guess what I'm asking you is, if you could turn the clock back, would you want to hook up with me again?"

"I'm a millionaire, many times over thanks to you."

"Yeah, well if you don't mind my saying, fuck that!" There it was again. "We all know that helps with the grocery bill but we also know it don't mean a God damn thing when it comes right down to what it's all about. I mean when we get in that grave we're all going with a different set of values, aren't we?"

"Oh yes." Tom replied with special meaning.

"Ever think about what you're going to say, to some of the questions I think you're going to hear, after you die?"

"I have. Many, many times."

"Then you think maybe we might get some questions?"

"Lots."

"But you profess no religion. How come you think like that?"

"I don't think religion has much to do with anything when it comes to thoughts like that."

"You down on religions?"

"Yeah, I guess you could say that."

"How come?"

"I think for the most part they're a bunch of pompous thoughts and regimens, schemed up by a few starry eyed zealots, to put on a lot of believers to keep them in line. Keep those poor dumb bastards laying some heavy coin in the collection box, on whatever day the local godman says is the one they should worship. I am so tired of all these religious people telling their flock what's right and what's wrong, I pay no attention to them at all. You know what Boss?"

The Old Man was paying close attention.

"What?"

"We've got over two hundred so called Christian denominations in this country alone, and every lousy one of 'em says they got the only true answer. Now don't you admire their balls. Doesn't it make you wonder if those stupid bastards ever look at their hole card? How can each one of them have the one true answer? There can't be two hundred, one true answers. There has to be only one. If there is a God, there can only be one God. Yes, you bet! I sure wonder how He figures all the shit that goes on, on this earth."

"You believe in God, Tom?" As close as these two had been all the years, it was a question that had never been discussed in depth.

"Yes, but I consider myself a passive agnostic. I believe absolutely in the existence of God, but I'm honest enough to admit that I don't know it for a fact. That's all agnostic means for Christ's sake. I don't know. Who does? The leaders of the great religions? Naw, hell no. They think they do, but they're like you and me when it comes down to the nitty gritty. They believe. I guess that's what ticks me off so bad with those bleeding deacons. Their belief somehow turns into a sure thing and if we don't join them in theirs we're the bad guys.

"What do you mean?"

"I'll tell you Mr. Alex, I don't think believing in God has one little thing to do with religion. No I think the business of religion has to do with religion. 'Matter of fact, from what I know and have read over the years it seems to me as though religion has stood right slap dab in Gods way, ever since man's been keeping score. Doesn't it strike you as the most hideous bullshit going, that whenever two nations decide to go to war and slaughter each other, up jumps the sanctimonious sons of bitches wrapped in the flag and religious banners and proclaim that God, the one God, the only God, is on their side? The devil is on the other guys side?" He paused to let his words sink in, continuing. "Come on now! These maniacs announce that the one True God is right there with 'em, and naturally wants these idiots to lead us to Him, and then on to the butchery. Christianity? What a joke! What a sick, sick joke. If we're hanging around waiting for the second coming of Christ, I sure want to be there when He shows up, and you know why I want to be there? Because I think He's going to be hot, that's why! You know what he preached? He preached love and understanding, that's what. He preached help your fellow man, don't hurt him, and really didn't go much beyond that. That'd be plenty good enough, and simple too. So what did all the wild eyed zealots do with that one? They murdered with it, that's what! Can you imagine the carnage that's taken place through the centuries in the name of Christianity and a bunch more religions. 'O ho, you don't believe in my loving God? Then for your disbelief how 'bout I rip your head off.' Somebody might jump up and say, 'Wait a minute. The Holy wars took place a long time ago. Then was then, now is now.' To which I say bullshit! Look around! What's happening? Same old sick shit, I'll guarantee you that!" His eyes went flat and distant like the old days. "Stupid Irishmen over there killing and killing in the name of God, too stupid to understand it's all about money. I don't want to hear the bullshit it's the masses doing that, against the wishes of their leaders. What about that pig eyed, big mouthed, super preacher that reigns supreme over there. If ever somebody deserved to be dead, it's that asshole. That hypocritical man of the cloth screaming his vile puke, whipping his blind followers along behind! The one thing pisses me off more'n anything is that God damn IRA. They're supposed to be so good? Real experts! Well if they're such hot shit, how come they haven't killed that rotten son of a bitch? Why's he still alive?" He paused, eyes glittering adding a subconscious afterthought. "I'll guarantee you if I'd been looking for him in the old days, he's gone?"

The Old Man was acutely interested in what Tom was saying, because an outburst like this simply was not his usual behavior.

"Well I'll tell you what I think, Jesus Christ wouldn't last on this earth anytime at all, if he were to show up. Those pompous jerks that lead oh so many churches would be in the front lines screaming, 'String Him up', and why not? They got a sweet racket going and they don't need somebody like Jesus Christ rockin' their boat. Man I tell you I do love those two black comics and the skits they're always doing on preachers. They got their number all right. "Let's all bow our heads and pray for guidance. Yes Lord guide me to their wallets, for that is truly the promised land." Now there's honesty at least, if not decency. It's a far cry from somebody like that evil rat bastard of a preacher that led his followers to their deaths down there in South America. Those poor blind innocent dupes, and the kids? The rotten son of a bitch killed the kids too? That's when I have to look the other way Mr. Alex, when shit like that's coming down." His white hot anger shimmered. "I can hear the old drums beating and I know in my heart I could kill someone like that easy, love every minute of it, and with absolutely no regrets. So instead of getting all riled up over something that's far away and out of my control, I look the other way."

"Yes Tom, I guess that's what we all do isn't it? We all have a tendency to look the other way. That's what made my old friend Huey Long so angry. Everybody was always looking the other way. That's what I used to tell Momma too, when I'd come home and find her in tears over some new insanity that had presented itself. 'You have to look the other way Momma." He was staring out the window again, rubbing Helen's head, brushing his tears away. "Don't you wonder who says we should look the other way, and when it's time to look back and come to grips with these problems?"

"Well I guess that's what our politicians are supposed to do." Tom added.

"Yes, well that's probably the sickest joke of all, don't you think?"

"How you mean?"

"I mean for the most part wouldn't you say the politicians of this world are now, and always have been, about the biggest assemblage of whores and opportunists you've ever heard of? I mean they've got to rank right there with child molesters...maybe a notch below. These slick dudes keep sliding out from under whatever rocks they hatched, get a press agent, jump in front of a TV camera, and smile that million dollar smile. "Vote for me folks and relax. I'm the sharpest, smartest, strongest, holiest, most honest man you have ever had the opportunity of electing. Then during the commercial break they're probably trying to hump the script girl behind the scene, just to keep in practice for what they're going to do to their constituents, as soon as the poor blind bastards elect 'em."

"How about your friend Huey Long? What kind of a man was he?"

"I'll tell you what he was Tom. He was about as honest a man as I've ever known. Kinda like a junk yard dog. If he was after your jugular you sure didn't have to guess about it. His enemies, and he had plenty of 'em, knew who they were. He'd look 'em in the eye and tell 'em, 'I hate your God damn guts', and they knew he meant it. He was a rough son of a bitch! Boy was he rough, but he didn't spend his time lying to people, and got what he wanted through sheer force of personality. He told 'em what he was going to do, asked for their support to help him do it, and spent the rest of his short life coming through for 'em. No Tom, I'm not saying all politicians are assholes because they're not. It's precious few who are worth a plug nickel, and that's the great tragedy. How do you tell which is which?" A sarcastic chuckle. "How far do you think a proposal would get to have all politicians take a lie detector test, before an election campaign? You know, a few questions indicating whether they want the office purely to steal from, con and rape the public, or do they have something of value to bring to the party? But I s'pose even if that came to pass the American people would prefer the cool dude with his slicked back ears and Chessie cat grin, to the one that passed his lie detector test with flying colors. I'll give you a classic example of what I mean. Twice, in the fifties, the American people had the chance to elect Adlai Stevenson president, and who did we get? Good old Ike. I'm not saying Ike was a bad guy, because he wasn't, he simply wasn't in the same league with Stevenson. He was a war hero, smiled pretty, couldn't put together an understandable sentence, and didn't rock the boat for eight years. Then came a steady procession of hustlers the likes of which I simply cannot believe. I think John Kennedy and Elvis Presley were two peas in a pod. They were on top! God damn were they on the absolute top of the heap, but I always got the feeling neither one of 'em could believe, or take seriously, the adulation they got from the mob. Saint John the Kennedy showed us the power of the old razzamatazz though. Sure I'm sorry he was killed. I'm sure he was a well intentioned person, but was he the best we had? I don't think so but I'd sure like to yank him out of his grave and ask him what in the name of God he had in mind getting us involved in Vietnam. Yeah I know Ike's administration sent the first advisors over there, but it was Kennedy and his four eyed hawks who really heated things up. Those miserable super intelligentsia bastards wouldn't have the balls to get in a snowball fight themselves, but boy were they hot shots when it came down to sending somebody else over there to die. Hold that flag and scream to the high heavens about the righteousness of the war." He paused knitting his brow quizzically. "Wait a minute, they called it something else didn't they? Police action.... Or was that Korea? Well whatever. What's in a name? Then Kennedy gets shot out of the back seat of his limo and what do we get to follow that act? Why we get old Lyndon B. "Corn Pone" Johnson sliding right on in there. That's the one I'd like to see drug out of his grave and shot. Boy you talk about one of histories premier hustlers, that has to be the one. I can forgive him being a hustler, but I'll never forgive him for what he did in that Vietnam thing. Gulf of Tonkin my ass! What a joke! What a lousy God damn joke! They stood right there, straight faced yet, and lied to us about the details of that set up, and everybody knew it pretty soon, so what happened? Nothing that's what, except to keep the lie alive with a whole lot more. Light at the end of the tunnel, they said? Oh sweet Jesus, there was a light at the end of the tunnel all right followed by the biggest freight train bearing down on us we'd gotten hold of for a long time. Can you believe the way we the people were lied to by those cunning bastards, and why? Tell me why! We'll never know, but I'll always believe we got in that thing up to our ass because of the massive ego that idiot had, and the blind support of those fawning sycophants he surrounded himself with, and that chickenshit congress went right along with him. Man I'm talking they laid right down for him, you know it? Pack up the boys and watch 'em die, but not, for Christs' sake, any of our sons. Let's get them deferred. They're too good for that shit. A phone call here, some grease there and voila', they don't go! The poor kids go! The black kids go in big bunches! The square kids who believe all the heavy shit about God and country, but those high line sons of bitches weren't about to go, not when they could get somebody else's son to die in their place."

The Old Man was clearly agitated and Tom wasn't sure whether he was really talking to him, or using him as a sounding board.

"You want a beer or anything, Mr. Alex?"

"No thanks, but help yourself."

Helen roused herself into a sitting position, watching Tom every inch of his trip to the refrigerator, and back into his chair opposite the Boss.

"I don't even know what you can say about Nixon, that hasn't already been said except I think we've been lied to again. They say he came from Whittier, California, but they gotta' be wrong. That man had to come from New Orleans. I think he'd much rather make a ten dollar bill under the table, on the sly, than twenty on top, straight up and legal. That's the way they do it in New Orleans, you know. Always have and probably always will. A city given over to the con. Too bad they can't claim Nixon as a native son, they'd have made a natural team. I'll say one thing about him though."

"What?"

"I'll bet he'd a been a good one, if he could have let the hustle alone."

They sat silent, each in his own thoughts while the gulf storm resonated with lightning, and resounding thunder.

"All of the people, some of the time." Alex broke the silence.

"Sir?"

"Oh you know, the old saying you can fool some of the people all of the time, all of them some of the time, but I swear to God Tom I think these slick bastards are reaching the ultimate which is conning all the people all the time. You know Thomas Jefferson had it pretty well figured when he said a democracy was the best government in the whole wide world, the problem was the people don't have the smarts to govern themselves, therefore the incessant con."

"Government and religions. Some combination." Tom was thinking out loud.

"Ain't they, and while it sounds like a blanket indictment, we both know there's plenty good people in both areas, but unfortunately they're not the leaders. I remember seeing a movie with Momma a long time ago that said it all, far's the churches were concerned. The two main characters were both priests. One a holy, devout man, much the older of the two. A good and saintly man but going nowhere because he wasn't aggressive, not a hustler. The other, his assistant, man he had the magic. Young, headstrong, great pious act, a politician in every sense of the word and while he couldn't hold the old guys cloak when it came to down home goodness, he did bullshit the big guys so he becomes a big guy himself. Now I ask you, what kind of a chance would Jesus Christ have today in that kind of setting?"

"Not too good." Tom answered, still wondering what this conversation was all about.

"I think you're right. He might show up and start asking a bunch of questions, like what the hell do we think we're doing on this earth? Why are we, as a species, always hurting or killing one another? How come somebody's always bleeding and dying? Where's all the blood coming from? Why do you lie to the people so much of the time? Must we forever be trying to put someone down, to make ourselves look good? Why put so much money into weapons of slaughter when it would be so much better to share that wealth with the really poor peoples of this earth. You know, teach them how to feed and care for themselves? Could we try and live by what He came to tell us, a long time ago? You know what I mean Tom? Yeah, yeah, I think He'd ask a whole lot of embarrassing questions, and I'll bet the leaders would be sitting in the back of the room sending folks up front to see if they could put the con on Jesus. Pretty soon the leaders would figure out a way they could frame this beautiful Man, and before you knew it they'd be working out a program to kill Him, and claim He was the antichrist. So they'd bust him up real good and tell the spiritually starved He was just another in a long line of hustlers, so they saw their Christian duty, and killed Him."

The Old Man was staring into the darkness, as if there was an answer there. Tom heard an involuntary sob come from him which caused Helen to snap into a sitting position, her flashing brown eyes riveted on him.

"That's what hurt Momma so, you know." He was crying because of the pain of both memories. "She was much too kind to understand how this old world works. She couldn't comprehend that the strong wipe their feet on the weak, and it broke her heart. Oh Tom she was such a marvelous person, she only had love and kindness in her heart."

"Yeah, I know Mr. Alex. I've known some powerful people in my time, and I'm sitting right here with one of them, but I think she was the most powerful person I have ever known. Nancy feels exactly the same."

"Powerful? How do you mean?"

"I mean the power of her love. She had the kind of love that could move mountains. Nancy told me how many times they worked together for people who couldn't seem to help themselves, and how Miss Marie never looked down on them. She worked with and for them and seemed always surrounded by an aura of love and compassion. How she especially loved the children, always intensely aware of their well being. She saw and felt suffering in others, almost as if she was experiencing it herself and did everything she knew to alleviate that pain. Never, in my life or Nancy's, did we ever hear her say anything ugly about another human being, and as you know I spent many hours with that lady when I came home. I still think she pulled me back single handed, but she'd never go for that. No cutting remark, nothing that would ever hurt someone, going out of her way instead to praise and say nice things about what might seem like trivial matters. I never saw her angry."

Tom was pleased with the sudden outburst of laughter this comment elicited from the Old Man, and waited for the reason.

"You never saw her mad?"

"Not that I could tell."

"Didn't I tell you about the time I bought her the new Mercedes, and was going to dump 'Ole Blue' the Chrysler?"

Tom laughed too, because he was so familiar with the story, and loved the idea of this remarkable, loving woman getting firm with a man no one got firm with. No one that is except his beloved Momma.

"Tell you what! Let's don't canonize her yet 'cause she knew how to get mad when the time came."

Tom thought he'd push his luck a little, adding.

"But you were the only one she ever got mad at."

"Yes, I suppose that's right."

"Well, I know why that was."

"Why? Why would she get so hot at me and nobody else?"

The Old Man's question was sincere but he didn't really care about the answer. It was an excuse to talk about his loved one of fifty plus years, and while it caused great yearning in his heart, it also brought satisfaction simply to celebrate her presence on earth.

"Because she loved you more than anything else. You were the great love of her life. She loved you more even than her children, which I know is hard to imagine but I believe it to be true. She told Nancy that, and of course Nancy told me. Those are the kinds of things that wives like to tell husbands. Nancy told me about one of the most memorable days she ever spent in her life, right over there at the house. Miss Marie and Nancy spent all afternoon one day, sitting on the porch, while she reminisced about your lives together."

"Did they? What'd she talk about Tom?" The Old Man wanted to hear about the woman who shared his life, and owned his heart. It was of no concern to him how old the news, a day before she died or thirty years, he wanted to hear about her.

"Everything. She talked about her childhood, which according to Nancy was a happy one, and then suddenly you came along and her childhood ended. I think she said you swept her off her feet."

The Old Man busted out laughing which pleased Tom. He knew with all of his money, his ability to buy any material thing in this world to give him pleasure, he was a sad and lonely man. Tom would have put on a clowns suit doing cartwheels through the yard, if there was any chance of bringing a smile to this eminently important person in his life.

"There's an old saying I've always loved Tom, because of the irrefutable logic involved. There's two sides to every story." He was laughing, obviously delighted with the thought. "She said I swept her off her feet?"

He was enjoying a tremendous laugh over this, wiping tears from his eyes. Helen seemed pleased too, bringing herself up to a sitting position, shoving her great muzzle under Alex's hand forcing him to pet her. It went exactly according to Helen's plan as the Old Man grabbed her huge head, hugging her close and laughing.

"You hear that Helen? Momma said I swept her off her feet? Christ Cher, I didn't stand a chance once I laid eyes on that beautiful Cajun gal. I couldn't even talk I was so damn tongue tied, but that sure as hell didn't bother her. She could talk like a machine gun, and did, which gave me some time to drop my brain in gear. Momma used to talk to you a lot too didn't she, when the two of you were working in the garden?"

He was holding Helen's head in his hands talking directly to her, smiling down in her eyes. Tom thought the dog was going to wet the floor, her short stubby tail a blur of enthusiasm. Her happiness was total over this unexpected attention, a happiness added to by her masters obvious good spirits.

"Oh Tom, Momma was a totally different young girl from the person you knew. Let's see now, you joined the family in 1939 and we'd already been married 16 years, so naturally she'd changed much in that period of time. I know the Momma you knew Tom, a great loving, caring, concerned person. Fun, lots of fun! God how she loved to laugh."

Tom got up, the pretense to use the bathroom. He thought he might lose his self control and didn't want that. His emotions almost never showed, most people considered him very reserved, but his beloved Old Man was having a ball going down memory lane, and the experience moved Tom deeply.

"But you know Tom, when I first met her she was a bubbly sixteen year old. Christ she was something, and would rather tease the hell out of me than anything. God, what a girl!" His eyes suddenly lit up. "What a figure too! Damn shame they didn't have beauty pageants in those days, 'cause we'd have a mantle full of trophies if they did. She was a real looker Tom, blond haired, blue eyed coonass girl. They don't make many of those you know. Wow, what a figure! Athletic, did all the sports available in those days, and it sure worked wonders for her body."

Tom hoped the Old Man would keep talking and forget he was there, because he was obviously enjoying himself so much at this moment. He hadn't seen him this happy since before Momma died. It was a joyous experience.

"Boy, hot damn, did she fire into me that day down in St. Martinville? I swear she was a walking, talking, hurricane. I couldn't even get my talker started, and man let me tell you for a coonass that's near impossible. I didn't think we were going to get hers stopped. Sassy lady had my number somehow and stood there working me over, with those gorgeous eyes crinkled up at the corners. Know what she was doing?"

"I think so." Tom was laughing too, because he could see the picture developing.

"Well I'll tell you what she was doing! She threw out the hook, baited it, waited to see if I took the bait, then sunk that thing all the way in this Cajun. Somehow that child knew I was a goner. She just stood there laughing her pretty little fanny off, enjoying the power she had over this dumbfounded coonass standing speechless in front of her."

"Yeah Boss, Miss Marie told Nancy the same thing. Said she fell in love with you when she first saw you sitting in your car, and was trying to figure out how to meet you, when you jumped out and started following her down the sidewalk. Nancy really laughed when she told me about it. You know it's pretty hard for us mortal folk to think of Alex George in those terms. Not that a man like you can't have those kinds of feelings, it's just that those of us who know you, can't imagine your being yanked around by a sixteen year old girl. Hope you don't mind, but we loved it. We could see the two of you there, her talking and you listening."

"Yeah well, that's the way it was and that's the way it stayed." Alex was still chuckling. "I'd of ripped my heart out and laid it on the table for that lady. I would have given her anything she wanted. I think she knew that." Suddenly shaking himself. "Anyway Tom, something happened to that wild and crazy lady. Soon's young Alex was born, she did an about face. I mean she went from being a devil may care, crazy young lover, to a dramatically different gal. It was like she was handed a brand new baby, and her adulthood at the same time. I've never seen such a transformation. Not that she wasn't fun to be around, because she always was. No it seemed she suddenly became aware there was a big old world out there, and there were people suffering in it, and that did something to her."

Tom and Helen settled back again, letting Alex wander through his pleasant memories. Helen was laying on the floor, a great concession to Tom's presence, her head across her masters feet dozing as best she could. Tom was up on full alert, trying to stay abreast of what the Old Man was saying because while he was glad Alex was enjoying his memories, he was also quite certain that was not why he was here.

"I suppose it was simply that, nothing more. Along with her new role as mother, came an even bigger role she probably couldn't have explained. First it was Alex. My God did she have a special place in her heart for that boy. I loved to watch those two together. Not doing anything special, you know what I mean Tom?" Not waiting for or wanting an answer. "It was beautiful watching them. They belonged together, like a matched set or something. I guess you might say their souls were on the same wave length, and it was a pleasure to sit and watch them. That's why she loved to go out in the boat so much, hopin' to get a look at the deer, but especially the does with their fawns. She understood that powerful attachment." He lowered his head suddenly, sobbing. "God how she loved that boy."

The rain hadn't let up a bit, coming down hard and the lightning had increased.

"The first time I got an idea how her mind worked was one day, probably 1929. I know it was before Mary was born. I came in the kitchen, and she was sitting at the table crying, real soft like, but different. You know Tom, it was the strangest thing but my reaction to her tears was always the same, extreme anger. That I should react that way pissed me off, because I knew it didn't help her, certainly not what was bothering her, but I never could control it. I felt that way simply because I did not want her to hurt. Oh I know that was silly, hell if you live on this earth you'll know pain, but even though I knew that was so, it didn't change my reaction. So I asked her what the matter was, and she looked up at me with those beautiful blue eyes swimming in tears and sobbed she'd just seen a whole family, adults and kids, searching through trash cans behind a restaurant looking for something to eat." He paused fighting tears a half century old. "I'd never seen such a look in her eyes. She said they had to eat garbage to stay alive, and that was horrible. I tried to explain we had a terrible depression in this country, the south hit worst of all, but it didn't matter, she couldn't handle it. Isn't that something Tom, she simply could not stand the suffering of this world. I spent most of the rest of our life together trying to shield her from that, but man I was not successful. It was a frustrating time for this coonass. You know I was such a brawler in those days. My means of handling hurt was to hurt whatever or whoever was responsible, instantly! Christ I can remember like it was yesterday, the day I picked you up off the road in Oklahoma. You sure didn't look like much, and I'm looking out the window fightin' tears because I knew exactly how you'd have affected Momma if she'd been there. You see what I mean, you lived around that lady and she got to you. Not on purpose, she never asked me to believe this or that, or see this or that, or do this or that. No I came to realize gradually that hers was that greatest power of all. She was love. Simple, selfless, powerful, driving love. I have never known anyone like her in my life. I think what I'm saying is she was about as close to a saint as I ever got lucky enough to meet."

Tom was intrigued by the great laughter following his last statement.

"If you're wondering what's so funny I'll tell you. I got a mental picture of Momma standing there giving me that look of hers. Level, cool, like I'd lost my mind for calling her a saint. Like most saints, she didn't believe she was that good." A long emotional pause. "But she was."

"Yeah, everybody who knew her, loved her. I know how much she meant to me, when I got back from the south Pacific."

"You do know where she was coming from then, don't you?"

"Oh yes." Tom whispered. He knew exactly where she was coming from. "Her son was gone. I was the new son."

"That's the way it was. She lost Mary, then her first born son, but an intense love like hers would not be snuffed out. Amazing isn't it? We lose something, and if we're smart enough to realize it we get something in return. Marie lost her children, and got you and Nancy in exchange."

Tom was thinking of all the time he'd spent in Marie's kitchen when he came back. Just the two of them, and while he never told her what he'd done as a Marine, she seemed to know it was horrendous. How many times did that soft, gentle hand steal across the table and take his, in some sort of spiritual attempt to take from him the mental pain and anguish he was going through. She touched so gently, the terrible scar that crossed the back of his left hand and her eyes filled with tears as she shared his insanity. He knew then she wanted his pain, but there was absolutely no way he would ever allow her to share that. Marie George would have died from sheer horror had she known what the hand she held had done, and Tom had experienced. She could not comprehend that human beings were capable of such things so she could only guess what he had been through. Gold Star mother was what Tom kept seeing. Marie had that in common with Jane Guidry and a quarter of a million other women.

'Why her? Why Jane? Why all the rest? Why am I here, in the kitchen with this woman, and not her only son? How could I possibly have survived and the others didn't.'

That transition period from consummate murderer to accepted member of the human race was the worst time of Tom's life. He knew beyond a shadow of a doubt he would not have made it without the wide variety of support he was given, and the overpowering effort of Marie George.

"You know something, Mr. Alex?"

"What's that?"

"Miss Marie's gone, and we're all poorer for that, but weren't you lucky having her all those years? Can you imagine not having known her at all? Over fifty years of memories of being married to a lady like that. Do you ever think how lucky you are, you know what I mean, thankful for having been with her all that time?"

"Oh yeah. You know that's exactly what she said to me when I went off the deep end after Mary died. She asked me if I didn't think we should thank God, instead of cursing Him, for letting us have her the six years we got to keep her. Man, damn, it was tough at that time to get close to those kind of feelings, but I have since come to understand what she meant. She was right, that's all."

Silence fell across them again as each man drifted in his mind.

"Excuse me Mr. Alex, I've got to empty the old bladder. Never could figure how two beers converts to two buckets of pee, but that's how it is with me. Can I get you anything from the kitchen?"

"No thanks Tom, think I'll have some dark roast coffee. Doctor says I shouldn't drink that stuff anymore. Says I'm too old. Wants me to drink decaf instead. Can you believe that, an old coonass like me reduced to drinking decaf?" He sniffed disdainfully. "So fuck the doctor!"

Tom laughed all the way to the bathroom. He loved the Old Man's stunning directness, a learned skill Tom had seen used so many times in business, to 'cut through the bullshit', as Alex George described it. He thought about the time they sat in a New York skyscraper, everyone acting so refined and discreet, their rapacious maneuvering going nowhere. Tom loved it when the Old Man's patience ran out asking the 'super slick boys'. "Okay boys, we've heard all the refined bullshit. Now what the hell you want?"

It had the same impact as if he yanked them out in the hall, like in the old days, and offered to beat the shit out of them. There was extreme nervous fidgiting while the cool sophisticates regained their composure, followed by a new directness.

As they got in their limousine and settled back, Alex George would invariably say to Tom. "Don't forget son, money talks! Bullshit walks!"

"Fuck the doctor!"

Tom loved it. He had absolutely no idea why he was here.

The Old Man watched Tom closely as he made his way back, thinking how supple his movements were. There was something about him that made Alex George think of tigers moving through the jungle. Fluid grace with an aura of restrained savagery. He knew much of Tom's story, because he had a hand bringing him back from whatever hell he was living in, when he returned from the South Pacific.

Alex loved Tom like the substitute son he was, and had no doubts about his utter devotion, and dedication. He knew, absolutely knew, Tom would do anything he asked, his loyalty beyond question. He killed a man for Alex, years ago. He put his own life in jeopardy at that time, obviously thinking nothing about personal safety. Like the mongoose and the cobra, his was blind rage at that time. Sixteen years old he was and someone was threatening his personal master. He killed one, maimed another, destroying their mission with his savage intervention.

'Wonder 'bout regrets.' Alex thought as Tom settled in his chair.

"How we doin', son?"

"Okay Mr. Alex. We've always been OK. How you mean?"

"You and me. How've things been with us. How've they been with you over the years? Don't want to talk about money." Waving his hand in dismissal. "We know about that. We also know if some little something had been different that day back in Oklahoma, we wouldn't be sitting here now, you and me. What if you'd delayed by one day, one hour, fifteen minutes coming over that fence? You told me you were scared when you got in the car. What if you'd decided to go around to the rest room at that diner, and took off down the road? What if you and Mahoney couldn't of made it, what if you couldn't handle the work? You know what I'm saying Tom? All the gears meshed and here we are forty plus years later. Would you say you've had a good life?"

"I'm sure you have no way of knowing...I mean absolutely knowing, what's in my heart and mind, not only right now, but all the time we've been together."

"Go ahead on son and tell me. It's some kind of important to me."

Tom was groping, and the Old Man knew it. He also knew the feelings were there but felt they should be articulated, for Tom's sake, and because of the reason for this discussion.

"Oh I suppose I could get starry eyed and eloquent, but I know you better than that." Peering into the darkness for the words. "There's been a lot of rags to riches stories in the past, but I doubt there's ever been one like ours. You ask how has it been? Well I'll tell you. If I could rewrite my life, with the exception of not knowing who I really am, who my parents were, I wouldn't change anything." Tom paused for a minute. "Maybe the viciousness of the south Pacific, but precious little else."

That stung the Old Man. Family was so terribly important to him, now and forever. His heart ached when he thought of Tom's predicament. They did everything they could to find out about his background, which was substantial because of financial capability, with no results. They got to that day they met in Oklahoma and could go no further. There was no place to go, a dead end. Detectives combed Oklahoma searching out the name Brooks and came up empty handed. He was, whoever he was. They could not lift the curtain that covered his past, so they had to settle for what they had, which was Tom Brooks.

"You say we have to overlook the money, and I understand what you mean. I also know it's there, and I'm dumbfounded at my wealth. How many men wind up where I am financially? I don't know, but I suspect it would be a tiny fraction of the whole population. That's something!" He started laughing at the thought of Nancy. "My wild and crazy wife probably couldn't even spend our money, and she's real good at that sort of thing."

Alex chuckled too, because he loved Tom's wife intensely, trying somehow to substitute her for his real daughter. He loved women in general, he thought they were simply the better of the species. They were a wonder to try and figure out, and when it came to love he thought they were a special gift. Nancy was so good to him too, trying however she could to help ease the pain of Marie's loss. She had no thought of trying to get Alex to think about anything else, just ease his pain.

"Well okay, like you said let's forget the money. I started out looking to you as more of a personal savior than anything else. Let's face it, my future was not what you would call bright when we met. You know really, it was more like you threw a line to someone who was drowning, I grabbed it out of desperation and you pulled me in. You are, and have been the most important man in my life. If I could follow Col. Carlson the way I did, into the places we went, because of my profound respect for him, I think you can imagine where I would follow you."

Tom wrestled with the words. He wasn't good at articulating his feelings, feelings steeped in unbelievable horror, so was finding slow going.

"You know Mr. Alex, I not only would follow you wherever you asked, I'd give my life for you in a minute. I don't even know how to explain my feelings for you, that's a difficult thing to do. I'm not going to put you in the role of God, but that's close."

He grew impatient with himself. 'Say it asshole, say it! You love the man, tell him.'

"I guess when you sum it up, what we're talking about is the fact that I have, and always have had, a deep love for you." God damn it wasn't really that hard, and he felt a whole lot better immediately for having said it. 'Although I do see our relationship as quite different from father and son. What it all comes down to really is, I owe my life to you. Without Alex George there isn't a Tom Brooks, not this Tom Brooks anyway. You can run that even further and say Nancy would never have given birth to Mary, and I'm real happy I didn't miss her. You and me Boss, the facts are there for the whole world to see. I think we've made one hell of a team. I would change nothing in our relationship."

Alex sat rubbing Helen's ear, she lay at his feet in a quiet state of ecstasy. He was silent for a long time. His heart full because of what this special person and long time aide said, letting the warmth of his words envelope him. There was less lightning and thunder but the rain came down steady.

"Thanks Tom. I appreciate your words."

Tom knew they were going on to another subject.

"What about God?"

"Sir?"

"How you feel about God, and this eternal struggle we always hear about? You know, between good and evil?"

"Don't know I've thought about it much. Guess a strong case could be made for the existence of a general condition called evil, but I don't know if I'm ready to accept the idea the two sides are drawn up all the time ready to go at it."

"You think it might be possible?"

"Might be. Lots we don't know when it comes to spiritual things. As a matter of fact I really don't think we, or our religious philosophers really know shit about those kinds of things. Like scrub baseball they threw it together down through the centuries. Well intentioned I suppose but how many of 'em had a straight line to God? I wouldn't dismiss any thoughts on the subject, out of hand though. You know when I look back on my life I can't really say I had good or evil in mind until it came down to thinking my acts over, after the fact."

"And then?"

"Well here again, it depends on the act. Could I rationalize the meaning of good and evil?" He was drifting away from the room thinking about his Marine Corps experience. "What I did in the South Pacific. Don't know about those. You think about that and you have to conclude killing is killing. The Marine Corps said it was all right for me to kill for them, therefore making it officially OK. They also told me if I chose not to I was guilty of a greater evil, cowardice. I'm good if I kill for them, and bad if I don't. These many years down the road I'd have to call that a perverse way of looking at things."

They remained silent for a while, searching their minds.

"I know it was a long time ago son, but what were your thoughts about killing that man out there on the marshes? You were only sixteen when it happened, how'd you feel about it? You mentioned you didn't give those experiences in your life any thought until after the fact. What did you think then? Any fear or regret? How about the man's family? Did you think about them?"

"Remember like it was yesterday, instead of so long ago. Young, couldn't appreciate the enormity of what happened. Wasn't concerned about the law or anything...didn't care. All I knew at that moment was somebody was trying to hurt you. I might have died right there if the man with the gun had been faster, but it didn't matter. You were sort of a God on earth to me and I wouldn't let them hurt you. Conscience you ask? I felt no pangs of conscience at all after it was over, never allowed myself to think of his family. At that moment he, and they, needed killing, and I was willing to kill them all. My biggest concern was not wanting Jane Guidry to know."

"I see. And the war? How about the war? How'd you feel about killing Japanese in the Pacific?"

"Oh now you're talking about a whole different ball game. That was such an extraordinary situation, beyond all accepted forms of human behavior. Everything about that area was like a scene out of hell." Tom was searching for the right words. "You know, I think you could take the most ardent pacifist that ever lived, put them in a situation like that, and if they see enough of their buddies reduced to garbage, maybe even sharing the same foxhole when it happened, their philosophical views would take one hell of a turn. If they could have seen the viciousness of the Japanese, and what happened to us as a result of that barbaric behavior, I don't think they'd remain pacifists long. Men mutilated by the enemy? I'm talking about heads, hands, feet, sex organs cut off simply for the sake of intimidation? Listen, murderous vengeance becomes the only motive in a situation like that. I suppose what's worse is the feeling that wells up inside you. You want to slaughter all the enemy by yourself. A one man job. I felt like a killing machine. I felt able, morally and physically, to butcher the entire enemy force by myself. You know what I'm talking about because you experienced the killing in France, although I don't think it was as barbarous as the Pacific. For instance when you friend Myron went down, how'd you feel?"

"Yeah. I was pretty young, and had never seen that kind of death before." Then softly. "When they killed Myron that day I went temporarily insane, and wanted to kill every German in front of me. Yes you're right Tom, circumstances dictate the action, and the afterthoughts. Funny business isn't it?"

"What's that?"

"Oh I don't know. Morality I guess."

"How you mean?"

"Well what happens if a person kills somebody. The law grabs him, then what?"

"Shit hits the fan?"

"Right! You bet. It's something the way we turn our morality on and off."

The rain was letting up somewhat, lightning and thunder fading into the distance. Tom was struggling with the conversation, sure the Old Man did not call him over for an exercise in philosophy.

"What I mean is every so often we get a bunch of politicians who can't communicate with their counterparts, any more. Their ego's won't let 'em. All those assholes are paid to do is negotiate with other nations, and every once in awhile the wheels come off and the whole process comes to a grinding halt. That's when we call out our youth to take over from the diplomats and send 'em over to kill and be killed. That's what gets me. This on again, off again morality messes with my mind because of the obscene hypocrisy involved. Uncle Sam, in this case, says 'Boys, we got some real trouble on our hands.' You notice the rotten bastards always make it in the plural. If they up and solve something themselves, I'll guarantee you they'll howl to the four winds their marvelous accomplishments, but it will be in the singular. Anyway they say, 'I'm going to give you this uniform, and some of the God damndest weapons you can imagine. I'm gonna teach you how to use 'em and kill the enemy with astonishing horror. Some of you boys I'm gonna teach to kill in extra special ways. Forget that stuff you been hearing since you were a pup, you know "thou shalt not kill". Don't pay any mind at all 'cause 'til we tell you different, that's bullshit! Actually you could say we're gonna teach you to be more murderer than soldier. We want you to kill big time, with ultimate skill. Don't y'all boys forget now either, we're the government and we're tellin' you it's okay. We need you! Why you're fighting on the side of God and He needs you.' Then after a period of time, when everybody has had all the slaughter they can possibly stand, and somebody surrenders, along comes old Uncle Sam again, grabs your weapons and uniform and says, 'Good going! Hey you really did swell! Sorry 'bout all your buddies that died, but it was for God and country.' Isn't that something? God and country? Too bad too, about all the mothers who'll never spend another day on this earth without thinking of their dead sons, knowing they will never, ever, see them again. The ones that went down blown to pieces by the remarkable killing machines the other side had waiting. Oh but what the hell, we gave them a flag, a gold star, and ten thousand dollars. That should help take care of their loss. Yes that's too bad, however it was war, and it's all over now, gang. 'So here's what we're telling you now boys,' says Uncle Sam, 'I want your uniform and weapons back, and while I sure do appreciate your help, don't you ever pick one of these things up again and kill with it. Not ever, because if you do, so help me God we'll bust your balls.' Ain't that sweet. They've trained and trained these kids to be the most up to date killers anywhere. Urge 'em on to greater and more glorious heights of murder, then blow the whistle and say, 'Hold it boys. It's over! No more'" He paused for a moment. "But wait a minute, how 'bout the guys that are different? Really got into it? You know, they call 'em war lovers? They're trained up to the level of a sophisticated machine, and all of a sudden somebody pulls the plug? These guys supposed to go back home like nothing ever happened? Jesus Christ, they train dogs like Helen here to be killers, and when it's all over they at least try to deprogram 'em. If that doesn't work they kill 'em."

He stopped suddenly looking at his younger friend.

"How 'bout you Tom? When you came back you were a masterful killer. What about those skills? How about your instincts and morality? You still what you were, or did that go away?"

Tom wasn't looking for that question, even though he'd given it much thought over the years. He knew what happened before, during, and after the war, not sure exactly where he did stand. He knew how to kill like few men have ever known, but didn't know whether that mentality was gone or not. He knew, over the years, how many times he'd thought of killing someone, for whatever reasons. He wasn't burdened with the usual pangs of conscience. He hadn't much training in morality as a youth.

"Did you kill Joe Thompson?"

Hardly heard, spoken so softly. The question came like a thunderbolt. Tom looked at him in total incredulity.

"Who!"

"Joe Thompson. The guy who killed my lady friend Sue, back in forty five. She'd just quit the life. The son of a bitch came storming into her house drunk, wouldn't take no for an answer and beat her to death."

His voice broke off in sobs as he spoke. Sue was a whore, there was never any doubt about that, but she was a special lady to Alex George. He was still enraged over it.

"His lawyer got him off on some bullshit technicality, and he was released. I wanted to kill him myself, I was so outraged. Then Thompson disappeared... flat ass, up and disappeared...gone. Never heard from again. You'd just come home from the Pacific. You remember? We had a long talk out at the camp about the situation." He shrugged his shoulders. "Then no more Thompson."

He paused a considerable length of time before asking.

"Did you kill him, son?"

The Old Man looked directly at him with a pleading expression. He wanted an answer. It was a matter of great importance to him in this time of his life. Helen had been awakened and was staring at him too. There was a long silence. A very long silence.

"Yes." His reply was as softly spoken as the question.

Alex broke into tears, confused tears, not sure whether he was weeping for Sue, or Tom. He'd believed ever since Thompson's disappearance that Tom had killed the man, but not until these many years had gone by, could he ask the question. The rain picked up again, a new line of thunder and lightning rolling in off the gulf. The three of them sat motionless.

After crying quietly for some time the Old Man added.

"You know, all these years I've wanted to ask you that question, and I couldn't bring myself to do it. Afraid to ask no matter what the answer might be, yes or no. Anyway, I'm glad I finally asked." Adding. "Even though it's a long, long time ago Tom, you must know how much I thank you."

"I...." Tom started to speak only to be drowned out by thunder giving them an opportunity to think, each glancing at the other in the lightning flashes.

"What?"

"I was staying out at the camp in the swamp. You remember, it was during my worst time. I knew how much Sue's death hurt you, and your feelings toward Thompson so I said to myself, 'Hey, what's one more? This miserable bastard deserves to die a lot more than the Japanese I killed.' So I got up out of the rain and mud and went looking for Joe. I knew when I went to Baton Rouge he was going to be a dead man, soon."

"Could I ask you something son?"

"Sure. Why not? Like you say it's ancient history now."

"How'd you feel about what you were going to do?" He cut his eyes around carefully. "We're talking premeditation. Did it bother you any? Any trouble with your conscience?"

"None, but then I was about as dangerous and as far from conscience as they come at that particular time anyway, after coming out of that murderous Okinawa situation." He wandered back in his mind. "I'd just come through three years of incredibly concentrated, savage annihilation and my conscience was all used up. So many of my buddies and friends were slaughtered all around me, my mind just took off. You know Boss, when I look back to those times, I figure I was truly insane. I killed with such skill and intense joy. It was a deeply satisfying experience for me to kill, and kill some more. I was so much into death...I had become a killing machine. Well anyway, after you left that night I sat there at the camp like a zombie. As I remember, it was a lot like tonight. Rain, thunder, lightning. I was squatting there in the slop, mud, and rain. I know it's hard to believe but I thought it was Okinawa all over again.... I actually wished it was. I knew what to do there. My God, we sat in foxholes over there that'd long since turned to chest high pools of mud. Must of rained pretty close to three months steady...had to drop supplies to us, there was so God damn much mud everywhere. Oh sure it quit once in awhile, but never long enough to dry up so's you could get any equipment up to our area. Dead bodies all over the place, Japanese and Marines. Too wet, and too dangerous to get 'em out, so they floated out there on a sea of mud. Looked like they were melting into the ground, and that's exactly what they were doing. No nightmare goin' was as hideous as that place. If there is a devil and a hell, no way could he come up with anything better. I seriously doubt there's ever been any place like that on this earth, at any time. You learn to unhook your mind in that kind of situation, or soon there's no mind at all, and if it goes, you get stupid and die. Anyway I was sitting out in the swamp and thought 'fuck it' I'd go on in and take care of Thompson, so I got in the old truck and drove to Baton Rouge. Found where he lived, and drove right on up to his house." Tom flashed completely back to 1945. "Knocked on the door...he answered...a big, mean looking piece of shit...hollered at me...says what the fuck do I want... did I know what time it was, and what swamp had I crawled out of.... I was really trippin' now...unreal.... It was like I'd come to tell him his dog had gotten loose or something. I knew he was dead when I was talking to him, I could see him dead, and I was calm as I'd ever been in my whole life. Told him I'd come to see him about the lady he killed. Can you imagine anything so God damn bizarre? He's never seen me before, and I walk up to his door, hair hanging down in my face all covered with mud and tell him I want to talk about the lady he killed? Said a good friend of mine didn't like it...I wanted to talk to him about it. He was mad, God damn mad, said I should wait right there, and slammed the door. I knew he was going for a gun so I pushed back into a palm tree bordering the sidewalk, and waited. It was all so natural, everything, even down to the palm trees. He comes back out, screaming something about a dead whore. Who gives a shit about a dead whore? Had a shotgun...came at the tree I was standing in, you know pushed back in the palm fronds? Stepped out smooth, like I'd been doing for three years, goin' on all my life...slid up close inside the shotgun barrel...he couldn't swing the gun around...shoved that knife in him one time and he was dead. The same knife that worked for me all through the South Pacific. Lucky thing it was raining as hard as it was, because nobody heard a thing. Combination of rain and thunder covered everything. No trouble loading him in the truck either. Grabbed his ankles and slid him across the grass like it was greased. Loaded him in the back of the truck, covered him with a tarp, and went back to the swamp. Same thing. Slid him out of the truck, across the mud into my pirogue...took him out to one of the islands the 'gators hang around all the time. Tied him under the water, tight enough to hold him down, loose enough for the 'gators to drag him down from there. No problem. Nobody came looking, and the 'gators did their work, quick. He was gone by sunlight."

They sat silently thinking back to 1945, searching for the right words.

"You want to know how it affected me Boss? How'd I feel about killing him? The answer was and is, no sweat, I can tell you that. If I'd kept notches in my knife, he'da been another one of those. No, I saw the situation two ways. He was a no good, rotten, son of a bitch who'd killed a decent person, no matter what she was. That, all by itself, should have been reason enough for him to die, but he also hurt you, and I wouldn't stand for that. He didn't deserve to live, so he died. I'd do something like that again, in a country minute. Comes down to the end justifying the means. That's always been one of your favorite sayings hasn't it?"

The Old Man nodded affirmative.

"Well it covered that situation completely."

Once again there was a long pause. Finally he asked tentatively.

"You'd do that again, did you say?" He probed.

"If it came down to it."

"What you think God thought about it, Tom?"

"Tell you Mr. Alex, I've spent much of my life since the '40's asking that question and I don't have an answer. Wish I did...might have an idea what to expect in eternity. Was it wrong to kill Thompson, but right to kill the Japanese I did...the way I did.... If so, how come? Who says? The government? They say I can kill for them, and that makes it right? They can regulate morality? Can government, made up of passing faces, faces incidentally that never seem to be around when it comes 'fess up time, order me to kill today and then forget it forever? Bullshit! I don't think so. No I don't have the answer to the God question. It seems to me the very idea of God would preclude killing of any kind, but I'll tell you one thing for sure I've noticed ever since becoming interested in the subject?"

"Which is?" The Old Man leaned forward.

"God must be mighty confused."

"Why?"

"For the reason we're suggesting here. Every time there's a war, both sides claim to have God with them."

Alex chuckled at Tom's last remark.

"Yes you're right Tom, you're absolutely right. Everybody gets into the killing don't they, and they all claim God's with 'em, but you know what I think?"

"No Boss, I don't."

Alex leaned forward and dropped his voice, like he was letting someone in on a guarded secret.

"Why son I think God's on the side with the most firepower."

Tom didn't answer, nodding agreement instead, more and more intrigued by the conversation, unable to figure why he was here.

"OK Tom, then let me ask you this?"

'Oh, oh.' Tom thought. 'Here it comes.'

He'd been with the Old Man so long he knew all of his nuances and whenever he said, 'Let me ask you this.' It meant the bullshit was over, he was playing hardball, coming straight down the middle.

"You think God helps people, or you think God helps those who help themselves?"

"I don't understand."

"How you feel about the Bible?"

"Don't know. I haven't decided what it is."

"What you mean?"

"I mean I view the Bible, and everything in it with passive skepticism. Never read it from cover to cover, pretty sure I never will, but I know enough about it to think it's as much historical fiction as fact. The Old Testament was obviously written by men of imagination. I suspect, long ago, something like these recorded events probably happened, then got stretched out of shape with the passage of time. That happens in the retelling of stories. The New Testament doesn't give me as much trouble. The various gospels obviously contain a high degree of cross checking and I think is more credible."

"But you will concede many of the stories in the Old Testament are historically true?"

"Probably. Many of 'em have been proven accurate."

"How about Sodom and Gomorrah? What do you think about that one?"

"Fiction. The part about the woman turning into a pillar of salt puts too much on my imagination."

"Yes, I think it taxes anyone's ability to comprehend, but that's not what I'm talking about. How about the destruction of the two cities themselves, could that have been true, you think?"

"Apparently it's been determined historically two such towns did exist and both were obliterated. Volcano apparently. They were there, and then they weren't."

"You remember the story real good?"

"I think so."

"Who do you think the two guys were that showed up in town, and looked the place over? Who were they?"

"Never really got into it, but I get the impression they were angels."

"Angels?"

"Yeah, saw a movie a long time ago, and they were depicted in the most sinister way I've ever seen. All through their part, you could see them plainly, but because of their hoods you never saw a face. It was the strongest, closest thing to a believable depiction of an angel or a spirit I've ever seen. Why do you ask?"

"Who you think busted the shit out of the place? Who burned it down, and turned the woman into the pillar of salt while they were at it?"

"God or the angels."

"Right! According to the good book one of the angels says, 'OK, I won't destroy the city you're going to.' You notice Tom he says "I" won't destroy. Then it says the Lord burns it down. Two versions at the same time, but there's a strong case these angels were definitely working for God, wouldn't you think?"

"Like I say I've never gotten that much into the Bible, but yeah, it sure looks that way."

"Well I'm not saying that's how it happened, because I wonder about the accuracy of those stories too, but we're given to believe that's what happened. God, working in concert with the angels, destroyed the two towns."

"What are you getting at, Mr. Alex?"

"I don't know. Maybe what I'm getting at is there aren't any of those kind of angels around anymore. Maybe what I'm trying to figure out is how far does one go with the notion that this, that, and the other thing are either God's will, or not. Maybe I'm trying to figure out if the beautiful fields, billowing over with crops, would have been so beautiful if God was working them all alone. If you see something really ugly, like Joe Thompson...no wait a minute, evil's a better word. What happens? Does God handle him, or do people?"

"We've got to pull on the oars, if that's what you mean. I haven't seen any divine intervention in the horrible affairs of mankind. Looks to me like we've always had to slug it out down here, alone. Bad shit's been going on in this old world for a long time. It still comes down to the point we mortals simply have to take the bull by the horns and act, if anything's going to get done. Is that what you mean?"

"Yes! OK! That's what I mean! Now then let me ask you this. Isn't it true that throughout history, politically speaking, there are always two extremes stirring shit? Aren't we forever victim to the whims, although extreme in nature, of what's referred to as the far left and the far right? Wouldn't you say that's true? You could use

Communism and Fascism, as examples. To make it more believable, you could say our own nation is constantly being tossed about by either those whose political persuasions line up on the left or right. Would you agree?"

"No doubt about it." Tom's curious reply.

"Okay then. Who's always starting these wars, big and little?"

"Either. Right or left."

"Yeah, and we're always besieged by the efforts of both. If they can't achieve their ends through normal channels like working within whatever system they're trying to penetrate, what usually happens?"

"Trouble?"

"Amen to that! You invariably get either a violent, militant faction on the left, or a violent, militant faction on the right, all shouting to high heavens their side's the right side. When they get enough power, stir enough shit, what then?"

"War?"

"You get an amen on that, too!"

Tom was watching and listening carefully because he knew Alex George wasn't playing any games, at all. He'd spent his entire life with this man and knew when he was angry. He was angry right now.

"Okay, we're agreed we have two extremes, always, everywhere in the world. So, now let me ask you the big question. After these sons of bitches with the power create war, who do they invite to fight the son of a bitch?"

"Us?"

"You got it! These assholes with their theories and wild eyed fervor whip everybody up in a lather, start a war, and then in the righteousness of their cause, conscript Tom, Dick and Harry to stop whatever they're doing with their lives, to come fight, bleed and die for, "THE CAUSE." By now they're all wrapped up in the flag and the certainty of their purpose, and tell these three guys, okay boys we started it, you finish it! Am I right or am I wrong?"

"It's always been that way."

"Yeah! You're right, it has! Okay so the militant right or the left's always startin' these inferno's and they get the good old piece lovin', don't rock my boat, let me do the business of living my life guys, to come in on both sides and slaughter the shit out of each other. Nobody's really mad at one another you know. How the hell could they be, they don't even know the other guy! No they're out there killing each other 'cause they got different colored suits on!"

The Old Man was really into it, fighting for words to explain the meeting.

"So how about this for a new approach? What if.... Just what if, someone were to come up with a new idea? Militant, violent, middle of the road? Now that'd be something, wouldnt it? Maybe not fight wars, but head off a lot of bad shit that normally gets smoothed over? Square things that've already taken place? You know what I mean Tom? Bad shit, like lots of things we've had happen."

"Not sure I follow you. Who you talkin' about?"

"Well Tom, what we've been talking about ever since you got here is basically what I mean. In other words what I'm saying is there were probably lots of guys, pretty much like you, that really got in to killing. I'm not talking about the ordinary soldier takes a shot in the direction of the enemy, ducks and hopes he doesn't get his ass blown off doing it. No I'm talking about the extraordinary individual who develops into a highly skilled killer...like you. The kind that doesn't shoot, duck and hope, but rather hunts down the enemy and murders him in cold blood. Yeah, I know most of your kind are dead, and that's a blessing, but some of 'em aren't dead...still have all their lethal skills intact. What if someone were to find these men and put 'em together? A group capable of swift, terrible, lethal action. Not talking about war, although I can see where they could serve a much needed function in that area. What about using a group like that to handle situations that can't get handled any other way? You think such a thing's feasible?"

"Sweet Jesus, Boss! Are you saying what I think you are?"

"Not too sure what I'm saying but I know things need doin' that aren't gettin' done. God isn't handling them! Judicial system sure as shit isn't handling them! In some instances you could say things might not be so clearly defined as to tell whether or not decisive action is called for, gray areas, but Tom sometimes you simply have to move."

Helen moved restlessly with the last clap of thunder, dreaming her elusive dreams.

"I guess what I'm talking about is kind of like what that guy over there in Texas did recently. You know Ross Perot, the computer man? When some of his people got nailed over there in Iran he wanted to get them out so he went to all the right people and said, 'Hey, I got this problem. Those assholes got a bunch of my people and I want 'em back. Can you help me?' From what I can gather he got a bunch of fast moves, double talk, and 'sorry, but we can't do shit old buddy.' Of course they said it in sweet diplomatic language, so you know what he says?"

"What?"

"He says, hey! They can't do it, I will! Gets some good men led by a Colonel somebody, and they go right on in and get those people back. Don't know, but I expect after all the smoke and bullshit cleared away he probably said look what we did! He wanted his people back, had the price, and got 'em. Everybody cheered."

He shrugged his shoulders and smiled, his hands outstretched, palms up.

"Same old shit huh kid?" He hadn't called Tom kid in years. "End justifies the means?"

"What is it you want me to do, Boss?" Tom asked, curious about the answer. He knew without giving it any conscious thought at all, he would carry out any wish Alex George might have.

"Don't know, but I'll tell you something. I got a whole lot of money, and lived a whole lot of life. Can't be too much life left for me, so I want to use that money taking care of things that don't get taken care of any other way."

He looked up suddenly.

"What time is it Tom?"

"I got nine thirty Boss. Jesus, where'd the time go?"

"Beats me son, but I'm tired. Me and Helen are goin' to bed. Call you later, we'll finish this conversation then."

CHAPTER 15

Tom spent the entire ride home trying to figure out what the Old Man was talking about. He knew some kind of final plan was being formulated in the long and full life of Alex George, but what. He also knew he'd gone through a few hours of rambling conversation that was obviously meaningful to the Old Man, but not to him. He hinted at many things during some of his soliloquies, but stated nothing definite.

'Why all the talk about spiritual matters?' Tom thought driving through the streets of LaFayette. 'Morality....Sodom and Gomorrah.... Angels....'

His wipers were on intermittent, the rain slowed to a drizzle. The glass would mist over giving everything an eerie, half world appearance, swept away by the next pass of the blades. Clear for a minute, opaque, then back to clear. Like the conversation he just left.

'Was it Momma? Was he only reminiscing? Why the emphasis about the anguish she'd endured because of her virtue. Tom had no doubts about that for she was truly a loving and humane woman.

'Only one like her I've ever known,' he thought, 'must be more like her. Wonder about the addicts of the world? Why do they deal themselves the agony they do? Are they cowards or do they really, truly see the world and life around them as an ugly experience? An experience they don't want to share? Do they know more than the rest of us and can't stand what they see? That's sure what Momma became over the years, an observer. An acute observer. The more she observed, the greater her pain. No booze. No narcotics. Nothing. She had to take life raw, like it is. Yeah, she was what Christ and the other gentle prophets talked about. She was about love. Marie George? Nobody like that lady. Never be again.' Thinking of her profound influence on his life. 'Power? I've seen power in all its forms. Survived 'em, but her selfless love was the most powerful of all.'

Tom had unquestionably experienced every nuance of raw strength. In business? Alex George was all the power he needed to see. The military? He watched the devastation. Beautiful islands covered with lush tropical vegetation when they landed reduced to splintered trash, after the slaughter.

'The guns, the guns?' He thought with bitter sarcasm. 'Need 'em to solve the international disputes don't we?'

He saw the power of Alex George's money for years, since leaving the Oklahoma home, and knew what could be done with that. He remembered, not without a degree of fascination, how easily Alex had handled the situation on the marsh, so many years ago. It was all so easy for him, but it wouldn't have been that easy without the money.

No, when it came to ultimate power, he decided it had to be love. Many things had happened in his life that proved that, things done for love of someone else. He thought Christ brought a beautiful message with him, love your fellow man. And Momma? Wow! She had the special light, all right. Yeah, love was her specialty, and she paid the price over and over again for being of such a mind. Life and the world kept rolling right over her, crushing her with its terrifying subtleties. Oh she had the strength to withstand the direct onslaughts all right, she weathered the twin storms that took her children. She had that going for her. No it was pain in the helpless she could not bear. To see the pain dealt those less able to handle it, was too much for her.

As quickly as Marie had entered Tom's mind, she left.

'What was it about? He covered all the bases, God, morality, politics, politicians, money, war and philosophies pertaining to it; the men who created wars and those who fought them. Killing and killers. How 'bout the ones who really get into it? What happens if they survive? Oh yeah that's a real ball breaker....'

*   *   *

He was only a kid, back there in 1942, when Colonel Carlson loaded his Raiders into the cramped bowels of the two submarines. Their departure marked the first American offensive operation of the still young war. It constantly amazed Tom, how people act in unusual circumstances. He remembered clearly his uneasy feelings as a passenger in that sub. Claustrophobia, somebody called it, but whatever its name Tom didn't like it. It had to be the closest thing to being in a tin can he would ever know. No windows, a couple of hatches out the top he wasn't enthused about, they were so tight, and of course no way of knowing what time of day it was, or what the weather was like. Seven days of cooped up submarine ride, and Tom wasn't fond of a minute of it. He was accustomed to the wide open spaces, working out on the rigs in Oklahoma and Louisiana, where you could see for miles in any direction.

"Where we going, Colonel?" One of the Marines asked the tall, gaunt looking New Englander as he passed through the narrow walkway.

"Huntin' son...place called Makin. Small island in a long chain. Our orders are to go in there and shoot it up good. Level everything we see, military installations, aircraft, kill as many of the enemy as we can. We'll have meetings soon to go over everything, you'll see what we're going after."

Sure enough, the Raiders had recently finished intensive training on an exact replica of Makin Island, and knew by heart what their objectives were. It was quite a trip, and having President Roosevelt's son with them, as executive officer to Carlson, made it even more exciting.

Tom remembered how insignificant he felt when the submarine surfaced, and they went over the side into the pitch black water. All he could see in every direction, were dark swells causing his imagination to soar, inventing many unwelcome mental images. It was the first time he really felt the rush of adrenalin, for like all young men going into their first combat it was an exciting, stimulating, terrifying experience. He thought he'd do well under fire, but wasn't certain. He sincerely hoped he wouldn't embarrass the Colonel.

In order of priority, Tom decided it would be good just to reach the beach because upon leaving the sanctuary of the submarine, they were in monstrous seas and high wind. Their outboard motors weren't made for these towering seas, failing immediately necessitating they paddle their boats in. It was then Tom thoroughly understood the meaning of gung ho, working together.

"Could you kill a man in hand to hand combat?" Was the question running through his mind right then, and while he'd already done so back home in Louisiana, he didn't know what to expect of himself now. Of course that was different, strangers hurting the Boss, and he reacted. Violently yes, but no one could have called it premeditated. This was a premeditated sneak attack with an entirely different set of rules, and Tom didn't know what his response would be. But then how could he, he was only 17 and just got off the boat.

The ride in to shore seemed an eternity to the young warrior, shivering uncontrollably, concerned whether he was cold, or scared. The Colonel told them any man who said he wasn't afraid going into battle, was either a liar or a psychopath, whatever the hell that was. All he knew was he was shakin' like a dog shittin' peach seeds. Christ how your mind could work for or against you. He laughed out loud at the thought, paddling the big black rubber boat furiously. His mind raced back to the rig in Oklahoma where he heard that saying for the first time, and his immediate mental picture of the dog. Good! Anything to get away from the unknown.

The boat rode low in the water, a howling wind driving waves that smashed against all sides. Tom tried to get lower in the boat, for warmth and protection from the spray. They came unannounced, without supporting gunfire, approaching the undefended side of the island. Unless the enemy had been alerted, there should be no resistance, and there wasn't. After what seemed an eternity to the young warrior, they finally reached shore before sunrise.

Tom learned later, the main purpose of this mission was publicity. Something to give the people back home as a morale booster, because to this point they certainly had been given nothing to cheer about. As such it was a smashing success.

In almost no other way could it have been considered anything but an exercise fraught with many unforeseen difficulties. Seek out the enemy and destroy him and his installations. Learn as much about him as possible, and develop their own practiced but untested guerrilla tactics. Tom did learn something on the mission he would never forget, however. Don't ever take on anything of importance without the best information, and equipment, necessary to do the job. The reason he learned this lesson so well was because he and his mates almost died in this first skirmish, a result of these requirements not being met.

There was much confusion upon landing and because of the failure of the outboard motors, the entire force was spread across the waters, tossed about and driven apart by the force of the seas. They wore black grease paint, which made it even more difficult to see one another in the half light of dawn, but finally managed to pull their individual teams together and move toward their objectives. They were relieved by the lack of resistance and apprehensive as to when the shooting would start. They didn't have long to wait.

Tom and his detail worked their way across the narrow island, met by the island defenders as they approached the opposite side. The resulting fire fights were short and furious, and the intensive training the Raiders received paid off immediately. They'd been drilled in discipline since boot camp. Discipline and a well conceived plan enabled them to fight their way across the island.

After the shooting started Tom's nervousness left him, much like when he was playing football for his high school team. He was always jittery prior to game time, emptying his bladder many more times than necessary, like a male dog pissing endlessly. When the football soared to its highest point during the kickoff, and both teams converged with mayhem on their minds his jitters left, replaced by an immediate sense of self preservation. Even though Makin was his first time under fire, he thought it was truly a most unusual event. Indeed, in later years, while thinking of the orchestrated insanity he found himself a part of throughout the Pacific, he changed his assessment from that of unusual, to the epic event of his life.

'Those bastards are trying to kill us.' He thought as they were being fired upon by a mostly unseen enemy. They had been warned on landing, by native islanders, that there were many Japanese snipers in the palm trees studding the island which was soon verified by intense fire directed at them.

"Jesus Tom!" His buddy yelled. "Where are they?" Hugging the ground while the bullets with their strange whines and thuds, tore small holes in the ground around them.

Tom saw the direction the sand flew after the bullets struck, backed up the line of trajectory, and discovered their source. It was one of many things he seemed to have an intuitive sense about, which became habit after much exposure to enemy guns, saving his life many times.

"Hey Bobby!" Tom whispered when the sniper let up. "I know where he is!"

"Where?" His friend was spitting out sand and dried grass acquired diving into their protective ditch.

"Palm tree! On the right! Only place he can be!" Tom rolled toward his buddy, whispering. "Do what I tell you, we got him. Not many places he can hide up there. He'll keep us here all day, or kill us if we move. I got the most firepower." Nodding toward his submachine gun. "Go down the ditch about 10 feet, stick your helmet real quick over the top. If he's there, he's gonna take a shot at it. If he does I'll blow the top outta the tree with this thing. Okay?"

As soon as his buddy was positioned Tom gave him a nod. He pushed the helmet up over the small embankment drawing immediate fire from the small caliber Japanese rifle. Tom answered instantly with the deep roar of the much heavier submachine gun. Even though he'd fired the weapon many times in training, he was amazed at the awesome destructive power of the weapon. He watched the top of the tree disintegrate, a rifle fall, followed by the body of the man he killed. The plan worked to perfection, Tom's first, but far, far, from last experience at killing an enemy soldier. At seventeen years of age he was feeling extra confidence over having shot the man out of the tree. He'd figured the situation out, killed his man, and was exhilarated over the experience. He didn't know whether it was because of the act of killing, or his ability to figure where in the tree the sniper was. He was also pleased with his handling of the submachine gun, an unstable weapon at best.

They fought their way across the island destroying everything in sight. Gasoline dumps, aircraft, barracks, anything important to the enemy and they did a thoroughly professional job. It was the afternoon of their baptism of fire that they were exposed to what was to become a common occurrence during the South Pacific war, the suicidal banzai charge. It was then Tom began to think about what was happening around him.

"God damn boys! Look what's comin'!"

Their big gunny sergeant hollered as they were making their way back across the island, to reach their rendezvous point. Tom looked with the rest far down the center of the narrow island, at a huge line of Japanese running straight at them.

"Banzai! Banzai!"

Was all Tom heard, while the line of Japanese soldiers charged their group. Officers among the enemy brandished their samurai swords, swinging them in murderous circles while the troops followed with fixed bayonets.

'Strange noise.' Tom thought, watching with disbelief as the tableau unfolded before his eyes. Shouts and screams of the hard running enemy wafted about by the sea breeze, a bugle blowing sounded eerie and far away, distorted by wind and distance. As they approached, the impact of their feet on the ground reminded Tom of the sounds he heard in the movies, back home, of the thundering hoofs of cattle.

"What are they doing?"

Someone asked in an incredulous tone.

"Different breed boys!" The grizzled gunny shouted. "Want to die for their Emperor. Those crazy bastards are comin' to give their lives, or take yours! Well all right! Let's show 'em what Marines are made of!" His years of training immediately evident. "B.A.R.'s on the ground! Spread out! Soon's these maniacs are in range, cut 'em down! Wait 'til you can reach 'em!" The B.A.R. men scrambled quickly. "Riflemen? Pick your targets! Squeeze 'em off! Remember, I said squeeze 'em off!" The riflemen moved apart, taking position. "Tommy guns in here! Mop up! You tommys'? Don't fire 'til I tell you! You got no range!" Then shouting at the whole group. "Keep your forty fives and knives handy! Any make it through, you'll need 'em."

Then in a booming voice, prompted by tension the gunny screamed.

"Gung Ho Raiders!"

Tom felt his skin crawl, right then. He'd heard that phrase ever since becoming a member of Carlson's Raiders, but never did it have the stunning impact of this moment. Tremendous slaughter was about to take place and it was unbelievable.

'Oh shit!' Tom thought through the incredible roar of the B.A.R.'s. 'Those stupid bastards are all going to die! What in the name of God they doin'?'

It was a strange thing to Tom, thinking about it later, he wept openly at the futility and stupid waste of life as the Japanese came screaming down the island. Funny thing, he wept then but later wasn't to weep at all. They were slaughtered as they ran. He'd heard the old saying 'like shooting ducks in a barrel' all his life, but never thought he'd be a part of such a senseless thing as this. They kept coming, the ones who could, and as they got closer the riflemen opened up, further shredding their ranks. Tom was dumbfounded by the grotesque motions of the running soldiers as they were struck by the powerful bullets from the B.A.R.'s. He didn't think it possible but could have sworn he heard bullets impacting. The pitiful few who made it even closer yet were met by a wall of submachine gun fire, his included. No Marine had to draw his knife, the enemy didn't get that close.

"Sweet Jesus!" Bobby whispered when the firing stopped.

The Raiders stood in total silence, overwhelming after the roar of the heavy guns, to view the results of the insane charge. Their weapons hung toward the ground. It was absolutely incredible. No one spoke, as they looked out over one hundred enemy bodies, silk scarfs on some of the officers fluttering in the sea breeze. They were all dead and dying and the dust from their charge was only just now floating over the shore, headed for open waters. Tom wondered if their souls were leaving too.

There was much confusion throughout the operation, starting with the fiasco of the boats and their reluctant motors, which caused their manpower to be spread great distances up and down the coast. There was also the lack of reliable intelligence concerning enemy manpower, so they never knew precisely what they were up against. They had no way of knowing if there were more Japanese left on the tiny atoll, and since they had accomplished all but one of their objectives, the taking of prisoners, they prepared to leave.

Their dead were left behind, Col. Carlson placing each on their backs, said a brief prayer over them, contracted with local natives to bury the men, and left for the waiting submarines.

The trip out was an unforgettable nightmare, the most grueling experience of the exercise. Immediately after pushing off from the beach, the motors died, because of large waves drowning out the exposed electrical parts. They tried every way they knew to protect them, but nothing would deny the incessant water which soon filled their rubber boats, making progress impossible. The men who were not bailing, paddled furiously, going nowhere because of the weight and ungainliness of the rubber boats, and frequency of the waves. It was pitch black which added even more to the mounting terror Tom and his comrades felt. Terror because they didn't know how many enemy troops were behind them, and an even greater fear of the pounding sea that seemed to be like a giant hand holding them back from the safety of their waiting submarine. To add even more anxiety, as if they didn't already have enough, there were the wounded who had to be cared for.

"Bail Bobby!" Tom shouted to his friend. "This thing weighs a ton! We're not going any...."

The raft like boat swung around in the pounding waves, lifted high in the air and overturned spilling all of their weapons, what supplies they had, and their wounded. Tom fought his way through the churning water, grabbed one of his wounded mates, and managed to catch the side of the boat. Working together, using the upward thrust of the waves they righted the craft and loaded their wounded back while each man tried to keep the thing headed out to sea, which by this time was also in serious doubt. The seas had turned them every direction so they weren't sure even where they were headed.

"Oh Christ, what in the hell are we doing?" Tom didn't know who the man was that said it, but he was aware of extreme panic on the part of not only that man, but almost all of them. This was not planned for, and it was truly their most desperate battle of the day.

"Bobby, keep an eye on those wounded guys!" Tom shouted into the wind. "I'm going over the side and see if I can haul this thing out to the sub!"

He stripped his heavy high top combat boots, shirt, pants, and went over the side in an attempt to swim the boat out. He was in the rough water pulling on a rope, hoping that would also hold the nose down and prevent further capsizing. It was only moments before they were swamped and overturned again to the complete frustration of Tom, who thought through sheer determination and his own considerable physical strength they would make it. They would, but not that night. After reaching a state of total exhaustion, unable to do anything more, the boat which had been righted again was pushed by the waves back on the beach from which it seemed they had left days before.

"You boys okay?" Carlson was asking, as he checked with each group.

"Yeah Colonel, but how the hell we gettin' out of here?" Someone asked.

"Don't know son." The Colonel hunkered down next to the frightened, exhausted Marine. "But I want you to believe one thing, if you've ever believed anything. We are getting off this island somehow. I don't know how just yet, but we are coming off this place. Now you men get some rest. We'll have a go at this thing again tomorrow."

Rest was an elusive thing for Tom, what with the days events still fresh in his mind, plus the uncertainty of not knowing if there were many, or any enemy troops left on the island. Exhaustion after the struggle in the surf, cold because of having no clothes, and mental fatigue from a day in combat, precluded anything like normal rest. He dug out, as best he could, a hollow in the sand to get down in and ward off the sea breeze which blew over his wet almost nude body, making his misery complete.

The events of the day clicked through Tom's mind as he tried desperately to force himself to sleep, knowing he could at least find escape there from his misery. He was surprised when suddenly Jane Guidry showed up at his temporary home, dug in the sand. She was standing over him looking down at his crude shelter, weeping.

'Oh hey Mama,' Tom said in his dream, 'don't do that. I'm okay. Didn't you hear the Colonel? Listen if that man said we're going to get off this island tomorrow, I'll guarantee you we're coming off this place.'

Her look of extreme suffering bothered the unconscious lad a great deal, because he loved her and didn't want her worrying about him.

'Come on now Hon', cut it out will ya. Hell I've been colder'n this on the rigs in the marsh, lots of times.' He could see she was looking at his near naked condition with deep and loving concern. 'Listen Jane,' he laughed, 'cause I don't have any clothes is no big deal. They'll give me a whole new bunch soon's we get back.'

She never said anything to the young Raider, just stood there crying, then disappeared down the beach.

'Boy I'll tell you what son, I do find you in some of the God damndest places...you know that?' Alex George was laughing outrageously at the sight of Tom in his hole in the sand, with almost no clothing. 'Will you look at yourself! Where the hell's your clothes? First time I found you, all you had on was a pair of overalls, and now scivvies?' He suddenly changed expressions to one of deep concern. 'Seriously Tom, I'm damn proud of what you tried to do out there tonight. Didn't work, but by God you gave it all you had. Jesus I really am proud of you, you know it! No whimpering or feeling sorry for yourself. Got a job to do and you gave it everything you had. Shit son, you make me real proud just to know you.' The dream Alex looked around before continuing. 'Say, I saw Jane Guidry back there, walking down the beach, seemed real upset. How the hell'd she get here anyway? Boy howdy damn, you boys in some deep shit here ain't you?' He was laughing again, obviously worried. 'Well Tom I told you these Marines do have a way of getting in serious trouble, but don't worry Carlson will take good care of you. That I'll guarantee.' He stood over Tom's sleeping body looking around. 'Kinda pretty here though ain't it?' He took a deep breath. 'God don't you just love the ocean? Big, huh? Well listen I got to get back home now, but I wanted to come out and see how you're doing. Looks to me like you're doing fine, soon's you get some clothes on. Take care of yourself Tom. Momma sends you her love.'

It was Tom's first experience with vivid dreams born out of exhaustion, but he was to know many more before going home to Louisiana. All manner of dreams caused by mind numbing exhaustion, and their nightmarish existence.

They got out the next day, after learning to their immense relief there were only two remaining enemy on the island. These were killed upon discovery, bringing the count to none. So while they had to wait until night again for the submarine to surface and take them aboard, at least they were spared the extra pressure of having to fight for their lives all that time. They carried their boats across the island, entered the water in a peaceful lagoon, and made their way out to the waiting submarines in much calmer seas. Tom took a different view of their transportation back, from the knowledge of safety afforded them by this means of conveyance. The ride back to Hawaii lasted another eight days, and they were flabbergasted by the hero's welcome accorded them.

"What's all the fuss about Colonel?" One of the Raiders asked their leader.

"Folks back home have been getting nothing but bad news since the war started. I guess what we did made a lot of papers in the states. Gave them some hope. Maybe even a lot of hope! Anyway, the spotlight's on us right now."

After a well earned rest Carlson's Raiders were put back into action on another dangerous mission, one earning them the deepest of respect from the rest of the Corps. They were to penetrate the interior of Guadalcanal, seek out the enemy force, kill as many as possible, and gather what intelligence they could about Japanese strength in the interior of the island. Most of the action that had taken place to this point was on the periphery, and the Americans needed to know what was going on in the interior.

"Jesus it stinks in here." His friend Bobby offered as they took their first steps into the thick jungle. Steps toward a journey through a different kind of hell. He was right, it did stink of the rotting debris of never ending ripe vegetation that fell, or grew, from every conceivable direction. What was to have been a cursory probe turned into 34 days of an experience that the survivors would never forget.

"S'posed to stink Bobby." They had become fast friends, forming a relationship so peculiar to men in combat. "This's real jungle, and everything adds to everything else, so what you get is this kind of place and the smells that go with it. The rain and heat causes everything to grow like crazy, and where there's no more room for it to grow, it falls over. Along comes the heat to turn whatever fell into a piece of garbage, so the whole place gets covered with that shit, and it stinks. Our swamps back home are pretty much like this too, different plants, but on the whole they do look alike. I don't know if we're going to run across any Japanese in here or not Bobby, but I can tell you right now there's bound to be a bunch of mosquito's, sharpening up their fangs, waiting to tear your ass up."

Tom was right about the mosquito's and almost all of them fell victim to the malaria their winged greeters carried. For most of the Raider's this was their first exposure to real jungle, so Tom had a distinct advantage in having experienced the Atchafalaya Swamp, back home in Louisiana.

"Christ Tom, what's in this place?" His friend Bobby asked a few short yards after they began their journey.

"What you mean?"

"Spooky, you know, any slithery creatures?"

Tom laughed at the mental pictures his young friend, a lad off a Kansas wheat farm, was obviously conjuring up.

"Yeah, some of those. We had alligators and snakes in the swamps, but you don't have to be scared of them none. Most of 'em want to be left alone. I 'spect if they could talk, you'd find they're more scared of you than you are of them. No Bobby, I don't think we need to worry about critters in here. What we need to be concerned with is Japs, because you can't see shit in a place like this."

They were back in the line, far back that is from the point which was where the Colonel was always to be found.

"Jesus Tom," the wheat farmer asked, "isn't that guy scared of anything? A Colonel walking point? I thought most of them'd be further back in the line than that."

"Yeah, well he's not like most of them. I don't think he has any fear whatsoever of death, that's why he walks the point. He's different Bobby, lots of the big wigs in the Corps don't like him."

"What you mean, don't like him?"

"Well you know how in boot camp and advanced training you were always taught a Marine officer was right next to God? Maybe even a notch above? You know there ain't no way you were gonna even think about questioning one of 'em?"

"Yeah?"

"Well Carlson doesn't go for that shit. He's always talking to us, explaining why he did things, asking what we think? Shit man, there isn't another officer in the whole Corps that gives a damn what grunts like us think."

Bobby felt better after the impromptu pep talk from his good friend, knowing what he said about the Old Man was true. Couldn't tell how old he was, because he was so damn skinny and his hair was cut so short. He did know Carlson fought in the first war so he had to be the age of his father, yet he never fell back in the line because he couldn't keep up. Bobby was the one having a bad time keeping up because the footing was so treacherous. There was always water everywhere, making the swamp as slippery as if it were covered with ice, compounded by the vines. They were all over, across and alongside the trails, reaching out to trip anyone who might be passing by, hanging from trees, making movement through them most difficult. They were also constantly harassed by the endless kinds of jungle vegetation growing everywhere. Huge leaves rubbing, slapping, cutting as they moved. The heat was the worst thing of all, rushing to 103 degrees with humidity to match shortly after the sun was up, sapping them of their strength in a few short hours. The daily rains that fell on them added to their misery. Some were slight but enough to turn their clothes into things that seemed to slide across their bodies. Others were torrential drowning everything under their leaden skies. Added to this panoply of misery were the strange shrieks and incessant chattering of jungle birds, making them nervous indeed as they worked their way through the miserable conglomeration.

"God damn mosquito's." Bobby spoke sharply as he slapped himself hard on the side of the neck. "You got 'em this big in Louisiana Tom?"

"Bigger." He replied softly. "Hold it down though, will 'ya. These jungles are full of Japs. We don't want 'em to hear us. Be real quiet, so's they don't jump out of this shit and surprise us.

"Surprise is the name of the game men." The Colonel fell back to spend time with each group along the trail, giving them small pep talks meant to buoy their spirits. "We know this jungle is full of Japs, but we don't know where or how many and that's why we're here. Be careful and quiet every minute we're in this jungle. We need to be on him before he knows we're here. Kill him and move on." Then earnestly. "How you boys doing?"

Tom knew he'd follow this man anywhere he might ask him, he was a leader of such charisma as to instill that sort of loyalty and faith in his men. What a strange mix he was, this Colonel Carlson. Definitely a man given over to a profound belief and trust in God, and yet one gifted in the art of the most vicious type of guerrilla warfare known to man. Murder by stealth. His Raider's knew more ways to kill a man than Tom thought possible. They used everything from howitzers to their trusted Kabar knives, to jiu jitsu with death administered by hand. He was a most unusual man, and like so many of that type appeared in the right place at the right time, this steamy jungle, in 1942.

"Okay men," their sergeant told them, "stay alert. We got a whole Jap force moving through the jungle right alongside us. I'm taking a patrol over there to find out what we're up against. You see a Jap? Kill him before he kills you. Watch everything and remember, "Gung Ho". If we work together, fight together, share together, we're coming out the other side together."

Jungle patrol was intense because of the foliage that could hide a company of enemy twenty feet away. Tom took to it naturally, because the swamps back home were an excellent training ground. He was comfortable with everything except his boondockers, which were too rigid for the terrain they were working on. He wished for some sort of tennis shoe instead, to maximize stealth.

He paid particular attention to his sergeant, a broad shouldered man, who moved without sound through the jungle, the left side of his body angled forward drifting silently through heavy vegetation. Tom picked that up instantly it seemed so natural, remaining with him the rest of his life. Through a crowd of people, in a darkened area, or hunting back home in the swamps and marshes, he walked at a slight angle, with the infantryman's slouched gait.

There was little sound, only the soft rustle of the vegetation they passed through, muffled in a few short feet by the dense jungle. Tom made sure his friend Bobby understood that silence could mean the difference between life or death, the Japanese or them.

They weren't out long before the point man raised his arm indicating stop, each man following his example until the entire patrol was squatting in the hot, humid, blindness of the jungle. Tom strained to hear what the point man had, sweat running everywhere, down his spine, between the cheeks of his ass, the sides of his legs, off the tip of his nose. It was like an oven and cooling breezes were unheard of. Then he heard it, a metallic clank, the first faint sounds of an enemy patrol.

'Canteen bumpin' something.' Tom thought, his nervous system on full alert. 'Two patrols close...lots of dead men...soon.'

The point man waved them up, until the four man patrol was laying in a line completely hidden from the approaching Japanese. "When we see the whole patrol, open fire." The whispered command. "Lead man's mine. Tom take number two. Bobby three. Down the line. More'n that figure who's your target's and kill 'em. I'll let the point man get far's possible, everybody get's a clean shot. Nobody fire 'til I do. You got that? Nobody." He crept forward like a natural inhabitant of this putrid stinkhole.

Tom watched in fascination as the Japanese patrol approached them, ignoring rules of silence talking animatedly, some even laughing. They were all going to die for their collective indiscretion. He stared with intensity at the man he was about to kill, thoughts crowding in. This was war, no bullshit about that. They were waiting for their victims like death waits for us all, and Tom was about to commit his first cold blooded, premeditated murder. It didn't seem to bother him at all. Couldn't see his young man all that clear because of the vegetation.

'Young. Probably my age. Short.' He thought. 'Somethin', huh? Looking at a dead man, who doesn't even know it. Doesn't know I'm here, doesn't know in a minute he's dead. Wonder what it's gonna be like? Feel like? The moment of death?'

As soon as the Japanese were totally exposed the hidden patrol opened fire with Tom still wondering about death as he fired, hitting his man directly between the eyes. He was amazed at the tremendous impact snapping the boy's head back, his helmet flying off in another direction. He died instantly, before his body settled completely into it's last configuration. The entire enemy patrol died so sudden there was almost no disturbance in the jungle. A few indignant screams from the tropical birds whose naps had been disturbed, followed by an unearthly silence. Each man had chosen his target well, sighted carefully and killed skillfully. As they searched the bodies Tom was intrigued by the restful pose his victim had assumed in dying.

'Looks like he's sleeping.' He thought, while looking at the photographs he found on his man. He checked the dead face on the ground, it matched one of the faces on the photograph. 'Must be his family. Picnic or something. Beautiful place. Family. Mother. Father. Brother. Good time....' Tom grew sad momentarily, looking at the boy's mother, knowing he had killed her son. She would never see that son again. 'Never again.'

"What did you learn out there, men?" The Colonel asked reviewing the action.

The ability to move with stealth seemed to be the most important thing. Each man realized how easy things could have been reversed with all of them dead, had they been the victims instead of executioners.

"The only thing I'd add is, search the next ones you kill for food. We don't have enough." Carlson continued. "If they've got it? You take it!"

The Raiders learned then what dire straits they were in for supplies, but they were trained in living off the land and that included taking supplies from a dead enemy. Between what they took into the jungle with them, what they could forage, and a few wild animals killed, they managed to survive the 150 mile, 34 day trek through the jungle. All but twelve of them.

Tom awoke one night to strange sounds coming from where his friend Bobby was sleeping. He thought it unusual, whispering across the darkness.

"Hey Bobby! You okay?" No answer. "Bobby, you awake?" He whispered and receiving no answer went back to sleep. He knew the guard was posted.

Tom awoke slowly, as light started sifting down through the heavy jungle canopy. He saw his friend lying in an unusual position, and as vision improved his attention was drawn to how still he was.

"Jesus Bobby!" Tom held his buddy in his arms, after confirming his murder, crying unashamedly, rocking him back and forth in some dim remembered motion. "Oh Jesus Bobby!"

The survivors were fully awake, stunned at what they saw, and full of rage.

"Who had the fucking guard?" Tom seethed, even after being told he too was dead. All the victims had their throats cut, dispatched with exceptional skill and in complete silence. It was Tom's first experience at losing someone close to him, but far from his last, each twisting his mind.

"Whoever did this, knew how to handle a knife." The Colonel said as he viewed the aftermath of the murderous sojourn. "Don't let their deaths be wasted on you men. Look what the enemy has done and remember what I asked you when you volunteered. Could you slit the throat of the enemy? Do you remember? Every one of you said yes or you wouldn't be here now." He stared at the group. "Well gentlemen that's how it's done. They crept in here last night and killed whoever was within reach. Some of you could have been victims as well, except for whatever made them select your dead comrades. Maybe you rolled over at the right moment. Maybe your position was wrong for a knife attack. No matter, our enemy was among us last night, and this is what he left. Stay alert! Double the sentries! Sleep two men to a foxhole, back to back. This is a terrible thing I don't ever want to see happen again."

Tom's mind started going sideways as he stood looking at Bobbie. He'd already killed two of the enemy he knew of, and probably more in the banzai charge on Makin, but this was different. His heart filled with murderous thoughts. He knew many more Japanese would die by his hand before this war was over.

They buried his dead friend in some nameless shithole of a clearing in the trackless jungle, continuing down the trail they were following. This time he was truly marching to a different drummer. Before he was acting out of obedience and reaction to orders. Now he was looking for Japanese to kill, understanding in some metaphysical way why he was here. He couldn't shake Bobby's face. He saw him on the trails and after darkness fell. Catching what frenetic sleep he could, his old pal appeared in many of his dreams. Sometimes they were in Kansas together, Bobby taking great pride showing him the endless wheat fields, stretching as far as the eye could see. Once Bobby, and Alex George, showed up together and the three of them had a fabulous night, leaving Tom with an empty feeling upon waking.

Their column moved alongside, but unseen by the much larger Japanese force's line, marching as it were side by side through the dense jungle. Carlson's genius at stalking became evident, weaving to the left of the enemy line, drifting back, paralleling on the right. The Raiders made ambushes and were ambushed in turn, each side developing their deadly skills as they traveled through the jungle together.

It was at this time Tom became expert at his own lethal specialty, the knife and murder by stealth. Drifting through the jungle with his Raider column by day, stalking, fighting, killing on the sly, ambush, harass, hit and run.

At night his was a far different game, stripping down to his shorts and undershirt, to prevent being entangled in the jungle growth. He took only his knife, crawling into the lines of the enemy paying them in kind for what they had done to his friend, and in the same manner. He was a good student, learning quickly how the human anatomy resisted attack with a knife, as he discovered in a near fatal foray one night.

He was crawling noiselessly into Japanese lines, when it appeared an enemy soldier was going to walk right over him if he kept coming. Tom knew he'd have to attack out of self defense, if for no other reason. Coiling into a crouch he waited, listening while his heart pounded, lunging out at the last moment, stabbing the man in the chest with an upward thrust of his right arm. He knew his opponent was terribly wounded, because he felt the warm gush of blood. His knife hit the heavy bone structure in the middle of the soldier's chest glancing upward and alongside of his head. He screamed in intense pain creating the need for swift action on Tom's part or possibly his own discovery and death. He recovered, sliding to one side of his victim swiftly, gracefully. Encircling the man's face with his forearm he gave it a powerful jerk as he cut his throat deep. Tom held the dying man tight to eliminate his escape or crying out feeling with his entire body the final convulsions of his victim. He was surprised at the vigor that went into violent death.

'Sounds like Bobby.' Tom thought as he dropped to his knees defensively, to evade or attack whatever might come as a result of this latest murder.

For the most terrifying effect Tom tried always to slide silently into an enemy encampment, find two soldiers sleeping together, cut the throat of one leaving the horror to be discovered by his fellow sleeper. He knew how he felt discovering Bobbie that morning, that a killer was that close to him, so he took special delight knowing the panic the Japanese would feel the morning after his visitations. He kept his knife razor sharp and the wounds he administered were deadly, but there is always the exception to any rule.

One of his raids was a nightmare caused by a missed thrust followed by a vicious fight in which the loser would certainly die.

Tom was alone, he always was. His type of slaughter was much better accomplished unencumbered. He could melt into the jungle, and even though within arms reach of his prey, be completely invisible. He wore the black grease paint they used on the Makin raid, locating a sizable tree beside the trail used by the enemy, and wait. It was while waiting to murder in cold blood his mind took strange trips, thinking many different thoughts.

'Strange shit,' he thought while waiting for the next victim, 'right here on this jungle trail I'm the designated killer for a couple hundred million Americans. They want me to kill the guy coming to kill me! Must make me a surrogate of some kind.'

His strange state of mind was brought to stunning clarity this particular night by someone approaching, as he became one with the tree, his knife encased in a grip of steel. He determined at the last minute there was more than one, and only had his knife to fight with. He moved quickly, silently, into the heavy jungle adjacent to the trail, laying flat on the damp hideous ground. There were three of them, availing themselves of latrine facilities, indicating to Tom a larger force down the trail. They were talking, laughing, lighting cigarettes while enjoying their bowel movement.

'Ten feet!' Tom thought. 'If I had something to shoot with, they're all dead!"

He was sure they could hear him breathing, the sound of his respiratory system roared in his ears. Sweat rolled off him, adding to the disgusting ooze of the jungle floor. It was almost as if they were aware of Tom's dilemma, taking an inordinate time with their toilet duties while he clung to vines and his knife, pressing himself further into the ground. It was then he felt the sharp scratching at his waist, causing him to recoil with maddening discipline. Cry out, make a sound and he was dead. He knew that. He rolled on his left side to nightmarish anxiety as he waited for something to follow. Nothing did.

'There.' Tom fought to breath normally. 'Fucker must be gone.' No sooner did he think it, than he felt many legs moving against his naked waist. He couldn't scream, he knew the consequences. He didn't know what was poking around his anatomy. Quietly, carefully, his heart pounding, he slid the blade of his knife in front of his chest, where the thing had moved, giving it a small flick. The soldiers were oblivious to his problem, shitting, chatting, smoking, for what seemed to him like hours, but really only minutes. Eventually they finished their efforts, a foul smell emanating from the clearing, and returned to their camp.

'Fucking land crab!' Tom thought. 'Can't believe a land crab would pick that time to walk on me.' He heard it rustling in the immediate area, trying to locate it with his knife when he heard someone else approaching.

Quickly, quietly, he rose from the dark sliding up to the large tree he'd used as a shield before. It was dark, but he could make out a single soldier dropping his pants in preparation for yet another elimination, on this bad smelling area.

'How they keep from stepping in it?' His thought.

Tom waited until his man squatted then stepped out from behind his tree lunging toward him slipping in the fecal matter of one of those who'd just finished. He fell to the ground next to the terrified soldier. Tom thought about that episode all of his life. He almost died because of a pile of shit.

"Haiee!"

The man hissed as Tom slid into him, both preparing for battle. There was no advantage and their death struggle became primitive in nature as they recovered from their initial shock, each prepared to kill the other. The Japanese soldier had a small entrenching tool, obviously to bury what his mates had not. It was his only weapon while Tom had his knife.

Tom's eyes were accustomed to the darkness, and he could see the man struggling desperately with his pants with one hand, while gripping his shovel with the other. Holding the knife low and in front of him, Tom lunged at his adversary who was ready, swinging the tool viciously, smashing the back of his left hand with numbing impact.

'The tree!' Shot through Tom's mind. 'Use the tree!'

He stepped behind it swiftly, utilizing it's defensive benefits.

All through the ensuing years he admired the courage of this Japanese soldier, because he had the courage to attack while struggling with his loosened trousers. Tom circled around the tree using it as a shield to ward off the vicious blows rained about him with that ugly spade. He was truly amazed that the man didn't start yelling for help, wondering if he could kill him quickly, or at the very least get away. He knew his left hand was broken, but had no idea how much blood he'd lost.

"Huuuh!"

He heard the soldier grunt as he swung, the shovel splitting the tree with hideous sound. After desperate effort, Tom feinted around the left side of the tree and as his opponent took a mighty swing, his foot caught in one of the vines on the ground, while losing his grip on his unbuttoned trousers. They wrapped around his legs twisting like a coil of rope, throwing him to the ground. Tom was on his back like a panther. It was over as soon as they hit, the enemy's shoveling tool twisting under his body, rendering him helpless, while Tom cut his throat with all the physical power he could muster. This was a new and different kind of deadly intent, coupled with pain and fear. He almost severed the man's head.

His hand was broken, but he was lucky to catch the flat of the trenching tool instead of the edge. He could have bled to death getting back to his lines.

Tom wondered for the rest of his life why the man didn't cry out. Maybe a sense of honor born out of an unknown Samurai predecessor. Maybe too terrified by the sudden appearance of his nocturnal attacker. Who knows?

The column struggled through those 34 days, making a name for Carlson's Raiders that would be recognized by all for years to come. They came out the other side stronger because of their nightmarish experience. They were estimated to have killed between 650 and 800 enemy, while suffering 12 dead of their own, a tribute to the training they received from their enigmatic leader.

Tom was acknowledged the best assassin the Raiders had by this time, killing frequently with whatever weapons at hand. Because of this natural instinct he seemed to drift further and further from accepting moral responsibility for his acts. They'd been given to believe the Japanese were something only slightly higher than animal, and it wasn't that he was bestial by nature, rather an average young man thrust into a brutal situation.

His life had changed too, from the joyous existence he'd known with the Guidry's, to the bizarre thing it had become. A series of random killings that didn't seem to serve any purpose, disjointed, surrealistic because of their surroundings. He came to believe, in a short period of time, there was no other world, no other life, only where he was at the moment. The men of his immediate company were all the family there was, and Tom never felt that with as much passion and pride as he did while marching through Henderson Field on their return. Trucks were available to meet them at the outer perimeter of the airfield, but Colonel Carlson and his Raiders wanted to show the world what they were made of. They marched in.

Tom felt a combination of immense pride in being one of Carlson's Raiders, and relief at having made that homicidal trek through the jungles. Even their unbelievable filth became an accepted part of their existence, filthy from wading the muddy streams. Clothing, bodies and hair caked with a horrendous combination of dirt, mud and sweat.

"Mama asked me to say a special hello, and give you all of her love." The letter from dark eyed Nancy Guidry was waiting when they arrived at camp.

"Paul finally talked Mama into letting him enlist and he joined the Navy." Tom was relieved over his choice, hoping against hope he would not be a Marine. He knew Paul was something special, maybe because of how Jane favored him, maybe because of his kind and gentle ways.

"You know Paul!" The letter went on. "He's going to be trying to help people no matter what. Guess that's what makes him kind of special. He's going to be a medical corpsman??? I hope I spelled that right. Anyway I guess he'll be the guy to give you aspirins and things. He says to be sure and tell you, you Marines don't need to get snooty with him, or he just might not open the bottle for you. Ha, ha, ha. He's through with boot camp now, and about to finish his corpsman???, training, so be on the lookout for him out there. In case you can't remember what he looks like, you can probably tell him by his halo. Well maybe he doesn't have one now that he's just a plain old sailor, but he sure will when he becomes a priest."

'My God, my God.' Tom thought reading the letter. 'When did I know him?' He thought how far apart they were now. The future priest, and the present angel of death.

"Guess what Tom?" Her letter continued. "I tried out for cheerleader, and darned if I didn't make it. Isn't that something? Most kids who get cheerleader are older than me, so I feel real good about it. Mama says I shouldn't do so much bragging. She says I might get the big head. I don't think so, anyway I sure hope not. I wish you were still playing football Tom, I'd like to cheer for you, but I guess come to think of it I can cheer for what you're doing now. Well Tom, Mama says I have to go to the store, so guess I'll say goodbye for now. She says to be sure and give "Brooks" her love, and that goes for all your other brothers and sisters here tooand then there's me. Hope I don't embarrass you Tom but I would like to say I love you, and I'm praying very hard for you every night, you don't get hurt."

It was signed Nancy. There was a P.S.

"Thought I'd put my picture in this letter. That's my cheerleader outfit. Isn't it dumb?"

Tom stared at the smiling dark eyed beauty, arms raised in some sort of cheer and was not unmindful she was growing up, fast.

'Praying you don't get hurt?' He laughed a different laugh from what this sweet girl knew. 'You don't get hurt out here, you get blown out of your shoes.'

He paused putting her picture in his billfold, wondering if a Japanese soldier might someday be holding it in his hand. The same soldier who'd just killed him.

The seven deadly sins seized the hierarchy of the Marine Corps, and Colonel Carlson was relieved of his command. A few short years later the maneuver would be known as kicking someone upstairs, to get rid of unwanted pressure. Carlson's unforgivable sin was his unorthodox training methods, which included the unpardonable discussions with every man in his outfit. There were those too who thought he'd listened too close to the Red Chinese Army philosophical line, and was forever tainted by the experience. Whatever, he was done with the Raiders, never to command again.

"This the thanks mother Corps gave him?" A hard bitten veteran of the long march through the jungles, spit out the words with contempt. "Well God have mercy on our souls if that's the kind of leaders we've got."

He was talking to Tom, but would have gotten more response from the tree he was leaning against, for he was lost in thought.

'Where would he ever find another leader like the Colonel? Who would he be? Would he know anything or would he be some green bullshit officer all full of Semper Fi, who didn't know his ass from first base?'

"Yeah, well fuck 'em." He startled the man talking to him, who didn't think Tom was paying any attention.

"Who?"

"The Corps! The Corps! Mother Corps! You think they give a shit about us, you got another think comin'! Dogmeat! Cannon fodder!" He moved off, never looking at the other marine.

"Who gives a shit? This is all there is anyway."

*   *   *

Tom ran across the beach that was disintegrating as he moved, shredded by murderous fire laid down by the Imperial army. The explosions of mortar fire were ear splitting, men blown to pieces by shrapnel ripping through the air. He saw one landing craft pull up to the beach, drop the unloading bow, take a direct hit from an artillery shell, and leap into the air, body parts blown in all directions. They were all dead, and didn't even get their feet wet. As in all these kinds of operations the beach was littered with Marine dead, dying, and wounded. Boats, amtracs, tanks, were scattered about, appearing to be like the junk they now were. Men ran up and down the beach diving for cover, some diving for eternity, shot dead while they ran. Acrid smoke, the pungent smell of cordite, and of course the sickening sweet smell of the jungle and bodies decomposing instantly because of the heat. The ocean breezes brought the odors they always do. Heat and sweat. Always the sweat. It was a living hell of a nightmare with the kaleidoscopic sensations of the...the what?

'They call it the Pacific?' Tom thought, incredulously. 'That's a sick joke. If this's peaceful...."

Loping across those vicious fields of fire, he noticed the knife on the dead Marine lying face down in the sand. "Ski" was all he caught on the man's gear, because he never stopped his strange paced angular gait, reaching down to catch the handle, pulling it from its sheath, never breaking stride. It caught his eye because of the unusual way it was made. Everything about it was special and lethal. Short, heavy, double edged blade, with one major feature, the hilt was fashioned into brass knuckles.

Even in that dense fire Tom recognized the terrible potential in this unique weapon which was never to leave him, not even back home to Louisiana.

"Give 'em hell, son.Dad." Was the inscription engraved on the blade of the knife, obviously done by a proud machinist father.

'Hope it wasn't his first trip ashore.' Tom thought staring at his new find.

It was created by an expert, with a heavy tapered blade made from high carbon steel counterbalanced beautifully by the weight of the knuckles of the grip. He understood better than its maker what a complete killing tool it was with its two edges, honed razor sharp, capable of delivering a lethal cut from any direction. The blade tapered forward, descending from all points on the surface to an extremely sharp point, thus making it an ideal stabbing weapon. The brass knuckles on the handle completed the deadly knife, making it a bludgeon as well.

'Well Dad,' Tom thought as he crouched in the momentary sanctuary of the jungle's edge, 'Sorry your son...whoeverSki out there's dead but I'll guarantee you one thing for sure boy. I guarantee you this knife'll be used like you intended.' His eyes went totally expressionless. 'Better I 'spect.' He cast his gaze around to the body on the beach whispering against the roar of the guns. 'Good luck, Ski.'

He continued his angular lope into the jungle.

"What do you think you're going to do with that thing?" Tom looked up to see where the question came from, discovering a new officer he hadn't seen before. "I hope to Christ you're not thinking about going in there." Shuddering involuntarily as he indicated the dense jungle. "That's bad news in there."

"If the Nips can infiltrate at night Captain, I can too." Tom answered. "This knife's the best silent killing machine I've ever seen and I intend to use at what it was intended. You see Captain it's what I do real good, infiltrate Jap lines, and kill anything I find in there until this war's over, or over for me. Don't see any reason why those slant eyed bastards should own the jungle at night, and we don't do anything about it except let 'em."

Tom wasn't looking at his interrogator at all, obviously chagrined at this pesky interference, anxious to resume his deadly trip. "I'm not afraid of the dark Cap'n, been able to see in it well enough up to now. Killed lots of the emperor's soldiers in the dark. Hope I'm not going to receive any orders now, that say I can kill only during the daytime, with a rifle, because in a war like this that wouldn't make a whole lot of sense. Now would it"?

The new replacement officer, fresh from the states, looked the tall, deadly apparition over, replying.

"Well okay sonny, but don't get yourself hurt with that thing."

It was getting dark, and the gunfire was lessening as Tom reached out taking the new Captain gently by the arm, looking into his eyes with the strange distant look of the surreptitious murderer.

"Hold on Cap'n, sir. Listen to me a minute, will ya'." His tone was almost a whisper. "You know I've been with the Raiders since they were born, back when Colonel Carlson was leading us. He taught me how to do what I do and I've been a lot of places doin' it where my government wants some killin' done, from Makin to this putrid sweat box. We did good on Makin, although we almost all drowned because some rear echelon asshole didn't know a God damn outboard motor from a kayak paddle. I killed Japanese on that island Captain, maybe more'n I know."

His voice was very steady, very low, as his eyes furtively swept the area.

"I went down a hundred and fifty miles of rotten jungle trail on the Canal with the Colonel, and I'll tell you something else, I'd of gone to hell with him if he'd asked. He's that kind of man, sir. You know what I mean? Had my buddy cut to death, laying not ten feet away. I've blown Nips up out of ambush, and had them do their best to try and kill me. I've murdered more men with my old Kabar at night, alone in the black jungle, than most Marines will ever see alive. I had the runnin' shits because of the garbage we had to eat on that trip, lost twenty five pounds from the time we went in until we made Henderson. So did everyone else, because we were living in a sweat oven and didn't have enough to eat. Had to ration ourselves on water to keep from dying of thirst. Attacked by every God damn bug there was on the island. Got malaria, dengue fever. Feet looked like two wrinkled prunes from being soaked the whole time we were in that slimy jungle, and they exploded when the sun finally got at 'em."

The captain was trying to figure whether this tall young man...or was he a young man, he couldn't tell. Should he be reported, or did he mean to harm him right there in the gathering dusk.

"Today?" Tom continued in his deadly monotone. "Why today I don't know how many Japs have taken a bead on my ass, tryin' real hard to blow it off. Lots of 'em have sir, but most of 'em are dead now and I'm not. Yeah, I'm gonna be running down these jungle paths Captain, 'til I make it to the end of the war or some Jap is rifling my shit to see what he wants to keep as a souvenir. I'd like to be runnin' down 'em with the Colonel, but mother Corps says we can't do that anymore."

Tom moved his grip lightly up the Captains arm, looking right straight through his spellbound audience. His voice had diminished to a whisper.

"Captain, my name is Brooks. Tom Brooks. I'm one of Carlson's original Raiders, and probably the best fucking marine in the south Pacific. Don't you ever call me sonny."

With that he released the stunned man's arm and disappeared into the jungle.

*   *   *

"Brooks you say? Yeah we got a man named Brooks. Why? Where'd you meet him? What'd 'ya want to know?" The grizzled Major looked up from his maps at the new replacement Captain.

"I think I want to put him on report, sir!"

The major listened, impatiently, asking at the end.

"Is that all?"

"Yes sir."

"Well before you do Captain, let me tell you something. Without a doubt that man's the best jungle fighter I've ever heard of." He gazed into the distance. "It's something we'll never know but I'd bet he's the best in the south Pacific, either side. That's what we're here for you know, although he gives it added flair. He's won the out and out respect of every man who ever fought with him. Grunts in the line who've never seen him talk about him like he was a legend of some kind, and I guess he's the stuff legends are made of. I wish I had a lot more like him, we'd all go home sooner, but I'll tell you something, for better or worse they don't make many like him. He's a natural born killer Captain, don't know how, don't know why, but I do know I'd rather be fighting with him than against him. You want to know what you can do about your little conversation out there? Why son you could probably put him on some kind of chickenshit report if you really think you should, but you'd have a pretty hard time making anything stick out here." Adding as he turned back to his maps. "Tell you what I'd do if I were you."

"What's that sir." Replied the eager replacement.

"I wouldn't fuck with him, Captain. I'd call him Brooks."

*   *   *

Tom learned shortly, to his horror, that Paul Guidry had been attached to a Marine division scheduled to go into battle soon. He was horrified because he felt the medical corpsmen had the most dangerous job in the war, far more dangerous than the grunt Marine on the line. They were always in the midst of battle, carrying only their medical supplies and a huge heart. No weapons, not even a God damn switch. Tom and his fellow Marines, felt the corpsmen were the bravest men they had ever seen.

"Wouldn't it be neat if you and Paul could get together while you're on one of those islands?" It was another of a continuous string of letters from Nancy. She was the correspondent in the Guidry family, but   always included what her mother told her to say to Tom. She told him what division Paul was with and he knew that outfit was due to go in on the next invasion. "I suppose you guys could even see some of those pretty hula hula girls while you're there in the islands."

Tom got a big laugh out of that, he hadn't seen any girls at all since a rest period in Australia. They were friendly enough, but he found it strange indeed that he still possessed his virginity. "A surrogate killer who kills for a nation of killers, that want the enemy dead." Well that's what he was all right, as good an assassin as there was in the Corps, he felt sure about that, and never been laid. Didn't make a lot of sense to this prematurely aged virgin, of twenty years.

The next invasion was a tiny island called Betio, a member of the larger atoll network called Tarawa. Paul's division was in the first wave to go ashore. Tom knew that, as he stood on the troop carrier watching the first waves of Marines being slaughtered in the surf.

"Hey Major!" Tom hailed his benefactor from the last island. "What's happening out there? Why are those guys in the water so soon? Jesus Christ Major, those God damn Japs are tearing those boys to pieces!"

The Major was stunned when he realized Tom had tears in his eyes, being of the opinion this lethal man was far beyond the ability to shed tears.

"They can't get the boats over the reefs, Brooks. They can only make it to the reefs and wade the rest of the way."

"Sweet Jesus Major, I gotta go! Gotta get in there." He was in a great state of agitation. "Can you get me a ride?"

"They're holding us in reserve now Tom. We don't go 'til they need us."

He knew his deadly Marine was searching frantically around the side of the ship, obviously looking for a way in, behavior so unlike him the Major asked.

"We'll get in soon enough, what's your hurry?"

"My brother's in that wave Major. He's a Navy corpsman and never been in anything like that. Jesus Christ Major," he broke into tears momentarily, regaining control quickly, "that boy wouldn't have the heart to throw a rock at anybody much less try and defend himself. He's not into that shit, you know what I mean. He's one of Gods own! Gonna be a priest after the war, he shouldn't be around that kind of shit." He started to cry again, angry frustrated tears. "God damn Major, I gotta be in there. I gotta be with that kid!"

"We'll get there Tom. We'll be there." The Major said softly as he took his premier warrior by the arm, turning his head so his own tears could not be detected.

Tom paced the deck of his transport, like the caged animal he was, never taking his eyes off the distant island. Everyone on board knew of the unprecedented firepower the Marines were meeting, stories of the horror drifting in like the wind. They heard about the command, "Land your men", given one battalion of 800 men, that were to hold position offshore until needed. The reply to that command was. "There's no one to land."

He walked miles that day on the deck of the transport, his nerves like a violin string. All sorts of thoughts raced through his mind, including going over the side and swimming ashore. He finally got his ride.

"Move this fuckin' boat man!"

Tom screamed at the startled coxs'n. It was D day+1 and the enemy firepower was still murderous. The number of dead Marines bobbing in the surf was unbelievable, and with all his experience he'd never seen anything like this. He couldn't imagine the roar of the guns he heard. It sounded to him like every weapon in the world must be on this tiny island, all firing at the same time.

'Well fuck em.' He thought, waiting only for this ride that seemed like an eternity to end on the beach. The tide was up sufficiently to go all the way in. His own mortality never seemed to be an issue with him, he simply didn't care. He'd learned the same sort of vague indifference to death from Colonel Carlson.

It was the same old symphony of slaughter only much grander than anything he'd ever known. The Japanese had every gun going from artillery and huge howitzers, down to their deadly Nambu machine guns and the always present snipers.

"Hey Pat!" Tom called to his buddy the minute their feet touched the hot sand. "Pat I'm leaving the outfit now, got to find my brother. If we're alive after this shit, I'll see you when it's over." He took off in his unusual loping gait, head low, abruptly changing directions every few feet, running down the shattered beach to find Paul.

"Think they're over there." He was answered by an intense looking officer. "If there's anything left of them. Over there to the right."

Paul's outfit had moved in from the beach a few hundred yards, and was being systematically annihilated by withering Japanese fire.

"Looking for a corpsman with this outfit!" Tom screamed into the ear of an officer. "Where are they?"

"God only knows! Look around, only be careful. These God damn Nips are everywhere, mostly buried in pillboxes, cuttin' the shit out of us. Not many left that came ashore with us. Look!" He yelled in Tom's ear. "There's a chaplain over there!" Pointing. "See him? He might know something."

Tom nodded his thanks jogging his strange zigzag style to the side of the chaplain.
"Oh yes son, I know Paul well. Used to talk a lot together. He's right over there...."

Tom turned in the direction the chaplain was pointing, his mind exploding as he saw row upon row of bodies awaiting their final destination. He found Paul among the dead, haunted forever by what appeared to be a slight smile on his face. Tom had seen many dead friends before, but none had the impact this did. His forehead stretched tight, and he had difficulty breathing. The roaring in his mind had nothing to do with the actual sounds of gunfire. He could feel only the most primitive rage, crowding out all rational thought.

"Oh Paul, Paul." He wept, whispering to his dead foster brother in the ear splitting roar of battle the dead boy had just left. "Why couldn't you have waited for me son? God damn it Paul, only a little longer? I would've done something...watched over you...killed whoever did this. Oh Sweet Jesus Paul, what's Mama gonna' say? You know how much she loved you." Tom was holding the dead Paul tight against him, kneeling in the sand rocking his lifeless body. "Oh Mother of God, why couldn't it have been me?"

"A friend?" The chaplain was asking, kneeling close, his lips next to Tom's ear so he could hear.

"My brother." Tom moaned still rocking Jane Guidry's oldest child.

"Well then listen to me, son! Please listen to me." The chaplain shouted. "You should be proud! Your brother died in the most beautiful cause of all. I know, I saw it!"

There was no reply from Tom, although he heard and understood.

"One of our men was down, horribly wounded, most of his chest shot away. He was dying out there by himself, screaming for water. No one would go! The officer in charge screamed don't go, it was too deadly. Paul went! He was holding the canteen to the dying man's lips when machine gun fire hit him in the back. They died together. Paul and the Marine he was trying to help."

Tom didn't react still holding Paul's body.

"Can you hear me, son?" The chaplain shouted.

Tom heard, nodding, his shirt wet with Paul's blood as he continued his rocking motion.

"Listen to me son! Listen to me! You must know and understand what happened here. Someday you must tell others about this. Your brother showed us the meaning of the word, love. He gave his life for love of another, probably a stranger. The Bible says no greater love has man, than to lay down his life for another. Paul showed us, by his example what that means. He didn't think about it, he did it! Oh my God son don't you see? Christ hung on the cross begging for water. Your brother brought it to Him."

Tom stopped crying, laid Paul's body back on the sand, looked through the chaplain's eyes with his incredible, distant stare, grabbed his machine gun and renewed his loping, evasive run back down the hot, murderous beach.

He found what was left of his company and with a renewed purpose, vengeance, entered into two days of unrestrained killing with cold blooded intent. He did nothing foolishly heroic, much too seasoned for that. He was everywhere in the slaughter at once, particularly intent on blowing pill boxes. He knew the machine gun that killed

Paul was hidden in one of those, so he used all the cunning and weapons at his disposal in a driven effort to destroy as many of the enemy as possible. He fought on and on throughout the remainder of the battle, sleeping only in naps destroying every Japanese soldier he could, until there was no more shooting.

In seventy two hours seven thousand men were dead. One thousand Marines, and six thousand Japanese.

'What was that Paul said back in LaFayette that night?' Tom was trying to remember. 'God was going to get him no matter what? Sooner on a battlefield, or later in an ordination ceremony. Guess He couldn't wait.' Suddenly thinking. 'My God what am I going to tell Mama? I can't be the one to break the news to her. Think I'll wait 'til I hear from Nancy, then tell them what I know."

The letter came.

"We just received word that Paul has been killed Tom, and are very sad. Mama hasn't come out of her room since we heard, she's so heartbroken. She really did love him so and while the rest of us kids knew that, I don't think any of us were jealous. She loves all of us, we know that, but Paul was her first baby and something mighty special to her. I take her food and do what I can to help, but I know God and she are going to have to work this out together. I also know she'll handle this in her mind, and we'll get back to something like normal. She's a strong person, always so happy and full of laughter. It breaks my heart to have to see her suffer like this. Papa's doing some better. He's going to work and that, but he cries a lot when he's home. We will miss Paul so much. He was such a fine person, and would have made an outstanding priest, but I guess God couldn't wait that long. Oh Tom, please be careful out there. I want you to come back to your cabin on the bayou. I want you to come back to me."

Tom wrote his letter to Jane explaining what had happened, and the exact words the chaplain had told him on that death swept piece of Tarawa.

"I know it doesn't help relieve your pain, Mama, but I think it's important you understand how he died. I thought it was a particularly beautiful thing the chaplain said about Tom taking water to a dying Christ on the cross. I wish I could have gone in with him Mama, but I didn't. We were in separate outfits. He was such a fine young man. I'm so glad I could call him my brother."

* * *

"Don't know about you Tom, but I'm scared shitless." Pat confided as they were about to disembark for the assault on Peleliu. "After Tarawa I can't imagine having the luck it takes to live through another. How about you Tom, you get scared too?"

"Hell yes, Pat. Colonel Carlson always told us any man says he isn't scared on these deals is lying. He said mankind's first instinct is survival, self preservation, and it isn't normal not to be scared."

It didn't bother Tom a whole lot that he didn't really believe what he was saying, knowing it did his friend Pat a lot of good having his fear shared. Tom had somehow come to the conclusion a long time ago that he would probably not survive the war, and for reasons he could never fathom didn't seem upset by this notion. He had seen so much death, of all kinds, it didn't appear logical to him that any of them could survive this brutal war. He thought about his different state of mind, through the years, concluding finally that his own personal lack of family and home must have had much to do with his indifference to his own death. That and the obvious fact he had become a war lover.

"Stay close, and low Pat." He yelled at his friend through the thundering explosions of artillery fire that greeted them as they approached the airfield. It was another of the endless arena's of death, that Tom and his fellows were ordered to take from the enemy. This one was especially murderous, a combination of vicious Japanese fire, 115 degree heat and no shade.

It took on a dreamlike quality, because anyone with half a mind could see there was no way to make it across the airstrip alive, such was the magnitude of the defensive effort. The sound had to be experienced to be understood. Whining sounds of incoming artillery and mortar fire, followed by the ear splitting blast on impact. Bullets zipped alongside as they walked, or ran in their slouching style. Tom thought it unusual that he could separate the various guns in this cacophony of deafening noise. The deeper staccato of Nambu machine guns, snapping rifle fire, muffled explosions of grenades, all happening at once and yet to him distinguishable. The one sight he could never accommodate was the streaking incoming tracer fire, appearing to be a white line of incredible speed and short duration, especially when ending with one of his fellow Marines crumpling to the ground.

The crushing impact of the bullet that hit Tom in the chest was a long expected shock. He had anticipated it for a long time, but was surprised at how hard it hit. The only thing he could compare it to was once when playing football, an opposing player hit him a powerful blow in the middle of his chest with his helmet, knocking him down, taking his wind in the process. He was wondering, as he fell, if this was when he stepped into eternity. He was calm though, simply wondering if he was fatally wounded.

"Oh Jesus Tom, not you. Shit man I didn't think they'd ever knock you down." Pat had seen Tom's body take the severe jolt, and was at his side immediately looking intently at the wound.

"What you think, Pat?" He asked, finding it difficult to breath.

Pat had his shirt open, staring in wide eyed horror at what he saw.

"How bad Pat?"

"Oh Jesus Tom it's right, dead, center. Those motherfuckers got you right dead center." Screaming. "Corpsman! Corpsman!"

"Listen Pat, those boys are all working their butts off." He was thinking of Paul and didn't want to be responsible for a repeat of anything like that. "Give me a hand back to an aid station? Take my rifle, and I'll hold this bandage. Doesn't seem to be bleeding all that bad, must of missed my heart or wouldn't be wondering about it at all. Where the hell is your heart?"

He knew, he was trying to lessen his friend's anxiety.

"Look Pat, I don't know what I got here." Tom was talking to his wide eyed buddy on the way back. "I'm not dead, so chances are I'm not going to get dead, so I'll probably be back pretty quick. If not I'll see you in Chicago or you come see me in Louisiana when all this shit's over." He noticed tears welling in his friends eyes. "Look

God damn it, don't worry 'bout me. You'll have all you can say grace over stayin' alive soon's you go back up. I'll be okay, I know that. Now promise me you'll watch your ass out there. Keep your head down. Run those dumb ass irregular patterns. Only don't let those slant eyed bastards kill you, you hear me? I'll get 'em to put a plug in this thing, and get back soon's I can."

He could not get Pat's last long look out of his mind, before he left the medical station to return to battle. Tom thought about it a lot while going out to the hospital ship.

"You're a mighty lucky man Brooks, do you know that?" The doctor asked after his surgery. "One inch higher and you'd have been a dead man. Don't know what you were doing, when you were hit, but I'd guess if you'd been exhaling instead of inhaling at that moment, you and I wouldn't be talking now."

"How soon can I get out Doctor?"

"Well Tom, we should get you out of here in about a month. I don't think we have anything too serious here, a simple gunshot wound to the lower chest." Suddenly he paused. "Isn't that the God damndest thing you ever heard. I'm standing right here telling you you've been shot one inch below the heart, and it's nothing too serious? This war's starting to affect my mind."

Tom watched his own progress closely, disturbed by his constant dreams of Pat. He saw him every time he closed his eyes, smiling, worrying, weeping, fighting, running, ducking, shooting, always asking with his eyes when he was coming back.

"Looking mighty good." The corpsman said while dressing Tom's wound about a week after he'd arrived.

"Jesus you're a lucky guy, you know that?"

"Yeah, I do. Listen, you think I'm okay now? Could I go back in the line now, if I had to?"

The corpsman looked at him, in total disbelief.

"What in the name of Christ is your hurry? You came within a whisker of being killed. You want to let 'em finish the job? Why don't you take it easy for awhile? You guys go through enough hell out there, as it is. I know! I went ashore with you at Tarawa." He noticed Tom's eyes tear up at the mention of Tarawa thinking he must have lost some buddies in that inferno.

"Did you know a corpsman named Guidry. Paul Guidry from Louisiana?" Tom asked.

"No, I didn't. Friend of yours?"

"Oh yeah. He was everybody's friend. He died there."

"Lots of 'em did, Tom."

"Yeah they did. Look!" Tom asked. "I need my gear, and I need to get the hell out of here. I got a buddy on Peleliu, and I'm worried about him. You understand? I'm afraid he'll get killed if I don't get back, so I gotta go. You know where my knife is?"

"Yes you crazy bastard." The corpsman's eyes were full of tears. "You were hollerin' so loud about that knife we took real good care of it for you, but I don't know why. You should be arrested for carrying a thing like that!" He took Tom's hand, looking right down into his eyes. He knew about the love these men on the line had for one another. "I'll get it for you Tom. I hope your buddy's okay when you get there. Hope he knows what kind of a friend he has in you."

*   *   *

"Gone! What the hell you mean gone?"

The doctor was real upset over Tom's empty bed.

"He's gone sir. Said he was through bleeding. He was worried about a pal of his up on the line, and I'll bet lots of money that's where he's headed right now.

*   *   *

"You still alive?" Tom grunted dryly as he fell down beside Pat, behind a slight rise they were using as a defense.

This was a relationship he was to think about many times through the years. Not only between he and Pat, but between most men who share the terrible demands of facing imminent death. It was far more than a buddy system, it was love in it's purest sense. Every man pulling for the rest. There was simply no way to explain that to the individual who had not experienced it. All the men in the line had was one another, there was nothing else.

"So, what'd you think of that one?" Pat asked as they loaded on the boat leaving the island. "Oh but then pardon me all to hell, I don't s'pose I should be asking you that since you were vacationing through half of it."

"It was tough enough Patrick, but like you say I did get a little time off.

They stared over the side at the receding island wondering what new hell hole the Marine Corps had in mind for them. They didn't have long to wonder.

CHAPTER 16

"Hey, what kind'a bull shit you call this?" A new replacement hollered as they went on the beach unopposed. "You guys been doing the Pacific thing all the time, like this? Hell, ain't nothing to it."

"What you make of it Tom?" Pat asked him, ignoring the boots comment. He'd seen this bravado before in green recruits followed later by many of the same young men defecating in their pants, and crying for their mothers in the heat of battle.

"Don't know," he gazed intently about, "s'posed to be lots of Japs on this island, and if they're not here they must be waiting. Probably dug in that hill over there like ants. We sure got our work cut out for us here, old pardner. Now don't forget what I told you, keep your ass down low and when you do move, make sure you give it the old pussy foot shuffle. We might be here for awhile Pat, lots of nasty looking holes in that thing for those slant eyed fuckers to hide."

They were in the line a short time, when the rains started to fall. Cold rains, some torrential. The real old timers who served in the first war said everything about this action reminded them of the trench warfare of that time. Both sides pinned down unable to make any progress, paralyzed in the rain and slop, trying to kill each other.

"Jesus Christ, Tom! How we s'posed to live in this shit?" Pat was bailing out their foxhole, a two man affair. It was filling as fast as he could empty it, using a long dead Marine's helmet to bail with. "I'm cold, hungry, wet and tired. We're stuck in this miserable armpit, going nowhere. I got to get out of here. We're gonna' drown in this hole if we don't." He looked at Tom . "Come on man let's take a walk and get the hell out of here."

Tom learned when conditions were as miserable as this, you went into your mind, and soul, to maintain sanity. He was beginning one of those trips now.

"Listen Pat, can you remember those great days you told me about on the beach in Chicago? You know, summertime, good looking girls up and down the beach. You remember?"

"Yeah, I remember. Why?"

"Colonel Carlson taught us a long time ago we could stand anything long's we didn't fold mentally. He told of being with the Red Chinese Army on what they called the Long March. It was a son of a bitch, marching, fighting, killing, disappearing, through thousands of miles of country, and all kinds of weather. They had no supplies, scrounging whatever to stay alive. When they killed an enemy they stripped him of everything, just to keep going. Food, guns, ammunition, blankets, anything. During the march the Colonel was in a column that was climbing a steep mountain, and noticed he was falling behind these raggedy ass guys. Guys that hadn't had a square meal in too long to remember, so he says, bullshit! If they can do it, I can do it and he did, right to the top. Then he said one of the soldiers was standing next to him breathing hard so he says to the guy, "How the hell can you keep this up?" You know what the soldier said to him?"

"What?"

"He says, 'if a man only has legs, he can't.'"

"So?"

"So, it's a mental trip don't you get it? That's what we got to do Pat, don't you see? We got to bear down and use our minds to tough this shit out, you understand?"

The artillery and mortar fire was the worst they'd encountered thus far in the war, turning the whole nightmarish scene into something unimaginable. Vegetation was long since obliterated leaving the entire area a sea of mud. Shattered trees with sparse limbs and no leaves, looked like weird sentries standing in the wind and driving rain, and were shot at many times in the night. The most mind numbing hideousness were the corpses, Japanese and Marine, that littered the area. Because of the ferocious fire from both sides, they could not pick up the dead who went quickly to decay and putrefaction due to exposure compounded by the rain. The smell in the area was unbelievable. A combination of rotting flesh, cordite, mud, human waste. Much of the time when subjected to the shattering enemy artillery fire, they had to use whatever means possible to relieve themselves, defecating in helmets, throwing the waste out of their foxholes adding to the overall stench. The area looked like something beyond imagining, a hideous war torn junk yard. Debris discarded everywhere, ripped C-ration containers, gunbelts strewn about, broken mortar shell boxes, plasma bottles with pieces of tape still attached marking the spot where a man fell, thousands of shell casings of every type. Adding to the grotesque horror was the incessant pouring rain, a rain that continued for days, covering everything with a sickly cold gray pallor. The single most excruciating thing the men had to bear however, was the never ending shelling. There was incoming Japanese fire and their own mortar and artillery fire passing over their heads going the other way. Each had it's own identifying sound. Some swooshed overhead, others sounded like freight trains passing, while still others seemed to rip the air with strange horrifying reverberations. The final ghastly touches were caused by flares bursting over the area at night, casting everything in a feeble green pallor. It was a scene right out of Dante's Inferno, with more terror added by the Japanese infiltrators who came in the night.

A few nights later Pat was standing in deep water his wet helmet pushed against his arm, sobbing. "I can't take it anymore, Tom."

"Yes you can Pat!"

His empathy took on an edge of rage, terrified he was going to lose his friend. Tom's apparent indifference to his own death was legendary but that did not include the death of his friend.

"You can take more of this, and you will take more of this. You know why?"

"Christ man, I don't care why." He was crying as they stood in the thigh high water of the foxhole.

"Bullshit, my Irish friend! Didn't you promise to take me home to meet your gangster friends in Cicero, when this shit's over? You said we could move right on in there and take over from those pussyfoots now that big Al's gone, didn't you say that?" He didn't wait for answers. "Yes you did and after what we've been through, old Patty, we'll show those badass guys what bad's all about. And what about the girls, the ones down on Lake Michigan you say're waiting for us? We're not going to disappoint them are we? I don't want to disappoint them! I want to make love to a girl Pat, I never have before." His stricken friend lifted his head to stare into the eyes of the savage killer. "How 'bout the Italian restaurants? You say they serve the best. Chicken and green noodles? God Damn Pat, that sounds good to me." He raised his friend's head, looking in his eyes. "I want to see all those places, you know that? I don't want to see any of it without you, son. You've got to show me around." He embraced the smaller man. "Don't leave me Pat, there's nothing else kid, just us."

"I'm not going to make it." Pat sobbed. He hadn't heard a thing. Tom kept his arms around his miserable companion, their wet helmets bumping as he pulled Pat close to him, while the pounding rain ran off their poncho's. His love for this man, right now, was as complete a love as he'd ever known.

"Yes you can Pat! Yes you can! God damn it I'm telling you, you can! We do this, and then Japan, and we go home! Chicago! How 'bout that kid?" He was holding his sobbing friend. "Come on, we made it this far, we'll go all the way. We can do it, you and me, you hear me? Those bastards can't kill me and you know it!" He held his fellow angel of death close, in the rain and mud, until he stopped crying.

"What time is it, Tom?" Aware he wasn't asleep. It was dark, raining in sheets.

"Early Babe. 'daylight soon."

"I gotta take a crap, and it won't wait. Be back in a minute."

"Okay but be careful. Be sure you let the guys in the line know who you are." He slapped his companion in misery on the back. "Make sure you get it all done while you're there too will 'ya, don't want you stinkin' up the place later. It smells just like a fuckin' rose garden around here now." He was trying to kid his friend into a different state of mind, drifting into something like sleep shortly after he left.

'Tom, Tom, this is horrible! This is the worst place I've ever seen in my life.'

Tom cringed when he discovered Nancy was in the foxhole with him. He didn't want her there it was so hideous. He loved seeing her though, and her red and white cheerleader outfit did do marvelous things for her figure.

'Mama's fixing rabbit sauce piquante for dinner Tom, can't you come home for dinner?' Suddenly smiling. 'Wait 'til you see the little kids, they've really grown. What do you say, let's go home now? I'll get you back real soon.'

Her face grew sad as Tom told her in his dream, he couldn't go with her now, but promised he'd be home as soon as the war was over. It almost broke his heart to see her tears, begging her in the hush of his dream not to cry, he was perfectly okay. Yes it was wet and muddy now, but soon the sun would come out and it was going to be nice. He asked her to wait a little, he wanted her to meet his friend Pat.

'Well, where the hell is he?' He noticed the Old Man in the corner of the foxhole, for the first time. 'Where's this Chicago guy?'

'Where the hell is he?' Tom woke with a start, aware he'd been dreaming but not how long. Pat was not back and it was getting daylight. The dismal morning light sifted through rain clouds, amid stirring from the rest of his company.

"Hey Larry!" He whispered to the man in the next foxhole. "You seen Pat?"

"Yeah, crawled through on his way to the crapper."

"Long ago?"

"'bout an hour. Wonder what's keepin' him?"

"Brooks comin' through!" He croaked in a strange half whisper as he struggled out of their slimy lodgings, sloshing through the cold mud in the direction of the latrine area. "Hold your fire Marines, Tom Brooks comin' through." They held their fire. There wasn't a man among them who would dare shoot at him.

Crawling, sliding, he made his way down the greasy incline leading to the area used by the men when they could get out of their foxholes. Tom drifted through the slop, moving with the considerable grace of the veteran foot soldier in dangerous surroundings. Japanese shell fire had lessened because it was morning and they didn't need the terrifying blasts to keep the exhausted Marines awake.

"Pat!" He shouted hoarsely from a crouch, his rifle in readiness. "Where the hell are you Pat?" The only sounds were the rain, wind and sporadic gunfire. 'Fuckin' weather,' he thought, 'can't see shit in this stuff. Where's that asshole? Hope he didn't go back to headquarters...know he's hurtin' but not that bad. They'll rack his butt if he goes in on a section eight.'

He moved further down the slippery path suddenly plunging headlong into the mud, his rifle pushed straight in front of him ready to fire. It was his friend he was prepared to shoot, hunched against a muddy bank, head bowed, hands in his lap, looking like he'd gone to sleep while defecating.

"What the hell's the matter with you, you dumb shit?" Tom was up, slipping across the expanse of mud that separated them. "Didn't you hear me hollerin'?"

Pat didn't respond as Tom approached, reaching his side.

"Wake up, you jerk?" He shook Pat's shoulder, transfixed in horror as his buddy's head rolled into the mud, helmet intact. At the same time his severed hands slid down his wet poncho landing in a puddle between his feet. Tom stared at Pat's headless torso and his blood felt like a raging fire in his veins. He wanted to scream in anguish but was much too much the true warrior for that. There'd be time for screaming later, he'd see to that, and none of it would be his. He'd heard about the Japanese practice of beheading Marines, but Pat was the first one he saw. Head, hands and many times the dead Marines penis was cut off and shoved in his mouth, a special kind of horror meant to turn an observer into a cringing, terrified coward. It didn't work that way with Tom. It didn't work that way at all.

"Fuck you Maline!"

He heard the voice way off, sifting through the driving rain, and he wept as he took his dead comrade's body down from its niche in the mud. This was his last and best friend, and he loved him completely. Pat had been hacked and mutilated by the Japanese, and while Tom had killed many men before, it was going to be quite different from this point on.

"Fuck you Maline! You find flend, Maline? Ha, ha, ha, ha. Fuck you!"

Tom didn't answer, his mind an inferno. One thing was brilliant in its clarity of the moment however. He knew absolutely in his soul, he would answer this aberration, in an unbelievably brutal way.

"Well how about that son, you got out of this shithole after all?" He arranged the body flat on the ground putting his head where it belonged. He was humming.

"Oh Patty dear, and did you hear, the news that's goin' round. Is that how it went, Irishman? Jesus Christ son," he sobbed, "you never taught me the rest of it. Is that all there is...?"

Tom's mind was disintegrating as he sat in the mud beside his dead friend's body.

"You know Patrick I don't know what the fuck it is, but I never seem to be in the right place at the right time. Do you know that? I mean first there was Bobby, then Paul, and now you." His glittering eyes swept the area, hoping beyond hope to locate one of the enemy. "You know something real sad too, I don't know how many dead faces I got in my mind with no names. Can you believe that shit? Humped with 'em, they're dead and I can't remember their names." He laughed out loud, a combination laugh and demented wail. "But I'll tell you somethin' for God damn sure, yeah. There ain't gonna be any more buddies for this fucking marine. Do you hear what I'm sayin'? No, no son. Hurts too much when you sons o' bitches die. Naw I've had it Pat, I'll go the rest of the way alone." He caught himself not wanting to upset his dead comrade. "Don't worry though kid I won't go yet. I won't leave you now, son. We'll wait right here 'til somebody comes up and gets you, then I'll be on my way."

He sat motionless in the rain beside his dead friend, then bent over slowly whspering in his ear.

"I'll settle this for 'ya kid. Yeah, yeah."

*   *   *

Tom had no idea what the word quota meant, but he put himself on a minimum quota of one Japanese kill every day. Some days were better than others.

"Where's Brooks?" The new sergeant hollered checking his men out.

"Not here Sarg'. Crazy bastard goes outside nights."

"What you mean, outside?"

"Hunts infiltrators, down in the draw, out on our flanks, everywhere. Goes into their lines. Comes back when it's light. Talks to nobody. Keeps to himself, fights on the line, makes his patrols, and goes out the wire at night. Never sleeps."

"Well as long as he's killin' Japs, who gives a shit? That's what they pay us for." The sergeant crawled back to his foxhole wondering about his absent murderer.

The draw between the lines was full of the bodies of the long since dead, the smell of rotting flesh permeating the grotesque surroundings. Tom was laying in the mud between a dead enemy and a dead Marine humming his tune from the Wearin' o the Green.

'Funny, we even got green flares to go with it. Wonder how the Irish got hooked on green anyway? Strange bunch of assholes, huh Patty, 'if you notice the Japs wear green too.' He was quivering with dry laughter as the situation became clearer to him.

'Oh Jesus Christ Patrick, can you guess what? We're wearing green! Our fatigues are green too, isn't that the shits?' He was beside himself with the irony of it, sharing the joke with a dead man. 'Assholes of the world must like green.'

The rain roared into his face and ears, but not his eyes. He feigned death laying with the corpses, his helmet tilted in such a way to keep his eyes out of the driving downpour. They sliced through the rain swept valley of rotting death. It was these eyes of death his fellow Marines could no longer look into, they were devoid of expression and bottomless. He came out on these forays armed always with a .45 automatic and his knife. The knife his most cherished instrument of slaughter.

The horror in the eyes of the men he had mortally wounded, just before they died, brought an intense sensual satisfaction to Tom. He especially relished watching the infiltrators steal their way across the stinking, disgusting draw, coming closer and closer until they were in striking distance. He would somehow spring up out of the slop, making a split second decision whether to use the gun or his knife. If the prey couldn't get his weapon around quick enough, Tom would smash the brass knuckles of the knife into the face of his quarry, shattering all underlying bones. He liked that, knowing what intense pain his victim suffered momentarily before he beheaded him with a terrible slash of the razor sharp knife, which is what he tried to do after completing each deceitful murder. After severing the man's head, Tom would inch his way across the draw if it took all night, carrying his gruesome souvenir to within throwing distance, pitching it into enemy lines.

Most of the men in his company shuddered when they heard him call early in the morning, "Brooks comin' in." They knew where he'd been, sleeping with the dead, fearful he brought some of their maggots with him. No one spoke to him about these ruthless forays, fearful he'd kill them too. There was no doubt in anyone's mind he was completely insane. Nobody murdered with the skill and relish he did, and laid claim to normality. They also knew that because of his cruel expertise, maybe the last man he slaughtered might have been the one coming to put them in their grave.

He buddied with no one, out of his choice and that of his fellow Marines because everyone figured him for a dead man. They thought no normal human being could carry on in this fashion thereby missing the truly obscene joke. This was the absolute zenith of abhorrent behavioral situations and the brutalities committed were done by men like Tom once was. Normal men adapting to the insanity of their surroundings.

Tom wasn't aware of it consciously, but death was what he sought, thinking in some convoluted way that was what he had become. Death. He'd long since reasoned there was no returning home for him, and accepted it. It didn't seem to him his kind should be allowed to go back anywhere, to live among normal people. How could someone like him ever be trusted to live among the sane people of his old world...whatever and wherever that was? Where was the place in life for someone like him, a superb and ruthless killer. He knew only how to pull pipe and kill men.

The dead men in the vile Dantesque draw told him that too, appearing in his demented dreams as they rose silently from their gelatinous heaps, in various stages of decomposition, gathering around him in the driving rain gazing at him accusingly. They were horrible beyond imagining to look at, but not for Tom, he was one of them. At night he lived among them, lying with them oblivious to the relentless rain and murdered while they looked on, laying back down with them after committing his heinous acts, waiting and dreaming. None of them harbored thoughts of ill will for this manic mortal among them, but a silent, ever silent consensus of opinion that he was much too deadly to be allowed back in civilization.

It was September 2, 1945 and the Japanese signed the surrender treaty. They'd had enough after the big bombs persuaded them not to prolong the carnage.

"Tom, come home. I need you."

The wire was from Alex George. Tom couldn't even remember him clearly. He'd pop into his mind for a flash, then Tom had to struggle remembering what he looked like.

"'bout the same size as that Jap I sawed in half on, on, some island.... Which one.... Who knows? Who gives a shit.... Maybe God keeps score.'

"We lost Alex, don't want to lose you. Please come home as soon as you can. There's no more shooting, they don't need you anymore. I do. I'll be waiting for you. Long way to go Tom. Let's do it together."

"Where's Brooks?" The replacement Captain for the long dead officer who wanted to put him on report asked, as he came through the area where Tom's outfit was bivouacked.

"That's him over there, Captain." Someone replied indicating a tree some distance from where they were. A solitary figure sat underneath, his back against the trunk. Tom made no move to get up and salute the approaching officer, who didn't mention the oversight. He knew who Tom Brooks was.

"Don't know who you know Brooks, but I got word to put you on the first boat out of here back to the states." There was no reaction, he wasn't sure Tom heard. "This order started from the CNO's office in Washington, so I'd say you got some pretty hairy chested friends somewhere. Anyway pack your gear, check in your weapons, and report to me in the morning 'cause you're on your way. Lucky boy Brooks." Tom turned his head slowly in the direction of the Captain, who wasn't sure he saw him.

"Been out here long, Brooks?"

"From the beginning."

"From the beginning?" He raised his voice. "Jesus Christ! Guess you do deserve to get out of here. You're a mighty lucky man to be alive. We're all lucky to be alive. Lots weren't."

"Yeah Captain, lots."

After getting Tom's orders processed, and taking him out to the ship, the Captain wondered if this killer was going to make it. Could he adapt, or would he have to be destroyed like most dogs of war?

It was easier staying to himself on the return trip because no one knew him, and after a few cursory conversational probes saw he should definitely be left alone.

He spent most of the voyage to the States standing under a scalding hot shower, trying to wash off the stench of death and decay. He was afraid it would follow him forever.

CHAPTER 17

"Hello Mr. Alex?" The voice seemed much, much older than the last time he heard it. "It's me...Tom, Mr. Alex. I'm back."

"Hey, hey Tom! God damn it's good to hear your voice! Where are you, son?" That was okay, Alex George could call him son.

"New Orleans. Just got off the plane."

"Oh damn Tom," Alex's voice was barely under control, "you don't know how good it is to hear you. I can't wait to see you. Apparently my call to Washington worked. Those Navy boys like to keep their oil sources happy. Well they sure made this one happy." Tom suspected something like that. "When you going to get here Tom, tomorrow night? How about we have a party, a welcome home party?" Followed by a long pause. "Forgive me son. I forgot there for a minute what it's like to come home from a war. I came home from one not too long ago myself. I know that's bullshit to somebody like us. Don't need that, not after where we've been. I was being thoughtless. Listen, why don't you go downtown and check into the Roosevelt Hotel. I'll have a room waiting there for you. Just sign for everything. They got everything you need right there, and I mean everything. You need anything Tom?"

He was in the phone booth, leaning his head against the glass thinking. 'Why is this man talking to me instead of his own son. I don't understand that. I just don't understand.'

"Hello, hello? Is this God damn line dead? Tom, you still there?"

"Yes sir, I'm still here."

Alex George spoke softly. "It's okay Tom. It's okay. Stay there as long as you want, I understand. Comin' home's tough after a war. Need any money?"

"No sir. Got my mustering out pay. I'm OK."

"Isn't that the shits," the Old Man was laughing and crying making conversation difficult, "I don't even know whether you drink or not, but at least you're old enough now. God knows any Marine that served in the south Pacific sure deserves it. Well whatever, but for your information New Orleans is the greatest drinkin' town on earth Tom, so if you'd like to go on a good old fashioned drunk, kind of blow out all the flues, for Christ's sake do it. Look I'm so happy to hear you I don't even know what I'm sayin'. When you get ready, come on home! We love you, we've missed you, and we're glad your back," adding softly, "and Tom...Momma's waitin' to see you."

"Okay Mr. Alex, I'll be there soon. Would you do me a favor?"

"You name it."

"Will you ask Albert Guidry to leave the cabin door unlocked in the back? You know, in case I get there in the night."

"Yeah, sure I'll ask him, but I doubt if it's been locked since you left. Yeah, I'll ask him." There was a real struggle for control going on with Alex George. "Okay, see you when you get here.... Oh and Tom?"

"Yes sir."

Alex George was weeping openly now. "I'm mighty glad you made it, son. See you when you get here."

Tom tried the night life from Canal street to the French Quarter but nothing was right. He felt completely out of place in these surroundings. After three years of intense personal involvement in ferocious slaughter the frivolity he found in the saloons was for the most part, stupid and meaningless. He gave it up as a bad job, and returned to his room at the Roosevelt.

The combination of general fatigue and alcohol led to fitful sleep and the beginnings of his sinister dreams. Pat showed up first, intact, indicating there was danger to Tom. There were no words, but an implied message that there were enemy troops in the closet of the room. He couldn't see them but Pat convinced him they were there. His entire being went to alert as he stared intently in the direction of the closet, listening, waiting. The first Japanese soldier to stick his head out of the closet was the first young man he killed on Guadalcanal. His victim said nothing, rather staring at the man who took his life as a matter of curiosity. Tom apologized to him soundlessly for killing him in the ambush, but that was the way of war. It could easily have been the other way around, if someone in their patrol had not been so careless. He was aware of the second soldier before he saw him, hearing that same hissing "Haiee" he'd heard so long ago. He crept out of the closet, clutching his trouser tops, armed with the same shovel. The smell of freshly dropped human waste seeped through to his nostrils and he woke, covered with sweat and a pounding heart. He was extremely careful not to let his unwelcome guests know he was awake though, especially the man with the entrenching tool. That's the one that smashed up his hand so bad, leaving the ugly wide scar as a remembrance of that night. Knowing he needed to be wary Tom slid quietly out of the bed watching the two like a hawk as he inched his way across the floor, toward his sea bag.

That was it, the sea bag. He hoped his heart would hold out until he got there, it was pounding uncontrollably. The first soldier seemed simply to be there, maybe as an observer or something, with no vicious feelings. Tom wasn't concerned with him. It was the second man that worried him. That son of a bitch damn near killed him back there in the jungles, and obviously hunted him down to finish the job.

The time it took reaching his gear seemed like an eternity, then he had to tip it sideways to the floor to open the top and get the knife. Thank God he didn't give them the knife, that was his. His and whoever 'Ski. He had to keep an eye on the dangerous man who was circling the room slowly, waving the tool, which made opening the God damn bag most difficult.

Jesus, finally, finally he got the top undone sliding his arm inside. Why'd he put it on the bottom? They wanted the big weapons back, he didn't have to put it there. Yeah, yeah there it is. Oh sweet Momma, the terrible thing felt so good back in his hand, no forty five to go with it but he should be able to kill this man easily enough with the knife.

His pounding heart smoothed out some now, he had his knife and was ready. Easing over to the floor lamp Tom made the final lunge, grabbing the chain, giving it a hard pull ready to slay the other occupants of his empty room.

He woke the next morning, laying on the floor under the bed, gripping his knife tightly. A careful search of the room after the incident revealed nothing, but the dream had been so real he thought it a good idea to put his sea bag in the bed and sleep on the floor under it, which he did.

New Orleans was of no interest to Tom, so he checked out the following morning and hitchhiked out of town, only this time his knife was on the top of the bag, loosely tied.

The scenery captured the returning Marine's imagination, noting all the way the similarity between the swamp like vegetation on both sides of the road, to that in the Pacific. Staring at the green topped drainage ditches following the highway, he thought about how many of those stinking algae covered waterways he'd crossed, especially in Guadalcanal, wondering each time if the ambush ending his life would take place there.

It was impossible to realize he was back home, in Louisiana. This was his home all right, although he'd spent more time as a Marine in the south Pacific, than a civilian in LaFayette. He didn't know what home was really, except it must be where someone loves you. He wondered if they'd love him now, if they knew what he had done? Was there any way they could tell what he had become? Would it show? Did he get rid of the smell of the dead he'd spent so much of this past year with? What would he say to Jane Guidry? His heart ached when he thought of Jane, and her dead son Paul. He didn't understand now, and never would in the future, why he was the one coming back. What a shame, about Paul, the priesthood suffered a big loss there.

"You in the South Pacific?" The driver of the Model A pickup was asking.

"Yeah." Tom snapped out of his mental wanderings.

"How long?"

"The whole thing."

"Jesus, you must have seen a lot of them Japs then."

"A few."

"Kill any?"

"Probably."

"Don't you know?"

"Hard to tell most times. Lots of shootin' going on. They shoot some. You shoot some. Maybe you hit somebody? It's hard to tell."

"Boy hot damn, wish I could've gone. Too young for the last one and too old for this one. Caught right slap dab in the middle." His knuckles grew white from the extra grip as he spat out the window, dangerously. "Shit man I missed all the fun."

"Yeah, that's too bad," Tom wasn't even thinking about the conversation, "it sure was fun."

He stopped in Opelousas to eat at a favored restaurant. Every time he came up this way in the past with the old man, they always ate there.

"Best damn roast chicken and duck in the whole wide world Tom." He became accustomed quickly to Alex's exaggerated claims, but found this wasn't among them. It was superb. "Don't know how they season it." He explained to the delighted young man with him, who could not have cared less how they seasoned it. He didn't know whether he had ever eaten anything as good as this. "I ask the waiter every time I come in, what's in it, and he gives me a sweet smile and don't tell me shit! Damn it Tom this's what you call shirt sleeve eatin', you know that?"

"It's run by colored you know." The racial comment came unsolicited from the man he asked for directions. "Lots of folks don't know that, but it's owned and operated by colored."

He was startled by the tall Marine with the strange eyes, as he picked up his sea bag asking. "Yeah? What color are they?"

He didn't wait for an answer. Having recently come through what he had, seeing life diminished to its lowest, a moment by moment proposition, Tom never could get into anything resembling racial discussions. A life was a life, color didn't mean a thing.

It was late when he finally reached LaFayette, and how true it was, what the Old Man said about coming home. It sure smelled good though, this south Louisiana town in early fall. He thought it smelled a lot like home, as he walked toward the Guidry house in his unusual, canted gait.

The gold star hanging in the window, brought back terrible memories of his last moments with Paul, on that blood soaked beach at Tarawa. He stood looking at the small banner hanging below the shade, listening to the screaming shells and deafening machine gun and rifle fire. Living the terrible heat and stench of the beach, smoke drifting about, while he knelt, holding the boys lifeless body. The words of the chaplain. That's what that gold star was to him, and would be, until it was taken down.

He'd purposely waited until after the family had gone to bed, because he was nervous about their first meeting. It bothered him, he didn't know what he was going to say to Jane when they met for the first time.

Tom went to the heavy bushes lining the Guidry's yard, drifting alongside them until reaching the extreme back of the yard. It was so natural, the stealth of the tall exMarine as he made his way to the unlocked cabin, and went to bed.

They came again that night, but he was ready for them, this time, his knife was under the mattress. They let him sleep most of the night entering the cabin shortly before dawn. These were the dead from the vile draw on Okinawa, Japanese and Marines. They were a disgusting lot in their various stages of decay. Tom asked them to go away, and stay away. He told them in the hush of the dream, he no longer wanted or needed their company. They'd served their purpose and he thought they should stay in their graves. The war was over, let's forget it. That's what he wanted them to know, but they weren't listening.

One of the rotting ghouls sat on the edge of his bed, bending over to see Tom better, causing his last eye, and the left side of his face to slide off, falling on the bed. He awoke with a start again, reaching for his knife while his pulse roared. It was some time before he could get the horrible dead out of his mind and their smell out of his nostrils, while listening to his heart gradually slow down.

"Always darkest before the dawn." Yeah that was the old saying and it sure was true, just as it was right now. He knew there would be no more sleep that night. Well that was OK he'd lived on cat naps for the last three years anyway. He'd already slept almost six hours, a great deal more than he was accustomed to at one time, so he sat on the edge of his bed and smoked until the light of dawn. He slipped on his fatigues and went out on the small porch, to watch the sun come up through the huge oak trees that lined the bayou. It was quite balmy.

The spring on the back screen door always squeaked and Tom looked up to see Nancy standing on the top step holding her hand to her mouth, staring directly at him. She came off the last step walking toward her Marine, who was completely engrossed in how much she had changed. She was a woman now, about that he had no doubts. She'd grown a head taller than her mother, which in itself wasn't a big thing because Jane was so short. She looked absolutely stunning to the veteran killer of men, still a virgin.

Nancy stood looking at her foster brother, confused by his far away look, taking in the damage she could see. The maimed left hand. The scar in the middle of his chest from Peleliu. Sores from constant exposure to rain on Okinawa in various stages of healing. It was his eyes that hurt her more than anything else. She'd never seen anything like them before, that seemed to hold so much horror and anguish.

"Hi Nancy." He sounded like the same shy boy that Albert brought home six years before. "Looks like I made it." He didn't know what that meant, it was merely something to say.

"Oh Tom, Tom!" She was immersed in tears incapable of understanding her emotion of the moment. Never in her life had she felt anything like this. Extreme joy at seeing him, great concern for the wounds he'd suffered, questioning how much change had taken place in his mind, and profound sadness because Paul was not here to share the moment.

"Tom."

It was all she could say, completely overwhelmed. She stepped forward putting her arms around him, her dark hair pressed against his chest. Hesitantly he put his arms around the beautiful girl, holding her gently, as he felt her body tremble with sobs.

"Thanks for the letters Nancy." He didn't know what to say or do, but he was acutely aware of how soft she was and how good she smelled.

'Must've just stepped out of the bath.' He thought, suddenly terrified lest she be able to detect the horrible odors from the draw on Okinawa.

Nancy could only nod her head in return, holding him tight, surprising the deadly object of her attentions by kissing him full on the lips. It was not the kiss of a sister.

"How's Mama, Nancy?" He was really trying, doing the best he could, but this most violent Marine simply had no experience whatever with women. Everything was pure reflex.

"She's doing fine now, Tom. It was hard for awhile, you know after we got the news about Paul, but her faith and your letter about how Paul died, really helped her through that time." She was still holding Tom around his waist, looking up in his face, her dark eyes highlighted by her tears.

"My God Nancy, you have grown." It was awkward, but the dark haired beauty knew exactly what he meant, feeling very much the female for knowing.

"Brooks!"

The shout from the back steps interrupted their welcome. Jane was standing on the back porch in her usual pose with one foot balanced on the heel, tapping furiously in the air.

"Brooks! Breakfast's being served and I'm not serving it down there." Then to her daughter in mock impatience. "Nancy, let go of that boy so he can get some clothes on." Her voice broke as she added. "Five minutes Brooks!" Turning back into her kitchen like nothing had happened these last four years.

The smile Jane Guidry elicited from Tom, was the first Nancy was aware of, and it made her feel good. "I'll wait on the porch Tom, while you get a shirt."

'What the hell's the matter now?' Tom thought listening to the familiar pounding of his heart. It felt like it had in the jungles, while he crouched waiting to kill.

Tom and Nancy walked slowly toward the back of the house, Nancy holding his hand.

'My God, could it be? Could it possibly be?' Jane asked her God as she watched the two young people. Had Jane known what God did, her emotions would have been entirely different.

"Look Mama!" Nancy was laughing and crying. "Look who I found down by the bayou!" Still holding Tom's hand as they stood inside the door. He looked for all the world like he did the first time he entered that kitchen in 1939.

"Guess what Brooks, the deal hasn't changed even a little bit in six years! No hug for Jane, no food for Tom! Now how do you like them apples?"

It was the first time in a long while he'd laughed out loud as he went toward the middle of the kitchen, and with one smooth motion slid a chair from under the table, picked his foster mother up, and stood her on it. He saw them now, she was a sassy coonass lady but the tears were there, and were not to be held back.

"Give me my hug, soldier boy, I haven't had one from you since nineteen forty one." The greeting was the same as with Nancy, only this was mother greeting son, home from the war.

Albert and the kids came trooping into the kitchen, each in their own stage of self consciousness. The littlest ones were not exactly hiding behind their mother's skirts, but they weren't making any bold moves either. Some of them couldn't even remember the returning Marine.

"Hey, hey Marine! Get over here!"

Albert had called the Old Man to let him know Tom was back, and he'd bring him to the yard after breakfast. He brushed aside Tom's outstretched hand grabbing him around the waist, in a powerful bear hug.

"God damn son it's good to see you." He released him looking at Albert, both had tears in their eyes. "Hey Albert, how'd Jane think he looks? Good huh?"

"Skinny Boss! She thinks he's skinny. She thinks she can fix that." He was beaming from ear to ear.

"Yeah, I'll bet she can." Turning back to Tom. "Come on inside Tom, we've got a lot to talk about."

Tom followed him into the office searching for the right thing to say.

"Sure am sorry about your son, Boss. I don't know what to say other than I wish it didn't have to be."

Alex cried for a moment, turning his swivel chair away in order not to embarrass Tom.

"Thanks Tom. None of us knows how these things work, you know what I mean? I guess God saw fit to take Alex, and for whatever reason. I don't know. Lots of boys went Tom. Lots of 'em aren't coming back."

"Miss Marie?" The question spoke volumes.

"Miss Marie?" His mood instantly reflective. "I still don't know where she came from, maybe passing by on a cloud full of angels and decided to get off here. Maybe He told her there was a wild coonass down here that needed a gentle hand. Hell I don't know, it's really something though. I do know she took Mary's loss far, far better than I did. When we received the news about Alex I was afraid it would kill her, but it didn't. She went to the well again? She's strong Tom, much stronger than I am. I want to help her when it comes to these enormous sorrows, and she always winds up helping me. Funny isn't it?" Suddenly returning to the present. "So how's everything with you, son?"

"Fine. I'm fine Mr. Alex." A man accustomed to dealing with men, Alex George knew that statement was pure bullshit. He could see clearly everything was not fine, but it was okay, at least he understood what he'd come through. He made the same journey, twenty seven years before.

"Yeah." He mused. "I did the same thing. I know how tough it is to make the transition from a battle field to home. You have to experience it to know what it's like. Looking at somebody you love across a table, catching a glimpse of someone you might have killed. I don't know where you've been or what you've seen, but I do want you to know, I understand." Leaning across his desk, looking intently at Tom. "I really do understand what you're thinking, and what you've been involved in."

They talked at great length, the Old Man studying his young friend carefully. Much was going on behind those eyes, and Alex wondered if he would ever learn what it was. He did know the South Pacific war was a particularly savage affair, neither side taking many prisoners. He could only imagine what a barbaric thing war must be without the taking of prisoners. The papers said six thousand Japanese dead on Tarawa, seventeen taken prisoner. That was a bloodbath.

Listening to Tom, Alex was aware he'd lost many close friends in those violent places. Nancy told him Tom had found Paul's body on Tarawa. Thinking that, he saw Myron lying dead in the field of wheat in France. He inhaled deeply, holding it to keep from crying out. His eyes were full of tears as he listened to Tom talk about all the meaningless bullshit he knew he was being told, to keep him from knowing the rest. That was okay, there'd be another time.

"Tell you what Tom, no sense in you being in a big hurry to do anything. You got a job here whenever you're ready. I got lots of plans for the future, yours and mine, but they'll wait." The tone of his voice changed suddenly, completely. "Some things won't wait though Tom." Alex dropped his head looking at the floor, pausing a long time while struggling for composure. "Miss Marie? She wants to see you. She knows you're back, she's waiting for you at the house. I know it's tough, but will you go see her?" Tom had never before heard him speak this way. He was pleading. "Take one of the cars out front and go on over to the house, she'll be there." His eyes were full of tears again. "She needs to see you, son."

Blowing a bunker, shooting, using the knife was much easier than what he was about to do. Alex George's wife had the reputation of being a near saint, a reputation she rebuffed but true nevertheless. Her kind of pain and suffering would be inconceivable to someone like this deadly assassin, coming to pay his respects.

The questions came in uncontrolled waves as he pulled in the driveway alongside the house on his way to the back. That's where she'd be, in the kitchen, it was her favorite room. The gold star in the window was almost more than he could bear.

'Hey God, you listening?' He could never decide if these short chats with God constituted praying. He wasn't that concerned. 'If you are I wish you'd let me know why I'm here, and her son isn't? I don't understand that? After what I've done, I come back and he doesn't? I gotta tell you I don't understand that at all'?

"Miss Marie?" He knocked gently on the back screen. "It's me Miss Marie, Tom Brooks."

He saw her coming through the long hall, alongside the stairs. It was a big, beautiful, old style wood house, high ceilings, cool even on the hottest days. It was peaceful there.

Her eyes too were full of tears as she opened the back screen.

"Welcome home Tom, it's so good to see you."

As her arms went around the recent butcher of men, confusing thoughts entered his mind.

'What is this? What strange, strange thing is this? This gentle, loving woman in the same world with me, holding me? How can that be possible?'

She hadn't changed much, still quite attractive, matronly, a little heavier maybe. Looked tired though, probably because of what she'd been through, but the same eminent tenderness. Just to be around her was some sort of reward in itself.

They sat at the oilcloth covered, round kitchen table and talked for hours. Her small French drip coffee pot filled many times. Tom hadn't had dark roast coffee since he left, and it was good. He saw her compassionate glance at the back of his hand and the terrible scar left from the shovel of the doomed enemy soldier on Guadalcanal. When she wasn't looking he put it in his lap or pocket, he didn't want to share with her anything of the dark side of his life she should never know. Later when his mind was somewhere else, she took his scarred hand in hers, staring at it with renewed tears.

"That's nothing Miss Marie, somebody found a football and a bunch of us were horsing around. Would you believe I went out for a pass and ran into a parked jeep. Really tore it up didn't I?"

No, she wouldn't believe, but she didn't tell him that.

"Do come and see me often, Tom. You look like you could use a little weight and my cookies might help. Do boys your age still eat cookies?"

'Boys?' He thought. 'Me? When was I ever a boy?'

"I suppose Jane will be trying to fatten you up too. Oh Tom, didn't Nancy grow up to be a pretty girl. She comes over often and we talk a lot. I do love her, you know." It was time for Tom to go, he didn't know why or where, but he knew it was time to go. He was no good at this. "Do come back Tom, I really want you to and if you'd like, bring Nancy."

Oh sure, that was it. He and young Alex were about the same age, and Nancy and their daughter Mary would be about the same age too. She'd lost her children so soon, she would naturally be interested in them.

The visitations of the specters and ghouls from Tom's immediate past increased in frequency and sinister intent. He dreaded the night because he knew they were coming, and while he wasn't afraid of them as such, they came to remind him of his abnormal behavior in the affairs of war. He'd gone far beyond acceptable behavior, even amidst the madness that was the south Pacific fighting. They would stand or sit in his cabin, turning their bitterness and sorrow toward Tom, asking silently why they were dead, while he enjoyed life. They brought the stench of their own decay with them, dressed in sloppy wet battle dress, fouling the cabin with their aura of disgusting rot. It was always the same, Tom reluctant to sleep, knowing they were illusions but despising their visits anyway. They stayed too long when they came and he was having more and more difficulty differentiating what was real, and what was dream. He'd had to bear these visits alone, fearful lest anyone discover his secret. Nancy did in a mind shattering experience.

It was a perfectly beautiful moonlit night, the kind usually reserved for young lovers, when Nancy first discovered Tom's gargantuan struggles with his past. Until this night she had no idea what was troubling him.

Her sleep had been interrupted by an annoying tug back to consciousness. She resisted, drifting almost to the point of sleep, then startled from drowsiness to fully awake, finally giving up the attempt altogether. The trip to the bathroom wasn't one of necessity, more something to do, thinking that might be the reason for her inability to stay asleep.

She checked her two small sisters, who shared the room with her. They were right where she wanted to be, sleeping. Returning to her bed she glanced out the window, freezing in fear as she saw the crouched man outlined so clearly against the tall, grass like bushes that surrounded the yard. With a pounding heart she watched his stealthy movements, still in a deep crouch, stopping for awhile, then inching toward the bayou. Nancy was about to wake her father to tell him of the interloper when he stood slowly, pushing the hedge back, until he reached full height. Nancy realized then it was Tom. Knowing there was nothing to fear from him she put on her robe, went down the stairs, and out in the moon drenched yard to see what he was doing.

By the time she reached the hedge he was nowhere to be seen, which caused her a little concern, but because of her ignorance concerning Tom's activities of the last three years, there was no fear. Had she known his mental condition she would have been horrified.

"Tom?"

It was really more thought than a whisper, the first time she called. There was no answer.

"Tom?" Louder now, but still no answer.

Thinking he might have gone back in his cabin, while she came down the stairs, she called to him through the screen, hearing nothing in reply. After entering the cabin to determine he wasn't there, she stood on the porch trying to figure where he could be, when she heard a slight water sound. Rushing to the bayou she peered intently in the inky black water, trying to find her elusive quarry when her blood froze at an unexpected glint of light on the surface a few short feet from where she stood.

"Tom, is that you?" She bent down to have a better look at the source of the glitter. "Tom, it's Nancy! Is that you?"

"Shhhhhh." It was soft, coming exactly from where she had seen the glint.

"Tom, what are you doing in there?" There was still no answer, only soft movement in the water followed by a lightning thrust of his arm, grabbing Nancy by the ankle in a steel grip.

"Get down!" He whispered out of the darkness of his watery refuge. "They'll see you."

She could see him now, following his arm from her ankle over the bank and into the bayou. He was pressed up against the bank, submerged, holding on to a root with his other hand. That hand also held his deadly knife.

"Who, Tom?" Her soft reply. "Who're you hiding from?"

"Japs! They're all over the place." He still held her ankle tightly, raising his head above the surface of the bank. That was when she saw for the first time the wild look in his eyes. She'd seen that look before, but only once, when she came on a dog that had been hit by a car. It was laying by the side of the road, terribly injured, rolling its eyes in unknowing terror when she reached down to help. She bore a scar on her wrist resulting from that effort where the terrified, dying animal had torn her flesh in its last agony. She was thinking fast, her heart and mind nearly exploding in compassion for this obviously wounded creature, that held her in an unrelenting grip.

"Tom," she loosened her robe letting it fall to the ground, "take my hand. I'm coming in with you." His response was good, and immediate, as he released her leg, took her hand, and gently supported her as she slid silently into the water beside him. It was cold, very cold, but she was unmindful, wanting only to help this man she loved so much.

Tom wafted between fantasy and reality, he knew who Nancy was, but could not understand why she was in this enemy infested area. It was like the time she came to him in that stinking, wretched, foxhole in Okinawa. He loved seeing her, but wanted her to go away.

"Where are they, Tom?" Nancy held the same root whispering in his ear. "I don't see them."

"Don't know. Bushes, maybe." It was a fantastic conversation in a like surrounding. Tom drew her close to him, aware in some distant part of his agonized brain how soft she felt, how nice it was to have her this close.

"I'll look Tom. With my hair they can't see me look over the bank. I'll be careful, I promise." He didn't answer but gave silent agreement by lifting her gently so she could see clearly the whole back yard. "They're gone." She whispered, sliding back into the water, "I know they're gone. They probably know we're ready for them and left. Come on, let's be quiet. Let's get out of here and back to the cabin. Will that be okay?"

They crawled on the thick grass back to the cabin, slowly, cautiously. The legendary south Pacific butcher, and the seventeen year old girl.

"Let me look in the cabin, Tom." She breathed in his ear. "I don't think they like me being here, and are probably gone. Those that haven't I'll ask to leave. Okay?"

"Yeah, okay." He was still whispering. "I'm right here. If they try anything, they're dead."

She knew looking at him now, pressed tight up against the cabin wall gripping that terrible looking knife, he was obviously skilled in these kinds of things. She didn't know what kind of skills they were but certainly recognized something deadly waiting to fall on its prey.

Upon confirming the Japanese had truly left, Nancy got him to go back to bed with the promise she would stay with him, watching while he got some sleep.

"I promise Tom, I'll wake you up the minute I see or hear anything. You've got to get some sleep now, you simply can't go on without sleep."

After restless, fitful attempts at sleep, all ending in explosive consciousness, Nancy got into bed with her wounded Marine. She drew the covers up around them, put her arms around him pulling his head to her breast, whispering softly through the night whenever he moved quickly. "It's all right Tom. It's me, Nancy. They're gone baby. Go to sleep." Each time followed by a reassuring hug. He slept fitfully the night through, dimly aware of that far away warm and comfortable sensation of his mother holding him the same way, her voice rumbling in his ear.

Jane was startled the next morning, when her oldest daughter came in the kitchen from the back yard, and could tell she had little or no sleep. Before she had the opportunity to say something regrettable, Nancy burst into tears running across the kitchen floor into the outstretched arms of her mother. Between exhaustion from no sleep, and her sobbing, she had great difficulty telling her mother the story of what happened, but finally succeeded.

"Oh my God!" Jane's eyes filled with tears. "Oh my God what have they done to him? When will it be over?" Her mind was going in a totally different direction than what it was only a moment before. "Is he asleep now Nancy?"

"Yes Mama." She was in tears.

"I don't want your father to see you like this, or to know what happened last night. Fathers think only one thing in matters like this, and that is sex." Nancy started to object. "Hush now, I know nothing like that happened, but being a man he wouldn't. Go upstairs and get in bed, and when he's ready for breakfast I'll tell him you have a cold." A part of her strange story sifted through Jane's fast moving mind. "My God child I didn't even ask, are you all right? I can't imagine going into that dark cold water. Do you feel okay?"

She was still crying out of control, managing to sob.

"Oh yes Mama. It broke my heart watching him look for the men who weren't there." She pulled away looking at her mother, her dark eyes flashed brilliantly. "I wanted to find them too! I wanted to find them and fight them with him! Do you understand that Mama?"

Her mother took her in her arms again, holding her close, crying softly. "Yes Cher, I understand. I do understand. I loved your father so much when we were married, I would have given up my life for him in a minute. That's what it is sweetheart, you love Tom. I know that. I've known that for years. Hush now baby, go on up to bed before Papa gets here."

'Please God, please bring that boy back to us.' Tom's foster mother prayed while preparing breakfast. 'Something terrible must have happened to him in that stupid war. Paul didn't come back to us dear God, and I accept Your will in that. I'm sure he's with You in eternity now and that gives me comfort, but Tom's different. We got him back dear Lord, but his mind seems to have been hurt so bad. Please God, I know love is great power. Please let her love, pull him back from wherever he is.'

It was one of many prayers Jane prayed, knowing her daughter was leaving the house every night to be with her warrior. She went to the cabin every night and either sat in a chair keeping watch for him, or if his dreams were too terrible held him in her arms while fighting off the ethereal visitors, until the last night.

"My God Nancy, what happened?" Alex George rushed around his desk when he saw the horrified, disheveled girl standing in the doorway to his office.

"Oh Mr. Alex." She was near hysteria. "I didn't know what to do. Where to go?"

"What is it, child? Is it Tom?"

She told the Old Man the whole story, between sobs, up to the final moment before he left.

"I was holding him in my arms last night. It was one of his worst. They kept coming at him all through the night. His friends, somebody named Bobby and a boy named Pat. He talked with them...on a farm somewhere." Fatigue and mental anguish were tearing her apart, bringing her sobs in a continuous stream. "Oh Mr. Alex, he cried so when he saw Paul again. He kept asking why it couldn't have been him instead." Her beautiful dark eyes widened in utter horror. "He asked Pat what they'd done with his head and his hands. Said he put them back where they belonged. Mr. Alex," she looked around furtively, whispering so no one could hear, "he told Pat he took care of the Japs for him. He said," she broke down completely in total agony, "he threw many Japanese heads behind their lines."

"Oh my God Cher." Alex held her close, trying to take some of her pain away, thinking. 'She's much, much too young for this sort of thing.'

"We were laying in bed...." Aware of what she had implied. "Mama knew I was there Mr. Alex. She knew we weren't doing anything wrong...."

"I know Nancy, I know. Go on child, what happened then?"

"He seemed to have quieted down, you know, sleeping pretty good when he grew restless again. I gave him a quick little hug and he exploded. He threw me clear out of the bed and was on top of me instantly, choking me with his left hand while searching for his knife."

The Old Man's eyes filled with tears, imagining the nightmarish scene involving these two young people he loved so much.

"I was pinned down, trying to breathe, terrified he was going to find that knife before he discovered who I was. He leaned far away from me searching for the knife, but still on top of me. I got his hand off my throat. I called his name, 'Tom, Tom, oh Tom. I'm Nancy. Please let me up Tom. I'm Nancy. I'm not Japanese. I'm Paul's sister Tom! Paul! Please let me up.' Something I said reached him and he stopped searching. He sat perfectly still, on my stomach, and seemed to be listening."

"What then Cher?"

"It was pitch black, and he was trying hard to understand where he was. He was sitting on my stomach, his knees straddling me, but not choking me anymore. His hand went up to my hair, feeling it all over my head, then he bent way over where our faces were almost touching. I knew he was trying to see who I was, and I said his name again."

"Did he recognize you then?"

"Yes! Finally! He asked if I was Nancy. He was whispering so soft I could hardly hear him and his lips were touching my ear. I said yes! I was Nancy Guidry. Jane's girl. Paul's sister. He jumped off of me and turned on the light."

Her sobbing reached the point of hysteria.

"Oh Mr. Alex if you could have seen his face when he realized it was me. I have never seen such horror and suffering in my life. He picked me up off the floor and held me while he cried. My God Mr. Alex he cried. He told me how sorry he was. He was dreaming when a Jap jumped out at him. It must've been the same moment I hugged him close and he thought I was the Jap. He was heart broken. I told him it was all right, but he said no, no it wasn't. It wasn't all right at all. He got his clothes on fast and I asked where he was going. He said he didn't know, but he knew he couldn't be around people anymore." She broke down in uncontrollable weeping.

"What then Nancy? What happened then?"

"Mr. Alex," her look of agony was too much for the Old Man to bear, "he said he was too dangerous to live with people. He said he'd killed far too much to ever be allowed to live among them again. He looked like he was dying, wild eyed, frightened. He said he shouldn't have been the one to come back, that God made a mistake. He said anyone who did what he had, should be dead. He looked at me so sad and said he wished it could have worked out for us. He wanted to tell me he loved me, I know he did, but he didn't know how."

The Old Man held her like he would his own daughter, thinking of her as such, at that moment. His heart was torn too, at the agony these two special young people were going through.

"Where is he now Cher?"

"I don't know. He grabbed that terrible knife and said he had to go back where he couldn't hurt anybody."

"Back? Back where?"

"I don't know Mr. Alex, but please find him. Please don't let anything happen to him. I love him so Mr. Alex. Please find him and bring him back. He's suffered so much already, I just want to love him and help him forget that horrible war."

So did Alex George. He wanted to help the boy too. He wanted many things for Tom, but locating him now was first.

Nancy told him Tom left before dawn, running down the long row of bushes that outlined the Guidry property, disappearing around the end heading down the street in the direction of the huge Atchafalaya swamp.

'Yeah, that's it,' Alex thought, 'what more likely place than the swamp. Pretty much like where he's been for the past three years. That's where he went.'

Alex drove in the direction of the swamp, stopping along the way to ask if anyone had seen him, finally locating someone who had.

"Looked kind of different he did, that's why I noticed him. Long loping stride, turned kind of funny. You know, like he was running half sideways. Looked like he was ready to go forever like that. Mighty serious lookin' too. He do anything wrong?"

"No, no. He works for me and I need to see him right away is all. Thanks."

He was moving down the shell road before he finished his statement.

'Boy this place never changes.' He thought as he slipped the boat into the inky black water. 'Looks like it did the first time Papa brought me here.' The outboard motor was a welcome addition to those old days of the paddle or pole. He moved swiftly into the main body of the swamp. He thought one of the boats usually sitting on the bank at the end of the road was missing, but wasn't sure. Tom was in this swamp, he was sure of that, and intended to find him.

"Tom! Tom Brooks!" Alex shouted into the gloomy surroundings. "Tom, Alex George here! Where are you?"

His only answer was a large water bird screaming in protest at this unwelcome interruption to its early morning feeding, large wings flapping as it flew somewhere else.

His camp was the first place he looked, because Tom had been out there many times in the past and knew where it was, but to no avail. He combed the waterways looking everywhere, finally spotting the missing pirogue on the bank of a small island. He drifted in shutting off the motor, floating in to the bank.

"Tom, you in there?"

Listening carefully, while trying to see into the dense growth of the island.

"It's me Alex George. If you're in there, come on out son, will you? I'd like to talk to you." He looked toward his left when he saw swift movement on his right. It was Tom, he felt sure of that as he stepped out of the boat onto the bank, heading toward the movement.

"Listen Tom, Nancy told me what happened last night. She's terribly worried about you, asked me to find you and bring you back."

He was struggling trying to make his way through the dense vegetation toward the spot he thought the movement came from. The light was only fair, slanting through the thick trees and vines illuminating everything in a strange muted way. He saw movement again in the opposite direction to where he was headed, wondering how whatever it was could be first one place and then another. It had to be Tom. Only a skilled jungle fighter could move like that.

"Hey Tom, I wish you'd come on out here and talk to me, 'cause obviously I'm not going to be able to run you down in there." Laughing. "Shit, I'm not as good at this as you must be and I'm sure not in good enough shape to be fighting these vines and things. How 'bout it Tom, come on out? Christ you must know we all love you. We only want to help...."

"Did she tell you what I did?" The voice startled him, he didn't know what direction it came from. "Do you know I almost killed her?" The voice quivered with emotion.

"Yes, she did. That's why I'm here. She didn't tell her Dad for fear he'd get things wrong, so she came to me. She may only be seventeen but she's a smart kid."

He was talking to the wall of trees and vines, that seemed to be where the voice was coming from, then he saw Tom move between some trees.

"She loves you Tom," he was pushing his way toward the area of movement, "and she told me about everything since you got home. That's what I want to talk to you about. Will you come out and talk to me?"

"I'm afraid to be around people, Mr. Alex." He was stunned, the voice came from yet another direction. "I shouldn't have come back. No, no. Too dangerous. I'll kill somebody, and not mean to. I should have been killed out there. That's what they do to a mad dog isn't it?"

The Old Man couldn't see him, but the voice tore at his soul. It was pure agony and despair.

"Tom come out and talk to me, will 'ya? There's no way I can run you down in there. I'll wait for you right here on the bank. Don't be afraid of hurting me son, because I'm not afraid of you doing that. Don't forget I can handle myself too. We have to talk though, and I don't want to do it looking at a bunch of trees. How about it, come on out here and we'll talk? Better yet let's go to the camp and talk. We got everything there we need, and can stay as long as you want. How 'bout it?"

He was startled when Tom stood up in full view, close to where he was standing. Nancy was right, he looked like a wounded animal. Wild eyed fear was obvious, with one added factor. This animal knew what his problem was.

"Okay Mr. Alex, I'll go. I'd feel a lot better about it though if you'd take this," offering the inscribed killing knife to his relieved pursuer, "I'd feel better."

Alex George was crying quietly as he towed Tom, seated in the stolen pirogue, toward the camp. The brutish south Pacific killer was sitting in a docile manner as they cut through the black water. Alex looked around, reminded of the times he'd pulled young Alex in a wagon. There was none of that innocence behind him now though, only vicious, violent, terrible death.

'My God what we demand of our youth. Go do this for us and then we'll forget it happened? Wonder who's responsible for this shit? God how I'd like them to be with me now. Love to see how they'd handle this. But that's bullshit, huh? People responsible for these things are never around when the shooting stops.'

"First things first Tom." They were sitting on the small porch of the cabin in the swamp. "Nancy's okay. Oh sure you scared the shit out of the kid, but other than that she's okay. I want you to know that, right now. That child does love you, like a full grown woman, and what she wants is what we all want. She wants you back with us, all the way. Do you understand?"

"Yes sir, I do." Answered in his low rumbling voice.

"But you're afraid you might have gone too far to make it back, is that it?"

"Yes sir, it is."

"Yes, well I was sure of that because of what Nancy told me."

His eyes grew wide with agonized fear. "Oh my God Mr. Alex, what did I tell her?"

"You were dreaming, just before she startled you. Talkin' to a boy named Bobbie. Something about his farm?"

"What else?"

"You saw Paul again. He was dead on the beach. You were holding him and talking to him."

"And?"

"A boy named Pat."

"What about Pat?"

"You told him you put his head, and hands, back where they belonged...." Tom got up from the chair he was sitting in, with a look of horror on his face as he walked to the screened outer wall staring out at nothing. The Old Man's heart was breaking, because he knew what an enormous load of guilt this boy must be carrying right now. Not only his savage part in the war, but the fact he had made Nancy a participant too.

"I can't go back, Mr. Alex." He was staring into the tangled undergrowth. "I'm too far gone to go back."

"Bullshit! Yes you can Tom! I'm telling you God damn it, you can! You're not the only man who's been changed by the primitive brutalities of war! You're not the first, and you won't be the last! You can make it back, son!" Alex was on fire with emotion. He was battling right now, for this boy to survive him. He had nothing left in children of his own. He'd fight for this one.

"Don't think so, Mr. Alex. I went too far."

"Because of the number of men you killed, or the way?"

"Both."

Alex launched into a long story of his own experiences in his war, including every man he'd killed and the barbaric emotions that controlled him at the moment.

"I was young, yeah and innocent too. I mean innocent. I was raised up around here where there was nothin' but hard times and lots of love. To be yanked up out of here and put on the killing fields of France was a son of a bitch. My friend Myron died our first day out and when I found him, my mind exploded. I was a powerful boy Tom, and when we made it to the German lines I jumped into their trench, and was face to face with a man much older than myself. The thought flashed through my mind he was no match for me, when he raised his rifle and I ran my bayonet through his throat." The Old Man's voice dropped suddenly at the memory. "His eyes were huge as he realized he was dying, but he was still standing. I pulled the bayonet out and smashed his face with the butt of my rifle." Alex burst into tears at the hoped for forgotten episode, now brought back to life, so vividly. "Oh Jesus Christ Tom, I didn't want to kill that man. I had nothing against him. He looked to be about the age of my Papa. I wish I could have met him some other way, some other place. Maybe we could have had a beer or something. Maybe we could have had a fist fight, or made love to the same woman but I killed him instead. Then I whirled around to see a young German soldier run around a bend in the trench and shot him straight through the heart."

Tom suddenly felt great compassion for the Old Man, temporarily distracted from his own sorrows, because he was sitting with his head hanging down weeping openly, unashamed, searching his soul for some sort of forgiveness, as he related his story.

"It's always the same shit, the old guys start the wars and the young ones have their lives changed forever, one way or the other, because we have to finish them. We go in and do what we're taught from birth is an aberration. Thou shalt not kill. We are taught that right out of the chute, thou shalt not kill and then the old farts put weapons in our hands and say, sic 'em. Don't you see what insane bullshit that is? What kind of an emotional roller coaster that is? Those assholes turn us on and off like a God damn light switch, only there's one hell of a difference. We remember."

Alex had no way of knowing what he was doing for his young protege, but by telling his own story he was opening a line of communication through identification and understanding. Before this day he had never told Tom any details of his own tour of duty with the Marines. That he was in the first war yes, but no details whatever.

"Don't you see Tom, I do know what you're going through. Don't you think I've thought of the Germans I killed, some while looking in their eyes, some over the sights of my rifle. They're with me all the time, but that was yesterday. It's gone son, and I can't do a God damn thing about it. I've forgiven myself, because I know I had no choice. But it's done with and nothing I might wish, will make it any different."

"Did you do the things I did?" Tom asked, still standing by the screened area.

"Yes. Yes I did. Maybe not the same way, but I killed!"

"Did you ever cut a mans head off?" The question was spoken so softly, he had difficulty hearing it.

"No son, I didn't, but you must remember we were fighting a different enemy. I know it's an obscene joke but we killed one another in a civilized manner. We didn't encounter the kind of savagery I read was a way of life out there in the Pacific, but killing a human being is a mighty bad thing no matter what." He paused. "Well most of the time, anyway."

"Most of the time?" Tom turned his head slowly.

"Yeah. Some people on this earth simply shouldn't be here. I don't know why they're here, but they are nevertheless. They're the sinister con artists. They fuck people over, hurt 'em, stomp the shit out of 'em, kill 'em, and somehow keep walking the streets. Some the state gets, imprisons or kills. Many walk the streets as free as you or I. They shouldn't be allowed to do that."

He told Tom all about his friend Sue and what she had meant to him, with no apologies for her lifestyle. He left out nothing from the beginning of their relationship to the time of her murder, emphasizing how much she had helped him, at the time of Mary's death.

"So you see Tom it seems as though we keep killing the wrong people. My old guy in the trench, probably most of the Japanese you killed, and a beautiful person like Sue. Murdered, all of them, and the murderers get off. Hers walks the streets because of some legality bullshit." Adding viciously through tightly clenched teeth. "I'd like to kill that motherfucker myself."

They spent the entire day talking, Tom's story coming reluctantly, a piece at a time until Alex knew what he had to know.

"What we have here Tom, is a situation where you did what had to be done. You simply adapted as human beings will, and when all accepted rules of warfare were dropped, somehow you understood that better than your buddies. Please don't give up on yourself, or consider yourself too dangerous for human companionship because I don't think you are. Yes, obviously you turned into a savage killer out there, but I'm telling you Tom, then is then and now is now. Let's get this thing handled and move on. I don't have anybody else now, kids that is, and you're the one I'm looking to fill that role. We're going to fight to bring you all the way back, and we're going to get on it right away."

"You mind if I stay out here for awhile Mr. Alex?"

"Think you should?"

"Yes sir, for a little while."

"Okay Tom, okay but let's make a two way deal.?"

"How?"

"Stay out here as long as you want. I understand that, but I want you to come and see me every day so we can talk. Will you do that?"

"Yes sir."

"And I want you to go see Mama everyday too."

Tom turned to his mentor. "I don't think I can do that Boss."

"You know I'll never tell her anything about what happened to you, Tom."

"Afraid something might slip out. She shouldn't know about that."

"Yeah I know what you mean, you read her pretty good. Don't worry though, I've only told her as much as I want her to know about the first war, sure never told her about what I did. No, I want you to see her every day too, for her sake and yours."

It started to rain as they finished their long conversation at the camp. Alex suggested they go back into town, get one of the old pickups at the yard so he could bring it back to camp, and stay as long as he'd like. He left Tom's knife in the cabin.

It was a long and terrible struggle, pulling Tom back from the brink of insanity but through his talks with the Boss, and his long afternoon sessions with Miss Marie he made his way slowly back to the world of normality. He got understanding and identification from the one, the purest of pure love from the other.

Miss Marie fought for his mind and soul with a tenacity usually seen only in the wild, that of a mother animal whose offspring is threatened. They met afternoons and talked for hours, this practice going on for nearly a year when it was deemed time and he was well enough to begin the fall term at school.

The setting was always the same, the kitchen, the two of them sitting across the oil cloth talking. Mama knew nothing about psychiatry but she was practicing it. He was her last chance at something like a child of her own. She would fight for this child.

Nancy was something else, she loved him with all her heart like a woman loves a man, helping however she could, waiting only for his complete recovery from his hideous experiences. She wanted to marry her Marine, right then. He wanted to marry her too, but not until he could trust himself not to try and kill her again, sometime in the night.

Alex consulted with, and arranged for treatment from, the best men in the field of psychiatry and asked Tom to see them, work with them, do whatever they said, which he did. He always did whatever this man asked or suggested he do, and why not? Alex George had literally given him life, twice. When he was well enough the following year, to go to Harvard School of Business he had the best in the field of psychiatry, waiting for him in Boston.

'Jesus what a struggle!'

Tom wheeled the big Lincoln in his driveway, hauntingly aware of the lady that waited for him. The same one that went into the bayou that night, and slid along the grass with her warrior to meet the enemy. Their enemy. The same lady he nearly killed so long ago. She was going to get a special hug tonight. He almost panicked when he thought about making her wait until he graduated from Harvard before getting married, but it was necessary at the time. He had to make sure he was all right before he would allow the marriage to take place.

'Thanks God for having her wait.'

He had tears in his eyes as he drove in the driveway.

CHAPTER 18

"Okay Tom, it's time to get movin'."

It was one week exactly since they last got together and Tom had not heard a single word from the Old Man, which was exactly what he intended. He had presented his views, and those of his beloved Momma, now it was time to act.

"I'm ready."

"Really?"

"Yes sir, I am."

"All right, but before we begin let me ask you something."

It was the Old Man he'd known all his life. There was a no nonsense, business like manner about him that Tom admired all their working life.

"I have to ask, even though I'm sure of your answer, what your degree of loyalty is to me"

"Total!" Tom's immediate answer.

"You're a wealthy man now, Tom. You can cut the cord anytime you want and walk on down the road, if you like. I know we go back a long time, you and me, and I can imagine how you felt toward me in the beginning. After all, you just left your old life stepping out on a new one, and I happened to be there. What I'm saying is I know, and appreciate, what a profound sense of loyalty something like that would bring about in most people, in particular in a fifteen year old boy."

"I'm a lot more'n fifteen now. Nothing's changed. Heightened, but not changed."

"Thanks, but I'm fixin' to ask something of you now that's far beyond normal expectation from any relationship, even one like ours."

"I determined a long time ago, I'd do anything you ever asked of me."

Alex George, visibly moved, looked at his protege.

"That shouldn't be any surprise. You handed me my life in the first place." Tom continued. "Our association would read like an unbelievable piece of fiction, if anyone took the time to write it. None of it would have happened if it weren't for you."

They were in the Shed, seated in the same chairs as the last meeting, Helen stared at Tom in the same distrustful way. The two men, one very old now, balding with a fringe of white hair, and his younger friend, were staring into the fire trying to articulate their thoughts.

"I'd give my life for you." It was softly spoken, as if thought aloud.

"You sure of that son?" There were tears in his eyes again. "It's important that you mean that literally, because of what I'm going to ask of you."

"Mr. Alex, I'm not the type of man who can say what I'm about to say easily, but the fact is I love you as no other person on this earth. No not even Nancy, although I suppose that's not a fair comparison. She's my wife, a woman, the mother of our daughter. My love for her is just that, a man for a woman. My love for you is completely different." He was searching for the right words to express his feelings. "This is something I've felt for years but for some reason or other couldn't say. Well neither one of us is getting any younger, so I want to say it now before one of us dies and the other regrets saying nothing."

The Old Man was staring at him intently, listening to the spoken words and those unspoken.

"I read about the loyalty of King Arthur's knights of the round table. They would and did give their lives for their king. I understand that. I understood how Gordon Liddy felt toward Nixon, when the shit was coming down. They hooted and ridiculed him, tried to bust his balls and put him in jail, but by God he didn't waver. I understand where he was coming from. I think he even made the statement, 'my king right or wrong.' I'm still amazed at the reception of that comment. They laughed at him and mocked him for his loyalty. I don't understand what's wrong with that kind of devotion. I think it says something about us as a nation, a bunch of fair weather friends. Well whatever, that's where I'm at and always have been as far as you're concerned."

"Be sure, Tom." He was leaning forward in his chair, a posture indicating exploratory conversation was over.

"I've never been more sure of anything in my life."

"Okay then, here's what I want. I want you to put together a small group of men, skilled and schooled in the ways of killing. You might call it assassination, but whatever it's only a word. I know the men I want, but I don't have the vitality to go out and find them myself." He paused. "You with me on this? You hear what I'm saying?"

"Yes sir, I am. I've been trying to figure our meeting last week, and I thought this was the way you were headed."

"You want out? You want me to stop?"

"No. I'll listen. Then I'll draw my own conclusions."

"Like I've been telling you, there's people on this earth, and in this country, that simply should not be allowed to live. Men, great and small, who heap suffering and death on their fellow men. These are the people I want gone."

He paused, staring into the fire before continuing.

"Paradox."

"Sir?"

"Paradox! Seems the longer I live the more I encounter paradox as a common, rather than uncommon proposition."

"How do you mean?"

"Do you remember the day you came home from the Marines and I sent you over to see Momma? Do you remember that?"

"Like it was yesterday."

"How'd she greet you, Tom?"

"She kissed me, and hugged me." His eyes softened. "And she cried."

"And what would you say about her, as a human being?"

"She was the most loving person I have ever known."

"What were you then, that day, when she held you in her arms?"

The old man sobbed involuntarily.

"A murderer. One of the deadliest creatures on the face of this earth."

"And she embraced you?"

"Yes."

"That to me is a paradox. A majestic, caring, loving soul, embracing the epitome of swift and terrible death in you. It was exactly that constant generous, worrying torment, over the weak of the world that finally got me to looking in that direction too. Well she's gone now and I'm not looking anymore, I'm doing. I don't have the time left. I'm too old for one thing and no longer have the arguments to talk myself out of what needs to be done."

"What you want me to do, Boss."

"Some special ones like you, survived the wars. Yours, Korea, Vietnam." He paused for a moment, adding. "Specially Vietnam. Those boys got fucked over so bad lots of 'em can't let go. What I'm tryin' to say is lots of men show up for every war, and a few become artists at it. Most of them die thank God, and that's a blessing all around because without tremendous help they just don't fit, but not all. Some make it back, and only God knows where they are right this minute. I'll know soon enough though because I've got the price." He raised his eyes slightly. "I got someone working on records right now. I want five of them to begin with and don't ask me why, it seems like a good number to start with. I want people who won't be hampered by things that hold most men in place. Wife, family, job, home. I want men who were specialized killers, because I don't think those skills are ever lost or forgotten. If they could murder a man, and justify it, for no other reason than he wore a different colored uniform, they're what I'm looking for. Like driving a car with a gear shift. If you ever drove one in your life, you never forget how. Well I want these men because their lives have meant nothing since the killing stopped and they'll leap at the opportunity to come out of mothballs and into action again."

"What about age? It's been a long time since the shooting stopped."

"Age don't mean shit! Intelligence does! These men aren't going to be storming anything that'd demand physical conditioning. It doesn't take much to pull a trigger, use a knife, or blow up a car"

"Yeah, you're right. So where do I find 'em."

"That's just it, you find the first, he finds the rest. The name of this game is secrecy."

"How's it work?"

"Not an original idea in this whole thing Tom. There's precedent, only a little different. Our identities, yours and mine, will be kept a complete secret from the man who does the choosing. His identity will be kept secret from the others, and theirs from one another. That's the way the Irish Republican Army does it, and obviously it works because Great Britain has never been able to crush those people for the simplest of reasons, she doesn't know who to go after. They grab an IRA man in one village, and don't have shit because he can't inform on the members in the next community. You know why?"

"No." Tom replied.

"He doesn't know who they are! They could rip his fingernails out, torture him 'til the end of time and he couldn't tell 'em."

"And that's what you want?"

"Yes. If any get nailed that's all they'll get. Even when working with the others, they'll be told up front never, ever, to reveal their true identity, and the reasons why. Then there'll be much less chance of getting caught."

"Less chance yes but what if they do get caught? What then?"

"How much we worth son?"

"Three and a half billion, last count."

"Got to convince our people there's more money backing this thing than some governments have. We'll have to assure 'em of the best lawyers money can buy. They must believe the money's there for those things." He spoke in a hushed tone. "When we find the men I'm looking for, those things won't present much of a problem."

"Why not?"

"Lots of reasons. First, your ability to convince the leader, that what we want is right. We want the vicious bastards who cause so much suffering and death to die. Simple as that. The ones who always seem to be above the law, or above answering for the horrendous things they've done, or had done."

"OK. Then what?"

"He takes it to the others, and they either believe or they don't. Remember Tom, we'll be looking for those who were exactly like you. Men who killed with extreme skill, yes and even enjoyment. Men who're approaching the twilight of their lives now. On the beach, so to speak. Killers, assassins, murderers all trained by Uncle Sam. Superb practitioners of the art of death, with the temperament and morality, or lack of it, necessary to do such work. These kinds of men Tom, will always leap at the opportunity for action. What the hell else is there for these poor bastards?" He seethed. "Turn the God damn switch on, applaud 'em. Turn it off and kill 'em if they can't shut 'er down. To hell with the manipulators boy, I'm going to put 'em back to work!"

"You don't think they'd have any fear of capture?"

"I'm saying I don't think the man I'm looking for would be that concerned about being caught. No, what I really think is that most of 'em are waiting for, longing for, their own death but want a punctuation mark at the end instead of just being erased."

"How do we finance it?"

"Momma's money." A wry chuckle. "Another paradox, wouldn't you say?"

"What do you mean?"

"She was always in on my financial affairs, right from the beginning...." He drifted only a moment. "So over the years her part of my income has amounted to hundreds of millions. She'd have given it all away long ago if I didn't hide it from her, and that's exactly what I did. Put it in foreign banks before they got to be such a fad, in case my financial holdings collapsed. We've got enough money there to finance most of the armies of the world." His eyes filled with tears as he continued. "My beautiful, lovin' Momma's money is going to finance something she never could have imagined."

"What do you intend to pay these men?"

"Well Tom, we'll have to see about that. You know, whatever it takes. I think the men I'm looking for would probably jump at the chance to be with us, and for little in the way of compensation. However I thought we could put them on some sort of income that would insure the necessities of life and some of the pleasures. It should be monthly, hold the leash a little tighter."

"Tighter?"

"Yes, tighter. I have no romantic illusions about this. Some of these men may decide they want out. If they're paid on a monthly basis they can go, and we can let them go. There'll be no hard feelings, and there will be no attempt on our part to try and make them stay against their will. We'll certainly never threaten them. If we can maintain total secrecy we don't ever have to fear one of them leaving and going over to the police."

"You've thought about the police, Mr. Alex?"

"I hope we can keep them off by this very secrecy. If someone gets too close we'll try money first, if that doesn't work I don't know what?"

"We'll have to kill 'em!" The old Tom suddenly returned, speaking softly.

"Oh Tom, I hope not."

"I hope not too, but I don't want you to have any misconceptions about that. Innocents will be killed, and that you can write in stone."

"Innocents?"

"Sounds terrible but these things always are. When you and I were killing men we were looking right at them, touching some of them. Honest and straightforward. Honorable at least, but how about the hundreds of thousands of innocents nations have slaughtered in this century with gas, shell fire, bombs, and bullets? How about the high line, high class bomber pilots that unloaded their bombs and flew back to base, a clean bed and a clear conscience. How many babies and their mothers did they incinerate? How many did we cremate in Hiroshima, a hundred thousand plus, but they got no names. Yeah, we'll kill some innocents too if they get too close. Wish that weren't so but it is."

The two men paused for a long while, each trying to take in not only what was being said, but how it was being received.

"I think the police might not be all that enthusiastic anyway Tom"

"What? Why not?"

"Because we'll be going after people usually beyond their reach."

"Like who?"

"People who have an out. Public sentiment in a liberal idealism maybe. Wealth. Shrewd lawyers. Personal power. The ability to bust anybody's balls. You know, the ones who always seem to be beyond judgment. The world's seen its share of these, most of whom are too powerful to answer for their wrongs. We're going to change some of that, to a greater or perhaps lesser degree and we're going to have the most powerful kind of help."

"Who?"

"The American people, that's who. I'll guarantee you public sentiment will be with us. You have my personal guarantee on that!"

"What makes you think so?" Tom was following the conversation intensely looking for every nuance, however subtle, indicating which way he was going.

"Because they're always on the side of right. Oh sure there'll be a horrendous hue and cry about this terrible thing coming down throughout the country. Mostly though it'll be bullshit from the same bunch that lets the majority suffer in order to protect the rights of the most offensive characters."

"The same middle of the road American that fights the wars?"

"And then some. The only ones you won't have with you, in sentiment if not in vocal support, will be that extreme liberal voice that's usually at the root of all the terrible things that go on in the name of freedom."

Tom knew the Old Man was right, he'd often thought many of the same things he was talking about now. It was something of a shock to bring them out in the open, and make definite plans toward putting together the ferocious group he knew it would be.

"Okay, I understand what you're saying, but how do you propose to put this group of men together and where are you going to find them?"

"If you're in Tom, that's your job. I'm much too old to do what has to be done, which is why I need your help." Again looking his protege in the eye. "Will you help me?"

"My answer is a qualified yes."

"Qualified?"

"Yes, because I want to talk you out of this, and will try. Failing that, I'll do anything you want me to do. I'm still curious though as to where you'll find the man to do this job?"

"Down at the local newsstand."

"What?"

"Get a copy of the Armed Services paper, and look for all the reunions listed. Then look for reunions of highly specialized groups, such as your old Raiders and go there. Look carefully and I guarantee you will find your man."

"How?"

"You will, believe me, he'll be there. I have no idea who he is or what he looks like, but he will be there. He'll catch your eye and you'll strike up a conversation with him and eventually have your man."

"Why not me? Why couldn't I put it together? I know all the areas you know. Organization, financing, planning and of course the ultimate."

"No Tom." He spoke softly again, pure love written on his face. "I've lost everyone, everyone in my life who has meant anything to me, except you. It would be too much if I lost you too. No, you find our leader and let him find the rest. They're out there Tom, men like you who developed one of the most amazing skills in the world, the administration of death. They seem to have been born to it and will never forget those skills, and many of them are sitting right this minute wondering what to do about them. Sort of like Patton. He felt he was born solely to fight WWII. He felt he was a reincarnated warrior brought back for the purpose of war. Who knows, maybe he was. He sure died immediately after it was over. Curious. Anyway maybe not consciously, but in the back of their brain lurks the seed. They have been death, and are waiting to be so again, now or in some other life."

"Do you believe that?"

"I do. I think we're all on an infinite voyage and what we don't finish this time, we'll do the next, but that's an entirely different matter. What we're talking about is the here and now."

"How many did you say you wanted?"

"Five, to begin with. Maybe one or two others, one for tracking and one driving and flying. They will, of course, all be expert at weaponry. Later if the program goes as I suspect it will, we can add more but five is the number to start."

"Who are the first?"

"I have a list in mind, which is the reason for the number five. I want Senator Anderson to be among the first." Tom's eyes widened. "He has brought so much suffering and death to many through his evil approach to power and how he uses it, yes and caused others to take their own lives. He has lied, conned, hustled and cheated and risen to great power because so many are reluctant to get down in the slime the miserable son of a bitch lives in, so he goes on and on twisting, perverting anything and everybody that comes his way. They call him the second coming of Joe McCarthy. One of those was enough. He's one of the original five."

"Original five? What do you mean five? What do you mean be one of the original five."

"I want this to start in such a stunning way as to announce to the whole country yes and the world for that matter, that we are here. We are in business"

"But five?"

"Yes Tom, and all together."

"You mean at once? At the same time?"

"Yes son, four of them will die together and be discovered together. The fifth man will die in his cell in the penitentiary the same night."

"Jesus Christ!"

"I want the message to get out, that we are here, operational and willing to take risks. I have a plan that will do that."

"And the others?"

"You mean who are they?"

"Yes."

"Manny Beatty, General Roberts, Carmine Palermo, and Ibn Faez."

Tom let a soft whistle slip involuntarily from his lips.

"And for the obvious reasons. Beatty's made a sick joke of the American labor movement through his policies of corruption and murder to get and stay where he is. How many men have been killed at his suggestion, God only knows. Manny needs to go. General Roberts? I'd like to kill that motherfucker myself. He's so typical of the kind of leaders we've had since the big war, maybe even before. Not men of honor like they once were but common hustlers like some God damn pimp. He hustled me and the American people during Vietnam. He hustled, lied, and led us down the primrose path which in and of itself is okay. But it is not okay when it causes a stupid war to go on and on for no purpose, resulting in the deaths of many of our boys. Screw him! He needs to be dead! This guy Palermo is one of the leading drug importers in this country, and while I know killing him will be about as effective as a fart in a hurricane, as far as stopping the flow of drugs into this country is concerned, we can at least serve notice we're coming after them. They kill our kids, we kill them. Ibn Faez, who should have been dead a long time ago, needs to be killed for two reasons. First he killed Congressman Shaw while he was running for President. That's a supreme insult to the American people all by itself, a candidate murdered.

By his act that son of a bitch said nobody could vote for Shaw thereby insulting the people. Can you believe that asshole would actually be paroled someday? I can't. I don't want that to happen, because it's not right. I'll be happy when I read about him in the paper. I also want everyone to understand we can reach anyone, anywhere, even in prison. He'll die the same night as the others."

"My God Mr. Alex, you've given this a lot of thought haven't you."

"Probably about twenty years Tom. Not these men, but the idea for such a group of killers has been with me a long time. Maybe even from the time I first read about Sodom and Gomorrah, or an eye for an eye."

"What happens if the operation gets traced back to us? I'm sure you've thought about that."

The Old Man burst into uncontrolled gales of laughter confusing his younger friend.

"Yes Tom, yes. Don't you see son, that's the most obscene paradox of all."

"Why?"

"Because, I'm suggesting we go after, and kill those who put themselves above the law."

"And?"

"That's exactly where I see us, above the law, but Tom, Tom," he was almost out of control laughing, "do you seriously think there's a rope out there strong enough to hang us, and our money?"

CHAPTER 19

The Old man was right, as he usually was. He'd long ago developed an uncanny skill for gathering information, summarizing it and proceeding in whatever way necessary. In this case he was all through talking, it was time for action.

Tom was on the plane for San Francisco, after taking a circuitous route to get this far. He piloted a company jet to Houston, a regular trip liable to no notice, boarding a flight to Seattle under an assumed name. Then another flight and name to San Francisco, thus starting the twisting path that was to be the standard from now on. He was getting accustomed to the dark wig, mustache, and horn rimmed glasses, purchased in New Orleans and donned at the airport in Houston creating a whole new appearance.

His normal color hair was salt and pepper, more white than the dark brown he started with and although he felt strange putting these new items on, he did agree with the Boss. They changed his looks immensely. It also amused him because of his excellent physical condition he seemed to drop twenty five years simply because of the dark hair.

'If Nancy could see me now.' He chuckled. 'My God I wonder what kind of a reaction I might get out of her if I showed up looking like this? Could be different? Maybe cause some excitement in bed. Wonder why that is? A trip to a strange place, a night in a different bed and we become inspired sexually. Well who cares why, guess it's great enough that it does.'

Renewed excitement? He laughed thinking of what a scolding he would get from his lady if she knew what he was thinking. A scolding followed by always tearful, and enthusiastic love making with the exciting and mysterious man she married way back in 1950. Tears of gratitude he'd been spared from death...how many times could it have been? Nancy was even more grateful that all of them working together had managed to pull him back from his state of mind, a sort of living death, or at the very least an outcast of society. He thought it had been quite an accomplishment too.

How could it be that fate had put all these marvelous people in his life. All of them desperately trying to pull him out of the grave. Grace of God, was what the Old Man always said. Undeserved favor! He couldn't argue with that.

He'd taken Alex George up on his suggestion, in 1945, to see Miss Marie as much as possible after the episode with Nancy in the darkened cabin and his subsequent flight into the swamp. The Old Man gained a new respect too, not that he needed it, but when he returned to normal thinking he concluded it took a lot of courage for

Alex to enter that gloomy swamp looking for him. Swamps had become his own personal and private garments, wearing them loosely, utilizing every subtle nuance of shadow and sound to murder out of their soft silence.

'He wasn't afraid of me, and I was.' Tom mused staring ahead. 'On the other hand I heard all over the oil patch he was a ferocious son of a bitch when it came to a fight. Bare fisted, love his only weapon, he came after me. Said I was the only son he had left, and would by God fight for me. Jesus!'

His eyes were heavy as time and place slipped by, drifting off to sleep.

'Those were some times though weren't they Tom?'

'How'd Momma got on this flight from Seattle?' He thought. 'Probably followed the hum of the jets and found me sitting here.'

Crystalline tears filled her eyes as she took his hand in hers, staring at the scar from the entrenching tool, long since turned white.

'But we made it didn't we?'

'Yes ma'am, we did.' He dreamed 'Couldn't have without you.'

'Oh I don't think I had much to do with it. It was Nancy and the psychiatrists back east.'

'Nothing would have happened without the love you gave me so freely, Miss Marie. The Boss knew that, that's why he made me promise....'

'Promise what?'

'To see you daily.'

'Why?'

'He knew what you'd do for me.'

'Which was?'

'Hold me up, pull me back, keep me from drowning. He knew you'd win with the power of your love, and he was right.'

'You give me too much credit.'

'You gave me my life.'

'What about all the others?'

'Oh yeah, they helped too. The Boss, the psychiatrists, Jane, Nancy. My God I couldn't believe Nancy. She went right into my nightmares with me.'

'Because she loved you Tom. Did you know she was terrified at the time?'

'Don't blame her. I tried to choke her to death.'

He wished he hadn't said that because the occupant of his dream suddenly had many more tears in her eyes.

'No not then.'

'When?'

'When you crawled across the grass, out of the bayou. She knew they were there too! She believed in your insanity. She had no other weapon so she was going to put herself between them and you. Use her body as a shield for you.'

'Like Paul?'

'Yes, like Paul. And like Paul she was willing to sacrifice her life for you.'

'Oh Miss Marie,' he thought the house dress with the scuffed shoes unusual dress for a plane trip, 'I'm so sorry you had to get involved with all that.'

'But why?' She had her big smile he always loved to see. 'You and Nancy were my children. I felt it every time you skinned your knees. Mary was forever skinning hers, even more than her big brother. I held them and hugged them when they were hurt, then they went away and I held you and Nancy when you were hurt.'

'I remember.' He responded softly in his dream.

'You look different.'

'Different?' He'd forgotten his wig and mustache.

'Younger?'

'Yes.' He laughed, suddenly remembering. 'Well I have a little something to do that requires....'

'Oh don't bother explaining. Probably more wild things Alex has dreamed up.' Her eyes teared again at the mention of her wild coonass. 'How is he?'

'Misses you Miss Marie.'

'Yes I suppose he does.' She picked up her huge old purse and started to get up. 'Pull that cord for me will you, I get off at the next stop. Come on now Helen,' it was the first time he'd seen the big Doberman, 'end of the line for us. Good luck Tom.' Her eyes crinkled as she gave him a kiss on the cheek. 'Like your other hair better.'

The hum of the jets droned back in as he tried to sort out his dream. Couldn't figure out, as his mind was reaching consciousness, how the hell she got Helen on board and since when did they put cords on planes to pull when you wanted off. Damn glad she didn't get more specific about what he was doing on this trip. He knew absolutely she would never, ever, understand it even though it was her compassion for the suffering that was responsible for this mission. He was partially awake, staring down the aisle looking for Momma and Helen unable to remember clearly why he was looking for them.

The plane was on its final approach to the San Francisco airport, the lights of the city shining like brilliant jewels followed by the glistening waters of the bay coming up fast, followed by the smoothing out of the huge craft as it gave a last great surge of power before touching down squarely.

'Damn good boys, those pilots.' He thought as they rolled toward his man, unknown to him at this moment.

*   *   *

He was there all right, just like the Old Man said. Tom spotted him soon after arriving. He read in the Armed Forces News about the SEAL convention in San Francisco, and it was from this group Alex George made his selection.

"They came out of the UDT boys of WWII, the most versatile specialists in guerrilla warfare going."

Alex George was responding to Tom's question of why the SEALS.

"Unbelievable physical conditioning, mental alertness, proficiency in weapons and explosives, and a belief in themselves and their commitments bordering on spiritual, that's what they're all about. I want our man to come out of that environment."

He wasn't exactly what Tom had in mind, when the search began, because of his size more than anything else. Slight of build, standing only about 5'7" and weighing less than 150 pounds. There was a svelteness about him though that caught Tom's eye, and he liked what he saw in the self assured manner in which the man conducted himself amid his peer group. His place in the crowd seemed to indicate the extent of his knowledge and influence but it was his eyes that attracted Tom's attention the most.

"Windows on the soul." Alex George called them. "Always watch the eyes boy, they'll tell you where a man lives, if you're sharp enough to read 'em."

Tom knew immediately the "Chief" had the eyes he was looking for. They glittered. Intelligent, lethal, and aware of everything that went on around him.

"Looking for an old pal of mine." Toms' made up excuse for being there after working his way closer and closer to him. "Met him on some chickenshit beach in the South Pacific in WWII. Weirdest looking thing I'd ever come across." He laughed, both at the mental image and what he felt was an excellent job of acting. "We were wading in to take the thing and there he was sitting on the beach, bigger'n shit. Looked for all the world like a frog! Big one! Had those flippers and goggles on. Christ what a shock! Scared hell out of me at first and I remember him laughing his ass off, 'cause I was so startled."

"What was his name?" CWO CT Evans is what his name tag said, he noted while sizing up his man.

"Johnson. Larry Johnson." Sounded as good as any other at the moment. "No idea what his rate was, unless it was tattooed on his ass, all he was wearing was trunks. And like I say, he was laughing when he said welcome."

"What outfit were you with?" Tom liked the way the man talked. Calm, smooth, self assured.

"Started with Carlsons' Raiders, wound up on the line with the First."

The Chief looked him over real close, commenting. "Man are you shittin' me, you don't look old enough to have served then. Did you say the Raiders? Weren't they clear back at the beginning?""

He was reminded his wig and mustache had taken years off his appearance, which is what he had wanted, but not to the point of losing credibility.

"I am, and we were," looking around, talking out of a cupped hand in an exaggerated manner like someone was listening, "but listen, if a guy my age is gonna' do any good with the dollies he's got to have all the help he can, and you know what they say, better things for better living through chemistry."

"Well I'll tell you something...what's your name?" Looking for a name tag that wasn't there.

"Oh sorry about that."

Much of this conversation took place in Toms' head before and during the trip, and with his background he wasn't rattled by much of anything. Most of his nimble wit he learned from Alex George, in the affairs of business. His conduct no matter what the situation, was of course a direct by product of his savage participation in the Marines. He concluded long ago that after what he'd seen and done, almost nothing in this world could ever shake him.

"Tom. Tom Glidden!" He wanted to keep his real first name, any other and he'd forever have to be on his guard not to get caught napping.

"OK Tom." He took his outstretched hand shaking it, both aware of the firmness of the others grip. "Whatever! I'd suggest you stay with it though 'cause you sure don't look old enough to have been with Carlson."

"Yeah, the ladies think so too!" Followed by suggestive laughter.

"Anyway I was too young to make it in WWII." He continued. "I enlisted on September 2, 1945 the day they signed the surrender on the Missouri. Joined the UDT's out of boot camp. Helped clean up a lot of the shit you guys left laying around, but I don't remember a Larry Johnson. We lost a lot of guys out there. It was treacherous going you know."

"Man I guess it was." Tom thought of the real UDT man he fashioned Larry Johnson after. He ran across him exactly as he said, amazed to find him sitting, laughing, watching the heavily armed Marines wade ashore. His only weapon was a knife, and a bunch of tools. A laughing Swede of some kind he guessed, with little more than courage in the way of equipment.

"Yeah, well the UDT's were brand new then, swimming around doing a hell of a job. Blowin' up shit so you guys could get ashore." The Chiefs' eyes took on a different light as he added. "We grew up after that though. Got a hell of a lot more sophisticated."

"I know."

Tom was sincere in this understated accolade for one of the most specialized military entities in the world.

"Kept getting badder and badder didn't you? Started off with swim fins and explosives and graduated to riot guns and murder in the jungle." He recognized the expression creeping over the Chiefs' face. "You out now?"

Like the Old Man said, Tom knew he'd found his man after asking the question. It wasn't only what he said, but how he said it.

"Yeah, can you believe it? I'm in good shape too, but the big guys decided I'd done enough time and said 'thank you very much for the best part of your life, and get out! You're gone.' And I was gone."

"You didn't want out?"

"Hell no! Those God damn SEALs were my life! My whole life! No offense to you, 'cause I know how you Marines feel about mother corps, but I'll tell you there isn't a sharper outfit in the world than us. We're the best there is!"

He meant it, the last sentence emphasized one word at a time.

"So they blew you out?"

"Yeah, sure did. Good pension, no excitement."

"Listen Chief, I'd like to talk to you more but I got one of those sweet young things lined up for tonight." He didn't want to overdo the first contact. "I'm in town on business but I'd like to talk to you more. I think we have a lot in common and I'm interested in your old outfit. You be here tomorrow night?"

He said yes he would and Tom left. This would have to be a gradual thing, and it was possible that CWO Evans might not be their man. He liked what he saw and while first impressions were truly lasting impressions it might be that Evans would be totally opposed to what they wanted done.

"Oh well," he yawned looking at the turned down bed, "a good nights sleep and start fresh in the morning."

*   *   *

"Hey Chief!" Tom spied him walking across the hotel lobby noting he was alone again, indicating many things.

"Hi Tom. Thought you were involved in the world of commerce today." Laughing. "Or did your sweet young thing take all the whip out of you?"

He really did look good. Tanned, trim and fit. Tom could see why he resented being put out of the service. From the looks of him, any military in the world would be delighted in having him on their team. Especially a man with the years of service and kind of expertise that were his.

"Got lucky. Took care of sweet thing last night, and no she didn't slow me down any. My man called me first thing this morning so we got our business taken care of right away...."

"Which is?"

"Which is what?"

"Your business. Not being nosy, but you never told me what you do."

"You know, you're right. No you're not being nosy, I'm a management consultant. You know, you got a problem with the management of your company, and old smart ass me comes in, hopefully with a clear head," the appropriate place for another suggestive laugh, "and shows you how to do whatever you want to do, better."

"Sounds like a hell of an interesting job to me."

It seemed like a perfect lead in.

"Well you know, if you're on the beach now, twiddling your thumbs trying to figure out what to do with the rest of your life, we might have something for you. Hell with the management experience you've gotten through the years, you'd probably fit right in."

"Yeah but you probably need somebody with different experience than mine." The statement was out of character for this otherwise confident man, indicating an emptiness or lack of purpose not visible before. "I can blow up things, or swim half way across the Pacific. I do sensational underwater maps and can grab a space shot out of the ocean quicker'n you can wink an eye. Had a bunch of jobs diving around the off shore rigs, but they all seem so dull after where I've been and what I've done."

" Yeah I suppose, but you'd have to have a discipline few men possess. That alone is a tremendous asset. Then your other specialties would be rare among men, wouldn't you say?"

The Chief gave him a guarded look.

"Yes, I suppose. What specialties would you be talking about?"

"All of 'em. From the little I know about the SEALS you guys must be the most decisive, dedicated, self assured men on the face of the earth."

"What do you mean, decisive?"

"Lots! What say we have a beer and find out."

The conversation rambled from where he was born and when, where he'd served, marital status.

"No wife. Tried that three times. Didn't work, any of them. Too fidgety I guess, them or me or both. At least that's what each one of them said."

Tom really wasn't surprised that most of what he was hearing seemed to be exactly what they'd hoped for, particularly the part about not being married. The Old Man wanted his man to be single. He wanted all of his men to be single, thinking it would be impossible to maintain the kind of secrecy he felt necessary, if there were any close attachments. How could a married man, or even a man with a steady lady disappear for varying periods of time without provoking questions.

There was something about the Chief's living in San Diego that seemed almost prophetic. San Diego naturally lent itself to being a never ending source of the kind of manpower they were going to need.

"Yeah they were still learning how to do it when I joined the UDT's. Like I said what we were about at that time was trying to clear away the debris of war, open up harbors and beaches. Got real good at it, when somebody decided we should go into more specialties."

"Like?"

"Like slipping up out of the water and doing strange things."

"Yeah," Tom replied, "I know what you're talking about. I developed in the war in the same fashion."

"How you mean?" He asked. "I thought they taught you Marines to be bad mothers from the time a green ass boot walked through the front gate."

"They do." He flashed back in his memory wondering if that was really him there in the jungles. "They do, but it's like anything else in life. Some people bring intensity to the things they do, while the other person might do what's expected and nothing more."

The Chief exploded with laughter, taking him off guard.

"I'm sorry, but I conjured up a mental picture of what you're talking about only in a different context."

"What?"

"Story about the guy that went through all the schooling there was in business administration. His old man was a self made millionaire and wanted his boy to have all the best education to take over the business. Graduates, first day on the job the old man asks the kid to show him what he'd learned in school by hiring his own new secretary. Interviewed three gals and the last question he asked each one was, what's two and two. Daddy asks what the hell that was all about when the gals left. Son says, well Dad the first gal said she thought it was four. Thought? Indecisive? Not sure of herself. Kind of a dumb broad to have around the office. Second girl said four. Definite, but not very imaginative, probably wouldn't be able to think on her own. The third lady said two times two was four. Two plus two was four, and two and two side by side was twnty two. Now this gal had imagination, would always give more than required on the job."

"So, who got hired?"

"The kids old man was all excited over this approach, said he was thrilled to see what technique's the boy had learned with all his education. So he asked, 'which one you going to hire.' The one that gave the straight answer, the one that gave the indecisive answer or the one that gave it all the pizzazz. That's when the kid tells him he's gonna hire the one with the big tits."

They laughed, while Tom welcomed the break in their conversation.

"Though you'd like that one, since you obviously like the ladies."

"Yes, well that kind of sums it up too. Lots of different reactions to the same situation or questions the final results maybe a combination of nothing, or something nobody'd ever thought of."

"What you talking about now?"

"Just that. Often times the end result is only just that, the end result. Nothing that went before it was intended to achieve the conclusion."

"We talking about the Marines?"

"Yes. What I mean is how some of us turned out after all that intensive training and brainwashing. Like some dogs will kick ass for a minute when you say 'sic 'em', scare the shit out of their opponent and run his ass on down the road. Others will run on down the road with whatever they've been told to 'sic', and kill it if you'll let them. You know what I mean?"

The Chief had a quizzical searching look. "Yeah I think I know what you mean. Some did what they were told and some bring more to the party than others. Sometimes to our discredit."

"For instance?" He was pushing to find out if this was truly his man.

"We were in Korea, during that police action," He took immediate note of the disgust emphasized on the word "that", "and the big guys needed a high ranking Korean officer to jimmy some information out of, so they invited us guys to go get 'em one. We'd become amphibious bad asses by this time, the best in the business at mayhem and murder, then disappearing. Hell, nobody could see us. We'd come out of the black water with black skins on, black grease on our faces and hide out in black shadows. I'm still amazed some of our boys got killed under those circumstances because we were good at making ourselves invisible. Anyway, we come up out of the sea, slip across a half mile of beach, kill the only guard we find, and ease on up to their command shack."

"No noise?" Tom asked.

"Not when I hit 'em." His answer was accompanied by a strange look.

"So we grab the general when he leaves the shack, tie his hands behind him leading him back out to our contact when we run across this enemy patrol. Down we go in the mud while these guys are walking by, and I'll tell you if they're still living today it's only because we were there for the general. We could have blown them all out of their socks. They didn't know anything about silence, acted like they didn't care. I got the general laying next to me when all of a sudden he tries to raise up. I jammed his face down in the mud so he can't holler at these guys and put my weight on top of the prick to keep him quiet. Seemed like it took those bastards forever to get by us, and the general's kicking and squirming while I'm holding him down, keeping my weapons ready in case these dumb shits hear anything."

"Did they?"

"Nope. Kept on going and when they were out of range we start to move. Everybody except the general."

"Dead?"

"Yeah, can you believe I drowned the son of a bitch holding him down. Pushed his face in the mud and killed him without even trying."

"How'd you feel about that?"

"Pissed! We had to go back again and the best we could do was a colonel and that's not what we wanted, although he was real cooperative. Gave us lots of information."

"Of his own accord?"

"Coaxed him some." The flinty reply.

"Coaxed?"

"Didn't fuck with 'em too long."

"You know I was never around any prisoners in the South Pacific."

"Oh sure you were." It startled him. "Only you guys called them dead men."

"So how'd you feel about that?"

"What?"

"Killing perfect strangers, because they had on a different uniform."

"It didn't make a shit to me. The big guys said kill these bastards. That's what they wanted, that's what they got."

"Do much of that?"

The look he received before his answer really said it all.

"Thirty years worth. That's what they paid me for and that's what I gave 'em. Taught the kiddies how to keep on doin' it."

"Now what?"

"You tell me. I'm on the beach. Lookin'."

"Yeah, I hear that. What do you think you'd like to get into? Management consultant interest you?"

"Sounds pretty dull to me. No offense!"

"None taken." He laughed. "Look, let me have a number in San Diego where I can reach you. I'll check the home office and see if they'd be interested."

"Where's the home office, Virginia?"

"No, Kansas City. Why Virginia?"

"Curious. Folks from Virginia contact me lots of times but I don't like 'em. Don't like what they do, how they do it, and who they do it for. They're the same scum bags that been gettin' us, guys like you and me, to do the killing for them forever. The same smooth talkers that keep stirrin' things up and then tell us to go 'sic 'em. The self same bastards that snuggle up in the flag and tell you and me how it's some kind of sacred duty to kill the enemy, then lo and behold we finally discover what it's really all about. They aren't wrapped in the flag man, what they're wrapped in is money and all the while they've been the most ferocious enemy we've ever been exposed to."

Tom was utterly amazed to see tears in his eyes.

"You know I really think I've been faded, fucked and laughed at. They taught me how to be something we don't even talk about in society, giving me the hustle all the time. They weren't the enemy." He pointed to the west. "The real enemy's always been the other way." Indicating the east.

"How do you feel about that?"

"What?"

"You know, killing a man because he's got the wrong uniform on. We didn't have any better reasons you know. You ever think about that? Did you feel justified in that or were you simply doing your thing?"

"Don't follow you."

"Well, I don't want to make a big thing out of this, but I really believe I killed more Japanese than any Marine in the war. I'm talking about Japanese that I was looking at when they died, either with these," looking at his hands, "or with small arms. I didn't start out that way, but I gradually turned into something that eventually caused me to be shunned by my own kind. My brand of slaughter was too much, even for them. Somehow I feel you understand exactly what I'm talking about."

Evans looked startled indeed at this comment by his new found acquaintance, aware of course he must have seen much action if he went clear through the South Pacific as he'd claimed. Now he knew. After looking in Tom's eyes during this last piece of conversation, he found the same awesome look he always found on the faces of specialized killers of any stripe.

Many Special Forces, most of his beloved SEALs, all the Lurps he knew in Nam. Men don't become devastating murderers, even with permission, without paying up in the eyes. He knew. He really knew what he was taking about because those eyes looked back at him in the mirror each morning.

"What are you talking about?"

"Something I've always wondered about, but been too busy with my life to actually go find out. I know how tough it was for me to return to normal life, and I had a lot of heavy duty help trying to make the switch. Lots of money invested. Lots of time and love invested by somebody else. She didn't know where I'd been or what my role in the war was but that woman cried over my soul, all the time pulling, pulling me back."

"Your Mom?"

"No, never knew her, my own mother that is. No this was an extraordinary lady who had a lot of selfless love and compassion and did everything she could to help me return to normal life, whatever that is."

"She dead now?"

"Yeah, that's what they call it but as long as anyone can remember her, she'll never be gone. Powerful lady Chief. By the way would you want me to call you anything besides Chief? You must have a front name."

He was surprised at the outburst of laughter his comment elicited.

"I hope to Christ you keep on calling me Chief because I'd hate to have to whip your ass for using my real name."

Tom laughed too. It was only said in jest and he knew it.

"Well you've set me up now so I guess you're going to have to tell me what the CT stands for."

"Would you believe Chauncy Tarkington." Followed by the most disgusting, "Jeeesus Christ. I don't know what my folks were on when they named me but it had to be potent. I was born in Natchez, Mississippi and those southerners do get hung up on weird names. In the beginning, when I first went into the UDT's some of the guys changed that to Chancey because I was known to take a lot of 'em. After I made my first grade of Chief, which was a long time ago now, it was Chief forever more.

Nobody dared call me anything else, because among the non coms I was almost always the boss."

"Not much of a southern accent?"

"No, my folks were killed in a car wreck when I was a kid and I was raised in Denver by an aunt. Left there at seventeen, joined the navy and you know the rest."

"No family? No kids anywhere?"

"No family, no nothing. My three wives decided early on, they didn't want anything to do with kids of mine, figured I was probably going to wind up dead pretty quick anyway and they didn't want to raise them alone. You know when I think about it, I think that was just about right. Met most of 'em in saloons of one kind or another, had a bunch of laughs, each of 'em a great lay and that was it. No substance, just sex."

"You miss anything?"

"About?"

"Ever wish you'd had kids?"

"Naw, I'm not the type. That life wasn't for me. No I think I wound up exactly where I should have, always dancin' along the ragged edge. Wondering where it was going to end. Hoping it would be different than it was."

"What do you mean?"

"Didn't want to die in bed. Now it looks like that's how it's gonna' be."

"Think you'd still like some of the action?" Tom asked.

"If it's the right kind."

"What'd that be?"

"Don't have the answer to that one. What I do best isn't in great demand."

"Yeah but what if there was? What if there was?"

"Depends. If I could get into something I believe in, something other than what the boys from Virginia keep talking about, I'd be a player in a minute. They want me to go places I'm not interested in, kill their enemies, not mine. I still think they're looking in the wrong direction."

"What you mean, wrong direction?"

The Chief looked thoughtful, considering his answer.

"Oh I don't know. Like charity. You know what they say, it begins at home."

"Charity begins at home." Those last words before the meaningless farewells, were going through Tom's mind as he flew the Lear jet on his last leg home. He was pretty sure this was his man but nothing specific had been said yet by either of them. Like the Old Man always said. "Just nibble around their asshole and let it fall out."

CHAPTER 20

"Sounds like our man all right."

They were back in the "Shed" with the real Helen in attendance as she always was when Alex George was about. He was keenly interested as Tom told him of his find, sitting on the edge of his chair, eyes shining brightly while Helen sat rigidly erect at his hand.

"And he was a SEAL?"

"Yes sir! Might say more like what they're about. Too young for WW2 but enlisted right after, served in Korea and lots of tours in Viet Nam."

The Old Man seemed surprised at his last statement.

"Lots of tours you say?"

"Yes sir. Said he didn't function good at home. There was something...he used the word mystical, about the draw the place had on him."

"Oh yeah. Your kind of men never come home 'til it's over. That's why most of you come home in a box...." He was remembering his own difficulty returning home after WWI, and the near loss of this man seated in front of him that he loved every bit as much as his own son. "Odds get 'em."

Tom nodded in the affirmative thinking about his mystical Colonel Carlson who long since died in bed.

"What's he look like?" Years rolled off the Old Man right in front of his eyes. He hadn't seen him this enthused over anything since Momma died. As a matter of fact this captain of industry, friend of the powerful, power broker himself had been more or less biding time waiting for his own death with not much interest in anything else.

Tom went into great detail over their meetings, answering all the Boss's questions that came at him like machine gun fire. What he looked like, his background, thoughts, age, everything he could possibly think of.

"How'd you get this?" The Old Man asked when handed the Chief's social security number and Navy I.D.

"I asked him for them. Took one of our application forms with no heading and asked him to fill it out."

"Just like that?"

"Well not exactly, but I told him I was a management consultant and thought he might fit in our organization. I'm sure he saw through my story."

"Why?"

"Because he wanted to know if my home office was in Virginia. He obviously thought I was CIA. I told him no it wasn't Virginia, it was Kansas City. Don't know whether he believed me or not, but I do know we had a real rapport going. Both of us been in some horrendous places in our lives, and we resolved a lot of our problems in the same way."

"You mean killing?"

"Yeah, that."

"I'll take this and get some more information on Mr. CT Evans, then we'll make our decision."

The Old Man took a long look at his younger friend.

"You sure about this?"

"About the Chief...."

"No son. You sure you can run this out to the end?"

"If it's what you want Mr. Alex, I'll take it all the way. I only wish there was some other way"

"Don't you know how much I agree? How much I wish this wasn't necessary at all? Oh yes son I do, but time and tide has shown me there's no other way. It's the legal system, the monetary system, and the whole damn system in general. If you know the right people, have the right kind of money, why you can circumvent any part of our legal system you want. Aren't the papers constantly reminding us of how delicate our people are? The people we put our trust and faith in? Why do you suppose good law men constantly fall victim to the call of the bribe? How come so many people are walking after the commission of some terrible crime, gotten off so much of the time on legal technicalities." Tears suddenly appeared in his eyes. "Like that no good son of a bitch that murdered Sue. No question really of their guilt but rather the smooth maneuverings of a talented lawyer can draw the jury down in the slime with him. Some caught cold with the goods, whether the goods might be a sack of narcotics or a dead body that they just made dead, but because a search warrant wasn't properly processed, or some such happy horseshit, they go free. No son that's not justice, that's chicanery. And how about all the rest that goes on, in the name of God knows what? Have you ever wondered why the politician invests hundreds of thousands in the job that pays thousands. Do you have any idea how Lyndon Johnson left the presidency with such an enormous accumulation of wealth? Not too many people are aware of that you know, and how in the world do you suppose he managed that? Well how the hell do you think? Did you ever notice who his pals were? Wouldn't want to buy a used car from any of that bunch. He always seemed to be surrounded by the slick dudes of the political and financial scene, and then of course with him there's always the really big unanswered question. The one lots of people want to know the answer to before they die."

"What would that be Boss?"

"Vietnam."

"Oh, I thought you meant the other." He replied softly.

"Yeah, well that too!" His eyes shimmered with intensity at the mention.

"What a gigantic sham, and was it because he really thought he was protecting the world somehow from those raggedy assed boys in the north, or was it because he had such a bloated ego he thought he had the chutzpah to pull off the end of a war that nobody seemed able to stop. Or was it because he really, truly believed we should fight that stupid thing for some high principled reason? Those assholes must have thought the American people were like a bunch of mushrooms. Keep 'em in the dark and feed 'em shit!"

Alex George was sitting with his knees spread apart, staring down at the floor, swinging his head back and forth as he searched each issue.

"I don't know son, this land of the free and home of the brave seems to have settled in to the great hustle. Doesn't seem to be high minded purpose anymore, and you know what I hate more than anything else?"

"No Boss, what's that?"

"My reaction when I hear some well intentioned idiot call this the greatest land in the world. Why that's such bullshit I can't hardly stand it, and what really pisses me off is that once upon a time we were. When I was young it was. I think up until the second war it was, and then it started to happen real gradual. Our leadership's changed from men of integrity to slick Madison Avenue dudes answering to the invisible string pullers, we've got now. People starving!" His voice disturbing Helen. "Our own God damn it, not some strange far off people, while our food storage facilities are busting at the seams! Educational system in shambles, slid from number one in the world to somewhere in the twenties. Ignorance, poverty, old people have to die in poverty stricken disgrace, people dying 'cause our money grubbing health system says, 'pay up front Baby or you get nothin'.' Two hundred and fifty thousand dollars for a God damn bone marrow transplant! Do you hear that, a quarter mil? Man are you shitting me? Those lecherous bastards going to charge a quarter mil to transfer something God gave out for free?"

Tom didn't like to see the Old Man get this inflamed, given his great age, afraid it might be too much of a strain for him to handle.

"Then there's the kids!"

Tears welled in his eyes immediately thinking of his beloved Momma, and her never ending search for kids who were hurting.

"Our kids're being slaughtered in their schools, homes and playgrounds by a horrible pox of drugs smothering this land like some huge malevolent blanket. We're just messing around with the problem while our kids become addicted with God only knows what kind of a terrible loss to our nation. How many politicians, doctors, businessmen and women won't make it to their potential because some rapacious bastards are loose in our streets, singing them their siren song while they guide them into addiction and death?"

He was really reaching, letting it all come out. There was great evil in our land, in his opinion, and he was going to do something about it.

"I want those boys in the worst way Tom. I'd like to kill 'em with my own hands, but that's out! I'll tell you one thing though...."

"What's that Boss?"

"I got the price! You hear me son, I do have the price! I got more money than there is and I can buy lots of things with it. Right now this is what I want to buy and if what we're about to do isn't right with God I hope He ain't watchin' while we're doing it. I'm not questioning Him, but man I've always wondered where He was looking while all those people were being slaughtered in the German death camps.

I'm not talking only the Jews, no, no, although they alone would have been plenty bad enough. No I mean all the people who died over there. What if I'd had the wherewith-al to slaughter those murderous bastards who were in charge of the killing, then and there? Wouldn't I have received the hosanna's of all civilized people? The battle cry I get from the church guys is that God allows. We do the doin's and He allows us to do it. Well I hope He allows on this one 'cause there's a bunch of folks here that shouldn't ought to be. I want 'em gone and I'm buying their way out."

"No denying you've got a strong point, Mr. Alex."

"You're God damned right I do, problem was I didn't know what was happening then but I do now. Now I can do something about this shit! I got the bucks and I'm puttin' 'em on the table. Why shit I didn't have a cryin' ass dime when I was born, and I'm willing to leave the same way so long's it goes for the right thing. Like I mentioned I'm not naive enough to think I can fix the world, or what we're firing up to do will, but let me tell you something, when enough bodies are found on the streets and everybody knows how they got there, know they're gonna' be more, we might make a difference before it's all over. We might've helped!"

"Then there's no turning back for you Mr. Alex?"

He wanted to make sure the Old Man was truly committed to his course, also checking to see if he was in control of his faculties. He'd do anything the Boss wanted, he simply wanted to make sure he was dealing with the real Boss and not some fantasy induced by old age.

"There is no turning back son." The reply was somber and obviously well thought out. "It's what I want done. It needs doin'. It's needed doin' far longer than anybody knows, and I repeat I got the price."

"Then I'm your man Mr. Alex."

"Oh yeah," tears suddenly returned to his ancient eyes, " but then you've always been my man, haven't you?"

*   *   *

It was a matter of only a few days when Alex George, oil tycoon and only recently committed merchant of death called Tom back to the "Shed".

"Jesus Boss, where the hell'd you get this?" He was looking at a complete background on CWO CT Evans, covering everything from his birth to this moment in time.

"Didn't I tell you money talks and bullshit walks. Well money did some talking here and now we know everything there is to know about our man. Yeah, he's one of yours." Pointing to the ream of papers. "If you'll look down there on the bottom of page six I think you'll be pretty interested in what it says about his weapon of choice."

Tom let out a long low whistle.

"Fuuuuuuck! Navy issue hand ax?"

"Yes, exactly."

"Now I know what he meant when he said, 'when I hit 'em, they stay down.' Jesus Christ, no wonder! I thought he was giving me some exaggerated horse shit because he isn't that big to be able to put people down with his hands."

"No son, it's what he's got in his hands when he hits 'em." He looked very thoughtful, tears glistening in his eyes. "Don't you see, he's another of those who've been trained and trained, and trained some more in devious murder." His tears returned as he added softly. "What do we do when we train our youth to kill in this manner? Kill while holding their victim in their grip. Kill with no mercy whatever." Hesitantly. "You still have the knife?"

"Yes. Don't know how many times I tried to get rid of it, but couldn't. Made a special trip out in the 'Chafalaya once to drop it over the side and couldn't. How could I?" He was still staring at the report. "This guy's got to be something else." He looked back at the report lest he misunderstood. "Navy ax? I'll tell you something Mr. Alex, this says he's our man if I'm a good enough salesman to convince him not only of the importance of the job, but how crucial it is we have the right man running the operation."

Tom looked up, stunned to see the Old Man holding his hand to his mouth in horror as he nodded yes, completely given to the monstrosity of what had to be done.

"You'll see him again soon?"

"I'll be with him tomorrow."

*   *   *

This time he flew the Lear to Orlando, rented a car and drove to Miami, boarding a nonstop flight to Los Angeles.

It started to come over him on the long cross country flight. It was all coming back, he knew it. He could feel the old band tightening around his head, while his mind turned in some sort of a two dimensional fashion like he'd seen on their computers. His eyes were going flat and he seemed to affect a death like calmness he knew always preceded the terrible swift action he dispensed so long ago...so very long ago.

It was the barracks cap that caught Tom's attention in his dream, as it rested on the knee of the dead Japanese soldier seated next to him.

'Where'd all the blood come from?' He wondered as he noticed the split toed shoes the dead warrior wore below the blood stained uniform. He recognized him immediately upon turning his head, staring into the dead eyes. 'Yeah. Oh yeah. Blew his ass up when he stuck his face in the gun slit of a bunker on Tarawa, right after I found Paul.'

The many years dead soldier smiled back at him, in his far eastern way.

'I bear you no ill will, American. It was war, we had to kill the enemy, what else could we do?'

'Yeah, well I'll tell you something, at that particular moment I'd have murdered my mother if she'd been in that thing with you. I'd just found Paul's body, you know? Do you know that? You murderous son of bitches shot his back out and all he was trying to do was help a dying man. I swear to God you'd not done it if I'd been there, it wouldn't matter how many guns you had, you'd of had to kill me first and your whole fucking Imperial Army couldn't get that job done.'

The bloody soldier smiled silently in reply.

'God doesn't make many like him, you know what I mean? I mean he was special. Loved everybody and loved by everybody that knew him. The most humble, peaceful man I ever knew. Going to be a priest you know until you sons of bitches shot all the life out of him.'

Tom started to cry, tears of agony and rage over the death of this good man gone all these many years, slaughtered again in his dream.

'You assholes killed him, but by God I made you pay!' Chuckling sardonically. 'Oh yeah, you paid all right. I wonder how many times you people did pay?'

The dead soldier indicated somehow in the way of dreams, they were not alone on the plane and it was then Tom noticed the plane was full of dead Japanese, many without heads.

'So, what did you expect.' He shouted in his dream. 'You cut Pat to pieces, sliced Bobbies throat and blew Paul almost in half. Did you think for a minute I'd let you get away with that shit without answering you in kind?'

The smiling soldier nodded toward the seat next to them that contained a bag, a sea bag he thought. He could tell from the general shape it contained the heads of those who had none.

'So what, asshole! So what! Yes it was me, you're God damn right, but you savages showed me the way. How 'bout Pat. How 'bout the way you killed him? He was kneading his hands, feeling the reassuring grip of the terrible knife and his automatic. 'Pretended your buddies I nailed in the draw was the one that did it, I'll tell you that.'

The dead soldier had a sad, disapproving look arousing even greater anger.

'Hey listen, don't give me any of that long faced shit. You guys showed me there were no rules to that war. Well I learned pretty good huh?'

There was no reply, only the smile. Tom thought he was mocking him.

'Tell you what you smug asshole, whatever you do don't be tryin' to lay any guilt trip on me now, you hear? I've been all through that shit and I don't need any more from you. Stick you face up again buddy and I'll blow another hole in your God damn head, so fuck you! Do you hear me? Fuck you!'

"Are you all right sir?" It was the pretty red headed stewardess, staring down into his eyes. "I think you were having a bad dream."

"Oh my God!" Tom said looking up into this most pleasant face. "Did I...."

Her look of concern turned into a hesitant smile, now that he was fully awake. "Don't worry about it, we hear dreams all the time in this job. Told him pretty good though, didn't you? Who was he, your boss?"

"No," He laughed with her, "nobody'd ever talk to my boss that way. No, no it was a guy I hadn't seen since 1944."

"From the sound of things I think he'd be well advised to stay away." She smiled broadly.

"Oh he will, Miss. He will!"

The extra caution of renting the car in San Diego was troublesome but the tall, aging exmarine felt it was worth the time involved, using the drive to gather his thoughts regarding the conversation that would take place.

In view of the fact the Chief had obviously been contacted by the CIA, and probably others, he might take measures to protect himself, thereby endangering everyone. He was taking every precaution possible, down to having the latest electronic equipment available to detect any kind of recording device close at hand. Avro Industries had some of the best minds there were in the field of electronics and where they were in many sensitive fields not only did they use devices appropriate to the situation at hand, they defended against them. There couldn't be too much caution going into this kind of venture, given its nature, and although he felt the Chief was what he purported to be and nothing else, he had to be careful.

"Well, I talked to the people in the home office, about you and your background and everybody seems to agree that you should be an excellent addition to our management team."

They were walking along the beach, at the special request of Tom, claiming a great love for the ocean and surf, especially because of his land locked surroundings in Kansas City.

"Don't get too many breakers on the Missouri river. Love to look at 'em when I get the chance."

His reason was security. The sounds of wind and surf would wipe out any recording device this relative stranger might have hidden on his person.

"You know Tom, I still don't know what your company does. Oh I know you say management consultants but that doesn't mean a whole lot to me. What is it you want me to do? What makes you think I'd be qualified?"

"Like I was telling you in San Francisco, we study companies, organizations and situations, look them over real good, find out what their problems are. Then we analyze the information and plot out whatever action necessary to rectify these troublesome areas, or people."

"People?"

Tom saw everything, especially interested in the way this man moved. He understood that kind of motion. On every beach in the world, footing was always less than the best, sand giving with each step but he seemed to glide across the surface, compensating subconsciously for the unsure footing.

"Yes people. We find all our problems rest in people. Often times, in this day and age of computers and high tech, it's easy to overlook the fact that everything still comes down to people. If the problem area is a really bad one, brought about by the wrong people, then what we have to do is recognize that and make necessary adjustments. That's why we're so interested in you."

"Why me?"

He was particularly pleased he'd chosen the beach for this conversation because they had a driving wind, one that he wouldn't have chosen to walk in otherwise, and the surf was even louder, each enormous wave crashing down with thunderous sound. No recorder was going to pick anything up over that, and even though the detection device his people in LaFayette had provided showed nothing at close range, he wanted to use all caution.

"We did a lot of research on the SEALS, and I hope you'll forgive us but we did an extensive background check on you too."

"How'd I do?"

He seemed more amused than upset, and Tom knew why. Nobody, after living a life like these two men had, could ever be upset by anything so trivial. They had looked into the face of death so many times, taking lives in the process that anything, everything in life after that had always seemed so anticlimactic. Having gone to the ground with so many of the enemy, holding them like a vise tight up against their body, feeling the shudders and spasms while they died of the violence these men had visited on them, nothing as mundane as a background check was ever disturbing.

"Both of you did extremely well. You know, before I came in contact with you I really didn't understand what you SEALS were all about. Don't get too much publicity do you?"

"No, we don't. The big guys want it that way. The kind of work we do best isn't going to be seen on TV, or for that matter discussed in the paper much." He took a sudden mental turn continuing. "We're kind of like the high minded citizen, leader of the community and all that shit. You know the person that's full of benevolence, love of their fellow man and has a loaded gun in the night stand. He'd be absolutely appalled if his fellow citizens understood what he had in his bedroom. Loves his fellow human, but will kill him if he stops in uninvited. Kind of a dark side for this guy. Well we're kind of a dark side for the Navy. You know your usual picture of a guy in the Navy is a tall thin boy that really looks good in his uniform. White hat, shining teeth, dance like a son of a bitch and the girls all love him. Well there's that, and there's us. The SEALS are the best guerrilla force in the world, bar none. Yeah I know that's a strong statement but I feel that strong about it. We can do anything from pluck astronauts out of sardine cans while they're bobbing in the water, blow up a whole city or a mailbox in that city, string communications, clear a harbor, track in the jungle, fight in the open, and kill anything that walks."

Tom saw the look, the special look possessed by those who have killed many times. He thought it very distinctive. Expressionless eyes, lids half closed, like maybe his soul had taken over forcing him to look at what he'd done for others. The others! God damn their souls!

"Yeah," the Chief continued softly, "we killed anything that walked down our path. We knew how and did it with gusto, or without a sound, whatever the doctor ordered." He stopped, turned around staring up into the face of the much taller aging Marine. "You know what I mean too, don't you?"

"Yeah I do, I really do. Fools with your mind forever doesn't it?"

"It does. Got a ticket the other day, for some dumb ass thing the cop said I'd done. Crossing a line I didn't know was out of bounds. Irritated the shit out of me but instead of being pissed because of the fine I was going to have to pay I was wishing I had my ax in my belt. You know what I'm saying?"

The tall man nodded his head in the affirmative.

"Makes you wonder what's going on, doesn't it? What really makes me wonder though is why they don't smoke us when they're through with us. Can you imagine letting something like me loose to walk the streets. You can't remove my brain and send it out to the God damn laundry. They showed me how to do it, and do it, and do it some more, always getting more sophisticated. Here CT, is what they said, we got some real special shit for you now son, you can kill a bunch more people with this stuff. Then they nod their God damn heads and say, good boy! Damn son you are really good at that mayhem you know it? And you know what's the worse part of all?"

"What?"

"We go for it! We get sucked down in it! When I hit 'em they go down and stay there and as perverse as it is I get a special rush out of it. I killed a man and I know absolutely the intelligentsia back in Washington that hired me on in the first place couldn't begin to do what I did. Yeah they'll pin bright colored ribbons on my chest and say what a great job I did but those mealy mouthed chickenshits sure wouldn't want any of the same action. Then after a while, short for you, long for me, they say adios momma! Great job baby, now go away and let's none of us talk about the past. What a joke, outstanding killers like me and you and it's down the road time. I don't know, something about the deal sucks."

It was time for a move.

"Ever think what a shame it is to let our talents go down the drain?"

"What do you mean?"

"I came back from the Marines, and to this day I don't know how I survived that except I sincerely believe I went through some deep metaphysical process. There was so much death and carnage around I somehow came to believe I was a direct by product of it. I don't know if you can understand this or not, and I don't want to sound overly dramatic but I came to believe I was death itself. Man when I waited for those infiltrators, at night down there in the middle of those decomposing corpses hiding in the pouring rain, I knew what a rattlesnake must feel like before striking, only more so. The rattler is simply trying to protect himself. I was there to kill something. I don't think I can really explain it but I'll tell you one thing for damn sure. I was operating on an entirely different plane than the rest of the guys."

"You mean you went out the wire lookin' for 'em?"

"Yeah. I had a short circuit. I found my last buddy after they'd cut his head off, his head and his hands. Meant to scare us, but it didn't work that way with me. I just shorted out after that and spent all my nights in that driving rain on Okinawa waiting for their night people to show up. They always did."

"What the hell'd you use, piano wire?" He was in the draw with him mentally, visualizing the scene based on his own past experiences.

"No, I found a knife on a dead Marine on some beach, and that's what I used. It's something else. Heavy, long, double edged and the hilt's machined into brass knuckles. Had the edges honed like a razor, could slice paper with it. A three way killing machine, stab, slash, or smash. So that's what I used, that and my fortyfive. Sometimes there was so fuckin' much noise, combination of mortar fire and driving ass rain, it wouldn't have mattered if you'd blown 'em up with a cannon, and you have to understand I'd gone sideways mentally. Well after they cut up Pat I figured we had a whole new ball game, so my rules said I'd lay out there with the dead and when one of the night people showed up I'd kill 'em. Loved to catch 'em square, hit 'em as hard as I knew how, which was hard. Practiced hitting trees with it. I could hear the bones going and I got that...rush did you call it?"

They were facing one another on the beach, moving back through time.

"Then the part I can't ever seem to understand."

"What's that?"

"Cut the heads off a lot of them. Spend all night crawling through that muck so's I could throw the guys head up in their positions so they could see 'em in the morning. Learned it from them."

"Didn't they see you, shoot at you?"

"I suppose, but I didn't care. I'd made the transition by then. I was death. I had no fear of dying. I was consciously and subconsciously expecting to die and really didn't give a shit. At that time there wasn't anything else. Everything was about death, theirs, ours, mine and yours. God damn I wish I could understand what exactly I was thinking about, in those days."

"Death."

"What?"

"You were thinking about death. Don't get me wrong, 'cause I've been exactly where you've been, but our entire essence, at that time, was the administration of death. What else? That's the part that gets me. What else is there under those circumstances? No milk of human kindness, only terrible, swift death. Do it to him! Do it quick, silent, disappear, and I'll tell you we survivors were good at it, otherwise we're not survivors. We're dead!"

It was obviously a conversation the Chief had going in his head many times, but probably never had the opportunity to run it with another of his kind.

"Then what do we do with all this training and talent when the paper's signed? You know what I mean. I mean you can't list these kind of skills in the want ads. Job applications don't have a place on 'em for that kind of shit. What do you do now that there's nobody to kill?"

Tom looked at the surf, his mind traveling further.

"Funny part is there's always more?"

"More! More what?" Evans looked at him.

"More people who really should be dead. I mean they've gone out of their way to earn it. The woods are full of 'em."

"What you mean?"

"I mean I killed a man, after I came home, because he'd killed a woman. She was a friend of a man who meant a lot to me. Guy was let free, partly because the woman was a whore and partly because he had a sharp attorney. He walked. I thought about it sitting in the rain one night and decided I should do something about that. Hell I knew way down somewhere you weren't supposed to do that sort of thing but I thought he'd earned his death more than any Japanese I killed in the South Pacific." He paused, the only sounds heard those of the crashing surf. "So I killed him, and you know what?"

"What?"

"I sure didn't care then, and don't care now. He forfeited the right to live and since nobody else was going to do anything about it, why not me?"

The two exslayers stood motionless while the Pacific pounded relentlessly. Tom saw the gulls wheeling about out of the corner of his eye and realized, for some strange reason, he couldn't even remember what his victim in Baton Rouge looked like. No face, just a body that smelled like booze, recoiled in its last moments of mortality, went into spasms and died while the killer held him. Seemed that way too, like the killer was someone else.

"Yeah I hear you. Why not us?" The response was from his subconscious.

"What'd you say?"

"What?" The Chief returned to the now, immediately.

"What you said about, why not us? I don't understand. What did you mean by that?"

"Nothing really."

"I thought maybe you had something in mind."

"Well I suppose I have had a few thoughts since they put me on the beach, more fantasy than anything else. You know what I mean? Kind of like what you were talking about there, about killing that guy back in 1945. I've thought about things like that myself."

Tom couldn't believe his ears, thinking this man he'd been stalking was waiting there all the time. Like he too had been thinking the same kind of thoughts discussed back in the Shed, but had nowhere to go with them. Maybe the funds weren't available for him, or maybe, maybe...?

"You stay in touch with any of your old guys?"

"You mean the SEALS?" The smaller man asked.

"Yeah."

"Well yes, in a fashion. I attend a lot of reunions and go to a lot of Special Forces gatherings too. Strong pension money and nothing else to do. We were pretty close with those boys, down through the years you know." He wandered away somewhere in his mind. "And then there's the others." It was barely discernible, almost like a whisper.

"What others?"

"What's that?"

"The others you mentioned. Who?"

"They all came out of Nam. Most of 'em dead, either over there, or by their own hand after they got back. Lurps!"

"Yeah, I read about them."

"Well I knew lots of 'em. They were a different breed of cat. Them and the tunnel rats." He grew distant again, going into that place these kinds of men inhabited. A kind of surreal existence. "Know where a couple of the super specialists live, in the physical world that is. Difficult to reach 'em though. Don't socialize much, you know what I mean?"

They stared out at the Pacific, each in a private part of their mind lost in thought. This conversation had gone far enough, and it ended on that last note.

*   *   *

The conversation played and replayed in Tom's head as he headed back to the Old Man. '

The Chief was exactly what they were looking for. Exactly! Wonder who the others were? From the sounds of it they'd taken up some other way of living. Needed to. Probably couldn't make the turn. Kill, kill, kill and go home. Who the hell they kiddin.'

The same angry tears rose up in his eyes again as he pondered whether the always present legions of four eyed bastards that whip up all these killing sessions called, what?

'What's the euphemism they're using now for war? Police actions? Active defense? Now that's dead cute. Love the preventive action line, and probably the greatest obscenity of them all, the Vietnam Conflict. Were those sick genius' still around? Yes, he knew damn good and well they are always around. Always stirring shit, starting wars but never to be found among the fighters. Too bad they couldn't do some of the fighting and dying!'

He switched channels in his mind wondering.

'My God how could he have been so lucky as to run this man down in such a short time.'

He knew the answer of course and chuckled thinking how carefully Alex George had put everything together for him, not the actual meeting with CWO Evans but the fact he knew someone would be there that would fit their needs. He must have been sitting in the Shed planning and investigating this course of action for a very long time. Probably ever since Momma died because he was almost never seen at the office anymore. Not that he needed to be there because he'd been the chief executive officer for many years now, groomed to take over total management of this enormous conglomerate anyway, all those years serving the Old Man like few are served in these times. It was a natural thing when he actually took the reins, but there was never any doubt who the boss really was. It was still Alex George and unless the infirmities of old age took his mind he was always going to be in command. That's the way it was, and Tom would have it no other way. He had no ego problem whatever when it came to matters involving Alex George.

CHAPTER 21

"So you two got to the point, did'ya?"

It was night and Helen was laying in a majestic fashion at the feet of her master. All four legs tucked under her body, head up, ears at rigid attention, the magnificent face staring at Tom.

"Oh yeah, we got there all right. I know where he lives, and he knows where I'm coming from. I wanted to talk to you one more time before I pop the question to him, but I'll tell you right now I'd be astonished if he turns us down. I think his life's over, according to the big boys, but I don't think it's over according to CWO Evans. I know the look Boss, I wore it long enough. He's got it. He was trained to do terrible things and now nobody wants him, but he's not through yet."

"He still think you're who you say?"

"I doubt it. I don't think he's ever bought who I said I was, but you know what?"

"No, what?"

"I don't think he gives a shit!"

"You don't?"

"No sir, I don't. I think he wants back in and will be ready to go the minute we convince him what we want is right. When I do that, and I can do that, we're on the way."

"Okay, tell you what. Wait a week, let it simmer, then get him on the phone, tell him to meet you in Kansas City. By the way, how'd you guess? I'm not losing my memory am I?"

"What do you mean?"

"Kansas City? That's where everything begins. Did I tell you that when we were talking?" The old Frenchman leaned forward while Helen maintained her icy stare.

"No sir, you didn't!"

Both Helen and Tom were startled at the spontaneous outburst of laughter, loud and long that rang out from the Old Man.

"How long we been together son?"

Now it was Tom's turn to laugh because he knew exactly what the Boss was getting at.

"Since '39." Then as suddenly, only with great seriousness. "Jesus Boss, where'd it all go?"

"Beats me. Seems like yesterday I was living down there by the fork in the road to St. Martinville. When could that have been? Early 1900's. Happiest coonass boy

God ever created, now here we are." Chuckling. "We've been together so long you know what I want before I get around to asking. Kansas City huh? Hit the nail right on the head and didn't even know you were swinging at it. OK kid, go for it! Nail him down and let's get on with it! See me before you leave though will you? I'll be contacting some other people to set things up."

The week seemed to go on forever because Tom was so anxious for this final meeting. He knew they would have to get everything handled between them, and he also knew it would take some time to get the other men. That would be his responsibility. Tom would have no part of that and very little part of anything from now on except contacting the Chief to inform him of the next target.

The $100,000 was earnest money on the part of the Old Man, and there would be substantial start up expenses. Tom wasn't a stranger to carrying that kind of money but for some reason or other he never felt comfortable with it. He wasn't afraid anyone was going to steal it, knock him on the head and make off with it. Tom never thought about physical harm coming his way. Why should he? He'd been there when all the really big shooters were trying to blow his ass up but didn't. He could not bring himself to anything like fear about his own personal safety, he just didn't like to carry that kind of money around.

The big jet was circling on its approach to Kansas City International as he stared down at the ground. Looked sort of dismal down there, cold, dark. Leavenworth federal penitentiary, just across the river from KCI didn't go by unnoticed either. He was aware. He tried to talk the Old Man out of the program. He really tried, not so much out of personal concern but fear for the Boss himself should they be discovered. Those concerns were removed by his smiling leader who reminded him once again that people with his kind of money don't go to jail.

"Fuck 'em." He said. "Fuck 'em son. Even if we get caught you think they want to put an old fart like me in the can. What they gonna do besides kill me."

He saw the expression in his younger friends eyes when he mentioned somebody might kill him.

"You wouldn't let that happen anyway would you son?" It was whispered, emotion packed. He knew what the words and thoughts entailed.

"No, I wouldn't."

"You and old Helen here. Right to the death."

                    *   *   *

The airport was enormous with the three terminal buildings sitting there, looking for all the world like inverted cups in the old shell game.

'Now you see 'em.' He thought. 'Now you don't.'

That seemed appropriate for this was exactly what they were heading into. He was about to create an invisible force of men skilled in the art of murder. A group more deadly than any the world had ever seen in such a compact organization, and strange as it seemed, he had no misgivings whatever about what was going to happen. He knew it was so far outside the norm as to be beyond belief. He also felt in his heart that the Old Man was right, it was something that had to be done. They had unlimited funds, it was a last project for the Boss and of course Tom would do anything he asked. That, was never in question.

Evans was waiting in the hotel lobby staring upward. He stopped and watched the former SEAL, transfixed, unblinking, eyes sweeping the area, up, down.

"CT! Good to see you. How's it going? Any trouble getting here." He was met by a strange look he couldn't define.

"Everything's fine." He indicated the chair next to him. "Sit here for a minute will you."

"Sure what's up?"

He looked toward the wall opposite them.

"Why that's where they all died."

He spoke softly, like they were in the presence of something awesome.

"You mean this's the place...."

"Yeah." Softly. "Seems like some kind of terrible waste doesn't it? Everybody having a wonderful time. Tea dance they called it. Husbands, wives, parents, heads of families. Big people, little people smashed like bugs. Dancing one minute, dead the next. Can you imagine that?"

"Jesus, I didn't think...."

"Hey that's OK. I mean it's just one of those things that happens, you know what I mean?"

"I do."

"So you drive up in a cab and ask God, 'Sir, how come those people were all blown out together?'"

"What's He answer?"

"Oh I 'spect He'd want me to know it was none of His doing whatever. Somebody screwed up and they died, not necessarily their time as we all like to say. No, somebody didn't do their job, and that's the way of the world. Time and tide seem to have a way of taking care of those things"

"Mostly time though don't you think?"

"Yeah I guess. Well listen let's don't start whatever we're going to do, on a bummer. Good to see you, and I'm hungry, what do you say we get something to eat. Know any good places? Hell you ought to, this's your town."

Tom studied the look that went with his statement.

"I know lots of places. What's your pleasure. Steak, seafood, chicken, barbecue?"

"Hold it right there. Did you say barbecue?"

"Only the best there is, is all. You like it?"

"God I guess so. Don't know what the hell's the problem on the west coast but nobody seems to be able to do good barbecue. Throw lots of sweet sauce on, and claim it's barbecue but forget it."

They drove on a circuitous route to the barbecue place, which was only a short distance. It was dark now and he felt he could see anyone following a great deal easier than during the day. He was still exercising extreme caution taking no chances whatever, at this stage in the game, utilizing the same kind of caution he used way back in the Pacific. He wasn't alive now because he had been some vacuous brained idiot charging machine guns with little more than courage. No, no his had always been a thinking game starting when he shot the Japanese soldier out of the tree on Makin, ending when he had the alligators of the Atchafalaya hide the evidence of his last murder.

"Without a doubt that's the best barbecue I've ever had." He was impressed and pleased after their meal.

"Yeah it is, isn't it? Kind of surprising too, the place I mean."

"Oh hell yes!" He laughed suddenly. "If this was San Diego, we'd have some chrome and plate glass palace to house food like this."

"Well this ain't San Diego. This is Kansas City and this is the best barbecue you're ever going to find. Different isn't it?"

"You live here long Tom?"

"Yeah I guess you could say that. Home office is here. It's close in time to everywhere in the country. Tell you what let me show you some of the town, we can talk and digest our dinner while we're rubber necking."

The drive was aimless, downtown, out to the Plaza, through residential areas back up to the Liberty Memorial, a memorial to the men of WWI. A complex of buildings housing memorabilia with a huge cement shaft rising many feet in the air. High atop a hill directly across from the old Union Station, a really beautiful setting overlooking all of downtown.

"Damn, this is something isn't it." CWO Evans was sincere in his appreciation of the scene.

"It really is. This is really quite some town. Used to be a wild son of a bitch too, back in the twenties and thirties. Why right down there," he indicated the area outside the massive, now dead Union station building, down the long lawn across the street and through the large parking area, "is where the great Union Station massacre took place. Ever hear of it?"

"Don't think so. How many got killed?"

"Some. Nothing like over there." Indicating with a nod of his head the hotel where they met. "Big deal at the time."

"Yeah, I can imagine." The question came like a shot. "What we doing up here?"

"Want to show you the city. Show you the city and talk a little bit before we go in the office tomorrow. You know, get our ducks in a row, so to speak."

Tom looked down at him in a somber manner.

"Go for it!" The Chief replied.

'Oh yeah.' Tom thought. 'He knows. He's known all along.'

"Yeah, Ok. I think we're through with the preliminaries, so we might's well get down to business."

"Which is?"

"I work for a group of people," that was correct, Avro Industries was one hell of a large group of people, "that are interested in instituting a course of action extreme in nature, by all accepted standards." That part not quite correct because the they he referred to was really he, the Old Man.

"Ok. I appreciate your words. I figured something like that. Go ahead."

"These people are vitally interested in making an effort to eliminate some situations existing in our society, and have existed in all societies from the beginning of time."

He glanced at the CWO Evans, both men leaning on the rail overlooking the city. "You with me so far?"

"I'm with you."

"Even though mankind has advanced through development and administration of laws, there are times when these laws either get out maneuvered or just plain steam rolled by one means or another. Cunning lawyers, powerful connections, bribery, murder. Organized crime specializes in that. There is and always has been that element of people who operate completely outside anything like accepted behavior. Let me use someone like a powerful labor leader, or the major crime figure like there's always been an abundance of right here in Kansas City. People who bring much suffering and death with them wherever they show up. You know what I mean, don't you?"

"Yes, I do." The quiet reply.

"This group wants something done about these people, and we need someone with special skills to carry out their wishes."

"Skills, like yours and mine?" He looked the exMarine square in the eye.

"Exactly. These people feel our country has a few men of our type, who are experienced in the administration of swift and final action, more or less shunned by society now that those times are over. More probably, than less. Oh we know they'll never be over for good, but people like us who have been...what was it you said, faded, fucked, and laughed at...." The Chief nodded looking out over the city. "Yes, well those are now put out to pasture, so to speak. We know of course when the next war comes and we need killers of this type, a whole new group of specialists will be trained and we're off to the races again. We want to find a few of those men and institute the plans we have in mind?"

"I appreciate what you're saying, and I know how careful you feel you should be saying it, but don't play games with me. Let's be direct." He pushed away from the rail and turned facing him directly. "Correct me if I'm wrong but what you're saying is you want some people dead! That I know! What I don't know is who, and why?"

"OK. Let's be direct, diplomacy takes too long." Tom was relieved to get it said in plain English. "We have a list of those we want to start with and while I won't give you names at this moment I'll explain to you why we want them dead."

"I'm listening." His eyes looked different.

"We want a certain labor leader who has spent a lifetime pillaging his own union, and the economy of this nation, crushing and killing anyone who's gotten in his way. He speaks of brotherhood and fellowship while his goons are breaking bones all around him. We have proof of many murders he's been directly responsible for, but because of his personal power no one has been able to put him in jail. We want him dead. Do you have any trouble with that one?"

"None! Go on." It wasn't more than a whisper.

"There's a major importer of narcotics...,"

"None!" He didn't let him finish. "Go on."

"A politician who seems to assault the law."

"What's he done?"

"You name it, it's in his book. We have reason to believe...no let me put that another way, we know this man has robbed, cheated, stolen and raped his way into the powerful position he holds at this time. We know of five people who have died, and many, many more who will suffer the rest of their lives because of his brutal, insensitive ways. He's bribed, corrupted, threatened, and killed, or at least had killed, with seeming impunity and gets more powerful as time goes by. Nobody wants to take him on."

"But you do?"

"Yes. He's too dangerous to stay in power, especially since he's looking for higher office."

"Which one."

"The oval office."

"Who else?"

"One who slipped through the net. This one we'll handle in another way."

"Who?"

"He's in the penitentiary serving a life sentence for the murder of a good man. Important man. Hope of his people. So they gave him life and one of these days he'll be walking with a piece of paper that says his debt's squared. It's not! My people feel he should have paid with his life and intend that he does. He won't be the obligation of the people we'll have on the streets. We'll handle him another way."

"You mean kill him in the pen?" The Chief asked, surprised.

"Yes, he'll die in his cell."

"Jesus, you people got some juice don't you?"

"We do. We have powerful contacts, unlimited money and determination. Lots of all three. We know what we want and the men needed to do it."

"You said five, I've only heard four. Who's the fifth?"

"Might be hard to take Chief, with your background."

"Looks like you guys are trying to touch all the bases, am I right?"

"We are."

"And what you want to do is let the country, and the world, know you'll reach anyone, anywhere, responsible for tremendous suffering and kill them?"

"Right."

"Then I can guess where the fifth guy comes from. There's one group that causes more agony than any of these pikers you've mentioned so far. A group that visits sorrow, death, and agony on people, not only in the now, but for the rest of their lives. I'm talking mothers of sons who are gone forever. They get to think about 'em every day forever don't they?"

"They do." He was interested in seeing how much the leader of their group had guessed.

"You guys want somebody to pay for visiting this kind of horror on many, many people don't you? Many mothers, fathers, wives, loved ones?"

"We do."

Tom was surprised to a degree, but not totally because he knew this man was an extremely intelligent person.

"You want the General don't you?" He swung around facing him.

"How'd you know?"

"Christ Tom, don't you think a lot of people feel exactly the same way? Don't you think at the very least the families of the boys that were killed in that pointless war feel exactly the way you people do?" He hung his head toward the pavement shaking it back and forth. "I don't know which came first with that son of a bitch, the lie or the perpetuation of the lie. It was always going to be over right soon, but right soon never showed up did it? I don't think I'll ever be able to understand the justice involved?"

"How's that?"

"Say a guy embezzles what, a hundred thousand? Everybody gets all up tight and slams his ass in jail for a long time. Then for contrast along comes some high line dude with stars all over him and embezzles not only horrendous sums of money in equipment it takes to hold one of those God damn charades, he embezzles lives too! Vietnam was lost before we ever got off the fucking boat, but the General kept the party going with his happy horseshit. Wouldn't you like to know how many good men died because of that bloated, egomaniac." Tom could have sworn he heard a sob from this special man. "Worse, how many men died there but haven't gotten around to stepping into their graves yet? I know a lot of those personally, and know about many more. You think I might be shocked because he's a military man, and I gave my life to the military? No way Thomas." His voice rose to a shout. "Fuck him! I'll kill him myself!"

It was all over. The only thing left was to iron out the details.

"You're in?"

"Yes, I'm in. I've always been in. What you're proposing is nothing new to me. I've always thought there has to be another way than what we see going on all around us. The slick maneuvering. Yeah I'm in! Tell me what you want done and how."

"Five men to start with, and we're not locked in to that figure. You will be in complete charge of the operation from now on. You and I will probably never see one another again, the reason being...."

"Security. I understand that."

"That's right. You don't know who we are, and your men don't know who the others are. If we lose people in this, we don't want them to have any idea who the others are or where they live. This program has worked successfully for the IRA for years and I see no reason it won't work for us."

"Agreed!"

"OK, it's money talking time. Come with me."

They walked toward the rental car as another vehicle drove up. It was very dark, except for what little light reached them from the Memorial. The occupants of the other car got out as the two men approached.

"Hey man, will you look at this now!" The voice seemed to be that of the leader. "Why we was just gonna steal your tires my man, but now that you two old farts show we might's well take what you got too, huh boys?"

"Yeah, yeah! God damn man will you look at that coat! I get the big guys coat." Another replied. "Hey Bubba the little guy ought to be about your size, what you think?"

"You dudes got any money on you? Watches? Jewelry?" The leader asked, assuming the impending robbery was a foregone conclusion.

The two intended victims had other notions though as they quietly drifted apart, all their past deadly skills at high intensity. They moved gracefully in opposite directions thereby splitting the hostile group. Their hands darted to their belts, unseen in the night.

"Why don't you come and see what we have? Why don't you come and take it if you can?" The voice was Tom's but he hadn't heard it since that rainy night in Baton Rouge. As if on signal both slid out of their topcoats effortlessly, at the same time the one called Bubba saw something and raised the alarm.

"Jesus Christ you guys, get in the car!"

"Get in the car?" His answer. "What you mean, man! We got 'em! They's five of us, two of them. Let's take 'em!"

"Get in the God damn car!" He was hurrying away. "I'm leavin', now!"

"Are you nuts man? Are you out of your fuckin' mind?" Another of the gang asked. "We got these mothers!"

"Jesus, Jesus, can't you see what they got? Get in the car and let's get outta here. They'll kill all of us!"

Bubba was screaming. He saw the glint of Tom's knife, somehow catching a view of the entire weapon. He'd never seen anything like it in his life. Even to this primitive lad it was terrifying. He swung his eyes toward the smaller man, stunned to see he was carrying a small ax flat in front of him, like a natural extension of his body. He was moving like a cat directly toward the group.

After they understood what was happening Bubba got them in the car, and they were gone quickly, none of them willing to get within reach of what they'd discovered. They watched the shabby car disappear around the divided road, almost out of control.

The two old warriors looked at each other for what seemed like a long time, but was really only a moment.

"Why you son of a bitch!" The Chief laughed.

"Me? Me a son of a bitch? What about you?" Tom was laughing so hard he was holding his sides. "I suppose you brought that thing with you just to whittle with. How do you whittle with an ax?" Indicating the small, deadly weapon he had in his hand. "Didn't trust me did you?"

"I'll tell you something Tom, never in my life have I been big on trust. No way! I suspect you weren't either, in the old days. That's probably why us two old dudes are standing here looking at each other right now. Who'd you trust in the South Pacific?"

"Nobody! Just me and this!" Holding out the savage knife.

The two warriors stood facing one another, listening to the far away drums, holding their terrible weapons. It was natural, second nature for both, ready to kill whatever was necessary.

"You gonna put that thing away any time soon?" The Chief asked laughing but not lessening his own grip.

"Yeah, but you know what?"

"What?"

"Feels pretty good doesn't it? Like skinny dipping after wearing a suit. You know what I mean?"

"I do. I do indeed." He replied as they put their weapons away, picked up their coats and walked toward the car.

Tom popped the trunk, grabbed the briefcase and asked the Chief to get in the car with him.

"And leave that ugly thing in your belt will you, what I got here isn't going to hurt you at all." He thought a minute. "Wrong! Come to think of it, what I got in here is probably the most deadly thing known to man."

He swung the case open revealing the $100,000 in cash.

"Gaaawed damn!" The Navy man exclaimed. "Where'd you get all that? You rob a bank on the way over here or something?"

"Nope, like I told you the people I represent have all the money we're going to need, now or in the future. Money's no problem. I want you to know that. We know...I know you are used to command. Command is management. This is a hundred thousand and we want you to manage it. There's much, much more where that came from?"

"What do you want me to do with it?" He asked.

"You'll have expenses. Lots of them."

"Yeah I know, but nobody's got this kind of expenses."

"You will. Take the money! Use it however you see fit. Take what you need for yourself personally."

"I don't get you...." He smiled in the dim light of the car. "By the way is it really Tom?"

"It's really Tom. Why do you ask, you think I'd shit you about that?" Tom was laughing out loud as he asked.

"In a heartbeat Tom, or whatever your name is." Both laughed hysterically. "In a heartbeat!"

"Remember though, this group is to be, and remain invisible. Only when we act will we be anything but. From this moment on I'll contact you in San Diego. You'll never contact me. You won't know how. You will never know who I am, or who I represent. When we have an operation going, I'll maintain close contact with you but it will always be either by phone or some other kind of communication. Keep your identity secret from the men you choose and above all tell them they keep theirs secret from one another. This should be explained, hammered home and understood by all your people going in, along with the reason for so doing. Keep nothing from them, tell 'em right up front and they'll give you their complete trust. You have any questions about what we want, or anything else?"

It really wasn't that complicated, the exSEAL had been accustomed to receiving orders all his life. Some of them, issued militarily, were exactly like what was being proposed by this tall man.

"Some."

"Let's talk about 'em then. Let's get it handled here because like I say, you'll never see me again. Not face to face."

"What do we pay these people?"

"You're entirely in charge of that. I suspect however, that we will all be surprised at what it's going to take to bring these men in."

"What you mean?" He sat with his leg up on the seat looking straight in Tom's face, wondering what he really looked like. He thought right from the beginning, in San

Francisco, something looked different. Now he knew absolutely he wasn't looking at the real man, whoever he was, at his side.

"We think there'll be men out there who would probably join forces with you for no money at all. We don't expect that. We don't for one split second suggest you even hint at such a thing when you contact them, but we know they're out there. When you secure each man, I want you to make your own deal with him. If he wants to be paid on a periodic basis? Do it. If it's annual? Do it. Do whatever's necessary and don't worry about your decisions. We have an in depth report on you. We know more about you right now than you probably do. Whatever you decide, at any time, will be OK by us."

He noted the raised eyebrows.

"Oh yeah. We can reach there too. Remember what I said, we have money, literally unlimited money, and with money like that goes everything. Anyway we know what kind of a man you are and with that knowledge we're entrusting the entire operation to you. You do the dealing, but we feel somehow that because of what we are asking, and from whom, there won't be a price tag."

"How 'bout defense money for anybody gets nailed." The question was obvious, anyone would ask.

"You know Chief I have a difficult time imagining any of our people ever getting caught. Do you know what I mean?"

The implication was there, powerful and unsaid. The men he wanted would simply never be taken alive. They would be like any other wild creature running from capture to their death. Many of them had been resisting life since their killing days anyway. Most of the ones he wanted had divorced themselves completely from society, not only wanting nothing from it but terrified to join lest they revert to what they were and kill someone totally innocent. They'd fight to the last bullet, that he knew, and would finish fighting with knives, bricks, fists or teeth. He knew unless they were rendered unconscious none would ever be taken alive. It was a legitimate question, the Chief deserved an answer.

"All you have to know is what I'm telling you now. If you could see inside my soul you'd understand I'm telling you the absolute truth. We're going after those people who always seem to be beyond judgment, for all the reasons I've mentioned. In a way this is just plain sardonic because the money behind us is such that I doubt we could ever be reached. There's too much for that to happen. The same thing applies to the men we want. If somehow they do get captured I promise you they'll have the best legal defense money can buy, and if that doesn't work I'll guarantee you they will have the best justice money can buy and we both know the blind lady with the scales can be had easily enough with a blank check."

Tom reached out his hand to take the small man by the elbow, looking him straight in the eyes.

"I'm not the person heading this Chief, I want you to believe that. I tried to talk them out of it, but their arguments were too strong. I'll tell you one thing though, they believe the system is breaking down and want to shock it back into some semblance of working order again." He fell silent for a moment, adding. "You know there's a school of theological thought that says mankind has had a battle going on ever since the jealous angels told God they wanted a piece of the action. They stepped up and challenged Him and He blew 'em out, starting a never ending war between good and evil. That's what we're going to be about, taking care of His end of things because He's not walking the streets. If that's presumptuous, screw it. That's the way we see it, and that's the way we're going to approach it, but we must have somebody to head the group and that's why we want you." Tom held out his hand. "Can we count you in?"

He thought for a long time, many thoughts racing through his mind. All the possibilities flashed by. The responsibility of command, the thrill of action, the power of weaponry. How to find the men they'd need, and their chances of avoiding detection. It seemed a long time, this moment of decision, but he took the proffered hand, shaking it, thus sealing the bargain as he replied softly.

"Yeah, count me in." Adding softly. "Jesus Christ man I am a warrior. It's what I am now, and all I've ever been. I need another war!"

CHAPTER 22

"A real moment of truth between the Chief and yourself up there on the...the, ah...what did you call it?"

They were in the Shed seated on the high stools at the end of the bar, Helen wedged uncomfortably between them. She was miffed at the seating, preferring the chairs they usually sat in while conversing. She could at least keep a sharp eye on Tom there, and doze while watching.

"War Memorial. An imposing thing and seemed like a good place for a meeting, or conversation like we were going to have."

"I'm not judging you Tom, but I am curious. Why the knife?"

"Not too sure about that myself Mr. Alex, except maybe I regressed a little preparing for our last contact." Tom's quizzical reply.

"If things had taken a nasty turn for the absolute worse, think you might have used it on the Chief?" It was an interesting point to the Old Man.

"Pretty obvious to me my subconscious was saying things I haven't heard for years. No doubt I took the knife along in case he surprised me and turned into something I wasn't expecting."

"Could you have used it, if that'd happened.?"

His answer came slow, as Tom thought it through. What if the Chief had come for the wrong reasons? What if he'd come to pry information out of Tom that would lead him or others back to the Old Man? If so, what then? Tom knew the answer to the question the moment it appeared in his mind.

"If I thought he meant to do us harm, I'd used it in a minute. Yes Sir." It was a statement of fact, stunning in its implication.

Alex George looked at his protege for some time before commenting.

"Then it's as I figured."

"What?"

"People like you and the Chief who developed...no that's not the word I'm looking for." He thought a moment. "No developed doesn't describe well enough, I think perfected is the word. Yes people like you with these highly perfected skills in killing, those instincts are always there, always alive."

"I thought about it too and apparently that morality, or lack of it, is always there just under the surface."

"Then if you were ready to kill the Chief, if need be, all the old feelings must still be there?"

"They must." He laughed.

"What?" The Old Man asked.

"Oh I don't know, but I think it's real funny, these two old warriors facing one another up there with their ugly weapons, listening to the beat of long ago drums in their minds. Listening and feeling, still under the spell of the adrenalin rush we experienced with the muggers, and both ready to kill."

"I don't understand? What's funny about that?"

Probably the fact we were armed with such deadly weapons, our favorite weapons, and the other guy wasn't supposed to know. Hell if those guys hadn't shown up we'd have never known the other guy was coming at least equipped for killing. Now we do." He paused a moment. "Now that I think of it I can see where he probably learned as much about me at that moment, as I did him. We already know all about him, but he isn't privileged in the same fashion with regard to us. He learned something that night that I hadn't planned, but it worked out perfectly." Tom burst out laughing again.

"What now?"

"We were having a drink afterwards and got to laughing about school days."

"School days?"

"Yes. We remembered there were always two boys could whip hell out of the rest of the class. They could beat everybody else, and knew it, but were never sure about each other. You know what I mean? With your reputation in the old days as a bar room fighter, you've got to know what I mean. Kind of a Mexican stand off until finally you have to get it on. Find out who's king of the hill, or king of the bar."

The Old Man remembered the times that kind of situation came up, which was often. Tyler, Lufkin, Oklahoma City, Shreveport, Lake Arthur, and lots more places with no names. Then there was the last one. The big drunk at the equipment show in Dallas. Alex really tried to get out of that one, but the guy wouldn't let him alone. Kept coming back until the only thing left was to whip his ass. He chuckled recalling H.L. Hunt taking all bets, the big guy was going to whip him. That was funny because Hunt lost a lot of money and thought it hilarious too.

"Shit Alex, I hope we're still friends but I just had to bet on that big bastard!" He laughed holding out his hand to the younger oil man.

"Aw hell no H.L.."

"Well I sure hope not. I'd never seen you fight before, and even though I'd heard stories about you I thought that big son of a bitch'd be too much for you. Thought I'd let him whip on your ass for a little while, then have my boys stop it. Hell I never figured you could handle him and thought I might pick up my expenses out of the deal with maybe a little something left over to get a pretty for the Missus. Now you got to say that was a good plan, don't you Alex?"

"Hell yes H.L., that's real thoughtful of you. How much did you lose?"

He laughed these many years later thinking how the oil magnate squirmed.

"Not too much son. Just a little bit."

"What you call a little bit, ten dollars?" The smiling coonass asked.

"Naw Alex." Hunt muttered, turning away. "Twenty."

"Shit, twenty dollars?" Alex was disappointed. "You're gonna let me get my ass stomped for twenty bucks?"

"No God damn it, twenty thousand if you got to know."

Alex was in hysterics then and now as he replayed it remembering his final comment to the storied tycoon.

"And I thought you were the king of the wildcatters. Shit! I'll never put my money on any of your wells with judgment like that. Yeah think I'll just call you Hunt, King of the dry holers." They laughed all the way to the bar.

"Thinking about the story I told you so many times about H.L. Hunt. Kinda bears out what you're talking about. So the Chief, he's in?"

"All the way Mr. Alex. All the way."

"All right! I know we can't put a time table on this thing, as far as getting his people's concerned, but what do you think?"

"He's mighty sharp, and knows a lot of people in his shitty war business."

"What you mean shitty war?" The Boss wasn't familiar with the phrase.

"People, groups, fighting outside accepted rules of war. They slip out of their cover, kill whoever they want and then disappear while you're looking right at them. The Japanese had a class called Ninjitsu's who were masters at this. I was expert at this type of thing, and even though I was trained by the Colonel, he had no idea as to what lengths his training would go. It's been carried to great lengths since I stumbled on my personal method of soft, silent, sudden death. Shitty war! No rules anymore. No, no! Well these are the people we need and he's going after them. Shouldn't take too long but you've got to remember he's got one hell of a tough job to do. Finding 'em won't be easy. Talking 'em into what we want might be tougher."

The Old Man reached for a sheaf of papers handing them to Tom.

"Here. Get these to him."

"What are they?" Tom asked.

"Names son. Names of people who have what we want. Special people who learned their lessons well. So well as a matter of fact the Chief'll have a hard time finding them. Some of 'em are right out in the open, and some aren't." Not many made the change you did Tom." The Old Man was deep in thought.

"No I'm sure not, but they didn't have the help I did, either."

He had the help all right, he thought driving home. He had the best professional help the Old Man's money could provide. The psychiatrists did all they knew how, in 1946, to put his mind in workable order again. Nancy loved him totally bringing his battered body into the effort through the physical lovemaking they introduced to each other. He'd been so many places, killed so many men and was still a virgin. How odd. Strange and beautiful were their sexual forays. Tentative, cautious giving way finally to complete abandon. Yes she loved him aggressively. She took care of his physical needs. And then there was Momma. She was the one who took care of his spiritual needs. Her love was powerful beyond words. She pulled him out of his mental shell, gently, lovingly but with a driving intensity that would not, could not, be denied. He was one of her children, she would fight as tenaciously for him, as would any mother of the wild trying to protect her young. Hers was the spiritual force that completed the struggle for the three sides of Tom Brooks. Mental, physical, spiritual.

Tom set up communication with the Chief whereby he could reach him on a one way basis. He sent him the list the Old Man gave him, the names of the special few. They were as they'd discussed in the early stages of their conversations, unattached.

That wasn't hard, most of them choosing to live alone in fear of their own savage behavior.

"Keep the line open Chief. I'll get in touch with you once a month until we get this operational." The parting conversation at the airport.

"And what if I need to get hold of you?" A logical question.

"Run an ad in the Wall Street Journal. Say you need more information to close the deal, and address it to Tom. My people want it that way and that's the way it's going to be."

"Kansas City, the home office? That's bullshit isn't it?"

"It is." Tom answered.

"Figured, but why the weird route to the restaurant last night? Hell we could've walked from the hotel over there."

"You noticed that?" Tom laughed. "How the hell'd you catch it? You never been here before have you."

"No, I've never been here before but you got to remember you're talking to a man who had to figure out directions swimming in the dark, under the waters of the world for years. Thought at first we were simply sightseeing, then figured you were watching for a tail. Am I right?"

"Boy I'll tell you one thing," he laughed "we got to have a lot of trust from now on 'cause we sure didn't have any at all, to begin with. Either one of us."

"Yeah, well you got to admit Tom, that folks don't get involved in these kinds of affairs every day, so caution is a natural thing."

"I know, Chief. I know." The somber reply as he stared at the strange wooden floor of the airport, wondering in the back of his mind who got rich on that one. "As a matter of fact, I know of no time in history anything like this's been done. I think it's one of those ideas whose time has come. What a shame. What a stupid fucking shame."

"You're right about that." The Chief was helping Tom stare at the floor, running many things through his head. "I doubt if it's a unique thought though. Matter of fact I know it's not. Thought of it myself many times."

"I'm sure lots of people have Chief, but what we're talking about is a project that takes tremendous planning, and organization. This takes contacts, the likes of which few people have. It also takes money and we have that. We're talking two different kinds of power here, financial and influential. Believe me when I tell you we have these, plus the main ingredient."

"Which is?"

"As terrible as it sounds, unflinching resolve and maybe a lot of luck."

"How's luck enter the picture?"

"Well what we are about to do will be one of the most stunning things to take place in this, or any other country in this century. Wouldn't you agree?"

"I would."

"We expect the support of the largest section of this country in the doing. The silent majority we hear so much about. We think when your crew drops the hammer you're going to incur the wrath of every voice and institution there is. The super lefties and righties will be hollering too, but when the public sees who you dropped it on, and the reasons why, I'll absolutely guarantee they'll be lined up solid behind us."

"You been reading Mao or Che?" He was kidding, and he was not.

"No, I haven't. Why?"

"Well your people must have been, because that's what both of 'em had to say about this sort of thing. You're talking about guerrilla warfare of a sort."

"You know, I hadn't really thought of it that way but I guess you're right." And he hadn't. Not from the guerrilla standpoint.

"You're damn right, I'm right! Christ that's what I was all about in the Navy, guerrilla warfare. I'll tell you something else, the most basic tenet of that school of thought is, you must have the minds and the hearts of the people with you. When you have that you have ultimate power, whether it's some guy picking coffee beans far off, or a brain surgeon in the building next door. It's all the same."

Alex George said he felt most of the people of America would approve this thing, especially in view of the scum, rich, powerful, famous, but scum nevertheless who would be the victims of their terrible effort.

"Look for the newspapers to rake our ass across the coals son. They'll give us the most heat. That's their thing, to give the public the down side of everything. That's OK though 'cause people will be thinking for themselves anyway. They may think what we're doing is pretty horrible, but they'll also think the loss will have been worth it."

The ad showed up in the Wall Street Journal around Christmas and Tom flew the Avro jet to Tulsa to call the Chief. It would always be that way at the insistence of the Boss. Caution was what he wanted, backed up by invisible walls of anonymity.

"What you got?" He was calling from a phone booth, somewhat surprised his heart was beating faster than normal.

"Your people, but I added something you didn't mention. Want to hear about it?" It was a natural enough question even though he was in complete charge of operations.

"Go ahead."

"Got the five you mentioned. Wasn't that much of a job to tell you the truth. The way you people researched made it much easier."

"So what's added?"

"You were talking about a straight five people, right?"

"Right."

"We need a tracker. That's the last time I'll use that word. In the future I'll refer to advance man. OK?"

"OK."

"Somebody we can send in to get all the information we need on these people."

"Agreed."

"I found her."

"Her!" The explosive reply.

"Yeah. She's perfect for what we want. Young enough to be good looking if she tries. Old enough to have been down the road and heard all the bullshit. Small enough she won't even be seen by those she's watching and listen to this will 'ya. She's a photographer, free lance. Isn't that great?"

"What's so great about that?"

"Don't you see Tom, she's got the balls, or whatever females are supposed to have to get right in there. Right in the middle of the action."

"So?"

"So she sees things, things people like you and me don't. She's got an eye for the whole picture, you know what I mean? You and I take a picture, what do we see? I'll tell you. We see the subject, period. She sees not only the subject but everything around, behind and in front of what she's looking at. This is a gal who can see your party get out of a car and tell you not only what he was wearing but also tell you what kind of car it was, who was driving, how many spokes in the hub cap and what color the building was he stopped in front of."

"Yeah. I see what you mean." He was thinking it over as he went. "She can disappear right in front of you."

"Yeah, only better."

"Better? How you mean better?"

"She's invisible standing right in front of you."

"Yeah, I can see how she could be. Where'd you find her? How you know she's OK?" Both legitimate questions.

"I found her at one of our conventions. Watched her maneuvering all over the place. Elbows, hips, sliding and shoving. Scrappy little broad. We had a speaker there that led one of the first groups of men into the death camps in Germany, can't remember which one. Wasn't listening that good. I look over at this pushy gal and am flat ass blown away to see her in tears. I mean lots of tears, so I started listening good to what the guy had to say. He was talking about the survivors, some of them Jewish women who had looks enough to wind up whores for the Germans. They survived.

Saw this little lady sitting at the bar after it was all over and she was still in tears. I asked her why and she told me. Told me her mother was one of those whores. Sixteen years old and showed up at the camp where they put her right in service. You know, tattoo and all. So when we set 'em free, her mom had no visible harm done."

"No visible harm?"

"All the horribly starved, dead and dying and she was OK. Came to this country, went to college, got a degree, worked for a few years, married a nice guy and had our gal for a baby, but she couldn't get that camp out of her mind. Big time guilt. The husband dies about five years ago and somehow her mom took that as another indication of guilt. He was dead, she'd survived. Our gal, Sandi's her name, Sandi fought like a son of a bitch to keep her mom on an even keel but she couldn't."

"She lost her?" A quiet question.

"Yeah. She came home one night and found her mom. She'd hung herself. Guilt. The poor lady could not get it through her head she had nothing to do with anything. Not being born a Jew, not being forced into prostitution, not being a survivor, nothing."

"So how'd you get to her?"

"If you were there, you'd know instinctively she's the one for us. You know we all got something that motivates us. Well revenge is her burn! God damn revenge is what she wants! She wants revenge for her mother! Somebody's going to pay, she wants that more than she wants to breathe. You know, get the big fish so they can't eat the little ones. I'll tell you Tom, she impressed the shit out of me with her violent attitude. Said she'd been covering all sorts of slime ball motherfuckers, and believe me when I tell you I'm quoting her exact words. She said they were the kind that brought her mother to where she had to destroy herself. God damn Tom she like to tore my heart out while she was talking. I mean she was heartbroken and almost out of control with her rage. She wants the killer whales to pay up for her mom so we took it from there. Same old shit, she doesn't know who I really am and doesn't give a shit, just so she's in, if you'll let her. She knows I'm not alone in this." He paused. "I know you put me in charge of this thing, but I thought maybe we had some extenuating circumstances here and wanted you to know."

"Appreciate that, but you're the man. If you say we need her, that's good enough."

"Thought you'd say that and told her so." There was an unexplained pause on the other end of the line. "She stood there smiling at me with tears in her eyes. She said you'll never regret this decision."

"Ok, you got everything in place?"

"I do, except for one thing."

"What's that?"

"What if some of our people decide they don't want to go after a particular prospect? What if they decide sooner or later they don't want to be part of our staff anymore? What then?"

"They're out. Neither eventuality should present a problem. If we adhere to our plan of total secrecy, it simply won't matter."

"Even if somebody goes over to the other side?"

"Even if. In the first place they'd be too heavily implicated themselves to do such a thing, in the second place I don't foresee any of these men turning in this fashion, and if they don't know who the others are they can't blow the whistle?"

"Yeah, your right."

"Tell them going in they're under no obligation whatever to stay for life. Make sure they understand that and I don't think you'll ever have a problem. We know who we're dealing with here."

"OK. We're ready then and will wait to hear from you."

"I'll get the information you need then and be back to you soon. Oh, by the way."

"Yes."

"Don't go overboard for the advance man, will you not?"

"Don't worry. She got to me with her intensity, nothing else."

He flew back to LaFayette thinking about the conversation.

'A gal for a tracker huh? More I think of it the better it sounds. Small, nothing distinctive about her. What'd he say, she's invisible standing right in front of you? Jesus, she could assume almost any dress, including that of a man and be a different looking person every time she shows up!'

He was definitely working up enthusiasm over this unexpected addition to their group. He wondered how the Old Man would feel about it.

They were sitting on the long porch, surrounding the Shed, enjoying some unseasonably warm Louisiana weather. Helen seemed to be especially appreciative laying in the direct rays of the sun, her body cushioned by heavy St. Augustine grass, enjoying the thermal effect on her dark coat, her long muzzle pointed directly at Tom.

"Well then son we're ready to go?" The Old Man seemed as enthused as Tom had seen him since the death of Momma.

"We are, although I still wish you'd abandon the whole idea."

"Why Tom, why?"

Although he was Alex George, powerful, domineering, The Boss, he respected Tom's opinion. They'd been through too much together for it to be any different. All the way from 1939 until now with enough jammed in to fill many lifetimes.

"Because, if for no other reason than what you want is against the law."

"Whose law, Tom? Theirs? We the people? Isn't that what the politicians use all the time as justification for everything under the sun? The people say.... The people want.... The people speak.... I don't want to hear any of that happy horseshit anymore because it's what they, the God damned flannel mouthed politicians want themselves. They don't give a shit about the people."

"Yeah, see your point. I guess your right?" It was spoken with a tone of resignation.

"I know how terrible the whole plan seems on the surface but anybody in their right mind would have to agree it's time. It's time for something like this, and we're the people that have what it takes to make it happen." He paused, continuing. "I love you too much Tom to ask you to be involved in anything against your will. If you feel you want no part of this, I understand and you can cut loose. Nothing will change, but I'm gonna pursue this all the way because of Momma." Tears appeared in his eyes at her mention.

"But don't you see that's the thing, Mr. Alex. She would be horrified at what we're proposing."

"Oh hell yes I know that son. I do know. I also know how much she endured because of the suffering and death caused by these same people." The tears were falling freely down his face, there was a terrible set to his jaw. "Well I'm all through watching these bastards thumb their noses at the law. It's pay up time, and they're paying."

"Then if you're going through with it, I'm going with you." Tom was moved by the weeping Old Man, and he knew him well enough to recognize total commitment when it appeared.

"All right then Tom," handing him a thick envelope, "here's where we start. Get hold of the Chief and turn 'em loose." He paused a minute. "Man damn, this old coonass has changed a little more than somewhat, huh."

His was an expression Tom had never seen before.

CHAPTER 23

"Hey Manny!"

The labor leader's massive bodyguard thundered at his chief as he was leaving for his usual Wednesday afternoon lunch spot.

"We got a little broad out on the steps wants a picture of you. Works for one of those hippy California magazines. You know, green belt, pure ozone, save a fish, or some such shit. You want me to run her ass off?"

The fat executive stuck his pig like face around the corner of the bathroom. Shiny scar tissue around his eyes, from his early days as a professional fighter, gave him a constant inquisitive look.

"Yeah, well run her ass off. Got no time for a lady photographer."

His words were acted on immediately, as the burly announcer started across the room to send Sandi packing.

"Hold it Pat, wait up a minute. What's she look like?"

"Little broad, like I told you. Got some shit muckeldun outfit on all those hippy assholes wear. Can't tell if she's got any tits or not." He turned to eject the intruder. "I'll get rid of her."

"Naw wait a minute, we got time to kill, let's mess with her mind a little. You know that high line lookin' dude in the office? You know the guy with the gorgeous hair? Get 'im, tell him we're havin' some fun with this gal, and get that plaque the boys at the smoker gave me. You know, the one that says what a great guy I am. We'll have some fun and tell her it's a special presentation I'm receiving. Tell him there's a hunnert in it for him if he does it up right." He started laughing. "I got another hunnert for you if you can tell me what size tits she's got before we're through."

"You mean you don't think I can do it, right?" Pat replied. "You don't think I can feel those tits before she gets out of here, huh?"

"Somethin' like that!" Manny answered. "Go on, set it up! Let's have some fun!"

"Come on in here little lady." The other bodyguard motioned. "You're just in time. So happens we got a little ceremony goin' on here, right now. Presentation for Manny, from the mayor. Civic stuff. Grab your gear and get some pictures. What's the name of your paper?"

"It's the...." She could see he wasn't interested, walking away from her as he asked. That was OK, she'd been through this kind of treatment many times before.

"Maybe these other two gentlemen could get in the picture with you Mr. Beatty." Indicating the thugs that served as bodyguards. "It would look better. You know, emphasize the presentation more."

"Hey! Not a bad idea, little lady." Manny agreed, visually searching her denim shirt to see if she did have nice tits. "You better get a feel of those things Pat, before she gets outta' here." In a whispered aside to his main man. "I want to know what she's got."

"Oh my God, I'm so sorry!" The mock ceremonies were completed as Pat smiled salaciously at Sandi after cupping his hand over one of her breasts. "I was only tryin' to help you with your gear. I'm sorry about that."

"No harm done," she smiled, strange thoughts flashing through her mind, "not the first time and sure hope not the last." Returning his knowing smile.

"Atta girl. Guess you California gals are kinda used to getting felt up all the time anyway, ain't you. All those TV commercials I seen about them half naked gals running around the beach. Guess that's the way of it out there, huh?"

"Heard only the other day the oldest virgin in California is a ugly third grader." Manny contributed. "'Zat right?"

"Never thought of it before, but you're probably right. How 'bout I get one more picture of the three of you together." The presenter had already been paid off and returned to his desk. "I assume you're all officers of the union?"

"Yeah sweet thing. Officers!" All three laughed crazily while she took more fast pictures. "OK little broad we got places to go. It's been fun, and here's a little somethin' for you to remember us by." Manny pushed the twenty dollar bill in her shirt pocket making sure he felt as much breast as possible. "Why'nt you have dinner on me tonight, or maybe even under me?" Accompanied by a chorus of laughter. "Let's go you guys!"

This interlude was over, they had places to go.

"What you think Pat, a thirty six?"

"Naw hell no, thirty four B maybe. Little tits!" They laughed hilariously as they left the office, not even casting a glance at the malevolent stare they were receiving from the small stranger with the photographic gear.

Harold Shelton and Pat Jordan were sent to Philadelphia to get Manny and bring him to the Arkansas location they'd picked as a central gathering point. He found Harold working on a shrimp boat out of Morgan City, a short distance from LaFayette. He was exactly what they wanted, and after the Chief spent a few days talking to him he agreed to join them. He understood the extraordinary precautions and the reasons why, but above all he agreed totally with the purpose of the operation.

"About time." Was his terse, and only reply when the Chief spelled out precisely what they wanted done, who they wanted it done to, and why. His record indicated a terrible ruthlessness toward the enemy, and a mystical indifference to death that was exactly what they wanted in their people. He'd served three tours as a Lurp.

"Spent so much time right up close to those NVA, we smelled like 'em. Started to look like 'em, too. Games? Man we played badass games with one another tryin' to see who could kill with the most audacity...flair. Came up their turn once. Little bastards ambushed us and blew the shit out of everybody, except me. Stayed alive playin' dead, laying under Smitty. Laid there for three days. Knew he wouldn't mind, he was all through using that body anyway. They wouldn't go away. Camped right alongside us and I couldn't move. Dead if I did."

His was that strange, distant look, eyes like the large whirlpools that eddy in the muddy Mississippi. Swirling, violent, beginning nowhere, ending nowhere.

"Smitty got to smellin' real bad. Didn't think I could handle it anymore when they just up and left. Funny though, you know it?"

The Chief asked what.

"Can't get Smitty out of my mind. Tried to for years, you know what I mean? I think somehow I loved him." His eyes, the Old Man said were windows on the soul that showed where a man lived, indicated Harold was pretty much out to lunch as far as soul was concerned. These eyes settled on the Chief. "That doesn't offend you does it?"

"Not for a minute Harold, not for a minute. I spent thirty years doing what you're talking about. I hear you."

Harold came back and tried everything he could think of to be a normal person but nothing worked. He liked to work the shrimp boats though, there was something about the smell of the ocean that made him as comfortable as he knew how to be.

Pat came out of WWII with one of the strangest stories from that murderous experience. He was a little on the heavy side, iron gray hair, medium height and a perpetual smile. His record indicated he'd been serving with Edson's Raiders on Guadalcanal, when he disappeared, given up for dead. Somehow, in the bloody night battle for which the Colonel received his medal of honor, Pat had taken a terrible blow to his head during hand to hand combat, and came to wandering in the thick, black jungle. He knew he was behind Japanese lines but because of the impenetrable thickness of that undergrowth had no concept of direction. He stayed there, until the island was secured, surviving in the most hideous manner known to man. After finding his way out he was hospitalized for a long time while they put his severely abused body back in working order. They never accomplished the same with his mind. He was a salesman now with no family, for the same reasons as so many of them. He felt he was not fit for human companionship, especially marriage. He was a walking, talking paradox. A smiling, apparently pleasant, psychopathic killer.

They met at the appointed time and place and went over Sandi's report, carefully. She'd done her work well, tailing the portly union leader relentlessly for two weeks. Sometimes she would be dressed to kill, high heels, tight dress and other times she might be wearing mens clothing, her hair drawn tight and wearing a hat. Her disguises were many and given her bantam size she was very hard to recognize. The Chief had done his work well also, because no one objected to Sandi. He'd told them in general what her motivation was, and that she was to be trusted completely.

"Fat dude?" Pat laughed looking at the pictures. "Fatter'n me even."

Harold wasn't laughing. He didn't laugh hardly at all.

"How you think we should take him, Harold?"

They'd decided there was no harm in first names, knowing how hard they would be to trace with just that. Harold? Harold who? First names they could and would react to, not having to figure out who was being addressed if they were to use phony ones.

"Sandi's got that all figured out for us. Right kid?"

"Yes. I've been following this pig for a long time now and know most all his moves, and habits. He goes to the same barber every Wednesday, last thing in the afternoon. It's probably the most vulnerable time in his routine, because it's in a small shopping center. No protection except for his two apes. Barber must be an old crony or something because it's not very secure."

"No place's secure if somebody wants you." Harolds somber reply.

"He's always got these same two goons with him, and you can bet both are armed."

"So are we, only we got something they don't." Pat added. "We know who they are, and they don't know we're coming. How do we get out of there?"

"Drive." Sandi's answer. "I've checked every possibility and this is the best. You have immediate access to the interstate, right out of the shopping center. I've gone over the route so many times I know it like the back of my hand. Up the ramp, off at the third exit, change cars. Back on the interstate the same way, to another exit, close by. Change cars again at that point and drive our boy right on out of town and down to where he's going to be living for awhile. Any problems?"

They shook their heads. There was no problem.

*   *   *

It was dark as the big Lincoln rolled up in front of the barber shop, in the small shopping center. The humidity and cold temperature made the tailpipe on the limousine appear to be pumping out pure smoke. They watched as Manny and his two bodyguards swaggered out of the car and into the barber shop followed shortly by the outside sign being extinguished and the venetian blinds lowered. It was six in the evening and as dark as it would get for the rest of the night. The other shops and businesses were emptying for the evening. They sat and waited.

"Takes about thirty minutes." Sandi's report stated. Vic, their driver was a young Vietnam veteran. He flew a small attack helicopter there, celebrated for doing so with wild abandon. He would race into a fire fight, hang there facing terrible enemy action while tearing everything apart in front of his guns, then dart away. The ground troops he was supporting had no idea who he was, but were always grateful when he showed up. Legends grew around his maniacal disregard for his own safety, some swearing they'd seen him follow the Viet Cong through the jungle forests.

"If I can't drive it my man, it can't be drove!"

Was his bright eyed reply to the Chief when approached.

"And if I can't fly it, it can't be flewn."

Cocky, smallish, and good looking. He knew no one could operate swift machines better than he. He was shivering.

"It's OK kid." Harold commented, his eyes glittering. "Nothing the matter with the shakes at a time like this. We're fixing to have a very famous passenger soon. S'posed to be nervous."

"Hell I'm not scared Harold, I've got the old pregame jitters, you know what I mean? Did wind sprints before I went out on patrol in Nam, to quiet my nerves. High strung I guess, but don't mistake it for scared."

"She say about a half hour kid?" Pat asked, like he was waiting for the next movie.
"Yes." The pilot answered.

"Then we'd better set up, huh Harold?"

Harold didn't answer, opening the door to the stolen sedan, getting the old rush as his feet hit the pavement. God damn the butt of the huge .45 automatic felt marvelous, just touching his lower ribs as he swung across the dark, wet parking lot. It was his favorite weapon, figuring if the bullet didn't hit his target, a near miss would knock him down from the impact of the rushing air.

'Big son of a bitch that bullet. Let's see, how'd that song go? Seems like only yesterday, ta da, ta da, a small cafe?' Boy did it ever and it was all coming back in a hurry. 'Fuck man, this is what it's all about, isn't it?'

Pat slid the riot gun, with the short pistol grip, under his rain coat for the walk to the side of Mannys' parked limo. He was exhilarated too, his walk changing into a bouncing motion, snapping up on the ball of his foot with each step. Yeah it was going to be all right, he'd get a little restitution and resurrection this night. The guy on Manny's left belonged to him.

"How's it look out there? Snowin' yet?" Manny laughed as the man who'd felt Sandi up, let the blinds back down.

"No but it's plenty cold enough to. Hurry up with the hair cut will ya' or we'll have to ice skate home." He answered

"Tell you what Manny," the barber said standing back admiring his work over the labor leaders shoulder as they looked at the newly coifed image in the mirror, "you ain't never gonna' look any better than that, my boy! No time! How long now, twenty five years is it? Why I swear between my barbering and your natural good looks I ain't never seen you look any better. Shit, you'll be the prettiest one at the dance." He looked to the bodyguards for reinforcement. "What do ya' think, guys?"

"Beautiful! You look just plain lovely Manny, now let's get the hell out of here! It's night time out there and I don't like walking you around after dark." The other hulk replied.

"Oh you don't eh? What you think, some of those shitbirds we put down in the last election gonna come get me?" He was laughing. "If you'll recall they're a little shorthanded now, thanks to you guys. They're probably still sitting home wondering what hit 'em! Ha, ha, ha! Here you go Bill," handing the barber a ten dollar tip, "you do beautiful work."

"Hey thanks Manny. It's my pleasure." The beaming barber replied.

The lead bodyguard had his hand on the knob pulling the door open as everybody smiled and waved at each other, stepping out on the sidewalk pulling the door behind them.

"He's a mighty nice guy, you know it. Knew his Dad real well when I first joined the union...."

He caught Harold out of the corner of his eye, and brain, as he stepped out the door, wondering where the man came from? Where'd the gun come from, he thought at the exact moment two horrendous explosions took place. One from Harolds .45 catching his man full in the face, the impact lifting his huge body in the air. The other blast came simultaneously from the riot gun aimed over the top of their Lincoln, tearing the second bodyguard's upper body out, blowing him backward through the plate glass window of the barber shop they'd just left. In a kaleidoscopic sequence the barber turned his head in the direction of the noise and shattering glass to rest his eyes for one split second on the deadly looking man who was going to kill him. He had his weapon aimed right now at the terrified barber, then snapped it up to fire at the lights still burning, screaming.

"Down! Down on the floor barber, or you're dead!"

Pat was pointing his riot gun directly in the face of the suddenly vulnerable labor leader, who knew beyond a shadow of a doubt it was his time to die. Manny could hear the car approaching but was much too terrified to notice anything more. The muzzle of the shotgun loomed enormously to the fat man as Pat motioned with it toward the car now parked next to them.

"In Manny. Get in." He was surprised at his own calm at this moment.

"But, but I...." He stammered.

"Get in you fat motherfucker or we leave you on the pavement with those two! What'll it be?"

Manny scrambled in the car, falling, hunching down in the back seat as Pat got in the front with Harold in back, his .45 pushed against Manny's face. With the muzzle touching his nose, Manny could smell the acrid odor of recently burned gunpowder which had killed one of his men. He wet his pants.

Tires screeched and Vic had them down the interstate, completing the multiple vehicle switch before the police had time to arrive on the stunning scene.

LABOR LEADER ABDUCTED

Headlines screamed, not only in this country but all over the world, because the brotherhood was international.

BODYGUARDS DEAD

They described the ruthless action resulting in the deaths of his two bodyguards.

LONE WITNESS SEES ONE ASSAILANT

The barber saw Harold, the papers explained, for the briefest of moments in the dark. He was worthless as a witness, completely shaken by the body crashing through the plate glass window, literally torn in half from the horrendous impact of 00 shot at such short range, coming to rest on it's back, his legs dangling over the suddenly windowless frame. That experience was then followed as he stared straight into those awesome eyes just over the muzzle of the huge .45. Those eyes were the thing Manny's barber could not forget. He'd never seen anything like them in his entire life. He was accustomed to the huge, mean faced men that always served Manny but never had he seen anyone with such an utterly malevolent visage as what he glimpsed in that moment.

*   *   *

"Mr. Brooks, the Boss is on line one." There was nothing unusual about this crisp, professional female voice referring to Alex George as the Boss. He'd been called that since his days as a driller.

"Hi Mr. Alex," Tom spoke casually into the phone. "You're calling about our latest investment?"

"Sure am." His noncommittal reply. "I'm not sure I expected the performance we got, but it was something wasn't it?"

"Yes it was. I know what you're saying, but sometimes those things take off in such unexpected ways, about the only thing an investor can do is hold on because he's in for one hell of a ride."

There was a long pause.

"Yes I suppose so son. What is it the gamblers say? You pays your nickel, you takes your ride?"

"Something like that, yes."

"Well I think that's what's happening here. We'll see. Let me know son, soon's you hear any more." The Old Man hung up without waiting for an answer. It wasn't meant to be curt, it was vintage Alex George.

*   *   *

Carmine Palermo would be different, that they knew. He'd lived long in the world of stealth, murder and guile and he wasn't going to be easy to take. They knew that because of the report Sandi called the Chief.

"He's covered day and night," her soft spoken words filtered through the telephone, "and his people are very nasty looking. I'm with him day and night and haven't figured yet when you're going to be able to get him but I will. I'll get back to you."

"Be careful, kid. I've read much about our friend. He's about as bad as they come. Don't draw any attention to yourself."

"Are you kidding?" She was laughing. "I went dancing with him the other night."

"You're shitting me?" His stunned reply.

"Well I didn't exactly go with him, but I did dance with him at some high class toilet, out on the beach. He likes the place, and goes there almost every night. Put on my tightest, shortest outfit, pushed my boobs way up with a cute brassiere and sat at the bar letting these guys see almost everything they wanted. One of his shooters asked me to dance, and I said no. I knew it was our boy doing the asking, so I gave him a real nasty turn down. They all laughed about that until he finally got up to show 'em how it's done, and of course I said yes."

"Jesus kid, be careful will you? You're s'posed to be the invisible one you know. Don't draw any unnecessary attention to yourself."

"How 'bout getting laid?" Laughing more. "What would you call that?"

"You are shitting me now!" Still stunned.

"No I'm not. Thought maybe I could get into his inner sanctum, see how things were laid out...." giggling, "or is that a poor choice of words?"

"Go on kid. Go on."

"No place to go really. We went up in this penthouse apartment and I found out it was his place to play hanky panky. It's too inaccessible anyway. Guards everywhere. Found out one thing though."

"What?"

"He just sells that shit, he doesn't use it. Offered me a whole bunch of it but I said no thanks. Don't use it. I'll stay on him, and before you say it, don't worry I'll be careful. I know he's a bad dude, and murder's a way of life for him. I'll get back to you soon's I find the weak link, and I will find it."

*   *   *

It was a beautiful Sunday morning, humidity quite low for Florida, temperatures in the 50's without a cloud in the sky. The surf was rolling in, both water and sky appearing bluer than the norm. Really a gorgeous day and everyone in St. Anthony's seemed to be in a special mood. The prayers from the altar were being answered with enthusiasm, hymns sung maybe a little different from normal. Father Cirone gave one of his very best homilies not unmindful that Carmine Palermo was in attendance and would probably be generous indeed in his contribution, when the offering was taken up. The good Father had heard rumors about Carmine, but felt they must be wrong. Didn't he, after all, show up almost every Sunday with his wife and son. Wasn't he obviously an adoring husband and father? And didn't he take communion on every visit to the church? No, no, these rumors had to be wrong. This was a good man whose reputation was being besmirched. Father Cirone wished people had more charity in their hearts and less invective.

He noticed the large priest in the pew directly behind the Palermo family, somewhat startled and miffed by his appearance. The polite thing to do for any visiting priest, and they had many of those in this beautiful vacation land, was to come to the rectory before mass and introduce themselves. Well maybe this one got lost and arrived late.

'Different looking man.' He thought delivering his sermon, but try as he may, couldn't determine what was so different about him.

Had he been closer to the strange priest he would have seen the now white, but still terrible scar that went from the inner part of his eye, straight down to his lip. On close inspection it took on an entirely different appearance giving an observer the impression of a perpetual sneer. The real sneer was on his soul.

The Chief went deep in the woods of northern Michigan to find him, doing so with great difficulty. Chris Stalling was his name, at least that's what the records showed. He'd been with the Marines in Korea, when only a boy, surviving the terrible conflict with the Chinese after their lines were over run in the freezing weather at the Chosin reservoir. He endured that only to wind up in Vietnam fourteen years later. He was just a kid, way back there when he lied about his age to join in the first place but after doing his tours in Korea and Nam, nothing was fun anymore. He got way up on narcotics there in the Nam, and when he murdered an enemy he always cut their ears off, which he wore in a necklace. His eyes were flat, expressionless, and there were no smiles. He'd gone totally Asiatic with an indifference to slaughter that shocked even his own jungle mates. Then there were his tours as a mercenary in Africa, where he killed for hire and did it with such ferocity as to keep himself always out of touch with his own men. They were terrified he might turn on them. Now he lived in the isolation of the north woods, aware after killing a man in a stupid barroom brawl, he needed to stay away from civilized people forever.

He sat directly behind the Palermo family. Carmine, his wife and son.

"Hey Carmine!"

The small person whispered to him as he stood in line to receive communion. He started to twist his head around, when the voice told him.

"Keep lookin' ahead, Carmine. Don't bother answering, do as I say and your wife and boy'll be OK. Take a look where they're standing. See who's standing next to them.

He turned his head to see the vicious looking priest had moved from where he was, to his present position next to his son. The bodyguards nearby were somewhat perplexed, when he moved next to them, but where it was a priest and watching the nun talking to him in the communion line, they thought it must be OK, knowing how Carmine felt about anything pertaining to the church.

"If you don't do what I tell you Carmine, the man standing next to your son will cut his throat, right now." The whispering continued. "Your wife too. Understand?"

He complied, nodding.

"Good. Do as I say, they live. You don't, they don't!"

More nodding.

"We're going to receive communion together Carmine, then out the side door. Let your hoods know to stay where they are. Give 'em an A OK sign. You got that?"

The nod was in the affirmative.

"Good. Do it right, your kid gets to vote."

The choir was singing as if inspired by this special day, the sun filtering through the gorgeous stained glass windows as the drug king was escorted to the communion rail by the smallish person. It would have been hard to tell whether it was man or woman speaking to Carmine, because of the nun's habit. The dress was dove gray with a white blouse and a smallish gray and white hat that covered most of the head, with a short veil that fell only to the neck. This worn by the fifth and last member of the newly organized band of killers that were the legacy of Marie George.

His name was Curt Henried, an atypical member of Alex George's group. He seemed to labor under some sort of vague death wish, living all his adult years in various kinds of terrible life threatening situations. He was quite small, five feet six inches, slim, perfect for what he'd become in Vietnam. Tunnel rat they called them, maybe the most terrifying job in that war. They went into tunnels the Viet Cong dug over the years, slithering along tiny passageways on their stomachs, killing anything they found in front of them, man, woman or child. There was no capture, only death.

Curt was born to this sort of thing. He was without conscience.

"OK Carmine, when we leave the communion rail walk over to the priest and shake his hand." He whispered hoarsely. "Old home week! Lots of teeth, then out the side door." Curt paused continuing. "Your man in the car's dead! Don't plan on him for anything. Do as we say, everything's OK. Don't? You, your baby and your wife die, right here."

Carmine moved exactly as instructed, indicating to his hoods with his eyes they should stay where they were as he moved to the pew occupied now by the terrible looking priest, shook his hand, leaned in to whisper to his wife they'd be right back and walked out the door alongside the altar rail into the beautiful south Florida morning.

"Hey Carmine!" One of his men hollered after them as they approached the parking area. "Want me to go with you?"

"Be cool Carmine." Curt whispered again. "Tell him no, or there's a bunch of bodies out here, right now."

The hood disappeared into the church after being told by his leader to go back in and wait with his wife. They could hear the voices of the choir as they got in the car and drove away with Carmine, his son, the priest and nun.

REPUTED DRUG CZAR SNATCHED

The papers locally, nationally and internationally gave it big play, because Carmine Palermo was a notorious celebrity of awesome repute, linked with almost anything and everything to do with the importation of drugs into south Florida.

BODYGUARD FOUND DEAD

They described the body discovered laying across the front seat of one of the cars used in the Palermo entourage, his throat cut viciously.

PALERMO SON FOUND

The small boy was put out of the car some distance from the tiny airport where Vic was waiting in the private jet they'd rented in St. Louis, and in a few hours they were in northern Arkansas.

"What is it you guys want?" Palermo demanded as they put on his blindfold and handcuffs. "You want money? I got plenty. How much you want? I know you're not cops. Not dressed like that. Tell me what you want and you got it, just let me out of this thing."

Chris put his face inches from that of the now terrified drug king answering. "If you don't shut your mouth, I'll put you out of the plane right now, the hard way, only you wouldn't look like much when they scraped your ass off the ground. Now sit back, shut up and enjoy your ride."

*   *   *

The phone rang in the Old Man's house, answered by his housekeeper.

"Yes Tom?" Their conversations now were always noncommittal.

"Second deal's down, we've sent the merchandise to the delivery point."

"Good. That's real good. Any hitches?"

"None."

"How soon do we get the rest of the program handled?"

"I'd say by the end of this week."

"That soon?"

"Yes. The really difficult part's down. Best to handle that first, and we have. It's just a matter of time before we conclude everything."

"Fine. Keep me posted." He hung up.

*   *   *

The General lived in a beautiful home on a tree lined boulevard in Savannah. Although built in recent years it looked like genuine antebellum, a tribute to the designing architect. The grounds were lush, huge trees, flowers and green grass complimenting the white house, generous in it's use of white pillars and back wrought iron.

Their knock on the door was answered by an old black man who seemed determined they were not to disturb the General at this time.

"No gen'mens," he replied to their request, "the General don' see no one this time of night. He be jus' befo goin' to bed and don' nobody never disturbs him then. Maybe you could come back in the mawnin', talk to the General then." He didn't like the looks of Harold and Chris anyway. They didn't look like the usual procession of distinguished visitors that came calling.

"I see. Yes that will be fine. Let me leave my card and maybe you can tell him we'll be back tomorrow." Harold handed a card toward the door at which time the old Negro opened it to take the offering.

"Hold it now! Hold it!" The old man complained as Chris stepped quickly into the foyer pushing the servant into the house while so doing, swinging him around clapping his hand over his mouth while holding the large knife against his throat.

Harold moved in quickly, closing the huge leaded glass door softly behind.

"Listen old man." He spoke softly. "Where's the General?"

"Don' know boss. Don' know." The old man was terrified, lying and obviously not about to tell these men anything they wanted to know even if it meant his death. Harold knew that. He admired his loyalty.

"Tie him up! Put him over in that closet! Gag him and tie him up, but don't hurt him." He leaned into the ancient face pushing his .45 against his temple. "You're a lucky old fart right now, I want you to know that. Anybody else answered that door'd probably be dead now. I know you're not going to tell me where the General is but I'll find him. Be quiet! Don't do anything silly. I don't want to kill you!" He nodded toward his vicious companion. "I don't want him to kill you! Do you understand?"

The old black man's eyes were large with terror and tears. He acknowledged nothing.

"Don't hurt him Chris. He's lived through enough shit as it is. Tie him good and gag him. I'll find the General."

The house was big, but not so big he couldn't find his prey in a matter of moments. He opened one of the large double doors leading into the study and found the General seated in a large leather chair reading a book. He looked up startled at the intrusion.

"What do you want?" The General asked, staring into his expressionless face. He remembered seeing this kind of face before, but where was it? "Who are you?"

"That doesn't matter General. I've come for you now. Get whatever you want in the way of a coat and let's get going." Harold put the huge .45 back in his belt, but the General knew it was there. He also suddenly recognized the look on the face. He'd seen that many times in the past, and knew it belonged to that special breed of man who seem to show up for every war. The conscienceless killer. He, and the other generals, got the glory these men fought and died for. He wondered from time to time what became of them after the smoke cleared. He knew about one of them, right now.

"I've been expecting you. I didn't know when and was beginning to think never, but I have been expecting you in the back of my mind. I didn't know what you'd look like or who you'd serve. Am I going to know that son? Am I going to know who you serve?" The General suddenly seemed to lose his usual proud military bearing for one of deep resignation.

"No sir, you are not!"

The eyes. That was it, the eyes. Yes that's where it all was, and it fascinated him those many long years he served in the army. Rarely had he seen those eyes, except when it came time to pass out medals. Eyes like these were never found in rear echelon areas. He never felt comfortable in their presence, feeling correctly, they were looking out at him in unspoken contempt. They'd been places and done things he would never know, much less understand, and yet he and all like him got the headlines for what they had done.

"May I go up and say goodbye to my wife?" He knew. He knew all along he'd been responsible to a large degree for prolonging the war, resulting in the unnecessary deaths of a great many men. Yes American men, but also North Vietnamese, and innocent civilians that died by the thousands.

"No General you may not, but I will wait if you want to write her a note." As much as he hated the man and all he'd been responsible for, at this moment he came as close to feeling compassion as he knew how.

The General wrote his note and the three of them left, vanishing in the damp night air.

FAMED VIETNAM GENERAL KIDNAPED

Speculation abounded and many were right on when they suggested the General was abducted by a Vietnam revenge group. There were panels of distinguished commentators belaboring in their usual endless droning what had happened to the General. What had happened to Manny Beatty and Carmine Palermo. Were these disappearances connected in any way? What they had to go on was so skimpy they couldn't tie anything together. The witnesses were of little help because of their terrible fright at the moment of the kidnaping. The barber, the old servant, the people in the church. None of them really knew what they were looking at while it was happening, so there were no descriptions, and the fact that they all simply disappeared afterward added to the overall mystery.

*   *   *

"I saw on the television last night Tom, the General was taken with no bloodshed." They were having breakfast together in the Shed, the Old Man cooking up a marvelous egg and sausage dish. "I'm glad about that."

"Yes sir," Tom replied, "he had the old servant there and our people took care not to harm him. They would have if he'd given them cause, but they didn't have to."

"Yes, well we have three dead already. The more we can hold that down the better I'll like it." He was behind the bar eating while Helen stared up at him waiting for her share.

"Yeah Boss, but I think you'd have to say they won't be missed. They were responsible for many deaths themselves."

"I suppose that's right." Thinking these words over.

"But you know Mr. Alex, what we're going to have here is a wild, barely controllable situation at best."

"How you mean?"

"I mean eventually we're going to have people dying in the streets because of our actions, and you can absolutely make book that one of these days innocent people are going to be involved. Our people are going to start up violent action somewhere, and something's going to go astray. Somebody's going to get killed. You are aware of that aren't you?"

"Yes, I suppose so." He answered quietly.

"This won't be much different from any other act of war, guerrilla or otherwise, and innocents die in all of them. I knew a fighter pilot who was strafing an enemy train in France. He flew that Mustang right over the train with all his guns wide open and there was a school yard full of kids just on the other side that took his fire full on. He has no idea how many kids he killed that morning," he leaned forward in his chair his eyes ablaze, "but he has wondered every fucking day of his life since then. United States forces have slaughtered civilians for years whether in the fire storms we created dropping bombs on German cities or the senseless murders we perpetrated in Vietnam in the name of search and destroy. Our troops killed anything that moved, and a lot they never saw when they swept villages with their automatic weapons full on. Thatched huts don't stop high velocity bullets. You must know that Mr. Alex. I want you to be prepared for that, because it'll happen to us too."

Tom knew it couldn't be helped and wanted to make sure his mentor did too.

*   *   *

The Senator was handled with great pleasure by both Harold and Curt. Sandi had done her usual excellent job outlining all of his actions in great detail. When he went to the Senate office building, how many people usually worked there. His eating habits, including when and where. What time he went home and when he visited the home of a certain woman friend.

"That's it!" Harold exclaimed, reading the report.

"What?" His smallish partner replied.

"Why Christ it's perfect. He's such a headline grabber, it's going to be tough to put the arm on him without killing somebody standing around, 'cause he's always got a lot of those."

"So? Who gives a shit?" Curt added.

"We do. The boss wants us to cut down on the body count we leave behind. We get a break on this one cause the Senator goes over every Thursday night, very late and they get in a little old fashioned lovin' until the wee hours of the morning."

"Anybody go with him?"

"No, strange as it seems, nobody. Not even an aide. I guess the son of a bitch doesn't known how many enemies he has, or maybe even thinks he doesn't have 'em. Anyway we can literally catch him with his pants down there, and take him without too much of a fuss."

Sandi's report was excellent down to the last detail including intricate details of the surrounding neighborhood. Streets leading to freeways, then on to interstates, taking them ultimately to the rendezvous point in Arkansas where the other three were now being held. Sandi had entered the house, her dark hair covered with a blond wig, wearing huge plain glass horned rimmed spectacles, on the pretext of doing a layout for one of the womens magazines. Her flattered and grateful hostess, took her everywhere in her home, while she busily snapped picture after picture. They knew in detail the exact configuration of the house, which she later assembled for the Chief, as if preparing a sales brochure.

"She didn't act suspicious?" He asked.

"No, not at all." Her answer. "Most people really get excited about having a magazine spread done on them. Usually you can get them to do anything and show you everything when you got them going."

Harold and Curt waited in the darkness, having decided to take him outside, when the Senator's car rolled up to a stop. They watched him finish his cigarette.

"What's taking him so long?" Curt whispered.

"Don't know. Looks like he's doing something with...."

"What?"

"Son of a bitch! I think the Senator's snorting coke."

"Yeah, that figures. At his age he probably needs all the help he can get when it comes to screwing." The car door swung open. "He's ready now, got a synthetic hard on and ready to get with it. Shouldn't be any trouble with this one."

Harold, the larger of the two stepped quickly out of the bushes approaching the Senator silently from the rear. He grabbed him across the mouth, shoving his .45 hard into the shocked mans ribs, causing an involuntary lunge which loosened Harold's grip.

"Who are you people?" Was all he managed to scream before being struck a crushing blow across the side of his neck with the barrel of the heavy weapon.

"Shut up, you high line sleaze, or you die right here! Do you understand me?" He whispered through clenched teeth at the stunned Senator.

"What's going on out here?" The smallish lady stepped around from the front of the house, alarmed by the sudden noise. "Who are you people? What are you doing to the Senator?" She demanded trying desperately to understand the situation.

'Scrappy little broad.' Curt thought as he moved silently toward her. 'Not bad looking either.' His mind raced on.

She saw him approaching at the last moment and turned to run toward the safety of her house, not quite reaching it when Curt delivered a crushing blow to the back of her head with his own heavy .45. He knew he'd killed her when he heard her skull collapse and felt a swift twinge of remorse, but only for a moment. After all how many Cong women had he killed in the tunnels? Plenty. They die or he does. He liked the way it'd turned out so far.

The van slid silently to the curb, with Vic at the wheel. Harold quickly opened the side door pushing the Senator in and across the floor, while the small woman's body was placed inside the home by her killer.

"I'll have you men swinging from the highest tree." The Senator threatened incoherently a result of the effects of the cocaine, the terrible blow he'd taken across his neck, and concern for the well being of his lady friend. "What have you done with Dorothy? You haven't hurt her have you? I demand that you stop this vehicle immediately and let...."

He didn't get to finish, staring cross eyed down the barrel of Harold's gun pushed hard under his nose.

"Listen Senator," Harold whispered through clenched teeth, "I don't know if you can appreciate where you are or with whom after taking your little pop just now...."

"I had nothing! I did nothing!" The politician objected.

"Let's go." Curt hollered as he leaped in the front seat, pausing. "Wait a minute. Senator give me the keys to your car!"

"I will not!" His belligerent reply.

"What do you mean, you will not!" Curt jumped out of his seat straddling the Senator's prostrate body. "If I tell you I want your keys, I want your God damn keys!" Ripping the pocket out of his overcoat in his fury, he seized the keys, running toward the car which he moved to the back of the house.

"OK let's go." He said to Vic. "Got the car and the lady put away. It'll be some time before anybody finds them and we'll be long gone."

"What do you mean you have the lady put away?" The Senator asked. "I don't understand what is going on here and I demand you release us both this very minute. I'll ask the authorities to go light on you if you'll stop this nonsense immediately. Take me inside, release Dorothy, and we'll do what we can on your behalf."

The van was already moving as fast as the speed limit allowed, Vic using great care not to bring undue attention to the stylish van conversion.

"Apparently you don't understand what's going on here Senator, but I'll be happy to fill you in, so maybe you can grasp the situation, shut up and sit back for a long ride." The smallish man resumed his menacing attitude with the still prone man. "The woman? You say her name's Dorothy?"

"Yes. Dorothy."

"Well Senator, Dorothy's dead. I didn't intend to kill her, but those things happen. She ran and I stopped her."

His eyes were immense with utter disbelief. He simply could not believe what he was hearing. How in the name of God could that beautiful lady be dead? That couldn't be the way of it. Who are these men? What do they want? He knew they had killed now and would obviously do the same to him if provoked. He decided to do as he was told.

The news coverage was huge now and while nobody knew what, or who was involved, conjecture was unlimited. Labor boss, drug importer, General of the army and now a United States Senator all whisked away amid violence of an extreme nature. What did it all mean? Almost everyone was convinced whatever was happening was a central plot of enormous proportions. Was it Castro again? Those crazy turbaned maniacs from the middle east? A definite possibility that was pursued endlessly, but it didn't really explain Manny and Carmine. If it was political in nature why these two, or could it be some sort of wild coincidence? Did labor rivals do away with Manny? That was a possibility, where was Jimmy Hoffa? And the Palermo thing? Could he have been abducted by a rival gang and if so, what for? Who did it? If they wanted him dead why hadn't they killed him and have it done with? The General and the Senator definitely smacked of political overtones but there was no word. Not one scrap of information pertaining to their whereabouts. All four of these powerful men had vanished from the face of the earth and nobody knew why. They were to find out soon.

*   *   *

Tom was walking with the Old Man in his gorgeous yard, Helen between them.

"I'm sorry the lady in Washington died." Alex George spoke softly. "Was there no other way?"

"Under the circumstances, given the people we have, I'm afraid not. Oh sure there was probably a thousand other ways, but at that exact moment, in that precise place there wasn't much of anything else he could have done. If she'd made it to the door before him, God only knows what might have happened. It's conceivable we might have lost three men and our entire program right there and we can't have that."

Tom was thinking of the four who'd died already as a result of their initial efforts. Three of them didn't matter, the woman was something else. How many more would there be, he wondered?

"No son, we don't want that." Pausing, suppressing an involuntary sob. "We've much too much to do."

He handed Tom a large envelope.

"See the Chief gets this. I want it carried out exactly as I have outlined and if any of his people don't think they can carry these instructions out, that's quite all right. As we have said from the beginning any time they want out, they're out."

Tom looked at the envelope, then the Old Man.

"Go ahead son," he said in a near whisper, "read it."

He read it in its entirety while the Old Man and Helen walked aimlessly about, all the while watching the expression on his younger friends face. There was no expression confirming once more what he'd thought ever since Tom returned from the south pacific. You don't turn something like that off, ever. There's no way.

"Exactly as you've said here, Boss?"

Yes, oh yes. Now he could see the eyes going flat.

"Exactly as I've said, son. Can you do it?"

It was a sincere question, knowing what a horrendous thing he was asking of this or any other man, believing as sincerely it simply had to be done, and the sooner the better.

"Yes I can, but are you sure?"

"I am son, I am. Anyway we can't turn back now, it's much too late for that."

CHAPTER 24

It was 10 in the evening, but it could just as easily have been any time of day, the news room of the Kansas City Star was such a dynamic area of activity. Phones ringing, people moving, doors opening and closing, the ever present smell of freshly brewed coffee and lights that burned on forever. This was the normal operation of a large newspaper in a major city in the United States. Amid all the hubbub, the small, smartly dressed woman who entered this domain was hardly noticed as she stepped to the receptionists desk.

"May I help you, Miss?"

It was the customary question, asked out of a sense of duty by an obviously harassed, overworked and indifferent young woman seated at the desk.

"Yes, please." Sandi replied. "I have some important information for Don McCormick and would like to ask you to give it to him." She smiled pleasantly. "Could you do that for me?"

"Sure honey. Lay it right there," indicating a small clearing on the corner of her overflowing desk, "and I'll get it back to him soon's I can."

"Would you do that? I know he'll be most appreciative, because it really is quite important. He is in, isn't he?"

"Yes, he's in conference with the boss but they should be through pretty soon. Just leave it there and I'll take it back."

"Thank you so much."

Sandi reached out to place the envelope on the receptionists desk. It was then the girl noticed the twenty dollar bill between the gloved thumb and the large manila envelope handed her by this pleasant lady. She slid open a lower desk drawer putting the bill in it, and rose from her chair commenting as she turned to enter the depths of the city room.

"For that you get special delivery. Want to wait for an answer?"

"No thank you," turning to leave while speaking, "he'll know exactly what to do when he gets it."

"Would you care to leave your name, Miss?" The receptionist asked.

"Oh my yes, thank you for reminding me, I almost forgot." She answered brightly. "Here, let me write it down for you." Writing leisurely on the pad handed her.

"Leslie Angeles?" She asked, checking to see if she was reading it right.

"That's right. Sounds pretty close to the big city, doesn't it?" Her smiling reply. "One of those odd coincidences between parents and husband. They liked Leslie and he brought Angeles with him so that's how it worked out. Thank you so much for your help. Perhaps you might enjoy a nice dinner on us in appreciation for your efforts."

It was fifteen minutes before McCormick returned to his desk, reaching for the insistent phone that was ringing as he approached.

"McCormick!" His usual terse answer.

"Don, this is Suzie on the front desk?"

"Yes I know, now what is it Suzie?" He was looking at her across the expanse of the huge city room, his mind still very much involved in his recently concluded conversation with the editor.

"An attractive lady left that envelope that's on your desk. Said it was real important you get it. Must have been too, you know why?"

"No Suzie," he was holding the envelope in his hand, "I don't know why. Why?" It was a typical answer for most working against the clock.

"She gave me twenty bucks to see that you got it personally." Miffed at his curt reply. "That's why!" The click of the phone was resounding.

'Twenty bucks?' He thought tearing the envelope open. 'What's so important it's worth a twenty to get Suzie to walk it back here?'

The letter read,

'Dear Mr. McCormick:

This letter is being sent to you because you have an outstanding reputation as a journalist, and because the Kansas City Star is one of the most respected newspapers in this land, with a long standing reputation for excellence in news coverage. For this reason we chose you to receive what would have to be a most newsworthy disclosure which is, what has become of Manny Beatty, Carmine Palermo, General Williams and Senator Howard.

They are dead Mr. McCormick. We want you to know why, so you in turn can inform your readers.'

"Jesus!" It was totally involuntary, as he read on.

'Manny Beatty, and his kind have made a travesty of the labor unions, since their idealistic formation in the first half of this century, twisting to their own personal perversions the efforts of millions of honest, hard working men and women. People who pay for the privilege of being represented at the bargaining tables by trustworthy men, supposedly looking out for their best interests. That's why the labor unions came about, and a good many men died fighting for what they believed to be a just and honest cause. It was a good cause Mr. McCormick until the rapacious breed represented by Beatty and his ilk, sunk their fangs into it, seizing power by force, and through thuggery, beatings, murder, bombings and arson, maintained that vise like grip. He was responsible for the beatings and deaths of many, personally issuing the orders precipitating such actions. The two men who were killed when he was taken, have murdered for him many times in the past. They will do that no longer. They murdered the union local president, and three of his followers in Phoenix, who had the temerity not only to cry out for honesty and decency in the management of union affairs, but was leading an effort to unseat those in power. No one could solve the car explosion, in which they died, and yet the whole world knew who did it and why. They killed the accountant in their own international headquarters who discovered the unbelievable theft of union funds, announcing his findings to the press and police.

He disappeared, much like Jimmy Hoffa did, and we'll never know exactly where. The woman in Los Angeles who died because she was the recipient of the accountants hard information, documents, papers, receipts and the like. That accountant must have paid a terrible price before he died to divulge her name to his inquisitors, knowing beyond a shadow of a doubt she would be killed as a result of his disclosure, These are only some of Manny Beatty's victims over the years, his rise to power and reign of terror covering many years. There will be no more.

Carmine Palermo was put to death because of, and in the name of, his many victims over the years. His has always been the same pattern of strong arm extortion and murder that we wink at and accept as a way of life here in America. This should never have been Mr. McCormick, nor should it continue to be. The selling of vice is something we must live with, for no amount of policing will ever clean up what must be an issue of morality. However when it comes to brazen wholesale importation of the stuff of addiction and death, the powerful drugs he brought into this nation; when it comes to our children being destroyed through their exposure to the mind numbing effects of something they have no way of understanding, only to submit ultimately to its powerful seduction. When these same children, yes and adults, turn to theft, prostitution, robbery and sometimes murder in order to keep their habit alive, then we believe is when something must be done. With Mr. Palermo's body you will find our down payment in this regard.

We have put General Williams to death as a tiny but long overdue gesture of defiance, contempt, and warning to those in our government who would proceed with the obscene, unthinking policies of war, declared or as happens so often in this cynical time, undeclared. Policies based always on ego and pride, out of hand. We see this everywhere and suggest to you sir, until we put these kinds of men and the thoughts they generate behind us, we will always remain hostile to our fellow inhabitants of this earth. Do you ever pause to wonder how many millions of people have been destroyed by the efforts of men like the General and the despicable hordes of sycophants surrounding all seats of power. Don't you wonder where this endless parade comes from and above all, why? How long must we be subjected to these vermin with their masters degrees and Ph.D's, pumping forth vile invective until the pressure becomes too much and we must start the killing machines again. Always we start them to the hypnotic chants of those who would not even understand the feelings and emotions of an area of slaughter such as a battlefield. Somebody simply has to be held responsible for these insane acts and almost never are, but isn't it strange that the ones who should bear the most guilt are usually retired instead to sumptuous homes, on exorbitant pensions, writing memoirs, reveling in the honors heaped on them. Are these kinds of people incapable of feeling? Doesn't it seem the ultimate vulgarity to have them forever appearing with veterans group, resplendent in their braid and medals, posing grandly as the leader of those they oftentimes unceremoniously directed to unnecessary deaths? Don't these people ever understand the kind of horror they have visited on untold millions of people? Their dead victims are actually the luckiest, but what about the survivors who must suffer their loss all the rest of their lives. Worse yet, what about the hundreds of thousands who are returned to us maimed, in body, or mind, or both. Some we put in beds and nurse forever, some we put in our penitentiaries to watch forever, and some we find necessary to kill so our society will be safe.

Were you aware Mr. McCormick that more returned Vietnam veterans have died by their own hand than were killed in the whole of the long stupid exercise in national pride? Did you know that? For some strange reason this doesn't seem to be commonly known, and the question is why? Why did the General, and other so called leaders keep telling us that the Vietnam war was always before coming to some sort of a vaguely promised glorious conclusion? Light at the end of the tunnel was the popular hosanna then. What light sir? What end? Why did he keep saying that the enemies will to resist was so severely eroded as to make our ultimate victory a surety? Is this what they teach our future warriors at West Point, to deliberately lie and mislead not only the country's leaders but the mass of people who only want these things to come to an end and disappear? Honors won't do for men of this ilk Mr. McCormick. Death will. If this seems extreme savage retribution to exact we can only direct you to the Nuremberg trials and their conclusions. You will be interested to know the General was expecting us, although he didn't know what form we'd take.

We had rather hoped, even though we realize that might be enormously naive given the history of man and his leaders, that in Senator Joe McCarthy we had seen the end of his type of political sickness, only to have it surface again in the person of Senator Howard. History books abound with tales of these treacherous individuals, a sad commentary of the frailty of mankind. It seems like some kind of horribly pathetic joke that we jail people of lesser standing than these, for infractions that would not even appear under the common light of close scrutiny, if compared to the record of the Senator. This man had carried out every twisted maneuver known, and invented even more in the field of deviousness. The suffering he brought to others, while enjoying the spotlight of personal acclaim has been the greatest mockery of all. Whores have more honesty than men like this will ever know, yet the world is full of them. Not as dangerous as this one perhaps, but there nevertheless. Whores at least acknowledge what they are, while this kind of man takes money, power and prestige under the table in the most brazen manner, all the while proclaiming his beneficence and efforts for his fellow man. We think in reality the Senator might possibly represent the most dangerous man of all in contemporary society, one who hustles, lies, cheats and charms their way to whatever top they may be aiming for. Books, movies, stage plays have been written about this type of devious pariah, and they keep rising relentlessly to the surface. It was his committee who started the witch hunts all over again, accusing, condemning, threatening, strong arming anyone who stood in his way, then speaking grandly to the ever present television cameras about his unselfish role as protector of the people. Why do men like this always claim to be acting for the people? They don't act for the people at all, they act for themselves. He has been directly responsible for the deaths of three men through suicide, who were his victims. He had personally ruined the careers and lives of many, many more, some of whom we know, many we don't. His is the greatest crime of all Mr. McCormick, a perversion of trust. We do not need his type and will do what we can to see that they don't go unpunished.

We are writing this statement so you can convey to the nation, and the world, that we are here. We know of the hue and cry that will go up from many concerning this terrible thing we do, but we will continue on our chosen path. Our regret is total that we find such a course of action necessary, but you will notice we have chosen only those who seem to be beyond judgment. Who would punish these men? No one, that's who. Their power is much too great to put them within reach of our laws, therefore in these kinds of cases we will administer our own punishment and it will always be death. No one will be too big, rich or powerful to escape our wrath. We can and will reach anyone at any time should their actions warrant our attention.

With that thought in mind Mr. McCormick, if you will call the warden at the Oregon State penitentiary and ask him to check the cell of Ibn Saud you will learn how far we can and will reach, and with what finality. We disagreed, as did most of the people in this land, with the sentence he received, especially in view of the man he killed.

The Reverend Stanton was yet another in a long list headed by no less than Jesus Christ. These good and loving men keep showing up on earth, only to be murdered by those who wait like the beasts of prey they are. A life sentence was not enough for a murderer of his type Mr. McCormick, especially in view of the fact Mr. Saud was to be paroled in the near future. He needs to die, not be released, and by the time you read this he will be dead. We can and will reach wherever we have to in the administration of our regrettably harsh punishment, and sad though it may be, our time has come.

We think our action has both historical and biblical precedent, not that even that will make our actions any more palatable. Understandable perhaps, but not acceptable.

If you will go to the front of your building you will find a large yellow rental truck parked there, with a padlock on the back door. The key is enclosed.'

He looked, there was a single key in the bottom of the envelope.

'Call the police now Mr. McCormick, have them open it for you and you'll find Manny Beatty, Carmine Palermo, General Williams and Senator Howard. They are dead, but they are there.

We want the people of this country to know we are among you. We want them to know we are a terrible force and from this moment on will deal ruthlessly in immediate death to those who seem to be beyond the law. We want the people to know we will harm only those who harm others, and have chosen these five men to demonstrate our willingness to act with terrible finality, and our indifference to what positions our victims might hold.

Tell the people Mr. McCormick. We are on the land.'

McCormick sat in stunned silence, his mind ablaze trying to figure what to do first. He exploded out of his chair running, like he hadn't run since college days.

"What the f...." The frightened Suzie exclaimed as he shot past her, slamming the swinging gate against the counter, pounding down the entrance hall area, down the steps to the street. The yellow truck sat waiting.

"Jesus! Jesus! Oh Jesus Christ!"

He never understood emotions, but he was crying now, staring at the large heavy padlock securing the back door. He had no doubt what was to be found inside. Thoughts blurred as they raced through his mind. What first, the boss? The police? How would he get hold of the Oregon State penitentiary and try to convince someone long distance who he was? How would he ask them to check this out? What if this whole damn thing was some smart ass joke? What then? But what about the four men? They had been kidnaped and were missing, about that there was no doubt. The whole world knew that.

He started with his boss, who sat reading the contents of the envelope for what seemed like forever to McCormick.

"What do we do, boss?"

"We get on the phone and check out Oregon." Looking at his watch. "It's ten thirty here...eight thirty there. We'll try going straight into the warden. Don't know if it'll work, but it's worth the try.!"

He reached for his direct line phone, punching numbers furiously until he found the Oregon State prison phone number.

"Yes, my name is Harry Hartman and I'm the night editor of the Kansas City Star, are you the person in charge of the prison?" He could feel the headache coming on. "Yes Hartman, and I have to talk to the warden, it's extremely important." A slight pause. "What about? I'll tell you this much and that is I have received information that one of your inmates has been murdered!" Pause. "Yes murdered!" He stared into the mouth piece of the phone in intense irritation and disbelief. "Hartman! Harry Hartman, God damn it! Kansas City Star! Kansas City, Missouri!" Adding. "Listen I'm sorry, I know you're only doing what you're told to, but I must speak to the warden. This is an unbelievable situation and I must speak to him." He listened. "Yes, yes call me back at this number collect." He gave them the number of his direct line. "Yes I'll be right here, waiting!" He slammed the phone in the receiver, kneading his forehead, aware of his developing headache.

"Look Don, I'm not ready to call the police yet but I'm not about to deny the truck contains what the letter says, either. Call down to the press room and have the foreman send a bunch of guys to stand guard around that truck. Tell him right now...no, fuck it, I'll tell him."

He ripped the phone off the hook, punching numbers ferociously.

"Bill, listen to me! There's a big yellow rental truck parked out front. It might be something very important so I want you to take every man you can spare for a while and stand around that truck!" He listened for just a second. "Look, have your guys stand around the truck, that's all. For Gods sake don't touch it! It isn't going to blow up! Just don't let anyone near it 'til you hear from me, or the police."

The private line rang, causing both men to start.

"Hartman!" It was short, but clear.

"Yes operator I'll accept the charges." A brief pause followed by, "Warden, as you know by now my name is Harry Hartman and I'm the night editor of the Kansas City Star. Warden I have just received a bizarre note, anonymous of course, that tells me where I'm to find the bodies of Manny Beatty, Carmine Palermo, General Williams and Senator Howard." Another pause. "What this has to do with you warden is the note says that right this minute Ibn Saud is dead in his cell in your penitentiary. I thought that would be easy enough to check out without our doing something foolish on this end. Warden will you please have someone check Saud's' cell to see if this is some massive hoax, something beyond my ability to comprehend?" More listening. "I know warden, I know. It is unusual, but I wanted to do it this way rather than ask my governor to ask yours. We can do that and you know he will, but why? Why can't you and I handle this over the phone? If it's true, the whole world's going to know about it tomorrow. If it isn't, only you and I need to know. Will you please have this checked out?" He listened more. "Thank you sir and please, let me hold this line open. I'll wait right here while you check, and please understand there'd be no reason whatever for you try and hide this from me. I'm the person who's bringing it to your attention." Pause. "Yes warden, I understand but remember if it's true it'll be impossible to hide from the press so there's really no reason to try and keep it from me." Listening. "This same note tells me exactly where the other bodies are but before investigating that, I thought it would be better to check Saud. We know where he is." He listened more. "Yes warden I will wait, and warden.... Thank you."

The street outside the building was dark and damp and the little paper hats the pressmen wore did nothing to ward off the cold. They stood on the sidewalk close by the truck, but not so close as to be harmed should it be a bomb of any kind. While they were standing there a sedan moved quietly by containing the soon to be infamous, Leslie Angeles. She was Sandi Myer again, different color hair, no glasses, wearing slacks, sweater and heavy coat. Suzie the receptionist would not recognize her now, if they were standing eye to eye.

"Yes warden, I'm here." Hartman answered. "How did it happen?" Nodding yes to McCormick who started to move out of his chair. "I see. No marks on the body. I see. I have no more questions sir because I know how much you have to do now. Thank you so much for your cooperation in this matter, now we know what to do on this end. Thanks again warden, and sir.... Good luck."

"Call the police Don, but tell them nothing until you get hold of the chief. I'm sure now, our boys are in the back of that thing out there but unless I get people here with really fuzzy balls, we do nothing! Get photographers out there and have them standby 'til the chief gets here. I don't want anybody besides you and me to know what's going on. Get the FBI down here, 'cause we're sure talking about their jurisdiction, and Don," calling to his reporter as he opened the door to leave, "before you call anybody be sure you make copies of that letter. They'll take it away from us immediately, so make sure we have copies!"

The rest of the night passed in furious activities starting with the arrival of the chief of police and the FBI. The truck door was opened revealing nothing until the light from their flashes revealed four bodies laid out neatly on the floor, covered with heavy furniture pads.

"Get those pictures developed and to the press room." Harry barked to the photographers, as he snapped the phone out of its cradle. "Bill whatever you got for a front page, pull it!" Slamming the phone down. "Don get to work on that front page. Give us a half page shot of the bodies in the truck. Give me individual pictures of each of the men and a bio. Spare nothing, just tell it like it is." He whipped the phone up again. "Suzie get in here quick. I want to ask you some questions before the cops get to you!" He slammed it down again as Don McCormick was opening the door to leave.

"Don?"

"Yeah Harry."

"Why us?"

He was intrigued by the slow smile he received, to this most valid question.

"Thought about that and my guess is these guys are scared of nothing. Think about it for a minute. We're Kansas City, the heart of the nation and what these people have shown the world is that they can, and will, act in an arrogant manner to prove their point. They snatched four of the most famous, or infamous men in the United States, transported them somewhere while the largest search in the history of this or any other country went on. Thousands of miles covered, four people killed in the actual kidnaping and now those four men dead out there. They murdered them and delivered their bodies to our front door." He paused breathless. "Do you hear me Harry? To the front fucking door! Man that took balls! I have no idea who or what they are, but I'll tell you one God damn thing, they're obviously not afraid of anything. They must have a lot of money to carry something like this out, and with Saud dead in his cell in Oregon they showed us what extraordinary things they can, and obviously will do. Their information must be limitless, which would indicate money again. They're obviously set up for a continuing program of the same, and do you know what?"

"No what?"

"If I was one of the bad guys, I'd be haulin' ass."

*   *   *

Every newspaper in the United States, and most of the world, was completely covered with the stunning news, the following day. Television networks had nothing but coverage of the gruesome event with a dizzying mass of guests, all decrying what had happened.

"We'll have these people apprehended shortly." The director of the FBI announced. "They left enough clues to keep us busy for days."

They left nothing. No clues, no evidence, no fingerprints, nothing. The Old Man had insisted they wear surgical gloves at all times, even when working together in the planning stage. There would be no way one of their number could go over to the side of the law, accompanied by some artifact containing prints. Rock ribbed secrecy was the order of every day, and all of their people understood that.

CHAPTER 25

The headlines of every paper in the world screamed the news of the five men, and their incredible deaths. Their executioners were immediately dubbed the Angels, exactly as the Old Man wished, suggested by the name Sandi gave when delivering the packet to Don McCormick. "Leslie Angeles".

"What do you think of the Angels, Archbishop? And why did they want us to arrive at this name?" The television anchorman asked the church leader.

It was the archbishops moment. He was supposed to be above vanity, a frailty of the common man, still, he knew the Cardinal would be watching.

"Yes, well I think great liberties have been taken with the concept of a spiritual messenger of Almighty God." It rumbled and rolled with exaggerated emphasis on the word almighty, God pronounced Gawd. "These people seem to be more modern day terrorist than celestial being who brings tidings from on high." It sounded good to the church man who looked splendid in his clerics garb, black suit, white Roman collar, red vest and gold chain. He was handsome too, a ruddy complexion contributed to by his regular evening libations, topped by a beautiful head of thick, wavy, pure white hair. "No I don't think I would call them angels. Murderers perhaps, angels definitely not."

"I see." The television personality answered, shuffling papers. "Do you think they were inferring angels spoken of in the Bible in reference to their visitation to Lot in the story about Sodom and Gomorrah?"

"Story?" It was the archbishops moment to rise to the defense of the good book. "If you mean the passage referring to the perusal by, and warnings of the angels for Lot to remove his family from that sinful city, no I don't. I don't think it could possibly have a thing to do with that. Those angels were scouting for God, and final retribution was to be His, not theirs. No I don't think that at all, unless this group has a convoluted notion of what the Bible says."

"What about the note with the bodies of the men in the truck, and what it said about historical and biblical precedent. What do you think they meant?"

"I really wouldn't want to comment on that, because I'm sure these people are far removed from any concept of Almighty God," he said it again and in exactly the same practiced way, "that to even suggest they might know anything about the Bible seems absurd on first blush."

"But your excellency," he always liked the sound of that, "there are so many direct examples of the wrath of God in the Bible, that maybe, just maybe, that's what these people are referring to."

"Such as?" His heavy white eyebrows raised indignantly.

"Such as the quote, 'Let no man deceive you with vain words: for because of these things cometh the wrath of God upon the children of disobedience.' Couldn't that be a possibility?"

"Anything could be a possibility when it comes to interpreting, or misinterpreting the word of Almighty God, yes. That's precisely why my church has taken the position for centuries, that it should not be read and interpreted by everyone." He regretted saying that immediately. "For instance where does what you read even infer angels?"

There was a pause as both realized the import of his answer. The anchorman delighted, and the archbishop appalled at what he'd disclosed. He was hoping now the Cardinal was not watching. He didn't do well on that last one.

"Nowhere Archbishop, but it does state wrath that we were speaking of."

"Well in any event I imagine if they referred to themselves, at least by the name the woman gave as the angels, that's what the press will call them until they're apprehended. Yes I suppose that would be a bit more sensational," smoothing his red vest, "but really, angels? No, no! Devils maybe! A leading military men, and a United States senator? Angels indeed!"

*   *   *

"Tom?" The Old Man was walking him to his car, parked on the long drive outside the Shed. "That statement you wrote to the reporter in Kansas City was done well. It sums up what we have to say, what we want them to know."

It was a beautiful midwinter day in south Louisiana and the two old friends stood alongside Tom's Lincoln, the Old Man shading his eyes as he spoke to his protege.

"Well writers, commentators and expert guests, not to mention every law enforcement agency involved are having a field day with it now." Tom replied.

"Yes son, I know they are." Still shading his eyes, looking off into the distance. "Plenty of outrage out there now."

"Well, we were prepared for that."

"Yes we were, weren't we." He didn't move, and Helen appeared to be grazing in the lush deep grass. "A shame about the Senator's lady. Could that have been helped?"

"If done again it could, yes." He was lowering his body into the large leather seat. "The man responsible for that came to us out of the Vietnam thing. Tunnel rat. An utterly terrifying job at best. They all carried basically the same weapon, the .45, because it was the biggest thing they could take down in those black holes. Many of them killed on sound, some on smell, almost none on sight because they worked in total darkness, but all of them...those that came back up...all killed on instant reflex. Something moved in those tight, tiny tunnels and either it was dead, or them. He was going strictly on reaction. If she had only stayed in the house she'd be alive today, but she blundered on to the scene and ran for the door, representing an immediate threat to the whole operation. He simply ran her down and swung that heavy gun when she reached the door, and she died. He didn't mean to kill her, or want to, but she was close to the man we wanted, and so she died for that. That's going to happen Boss, in this or any other action involving chance spectators to what we're doing. Wish it wasn't so, but the people we're after are going be taken whenever and wherever."

"Taken? We don't want any more taken at all. This was strictly to get the attention of those the law can't, or won't."

"Yes I know Mr. Alex. What I meant to say is many will be under heavy armed guard, at the time we take them out, and you can be assured those guards will always die too. I wouldn't call them innocents, but there will be others." He started the large engine. "Anyway, there's no turning back now."

"I know Tom. Seems a pity though doesn't it, that something like this has to be done," he stiffened and drew himself straight, "but it has to be done."

"When?"

"Soon. I'll call you." He put his hand on Tom's arm, tears glistening in his eyes. "And thanks for your support. I don't know what I'd do without you."

Tom looked at him in silence for a long time.

"You'd have done this without me if I'd refused though, wouldn't you?" He stared up into the ancient face for his answer.

"Yes son, I'd have done it without you."

"Knew that, but I couldn't let you. We've been in this thing together since Oklahoma and I'm in the rest of the way." He touched the Old Man's hand affectionately. "Take it easy for awhile, call me if you need me?"

The old man stood with his sleek Doberman. He waved at the departing Lincoln.

*   *   *

The word flashed down the news wires that the four men had been shot at point blank range in the head with a .22.

"A hollowed out .22?" Don McCormick asked. He'd been allowed to stay with the bodies all the way through forensic examination. "Lot of damage?"

"Yes. When the bullets smashed into the skulls, it flattens and destroys all brain tissue it tears through. There was no chance it couldn't have killed them, but they were obviously dead men from the moment they disappeared."

"What you mean?"

"Just that anybody who could do this to four men, together...."

"Wait a minute!" The reporter threw up his hand. "Wait a minute. You mean at the same time?"

"At the same time, and as I was saying the men who did this are obviously capable of killing any time." The doctor added.

"Why men? What makes you think there was more than one?"

"Two reasons. One I know, the other I surmise."

"OK?"

"Each of these men has been shot in a different spot, from a different angle, indicating varying heights. One of the killers is obviously left handed, from the entry of the bullet in Palermo's head. He's probably the same man who killed the senators lady, because the lower left side of her skull was crushed. Again, left handed. I'd suggest they were killed probably facing each other. You know, seated in a circle, where they could see the others, as indicated by the eyes of the Senator and Beatty."

"What do you mean?"

"They were looking up, obviously horrified at what they saw."

"Which was?"

"It's only a guess Don, but on the basis of what I see I'd say each of them were looking at an individual killer."

"Jesus Christ Doc! You mean shot in the same room at the same time by four different killers?"

"Yes, but that's only theory you know. I know how they died and approximately when. I know the physical angles of entry of the bullets. I can guesstimate the height of their killer, but I leave the rest up to you and the police."

"Bullshit Doc! You can't lay something like that on me and leave me hanging. What the hell you mean individual killers?"

"Well, it's only a guess on my part, but I think we've got something here that this nation, or the world, has never seen. Executioners pure and simple, who killed at the same time, while looking at the others so there's absolutely no chance any of them will ever inform on the rest. These angels, or whatever you want to call them, are in business Don, and my prayers go out for whoever they want, because they will get them. Look at Ibn Saud for Christs' sake, dead in his cell in max' of a poison tipped dart. Who the hell did it? Who knows?" He paused, his brow furrowed. "I'll tell you something else."

"What?"

"I'll bet you never see any more disappearances. I'll bet from now on whoever they're after are dead in the streets, and no suspense about it."

"What makes you think that?" The reporter asked.

"Oh Don, people that kill like this? They'd as soon kill you on 12th and Main at high noon as any time. Don't know who they are Don, but I'll tell you something. We've got some very, very, heavy mothers on our hands here."

*   *   *

The smallish man sat in the cramped dinette drinking coffee, reading his paper about the dead men in Kansas City. He admired the efforts of the police as he reached for the cup with his left hand. Palermo had been his to execute, and the paper stated correctly he shot him with the gun in his left hand.

The kids called him Lefty growing up, but with respect because he proved time after time deserving of their approval. He was not only willing to do those things considered fearless among school boys, but was also ready to fight any of the larger lads, at any time. He lost most of the time, but was renowned for his determination.

He kept getting up, as he received each beating, until his adversaries walked away, out of sheer frustration. The tenacity with which he was driven was the same found in many short men, an attempt to show the world they could, and would, stay with the best of them.

He was immediately attracted to the Chief because of his diminutive size, but he also knew size was all the Chief was lacking. Fearlessness, an easy thing to recognize for those who possess it, had nothing to do with braggadocio.

Curt went to Vietnam recognized by his officers and enlisted men as what he was, utterly without fear. He attacked basic training with an abandon, and fought any man, anywhere and at any time. He lost most of them, because of his lack of size, but every one of his opponents knew absolutely he would have killed them had he been armed.

He was among the first American troops to come upon the infamous tunnels of the Viet Cong. Tunnels dug over a period of years, and volunteers were needed to go down them after losing many dead to sniper fire emanating from these honeycombs.

"Weird down there, man." He thought as his mind raced from the newspaper and mention of the left handed assassin, to the thought that being left handed probably saved his life many times. Sure they dropped grenades down first but those tunnels had more twists and turns than you could imagine. All any gook had to do was get around the first bend and he could heave grenades all day and not hurt them. That was when he went down.

'Hot! God damn it was hot and stunk too.' He thought. 'Things seemed to go forever. Tunnels, drops, turns, alcoves and rooms. Whole families down there.' Like the one he shot to pieces when he suddenly dropped into what served as their living quarters. 'Yeah, saved my ass many times because I was always working with my left hand, rollin' out of the line of fire when it came. When they started shootin'...must've been firing down the wrong side.'

He caught a plane out of Kansas City flying to his new home in the desert of southern Arizona. Deplaning at Tucson, he drove the remaining miles that took him close to the Mexican border where his mobile home sat out in the desert. He had plenty of money now to do whatever he wanted, and what he wanted was to drink Tequila, screw beautiful Mexican women and read. He loved to read, drink, and fornicate, and had the time now to do all he wanted.

He felt kind of bad about the lady in Washington D.C. he'd killed, but not so bad he was losing any sleep.

'Too bad.' He thought. 'If she hadn't been there she'd still be alive but she was.' He thought a moment. 'Wonder what kind of a lay she was? Pretty good to have the senator coming by on a regular, scheduled basis.' He laughed to himself. 'Don't guess he was the first or the last to get it over some broad.' He suddenly laughed, shouting. "That's it! That's it! Oh yeah, God damn that is it! I want to be up in the saddle bootin' home a winner when I die! What a way to go! Screwing my brains out one minute, looking around eternity the next. Hey yeah man, that will work!"

*   *   *

"So what do you think Helen? It's so nice out here today, let's walk a little, soak up some sun."

To an observer it would have been a pleasant scene to see, the beautiful mahogany colored animal prancing one minute, running the next in long graceful strides overjoyed at the thrill of being outside and alone with her only love. There was great celebration of a sort, when Tom or anyone else left, she didn't want to share Alex George with anyone. She sped back and forth across the luxurious lawn of lush St. Augustine grass, stopping suddenly, front legs and paws down flat on the ground, rear end high in the air, short stubby tail wagging furiously, checking to see if he was watching her, and he was.

"Go Helen. Go!" He laughed joyfully, throwing his arms in the air urging her on. "Oh go baby! It was God Himself gave you those magnificent wheels! Use 'em sweetheart! Say thanks to Him! Use 'em!"

She entered the game joyously, trying to outdo herself with each breakneck burst of speed. Helen was ecstatic, gamboling for her master, cutting, diving, stretching her legs to their maximum, streaking the full length of the lawn, appearing airborne at times, turning ever tighter corners around the massive oak trees until the angle of her body overcame gravity and she rolled in a flurry of ears, legs and joy, all to wildly enthusiastic support from the Old Man. She raced behind the lattice work around the bottom of the back porch of the main house disappearing for a moment, then reappeared literally flying, skidding to a halt at his feet placing the ball in her mouth in his hand. Her long muzzle nudged his hand insistently as she rolled her huge brown eyes, inviting him to throw it. She'd chase it to the moon for him if she could.

"Oh it's game time, huh babe? Well you know I'm a real old fart now but we'll give it a try." Whereupon he rolled it a little way across the grass snatched immediately by his constant companion initiating yet another crazy abandoned run. Somehow, in her way, she knew he was old and feeble, unable to join in her romp. That was OK, she'd romp for both of them, finally arriving at his feet holding the ball gently between brilliant white teeth, separated by a vivid red tongue panting furiously, completely winded but willing to go on forever if he would.

"Helen, Helen, Helen!" He was weak with laughter. "Oh Helen wouldn't Momma love to see you now?" He took her head in his hands, scratching behind both ears. "You are a funny lady you know, and Momma loved you so." He paused momentarily as he left the present. "Oh but she loved everyone so." Drifting in thought. "Why baby, I think she was love itself."

The winded dog stared at the old man as tears coursed down his face as he looked at the vision of beauty and grace that once was his late wife's constant companion. Helen was instantly affected by his change in attitude, dropping the red ball letting it roll up to his foot, shaking her head in the manner of a race horse wanting more. She knew it wasn't coming. The old man in the heavy white cable knit sweater, baggy brown trousers and his dog, walked slowly over to the lawn chairs at the end of the property. He sat down gingerly with Helen seating herself on her haunches, fully erect, immediately in front where he could pet her if he would.

*   *   *

"How long you gonna' sleep?" The terrible looking man, gently nudged the large black Labrador curled up at his feet in the bunk, which sat in the corner of the smallish one room cabin. "Wonder what time it is anyway?"

Someday he'd get a clock, or a watch, but not now because he didn't care either what time it was or what day it was. They all seemed pretty much the same to him anyway, and somehow, even though he spent little time thinking about it he knew one of them was going to be his last. He didn't give a shit.

Chris and his dog lay dozing, drifting in the state somewhere between awake and asleep. The cabin was deep in the northern Michigan woods, surrounded by thick forest, covered with a dazzling coat of white snow. It was a vision of peace and beauty as it sat in the woods letting the thin plume of smoke rise through the trees and into the sky. He knew this was as close to heaven as he could imagine qualifying for, but had no regrets in that regard. His whole life had been involved in violence and death starting with the racial gang wars on the streets of Detroit when he was a boy.

There was no love in this family and it was like he showed up one day, and started living with them. His people were hard working Polish immigrants, and his old man worked for years in a Chrysler assembly plant. He worked hard during the day and drank all the rest of the time, handing out savage beatings to all his kids at every opportunity until Chris finally just stayed away. It was a dismal city, a dismal family, and an equally dismal life, devoid of caring or love. Even his mother was too defeated by the mind numbing conditions around her to dispense anything like love.

"Killed that black son of a bitch, you know it." He mumbled to his dog through his dreamlike state, watching the replay of his first murder take place on the rough hewn ceiling. "But just barely."

Chris could still see the tall thin black youth running desperately through the darkness, trying to evade the iron pipe he grabbed somewhere. The boy was looking over his shoulder, with the wild eyed look of desperation Chris was to become so familiar with over the years. He never saw whatever tripped him, sprawling out on the pavement with his enraged white adversary descending on him swinging the pipe in great roundhouse blows. As it was happening Chris was aware of a distant vision of his father, but it was never quite clear to him. The first blow broke the fallen boys arm, the second smashed the knee he'd drawn up in a defensive motion and the third crushed his life out as his skull folded under the terrible blow.

"Had it to do over again I'd coat the walls of that alley with his brains. Think I was afraid the nuns'd find out anyway. Sister Katherine especially. I think she was the only person I've ever known that loved me and I didn't want her to find out so I took off to the Marines and Korea."

He nudged the black dog who looked at him through blood shot eyes.

"That's where I got this, you know." Pointing to the terrible scar that ran down his face from his eye, across his lips, stopping at his chin.

The dog looked, saw nothing he hadn't seen before, and nestled his head back down in the heavy covers.

"You don't even give a shit do you?" Chris laughed giving the dog a playful kick, answered by a low growl that meant he was not to do that again.

"Tough guy eh?" He grabbed the dog by his muzzle shaking it vigorously. "You're sleeping with a tough guy, you know that? Why I'da been dead a hundred times if I hadn't been a tough guy, like the time that Chink slid over the edge of our foxhole in that fierce cold and gave me this," indicating the long terrible scar, "with the butt of his rifle. Jesus, what with the cold and all I thought he'd knocked my God damn head off. My face at least."

The dog stirred, wanting quiet so he could get back to sleep.

"No big deal? You figure I'm ugly enough, so what's a busted face."

The dog had enough and got down with a great display of irritation, shaking his coat out, laying down to scratch vigorously, followed by a huge yawn. His lethal bunkmate laughed out loud.

"Get up here you asshole." Chris commanded, while holding open the covers so he could jump in to his favorite place in life, under the covers with this strange man he loved so much.

"Nice huh?" Chris hugged the big dog, who was enjoying the warmth. His mind wandered, speaking in a low tone to his only friend. "Talking 'bout nice, I gotta tell ya' it was some kind of nice being back in action." The dog stirred which Chris took for an objection. "Hope you didn't miss me too much while I was gone. Hell, I looked all over for the kennel I left you in, I knew they'd keep you in a nice warm cage." He paused, continuing in an ominous voice. "They aren't shittin' me are they? You do stay in a heated cage don't you?" Chris didn't like that thought, as he hugged the dogs warm body to his. "Naw they wouldn't dare keep you in the cold. Anyway like I was sayin' it was great being back in action, and especially doin' what we're doin'."

The dog didn't have a name. Chris never got around to giving him one.

"But I never felt so good about it as with this bunch. We took out a bunch of real heavy dudes that should have died a long time ago, but nobody had the balls to put em' down. Felt good I'll tell ya' but I might have lost my touch a little bit. 'Member me telling you about that Chink that busted my face wide open? Well when he quit rollin' I almost cut his head off I was so God damn mad. I mean I was on him and cut deep with that old Kabar of mine. Only thing holding his head on was his spine. Cut a lot of throats since then, always the same way, but that slime ball hood in Florida, you know the one guarding Palermo's cars? I don't think I much more than scratched him a little and he up and died. Glad he did though, you know it, 'cause I think I need a little practicin' up. No problems blowing up the senator though. He was long over due." He pulled the dogs face up close to his staring into the huge bloodshot eyes. "Man God damn, I don't have any idea who I'm working for, but I'll tell you one thing, they've found themselves some real bad folks. Nobody, not even one of 'em so much as flinched when it came time to execute those guys, and that's really something. Not many guys could do that you know."

He hugged the dog up tight beneath the warm covers.

"Hey, what say let's get some sleep. I'll take you ice house fishing later."

*   *   *

"You know Helen," Alex spoke to her all the time and although he was told dogs couldn't understand, he never believed it, "this is really strange, isn't it? You know what I mean, the part about doing this thing because of Momma. Yeah, yeah, I know she'd be appalled at what we're doing but then on the other hand, she was even more heartbroken over the terrible things done by those people specifically and their kind in general. That's something I never did learn to handle, you know it? I never could stand her hurt and tears. Wanted to do something. Smash something! Hurt somebody!"

Helen was intense listening, saddened by the weeping man in front of her.

"When she cried over things that went on in this old world, I didn't know what to do, her tears enraged me so. Not at her though." Giving her a reassuring scratch. "Purely out of frustration and inability to help her, I'd go out, find a fight and beat the shit out of somebody to let my rage out. When my brawling days were over I had to stay and see what I could do to help her through her pain." He recoiled at the thought, his voice choked by emotion. "She had much too much of that you know."

The brown eyes were riveted to his.

"Yeah God damn, she had a lot of that. So what I'm trying to do right now is see to it that some of these people who dole out misery and suffering to others, will just have to pay the piper. Well in this case, I'm the piper and I can do that you know Helen. Yeah, yeah, and since I'm running out of time, and God doesn't seem to be doing anything about it, I guess I will."

*   *   *

The panel of experts were assembled in front of the camera on the network television special, moderated by the old king of the medium, now retired.

"It would seem to me what we have here is something different than we've ever seen in fact or fiction." The ex-director of the FBI commented. "I know of nothing in history that could shed any light on this situation with the possible exception of the death squads, in the Buenos Aires police department itself, back in the early sixties."

"And who were their victims, Director?" The mellifluous moderator asked.

"Criminals, of various stripe released through disparate legal procedures usually imputing guilt of some sort to the police who'd worked so hard to apprehend them. After enough of this these same police simply took the law into their own hands executing those they felt were guilty. There was no doubt what they were about, because they threw their victims bodies on the steps of the various courthouses that had only recently put them back on the streets.

"Yes Mr. Director," the aging newscaster, a member of the august panel interrupted, "but those men were all criminals. Wasn't that so?"

"They were."

"Well while we do have a notorious suspect in criminality in Carmine Palermo, the others have never even been close to indictment for any crimes. In other words what we're talking about here are some high ranking people...."

"What you got here are some mighty dead people who've handed out a lot of misery and gone their merry way because they were too damn powerful to be touched." The hard bitten New York street reporter, a panel member interrupted. "The thing is you may not want to admit it but you absolutely know there's lots of people right this minute who aren't the slightest bit unhappy these men have been killed. I know what I'm talkin' about! I talk to the guy and the gal in the streets, and believe me when I tell you there's no tears being shed over this happening down there."

"Do you mean to say there are actually people out there who condone what's happened?" The pompous senator leaned in the direction of the reporter.

"Oh yeah senator, and then some."

"But my God man you're talking about a member of the United States Senate, and one of our most famous, and I might add most heavily decorated generals, not to mention the leader of one of the largest unions in the world. What of them? Won't they be missed?"

"Not by the people I talk to, senator." He leaned back in his chair.

"Who in Gods name are you talking to, maniacs? Criminals? You don't seem to be in touch with reality...."

"Look senator," the reporter was using his cigar as a pointer, "don't get down on my people because I'll tell you something I don't think you know. They are America, not your hot shot power brokers, or big time hustlers! You won't find any millionaires down there or influential politicians. Naw hell no, what you will find down there is America and they don't think Beatty was any thing but a God damn murderous thief!" He nodded toward the moderator. "Sorry, but if you live there you do take on the language of the street."

"But...but he lead a union that numbered in the millions!"

"Yeah and Hitler led a nation numbering more than that! So what! What's that mean?" The reporter never liked the senator and was baiting him.

"Would you compare these men to Hitler?"

"Listen senator, I'd compare these men to Hitler, Stalin and Rasputin all rolled together...."

"YOU WHAT?" The politician's apoplectic response.

"You heard me senator. I don't know what kind of games you guys play in the senate, but don't try and play 'em with me. You know these guys have been reported or suspected of some of the greatest crimes imaginable but because of money, power and prestige have been untouchable. There's nothing new about this sort of situation, it's been going on since the dawn of mankind. You guys in the senate deal in it all day, every day in your cloak rooms. You know what I mean, the old swaperoo. You give me this dam and I'll give you that defense contract. Help me crush this man, and I'll do the same for you. Christ senator, Caesar and his mob were doin' it way back then, and nothing's changed. Substance maybe, but not style. Well I'll tell you, it looks to me like finally, at long last, somebody's pretty hot about it. I don't have any idea who they are but they ain't kidding around" He sat back puffing the cigar.

"But the general? What about the general?"

"Oh come on, let's quit the game? I don't know how much responsibility the general bore for the continuation of Vietnam, but lots of folks think he was in for a lions share and if he was...." He inched to the edge of his chair. "Go along with me on this for a minute senator. If he or anybody else was responsible for unnecessarily prolonging that awesome, obscene exercise in stupidity. If he or anyone else kept feeding the bull hockey publicity fires that resulted in many, many more people dying, don't you think that might heat up some folks? Heat 'em up bad enough to want to mete out some punishment of their own. Don't you think that's possible senator?"

"I'll tell you what I think sir! I think you are an irresponsible ass who should never be allowed to touch a typewriter! I...I...."

The reported had him and loved it as he asked.

"Now wait a minute senator, wait just a minute! Let me get this straight so I can report it right. You want to take my typewriter because you don't like the truth? One of your club members in the senate gets blown up and you're going to get even. Is that it senator? If that's it sir then you are also saying you would deny me one of our most basic freedoms? Freedom of the press?"

"Gentlemen I'm sorry, but we've run out of time." The revered newscaster droned. "I'm sure we all would like to continue, but it seems we are out of time. I want to thank...."

*   *   *

He reached out a hand to touch her, met immediately by her up thrust head longing for that same touch.

"I got the price for what it takes, you know, and what the hell, it's long past due. Oh don't get me wrong sweetheart, I know we're not going to right all the wrongs in the world, but I do think if we keep accepting the evil that goes on around us...you know what I mean, look the other way, why it seems to me as though we become part of it. You know what I'm sayin' Helen? Like Hitler for instance. He shows up doing his dumb ass strut and the leaders of the world laid right down for him, can you imagine that? Everybody kept giving, bending, bowing, scraping and kissing his ass, while he was pushing his poison across the world and the way I see it these same people wound up cooperating in his conspiracy to rule the world. Nobody knows how many people died because of his bullshit but the experts figure around twenty million. You got that Babe, twenty million human beings! Now what if we had a magic crystal ball that could tell us how he was gonna' turn out? What then?" Helen had no answers but she was listening. "Well I'll tell you what, somebody would have killed him when he was a pup, and then all those millions of people who died wouldn't of. You know what I'm sayin'?"

She didn't but she was trying.

"Even young Alex would be sittin' here with us today, if that war hadn't started, but it did and he isn't."

He paused momentarily trying to see what Alex, Jr. would look like if he were still alive. All he could see was the broad, smiling, handsome young face in the picture upstairs. The one with his helmet and goggles.

"That makes me angry sweetheart, and I guess the only thing that's going to douse that anger in this old heart is death itself." Adding. "Mine." He thought a moment. "But there'll be a bunch go before I do."

*   *   *

The temperature was balmy as Harold sat at the rear of his new air boat, purchased with funds received for his services rendered. He wasn't much of a mixer, like most of the others, preferring to stay by themselves, so what he called home in the Okefenokee swamp of southeastern Georgia was almost perfect. It reminded him so of much of Vietnam, and there was something indescribably beautiful about the immense, brooding damp world it contained. With his new boat he could travel great distances at high speed disappearing whenever the mood struck him, and it struck him quite often.

He was tall, thin and rangy, with long straight blond hair and dark brown eyes that almost never smiled. He didn't have much to smile about after subordinating his body, mind and soul to the military effort in the sixties. He complied in a most unusual way and his mind took a turn for the absolute worse, a result of his multiple tours in the southeast Asia hell hole that was Vietnam. It was strange somehow, but upon first casual glance Harold looked somewhat Oriental because of his flat facial features and a complexion given to darker tones. He did three tours as a member of long range reconnaissance patrol groups that came to be known as Lurps, and paid for it by ostracizing himself from his fellow human beings.

It was Harolds cold, flat, deadly eyes under the wide brimmed hat and over the top of the .45, that Manny Beatty's barber had seen.

'Wonder if I'm going pussy.' He mused as he flipped the long line from his casting rod and watched it settle a few scant feet from where he'd aimed. 'Still don't know why I didn't blow him up.' Referring to the terrified barber. 'Know one damn thing though, with reflexes that slow it wouldn't do for me to be making any more patrols in the Nam. One of those gooks see me looking at him over the sights and not shootin' and I'm a dead son of a bitch.'

He thought deeply about that, vowing not to make the same mistake again. Oh sure the barber had been much too terrified to make anything like an identification, but there was the possibility, a result of his hesitancy to pull the trigger. Harold shifted the rod into his left hand and opened his tackle box to view the huge weapon he killed the bodyguard with, but failed to fire at the barber. He never went anywhere without it and especially now that he was back in action again, with the constant possibility that somebody, somehow, might be tracking him right into the swamp. It was as vital a piece of equipment as his own heart. Many, many times he'd sighted over the top of the huge weapon at an alligator, but could not pull the trigger. He shot up a lot of cypress trees though, but that was to be expected, because he was forever reverting to his Vietnam experience.

Nights were best for that, although he would slip back in time whenever the notion struck him, and it was always the same. He'd look for a strange island in the trackless swamp, his boat gliding soundlessly into the bank. Then he'd remove his soft brimmed jungle hat and quickly replace it with the old bandana that had once been part of a parachute. It was like an old friend and came with him all the way. He put the one earring in place, always in his right ear, smear his face with black grease paint and slip quietly over the side to enter the dense jungle. It was a test to see if he could penetrate the leaves and vines without a sound and he was expert at it. When he ran on the cottonmouth water moccasins, he'd stop everything he was doing and watch their silent maneuverings until they moved out of sight. He wanted so much to achieve their perfection at stealth, admiring them as they passed from view. His equipment was much the same as Tom's, back in his south Pacific days, except the knife he carried was for throwing as well as stabbing, and there was the .45.

It was only an exercise, but one played out with deadly seriousness. The jungle floor felt good to him somehow, probably because it had afforded him so much protection in the past. It would take a lucky bullet to find him in that position, crawling like the snakes he admired, because his silhouette was almost non existent, yet he could see everything ahead of him. Sometimes he would rise up swiftly, throwing the knife with deadly accuracy, sinking into a tree that had suddenly become one of the enemy. Other times he'd slither around an obstacle confronted by an ideal cypress tree with the right sized outcropping that resembled a human head. He'd open up with his .45, blazing away until the clip was empty, the intent being putting all bullets fired in the tight confine of the target.

'Totally Asiatic.' His sardonic thought. 'But what the hell, it's what I do.'

Harold had a deep mental struggle going on and was astute enough to know that, because even though he had become but a notch short of a homicidal maniac, he was also an extremely intelligent man. That intelligence was precisely what brought him through everything, and to whatever moment he was living in. He knew he was, what he was, because of his time in the service. He had been ordered and encouraged to kill as many of the enemy as he possibly could, until such time as the war was over or he'd been killed himself, making it over in any case. Then they pulled him into the Lurps and the rest was history.

'Wonder if I get another chance?' It was one of those kinds of thoughts most men are forever running through their minds. 'I should you know! Once upon a time I was a regular person like everybody else. Had folks, went to school, girl friend, football, guys on the corner.... Girl friend? Wonder what became of her? Probably married one of those normal guys, got a bunch of kids and all settled in to what they call a typical life. Bet her husband would be pissed off if he knew I popped her cherry.' He almost smiled. 'Wonder if I had kids what they'd look like? Wonder if I get another chance when this life's over? Oh well, who gives a shit, it ain't over yet.'

He was sitting in his boat drifting, on one of his sojourns in the backwaters, his mind far away when his peaceful interlude was suddenly interrupted by gunfire. He dropped to the bottom of the boat soundlessly shutting down all thoughts except one. Where was the gun that had been fired?

He took the boat into the closest bank, grabbed his .45 and leaped onto the island, standing motionless listening with heightened intensity. Listening for the next sound which wasn't long in coming as a thrashing noise from the dense underbrush. Harold's senses were on full alert, no longer in the Georgia swamp, but back in the steaming jungles of Vietnam. His entire body responded as he waited for the source of the noise to show itself so he could kill it if necessary, and it did in the form of a small swamp deer. A little female that had been shot in the front leg breaking it, which made her thrash about as best she could. She flopped out of the jungle and into the water swimming the short distance to the opposite bank where he stood.

"Hey little deer, let me give you a hand." Harold was in the water struggling with the small creature, who was terrified. She'd been shot and now found herself in the grip of one of those things that showed up once in a while. Her huge brown eyes rolled, terror filled as she tried to get away from his tight grasp.

"Look you little fart," he was fighting for all he was worth to help her, "hold still and I'll give you a hand. Not going to hurt you baby, but I sure would like to help." Harold whipped his headpiece off tying her front feet together, at the same time pulling his shirt off, fashioning it into a rope like device securing her back legs.

"Hey mister!" Harold was waiting, listening to the hunter stumbling through the dense undergrowth. "Mister I think that's my deer you got there."

Harold stood up staring at the man with his eyes no one could describe. It wasn't only that they were deep, they appeared to have no bottom at all. When you looked in them it was like looking into a still, dark, tidewater pool that defied all understanding of what was beneath the surface. It was then the hunter noticed the .45 hanging loose in the hand of this strange looking man. He wished he hadn't tracked the deer to this side of the island.

"Did you say...your deer?"

Harold asked with a menacing, expressionless visage, steeped in pure malevolence. He raised the .45 sliding the carriage back casually, yet indicating to the hunter the weapon was ready to fire.

"Must be some kind of mistake. I shot this critter." His eyes flickered in the direction the imaginary ejected shell traveled. "If you'll look there," indicating a spot in the weeds, "you'll see the shell. Come on over, take a look for yourself?" His voice was utterly terrifying in sinister intonation to the already shaken man. The hunter stood on the bank opposite Harold and the wounded animal with a strange sick smile on his face. He knew nothing about Harold but he knew absolutely he wanted to be gone from there.

"Aw no thanks. Listen it's probably one of those once in a lifetime things." The nervous hunter replied. "You know, both guns going off at once, sounding like one? Hell I probably missed anyway. I'm not the best shot in the world."

"I'm an excellent shot, almost never miss. Had this in Nam with me all the time I was there." Holding up the monstrous weapon. "Used it a lot. Would you like to see the empty shell?" Harold asked again.

"No, no! Hell no!" The hunter wanted out of the area. "Shit I know it's there. Saw it flip when you pulled that thing back. Nope, that's your deer all right. Not very big is he?" He really wished he hadn't said that, what if the weird looking guy was sensitive about the size. "Look, wish I had more time but got to be gettin' back to my buddies."

Gathering a little bravado. "There's a whole bunch of them on the other side." God he hoped the odd looking man with the earring believed him. "Well nice talkin' to you and see you later, now."

He disappeared, thrashing his way back to the other side of the smallish island. Harold watched, making sure the last thing the man saw when he turned for his parting glance, was the oriental looking man standing on the bank staring directly at him with the flat expressionless gaze.

"Come on little deer," Harold picked her up as gently as he could, "I got the right place for you." He laid her on the front of the air boat to lessen the fright he knew would be hers upon starting the engine. "We're gonna see if we can get that thing fixed and while you're mendin' you can live with me. Would you like that?" She was in shock and he knew it, talking in low soothing tones meant to calm. "I need a tenant at my place little critter and you ought to do fine. Why hell who knows, me and you might get to be real good friends."

They sped across the waters shallow and deep, going home. The one he'd chosen, the one she hadn't. The killer hired by killers who wanted killing done, and the small wounded deer.

*　　　*　　　*

"Hey gimme that God damn wrench will ya'? Hurry!"

Vic only had one speed at any given time except when asleep. Fast. He called it balls out, but by whatever name he seemed always to be hanging on the ragged edge of self destruction in his manic pursuit of faster, wilder, more, watching whatever scenery there was at any given time scream up in his line of vision. He never was sure which came first, this almost religious fervor for hurling his body through space or what he felt was the greatest experience of his life, flying that Cobra in VietNam.

"Man, God damn you talk about a rush, that was it! Know what I mean? Jeeeeesus! Talk about exciting!" He usually came out of his chair if he was in one, pacing. "Loved to drive that God damn Cobra, balls out, right on up to the trees. Shovin' her! Sliding her! Driving her, then hang her up there, blowin' those gooks right on down their paths. Man that's where it's really at, you know it? Oh you can drive these roundy rounds and get a little something out of it but it sure don't measure up to that over there. Hundred and sixty knots on a line and slide that hot dude right into the action. Hang 'er up there and guess what? Yeah, yeah, you got it! Then we'd have us a shootin' match, me and my gunnery guy and those little bitty assholes trying to shoot my eyes out." He usually drifted a bit at this point. "Wonder how they got those little guys to do that stuff?" He never waited for the question, what? "Why man they'd stand down there in their chickenshit paths in the woods and blaze away at me with their AK's or whatever. Hell, I bet they'd challenged me if they'd been B.B. guns." Once in a while his eyes would mist over, remembering. "They were some kinda real tough little guys, let me tell you! Weren't scared of nothin'! They'd be down there choppin' up our guys, I'd get the call and run their butts up those paths, hang 'er up there and watch a bunch of those itty bitty guys turn to liquid when we hit 'em with the mini's.

Get the picture I'm talkin' about? Jesus, you talk about action! I know I must have been trippin' at the time, but I swear a time or two I took her right up the path after them. Don't know how the God damn rotors made it!"

He drove the race cars now, except when his sponsor let him fly his Lear. That was his thing, speed. Grab the jet, fly to the desert and bring it screaming down from 40,000 where the private jets flew. Balls out he'd skim across the desert, almost out of his mind with the thrill of power and motion. Stamping on the floor, skimming a few scant feet from instant destruction, screaming. "Go you son of a bitch! Go!"

Then the tears would come, born out of raw emotion, as he looked for more speed putting the belly closer and closer to the ground until he heard the sage brush smashing into the underside.

"Ha, ha, ha!"

He screamed with laughter the time he caught for a millisecond the sight of the jack rabbit frozen in his tracks, for all the world appearing to be holding his two small forepaws over his eyes as Vic and the Lear nearly lifted him off the ground. He'd yank the nose up, twisting, rolling, maneuvering violently as he tried to remove all the rivets, wringing the aircraft out every way he knew how. Speed and prospective doom were what made the young man function. There was no way he could get enough.

"Oh Jesus, not Vic again."

One of the drivers commented after he was informed Vic was to share the track with him and the others that night.

"Man God damn, that one belongs in an asylum, not on the track I'm on. Oh it's not that he's a bad driver," in response to the unasked question, "'cause he ain't. He's as good as they come. Sometimes I wonder how tight he's wrapped though. No it's just that the son of a bitch doesn't know anything like...what? Like caution? Don't get me wrong he ain't reckless, at least in the legal sense, but I'll tell you what, when that man gets down in one of these Indy cars, a real different light comes up in his eyes. You know what I mean? Don't ever try and bluff him, and you sure don't ever try and cut him off in the turn 'cause I'll absolutely guarantee you he'll drive right on over your ass. It's like the boy's possessed! Shit, who knows? Maybe he is!"

Vic didn't win all that many races because it was a rare machine that could last a full race with him. Most owners didn't want to give him a ride knowing that. He was an outstanding driver except for the fact he kept bringing those unbelievably expensive machines back to their owners in a sack.

"Yeah, I know. I know!" His sponsor, a wealthy car dealer told those who questioned his choice of Vic as his driver. "He'll bust my ass clean up, tryin' to keep cars under him, but one day we'll find one that'll do it and that's when we fill up my mantle at home. Besides, it's my God damn money. I earned it, and think I got the best driver alive!"

Vic was a ladies man of the first order too, for the very reason his was such a wild, abandoned approach to life, love and the pursuit of his happiness. The ladies found him irresistible in a bad boy way. Handsome, smiling, laughing, always looking for the next thrill, and there were never enough of those. Black curly hair, broad muscular face, well built, possessed of great physical strength, which he used with consummate skill in the manipulation of the various craft he drove to the edge, obviously willing to destroy his body in a moment in his quest for speed, equally willing to fight any man with his fists.

The Old Man made a one in a million choice in Vic, and the Chief made an excellent presentation to bring him into the fold. Vic listened carefully as the Chief covered all the points. The object of this new organization. Who the first victims were to be. The reason for absolute secrecy. Vic heard the message one time, making his decision on the spot.

"Looks like you boys might need a quick ride out of your deep shit. Am I right?"

"You're right, and the people I work for think you're the best ride there is."

"You're people are right, my man. They must do their homework, 'cause I am the best there is!" Flashing his biggest smile, meaning every word.

"I believe they are Vic and I know we need you, or somebody like you...."

He was smiling again.

"There ain't anybody else like me! You can look wherever you want, but I'm tellin' you there ain't anybody else out there like me, as good as me. Nobody's been where I've been and done what I've done. If there is I haven't met 'em yet."

"We know that Vic. We know you've looked at the end of the line many, many times and kept coming back. We think you know what you're doing."

Vic broke out in a broad smile ending the interview.

"Do you? Come on with me...what was it, JB?" Not waiting for an answer because he knew it didn't mean shit anyway. "Let's take a ride."

The Chief was to remember that ride, all the rest of his life.

*   *   *

The old man had quit talking, his dog on full alert waiting for whatever came next.

"Wonder who figures everything out don't you kid? I mean God must be in there working on stuff, but you can't tell me there's any way He arranges for those twenty million to die. I don't believe He's into that kind of shit. So then you got to sit down and think about it. You know? Like we're doing right now."

Helen responded to inclusion in the decision making process, by a nervous shifting of her front feet as she sat attentively, listening.

"No I think it comes down to Him putting us here, wanting us to work out our own destinies. Sending somebody once in a while to remind us what we're here for, like to love one another and not kill each other. Problem is there's lots and lots of folks that not only don't want to hear that message, they want to kill the messenger."

The Old Man fell silent for awhile, gently stroking the long muzzle insistently pushed under his hand. His was a journey of eighty plus years as he sat analyzing what had happened during that time, and his present course of action resulting from that accumulated experience. He was staring at a wall of greenery that formed one of the borders of his property, pale in it's coloration in this winter month but unaware of anything he was seeing with his eyes, everything he saw in his mind.

"You remember when Mary died Helen, and I became totally insane in my rage?"

Helen didn't remember because it took place more than forty years before her birth, but that was OK, it didn't have to do with her participation in the story anyway.

"I was very, very angry with God." He laughed a bit at the memory. "Why I even called Him out, can you believe that? In my insanity, I put all the blame on Him like he had that little girl die to hurt Momma and me on purpose. Couldn't see the justice in that and wanted revenge. Revenge from God. Silly wasn't it?" He chuckled at the thought. "But I was out of my mind with pain." He paused again. "Only thinkin' of myself though, you know it? Christ I loved that little girl so much I could only think of my pain, forgetting Momma's entirely." He shook his ancient head slowly. "Selfish, selfish, selfish, huh babe? Yeah, well that's where I'm still coming from I guess. Selfish. My way, or no way. I just want these people who deal in pain and suffering to the helpless, to answer for their actions so it can be said somebody noticed. Well we noticed. I want to stop some of these killers while I can, and if in so doing...I mean if in killing these same killers to keep them from killing others we become part of the same evil, than that's the way it is."

*   *   *

Pat was leaning against the fender of the shiny new car on the sales floor, of a large dealership in Seattle, smiling. He was always smiling, even when doing work like that recently discovered in Kansas City. Of the whole group, he was the really different one. There was almost nothing about him that added up, given his aptitude for viciousness. One could stand and look at him all day, and never see it.

He was approaching sixty now, but looked years younger because of his blond hair and fair skin. He wasn't fat but as he said himself, pleasingly plump, built in a peculiar fashion, somewhat along the lines of a pear. His head was small for a man his size, which was around six feet. It sat atop a strange looking neck, bull like, appearing to be wider than what it supported. The neck flowed into narrow shoulders, his torso broadening as it descended. Lump, he laughingly referred to himself, occasionally putting the lie to his entire physical appearance by his performances in dexterity, always to the astonishment of his fellow salesmen.

"How many quarters you got?" He'd ask, smiling. "Need six of 'em."

"Why? What you gonna do?" One of the many questions.

"Stack 'em up in a row, on the back of my hand. Give 'em a little flip in the air, then grab 'em one at a time before they hit the floor."

"Bullshit!"

"Want to bet?" Pat smiled.

"Naw bullshit!" This stated with great caution. Commission salesmen rarely challenge the other mans game, usually a preconceived con born out of boredom while waiting for the next customer.

"Tell you what," still smiling, "whyn't you try it yourself. Here, try it with three. Let me show you how." He'd give the coins a gentle toss off the back of his hand, picking each coin out of the air cleanly. Smiling, handing the coins back. "Your turn."

He always worked with men at least thirty years younger.

"Give me those God damn things. Old fart like you can do it, I can too." The young good looking salesman ordered. "I'll show you how."

He got the first two, sending the third skittering across the floor to shouts of ridicule from the others.

"Now now boys, musn't ever laugh at a man for trying." Pat admonished. "Especially if you're not willing to do the same."

"By God I'll bet you can't do six." The man with the failed attempt replied.

"I can, but I need enticing." Smiling, while the bet was being made.

Pat would remove his coat, to free himself of the bind of the garment. Placing the quarters on the flat of his hand, he'd give them a long graceful toss in the air followed by blurred hand movement, grabbing each in a series of lightning like jabs. He was inevitably accused of chicanery, when no coins hit the floor, and always had to roll up his sleeve before the repeat performance in order to convince his viewers he did nothing crooked.

"Jesus, for an old guy you move quick." A wide eyed spectator commented.

"Do, don't I." Pat smiled as he counted his winnings.

"How the hell you do that?" He was asked.

"Don't know really. Always did move quick. Catch flies between my thumb and finger...on the fly."

"You ever box?"

"Not for money." Pat's reply.

"But you have fought?"

"Now that's totally different, my boy."

"What you mean?"

"There's a difference between boxing and fighting."

"Semantics?" The young man asked.

"Weapons." Pat replied.

"Been around a lot of weapons?" The unwelcome question, as Pat's smile lessened.

"Some." His reply as he walked across the floor to greet an incoming customer.

Some was the understatement of the year for the outwardly pleasant salesman, his life having been a continuing series of one war after another, interrupted by stints in the sales field. After wandering out of the Guadalcanal jungle, leaving a special part of his mind behind, it seemed as though he was forever involved in terrible actions of one kind or another.

Maybe if he hadn't stayed in the Marine Corps reserve after WWII, Korea wouldn't have happened for him. Maybe things would have been different all the way down the line. He might have been able to stay away from the brutal life he descended into from time to time.

'Man,' he thought wandering into that part of his mind, 'I might have been a whole other person than what I am.'

What he was no one was ever allowed to see, which was the reason for the ever present smile. He felt at times like he was barely hanging on the edge of what? Sanity? No that word couldn't possibly cover where he was coming from. There was some kind of inexplicable savagery that cut through the middle of him that had to be let out once in awhile. When he thought about his life he felt as though parts of it happened to someone else. There was simply no way he could be, and do, the things he was and did back there in the jungle. He sought revenge for those things later in Korea and found it, but never enough. He even tried in a special way to find forgiveness in God but came away from that experience, worse that before. It came to him that God could offer, what he wasn't capable of himself. Forgiveness. It was much too much for Pat to handle, so he didn't. He simply turned his back on that possibility. Selling was a career that allowed him to come and go when he wanted, whenever his mind went too far astray. Pulling up stakes to take up professional murder again for whoever wanted it done. Governments, kings, dictators it was all the same to Pat and legends grew about the smiling man with the murderous ways. Sometimes when his conscience descended in unmerciful pressure he would succumb, put on old clothes and step into the ferocious bars all major cities have. He was looking on these forays, looking every time, and always found someone who felt pretty much the same way about life as he did and wanted to hurt anybody on general principles. Pat qualified as anybody, especially because of the ever present smile. Loud obscene language would follow and Pat would always let his adversary make the first hostile move, sometimes with weapons. His blinding fast hand action would come into play, and many a nameless, faceless man died in an equally anonymous back alley.

No one who observed his beaming countenance immediately after these killings, ever had the slightest notion what prompted his smiles, and neither did Pat really. It was what he did until time for his next victim, or that moment he longed for in his secret heart of hearts. His own death. He thought about it a lot concluding without too much distress that he must be truly insane, totally or partially. The surprising thing was that even in the face of his own terrible judgment he didn't seem to give a shit.

Guadalcanal? Yeah, that's where he left the best part of his mind, no doubt about that, but Korea, the various mercenary operations he was part of, and those fetid, horrifying jungles of Vietnam where he found himself at the age of 40, why they all added up to the sum of what he was now, and what he was now was homicidal.

He was made to order for these new "Angels" as they were called in every reference made to them by the news media.

*   *   *

Alex paused a very long time, staring, thinking, remembering much that had gone on before, while Helen remained seated. She occasionally worked her front feet up and down nervously, alert, knowing the conversation wasn't over. It was Ok, she had plenty of time.

"You know the one thing that bothers me the most about this whole thing is bringing Tom into it. I know the man would do anything I asked, whenever I asked, but I don't want him in on that basis. He shouldn't participate on the basis of my wishes alone, but I have a hunch he sees the need for what we're doing."

They sat silent for a while, Helen never taking her eyes off the Old Man. She was listening, but what she was hoping for more than anything else was the chance of another wild ass romp in the yard. She didn't get to do that much in the way she wanted, which was with the very old man as an observer.

"Tell you what though Baby, we sure have the right people working for us. Those five, and the girl." He paused thinking about Sandi. "She's the strange one though, you know it? The others were waiting for us, another killing situation or death to come along, but this girl is something quite different. Wonder what she's really like?"

*   *   *

"Look Sandi, I don't want you to get involved in that strike thing back east." The editor of the small liberal publication was telling the slight girl in front of him. "Those mine owners are mad, and you know the miners are bad news. They've bombed, shot at and beat anything that comes within their reach, but the worst part of the whole damn thing are the miner's wives. Those gals are possessed! Nothing's safe around them! No, I really don't want to see you going in there."

Sandi looked at the well meaning editor with something akin to pity.

"Sol, I've already been places that make this one look tame by comparison, and your tough wives don't mean shit to me. I've covered and photographed everything from wars to weddings, none of which I've been invited to. You know that thing up there in Belfast isn't exactly what you'd call a picnic with all those crazy ass Irishmen, and women, trying to kill each other and especially the strangers that get in their midst. I went there didn't I? Got nominated for a Pulitzer didn't I?" She thought for a moment. "Didn't get that one though. Think I should have put a little more into it, if you know what I mean." Her eyebrow arched.

"What you mean?"

"Nothing!" Her hot reply.

"You think you could have changed the judging if you'd played footsie with the right people?" He challenged.

"Hey, I didn't say that but now that you mention it maybe I should have." Laughing.

"Horse shit! If you ever get one of those things I hope you earn it on your work and not your back."

"Whatever, but you got to admit I don't do bad there either." She challenged.

"Sandi, did last night have anything to do with this assignment?" He leaned across the desk. "Did it!"

"Of course not," she lied, "you had to do with last night, lover boy." Laughing. "Candy is dandy, but liquor's truly quicker, huh?"

He relaxed a bit, sitting way back in his chair.

"I've heard that. So you're telling me I got you drunk and took advantage of you."

"Horse shit, also!" She laughed out loud, making the man a bit edgy, thinking she was laughing at him and not with him. He was right but didn't know it. She had used him as she was to use so many others. "Who do you think was doing the old pelvic rub out there while we were dancing, you? Not so my man, me! You and the night and the moonlight were responsible for that and since it felt good I thought it'd be in order to do it. Isn't that the battle cry for this time in our century? If it feels good do it! Well it did, and we did, and that's all there is to it. Now please for Christ's sake don't get all prudish and pushed out of shape on me, and tell me anything's the matter with that, will you?"

He leaned back in his chair staring at the ceiling.

"It was kinda nice, wasn't it?"

"Yeah, it was. Now how 'bout it? Do I get the job?"

"Need to think a little more about it." His reply.

"What's to think? If I can go into Beirut, which I did, and get along with those psychopathic camel jockeys which I did also, I sure ought to be able to handle a little pissy assed job in the hills of Appalachia."

"Let me ask you something Sandi? Did you really sleep with that banana nose head of the Christian militia, like I heard? Is that how you got to go everywhere and photograph everything you did?" He leered.

"Hell no, I didn't sleep with the guy!" His question irritated her. "I don't just sleep with guys you know. I screwed his God damn brains out, that's what I did! What business is it of yours anyway, you writing a book on me or something?" Her pretty jaw was set, ready for a fight.

"No, come on now Sandi, don't go gettin' all pissed off. I heard a lot of our other photo journalists weren't too happy about the fact you could go places they couldn't."

"Yeah? Well all they'd had to do would be get on their backs and they'd been right there with me." She laughed.

"That doesn't bother you?" He was serious.

"Hell no it doesn't bother me! Why should it? He got what he wanted! I've still got what it was he wanted! I got what I wanted and you got what you wanted. That's called everybody wins!" Defiance in her voice and attitude.

"OK. OK!" His hands went up in a gesture of surrender. "So what d'ya say, am I on? How 'bout we have dinner again tonight and think about it my little chickadee?" He pretended to be twisting a long villainous mustache he didn't have.

"You're on Sol, and when I get through with you, I'll have either the job or your balls!" She jumped out of the chair not waiting for an answer. "Be ready about eight. I'll pick you up at your apartment. Who knows we might even have a little aperitif before we get started." Both laughed knowingly as she closed the door behind her.

She thought a lot about her role in the affairs of the Angels, approving wholeheartedly as the plane droned on toward her assignment in West Virginia. She'd screwed Sol the editor into complete submission as she'd promised, and got the assignment she knew she would. She was outstanding at screwing, excellent at photography, and had learned to be afraid of absolutely nothing, in the pursuit of her craft. It took chutzpah to mix it up with the hordes of people she always found on her various assignments and if she had nothing else, she had that.

Actually she knew better than that too, the part about having nothing else, aware she'd been blessed with many excellent qualities. Intelligent, seemed to have been born that way, but also blessed or cursed with a driving Jewish Momma. She smiled at the thought of her.

"Any reason my daughter the scholar isn't getting up this morning?" Her usual question if she slept late. "You don't get to school on time scholar, and maybe you wind up like your mother."

That hurt Sandi so bad when she said that, because she knew what it meant, where it came from. Her heartbroken father told her on one of the numerous occasions her mother had been taken away to have her mind tinkered with. He sat in the living room crying, when Sandi drug the information out of him. She knew about the death camp since she was quite small, the tattoo was there although she tried desperately to cover it, but she didn't know how her mother survived and could remember the strange feeling that came over her when her Dad told her, between sobs. It was like someone had removed all of her blood and replaced it with scalding hot water. The skin tightened across her forehead and she couldn't breath. She wanted to do something savage. Something! Anything! But didn't know what, or to whom. She loved him too and wanted so badly to be able to relieve his agony, but there was no way she could reach him so she just tried to love him as much as possible. The problem was they wouldn't let her in to their nightmares, so she had to stand by and sometimes wade in to their agony, fighting savagely for their survival.

There was no way she was going to wind up like her mother, death camps having been out of business as long as they had but she agonized over the still pretty woman, who tried so hard to be unattractive. It hurt her to her soul the way the woman spent all her life putting herself down over something she had nothing to do with.

"Do you see?"

It was like yesterday when her mother sat on the couch in their small apartment after returning from the funeral services for her father.

"Do you see Sandi? God is punishing me for my sins!" Weeping uncontrollably. "He knows what I did in those camps and He's going to punish me for that, so He took your father." She wept more, in total agony. "I don't know why it couldn't have been me. If God is angry with me, why doesn't He take me? I'm the one He wants. Not him! Not you!" Her eyes rolled in horror at the thought of Sandi.

"Momma!" Sandi knew hers was a last ditch battle, and she fought it out of desperation and love. "God isn't mad at you for what you did, don't you understand that? Don't you know how much He must love you, one of his very own? Why can't you let the notion of an angry God go? That's bullshit Momma! If there's a God at all He'd have to love you as much as the Rabbi in the synagogue or the Pope in Rome. You're His, can't you see that? You belong to Him! Do you think for a minute that God or anybody else blames you for what those pigs did to you? He didn't take Daddy to punish you Momma! Daddy just died, that's all! Please don't put any more into it than that! Please let all that go will you? You've got me, we can go on together from here!" She dropped on the couch embracing her mother in a protective manner. "Come on Momma we can make it, you and me! We can make it together!"

Sandi's mother tried but she couldn't make it, or wouldn't, and something went sideways in the mind of the young photo journalist when she found her hanging in the bathroom. Her promiscuity didn't happen all at once, but it did happen. She equated it somehow with getting even, taking special pleasure out of screwing men strictly for her own selfish reasons. How many Sols, how many banana nosed chieftains had there been?

'Who knows?' She thought as the plane raced on. 'But I know one thing for sure, somebody's going to pay! I will, by God, get even!'

CHAPTER 26

"McCormick!"

He wasn't being rude, he was simply trying to cram as much work as humanly possible in a given day, and there was never enough time.

"Mr. McCormick?" The tone of the voice demanded his immediate attention.

"Yes! Don McCormick! How can I help you?"

"Mr. McCormick I represent the people who recently contacted you? You know, left the truck out front?"

He knew intuitively who he was speaking to and felt the skin crawl along the underside of his collar. Nothing was said directly, of a threatening nature, but he used the word ominous to describe it.

"I suppose you're going to tell...."

"No Don, I'll never tell you anything, that really wouldn't mean a thing now would it? It would be too simple for any and every crackpot in the world to call and tell you, after every killing, they were us. No, when we want you to know we're the ones responsible for someone's death, we'll show you rather than tell you."

There went the feeling again. He didn't bother recording or having the call traced. He knew it wouldn't last that long.

"You will always know it's us when you receive a duplicate of the original key to the truck we left with you. Rather than a written or phoned message which means nothing to anyone, we thought it best if we sent you one of these every time we move. That way there'll be no doubt. I wanted to let you know this. Our means of contacting you will be varied, so as to leave as difficult a trail as possible."

"You mean you're going to stay in contact with me?"

"That's right." The soft reply.

"Why me?" McCormick asked.

"Why not you? If not you, somebody else."

It was the Chief calling.

"You, because you are a reporter of note, and the Kansas City Star because of its reputation and location in the middle of the United States. We're not indifferent to those who hunt us, but we expect to move freely. We're good at what we do, including evasion. We may lose some of our people dead in the street, but even when that happens you will have nothing more than a body on your hands. Identifiable perhaps, but no associations drawn."

"What do you want me to do, when I receive the key?"

"That'll be up to you, but I'd imagine you'll call the FBI, and then put it out on your wire service immediately."

"That would be procedure. When will I be receiving a key?" He didn't know why he asked that, totally aware his part in the arrangement was that of a human transmitter. Questions were not his to ask.

"Keys." The soft reply.

"Keys?" McCormick's startled reply.

"Yes."

"Who?"

"I'll tell you this one time only because both are dead as we speak. Both in different parts of the country. You'll receive the keys in the mail. One with the name Ransom, the leader of the super secret white supremacy group known as Free America. The other will have the name Narangi."

"Jesus Christ! You mean the black agitator on the west coast?"

"Yes. That one."

"Deveraux Ransom too?"

"They are gone now Mr. McCormick."

"Son of a bitch!" It was pure reaction. "Both sides of the fence at the same time?"

"Exactly. You've hit on exactly what we want known. We do not, and never will take sides on any issue, but if those views become deadly to others, the perpetrators will become of interest to us."

"You mean they're dead?"

There was a pause.

"Yes. Anyone who decides for whatever reasons, to wreak havoc on those less able to care for themselves, we will kill at our discretion. Those extremists who are forever shouting hatred, suffering and death at someone different from them. As we have shown we are violent. Violent and deadly, but we will never harm anyone unless by their actions they seek to harm others. We have waited as generations before us, for something like justice to descend on these people and it doesn't, not to this time. It is happening now though, and will continue until we decide it should stop."

The click of the phone as it was hung up was resounding, McCormick sitting in a state of stunned disbelief. He couldn't believe he had been chosen as a central clearing agency for these people. It seemed like five minutes before he hung up the phone, but was actually less than five seconds. He slammed the receiver down and raced to the wire service machines checking first one than the other. There was nothing.

"Get me this guy Ransom's phone number. Where the hell does he live? Alabama? Georgia? Get him!" His terse demand to the fledgling reporter standing by.

McCormick made many hurried phone calls before he got the odd voice in Los Angeles.

"Who did you want to talk to?"

"Narangi, or whatever the hell his name is!"

"Who'd you say you were?"

"Wait a minute. Who the hell are you?" McCormick was at a boiling point.

"Lt. Aaronson, LAPD. Now I want to know who I'm talking to?"

McCormick identified himself again, slower, going into great detail why he was making the call.

"I'm the one that got all the publicity regarding the Angels. When they left the four bodies outside?" It seemed identification enough. "I got a call from them and they told me Narangi is dead. Am I to assume you're answering the phone because what I've been told is true?"

"I'd rather not answer that McCormick."

"Hey can we cut the shit, is it true or isn't it? I'm telling you what I know now, so don't hold out on me! Why else are you there?"

"Hold on a second will you?"

There was a long pause as the Lieutenant put his hand over the receiver. The hand was removed momentarily to the sound of loud voices, then back again.

"OK McCormick. Spoke to the chief and he says OK. Yes. Narangi's dead, along with three of his bodyguards...no make that four. Looks like they came out of the house to get in the car and found the driver gone. Have no idea why they didn't get suspicious, but they got in the car, hit the starter and God damn near blew this end of LA out to sea. There were absolutely no survivors. I'm talking about a huge explosion and whoever rigged it really knew what they were doing. That Mercedes came apart, and so did everybody in it. We found the real driver and he was dead. Couldn't figure out what killed him at first, found him face up a short distance from the car. Rolled him over and then we found out."

"What?"

"Whoever did it was an absolute artist, turned his lights out! Man I'm tellin' you they shut him down, and I mean right now! Hit him an unbelievable shot with something small and sharp. Coroner thinks maybe a small ax. He said it'd be like turning off a light switch, for the person taken out that way. Hit the driver one time at the base of the spine and that's all she wrote. I'll guarantee you he had no idea what hit him, it was that expert."

"Thanks Lieutenant. I appreciate your telling me."

"That's OK...Don is it?"

"Yes, Don."

"Well Don I don't know how you got on such terms with these people, but I think it would be in order to suggest you be careful. It's pretty obvious whoever they are, they'll kill anything or anybody they don't like, and do it in a minute"

"Thanks Lieutenant. I know that, but I don't think they intend to do me any harm, only those they think need it."

They finally located Ransom's phone number in Alabama but had no success getting an answer. In desperation they called the sheriff of Ransom's home county.

"He went over to Georgia to take care of some things, Mr. McCormick. Told me last week during a break in an interview he was giving some gal. Said he was going to get in a little fishin' with some of the boys while he was there."

"Can you remember where sheriff? Where, and with whom?"

"Sure, some boys down Waycross way. Why? What's goin' on here anyway? Why you callin' from Kansas City?"

McCormick told him about the phone call, the bodies in Los Angeles and that Ransom had been included in the conversation.

"You mean somebody's killed ol' Devereaux?" He shouted in the phone.

"We don't know that sheriff, but our guess is he's dead right this minute."

The word wasn't long in coming that Devereaux Ransom and two local leaders of the Free America movement had been found on a small island in the Okefenokee swamp, shot to death.

"I'll tell you something Mr. McCormick."

The commander of the Georgia Bureau of Investigation was on the phone. McCormick's entree to privileged conversations was completely established now, in view of his selection to receive word direct from this terrible group. The rest of official America knew it.

"Whoever did this moves like the night itself."

"What you mean?" McCormick asked.

"All three of these guys were found shot to death in their chairs. Two of 'em laying on their sides but still in their chairs, the other one sitting there looking like he was asleep. Fortyfive it was, and phenomenal shootin' at that. Figure they must of been shootin' the shit, sitting around the fire when somethin' invisible damn near tore 'em to pieces."

"Invisible?"

"Invisible! These guys apparently didn't move. Hell they had guns, and lots of 'em. Always were armed to the teeth because of the business they were in, but they didn't have a chance to use 'em. They just sat there and died."

"So what do you think?"

"I'd almost think maybe black folks killed 'em, God knows most every black person in America'd like to."

"Why black? Because they weren't seen?"

"Yes. These guys were looking right at whatever or whoever killed 'em, and didn't see 'em. Real spooky. We'll nail 'em though I'll tell you that. Maybe these guys were up to shit folks don't like, but we got laws! Them or nobody else can run around the country killin' people. We'll get the sons of bitches!"

"Good luck, but your killer's probably on the other side of the country, or world by now."

He hung up as the letter was placed on his desk. It contained two keys.

*   *   *

"Hey little deer."

Harold reached over the top of the makeshift pen made for the small deer rescued from the hunter. She knew him by this time and welcomed his visits, always accompanied by good things to eat and strange but welcome scratching behind the ears. Her leg was doing fine in the expertly made splint and she looked much better, fatter than when he brought her home.

"Hope I didn't bother you goin' out last night, but I had a job to do."

He was covered with the black grease paint he used whenever he went "Asiatic" and slipped into the swamps to let his mind run sideways for awhile.

"Strange shit peewee." Her dainty head was lifted along the line of his forearm, accepting her ear scratch while sniffing and licking the welcome salt off his arm.

"Working mighty close to home?" He laughed. "Glad I'm not on a mileage basis. You know, so many cents a mile? Those guys were down the line, maybe forty miles or so. General was close too." He thought a moment. "They wanted to send some help on this one, but no need for that, specially with the report. Knew all about their island before they got here. Knew when they were comin', how many were comin', everything laid out real good. Tied my boat a couple of islands down the line, took my foldy up boat, paddled to their island and waited."

Harold was sitting on the ground inside the pen, rubbing the black paint off with a piece of toweling while talking to his attentive deer.

"Still got it though. They never saw what hit 'em, much less me. Funny too. I must have been watchin' 'em an hour before I took 'em out. They looked right at me lots of times, but all they saw was the jungle." He grew distant. "They don't see that any more."

*　　　　*　　　　*

A letter appeared with the keys.

'By now you know about the two latest additions to our list. We are aware of the seemingly impossible task of going about our business without appearing to be a part of the lunatic and dangerous fringe we intend to eradicate. That's ironic too because we are trying to bring something like balance to the fabric of our daily lives, so we find our measures necessary. Extreme? Yes. Nothing is more extreme than the sudden death we deal in, but only because every other method seems to have been tried and tried to exhaustion. If in so doing we must incur accusations as to our own mental stability, then so be it. We know who we are, and why we are.

Messrs. Ransom and Narangi are dead because of the vile poison both espoused. Ransom would roll back the clock and reimpose slavery, responsible for innumerable beatings, burnings, and deaths, either on the basis of his own direct orders or the result of his thoughts. Narangi on the other hand would have all blacks take weapons, rise up and kill the white man. This sickness must be eradicated too. This kind of extremism should not be allowed to continue, but because of our constitution, it goes on and on.

We cannot, and will not, allow this perversion to continue. It has gone on since the beginning of time and must stop somewhere. The idiocy involved behind this discriminatory hatred is really beyond comprehension upon close scrutiny. We have never been able to understand how any thinking human being can possibly conclude they are superior to another simply on the basis of color, and color alone. The thought has prevailed since the dawn of time, but there is no reason for it and we leave these men as examples of our intensity of purpose to stop those, who would stop others. We are completely aware of the impossibility of our task, but feel what we are about is so long past due as to preclude any need for elaborate explanations.

"Angels", you call us? Perhaps! There were good and evil angels to begin with, according to myth, and many believe nothing has changed, since time began. Good and evil split at the dawn of creation, and have been in constant conflict since. Why is it that what is perceived to be forces of evil always seem to have the upper hand, not only in the administration of hurt, suffering and death, but in the fostering of philosophies that instigate such action? They seem always able to do their terrible damage and walk away unharmed, protected by laws their kind have introduced. Could it be because the other faction, that representing good is just that, too good to stop this endless evil? They seem capable of administering death and destruction at any time, yet those who would live the life "Others" have suggested, are too good to stop them. They are the ones who listen to the admonition of turning the other cheek. They are the ones who pay, and pay, and pay, in the name of Christian charity and love, all the time being raped and pillaged by those who don't suffer the same constraints. We are determined to be the difference, placing ourselves between those who dispense suffering, and those who are too good to do anything about it. We think something should be done about the situation and are determined to do so.

No longer will we attempt to explain our philosophical position in these matters, we have done that. When we leave our victims in the future we will tell you why they died, nothing more.'

The message was on the wires immediately, flashed to every corner of the world.

*   *   *

"The paper said Narangi's one bodyguard died instantly of a blow at the base of the spine from a small, sharp instrument. Something like an ax?" Tom had called the Chief.

"It was an ax, not something like. Why?"

"I didn't know you intended to go into these things yourself, that's all. I thought you'd bring someone else in."

"Yeah I know, but I feel the same as you, and have no problem with the work. I've sent a lot of people on their way, who deserved it less than the ones you've chosen. No problem here. Any there?"

"None whatever. Just took me by surprise. Recognized your work when I read the paper and was intrigued."

"Well you know what they say, don't issue an order you can't carry out yourself. I had help though, brought the Seattle man in." He chuckled.

"What's funny?" Tom asked.

"He was. Asked why I had him come down, as an observer? Wondered if I brought him down strictly for an exhibition."

"Why?"

"Because I rigged the explosives, and took the guard out which didn't leave him much to do. He was miffed." The Chief retorted.

"He the one that smiles all the time?"

"Yeah, he's the one."

There was a pause in the conversation.

"You have anything for us now?" The Chief asked.

"We do."

"What is it?"

"A tough one."

"You going to tell me, or do I guess?" He laughed.

"You'll have the instructions in the mail tomorrow and remember what we said in the beginning."

"Which was?"

"Anybody, and that includes you, don't want to go in, it's OK. Lots of risk here, more than any thing we've done to this point, so we'll understand those who refuse. Much planning will have to go into this one so we want you to get your advance person in there. Take all the time you need."

The Chief hung up wondering who it was and why there was so much risk involved. He found out the following morning.

The letter read.

'Our man's name is Clarence Wilson, a name you should know. In the event you don't, he abducted the two young girls from the shopping mall in Phoenix and drove them into New Mexico, raping first one and then the other. His sadism grew as each mile was traversed, culminating with his savage sexual abuse on both girls involving various instruments he carried in the vehicle. He blinded one of the girls, disemboweling both, hopefully after they were dead but possibly before.

The actual murders took place in San Felipe county so the trial will take place in the city of Jackson, New Mexico. We wish to end that trial abruptly, in our usual manner, and want Mr. Wilson put to death with great vigor before you leave.

This will be our first attempt to circumvent the judicial process while actually in session. We hope to illustrate that some crimes are simply too heinous to consider giving the perpetrator an opportunity at trial, with the real possibility of something less than a death sentence being handed down. There will be many police at the trial and for this reason alone we will understand if any of our people don't want to participate. Those who don't, will be held in high regard by us and their decision will be honored. We want you to move on this request upon receipt of this letter, and send your lead person immediately.'

It wasn't signed. They never were.

*   *   *

"Ok," Sandi was on long distance, "I'm through here. See you in Dallas tomorrow morning."

The Chief found her in the Dallas-Fort Worth terminal taking her on a circuitous route to the parking lot and back again, catching a cab.

"Where to chief?" The cabbie asked.

That startled him momentarily, realizing just as quick he meant nothing. Obviously that's what the cabbie called every fare.

"Drive." He ordered.

"Anywhere?"

"'Til I tell you to stop."

He exercised great caution, because the police of the world were looking for them now. After traveling some distance, they got out in a suburb of Ft. Worth, and he told Sandi what her next assignment was, where and why. He'd seen many people way up high on narcotics before, cocaine mostly, and was struck every time by the luminescent quality of their eyes. Sandi's glowed in exactly the same fashion when the Chief explained what Clarence Wilson had done.

"Oh yeah. I'll be on the next flight out of here for Albuquerque." Her eyes were aflame. "How old were the girls?"

"Sixteen. Kids. Probably being smarty pants to impress each other. You know, dare you sort of thing? They got in and went for the ride of their lives."

The brilliant glow gave way to tears as she watched her sixteen year old mother being pressed into service as a screwing machine. Even at that those pigs didn't murder her. Maybe better if they had, but they didn't. They didn't do what this maniac did.

"You know Sandi I'm no more aware of who we're working for than you are, but so far I can tell you I have no problem whatever with their choices." He'd seen her tears before and they made him uncomfortable.

"No, no." A hollow whisper. "I know what you mean. None of these creatures I wouldn't gladly kill myself. This one in particular."

Sandi looked straight in the Chief's eyes.

"I want no money for my part in this." It didn't occur to her in this moment of white hot rage, that they weren't paid by the assignment anyway, she only knew she didn't want any money for this one.

"OK Sandi, I'll tell 'em." He looked deep in her eyes. "You won't try and do anything yourself would you?"

"Like kill him myself?"

"Yes."

"Jesus, how I'd like to, but I realize you've got experts for that. No, don't worry, I'll go in, find out what you want and then split." She looked away. "No chance I could be a part of the action?"

"No Sandi, there isn't! The way I see it you've got to be the most important member of this entire operation. I'm not saying that because I know what you're feeling right now. I'm saying that because I mean it. We got some very special people with us, people who are probably the best at what they do in all this world. No contest really because there wouldn't be much competition, but what I'm saying is they are God damn good! They do what we ask of them, and go away until we ask them again. Even at that, and I don't want you to think I'm denigrating them in any way whatever, but even at that they are shooters in the final analysis. Your job is oh so much more than that. You are our eyes, ears and brains. You are the one person that lays everything out so we can do our work."

She thought about the friend of the now dead Devereaux Ransom she allowed to paw her over, in the course of getting the information she did. He was laughing about the group of blacks his "boys" had beaten the previous night in the service station at the end of town. Hemmed them up in the service station with their cars and trucks and beat them with ball bats and chains. Beaten because of their color.

He thought that was funny and what should be done to all of them, wherever they were. Jews too, he added, thus making her job so much easier. Thank God he got totally drunk, provided her with much vitally needed information and passed out before he got around to taking her clothes off, but if he had taken her to bed she'd been right there, screwing his brains out. She could do that now, paying an old debt.

"Please don't do anything that would put you in jeopardy, I wouldn't want to try and replace you. Nothing happens until you come in with your information, and the success or failure of what we do depends primarily on you. So even though you might have a particular interest in the outcome of a given situation, such as this, you must realize you can never do anything foolish."

"I know that, but I can dream, can't I?" He knew the contents of those dreams, and understood the reasons why.

CHAPTER 27

"Name's Mary Ryan! Photographer! Covering the Wilson trial!" She beamed, holding her hand out to the janitor of the county courthouse, a large easy going man. "And you are?"

"Harry. Harry Simpson." His uncertain answer.

"Well Harry, when I cover big events I look for something different. You know, an angle no one else is going to think of, and that's why I came looking you up."

"OK Mary." It sounded reasonable to him. "How can I help you?"

"Well first off let's go out front and get pictures of you and your building." He liked the sound of that because that's exactly how he felt about his job. It was truly his building to care for and watch. "Then you can show me around so I can get the lay of the land, how everything functions. How many floors you got, jail facilities, do they cook there or what? You know, stuff the other guys don't get. That's what makes my work different."

"Sounds good to me Mary, where do you want to start?"

"How 'bout the front door!" Her laughing answer.

It did sound good to Harry, he could visualize a large layout in a national magazine and featuring him. He got into the task of showing Sandi around, fueled by her infectious excitement.

"Well okay, there's the front door." He pointed while Sandi ran down the front steps.

"Hold it Harry! Hold it right there! I want that shot, you pointing to the building like it was yours." She was shooting the 35 mm as fast as it would go on full automatic. Harry liked the little winding sound he'd heard so many times on TV, and in the movies.

"I guess, come to think of it, it is sort of my building." Pausing. "Me and the rest of the taxpayers that is, but I'm the one takes care of it." He was starting to swell a little with importance.

"Oh Jeez, Harry. I forgot to ask if I should talk to your Boss about this first. Who might he be?"

"I'm the God damn Boss Mary, we don't need to ask anybody." Harry was hooked.

He went about this business with great self importance. He wasn't being cocky, but he definitely was the expert at what this lady photographer wanted to know. There sure wasn't anybody else in town could show her as much about the building as he.

"This is where the trial will be held, little lady. Don't s'pose it's much to you...."

"Oh not so Harry, not so." She played her part well. "I swear I don't see how you keep this big building looking so nice." Smiling effusively she added. "Do they ever allow you to go home?"

"Well every once in a while, they do." He laughed. "Naw I figured you probably seen a lot bigger courthouses in your day, and this probably ain't much by comparison."

"Oh now, you're being modest Harry." She never stopped moving, photographing everything. "Harry, do me a favor. Sit up there behind the bench will you? You know, where the judge is going to sit? I want pictures of the whole place, and you'll give them perspective."

"My God Mary, how many pictures do you shoot on one of these assignments?"

"Hard to say Harry, maybe five hundred, maybe a thousand." Sandi commented, shooting everything in sight.

"Jeesus! How many do they print?"

"Five if I'm lucky, that's why I want to try and get you in." She smiled sweetly at the now Judge Harry.

After taking pictures of the contents and structure of the courtroom Harry took her on a tour of the rest of the building, so she could photograph the judges chambers, and all rooms leading off the main part of the building.

"Are the prisoners kept in another building?" She asked while taking more pictures, facing away from her guide.

"No hell no. What you think we got here, a big city operation?" He laughed. "Prisoners are kept in the basement, by the Sheriff's department." He paused a moment indicating stairs outside the building that lead into the basement area. "Come on down here and I'll show you what I can." He thought he should explain that was not his bailiwick so Sandi would not think less of him for being more or less excluded from that area.

"Wait a minute Harry, we got time to see that later. How 'bout the second floor?"

The would be famous janitor was in to his job of tour guide, showing the magazine lady every nook and cranny of the building while she engaged him in casual banter, shooting everything in sight. She knew she had the makings of a magnificent montage that the Chief and his men would rely on totally, if everything kept going like it was. She was only doing what she did for a real living but for entirely different reasons. Money was not among them.

"Wow! This building's the tallest thing around isn't it!" She exclaimed looking out from the cupola that sat on top of the building. "Let me get a picture of you by the door there."

"What the hell you want with pictures up here Mary? You can't see anything else can you?" Harry asked still out of breath from the steep climb.

"Harry," never taking her eye away from the camera shooting downward and in all directions showing the ground and all streets entering the square, "you never know what's gonna' turn these editors on. You know what I mean? Why hell once I had a picture that I'd meant to throw away because it was so shitty but one of my editors grabbed that thing and it went on the cover of Life magazine."

"Life magazine? The cover?" Harry was impressed.

"Yeah," she wasn't impressed continuing, "and he threw one in the shit can I thought was the hottest thing I'd ever done, so you see, you never know."

After filming everything in sight they went to the basement area, entering the lawmen's domain.

"You can't bring that thing in here lady." The deputy on the desk told her.

"But Tim!" Harry implored.

"No buts about it Harry. Sheriff said no pictures down here and that's what he meant?"

Sandi had been through this before, figuring she wouldn't be allowed to photograph the area, but also not listening to the heated argument taking place between her new found friend and the deputy. She knew that was going to happen and took advantage of the moments photographing everything she saw in her mind.

'No problem.' She thought, concentrating on every detail. She had long since learned to see things like the camera did, that's what made her such a great photo journalist. 'Desks out here. Prisoners down the hall there. Afternoon, two men on duty. Sheriff gone. Got to find out about him.'

As if on cue the door opened and the sheriff hurried in appearing preoccupied.

"Sheriff," Harry was making the introductions, "this here little lady is Mary Ryan. Mary Ryan?" It was the first time Harry really heard the name. "Jesus that's Irish ain't it?" He rushed on. "She's covering the trial for Life magazine, only from a different angle...."

"Hi, sheriff," Sandi interrupted, snapping the harried man out of his day dream while offering her outstretched hand. "Mary Ryan. Looks like you got quite a story on your hands here and I wanted to get some good pictures which Harry here has helped me with. Lots of attention on this one, looks like. You gonna keep Wilson here during the trial?"

The sheriff looked her over closely and liked what he saw. An attractive blond haired girl with gorgeous green eyes and a lovely figure.

"Tyler's the name ma'am. Sam Tyler." Shaking her hand longer than usual, which she noticed. "Yes ma'am...."

"Look Sam, call me Mary will you. I know you folks go in for better manners than us city dwellers but every time some one calls me ma'am I feel like I ought to be in a whorehouse."

Everybody laughed explosively, not expecting anything like that from their small attractive guest.

"Well we got no whorehouses here, so I guess Mary it is." He was quite handsome when he smiled, and he was smiling now. "Now where the hell were we?" Laughing still.

"Wilson?" She asked again, turning on the charm. If the sheriff wasn't married he'd be duck soup, she knew that. If he was, it might take a little longer.

"Yes, Wilson. He would be the reason you're here." He was stalling and she knew it, enjoying every moment. She was definitely in control here.

Sheriff Tyler seemed lost in thought and the small good looking lady in front of him knew why, giving him all the time necessary to figure how to get her in his private office.

"I got calls to make Mary," it came to him, "why don't you come in my office and wait? We'll get back to you in just a minute."

'I bet you will.' She thought as she smilingly complied, aware of Harry's consternation.

"Thanks Harry!" She called as she was taken in tow by the sheriff. "I'll look you up tomorrow." His face lit up in a big smile. "I'm here for a while anyway, and we'll get together again. I sure do appreciate you showing me your courthouse." His smile spread, as he accepted the look of appreciation from her and envy from the others.

*   *   *

"What you got?" Tom called in response to the Wall Street Journal ad.

"Ready to go here. Advance man did a superb job. We know more about that place now than the natives do."

The phone calls were always noncommittal.

"Got enough people, this's going to be different?" Tom asked.

"The whole gang, myself included." His reply. "After I told 'em the nature of this situation each not only volunteered, but insisted on being part of the program."

"You know that's amazing."

"What?" The Chief asked.

"My boss thought it would be that way. 100% involvement." Tom offered.

"Yeah, well he was right." His jaw tightened. "I had a hard time convincing the advance crew their job was over when we received the information, and you should see the information. We got one huge picture of the entire location. Anyway the advance crew wanted to be part of the final effort, there was such intense feeling this was exactly the thing to do in this market."

"Yes, well you did the right thing keeping them out. Good market research people should stick to their area of expertise and leave the final effort to our field crew." He didn't want Sandi anywhere around Jackson, New Mexico when the shooting started. "What do you need special?"

"Some vehicular items, but our Director of Transportation is on top of that." The Chief answered.

"When's your crew get together?"

"We're together now. Three weeks before kickoff so we're working daily on everything to make the smoothest presentation possible. Some problems because we've never had an operation this size before, but by kickoff date we ought to be able to field the best campaign we've done to this date."

"Sounds good. I'll talk to you next week." Tom was ending the conversation. "Let me know whatever you might need. How you fixed for money?"

"Fine. Money's not too important in this contest. Belief in what they're doing is." The Chief closed. "Tell the boss everything's gonna be OK."

"Thanks, he'll appreciate hearing that." He hung up and flew back to LaFayette.

*   *   *

"We got total involvement, Mr. Alex." Tom stood before the seated billionaire. "Every one of our people wanted in. Funny isn't it?"

"What?" The Old Man asked.

"This whole thing seems to be going together exactly like you had it pictured in your mind."

"You mean our people? The angels?"

"That too, but what I really mean is the fact that a group of this kind was obviously waiting to happen and you knew that."

"Only because of you Tom." Alex George replied softly.

"Because of the killing?"

"That's right son. You remember when we had our first talk and discussed that?"

"Yes sir."

"Well long ago I concluded that all the real warriors of each war don't die on the battlefields but must wander all the rest of their days. If not geographically, at least mentally. They are a resource Tom, make no mistake about it but the kind of resource nations hide until the next area of the world goes up in flames. Then drag 'em out, or even better yet create new ones to step into those flames and do what they seem to have been born to do. I knew they were out there because I'm sitting here lookin' at you. You played the game and invented some new twists and here you are, so then what?"

"What to do with the talent?" Tom asked.

"Yes." The Old Man's eyes misted over as he stared up at his long time friend. "They got to tough it out 'til they die. Mostly alone because they don't fit anywhere." He paused, rubbing Helen's nose. "So they drift off and hide from the society that asked 'em to kill." He shook his head slowly. "Terrible, terrible irony."

"That they have to live apart from the rest of the world?"

"What was that?" The Old Man looked up.

"Ironic they have to hide out for the rest of their lives?"

"Yes, well that too, but I was really thinking of the irony that Momma's memory is the driving force behind the whole operation. The sweetest of sweet love. The one responsible for the plan in the first place. The spiritual leader of as ferocious a group of killers as has ever existed? Don't you find that paradoxical, to say the least?" The question was intended for Tom, but the Old Man was looking in Helen's eyes when he asked.

"Of course, but you have precedent all through time."

"How you mean son?"

"Well as much as you loved Miss Marie I know you wouldn't equate her with God, would you?"

He thought long before answering.

"No, even if I wanted to I couldn't. Why?"

"Because millions and millions of people have been slaughtered on this earth since records were first kept, and a huge percentage of them died in the name of somebody's God. God always on the side of the conquerors and if they claimed what they did was for Him, then maybe it's OK to do what we're doing not necessarily in her name, but because she saw the suffering and made you understand."

Neither spoke for awhile, Tom finally breaking the silence.

"How do you think she would have felt about Clarence Wilson and what he did to the girls in the back of his van?"

"We know the answer to that one don't we son? It would have broken her heart." His answer after a long pause. "Be sure you keep the girl out of that affair, and Tom?"

"Yes sir."

"Ask the Chief to have his men shoot only if they have to. This'll be a tough one and I'm afraid some people are going to die that shouldn't, so please let's use restraint."

*   *   *

The Chief located a desolate piece of Nevada desert and brought all five of his men together for the first time.

"You all know the rules, and we want you to adhere to them. No names. First names okay, but nothing else. We told you this going in and why. Security. One of us gets captured he's got nothing to tell. No past affiliations like branch of the service, where you served and when. Nothing that will expose us in any way. I know you understand that because I covered the subject with each of you, up front."

All nodded, while the Chief marveled silently at the awesome group assembled in front of him. Normal human beings once, anything but now.

"We got three weeks to train for this thing. I want each of you to give me everything you got during that time. We need firepower and hope to shoot only once, but we're going into an area where there'll be heavy security. Three weeks may be a little or a lot of time to get ready, but I want everybody except Wilson to leave that place alive, so let's give this time our complete attention."

They practiced day and night, working on timing, logistics, camouflage, withdrawal, the building. Sandi's countless pictures were unbelievable and they were blown up and pieced together on boards in the large tent that served as headquarters for the operation. For as diverse and dangerous a group of men as they were, there was no trouble between individuals, all participating to their fullest during the day and staying to themselves at night. Only once during the three weeks was there anything like displeasure with the proceedings. They drew straws for the task of killing Clarence Wilson. The short straw wins.

"Shit!"

Harold knew his wasn't short, followed by a series of equally profane comments until Curt held up the winning straw with a look of joy.

"Hot damn I got that son of a bitch!" He hollered. "Hooeee I got it!"

He whirled around, eyes glittering, looking at the Chief.

"I know you got the best there is at what we do right here, right now, but I'll tell you something! I'm gonna be the best on that day." He looked sad for a moment, adding. "God damn I wish I could talk to him a little, before I blow his fucking face off!"

Sandi came back to Jackson a week before the trial, to ply her womanly wiles on a very willing sheriff. Through subtle, and not so subtle questioning she discovered security would be much less than they thought. Because the murdered girls were not from the local area passions weren't running as high as might be expected. No one even suggested lynching the suspect, much less making a public outcry for the same, so the five state highway patrolmen, and their cars were the only addition to the small Jackson law enforcement group. Ten in the sheriff's department, six local police and five highway patrolmen. A total of twenty one.

"Shit man, that shouldn't be much of a hurdle." Harold commented in his soft spoken manner. "Hit 'em hard up front, ought to be over before it starts."

"Yeah it should, but we want to keep honing right up to the day. In and out, the whole thing over in minutes. Our people don't want anybody hurt except Wilson, so we got to stun 'em, blow him up and get gone before they know what's happening."

Jackson was a typical high desert small town, lying a few short miles from a rugged range of mountains. The community was built in the main on the east side of a small river, with large lovely homes on the west side, away from town and across the small river to enjoy the gorgeous panorama provided by facing the mountains. One road, blacktopped through the residential area and turning immediately into gravel, ran across the desert to the mountains. The main part of town was built around a square dominated by the two story courthouse. They owned the key to it now, thanks to Sandi. She made an impression of the one the sheriff carried on his ring of keys attached to his belt, and since he wasn't wearing his belt or anything else at that moment it was no problem.

The trial was scheduled to start on a Monday morning, so the Sunday night before Chief CT Evans and his group, now known world wide as the angels, slipped quietly into the small community.

For an expert like him it was an easy matter loading the supports of the bridge leading out of town with his beloved C-4 plastic explosives. Plastic was his favorite and most versatile tool of destruction, while a member of the SEALs and he'd blown many an obstacle under a variety of circumstances.

"We get to the other side I'll drop that thing in the middle of the river," he told his people during their training, "then we can take our sweet time getting out to where the plane picks us up."

"How far's that?" Pat asked, smiling.

"Kind of a rise out there about three miles from town, and he's going to pick us up on the other side."

"Can't be seen from town, huh?" Curt asked.

"Right. Our man will come in low, low. Don't ask me how 'cause that's his baby, but I know him and I'll guarantee you he'll be there." He chuckled some. "Anybody afraid of flying don't worry about it because in order to avoid radar detection our man will be taking us across the desert floor about six inches up, around five hundred miles an hour."

"Six inches?" Chris cocked an eyebrow at the Chief.

"A small exaggeration, but we'll be traveling fast and low."

They entered the dark courthouse in the middle of the night, careful not to make a sound lest the sheriff's department downstairs hear them. All wore the garb of the surreptitious killer, dark turtle neck sweaters, dark knit caps, gloves, trousers and shoes, faces smeared with black grease. Anyone coming across them accidentally would have been terrified, just looking at them.

"The girl will knock on the storage room door, when they bring Wilson into the courtroom. We wait five minutes then you all know what to do."

Curt and the Chief, seemed to be the only ones with a nerve problem, both for the same reason. The whole operation was his responsibility, he wanted it to go flawlessly. Curt on the other hand was tense out of an intense desire to get on with it. He was looking forward sadistically to bringing Clarence Wilson's life to an end.

"Hey man we appeal, that's all." Wilson smirked for the newspaper reporter. "Look I'm sure I'll be found innocent anyway because I am, but if not we appeal. Why shit, by the time we get through appealing most folks'll forget the whole thing anyway. Hope they're not dusting off the chair in the gas chamber at the penitentiary for me 'cause I sure don't expect to be usin' it. Who were those girls anyway?" Accompanied by a big wink. "I didn't get to 'em whoever they were."

When his van was found it contained some of the girls clothing, much of their blood, and a grinning, denying Clarence Wilson.

"Who the hell locked this thing?" Harry the janitor was trying to open the door to the locked room containing the forces of Alex George. "I didn't lock it, who the hell did?"

They couldn't see who he was talking to, but he was only inches away from more firepower than he could have imagined.

"Hey Harry?" The Chief recognized Sandi's voice. "Harry, give me a hand with some of my stuff here."

It was five minutes to ten, the trial scheduled to start at ten.

"When they bringing Wilson up?"

"S'posed to be ten, Mary." He tried the knob again. "Don't remember locking this door."

"To hell with the door. Look I got some stuff out there in the back of my car and I need a hand with it, can you help me?"

"OK Mary but I'll be God damned if I can ever even remember seeing that door locked." The door shook one more time. "Probably the sheriff. Where's your car?"

"Outside...."

Their voices faded away as the gutsy girl led her admiring janitor away.

The knock on the door wasn't really necessary, only as a reminder. The men inside the locked room could tell by the commotion, their man was entering the courtroom.

The level of intensity rose to a high pitch as the heavily armed group stood by the door their weapons at the ready. Harold, Pat and Curt were carrying shotguns, Chris and the Chief each had small machine guns.

"Go!" The Chief murmured through clenched teeth and the door came open like it was blown off it's hinges. They moved like the well trained team they were, hurrying on whisper quiet crepe soled shoes, each to their own assignment.

"Hey what the...."

The deputy had no chance to finish his statement catching the butt of Harold's shotgun in the head, dropping to the floor like a stone. Two highway patrolmen were taken completely by surprise, so stunned by the sudden appearance of this awesome and lethal looking group. They knew an attempt to go for their weapons would be exercises in futility, so they wisely chose not to. The Chief ran to the stairs leading to the sheriffs department below, hurried down them taking the two deputies on duty by complete surprise holding them at bay with the small machine gun.

"Who the...." One asked his hands in the air.

"The angels!" The Chief answered quietly. "Don't want to hurt anyone except Mr. Wilson. Get in the cell area."

"The Angels? The ones in the paper?" The younger mans eyes were wide with fright and wonder.

"Yes. Now move, but before we do put your weapons on the floor. Don't do anything foolish because that asshole upstairs isn't worth your life. Put them on the floor and get in back."

Chris moved to the front of the building standing right inside the door, watching the troopers out front making small talk while sitting on the fender of one of the cars.

The doors to the courtroom burst open violently, slamming against the wall as Harold and Pat entered with concussion grenades. The Chief rigged them with instant fuses. Both rolled to the base of the stunned judges bench exploding with enormous sound, smoke and flash, while Harold and Pat screamed.

"DOWN! DOWN! GET DOWN!"

As they screamed the terse command they fired their heavily loaded shotguns repeatedly into the wall directly over the heads of the jurors, the judge and the spectators, all digging desperately for the floor.

Wilson was stunned as the rest, unable to comprehend what was happening, his head reeling from the concussion of the explosion. He rose and turned barely in time to see the smallish man dressed in black with black face, hurrying toward him. Curt wore an expression of maniacal glee while leveling the cavernous barreled sawed off shotgun at him, and he heard for a split second the blast of the weapon blowing his face, head and life completely away.

Chris stepped through the door pointing his machine gun toward the troopers, all of whom had reached for their guns as a natural reflex to the explosions inside the building.

"DON'T!" Chris screamed at them. "DON'T!"

The Chief ran to the front lawn with Chris. He'd secured the sheriff's department, destroying all means of communication before leaving.

"WE'RE THE ANGELS!" He shouted. **"DON'T PULL YOUR WEAPONS OR YOU'RE DEAD!"**

One of the troopers looked at the two machine guns pointing directly at them.

"The angels?" He asked.

"Yes!" The Chief answered.

"My gun's on the ground." He removed his pistol gingerly with thumb and forefinger, dropping it where he stood. The others did the same as Chris and the Chief kept their stony gaze on them.

'Knew it! God damn it I knew it.'

Harry was very upset over what was taking place, he was afraid his beloved courthouse was being blown to the ground, the noise was so deafening in the halls. He pulled the large revolver from under his coat as he hurried to the front of the building.

'I knew there was going to be some shit the minute they brought that son of a bitch in here. Why the hell they didn't take him to Gallup or someplace is beyond me? Now look! Just look! They're blowing my building to pieces.'

Harry had no idea whatsoever who Chris was as he fired his revolver hitting him in the kidney, unaware even of the horrified expressions on the highway patrolmen. That was the last thing Harry saw as he was shot dead on the spot by the Chief, who was standing off to one side.

"Hook 'em up!" The terse command from the Chief as the other three moved hurriedly out the door, across the lawn, each firing their weapons at the tires closest to them on the waiting police vehicles. They stood in a terrifying circle as Harold picked Chris up off the ground.

"Go on!" Chris admonished. "Get out of here."

"Can you walk?" Harold's short reply.

"Who gives a shit, man?" Chris gasped. "'...hollowed me out. What'd he have?"

"Big, whatever." Harold answered as he helped the mortally wounded Chris with great tenderness. It was always the same, no matter where. They were back on the battlefields now. He loved this dangerous dying man simply because he was one of theirs.

Harold and Pat joined him, carrying the dying Chris to their waiting car. The others stood their ground hardly noticing the small blond girl weeping over the deaths of her friend Harry, and the impending death of the large man in black. She didn't know him, but the stupidity of these two men dying over that vile man who now lay dead in the courtroom, was yet another in a long list of enormities she'd had to bear in her young life.

They sped through the small town, with many onlookers because the whole town, or at least that part of it in the immediate vicinity of the courthouse had been alerted by explosions and gunfire.

"Who the hell were they?" Someone asked a trooper.

"The angels." The quiet answer.

As their stolen vehicle sped over the small bridge the Chief pushed the detonator. A tremendous explosion dropped the old wooden structure neatly in the stream that passed for a river.

"How's he doin'?" Curt asked from the front seat.

Harold was holding Chris with his head on his lap in the back seat grimacing for him at every bump. He shook his head in the negative.

"Hey pardner." The dying man whispered hoarsely to Harold.

"Yeah, I'm here. What you want?"

"My dog, man. My dog." Chris muttered.

"Yeah. OK. What about him?" Harold asked, his head close to that of his comrade.

"See he gets out the kennel, will ya? Jesus don't let 'em smoke him...only friend I've got, you know what I mean?" Blood was foaming on his lips.

"You get him out." Harold lied. "You're gonna' be all right." They were whispering against the noise of the wind screaming outside of the car.

"No, no." The cruel looking man protested softly. "It's OK. Been waitin' for this one...long time. Don't belong." He faded into unconsciousness then back. "Get the dog, please?" He had tears in his eyes.

"Yeah I will." Harold held him gently as they raced across the desert floor for their rendezvous with Vic and the jet. "Who are you? Where's the dog?"

He bent way over to hear the dying man's last words, pulling him closer as he sat back in stony silence.

"Blow it! Burn it!" Were the Chief's terse words as they saw the jet come in very low. "Leave him! He doesn't need a ride out!"

Harold pulled the .45 from his belt staring down the barrel while eternity rolled before his eyes. He shot Chris once in the head, before blowing up the car, then stood looking away while the plane approached.

They got in the jet the moment it stopped, each moving to their designated seats while Vic sent the small craft screaming down the road lifting it off the ground. He maintained this dangerous height while negotiating the twists and turns necessary to leave the area without gaining altitude. Radar couldn't find them that low. Harold saw the plume of smoke rising from the desert floor and his eyes filled with tears thinking about the vicious man on the back seat being destroyed by that fire. Vicious because of circumstances over which he had no control. Too dangerous to keep company with his fellow humans, concerned while dying about the welfare of his dog.

"Ok now, huh Chris?" Harold wept into the small round window.

A short ride to a remote area outside El Paso and they were all on their individual ways back home.

The news flashed over the wires and television news networks that the angels had struck again, only this time with different results. The death of an innocent, although involved person in Harry the janitor, and the stunning disclosure of the loss of one of the angels. This discovery led to more avid interest than the murder of Clarence Wilson.

Everyone knew who he was. No one knew the identity of the man burned to a crisp in the fire.

*   *   *

'The reasons for Wilson's death go without saying Mr. McCormick. Heinous crimes like his should not be dignified by virtue of a trial in a court of law, by a group of his peers. Men like that don't have peers. We are sorry about the loss of the other two lives, the janitor of the courthouse and our man, but these things we

must endure. You may tell the world we will strike with swift determination whenever the situation warrants, and in the case of the murdered man in Jackson, New Mexico his crime certainly justified in our minds the means employed to bring his life to an end.
Enclosed you will find the key.'

He knew the letter was coming, because of the action involved and the fact that this was such a public thing. It was the first time the angels had struck in public, thus demonstrating their willingness to pull off the audacious.

The newspapers of the United States and most of the world told of the stunning swiftness and precision with which the raid was carried out. They also told of the exhaustive, futile efforts of the forensic people to try and determine the identity of the body found in the car, burned beyond recognition.

While the newspapers and police worked furiously in an effort to solve the identity of the charred body, the Old Man summoned Tom to the Shed to discuss the latest events.

"Another onlooker died?" He asked.

"If you're talking about the janitor Mr. Alex, I wouldn't classify him as an onlooker. He came to the courthouse armed, and shot our man in the back while he was holding the troopers at bay. Neither of them knew anything at all about the other and while it was one of those sad, stupid things that always seem to be happening, it could not have been avoided." Tom replied.

The Old Man thought for awhile as the three of them sat quietly in the large room. Tom, his mentor and Helen. Finally Alex George looked at Tom.

"Did we really shoot our own man in the head, like the papers said?" He asked his head hanging to the floor.

"Yes sir, we did." Tom's soft reply.

"Why? Why did we do that? Why didn't we put him on the plane and bring him out of there? We had plenty of time didn't we?" Tom knew he was crying, he cried much in this stage of his life.

"I asked the Chief, and he said the man...."

"Please son, his name. For God's sake use his name!"

"His name was Chris. The Chief said he wouldn't have survived the hop to El Paso, he was that close to death. Matter of fact he thought Chris was dead when shot by our man, but in case he wasn't, they didn't want him to be burned alive in the car." Tom continued.

The Old Man sat weeping while Helen glared at Tom like he was to blame.

"Think it's worth it?" Alex George looked up at his protege. "Think all these people dying are worth the effort?"

Tom looked at the Old Man in disbelief.

"This is what you wanted isn't it?" He asked quietly. Again there was a long pause while the old man thought out his answer.

"Yes Tom I suppose, but I don't think I reckoned with all these bystanders dying."

"I know Boss, I know but we discussed that in the beginning and we both acknowledged the possibility. I told you I thought some would die, but with this kind of action there'll always be that risk."

Neither spoke for awhile, Tom finally breaking the spell.

"I'll tell you one thing though, the program seems to be developing like you said."

"How do you mean?" Alex asked.

"People seem to be right with us, man in the street type interviews verify that. The people of the nation are solid behind us. That comes out more all the time, and even some of the notables interviewed on various talk programs are starting to come out of their shells discussing openly their support of our actions. Most people don't like these vicious murderers afforded the luxury of a trial. Why even the lawmen out there in New Mexico laid down and gave us no resistance whatever when they found out who we were. That's got to tell you where their hearts were, and probably are at this moment." Tom paused in his conversation, continuing. "No I'll tell you Boss, I wasn't fond of this idea at all when you first proposed it but the further we go the more I can see not only the wisdom in this, but the absolute need."

"You think the program's working?" He was searching his soul at the moment.

"Not a shadow of a doubt." Tom answered.

"OK. Guess we finish what we started."

"Finish, Boss? I don't understand what you mean finish. You mean continue don't you?" Tom queried.

"Yes, you're right. Continue's the word." He thought again before adding. "Wish those men didn't have to die though."

*   *   *

The veterinarian in the small animal hospital wasn't happy about the request made by the deadly looking man at the counter.

"You say Chris is dead?" He asked.

"Yes. Brain hemorrhage. Last week. Before he died though he asked me to come here and get his dog. He knew he'd have to be put to sleep otherwise. You know how he felt about that dog."

"Yes, he was fond of the animal." The vet answered.

"Yes he was." Harold centered his fathomless look on the smallish man. "May I have the dog, I have a long way to go."

"Which is?" He no sooner asked the question than he wished he hadn't.

"Bay City." Harold answered, telling the man with his eyes to get the dog, and soon.

The huge plane lifted off the runway at the Detroit airport, the black dog lying comfortably in the baggage compartment in his strange small cage. They were bound for Jacksonville, Florida where Harold left his car before making good on his promise to the dying Chris to get the dog. Harold stared out the window, trying to figure out how he'd arrived at this point.

His vicious past, coupled with the hopelessness of his future all crowded in on him along with his thoughts about the dead man he didn't even know, on whose behalf he was doing what he was doing. What a trip it had been thus far in his life, coming from a normal childhood to a murderous war, becoming an expert killer involved in nothing but the business of death. How the hell did it happen? Somehow it all seemed so futile, so sad. He wept as he thought of Chris's dying request to take care of his dog. A request from a man so dangerous and yet had the depth of feeling for the nondescript looking creature riding below to beg for mercy for him, while he was dying.

'Who makes the fucking rules?' He anguished staring out the window with tear filled eyes.

The next day Harold walked his new friend on a leash showing him around, introducing him to the small swamp deer that no longer wanted to go back to the swamp.

"So what you think dog?" Harold asked, a slight smile on his face. "Freezing your nuts off yesterday in northern Michigan, baskin' in the warm Georgia sunshine today."

The dog stood wagging his tail slowly, looking at his new benefactor.

"No name huh?" Harold asked, a wry smile creeping across his face. "What say we call you Chris?"

CHAPTER 28

"I want an all out assault on the drug community in south Florida, Tom." The Old Man offered him a packet. "The name's are on this list."

They were sitting on the porch at the Shed.

"All out?" Tom asked.

"Yes. Terrifying, swift punishment. I want as many to go down as possible, and on the same day." He paused. "We won't get them all, a matter of logistics as I see it. We can chart their habits, but this many...and keeping that close tabs on them.... No. Send Sandi in now, she'll do as much as possible and we'll improvise."

The Old Man handed Tom the list, eliciting a long low whistle.

"Jesus, this is a list!" He exclaimed.

"Yes it is, and I want it carried out with great vigor. Extreme violence." His eyes clouded over, as he added softly. "You know Tom it absolutely broke Momma's heart, all the suffering and death these people caused. She never could understand why they had to sell drugs to the kids. Adults were one thing, impressionable kids ready to take a dare, another. Bright young people with entire lifetimes ahead of them reduced to thieves, whores, some even killers themselves and for what? So they could pretend they were somebody else for a brief moment, while the drug does it's work? And the deaths?" He looked into Tom's face. "You know we never see numbers on the deaths involved because of these drugs, unless it's a celebrity. How many a year do you think die because of this shit?"

"Don't know, but I imagine it'd be a great many." Tom replied.

"Yes, yes. A great many. Nobody seems to know the numbers, but everybody knows it's a great many, that's why I want this action taken."

There was a long break in their conversation. Helen took advantage of it by laying her face in the old man's lap. He scratched her ear.

"I'm an old man now son, really old and fully aware of my situation. Far past the expected life span, and with each passing day I seem to be more aware of what a singular gift life is." He paused again, continuing. "Why, when we go out driving and I see all these bright beautiful kids, you know the high schoolers and the kids over at the University, I can't help it Tom, I get tears in my eyes. You know what the tears are about?"

"I can imagine." Tom was a good student and even though Alex George was a great age, he listened with the attention of a loving pupil.

"What they're about Tom, is excitement over their lives. Why my God son, when I see these kids, all full of life, piss and vinegar, I get carried away with emotion thinking about what's ahead for them." His tears ran freely. "A life son! A life! What an utterly amazing thing! I've been where they're going and when I think about the trip I get worked up...excited.... Just thinking about it."

He looked at Tom again, tears shining in his eyes.

"Think about the potential in each and every one of those kids you see. Joys and sorrows, triumphs and defeats, loves and busted loves, all jammed into a fleck of time. Jesus Christ Tom, it's exciting."

His mood changed abruptly, hissing his words through clenched teeth.

"Then along comes the God damn dream merchants...death merchants more like it, stealing some of these lives. God Himself gave the kids this beautiful gift and these rotten motherfuckers come and take it away!"

He was getting upset and Tom didn't like that. Neither did Helen.

"Well I've had all that shit I can handle for this lifetime. I know we can't get 'em all son, but by God we'll deal out some unbelievable punishment. Some of those rotten bastards are going to pay in full. The ones we don't get are going to be lookin' over their shoulders for a long time to come."

"When?"

"Now! Right now!" He was sobbing, his face to the sidewalk. "And Tom?"

"Yes sir?"

"Tell the Chief to be careful. We only want who we want. You know what I'm saying?"

"Yes sir, I do!"

Tom left town the following morning to contact the Chief.

"We'll focus on the drug community. Let them know we're not restricted by any law. We know who the leading figures in this thing are, and we want them handled in the usual manner."

"Got you." The Chief answered. "I'll send our people out immediately."

"Thanks. This's different. It'll take precision. We want maximum results. It's a market we have to penetrate, so our efforts will have to be massive and swift." Tom offered.

"Ok. I'll move when I get the list." The Chief hung up.

'Gotta get hold of Sandi first thing in the morning.' He thought walking toward his car. 'Wonder what they're up to this time?' His mind went on another of it's lightning like trips encompassing many things, returning him where he left off. 'Well whatever, there's no dull moments with these people.'

His mind encompassed situations in a different way, like a great bosom of thought in which ideas, plans, action and solutions immersed themselves. Instead of thinking in multiple choice terms, he thought in complete realms of possibilities, a style he could never quite understand, even though it was his own. Maybe it wasn't though? Maybe his many years of operating in, and becoming part of various oceans had something to do with it.

"Need to see you tonight, Sandi." He called the next morning. "Got a big operation and you'll have to leave immediately. I'll meet you on the beach, the usual place, about seven."

As he approached he saw her standing on the boardwalk staring out to sea, lost in thought.

"Hey kid." He startled her. "You lost or something?" Smiling as he drew near, immediately aware of her tears.

"Oh hi." She covered up quickly. "Taking in the sounds and smells." There was a long silence while he waited for her runaway emotions to catch up. "Really something, huh?"

"What?"

"Everything." Her tears ran freely and she made no attempt to hide them.

"Yeah kid." He put his arm around her shoulder hugging her tight. "Yeah. Know what you mean. Everything. It is really something."

The Chief didn't want to get into her mind so they stood there staring out to sea. He could feel her body shaking with emotion and drew her closer, aware without a word being spoken, the nature of her sadness.

"Well fuck it!" She muttered through clenched teeth, flipping her cigarette in the air. "Let's go! Let's see what you got!"

They drove down the coast to another area where they walked the beach again, the Chief always alert to see they weren't followed.

"You OK now?" He asked with genuine concern, after they'd walked some distance in silence.

"Yeah, yeah. I'm OK now." She laughed, her eyes filled with crystal tears. "Took a little trip back there, but I'm OK now." Smiling broadly. "Where'm I going?"

"Get out your beach wear kid." It didn't seem to fit her general makeup but she liked for this strange, exciting man to call her kid. She knew it was a term of endearment and didn't take it lightly.

"Why, we going swimming?" The tears were mostly gone, replaced by a wicked gleeful look as she reached to undo the top buttons on her blouse. "We don't need any beach wear for that you know, unless you old farts are too modest to skinny dip!"

He grabbed her hand stopping the impromptu strip, laughing out of joy at her total lack of inhibition, and real pleasure that wherever she went on her excruciating mental excursion, she was back.

"Listen, will you quit that and behave yourself?"

They were struggling gently on the beach, she was trying to disrobe and he was trying to stop her.

"Jesus this is truly the age of Aquarius isn't it? You right now kiddies don't want to leave your clothes on, do you?"

She took his hand that was trying to keep her blouse buttoned, and placed it directly on her breast, kissing him suddenly, long and deep. Evans pushed away slightly but she wouldn't let go, and he really didn't want to anyway.

"Jesus kid, or should I call you Miss Sandi after that?" He was somewhat rattled, hoarse, and his condition charmed her all the more. "I don't think this is what the people we work for had in mind when they hired us on, you know it?"

"Maybe not, but I'll bet they wouldn't begrudge us a few minutes of our own time." Her smile was gone. "What do you think?"

"Probably not, but I don't think we should get involved like this, do you?" He replied.

"Yes." She was staring directly in his eyes as they stood holding one another. "Yes, I do."

"But I'm...." He started to protest.

"Look," she paused, "please don't give me that old line about you're old enough to be my, blah, blah, blah, will you? I don't care about that! I don't want to hear it! I have some strong feelings that show up whenever you do, and I can't seem to control them. I can't help it, that's the way it is." Her eyes were asking him in yet another way. "I want to do something about those feelings and don't want to hear any of your objections. Christ, in our business there might not be any tomorrow! We've got to grab it now! You see that don't you?"

Sandi had a soft look in her eyes the Chief found devastating. She pushed him away, making a great show of opening her purse, rummaging through it, removing her wallet, inspecting its contents.

"What...." He started to ask.

"Guess what?" She smiled wickedly. "I've got one hundred and twenty bucks, cash money..." searching more while he stood dumbfounded, "Mastercard," more looking, "Visa, and a whole lot of desire." She took his arm firmly walking him toward the car. "With all of this," patting her purse indicating the items mentioned, "we ought to be able to get a room for awhile, and just so's you don't go getting all defensive I want you to know I am, by God buying! That way your conscience..." giving him an impudent stare at her poor choice of words, "will not give you a bad time over seducing a sweet young thing like me. There's a nice motel back there, we passed it a minute ago, and that's where I'm taking you right this minute."

The Chief drew up a little.

"No, it isn't going to be like the rest," she said softly with an entirely different expression on her face as she lead him gently toward his parked car, "this is going to be the way it's s'posed to be."

"I'm still curious," the Chief asked after the unbelievable sexual experience with Sandi was over and they were laying in bed in the darkened room, "why me?"

"Hell, I don't know. Maybe I'm tired of screwing guys for whatever I can get out of 'em. Information, favors, everything but money or love."

She felt him stiffen a bit on the word love.

"Now don't go getting all scary on me 'cause I'm not gonna' get into the subject of love here." She laughed reaching over, touching him gently. "Christ, I don't even know who you are! It'd be pretty stupid for me to fall in love with a guy like that, now wouldn't it?"

"Yes Sandi, it would." He held her hand across his chest. The tenderness in his voice and gesture, bringing instant tears to her eyes.

"So...see what I mean? Love, the way it's s'posed to be is out, but I sure don't see anything wrong with trying to steal a moment...pretend a little? That's all we're doing. I don't want anything from you, and am fixing to go on another job for you, so it's a lead pipe cinch there's no strings attached."

She slid on top of him, in the most sensual of movements, stretching her naked body full length on his.

"You do pretty good for an old fart though, you know it?" She teased, her hair falling down, framing his face. "If you've got any strength left what say we try something a little different?"

They laughed raucously and pretended, each to themselves, that this was the person they loved.

"Jesus!" Sandi exclaimed during a break in their love making, a break in which they were sitting side by side, knees up under the sheets acting like old lovers. She was reading the list he'd brought for her. "All these people?"

"Gonna' try. We'll miss some, we know that. That many names, somebody's bound to slip through." Her bed partner answered.

"Why so many, as if I didn't know?" She was smoking, reading the list.

"For the reason you suspect, I'd imagine, although we don't go into it that much. We never do. They tell me who, a brief why, and we're in business. They said drugs...these are the people...and we'll leave it at that."

"Who are these people?" She asked.

"What people?"

"The ones we work for."

"Are you kidding me?" His unbelieving question. "You've got to be kidding." He grabbed her arm, rougher than he intended. "Listen, I know you didn't mean that the way it sounded so we'll forget you asked, but two things I don't ever want to hear from you again are who do we work for, and what are they like. You knew going in secrecy is what it's all about. That's written in stone Babe! Nothing's changed, and it'll never be any other way."

"Well OK, you don't have to get all huffy about it." She pouted.

"No listen kid, I mean it. I don't even know who they are." He stared into her eyes. "I hope you believe that!"

"I do, but you can't blame me for wondering. Bet if the truth were known, you do too?" Still petulant.

"Well since we're all snuggly and hiding nothing..." they laughed at the obvious comment, "of course I wonder about them. I know what they want, have no problem with that, and I'm in complete agreement with their program." He thought for a moment. "I know one thing for sure though, and that is they must have a great deal of money. That's pretty obvious from what we've seen so far, but I really want you to believe me when I say I do not know, nor do I want to know, who they are."

He was met with hilarious laughter from this talented, attractive, complex girl.

"What?"

"Look at you!" She laughed.

"What about me?" He asked looking in the mirror at the end of the bed, at which point he joined the laughter. His reading glasses were perched on the end of his nose. He was wearing a stern visage, and absolutely nothing else.

"OK Mr. Professor," she giggled, removing his glasses reaching to turn off the light, "two can play at this game, you know. Your lecture's over. Now I'm the teacher and here's what we're going to do. We're going to have to do this over and over and over again, until you get it right."

"Oh mercy!" The Chief's mock, pained reply.

"Oh come on now, you know there'll be no mercy." She whispered up at him in the darkened room. "We're seeking the answer to a very old, hypothetical question, right now."

"Which is?"

"In this case? How many times will fifty nine go into thirty two?"

Their exhaustive research into the answer over, and unanswered, the Chief took Sandi to the airport the next morning.

"Listen little one." He admonished as they said their goodbyes. "Be careful down there will you? We're dealing with some bad people, as ruthless as any breed ever set foot on this land, and what they've got they intend to keep, at any price."

She smiled, appreciative of this exciting man's concern for her, warmed by him calling her 'little one'.

"Don't worry, I'll be careful." She stepped toward the passenger loading ramp, stopped suddenly turned giving him a firm kiss full on the mouth. "You know what?"

"What?"

"I think we found the answer to the riddle."

"What riddle?" His mind was back on business.

"You know," she teased," how many times will fifty nine go...." He stopped her at that point, placing his hand gently across her mouth.

"Shush." He looked around with mock concern, returning to her eyes. "What's the answer?"

"Lots!" They laughed together." You don't do bad at all you know, for an old fart."

Sandi went to south Florida, tracked her people, took her pictures, sent her reports.

"The best way is get the street scum, pushers, dealers, the like, handled swiftly." The Chief was discussing the matter with Tom. "We have exhaustive and excellent information on the people higher up, most of whom can be found quite readily, either because of their habits or habitats. These go from trigger happy Latino's, all the way to judges, people we can handle with no problems. They have scheduled habits. In order to take as many out as feasible what's needed is lightning like action, getting as much handled in the shortest time frame we can. I'll take care of many of them with explosives. In their homes, places of business, boats, cars, wherever we know they'll be at a given time. I'm going in now to get that handled, then once I've got those in place we can wait as long as we want."

"Looks like you've got it under control."

"Yeah we do, but I'll tell you something right now."

"Yes?"

"This is going to be a bloody son of a bitch."

"I know. That's what we want. Tear 'em to shreds and leave. We know we're not going to stop 'em, but they'll be nervous as hell in the future."

"OK! You people are calling the shots."

"Yes we are, but thanks to you and yours they get handled. Oh...."

"Yes."

"We're sending another list we'd like your advance man to get on right away."

"What? Where?" His incredulous answer.

"Seattle! The moment you finish in Florida, get your people up there."

The Chief hung up astonished, aware he was involved in something larger than even he had anticipated.

* * *

Warrant Officer Evans and his group were ready in a short period of time, putting the stunning operation in action.

It was a typical south Florida day, blustery, heavy rain laden clouds scudding hurriedly across the peninsula shedding their contents on the already wet area. It smelled like south Florida, damp, musty, hot.

"Ramon, my man!" The pusher greeted his customer with great ebullience on the street where he did his business, unchallenged by friend or foe. "How's things with you, Ramon? Another one of them hot nights, don't you think my friend?"

They were intent on their business, the customer anticipating his departure from reality, the Latin pusher his expected profits. They were much too preoccupied to notice the late model, low slung sport car rolling to a stop a short distance from where they stood.

"Yes sir!" The pusher smiled effusively as the tall thin man approached rapidly. 'Well dressed. Businessman perhaps? Another referral?' He thought. "You came to see Felipe here?" He felt expansive, on top of things. "How might I be of service to you, my friend?"

"You already have Felipe. You already have!" Harold walked swiftly toward Felipe. He was wearing a white linen suit, unbuttoned at the waist. His white panama hat sat exactly square on his head accentuating his eyes. Eyes with the look of eternity.

"Then...." Felipe's conversation, life and the life of his customer ended abruptly as Harold slid the .45 out of his belt in a smooth motion firing exactly twice, hitting both stunned men in their foreheads. The area was cathedral like in its silence, as the man in white stepped back into the car nodding to the driver who accelerated down the broad boulevard leaving the two dead men staring silently skyward.

The scene was repeated simultaneously by each team, moving swiftly to the next target repeating the same action, hammering on and on with relentless precision. It went exactly as planned, the first wave to go down were street people dealing in consumer sales, then suppliers put to death by whatever means, usually heavy automatic weapon fire. The approach was the same everywhere. No warning followed by awesome firepower. Word of the horrendous slaughter went out by whatever means possible.

In the ensuing frenzy people in the hierarchy of the drug world died rapidly as they were blown to pieces upon entering their cars, boats, homes, businesses. They were slaughtered wherever they sought refuge, having their lives brought to an end in a terrible orchestration of death, all engineered by the Chief at the behest of the Old Man, in memory of his adored Miss Marie.

The teams of killers were unmerciful as they made their way about the city destroying with great quickness any and all they could find on their lists. When the hunted were in groups, they died in groups with the angels coming together in stunning precision, moving to the slaughter. As soon as the police were informed about one killing, dispatching cars to the scene, they learned of more on the other side of town.

"What's happening?" The chief of police asked in utter disbelief as reports rolled in like the tide. "Who is it? What's going on? Who's behind this?"

His top aides were lined up in front of his desk, none able to give him anything like a plausible answer.

"Rival mobs?" One offered.

"Who?" The shocked chief asked. "What mobs?"

"Jesus Chief we don't know. Columbians? Cubans? The Mob? Who the hell could it be, with that kind of firepower and planning...." it was as if they all had the same answer simultaneously.

"Oh my God," the chief cried out, terror in his eyes, "it's them?"

They stood staring at one another as the room disintegrated in an ear shattering explosion, killing everyone assembled.

The terrible carnage went on and on, into the night, finally stopping in the early morning hours.

*   *   *

SOUTH FLORIDA RIPPED APART

The headlines read on the paper the stocky man was reading in the small restaurant in New York City.

"Man I'll tell you something," it was the tough reporter who'd challenged the senator on the television interview, "those angels are something else! They don't much give a shit where the chips fall, do they? They go after somebody, boom, and that's it! Always the same too. Cops hung up over technical bullshit, these guys aren't. That thing down there in south Florida really spells out where they're coming from don't it? Some kind of a slaughter huh? Took out everybody involved no matter what their name was, or how big their check books. Chief of police, and his people! Blew 'em up in his office. Anybody, everybody, all in on the action. Blew up the God damn judge when he tried to split in his boat." He laughed wickedly. "Tell you something. I'm sure glad I wasn't there! Those boys might find out I pad my expenses and take me out on general principles."

There was almost nothing else to be found in the newspapers and television reports of the nation.

*   *   *

"What in the name of God do we have here?" The director of the FBI demanded of his assistants. "Is anybody working?"

He was far beyond his usual quiet demeanor, losing control in frustration and anger.

"Can we get a handle on this thing or what? We're being made a God damn laughing stock by these..." he sputtered, he didn't want to call them what was on everyone's lips, "these so called angels! Well gentlemen I'm telling you, I've had enough of this shit! I want action on this! No, let me rephrase that. I want everything we've got on this! Why my God, they move around and kill with impunity, like they have some special license to do this sort of thing. They even murdered the chief of police and a judge...."

"Ah, sir...." The timid approach.

"What?"

"The information, sent the reporter in Kansas City? That fellow McCormick?"

"Yes...what about it?"

"The message he received was that those people, the police chief, the judge, the bank president, all the rest...."

"Well speak up man! What about them?"

"They were all part of the drug picture down there sir? Intimately involved." Apologetic in tone.

"What are you saying to me?" His voice was rising in anger.

"They weren't killed accidentally sir?" The assistant wished he'd never started the discussion.

"What are you saying to me man?" He screamed.

"Only that these...."

"Say it, God damn it! Say it! These fucking angels!"

"Yes sir, them. They only killed those directly involved in drugs."

"What's happening around here?" He rolled his head and eyes, insanely. "Are we on the same page? Are you getting the same information I am?" He screamed.

"Sir?"

"What about the judges family? They were on that God damn boat too, you know! What about the people who were buying when the shooting started. They were killed too you know!"

"Yes sir, they covered that in the letter to McCormick. They...."

"Shut up!"

"Sir?"

"Shutupman, don't you see what's happening to you?"

"No sir, I don't!" His assistant was upset now, being talked to like a lackey.

"You're being taken in like all the rest. What did the New York Times say this morning? The man in the street gave seventy per cent approval to what these murderers are doing? Seventy God damn per cent!" He was apoplectic. "They murder with impunity, enjoying the approval of their peers while the whole world is laughing at us and our inability to apprehend these people."

"But sir, we have every available agent working on this, as do all the rest of the law enforcement agencies in the nation."

"Great! That's really great, and let me ask you what do we have so far? Bullshit, that's what! A body, charred beyond any hope of identification out there in New Mexico. That tells me something about these people."

"But...."

'Ah yes, but. But, we take a forty-five bullet out of his head, and that matches the one that we took out of Manny Beatty's bodyguard, which just happens to match what we took out of the white supremacist in Georgia, and I know we'll take out of many bodies down there in Florida." He paused to bring his runaway emotions back under control. "Look what I'm trying to say is that we are dealing with such an entirely different thing here I think we're losing it out of sheer frustration. We've never, ever had anything like this, in the whole history of the bureau and it's infuriating. Do you know what I mean?"

"I think so sir?" The tentative answer.

"What I'm saying is whoever owns that cannon just doesn't give a good God damn. If he did do you think for a minute he'd keep using the same weapon? Of course not! He murders with total abandon, not even thinking about the consequences and do you know why?"

"Like you said...."

"Like I said, he doesn't give a shit if we catch him and kill him. He's telling us that, although I suspect we'll never catch that one alive."

"How many dead are there in Florida, sir?"

"We don't know yet, but we do know the count's fifty now and rising. They knew exactly where these people were to be found, went there and slaughtered them. I'm sure the final count isn't in yet."

"Sir, what about the judge? Why his whole family?" The aide asked.

'I'm sure these Angels had no idea they'd be with him. They've never done anything like that before and I'm positive had nothing like that in mind."

He was absolutely right, the boat had been an unknown to the judge's family, but in his moment of panic, he inadvertently led them to their deaths. The explosion was timed to occur minutes after ignition, when the boat had time to be far away.

*   *   *

The phone rang in Tom's LaFayette office.

"Mr. Brooks?" It was his secretary, a note of urgency in her voice.

"Yes Jeannie."

'I'm sorry to disturb you. I know you told me no calls, but Mr. Alex is on the phone and wants to talk to you right away."

"Oh that's OK, put him on."

"Mr. Brooks?" She hesitated.

"Yes?"

"I've never heard him like this before." She started to cry.

"What Jeannie? What is it?" Tom asked.

"He was very abusive."

"Alex George?" It was an astonished question.

"Yes sir."

"Put him on kid."

"Brace yourself Mr. Brooks." The warning was out of concern for Tom, she'd been with for years.

His mind raced in the moment it took to get the connection, arriving swiftly at what he knew to be the problem.

"Hello Mr. Alex, how are y...." He had no chance to finish the greeting.

"Tom, drop whatever you're doing and get over here right now!"

"Is anything the matter?"

"Not unless you're totally insane, nothing's the matter. If you're not, and I hope you're not because you're at the helm of a mighty big company, you know somebody fucked up! Now hang up the God damn phone and get over here." His voice rose to a shout. "Right now!"

The skin crawled along Tom's neck as he heard the resounding click of the phone being slammed down. He'd been with this man since 1939 and had never been spoken to like this before. He didn't like it.

CHAPTER 29

Tom decided on the way over to the Old Man's place to take his verbal pounding, let it slide off his back and forget it. Many times over the years he saw Alex George come completely unhinged and knew from experience when he was through blowing his stack, whatever the problem, it was forgotten immediately. He told Tom years ago that the dumbest, most counter productive thing he could imagine was holding a grudge.

"Blow it out and forget it son," his advise, "'cause the dumbest God damn thing I know of is letting the other guy run my life."

"What you mean run your life, Mr. Alex?" Tom asked on that occasion.

"Just that! Can you think of anything more useless than hating some guy, even if he is a son of a bitch, long distance? I mean sit here and get all worked up over something a guy does to me in a business deal." He broke out laughing, continuing. "So he lets me have it in the shorts, so what? He sure didn't get any cherry, you know what I mean? You don't get in life where I am and not have to take a screwing now and then."

"Who was he?" Tom asked innocently.

"Nobody! An example! Resentments? Forget 'em! They stink! Waste of time and emotion. Most stupid kind of self abuse I know of and I don't want any part of 'em."

'Hope he still feels that way.' Tom thought as he pulled into the drive leading around the main house.

"In here Tom!" The Old Man shouted from inside the Shed. "Come in!" There was urgency in his voice.

"You got the dog?" Tom hollered into the large room, as he always did whenever coming to visit. He never trusted the large mahogany colored creature, even though Alex tried to convince him she would not harm him.

"Yes, yes! Come in here!" It was a command, not a request.

Tom's eyes quickly became accustomed to the dark of the huge room, finding the two of them seated on a far wall.

"I don't like this! I don't like this at all!"

The Old Man began his diatribe without the niceties of greeting. Tom knew he was in for a fight, no doubt about it. He'd heard over the years stories about the brawling episodes in the Old Man's earlier life, familiar enough with them to know when he fought, there was no slow circling of his adversary. No, when it his was time to fight he was like a mongoose, with tunnel vision, moving directly in to his opponent, unmindful of anything around him. On making physical contact his commitment was total. Either he or his opponent was going down. Absolutely nothing was different when the arena of contest was business. He moved with a lightning directness that was awesome indeed to behold. They were going to go to it now, of that Tom was sure.

"Is that Chief of yours completely out of his mind."

He launched his attack as his eyes danced across the room, the far wall and then directly into Tom. When they landed on him, Tom was aware of the impact. He knew it was psychological of course, but it was there and real.

"I don't understand Mr. Alex?"

Tom understood all right. He was trying to buy a little time to bring his emotions under control. He was after all approaching 60 years of age, the CEO of Alex George's vast financial empire, and unaccustomed to receiving verbal abuse from anybody. He needed the time.

"Now why would you say that Tom? You know God damn good and well what I'm talking about."

"Florida?"

"Where else!" He was livid.

"We gave them their targets?" Tom reminded him.

"We did, didn't we?"

"They did what we asked. Was it excessive?"

"Yes God damn it, it was!" Tom felt had it been forty years ago there would be a fight at hand, right now.

"The judge's family?" Tom knew.

"Go to the head of the God damn class! You got it right the first time!" Alex spit the words in reply.

"But Mr. Alex...." Tom's anger rose. They'd been through this before.

"Don't give me any of that Mr. Alex shit!" The conversation was out of control and they'd just started. "Yes I wanted the place blown up, but not innocent people!"

"Yes, yes I know that!"

Tom was trying to overlook the stinging barbs thrown his way. He knew he was dealing with great passion out of control, and age. Alex George was well into his eighties now and his emotions had a way of slipping away at this stage of his life.

"We knew the judge had kept the boat secret from his family. He used it to meet people with payoffs, and he used it to entertain and get laid a lot. Sort of a floating whorehouse. We had no idea...."

"We?"

"The Chief! Everything we had in the way of intelligence said it was a secret plaything."

"Then your intelligence sucks!"

"Our intelligence is the best there is!" Tom defended, displeased his judgment was being challenged.

"Bullshit! The judges wife and kids are dead aren't they?"

"Yes, but...."

"Yes, but we fucked up! Am I right?"

"Look Mr. Alex. Our gal spent considerable time on that one trying to figure where was a good place to take him out. She even got in on one of the boat parties to get the lay of the thing."

"She was probably the lay of the thing."

"Maybe!" Tom was getting very angry and didn't want to. "Maybe she was. Maybe she did! I don't know that and neither do you!" He pointed his finger at Alex in a stabbing motion causing Helen to rise slowly. "I don't think either of us has the right to question her at this time. Her life's constantly on the line, not ours! That gal has put it all on the money for us so far, and I'll be God damned if I'm going to listen to any second guessing! We weren't there! She was! She's never given us anything but the best information. She asked the judge if he took his family out on that boat and he told her no, they didn't know he owned it and what his family didn't know wouldn't hurt them."

"No, but it would kill them!"

Tom was losing patience.

"We had no way of knowing the low bred asshole would switch patterns on us and load them up when he was trying to get out of our reach. The rotten son of a bitch was probably using them as a shield, consciously or subconsciously. He knew there were people dying right then, and that he was part of the picture. The boat was rigged by the Chief himself, and it blew like clockwork. We're all sorry about what happened, but we went over this a long time ago. We knew the risks going in, and decided they were part of the action."

"All that's fine and good." The old man was cornered by his own words. Tom did try to talk him out of this in the first place, suggesting the possibility of innocent bystanders dying. "But they told me we had the best people there were!"

"We do! We do! That's why we've got to keep going!" Tom had converted. "Can't you see what's happening right now? Jesus Christ Boss, it's exactly as you predicted!"

"What is?"

"Public opinion! The people! The real people of this country are with us. Not all, but according to the New York Times seventy six per cent interviewed say they approve of what we're doing. They almost always hang a proviso in there and say they wish it wasn't so. They wish we didn't have to exist, but if it takes slaughter in the streets to get back on track, then so be it. Everybody knows we have to send our boys packing periodically to weird places, places we have to go look up on a map because we never heard of them before, and then ask them to slide down strange jungle paths, or strange streets and blow the shit out of things. We do that periodically, always looking somewhere else. Well the people have finally had it! Don't you see Boss, we got the momentum! Let's keep it!" He hung his head low and shook it. "Yes I'm sorry about that judge...." another pause as he shook that thought, "hold it! I'm not a God damn bit sorry about him! We wanted him! I only wish he hadn't taken his family with him! We didn't want them! You know that! I know that! The thinking people of the world know that!" He paused momentarily searching frantically for the right words. "Our troops never meant to burn those babies down to the ground in Vietnam with their horrible fucking napalm, you know that, but they were there weren't they? When we incinerated Germany it wasn't those beautiful blue eyed German children we were after was it? No, God damn it! How about the other innocents we slaughtered in villages and towns wherever we've gone? Did we kill them on purpose? No! They were just there!" Tom felt the old murderous ways coming back as he spoke. "They gave and give us the guns and say kill those bastards, but they never tell us about the wives, children, and parents of those bastards that are going to die in the doing! No, no! Well fuck it Boss, I'm telling you we got something rolling here! You laid it out! You said nobody in the history of the world had ever attempted what we're doing! You said violent, militant, middle of the road! Those were your words, not mine and it's working, don't you see that? We got it in place and working! Please, please, don't fool with it! We're not going after innocents in the deal but when we go large scale, some of 'em are going to get in the way. You know that! You knew that! The people know that! Don't lose heart now. You started something big, and I think as horrible as it sounds, something good. Let it go on!"

Tom stopped suddenly, he knew it was time to put the icing on the cake.

"You think maybe a few less kids'll die because we put away some of the rotten bastards that take their money and their lives. How about that Boss? That's what you wanted! That's what we're doing! You know how it ripped Miss Marie's heart every time some kid died 'cause they either got a bad load, or a big load of that shit. Think she'd feel any different now?" Tom was breathing rapidly at the end of his diatribe.

They sat motionless as Alex George ran all he'd heard, and all he knew, though his mind.

Slowly, reluctantly he answered. "Yeah you're right Tom. I know you're right. It's just that I hate the way that thing turned out." He idly fondled Helen's ear, suddenly returning to normal. "Yeah son, we are on the right track! Sorry about the outburst! Tell the Chief to put the thing back on track up there in Seattle!"

Tom rose to leave, aware the conversation was over.

"Oh and Tom?"

"Yes sir?" He stopped, turning to listen.

"Tell the Chief to use as much caution as possible to keep from hurting, or killing the wrong people?"

"You know I will."

"OK then, turn 'em loose."

He phoned the Chief as soon as he could.

"Yeah I know, I feel terrible about that but you got to know if we were planning it again, I'd do it exactly the same way. I did that, and when it comes to demolition work, I'm as good as there is in the world, I'll guarantee you that."

"I believe it." Tom replied.

"That boat went up exactly when and where it was s'posed to, the only thing was he had passengers on board that didn't even know the boat existed. That, I didn't count on."

"I have absolutely no doubts about you, or your people. It was a shock and we don't want it to happen again." Tom paused thinking how much he must sound like the Old Man. "I told our people we don't want things like that happening, but we do have to expect them with that much violence taking place." He paused, adding. "You getting ready in the next market?"

"We are. We'll have our people on the streets as soon as we get our preliminary report."

"Then when you're ready go for it. It's quite a mart, although it doesn't get the publicity the others do." Tom added before hanging up. "I want you to know one thing for sure. I admire your work a great deal. I only wish...."

"Yeah I know," the Chief replied, "but I also know how this whole thing's gotta' work. I know what you're sayin' though, and appreciate you telling me. You know where I'm coming from. Where I've been. What I do.... We've been there. Couple of old fire horses, straining to get back into harness, wouldn't you say?"

"Yes, yes that's exactly what I'd say."

"Sure you would and you know why?" The voice sounded further away.

"Wondered about it for a lot of years." Tom spoke softly into the phone.

"They didn't kill us when they had the chance."

Tom was still holding the receiver, long after hearing the click when the Chief hung up.

'They didn't kill us when they had the chance.' He thought as his mind raced back over forty years. Back into the hot, fetid, rotten smelling places his country kept sending him to.

'They had every chance in the world to kill me and they couldn't get it done. Kept killing everybody around me and couldn't bring me down.' His mind floated in the area that was his Marine Corps experience.

'The colonel? Fantastic man. Bobby? Where the hell was he from? Farm boy? Yeah, yeah. Paul? Wonder what he'd look like now?'

He chuckled thinking about how he'd probably be fat, white haired and beautiful in his innocence and love for his fellow man. He broke into tears as he walked the street away from the phone booth.

'Oh Paul,' his head rolled to one side in his anguish, 'why, God damn it, didn't you wait? A little more? I'd of killed 'em son, if you'd only waited. I'll guarantee you that.' He caught himself in mid thought. 'Listen to me will 'ya. Sorry about that. Hell I know you're OK. Been OK since fortyfour. Probably sittin' right there with your Boss too, huh son? Maybe not? Maybe He had another job for you. He couldn't pick a better man.'

He walked down the wet sidewalk laughing out loud as he caught sight of his long since slaughtered friend Pat, leaning against the street light smiling.

'Why you son of a bitch!'

Tom laughed silently as the years disappeared as he approached the shade of his dead buddy.

'Fucking with me all the time, weren't you?' Both chuckled at the thought. 'Got you out though didn't it?'

Pat's ghost like smile intrigued Tom as he kept walking. He just smiled, Pat did. He didn't speak, but as Tom approached his smile suddenly disappeared, replaced by a look of such horror to make the tall graying man move swiftly, gracefully, toward the subtle protection of the building. As he did, his gait changed effortlessly, subconsciously, into an unusual oblique gliding motion.

'Where is it?' He thought as he approached the area of terror, reaching for the knife that wasn't there.

"Hey mister," the loiterer asked, "you got a match."

Tom swung about suddenly, facing the man who wanted instantly to be somewhere else. Never in his entire life had he seen anything like the terrifying spectacle that presented itself in the form of Tom, cranked back in time forty years. Murderous look in his eyes, lips drawn tight across slightly bared teeth. This lad had never seen anything like it, pounding down the street as fast as he ever ran in his life, not even daring to look back over his shoulder to see if his deadly chance encounter was in pursuit. He was, but for only a few brief steps when he caught himself and made the quick journey back.

'Hard to make a silk purse....' he thought as he left the area.

*   *   *

The operation in Seattle was to be the same as south Florida, hit and run. Shoot and kill, then disappear to do the same thing a short distance away. In every technical sense of the word they were a classic urban guerrilla force. Small in number, deadly in intent. Sandi did her usual perfect job of surveillance, using extreme caution to prevent a repeat of what happened in south Florida.

"You coming up here to get what you want?" She giggled into the phone, smiling broadly at the double entendre.

"That'll wait." The Chief answered, thinking he couldn't let her off at that. "Meet you at noon. Maybe we can remember what we're supposed to be doing." He smiled into the phone.

"Spoil sport." She pouted long distance.

"Yeah, well what we really don't need are affairs of the heart to complicate things."

"Does it say in the manual anywhere we can't have a little affair of the body?" Mocking his stern tone of voice.

"All right now, behave yourself and let's get back to business?"

"OK. Seriously, I think you should come up here to look at this situation. One phase of it should be simply stunning in it's impact on everything." A sudden shift in her tone and intent to one of business. "We have a unique situation up here and I want you to see it so you'll understand what it's all about. It appears to me you might want to do something special." There was no nonsense in her voice at all.

"OK. I'll call you when I get there." He said.

"Still don't trust me." She asked.

"No, that's not it at all. We know our competition is trying hard to put us out of business and we want to do everything to make their job as difficult as possible."

"I'll be waiting for your call." She hung up.

The strange passenger conveyance at the Seattle airport was making its long circuitous way to the main terminal building as the Chief pondered what might be in the offing.

'If that little shit got me up here to jump in the sack with her I'm going to kick her butt.' He thought.

They met in front of a large hotel, taking an elevator to one of the top floors, moving quickly to another, then down to the lobby, affording them many ways to exit the building. They hurried down a side street to his waiting car.

"OK little one," she really liked that name, "I'm here. What you got?"

"Let me drive and I'll show you." Her reply.

They changed positions in the front seat, with Sandi driving swiftly to one of the outlying neighborhoods, where she stopped.

"OK. What?" The Chief asked.

"Over there." She replied. "See that bar?"

"Yes. What about it? What's the story?"

"Like the information we received from them," indicating Tom and the Old Man, "this place is a known beehive of illicit activity. Mostly drugs, but a lot of murders and every kind of rotten business you can think of are planned in that little building. Probably more narcotics transactions take place in that establishment than anywhere on the west coast. I've spent hours getting information on that place and I'll tell you something, it's bad!. The cops can't prove it, but they think more heavy shit comes out of that place than any where else in the Pacific northwest. Murderers and drug dealers on a major scale are in there all times of the day and night. Cops don't know how many murders have actually taken place inside that building, but they think the answer is plenty. Nobody's bringing them any information."

"You been in there?" It was more statement than question.

"Yes"

"And?"

She was silent for some time.

"And?"

"It didn't turn out good." She replied.

"What you mean?" He looked her straight in the eye.

"They don't live by any rules in there." She was distant.

"What happened?" His jaw muscles were working.

"I got roughed up." She answered.

"What did they do to you." He demanded.

"Look," she responded, "whatever happened I asked for by going in there like a dumb shit."

"What did they do? Did they...."

"Yes, they did! Those bastards take what they want, and I guess if a gal's dumb enough to walk in the place, she's fair game." She was her old hard bitten self, but burst unexpectedly into tears.

"What?" He asked.

"Nothing I won't get over." She hissed.

"I want to know Sandi." He was gripping her arm.

"I was raped in front of the rest." Her eyes were wide, staring straight ahead, brilliant in intensity.

"Oh Sandi." He touched her arm.

"Forget it!" She replied, angrily. "They didn't get any cherry. I'll be all right soon enough. Humiliated more than hurt."

They sat silently staring at the insignificant looking brick building with the smallish windows. The Chief's mind and emotions turned to ice.

"This the motorcycle gang?"

"Yes."

"OK. When's the crowd arrive?"

"Anywhere from eight on."

"And what's the name of the man who did this?" He asked softly.

"Why? You're not going in there alone are you?"

"No. His name?"

"They called him Mike. Big guy, beard, leathers, smelled bad. Earring in the left." She looked at him beseechingly. "Please CT don't go in there alone. He didn't get anything that hadn't been had before. I'm OK, my feelings and pride were hurt."

"We'll come back tonight, when the clan gathers. I want to see what this guy looks like." He started the vehicle. "Don't want to make any more mistakes."

They returned in the evening, sitting in the rented van so they could have the best possible vision.

"There he is." She whispered, her hand on his arm.

"The big guy with the red bandana."

He said nothing, watching the large man exchange banalities with his entourage while sitting cross legged on his bike.

"You're sure?" He asked, almost a whisper.

"That's him." She replied.

"I'm taking you back to your motel." He was climbing through the van to the drivers seat.

"You'll be careful?" She asked.

"I'm fifty nine years old, little one. That whole time's been a continuing series of one tight situation after another. I could have been killed when I was 18, out there in the Pacific blowing all that shit out of the water and many, many more times since then. I have never, ever, done anything foolish in my life when it comes to this kind of business. Don't you see, that's how I got to be fifty nine. I'm as good as there is, and some bad smelling biker isn't going to change my record now." He reached across and touched her gently. "Yes, I'll be careful."

He waited patiently, as he'd done so many times over the course of his life, waited for the man called Mike to exit the building, which he finally did. Mike and his lady rode his bike through the night, too drunk to notice the small black sport car following at a discreet distance. They saw nothing as they pulled up and parked in front of an older home, with a porch supported by the large square wooden pillars popular in the twenties and thirties. They saw nothing, too intent on their lust of the moment, each pawing the other as if there were no tomorrow. For one of them there wasn't.

The Chief waited for them to get into the house, giving them enough time to rip their clothing off. He thought in a livid, bizarre way the man called Mike must be entering her at this moment. He'd let them continue for awhile suspecting Mike would need considerable time to achieve orgasm, waiting, waiting until he thought the time was right. Telephone and electrical lines were already cut. The house was completely isolated.

He moved across the porch, one violent kick with his black soft soled shoe, and the door to the old home flew open into the living room to the sound of shattering glass. The Chief stepped immediately inside the empty doorway and pressed up against the wall. He would have been impossible to see by an alert mind, dressed as he was in black trousers, black turtle neck sweater, black knit watch cap, his face completed covered in black grease. Mike had nothing like an alert mind as he lurched into the darkened room enraged because his act of fornication had been interrupted, at the worse possible time.

"Who the fuck is it?" He bellowed.

No answer.

"Where's the God damn light switch?" Mike shouted.

"What is it, Mike?" The woman asked terrified.

"The light switch?" He screamed. "Turn it on!"

"They don't work!" She called out, desperately trying a wall switch. "The lights don't work, Mike!"

The small, nearly invisible man stepped across the door quickly, moving away from his obvious second position.

"Who are you you son of a bitch?" Mike yelled as he grabbed a chair using it as a club while charging the spot he'd seen the figure move to, now vacant.

He swung the chair in roundhouse fashion, smashing it into the wall, at the same time experiencing the last electrifying sensation of his life. The Chief moved swiftly behind the drunken man, swinging the small navy ax with greater violence than ever before, burying it at the base of Mike's spine, severing the spinal cord which resulted in his instant death. The large man dropped to the floor without uttering a sound, while his naked companion ran through the room directly into the black figure still sharing the room with her. Her mind disappeared as she stood, held by her arms not a foot away from the silent killers face. She saw nothing, only an outline, totally black.

"Did you...." Sandi asked.

"I did. Mike won't ever do anything like that again." The Chief answered as he climbed out of his night clothing.

He went over the information the astute young woman had gathered, the papers and TV full of speculation as to who was responsible for the unbelievably ferocious way in which the man died.

"We have to hurry." He told her. "I'll get our people in here and we'll dismantle the place, like Florida. Don't know how sharp the police will be, but they were fascinated at what happened to the bodyguard in LA. Maybe they'll think coincidence but whatever, we've got to move. Go home kid, you've done your job."

"Why'd you kill him?" She asked as they were driving to the airport.

"He needed killing. He was one of the leaders of this scum and he needed to go. We'd of gotten him sooner or later." He answered.

"That it?" She asked again.

"No, that's not it." He replied. "No way I'd let somebody else bring him down after what he did to you." He reached across the front seat and hugged her to him. "I don't allow those kinds of things to happen to my friends. You're my friend and he wasn't." He rubbed her hair affectionately and felt her body give in his direction.

*   *   *

They came into town quickly as he said, with the same devastating firepower, absolute lack of mercy, and homicidal results.

It was decided the bar serving as headquarters for the biker gang with the cruel record would be the first hit. Always heavily populated with vicious people responsible for mayhem and death, it represented a natural starting point.

The van, with Vic at the wheel, slid quietly down the back alley until reaching the back of the building. He parked it against the door, flush along the back wall, eliminating an escape route that way. At the exact same moment Harold, Pat and the new man stepped quickly from a car in the front.

They moved through the front door in unison, all three wearing long raincoats which were not unusual for this rainy part of the country.

"We told you motherfuckers everything we know about Mike!" One of the men seated at the bar shouted to the three, mistaking them for police. "You got a search warrant let's see it, if you don't...."

He pushed away from his position at the bar sending a signal to the rough assemblage, all of whom rose simultaneously as an intended threat to the unwelcome intruders. The room was about seventy feet deep, bar on the right, tables in the middle, booths on the left. Pat stepped smilingly to the right, Harold to the far left with the new gunner taking the middle as all three suddenly and without a word, whipped out sawed off riot guns from under their coats.

"Jesus!"

One of the habitues screamed as the killing started, hammering on and on relentlessly. Their fire orchestrated for maximum efficiency with Pat blowing everyone in the booths to sudden deaths with the terrible heavy buckshot loads. Harold did the same, the bar was his target, thus developing a murderous cross fire creating a deadly no mans land in the center, which was being systematically blown to shreds by the new man firing down the middle.

Some ran toward the guns while others tried to escape seeking refuge anywhere they could. Harold stepped swiftly through the carnage when the shotguns ceased roaring, drawing his .45 heading for the back area where he saw one man disappear. Two shots from his heavy caliber hand gun and he was back, speaking softly into a hand held walkie talkie.

"Let's roll, Vic."

Harold nodded toward the new man who moved quickly to the back door, through it into the van, and off toward their next victims as Pat and Harold stalked what was left of the interior of the building looking for survivors. Pat found the bartender crouched behind the bar.

"Oh hey man," the terrified man hollered at the strange smiling face looking down over the top of the bar, "I didn't do nothing, these other fuckers...."

It was as far as his conversation went, as he took the memory of Pat's smiling countenance with him, to his death.

"Go!"

The Chief said as he left the building having set his explosives quickly. They drove up the street as tremendous blasts ripped the building, a huge fire ball rolling across the street as the building went up in flames.

They dispersed in various directions, all with the same intent. The gunfire roared over the huge city until there were no more targets, slaughtering with terrible precision those wished dead by two men they didn't know. When the gunshots were stilled all the Chief's men left the city, disappearing in the soft Pacific rain.

*   *   *

"No use wondering what that was all about."

The chief of police commented to his assembled department heads.

"A little late but here's the report from the coroner in Los Angeles. The wound that killed Mike was the same, in exactly the same spot as the one killed Narangi's bodyguard in LA. The son of a bitch swinging that thing has a surgeons touch, I can tell you that. Unique, quick, quiet and about as final as anything I ever heard of. I suppose that reporter guy in Kansas City'll be hearing from them pretty soon now."

He spoke with a note of sad resignation realizing they were going to find the same kind of clues as the rest of the law enforcement agencies across the nation had.

None.

*   *   *

McCormick did receive the message, discussing in some detail what reasons they had for shredding the same element in Seattle as they'd done in south Florida.

'Make no mistake about it Mr. McCormick, as stated before we are not naive enough to think we are going to stop the despicable acts these kinds of people perpetrate. At best we know only that the people involved so far will never foist their death dealing influence again. We hope others may have pause about their own activities, as a result of the example of our determination to see to it these acts don't go unnoticed.'

'Whether you or the public choose to believe it or not, we sincerely regret the need for our extralegal means of dealing with these situations, but we want known our determination to stay on our chosen path. We will continue in our efforts until our cause is realized to some degree or our entire number is dead.'

McCormick read this latest note with mixed emotions. He wasn't without some measure of admiration for the audacity, and purpose, of this strange new force on the land. He spent much time wondering about the makeup of the killers themselves.

'What an awesome thing,' he mused, 'where do they find the people to murder with such an obvious lack of feeling? How many are there?"

The Director of the FBI was in his usual state of rage over his agencies inability to find anything in the way of a positive clue. Network television news was devoted heavily to the Seattle murders, inciting yet another round of programs devoted to speculation as to the makeup and direction of this unprecedented movement facing the nation. Public opinion was on the rise as far as approval of the results of the angels actions were concerned, almost all interviewed demanding anonymity.

*   *   *

"You seem to be a staunch supporter of this group of murderers." A network talk show host charged the outspoken New York street reporter.

"Don't know's I'd go that far, my friend." His gimlet eyed reply.

"Well you keep reporting in your columns the man in the street isn't too upset about what's happening." He taunted.

"They're not!" His terse reply.

"But the way they kill?" The next question.

"What do you mean the way they kill? Dead is dead! How you think they should do it?" Sarcasm dripping.

"I don't think they should do it at all, certainly not the way they pulverized that hangout in Seattle. Shot the place up totally, probably killed everyone in it before they blew it to bits, then burned the whole thing to the ground. Why that's medieval! Surely you can't condone that sort of thing, do you?"

"Hey, listen!" His sarcastic reply. "I calls 'em the way my folks out there see 'em! I ask questions, listen, and write the answers these people give me." He paused. "Support, you ask me? I don't think I'd say that, but I have to tell you the fact that these people exist doesn't surprise, or disappoint me even a little bit. I've been expecting them."

"My God man how can you say such a thing?" His eyes wide, forehead knit with feigned innocent anger.

"Hey, you kidding me or what?" He stabbed in the direction of his TV host with his unlit cigar. "Don't you know things have got out of hand in this land of the free and home of the brave in recent years, or do you guys up here believe the slick crap put out by whatever press agentry? You shucking and jiving me, or don't you red hot news people up here in these towers of enlightenment know what's going on down there on the streets. They pipe this drivel they want you to believe and report up here, or what?"

"Wait a minute," the host interrupted, unaccustomed to having his thoughts challenged.

"No you wait a minute partner...."

He was sitting on the edge of his chair, dark curly hair hanging down in his eyes, coat unbuttoned, tie akimbo, shirt straining at the buttons trying to hide a large belly built by the booze he was famous for consuming.

"I'm sick of this pious pap you people keep pumping over the airways. How awful! How cruel! How, whatever the hell you can think of to milk a few tears out of your audience! Well I want to tell you something my friend, the people found dead on the streets so far, are not going to be missed...."

"But, but...."

"But, if you guys'd do your homework you'd know except for having their professional pride shook up the police agencies of this country are privately pleased as punch these rotten bastards are dying."

The host, as well as millions of viewers were astonished to see the hard bitten cynic with tears in his eyes as he continued.

"Dame justice? Why God damn man why do you s'pose she's wearing her mask? Impartiality? Horse hockey! Don't you believe it! That lady's trying to hide her tears because her people are dying in the streets, in their homes, by their own hands because the rotten bastards.... Don't do that!" He was enraged when the host held up his hand in opposition to his harsh words. "Don't ever do that to me when I'm talking about the common disgrace of this nation. Don't ever try and deny what's happening out there, unless you're too insulated or stupid to know our death toll is a sickening shame to this best of all nations."

He spit those last words out as if they were garbage that had found its way into his mouth.

"Don't you know what a sick joke we've become as a nation, and before you get all huffy and suggest if I don't like it I can go to Russia, save your breath! I love this country too much to have that insane line used on me! If I didn't love this country and the people in it don't you know I wouldn't care about these people dying in their homes and the street, but I do care man, that's why I'm telling you somebody just had to come down the pike in this fashion. I know that! The cops know that! Don't you know that? Don't you know if you got the price in this land of the free and home of the brave, you can do anything you want? You can kill by whatever means you want to employ, and if you got the bucks one of these really slick lawyers will come right on in and set you free."

He broke into insane laughter.

"The truth will set you free? Maybe so my man but not near like a real slick lawyer hummin' a few bars of his version of justice. You know what I mean? Making things up as he goes along! Charm the pants right off the jury, get his scum off scot free and sashay right on out the building, flippin' dame justice the bird as he passes. I'll tell you something partner." He said to the wide eyed TV personality. "I'm not about to lose any sleep over these people who're getting killed and I'm not about to lose any sleep over the fact these angels are invisible, except when they blow some disgusting scum into the next world. I'm not alone either baby, watch the papers, you'll find out where the sentiments of the people in the street are!"

"My God man are you saying they don't want these people apprehended?"

"Yes! Yes that's what I'm saying, yes! Read my lips. Go to the head of the class! Yes!"

"Well then what about you? Don't you want to see them caught?" His answer was slow coming.

"No. Not really."

*   *   *

The nation was divided, as displayed in the heated exchange between the two on network TV. Television commentators in the main reporting, preachers condemning, groups of all stripes split dramatically in their opinions concerning these ferocious, relentless, killers.

WHO ARE THE ANGELS??

Headlines throughout the world asked as the gunners kept at their grinding dispensation of death.

Alex George sent for his Chief Executive Officer, in Avro Enterprises as well as this newest venture. The one so far outside the norm of anything and everything the world and civilized society deemed acceptable.

Tom went to the Old Man's house to hear the latest turn of sentiment. He wasn't long in finding out.

"Sit down Tom."

Tom was relieved to see whatever the mood he was in, at the very least he seemed to be in control of his emotions. Not like the last visit at all. He sat without the usual small talk of greeting, indicating by his silence he was ready to listen.

The Old Man sat stroking Helen's neck and back, as she stood attentively by his side.

"I don't know son."

He said, staring out the window at his side. There was a long pause as he continued staring. Tom was willing to wait. Patience was a virtue he was long on, having learned the patience of all killing animals, back there in the jungles of the south Pacific.

"I don't know about all this."

"What's that Boss?" Tom asked quietly.

"Just about everything I guess, and nothing."

"I don't understand?" Tom answered.

"Well we're doing what I wanted done, but now that we're in it I wonder?"

"About?"

"A confusing mixture of thoughts. I know these pigs we've had our people handle have no business, or right, on this earth and yet...." He left it hanging.

"You find our methods too strenuous?" Tom thought he'd help him in his line of thought.

"Well, yes."

"The operation in Seattle too much?"

The billionaire stared out the window more.

"It was extreme violence son."

"It was Mr. Alex, and it was intended to be. Nothing that took place there wasn't thought out well in advance."

"But the thing I don't understand Tom is why the need for such devastation. Many of those bodies are still unidentified, they were so totally destroyed." He lingered a moment, continuing. "After all, how many times can you kill somebody?" Still staring.

"Yeah, I know Mr. Alex, but there's only one way to look at it. If you're going to strike? Do it! Don't mess around! Do it!" He hesitated momentarily. "Man I'll never forget seeing Bobbie's body in his shallow foxhole. Bobbie, do you hear? My buddy, with his neck cut clear across, and deep." He hung on, feeling his repressed savagery rising to the surface. "Why did that Jap choose him instead of me? Hell, I don't know. We were maybe six feet apart, but the Colonel made us stand there and look at those bodies, Bobbie's and the others. He told us, 'you men let up a little and that's what you'll look like.' I can still see Bobbie's body! I can still feel the shock! I was stunned and my blood turned to fire, as it is at this moment while I tell you about it!"

"Yes I understand what you're saying Tom, but what's that got to do with what our people did in Seattle?"

"Burn 'em Boss, that's what!" His anger was still riding high after seeing the forty years dead Bobbie. "Can you still remember seeing that kid Red, go down in that nameless, chickenshit wheat field over there in France?"

The Old Man hesitated.

"Yes. I remember." Tears shone in his eyes as he looked back over seventy years. Softly adding. "I could never forget that."

"Do you know why Mr. Alex?" He could see the old man immersed in tears at the mention of this long ago episode. "Well I know why! You learned something, at that moment, that every combat soldier history has ever known learns immediately. Maybe you don't like that guy next to you but you better by God love him, 'cause he's all you got right then. You might whip his ass in the barracks, but when he gets killed while you're runnin' across that field, why that's a whole different thing. You see Red whipped off the God damn ground by the impact of machine gun fire, his rifle flying. You ever going to forget that Boss?" Tom's voice rose in rage. "You ever going to fucking forget that?"

The Old Man was amazed at the passion in Tom's voice. Emotion was something he almost never displayed.

"No. I never will."

"Did they put the frosting on the cake for you when they slaughtered Myron?"

"They did." He was given easily to emotion with his great age, weeping freely at the mention of his old "silent partner".

"You got pretty crazy right after that didn't you?"

"I did."

"You remember that shit, don't you?"

Alex George was dimly aware his no longer young but younger, friend was speaking through teeth bared in his animalism of the moment.

"Yes, I do."

"You're God damn right you do! When do you think I'm going to forget Paul's blood on my fatigues? A half hour after I die, maybe? When do you think I'm going to forget Pat's head falling off his body when I reached down and shook him, sitting in that miserable mud hole. Same fucking time, that's when!"

He was crying too, completely overwhelmed in his emotional involvement, and the reasons why.

"So fuck 'em! We're not out there trying to murder these assholes with style and grace! Naw, fuck 'em! Blow 'em up! Burn 'em down!"

Tom's feelings had run away completely, indicating to him later, upon thinking about the emotional scene with the Old Man, what a fragile, borderline grip he really did have on his sanity.

CHAPTER 30

The year continued at a slower pace than the stunning way it had begun, with the savage strikes lessening some.

Sandi performed flawlessly in all her assignments, using a wide variety of disguises occasionally, and sometime none at all. She was invaluable because of her brilliant, incisive, mind and eye, as she went about the terrible business of the Old Man.

The Chief ran the small group in military fashion, with the one exception. All of their people had the option of refusal on any assignment, none were sought but the deal going in gave them that alternative. His qualities of leadership were such that no one challenged his authority, or decisions regarding operations, because they all knew he was one of them. None of the others had his specialized skills in planning, direction, and execution of their assignments, and none possessed his mastery of explosives and chilling proficiency with the vicious, navy ax. He was truly what Alex George had in mind when he created this small force of conscienceless killers. They moved quickly and in deadly manner across the length and breadth of the land, murdering with stunning swiftness, then disappearing like phantoms.

Among their victims was the corrupt mayor of the small western town, responsible for the deaths of many in his community. Some at the hands of personally appointed and directed police, some the result of blatant murder so obviously done at his behest by person or persons unknown. It all had to do with the usual motives, money and power. His death occurred in a terrifying strike by the men who came for him.

He was eating dinner that night, in a restaurant and supper club that served as his unofficial headquarters, and from which he ran his small empire. No one paid any attention to the two men who entered and sat down for dinner across the room. They looked like traveling salesmen enjoying a respite from the endless miles of driving necessary to travel anywhere in the state. They ordered steaks, ate them quietly and hardly spoke while dining. After finishing dinner and receiving their checks, they paid the waitress, left a sizable tip, rose from the table and walked toward the door. One of them stood waiting while the other appeared to be heading for the rest room.

The mayor glanced up from his dinner to see Harold striding down the open area between tables, walking directly toward him.

'Curious looking man.' He thought as he realized in chilling horror that Harold was drawing his .45 in a strange, graceful sweeping motion. There were no words spoken as Harold fired twice, the first bullet striking the mayor in the chest, the second in the middle of his forehead.

It was staged for maximum impact, their purpose to shock the public dramatically, into awareness of the wrongdoers violent demise. The horrendous roar of the large caliber hand gun stunned the diners into terrified silence as they watched Harold return to the front door.

"Don't leave until the police come." Harold announced to the paralyzed diners, as they left. "We've set explosives at the doors."

These shocking episodes always worked as planned, everyone having a different description for the chilling man who spoke to them from under his wide brimmed hat. Middle aged, some called him. Dark or different colored skin others said. Tall, rangy, raw boned a few decided. The blast of the huge gun worked its frightening magic on the diners. Out of confusion and terror, each witness wondering if they were next, few dared look at him and those who did look found it impossible to describe his eyes.

"You had one of the most vicious and corrupt officials in the nation in your midst, and now you don't. You could not or would not remove him legally, so we have removed him our way!"

Harold turned and left leaving the patrons of the dinner club paralyzed in fear. No one ever saw the small plane waiting off a side road, a short distance from town. They were gone as suddenly as they'd come.

The doctor who ran the phony cancer clinic in the deep south playing on the fear of those given death sentences by their own doctors was next. His offense was simply that he fleeced the desperate dying, fed them placebo's and sent them home to die minus their money.

The nurses who found his body in the examining room, stabbed to death, described his last patient as a smiling man of indeterminate age. That was unusual because they almost never saw smiles in that place of the dying.

The judge in a northern city who by his misplaced pride, literally killed a most valuable informant. A man whose testimony helped bring many international drug king pins to justice thereby taking some pressure off the streets for a while. The judge was angered by his inability to sentence the informer because of a plea bargain agreed to by all, including himself, so he sentenced the man to a local work program instead, his hours regulated like clock work thus setting him up for the inevitable murder that followed. The judge was found dead, murdered in much the same fashion as the informant.

The Angels, as they were now known by everyone, stayed constantly busy at the never ending job of gunning down any and all they could find in their sights involved in the drug trade.

"It's become such a runaway situation in this country Boss, it seems to me we should keep the pressure on. They know our judicial system isn't going to get them, and even if it does, the risks are definitely worth the taking."

Tom was talking to the Old Man who was growing more distant each day.

"These people have more cash money than anyone I know of and they don't mind for a minute spending it on bail, which they are willing to forfeit and then run for it. When we get to them they don't run anymore."

They kept hunting and killing in streets, night clubs, cars, homes, wherever they found those on the lists of Tom Brooks and Alex George.

"Mr. Alex." Tom's eyes glistened. "I want this one real bad."

"Who you got?" The Boss asked.

"One of those sick preacher types the world seems to be full of. Can't tell without a crystal ball, but I think we've got another Jim Jones here."

They thought for a moment, wishing somehow they could roll back the calendar to 1978. When Tom allowed himself the luxury of fantasizing about that Guyana thing he would subconsciously revert to where he was in 1945, an unrestrained psychopathic killer who went about his murderous business legally, with the blessings and hosanna's of his country and government. How many times he wished he could have put his hands on that maniacal preacher before he led his followers to their deaths in that hot jungle, that so quickly laid claim to their mortal remains. He couldn't allow himself reflection time over that particular situation, because invariably the next person to speak to him would be confronted by icy, suppressed rage.

"Who is he?"

"Reverend Billy Taylor, he calls himself now." Tom replied softly.

"Oh? What did he used to call himself?"

"Kenneth Sanderson of Omaha, by way of Wichita. Joe Delaney, of the Illinois State pen, by way of the Ohio State pen. Paul Helmann, by way of the Portsmouth naval correction center, by way of God only knows."

The Old Man agreed with this one immediately.

"You've researched him thoroughly?" He queried, distantly aware the decision making process was changing.

"I have, and if ever there was an evil one this guy's it. He'll stand right in there with Jones, that ridiculous swami with the towel wrapped around his head up there in the Pacific northwest, and all the rest."

"What's he doing?" Alex George asked.

"Same old shit. Blows smoke up everybody's ass, giving them the "God has instructed me" line while he's ripping his followers off, personally screwing all the good looking women that fall into his web. Whispers God's will while he's humping these poor psychotic creatures. Been numerous suicides from these vulnerable, gullible women. He's got the usual paranoia, surrounding himself with many bodyguards, all heavily armed. There've been disappearances from the ranks of his followers. One man in particular, husband of another of the reverend's conquests, was found beaten to death in a back alley of a neighboring town. He'd threatened to go public with his findings."

They sat in silence for some time.

"You wonder where they come from don't you son?" The Old whispered.

"Yeah, you sure do."

"It goes on and on doesn't it?"

"It does. These phony assholes keep playing to the same kind of people, beat up by life and the shit they've been dealt. Talk about your con men, these bastards rank with the best of them, and now so many of them are pumping out their puke on television, to millions of the same kind of person. Same old shit, blubbering, giggling in their righteousness. Always so clever, and always so right because God told them so."

"They've been around forever."

"They have, and you have to let 'em go. Religious freedom is why this country got started, but I'll tell you we don't have to let the reverend Taylor keep getting away with his immense evil, pulled off in the name of God. Bull shitting the folks is one thing but it's too much, when rape, robbery, dope, prostitution and murder are included in their ministry. That's his bag and he's got to go. We need to see to that."

"Sounds like you've got a good case. You know how I've always felt about these holier than thou pricks. I got no objection whatever. Where's he live?"

"He's got a commune in upstate New York. Same old shit, you know. Gets his victims up there in his pristine woods, hypnotizes them with his garbage, then cuts 'em up at leisure. Empties their minds first, their pockets second."

"Easy one?" The Old Man asked.

"Wouldn't say so Boss. He knows what he is, so he's surrounded by heavily armed people. When he goes down, some of his disciples are going to have to go with him."

"Seems fair enough. If they really believe in him, they might's well follow him into the promised land."

"Yeah, I'll guarantee you that's where he's headed!" Tom answered as he left to get the word to the Chief.

*   *   *

He discussed the reverend explaining their reasons for wanting him dead. Options for refusal were always left open.

"I'll get right on it."

It obviously met with the Chief's instant approval and support. There was a note of excitement in his voice, something he almost never displayed. Steely dedication and single mindedness of purpose were his hallmarks, but this seemed to pique his interest in a special way.

"We'll have to get inside." Tom suggested.

"I'm sure of that."

"This is a mighty dangerous man, and situation. She needs to be careful. He's such a rotten fraud he's suspicious of anyone who gets near him. I don't want her to be another unmarked grave up there, so warn her big time, will you?"

"I'll tell her. You're words will mean a lot to her." He was impressed by Tom's concern, and knew Sandi would be too.

"Good! She's important to us. We don't want anything to happen."

"I'm on the way." CT commented as he hung up.

He called Sandi immediately.

"What do you have?" She asked when they met.

"A tough one."

"So?"

"Preacher man. Name's Taylor."

"Billy Taylor?" She was instantly receptive.

"Yeah, that one. You know him?"

"Don't know him, but know all about him. When you want me to leave?"

"Whoah! What's the hurry. I haven't told you where yet!"

"New York?" Her reply.

"You do know about this guy." It was a statement, not a question.

"Him and the rest." She answered.

"The rest?"

"They been around for a while you know." Her eyes blazed.

"Not like this they haven't." He replied.

"Oh I don't know. Hitler was one helluva preacher, wouldn't you say? Wouldn't you say he was probably the best ever, since Jesus?"

"Different message, but you've got a point." He wanted to evade what lay behind her sudden fervor.

"Oh yeah he was." The light remained. "Can you imagine how and where he got started?" She spoke in a hushed tone.

"Don't think I ever gave it much thought Sandi." He didn't want the discussion going this way. He knew how painful it was to this driven woman.

"I have!" The tears were not to be denied. "Don't you s'pose he started humming his vile shit back there in the twenties? Hummin' it to anyone who'd listen? Oh sure he did. Sort of like whispering in someone's ear while you're making love. Don't you think that's how his venal poison started? Lo and behold he found out those poor depression ridden sons of bitches wanted to listen out of desperation. Listen to anything, anyone who might show them a way out of their misery? He had a ready made audience all right, and got stronger and stronger as he went on hummin' his deadly tune. The hum went to a song, and the song became an anthem. Why my God man how 'bout when he had all those hundreds of thousands of believers lined up shouting their hosanna's and amens in reply to his sick shit. Jesus Christ CT, where were you then? Where were all the gunners then?"

"Come on Sandi, don't get into that. I know how much it hurts you."

"You're right, it hurts! It cost me my whole family years after the fact! It cost me that, and whatever kind of peace of mind I might have been able to know in this life." She lowered her head trying subliminally to hide her feelings of the moment. "What I want to know is, where were you God damn gunners when that sinister monster was walking the streets?"

He spoke softly hoping to stop this before it went too far.

"We weren't born yet Sandi. I guess though if there was any one man responsible for giving my kind birth with his thoughts, words, and actions, it would be him. Passed 'em on to the next generation of power brokers and they'll pass 'em on to the next. My kind's born out of that deviousness, death and destruction." He paused a moment, adding. "I don't think people realize that yet. They learned something after Nam they weren't aware of before, but I don't think they know we're still out here."

He thought a moment adding.

"The gunners you ask? Where were we? Why we were in the womb, waiting. Might have grown up normal, we were normal kids, but what we are now is a result of their messages. They, the Hitler's, Mussolini's, Chamberlain's, Roosevelt's, Stalin's, they started it and like forever more, turned the slaughter over to us demanding we stop it. Demanding we slaughter our opponents, and then demanding we disappear when it's over. Most of us did, only we were blown away instead of going away. Most, but not all. We, the so called angels, we're the survivors of that breed Sandi and we'll always be in demand."

"You're God damn right, my man." She seemed taller than she really was. "Let's get me out of here, right now!"

There was no real hurry, their advance information was such they knew everything had to be carefully planned. She approached the assignment with religious fervor, and for a very simple reason, she wanted the Reverend Billy Taylor dead. He represented in her mind, that which destroyed her mother.

She appeared first at meetings held by the cult in Albany, meetings intended to recruit. Her unique message of misery, sorrow and inability to cope with life in the real world came quite easy. Few facts of her life were changed, and in her driven manner she held back absolutely nothing, indulging in a dual mission. She stalked the reverend like the skilled huntress she had become, but also honed untapped skills in relating her story with emotional abandon. Sharing sessions were sometimes devoted in their entirety to Sandi as she let all of her pent up emotions go, like some great dam bursting. It was always a stunning performance and exercise, establishing her as a new cult superstar.

"We'd like you to join us at our camp Sandi?"

A group leader asked, aware he had someone here with a story placing her in near celebrity status. Anyone with a story like hers the Reverend Taylor would want to have close to him. If the stories the missionary had heard about the Reverend were true, he'd probably like to have this good looking woman close to him under any circumstances. He felt sure those rumors were not true, but just in case he might be able to pull off a double coup.

"You mean with him?" She asked breathlessly, propelling her acting skills to yet another level.

"Yes. I've spoken to the Reverend about you and he would like to have you join him at headquarters. He feels you have special need for his ministrations. He's heard your story from myself and others."

Sandi couldn't believe it might be this easy, whisked to the sanctuary in the woods along the Canadian border. She was amazed when she saw the huge mansion in the middle of the woods, surrounded by deep snow adding to it's beauty.

"Belonged to a robber baron who built it around the start of the century." Her escort told her as they entered the property. "He liked his privacy and built to preserve it. I don't know how the Reverend found it but he did and here we are." He was nearly overcome with his own eloquence and depth of feeling, as they drew near his spiritual leader.

"You will be shown to your quarters Sandi." The official greeter informed her after her welcome was out of the way. "We'll have dinner in the great hall this evening at six." He was nearly moved to tears as he added. "Oh child you are so fortunate, Reverend Taylor is going to join us." He fought to keep command of his emotions. "You'll never want to forget this night."

He disappeared down a hall, obviously overwhelmed as Sandi was taken to her room. Her guide was a lovely young girl, with a strange vacuous stare.

"When you hear the chimes, it will be time for dinner." The girl told her upon leaving. "I'll escort you to the dining room. We call it the great hall."

"Yes, I was...." The girl was gone before she could finish.

Sandi was impressed. Nobody in their right mind could help but be impressed with the sumptuous decorations. The interior halls of the entire mansion were dark mahogany paneling, beautiful, but adding to the somber atmosphere. Her bedroom was large and comfortable, with walls done in a light blue textured wall paper.

'Wonder what takes place in here, as if I didn't know.' She thought after waking from a short nap. The knock came on the door almost the moment the chimes pealed their soft announcement.

"What's your name?" Sandi asked her escort of earlier.

"Rachel." Her quiet reply.

"You been here long Rachel?"

"I don't know, really." It was hard to hear her, she spoke so softly.

"What do you mean you don't know?" The huntress asked.

"I really don't know. I pay no attention to time." They were heading toward the broad stairs. "It's not important. I'm with him, that's what matters."

She led the way down to the huge foyer she entered earlier in the day, then turned off through a set of double doors that opened into an impressive dining hall.

"Please sit here." Rachel asked indicating a seat midway down the row of chairs on one side.

The room filled rapidly with the many diners privileged to sit with the master, a quiet but lively conversational hum taking over the hushed surroundings. There were many introductions, all basking in the warmth that membership in the inner sanctum brought with it. Suddenly everyone became quiet as four obviously armed men stepped quietly into the room, each going as if on signal to a corner where they stood with their backs to the wall, staring icily at the gathered disciples.

'Heavy duty shit.' The newest of disciples thought as the Reverend Taylor made his entrance to the sound of chairs pushed back while everyone stood. Sandi followed suit standing in her dark skirt and white blouse, gathered attractively around her small waist by a broad belt. She had the top three buttons unbuttoned displaying discreetly a hint of cleavage, neither flamboyant nor subdued. Her dress would have been acceptable in any corporate boardroom in the United States.

"Please, please be seated." The reverend said softly with half closed eyes. "Let us take a moment now to give thanks for our assembled friends," he cut his eyes around the table letting them come to rest on Sandi, "new and old."

She didn't hear the prayer, too engrossed in the appearance of this cunning, charismatic, manipulator. His head was bowed, and she noted how impeccably dressed and coiffed he was.

'Look at that asshole', she thought, 'not one God damn hair out of place. Not one! Right amount of body to look good without being flashy. Hair line shaped to the collar. Snow white shirt open at the throat, freshly starched, set against a rich midnight blue sport coat. Soft, soft gray flannel trousers. Bet the shoes are right too.' She was acting the role of the human camera, marking everything. 'Glasses perfect, rimless, just right, pick up the light, accentuate the hair.' She paused in mid thought as her intense hatred rose to an almost unbearable pitch. 'Sandi baby, that hair isn't gray, it's silver. And look at that sweetheart', she was having a private party in her head, 'a pencil thin mustache. Jesus he looks good! Bet he smells good too!'

The mood was disrupted by a chorus of amens filling the great dining hall.

'Show time sweetie!' She thought shifting moods, searching for the prevailing feeling in the room to adjust accordingly. No introductions were made, but she knew he was aware of her presence as his eyes paused on her many times during dinner.

"So you are our newest guest?"

He spoke to her as he approached after dinner was over, taking her hand in a smooth motion. She thought of him as not so much walking, but maybe flowing was a better word. As he made his way around the room speaking softly with various members of the group he was followed constantly by the bodyguards.

"Yes, I guess I am."

'Act, bitch!' She hissed in her mind.

"I can't tell you what a great honor it is for me to be here Reverend. I only hope I can be worthy."

"Yes, yes Sandi." He knew her name, no introduction was necessary. "We can only hope, any of us, to be worthy. It was the apostle Paul you know, who said we all fall short of the glory of God."

'Slick!' she thought.

"It couldn't be said better." She answered.

"No Sandi it couldn't." He didn't release her hand and she was aware of it's softness and the scent of talcum powder.

'Knew it,' she thought, smiling angelically, 'the son of a bitch smells good!'

Her skin crawled as her hand rested in his but he didn't know that. She'd been schooled with, and by the best in this form of deception.

'Mata Hari, don't fail me now!' She thought.

"We're so happy to have you with us, my dear." His eyes fell delicately to where the folds of her blouse met, barely revealing a gentle rise. "Please forgive me now won't you, but I must share with the others."

The whole room circled around the Reverend to sit at the feet of the master, in and listen in rapt attention as he gave his homily for the night. Seemed appropriate enough to the representative of the deadly group stalking him at this exact moment, that he chose this night to preach on sharing.

"In order to keep love, one must give it away." It sounded like he was purring. "If we can't give our love freely to others, it's as if we have no love at all." His half closed eyes slid lightly over Sandi as he spoke. "No man should we refuse, when his needs are that love we possess."

'That smooth son of a bitch is propositioning me, right here! Right in front of the gathered brethren he's hittin' on me.' She thought, wondering how long it was going to take him to get to her.

He droned on as Sandi tried desperately to grab bits and pieces of what he was saying so she could have something to comment on while he was making love to her later in the evening, or whenever it happened.

'Never screwed a preacher!' She thought. 'Wonder what you're s'posed to do?'

It was later while Sandi was getting ready for bed the expected soft knock came on the door. Her mind raced with all sorts of possibilities and conversations as she walked to the door, a door with no lock.

"Oh Reverend Taylor!" She exclaimed as she opened the door.

"I thought I would check to see if you're comfortable." He asked. "Do you have everything you need?"

"Yes. Yes I do." She was struck by the fact he was making no move whatever.

"Good." He purred. "We are so pleased you've seen fit to join us, Sandi. Have a good nights rest, we will look forward to seeing you tomorrow."

"I'm the grateful one Reverend. Just to be here with you," dropping her eyes demurely, "is a great privilege, and one I'm so thankful for."

"Yes Sandi, gratitude is something we all should be aware of and give constant thanks to a generous Creator."

It was then she noticed for the first time his half closed eyes and tendency to drift in his speech. She was absolutely certain he was on some narcotic.

"Until tomorrow then?" He said as he started to drift down the long hall. "I'll remember you in my prayers."

"Thank you Reverend." She whispered after him as he disappeared in the gloom of the dimly lit corridor.

'Smooth son of a bitch,' she thought closing the heavy door, 'either knew I was expecting a move or too popped up to give a shit. Maybe one thrill at a time's enough for him.'

Rachel came to her door in the morning to take her to yet another dining area. Her strange demeanor intrigued Sandi making her wonder where she was coming from. Narcotics, bent mind, maybe even possessed by the kind of faith so many of the zealots she'd been exposed to over the years seemed to have.

"Are you happy here, Rachel?" She asked on the trip downstairs.

"Yes." The barely audible answer. There was no elaboration.

"Married?" It was a natural question with no hidden meaning.

"I was." The soft reply.

"Is your husband here?" They were approaching the top stair.

"I don't know." She seemed confused. "He was."

"You don't know?" It was suddenly much more than a casual conversation.

"No. This is where you will have your breakfast." She left abruptly.

Sandi had her breakfast with the others, but without the Reverend. There was no way she could get Rachel's words out of her mind. Her day was spent attending various meetings and prayer sessions, all the while aware of the powerful brain washing being dispensed to everyone there.

The soft knock she'd been expecting, came about a week after she arrived. It was Reverend Taylor dressed for the action he obviously intended having this evening, with his new disciple.

Smooth was the only word she could use to describe his technique. A combination of biblical exhortations, coupled with sexual banalities accompanied by constant touching, kissing and stroking as he lifted her gown, probing the private parts of her body. She'd been through this routine many, many times with every stripe of man imaginable, but never a so called churchman of any rank, much less a personality of such renown as this.

The event was certainly unspectacular, by her standards, attended by incessant murmurings of the obviously drugged leader. She was aware of his difficulty reaching orgasm, thinking his drugged mind was not able to reach where he needed to be without some degree of exertion. Sandi's act included finely honed sexual skills, all of which she used to help him get where he wanted to go.

The following night at dinner he was his usual calm self acting as if nothing had happened. The routine was exactly the same, the homily different, this one exhorting them to be willing to sacrifice everything for the love of God. Nothing, according to the Reverend, should be ever held back indicating to her there was to be more of the same tonight. She was partially right.

They were in her bed, an unsuccessful attempt at fornication out of the way when a gentle knock came on the door.

"Come in Rachel." He answered softly. Sandi was stunned.

"I have asked Rachel to join us Sandi. She has truly God given talents beyond imagining, and enjoys sharing her gifts with others."

He turned to the girl standing in the room, lifting the covers as he asked her to join them. In the half light of the darkened room Sandi was astonished at Rachel's voluptuous figure as she loosened her robe, letting it fall to the floor, revealing her completely naked figure as she slid into bed with them.

The Reverend turned his attention, and probing hands in the direction of the new arrival bringing her to a state of heightened passion almost at once. He quietly left the bed but not until he had urged his two bed partners to share what it was they had at that moment.

Sandi was completely unprepared for this, responding as best she could under the circumstances. A lesbian experience was not new, there was the female editor in New York that had challenged her to try it, and she found it had its moments, but this was very, very different. Rachel was all over her body in a quick series of moves which under different circumstances might not have met with her total disapproval. It was only shortly after they'd begun the Reverend turned on the light by the side of the bed sitting in a chair while he watched with half closed eyes. That she wasn't used to at all. It was an abandoned performance by the shy Rachel, which she finished in spectacular fashion with the aid of a sexual device handed her by Taylor.

"Rachel, Rachel, Rachel." He whispered as she lay back exhausted by her efforts. "Why didn't you make Jimmy see what he was doing? He could be with us now too, but no." The drugged spiritual leader laid his head back on the chair, adding. "He had to leave us, only to be found where he was. Such a loss."

It was all he said, but it spoke volumes to Sandi while she shared the room, her intimacy and body, with the two anesthetized zealots. Or was Rachel truly a member of the cult? She seemed to stay quite apart, never eating with them or attending the various group sessions that were such a prominent part of the operation. They met in the hall the next day, Rachel apparently unaware of what had happened.

'That's it! She's insane!' Sandi decided after the wild sexual foray that had taken place in her room that night. 'She doesn't know where she is, or who she is!'

It didn't take long to confirm her suspicions, at least circumstantially. Rachel's husband Jimmy had grown disenchanted with the cult and especially the Reverend Billy's insatiable appetite for sexual favors from his wife. Obviously he had protested, threatening to expose Taylor and his whole operation, disappearing immediately.

'Lots of woods out there.' Sandi thought as she looked out her bedroom window, much aware of the many mysterious disappearances rumored. She wondered how many bodies they held. The bodies of detractors from within his organization. 'Shouldn't be for long though.'

The thought was a pleasant one. She had grown to hate the man even more than she thought, finding it increasingly difficult to hide her true feelings towards what she felt was a monster of the greatest stripe. She managed to get away from the estate to call the Chief, at the end of the first month, a month given to more wild sexual encounters with Rachel, who's sanity she no longer wondered about, and the ever present Reverend Taylor. This man she also considered insane, but in the most sinister sense of the word.

"I'll tell you one thing CT," she offered, "he'll be tough to bring down. He's always guarded by at least four men, all carrying. Try as I have, I can't get anything like a handle on a regular schedule. The exception's the one time a week he goes into Montreal, otherwise there is no pattern."

"Then we take him out on his weekly trip, kid." Her heart ached to be with him while talking long distance.

"Don't go back there Sandi. You found out what we needed to know, I don't want you in there any more. I'll be in Albany tomorrow, we'll set it up. Give me a number where I can call you."

It was the longest twenty four hours in her life waiting for his call which finally came, with instructions to meet him downtown.

'I can't be in love with this guy.' She thought as he walked toward her. 'This kind of business doesn't lend itself to involvement.'

She loved to watch him from a distance when he wasn't aware, because it was like observing a creature of the wild. He stepped surely but soft, almost a gliding motion, leading her to wonder if he left a footprint. Steel gray eyes with which he swept his field of vision constantly, while his well trained mind took in everything he saw, computed it and arrived at decisions. She couldn't believe he was his true age, because of the way he moved, alert, ready to handle anything. He was the epitome of the most dangerous animal on earth, man with murderous intent.

"Colder'n a whores heart." He murmured in greeting, causing her to laugh out loud. She was obviously in love with the man although both knew that was a state they had no business being involved in. What a greeting!

"It gets cold in this part of the country." Her reply. "The locals say it gets cold enough to freeze the nuts off a John Deere cultivator." Her eyes crinkled up as they stood smiling at each other.

"Well tell you what," he exclaimed, "let's go find some heat. My blood's too thin for this shit."

"My place?" She teased.

"No!" His abrupt reply. "We'll find a restaurant, and lay it out there."

He was visibly saddened when Sandi told him of their abnormal sexual forays. He didn't think she should use her body as a pawn. It seemed to him that couldn't help but add to her outsized load of guilt, something else he would like to stop. He deliberately skipped that phase of the story with a tiny portion of his mind storing information in that regard. Reverend Taylor was being subliminally and consciously targeted for severe treatment.

The Chief was in total operational control of the affairs of the horrendous group the world had accepted as the Angels. Whoever he wanted in the way of personnel was his choice, unless the individual turned him down. They never did. He knew how it had to be done. He would need Vic to drive, and Pat to kill.

"He goes to Montreal every Friday." The Chief was telling Vic and Pat. "We take him on this little road that leads to the interstate. We blow him and his people up, and split. There should be massive confusion because we'll be so much closer to Canadian jurisdiction, even though we'll still be in the U.S."

"How?" Pat smilingly asked.

"Our only chance at the sick bastard is in his car, on the road. His gunners will be too alert to try and kill him from a car."

He looked at Vic taking it all in, memorizing the route.

"How you feel about a truck, it's the only thing that'll work?" He stared across the table at their genius at transportation.

"Got wheels on it?" His terse reply.

"How ever many you need."

"Got wheels, I can handle it." He wasn't smiling.

"OK. Tell me what you need and I'll get it for you. What we'll do is come down the road behind the Reverend and his car. When we get to this stretch," indicating an area on the map close to the interstate, "we'll pass." He looked at Vic again. "We'll be driving on ice and snow, no doubt. Can you handle it?"

"Got wheels on it?" He meant it. He still wasn't smiling.

"OK, I got the message! The back of the truck will be covered with a heavy netting type material, maybe something like fish net. We have to be able to see them, but they can't see us." He paused. "Not until it's too late that is. I'll have a rocket launcher and when we get around in front of them I blow the Mercedes up."

"What you need me for?" Pat asked, his smile lessening.

"Mop up. We'll have machine guns for that. Flak jackets and machine guns. If we don't get 'em with the rocket, we kill what's left with machine guns."

"Afraid you just wanted me along for the ride." He beamed. "What kind of machine guns?"

"Thompsons." His reply.

"God damn, that's great! I've had a love affair with that thing ever since boot camp. Sure clears a big path doesn't it?" He was obviously pleased.

"Should push what's left of that Mercedes down the road, if we have to use 'em."

"Oh I hope so. I hope so. I don't like the Reverend at all you know."

"You need chains?" He asked Vic.

"No. I need a small, short bed, stake body with duals. Got four tires on the ground in back I can take it anywhere. I'd like an older model with the biggest veight we can find."

They went over their route many times, working on logistics and timing. The truck worked beautifully, each man taking turns riding in a car behind, trying to see if the casual observer could see its' deadly cargo. They couldn't.

Friday came and so did the Reverend Billy Taylor.

"OK boys, hook 'em up." It was time, the Chief and Pat got in the back of the truck, with Vic driving. It was a long drive and a longer wait in the subzero cold. The Reverend was running behind schedule.

"There he goes!" Vic called through the sliding glass window as he dropped the truck into gear accelerating smoothly out of their position on the side road, navigating carefully the turn onto the larger road. It was all ice and snow.

No matter how many times they'd gone into action, their nerves were like violin strings on any killing mission. Death was not easily dispensed, even by these proficient killers. Pat was acutely aware of his shivering, indifferent whether the Chief knew it or not. He was cold and tense, tightening his muscles constantly to overcome the feeling. They felt the truck swing into the main road that led to the interstate, the rear end sliding as they made the turn.

"Quarter mile behind!" Vic called back.

The Chief busied himself with the rocket launcher, loading, balancing the heavy weapon on a box put there for the purpose. His eyes glued to the rear of the truck.

"Hundred yards!"

"Go!" The Chief called out.

He felt the truck accelerate, moving to the left side of the highway to pass. They stayed out long enough to see the black limousine dropping behind them on their left. Vic pulled the truck smoothly, cautiously back into the driving lane placing the Reverend's vehicle directly behind.

The Chief was down on one knee sighting over his deadly launcher at the five occupants of the limousine when Vic screamed.

"Jesus!" The truck went into a crazy slide. "Jesus!" He screamed again.

The two in the back of the truck watched the Mercedes lose control completely, the back end of the car fishtailing as the driver responded to something they couldn't see, their vision cut off by the back of the truck.

Everything happened in kaleidoscopic fashion, and even though they were used to that sort of action, it was difficult to put together later. The Chief was thrown against the side of the truck just as he was ready to fire, the heavy box he was sighting on thrown against his arm and chest causing him to involuntarily pull the trigger. The rocket was launched with a terrible blast of sound and smoke, the projectile ripping through the canvas side of the truck.

They were passed at exactly the same moment by a huge vehicle out of control. It was tilting over on its side as it slid toward the ditch after the rocket slammed into it, exploding with stunning sound.

All he saw were the words "de Sione", the end of something his mind didn't want to compute. His subconscious told him it was a school bus but somehow in the insanity of the moment he couldn't, or wouldn't handle that. He fought to right himself, as Pat sprawled behind him, struggling to regain his feet.

'Kill those motherfuckers'. He thought, watching in his peripheral vision the bus turn over on it's side, soft white snow spraying out in a wide wake.

"Merciful Jesus!" Reverend Taylor screamed, unable to understand what was happening. The occupants of the Mercedes were aware of the sliding vehicles, but they could not understand the explosion, unaware a weapon had been fired from the truck directly in front.

"Give me the rocket!" The Chief called to Pat who had regained his feet, handing him the small deadly projectile.

He reloaded in an instant, scrambling to the rear of the small truck sweeping the netting aside in full view of the Reverends party. He fired his second round at near point blank into the black car, watching it lurch from the explosion, doors flying open, the instant wreck crashing back to the ground immediately.

"Go Pat!" He screamed.

The smiling heavy set man moved with unbelievable grace out of the back of the truck, toward the shattered automobile. As he moved one of the bodyguards who'd been thrown out, rose and shot the ancient warrior in the head, killing him instantly. The Chief was aware of Pat's smiling countenance, laying in the snow his face turned toward him as he passed. He shot the bodyguard who'd killed Pat, rushing by him toward the back of the smashed vehicle where he pulled a door open, machine gunning all the bodies he found inside. He fired in maniacal rage, especially pleased as he watched the Reverend Taylor's face disappear under the impact of the heavy caliber bullets at point blank range, until his entire clip was gone. He would have kept firing but there was nothing more to shoot.

Vic raced down the side of the truck, as the Chief ran toward the overturned vehicle, its wheels still turning. He jumped off the embankment onto the side of the bus, horrified when he understood the sign said "Notre Dame de Sione". He saw the damage done by his heavy weapon as he ran down the top of the crippled bus, children lying all about inside. It was then he saw the flash of light blue, firing memory neurons, and turning his blood to ice water.

"What?" Vic screamed into the enraged Chief's face.

"Come on!" He yelled at Vic jumping down, running toward the truck. "Help me load Pat!"

Vic obeyed silently as they struggled with the dead weight, sliding his body along the glass like surface, lifting him into the back.

"Get out of here!" The Chief commanded.

"I can't leave you!" He replied.

To his astonishment the Chief pushed his automatic in his face as he screamed.

"Go Vic, or you die here! I've got to help those people...." indicating the bus. "No time for you.... Go! Find somewhere to dump Pat! Get gas! Burn him! Leave nothing!" Once again leveling the weapon in his face. "No time boy! Get out of here!"

Vic knew absolutely the Chief would kill him in a second if he didn't do as he said, but he had to ask.

"What'll you do?"

"Stay here 'til we get help. Nobody'll see me, too much confusion. Now go!"

As Vic started the truck he saw the Chief in his rear view mirror leaping on the bus, smashing at the windows with his heavy black shoes. The girls were in a pile on the bottom side, screaming, crying, bleeding. Many wounded. Many dead. He ran along the sides of the seats toward the back, bracing himself against the last seat smashing the door open with the force of his heels.

He saw her up front, the light blue. He knew she was there. He knew who she was, the color of her habit emblazoned on his mind, but he couldn't dwell on that. Not now.

"What happened?" A motorist called into the back of the overturned bus.

"Wreck! Get help!" The Chief screamed as he helped the girls who could walk. "Go, God damn it! Get help!"

The man disappeared, impressed by the tone of command in the voice of the deadly killer who was so desperately trying to get the innocent load of dead, dying and injured out. No one had any idea what had happened, or who to blame.

The girls in their beautiful dark blue caped uniforms lined in scarlet, now torn, disheveled, some covered with blood, made their way out haltingly.

"Sister's in front." One of the stunned girls murmured as he helped her out.

"I know. I know. I'll get her." He ran to the front as soon as all the girls that could get out, did.

'Oh my God'.

His mind erupted at the sight. He wept instantly for the first time in years as he stared down at the crumpled figure. His whole life had been one series of killings after another, but he'd never hurt anyone like this. Her beautiful sky blue habit with the stunning white trim adorned by the crucifix, was now marked with her blood as she lay on her side.

'Oh my God'.

He fought to get her seated upright, noticing the blood on the left lens of her glasses, a wisp of blond hair sticking out of the white headpiece.

"Can you hear me sister?" He asked the stricken woman.

"Yes." The barely audible reply. "The girls?"

"Let me help you out of here?" Ignoring the query.

"No." She whispered. "The girls?"

"We have some out." He whispered.

"Some?" She asked.

"Yes sister." He was answering obediently now, that's how the nuns taught him so many years ago. "Some are dead." He sobbed.

He held the dying nun, young, pretty, a slight smile on her face.

"Then we can go together?" Her eyes closed gently.

"No Sister! You can't go!" The leader of the ferocious band wept openly. "Oh sweet Jesus Sister, don't go."

"It's all right." Her head bowed gracefully. "He'll be waiting for us."

CWO Evans laid his head alongside hers, hoping, wishing it was he dying, not her.

"Sister, can you hear me?" His eyes rolling in agony.

There was no response, then she answered.

"Yes."

"I didn't mean for this to happen. Can you forgive me?" He held her soft hand gently. "Will you forgive me?"

"Yes."

It was so soft he had difficulty hearing. She died in his arms.

CHAPTER 31

"I'm gone Tom, for however long it takes."

"What, in the name of God, happened?" Tom asked.

CT paused before answering. Tom knew why.

"I was ready man...knee on the deck...Mercedes square in my sights." He spoke softly, almost a whisper. "Swerved...threw me...slammed rocket to the side...jerked the trigger...fired through the canvas." Another pause. "No idea anything was there...couldn't see. Fired...explosion...saw the bus for the first time...." he struggled for control, "as it slid past. Didn't know what it was. Took out original objective. They killed Seattle man...." He hissed through clenched teeth. "I killed...every...fucking...one...of them! Got him out...and vehicle. Stayed with the bus...went with 'em."

"You mean, to the hospital?" Tom found that incredible.

"Yes." The answer was delayed again, indicating his extreme agony. Tom knew he was fighting for control. "No problem...too much confusion. Said I was riding snowmobile...saw everything. They believed me...no reason not to."

This followed by yet another interminable pause.

"Was with her...in the bus...when she died."

Tom put his forehead against the cold glass of the phone booth, weeping as he shared the Chief's despair. There was another excruciating period of silence.

"Goin' away now."

"Where?"

"Don't know. Got to think."

"Will you be back?"

"Don't know...." Another pause. "Maybe.... Maybe not...."

"CT?"

"Forget it Tom...there aren't any words. If I make it through this, I make it through myself."

"I'll be waiting to hear from you."

"You know how to get hold of Harold?"

"Yes."

"He's the best. Anything comes up...get him. You don't hear from me in a week or so, you never will...then Harold's your man. He knows that...we've discussed it."

Each man gripped his phone, no words spoken, the silence finally broken by the Chief.

"Tom?"

"Yeah?"

"Hell of an idea." Pause. "Sure wish...."

"Yeah, yeah!" Struggling for control. "CT?"

"Yeah."

"Hope you make it back."

"Yeah well...we'll see." He answered quietly. Their connection was broken.

Tom's fight wasn't over. He knew the Old Man was waiting.

*   *   *

"I just don't have the words for you Boss."

The Old Man was in tears, open, unabashed.

"Does anyone?" He asked.

"I know now how it happened."

"Well then would you tell me," he sobbed, "so I can understand?"

Tom related the story exactly as the Chief told him. It only took a moment.

Alex George sat, arms on his legs, staring down at the floor where his tears fell. He'd known terrible suffering in his long life, but never anything like this.

'Even Mary....' He thought. 'When was that.... When the hell was that? Momma? God how that hurt. That's when it was over. Now this.'

"Do you think God...." He begged Tom.

"She could." Tom offered.

"What do you mean, she could?" He sobbed.

"The Chief was holding the nun in his arms when she died." He was struggling. "He asked for her forgiveness."

"And...." His voice hollow with emotion.

"She said...yes." He whispered, his head lowered.

They sat in total silence for what seemed an eternity, before either spoke.

"Paradox." The Old Man murmured.

"Sir?" Tom asked.

"My whole fucking life seems to have been one long, terrible, God damn contradiction."

Tom waited.

"Tried all along to do the right thing... you know what I mean...." He shrugged his shoulders. "Kept losing people. Papa, when I was a boy." He was entering the yard of seventy years ago. "Should have been with him...." He stared straight through Tom. "I'll guarantee you he wouldn't have died, not that day anyway... but I wasn't. How come?" He lowered his head shaking it slowly. "My old friend Myron.... Can't even remember what he looked like? Huey.... Man, God damn I don't know.... I just don't know. Ever wonder those things?" He looked imploring.

"Three times I'll never forget." Tom replied.

"South Pacific?" The old man was wandering.

"Yes."

"Mary?" His eyes filled with tears again. "Mary. My boy Alex. Sue. I got all the money in the world and a tough son of a bitch to boot...and I couldn't help 'em."

He could barely be heard.

"I know."

Tom rushed back through the years and saw Paul's blood pooling on his green fatigues, as he held the dead boy.

"Momma?"

"I know." Tom was still holding Paul's body.

"The little French girls in the bus.... Amazing! Notre Dame de Sione you say.... Sister Celeste was it.... Wonder why?"

Alex George needed some answers.

"Have to wait on that." Tom answered.

The silence grew longer. The Old man finally spoke.

"Tear 'em down son."

"Sir?"

"The angels! Tear 'em down! Now!"

"OK Boss."

He hardly heard what the ancient tycoon said, much less had any intention of complying.

"Go now Tom. I'll call you."

"OK Boss." He started to leave and stopped. "I'm going to the swamp. Be back tomorrow some time."

"Yeah, yeah. Do that. I used to do that...helps."

*   *   *

"Mr. McCormick?"

The Chief's sudden appearance out of the shadows of the back seat caused such terror in the newspaper man he had difficulty breathing. It was so utterly unexpected and frightening, he was amazed he didn't lose control of the vehicle.

"What? Who are you?" His frightened reply. "What do you want?"

"I'm not here to hurt you, or want anything from you. Act natural. Just drive." The voice was not threatening, yet had a quality about it that told the reporter to do exactly as he was told.

"Where do we go?" He asked his ominous passenger.

"What time are you expected home?"

"No time. Whenever." He swallowed hard. "One in the morning...now, it doesn't matter...wife's asleep. Any time."

"Good. Don't be frightened. It's just that I must talk to you, and I require your undivided attention. Whatever you do, don't move...do not look around."

"I assume you're armed?" McCormick asked.

"Heavily." The short reply.

"If it's money...."

"I'm sure you know without a doubt who I am, and that I don't want your money."

"I thought something like that. Where do we go?"

"The War Memorial."

McCormick felt his skin crawl and hands grow damp driving up the steep Main Street hill, then turning into the long dark mall.

"Pretty dangerous up here at night." His frightened comment.

"You'll be in no danger Mr. McCormick."

"You're one of them, aren't you?" He asked, feeling the strangest mix of emotions he'd ever known in all his life. Terror, curiosity, security.

"I am." Another short reply. "Park over there."

He indicated the location with his black gloved hand. It was all McCormick ever saw of him.

They sat silent in the darkness, the newspaperman gripping the wheel, while the Chief sat in the deepest darkness of the right hand back seat.

"You're voice? It sounds familiar. Have we spoken before?"

"Yes, but that was about other matters, now I'm here to speak to you." He paused. "They don't know I'm here."

McCormick knew his passenger was under great emotional stress.

"You were there?" McCormick asked softly.

"Yes."

"Were you the...."

"Yes." He whispered. "That's why I'm here. I fired the rocket...had no idea the bus was around...much less alongside our truck."

"The girls said their bus came down a long hill leading into the road you were traveling. They said their driver couldn't stop and went into a long slide, hooking around the outside of the other two vehicles."

"Read that, doesn't help." Another long pause.

"How could you leave them?" His question startled him given the circumstances, but he was a reporter. There was no way he could not ask.

"I never left them." The answer stunned the reporter, and the anguish it contained.

"You mean you were the...."

"Yes...told them I was snowmobiling...saw everything... confusion...so many dead...so many dying...knew I wouldn't get any attention. If I did...."

His voice trailed off. McCormick understood. If he'd been noticed, whoever made the discovery would have been in great jeopardy, if not dead.

"But my God man, why?"

"told you...never saw them...fired through the canvas...didn't know they were there." He paused again, continuing. "Haven't slept or eaten since the... since." Another pause. "Killed many men in my life...only God knows how many...it's what I do. I never, ever, killed a...." His voice broke and they remained silent, McCormick not daring to say a word at that emotionally charged moment. "...child." His was exquisite agony out of the shadows. "I have never, ever killed a...nun." He whispered, trying in some subliminal way to hide his guilt from God.

"You were the man the girls said was holding her?"

McCormick thought there would never be an answer.

"Yes." It was half hollow whisper, half agonized sob.

"Did she know?"

"Yes... I asked her forgiveness...asked her to pray for me."

McCormick's mind reeled with emotion.

"And?"

"Said yes...yes, she'd pray for me...yes, she forgave me."

"But you can't forgive yourself?"

If the reporter had dared look around he would have seen the specialist in murder holding his gloved hand over his mouth, stifling a scream, eyes wide in horror.

"No."

Half whisper, half choked sob.

"I can certainly...."

"No! No! No you can't! Be quiet...." He whispered. "No God damn it, you can't.... Listen...."

They sat in silence while the Chief fought his emotions under control.

"Thought of giving myself up...." His head bowed. "What good.... Thought of nothing but killing myself.... Oh yeah," A dry chuckle. "I could do that.... I am the expert you know, done it so God damn many times...what would that accomplish? Another body? To what end?" He paused again before continuing. "I'm here at risk...to speak to you in person.... I know you could never understand my kind, I don't ask you to. Yeah, I kill, but I'm not evil." He stopped, adding. "Paradox. Yes I'm a killer...but not evil...terrible accident. Killed the preacher, yes...biker and many others in Seattle, yes...blew up half of Miami...bodyguard in Los Angeles, yes. Gladly! Happily! I'd do it again in a minute!" He gripped McCormick's shoulder. "But man you must know I don't kill people like those...." His voice trailed off.

The reporter shivered remembering how some of those men died.

"They had it coming McCormick, and you know it. I'd be happy to take 'em all down. They've no right to live. You don't have to agree with what we do, but God damn man you've got to admit the people we've removed from society won't be missed."

"Strange, but I do agree." He reflected aloud. "Guess it's not that strange though. Most people feel the same way."

"...going away now McCormick," he whispered in the reporters ear, "but I wanted you to hear from me in person, how very, very sorry I am for what happened. I'd trade my life in a minute, for any one of theirs," he was weeping and McCormick had the impression he was screaming in his ear without raising his voice above a whisper, "but I can not, bring...them...back."

McCormick drove his surreal passenger to a large hotel nearby, careful not to look at him as he got out. He didn't want to be able to describe him to the police.

"McCormick?" He was closing the door.

"Yes."

"Write in your paper I came to see you. Write what I've told you. Tell them I'm the leader of these men. They must know to what extent I've gone to acknowledge my deep sorrow."

"All right. I'll do that. Could I ask you one thing?"

"You can."

"What will you do now?"

"Think...decide...." The door closed, the leader of the angels disappeared.

*   *   *

Vic was shaken into reality by the sudden ringing of the telephone.

"Get a 'copter! Pick me up at the usual place!"

He recognized the Chief's voice immediately.

"How'd you get out?" Vic asked.

"Long story. Pick me up tomorrow! Same place."

"I'll be there." The click indicated the conversation was over.

*   *   *

"Why didn't you call the police." His editor regretted asking the question the moment it was out of his mouth. He would have done nothing different.

"Didn't know...."

"Aw shit, forget it. That was a dumb question. You did what anyone would have. Terrified?" He asked.

"Yeah. At first. When he came out of the back seat I thought my heart would stop. Then he told me who he was and I knew all I had to know. I had a deadly passenger. I'd have done anything he asked. He didn't want anything though, except to tell me his side of it and hope for forgiveness."

"Big order."

"Sure it is, but if you could have heard the man you'd know the intensity of his pain."

"I can imagine...." The editor replied.

"NO, GOD DAMN IT! NO YOU CAN'T!" The swift, angry, shouted reply.

"What?"

"Oh I'm sorry, but that's what I said to him. Like he just had his dog put to sleep or something." McCormick was crying. "I can imagine your sorrow, and he said through clenched teeth there was no way I, or anybody else could imagine his sorrow. He said no one could possibly imagine." He thought a moment adding. "He's right Boss, none of us could you know."

The editor thought a moment. His reporter couldn't see the tears in his eyes as the man touched his shoulder.

"Yeah, your right. Hey, write it like he told you, Mac. Fuck it! Let the chips fall where they may. For better or worse the public's going to judge him anyway. If he meant what he said he's probably dead now."

He turned away quickly.

"Write it!"

*   *   *

"We're going where?" Vic asked the Chief as they rose into the sky.

"Fifty miles out."

"Then what?"

"I get off?" The Chief replied.

"What?"

Still shaken, from when the bus was blown up, Vic didn't want to play any games. He had to burn the truck with Pat's body in it. He'd never done anything like that before.

The Chief was changing into swim gear. Heavy underwear, thick rubber suit, gloves, goggles. He was under desperate mental stress, and not good company. Vic decided to take him where he wanted and forget the questions.

"Far enough?" He shouted over the roar of the engine a short time later.

The Chief nodded signifying with a downward thrust of his thumb they were to go to the surface.

"When you want me to come get you?" Vic yelled.

"Don't bother! I know the way!"

Chief Warrant Officer CT Evans jumped out of the door, into the Pacific.

Vic watched the ex-SEAL bobbing in the swells, until he became so small he lost him. He calculated mentally where he might be in one, two, three days, if he was still alive.

The Chief was really in his element now. He rose and fell with the gentle swells. If there was a solution to be found for this extraordinary man, it would be found out here.

As soon as Vic and the copter left his vision he truly became part of the Pacific ocean, letting it take him, mind, body and soul with the drift. Passive. Floating. He waited.

*   *   *

Tom went directly to the Shed, after returning from the swamp. He knew the Old Man would be waiting for him there. He was.

"OK Tom, get on with it! Destroy the outfit!" He almost sounded like the warrior he once was.

"Been out there thinking Mr. Alex." Nodding his head toward the great Atchafalaya swamp. "This is a terrible thing that happened, but I don't think we should destroy what we've put together."

"You don't, eh?" He might be old, but the spirit was still there. "Well I got news for you old friend, I don't much give a shit whether you think so, or not! I'm telling you take it down! Now!"

"Mr. Alex, we went through all this when you asked me to put it together. I tried my dead level best to talk you out of it then. We discussed the chance of innocent people getting killed. You knew the possibilities. I thought we concluded we'd have to live with that if it ever happened."

"I don't give a good God damn what we decided then! I'm deciding different now! I will not have anything like this happen again." He raised his ancient body out of the chair. "Tear the God damn thing down!"

"Yes, yes." Tom answered. "Nobody wanted that to happen, but it did. The only man who knew what was happening at that moment was our driver. He was the only one could have seen that bus slide around the truck. It was more of an act of God than anything else."

"AN ACT OF WHO?" He was totally outraged. "Do you want me to be-lieve God decided right then that those girls, and the nun should die by MY hand?"

His fury was complete. Sensing trouble Helen was as alert as she'd ever been, her body tensed like a coiled spring.

"I don't think God had their deaths in mind when they left the convent in Canada. I think He had something more like an educational visit in mind." What was left of his chest muscles grew taut. He wanted to fight. "Don't give me that act of God shit, will you not!"

"I only meant...." Tom tried to reason.

"I don't care what you meant!" He raised clenched fists to the ceiling. "Those beautiful people are dead! Don't you understand they died with that God damn scum, and I'm responsible for it! I can't stand it! What a horrible thing! Loving innocence dying alongside consummate evil!" He wept briefly, finally screaming. "OBEY ME TOM! DESTROY THE GOD DAMN ANGELS. NOW!"

"Wait a minute, Mr. Alex. I know you're incensed, everybody is. The Chief's trying to work his way through this tragedy now. We could disband, but I wish you wouldn't do that yet. Can't we sit on this for now? God knows it's a monstrous thing, but didn't we agree it was time for something like this? Didn't we decide this country's suffered too much because of all the wrongs that go on in the name of some kind of perverted freedom? Didn't you and I discuss, right in this room, the possibility this nation just might not be as grand as everyone would have you believe, falling behind in everything because we've lost values once sacred?"

Tom was breathing hard. He was not only pleading, he was selling as hard as he'd ever sold.

"Don't destroy this thing Mr. Alex! We've got what you wanted! We've got the approval of the people! We'll have it after this blows over. Did you see the story by McCormick up there in Kansas City? The Chief risked talking to him in person to explain his actions. Did you see that article Boss? There's absolutely no doubt where McCormick stands although he can't come out and say it. You can't say 'we're glad our scum are dying in the streets.' You can't say that, even though it's true! We got to play the double standard, two face game! 'Let due process take care of 'em,' and really mean let's get 'em gone! Anyway.... However.... Well that's us Mr. Alex. We're the anyway! Too bad, yeah. Really too bad that's how it has to be, but there isn't any other way! Please, think about it for a couple days? Don't destroy out of sorrow, what you wanted put together so desperately." Tom was shouting.

"TEAR 'EM DOWN!"

Alex George looked his long time protege' directly in the eye.

"Take 'em down now God damn it, or else!"

*   *   *

The Chief rode the swells sometime in the dark of the third night. He'd been in the water two and a half days now, reaching the state of mind he came seeking. Nothing else existed, just him and the Pacific.

She came like he knew she would, in the deepest part of the night. Oh yeah, he knew she'd be here, and here she came. He saw the beautiful white head piece first, coming from behind a swell some distance away.

"Sister Celeste! Over here Sister! I'm over here!"

He shouted into the gentle wind and sea, immediately sorry he'd attracted her attention. He turned his back to her in the hope she wouldn't be able to see him because of the black head piece to his wet suit. But she was Christian love itself, no way would she be denied. She knew he was there, drifting directly toward him.

'What a radiant smile'. He thought, waiting.

He knew she wouldn't be refused. He knew she would not be deterred in any way by what he might try to do. After all, she was why he was out here. He knew all along, she'd be there. He couldn't see his black gloved hand in front of his face in the dark of the night and the sea, but he could see her.

'Why are you here, Mr. Evans?' She asked silently, smiling gently.

'Because of you Sister.' His thought. He didn't even wonder how she knew his name.

'But I'm just fine. You must know that. Don't you know I'm with Him.' She replied, rising and falling with the swells, her large rosary floating on the surface.

'Yes Sister. I know that.' He was weeping like he hadn't since childhood.

'The children then?'

'Yes.' He whispered his thought.

'Oh you shouldn't Mr. Evans, they're all so happy.' She beamed. 'You will be too when you join us.'

'When will that be?' He wanted to know.

'When it's time.' She smiled. The gorgeous head piece looked especially striking against the backdrop of the starry sky. 'I must go back to the girls now. Will you be all right?'

'Yes Sister. I'll be all right. Thank you for coming.'

'Then goodbye Mr. Evans. We'll look forward to seeing you again.'

She disappeared over a long rolling swell as he shouted in the darkness.

"Sister! Sister! Will I...."

She was gone, followed shortly by the Reverend Taylor who circled the bobbing warrior. Circling with a half leer, eyes mere slits.

"Hold it, you God damn son of a bitch!"

He screamed as he struck out in a powerful stroke.

"Hold it!"

His fresh water tears felt somehow consoling as he rode the swells, swimming in the trough. He reached down to make sure the knife was strapped to his leg. It was.

Reverend Taylor drifted down the back side of a large swell while CWO Evans turned the water white with his frenzied strokes.

*   *   *

"Have you taken steps to dismantle this thing?" The Old man asked when they met three days later.

"Yes sir, I have." He lied. What was the matter with a lie at this time in their relationship?

"You haven't, have you?" Alex George hissed.

"I have! I am! The Chief's gone so it'll take a little time to get it done, but I'll do it." He had no intention of doing it. He saw the need.

"I don't think so Tom, but it's OK. I'm drafting a letter right now to McCormick telling him the whole thing. Who I am, how we put this thing together. How we found our people. What kind of people they are. Everything." He sat looking at Tom.

"Will you let me read it when you get through Boss?"

"Yeah. Sure son, I can do that. I won't mention your name, or theirs. Just mine."

"OK then Mr. Alex. I'll be back tomorrow night. We'll put it together then."

"Good son. Glad you see it my way." He thought for a bit, adding. "Hell of an idea though, wasn't it?"

"You know that's exactly what Evans said when I spoke to him last." He closed the door gently as he left, the old man was already dozing in his chair. "Sure was, Mr. Alex. It sure was."

* * *

"Harold?" The voice was quite soft.

"Yeah?"

"CT's gone for a while you know."

"I know. He told me."

"I'm the man...."

"Yeah. I know. He said you might need me."

"I do."

Harold felt sure the man was either crying, or trying desperately to maintain control.

"This is an emergency."

He was sure of it. The stranger was crying all right.

"His name is Alex George...knows who the Angels are... LaFayette, Louisiana...Doberman with him always...bring shotgun... heavy load."

THE END